THE BRITISH YEAR BOOK OF INTERNATIONAL LAW

THE BRITISH YEAR BOOK OF INTERNATIONAL LAW

2000

SEVENTY-FIRST YEAR OF ISSUE

OXFORD
AT THE CLARENDON PRESS
2001

OXFORD
UNIVERSITY PRESS

Great Clarendon Street, Oxford, OX2 6DP
Oxford University Press is a department of the University of Oxford.
It furthers the University's objective of excellence in research, scholarship,
and education by publishing worldwide in

Oxford New York
Athens Auckland Bangkok Bogotá Buenos Aires
Cape Town Chennai Dar es Salaam Delhi Florence Hong Kong Istanbul
Karachi Kolkata Kuala Lumpur Madrid Melbourne Mexico City Mumbai
Nairobi Paris São Paulo Singapore Taipei Tokyo Toronto Warsaw
with associated companies in Berlin Ibadan

Oxford is a registered trade mark of Oxford University Press
in the UK and in certain other countries

Published in the United States
by Oxford University Press Inc., New York

First published 2001

British Library Cataloguing in Publication Data
Data available

Library of Congress Cataloging in Publication Data
Data available

ISBN 0–19–924692–0

1 3 5 7 9 10 8 6 4 2

Typeset in Imprint
by Interactive Sciences Ltd, Gloucester
Printed in Great Britain
on acid-free paper by
Biddles Ltd., Guildford and King's Lynn

Editorial Communications should be addressed as follows:

Articles and Notes:
PROFESSOR JAMES CRAWFORD
Lauterpacht Research Centre for International Law,
5 Cranmer Road, Cambridge, CB3 9BL.
JRC1000@hermes.cam.ac.uk

Books for Review:
PROFESSOR J. G. MERRILLS
University of Sheffield Faculty of Law,
Crookesmoor Building, Conduit Road,
Sheffield, S10 1FL.
J.G.Merrills@Sheffield.ac.uk

The British Year Book of International Law is indexed in *Current Law Index*, published by Information Access Company, and in *Legal Journals Index*, published by Legal Information Resources Limited.

MRS C. A. HOPKINS, OBE

With this volume of the *Year Book*, Mrs Cherry Hopkins of Girton College, Cambridge is stepping down as Assistant Editor. She has served in that capacity for no less than 27 years, since volume 47 (1974–5). The regularity of the *Year Book* since that time, the consistency of its presentation and the excellence of its indexes are all very much due to her dedicated work. It is pleasing to record that she was, in 1998, recognized in the New Year's Honours list with the OBE 'for services to international law', amongst which her contributions to the *Year Book* stand high.

I.B.

CONTENTS

EXPEDIENCY IN THE DECISIONS OF THE INTERNATIONAL COURT OF JUSTICE*

By MOHAMMED BEDJAOUI‡

Introduction

An international court is above all the practitioner of the application of international law. The function assigned to the International Court of Justice under Article 38 of its Statute is to 'decide in accordance with international law such disputes as are submitted to it'. To that end, it applies international conventions, international custom, and the general principles of law, without forgetting to draw inspiration from learned doctrine as and when appropriate. There would therefore appear to be no room for any paralegal or metalegal action by the International Court closely or even remotely akin to the elusive concept of expediency.[1]

It may therefore seem strange, not to say provocative or irreverent, to set out to investigate the possible role of expediency in the decisions of the International Court of Justice, when these decisions are presented as being a pure product of the application of international law, and must necessarily meet the standards of this seal of high quality. It may also seem that I am following fashion in this age of '*glasnost*'. Yet in fact the question as to whether the decisions—or 'some' of the decisions—of the International Court of Justice conceal a hint of expediency is neither malapropos nor inspired by fashion. The possible replies to this question would, I believe, generate greater understanding and trust on the part of States and doctrine with respect to an institution conceived as a cornerstone of the system for the peaceful settlement of disputes put in place by the United Nations Charter.

Law is the science of security. The legislator, the administrator and the courts all contribute to this security. 'The function of adjudicating' thus seems simple and reassuring in the light of this end of the law, striving to protect established relationships. To achieve this, all a court has to do is read the concrete case submitted to it, applying the set of legal rules relating to it. 'Ultimately', one author writes, 'a system of law designed

 A French (less complete) version of this article will be published in 2001 in *Essays in Honor of Professor George Abi-Saab*.

‡ Judge and former President of the International Court of Justice.

[1] The word 'expediency' possibly does not correspond exactly to the French expression '*opportunité*' that I had in mind when I drafted this article in French.

on the basis of the sole ideal of legal security would dispense with the need for any judgment, replacing judges with computers'.[2]

Yet in fact we are far from the automation of the 'function of judging' reduced to programmed behaviour in the national and international order alike. One might even wager that a 'syllogisms machine', a 'machine for stating the law', a 'judging machine', will never be invented. For various reasons which will be set out below, and in certain circumstances, legal security, which is not just necessary but essential, is nevertheless not enough. It sometimes jeopardizes the very order it is supposed to bring about and becomes a potential factor of instability. In that case, the requirements of legal security must be able to reconcile themselves expediently with other values, such as the feeling of what is equitable or reasonable.

By the strict application of a rule of law, always supposing one exists for each case and that its application is automatic or easy, an international court can guarantee legal security to the State that prevails, upon completion of the court's deliberation. But it does not have the power to bring about this legal security *in concreto*. It therefore feels a duty to do its utmost to bring about its concrete realization. In short, an international court is not exclusively a dispenser of legal security. It is also one of its functions to extinguish a dispute, not to fan the flames of it. The judicial function is bound up with security, but also with peacemaking. This is one of the reasons for thinking that courts and judges can never be replaced by automatons.

We shall therefore try to look a little more closely at the various operations which bring into contact a concrete case and the corresponding legal norm to resolve it, in other words, try to analyse the operational route taken by the International Court in its passage from the external world to the legal world, with a view to discerning whether, and, if so, when and how, elements of expediency surface in its decisions.

Yet before considering this task of the legal interpretation by courts of international reality, the meaning of 'expediency' must first be ascertained. The language dictionaries are no great help. They merely tell us that an expedient decision is one which is opportune or which suits the specific case perfectly. '*Opportunité*', the French equivalent of 'expediency', denotes something which occurs at just the right moment. The *Petit Larousse* speaks of the power afforded for taking the initiative in certain measures. What is expedient is what is advantageous and occurs reasonably and suitably or which fulfils a certain expectation. Anyone consulting international law handbooks and treatises, in any language, in the hope of finding the words '*opportunité*' or 'expediency' in the index, with convenient references to helpful analyses in the text, will surely be

[2] C. Perelman, 'Les notions à contenu variable en droit. Essai de synthèse', in *Les notions à contenu variable en droit*, Studies published by Chaïm Perelman and Raymond Vander Elst, proceedings of the Centre national de recherches de logique (Brussels, Bruylant, 1984), p. 363.

frustrated. To the best of my knowledge, no work, or specialized study, deals with expediency, the exception being a brief reference in the work by Shabtai Rosenne devoted to the International Court of Justice.[3] So expediency would seem to be an aspect of the 'inner sanctum' peculiar to international courts, which is kept safe from the curious or prying eye of doctrine.

Works on administrative law, on the other hand, do deal with the matter. '*Legality*', writes Professor Chapus, 'is not all that counts. *Expediency* is also important. It would be distressing if the requirements of the principle of legality were so unwaveringly strict that too often they forced inappropriate behaviour on the administrative authorities. When they have discretionary power, it is precisely the freedom to assess what expediency recommends that is vested in these authorities.'[4] What this author writes about administration might be applied, *mutatis mutandis*, to the International Court.

Discretionary power and expediency are in fact quite intimately linked. Both of them, it should never be forgotten, form part of the tissue of legality, which is what distinguishes them both from arbitrariness. When a legal norm gives courts the choice between two or more solutions, all of them legal ones therefore, it gives them latitude or freedom of decision, whence comes what is termed their discretion or discretionary power. Thanks to this freedom, firmly framed by legality, courts seek to make the most expedient decision possible. Sometimes they are successful. Contrary to arbitrary power, discretionary power is thus nothing other than the ability of international courts to take a decision freely but legally. They act within this framework in order to meet the requirements of the sound administration of justice and not in deference to concerns foreign to their legal duty.

However, a certain deviation from this course may arise, which can be checked and is in no way to be scorned, steering courts less in the direction of the *expedient decision* than in that of the *decision of expediency*. In taking their decision in accordance with legality, they use the resources of legal technique to avoid a solution which risks being misunderstood and not well received, and to choose the solution which best seems to them to satisfy the circumstantial factors surrounding the case submitted to them.

A decision dictated by expediency is therefore one which, while remaining legal, is inspired by feelings of appropriateness, wisdom or prudence. These are suggested to the International Court by its desire to

[3] Shabtai Rosenne, *The Law and Practice of the International Court* (2nd rev. edn., Martinus Nijhoff, Dordrecht/Boston/Lancaster, 1985); the general index refers to pages 91, 436 and 588, even though these pages do not give any real picture of this matter. In the third edition in four volumes of Rosenne's work (*The Law and Practice of the International Court, 1920–1996* (Martinus Nijhoff, 1997)), the word 'expediency' has vanished from the general index.

[4] R. Chapus, *Droit administratif général* (10th edn., Paris, Montchrestien, 1996), vol. 1, p. 963, para. 1074 (emphasis in original).

promote justice and peace between States. This is not a question of a decision actuated by bias or partiality, certainly so far as the International Court of Justice is concerned. Considering that there are fifteen judges from different backgrounds, it is out of the question that they could simultaneously be biased in the same direction.

A decision of expediency may consist in a particular legal solution or simply in a more appropriate and better-adapted formulation of a classical solution, or in the justification of the operative provision of a judgment thanks to a specific choice of grounds, rejecting or avoiding other grounds for decision which might be, abstractly, just as valid.

But expediency may have one or more further roles to play. When the legal norm is deficient, obscure or inadequate, or when its rigid application risks producing an unreasonable solution, an international court, in order to avoid declaring a *non liquet*, appeals to equity. In this case, the decision of expediency is that by which a court seeks to adjust the abstract norm more effectively to the concrete case.

Expediency thus appears as the faithful but often discreet companion of applied international law. In almost every legal decision, it claims a place which varies but which, however tenuous it may sometimes be, is nevertheless inevitable in every judicial treatment of the norm with respect to the facts of the case. But care must be taken not to lose sight of the fact that expediency is neither opportunism nor arbitrariness. In the context of their own powers, many international or domestic institutions share with the International Court of Justice the peculiarity of having a power of appraisal on grounds of expediency. But in no way does this power conceal a manifestation of arbitrariness. All administrations risk becoming arbitrary. But it would be absurd to have to recognize that a court, in other words, a body constituted precisely to thwart arbitrariness, had this 'right to err', for all that it is such an integral part of the infirmity of human nature. Therefore what one author calls 'a new form of pseudo-judicial arbitrariness' cannot conceivably be accepted.[5]

The aim here, and it is a difficult, even perilous undertaking, is to reveal—yet without exaggerating or understating it—this element of expediency, which is almost inevitably present in virtually any international legal decision, even one apparently founded on the strict application of international law. To realize this is not to knock international justice off some imagined pedestal; it is above all to give it a human face, to give it dimensions which in the end are acceptable, just as the common human condition is accepted. To realize this is also to make

[5] O. Pirotte, 'La notion d'équité dans la jurisprudence récente de la Cour internationale de Justice', *Revue générale de droit international public*, 77 (1973), pp. 92 ff.

everyone appreciate the effort made by an international court to make its decisions humanly acceptable. It is ultimately to underpin the respect due to its decisions and the credibility of the justice it delivers.

I shall begin my consideration of this theme from two angles:

(1) The norm, the order, the command of the legislator which the court must apply may be non-existent, incomplete, imprecise, indeterminate in its content, vague and hazy. Here, it will be found that the corpus of international law is incomplete. This has two consequences:

a) first, that there are technical limitations on the application of the international legal norm which the court is required to apply,

b) second, that, given this finding, there are only two possible approaches:

— to push international courts in the direction of *non liquet*, which would be disastrous, or
— to note the existence of an area where such courts have discretion in ruling on a particular case.

Hence, the limitations on the duty to apply the norm also have a by-product: the right to apply discretionary power.

(2) Given this by-product of the function of ruling according to the existing normativity, how do courts use their discretionary power? It is this second question which needs to be answered.

The following two-phase approach may be adopted:

I. The limitations on the judicial function in the application of the international positive norm.
II. Opening the judicial function to the field of expediency; discretionary but not arbitrary power.

Let us therefore consider these two points in turn.

I. The Limitations on the Judicial Function in the Application of the International Positive Norm

The aim here is to show that one cannot, always and in all circumstances, strictly and exclusively apply the international legal norm. Rather, there are areas of discretion for an international court, and the question becomes one of discerning the limitations on this judicial function. These are of several kinds: they may stem from the court, the legislator or the litigant.

1. *The Limitations Stemming from the International Court in its Human and its Legal Aspects*

A. *Limitations stemming from the human condition of all judges*

It is not my intention to lose any time probing the hearts and minds of international judges to assess the degree of subjectivity there is in their judgments as *human beings*. I readily leave this task to certain authors, jurists, or sociologists to use this approach for creating a 'standard profile' of the international judge. I am thinking, for instance, of Professor Lyndel Prott, whose legal doctoral dissertation at the University of Tübingen, entitled *Der internationale Richter im Spannungsfeld zwischen Rechtkulturen*, was published in English under the title *The Latent Power of Culture and the International Judge*, or of Professor Rüdiger Lautmann's *Soziologie vor den Toren der Jurisprudenz*.[6]

In Chapter II of her book, Professor Prott suggests that the judges of the International Court of Justice have split into groups which vote together in the same way in various cases, owing to a common view of law, ties of friendship and similarity of professional experience. In Chapter VI she states that the training acquired by the international judges in the various national legal systems has an influence which is particularly easy to detect in the case-law of the International Court. The approach to solving a case, the style of the judgment, the nature of the remedies they consider possible, all this, according to her, is 'programmed' in a certain way by the judges' basic and professional legal training.[7] Methods of interpretation, questions of procedure, judicial philosophy, the style of the judgment thus allegedly borrow something from the national professional background of the judge.

If there is any truth in this, it should not be exaggerated. What is certain is that, just like anyone else, the international judge is 'situated'. By this I mean that the judge has a 'position', in the sociological sense, which confers a status and assigns a role, yet a position, status and role that the judge cannot occupy or perform while completely erasing origins, education, and training. In these positions, statuses, and roles, the judge will adopt personal standards of behaviour, the fruit of the culture of his or her origins, but also of what colleagues, friends, critics, expect of him or her, and also, after all, of what may result from his or her various roles as all at once judge, member of a club, a family or a church. If one wishes to go down this avenue, it should be noted that the role of the international judge is also partly fashioned by the judge's working 'colleagues', as well as by his or her 'transmitters'. The national cultural

[6] L. Prott, *Der internationale Richter im Spannungsfeld zwischen Rechtkulturen*, translated into English as *The Latent Power of Culture and the International Judge* (1979). See also L. Prott, 'The Role of the Judge of the International Court of Justice', *Revue belge de droit international* (1974), pp. 473–507. See also R. Lautmann, *Soziologie vor den Toren der Jurisprudenz* (1971).

[7] L. Prott, *The Latent Power of Culture and the International Judge* (1979), p. 191.

experience blends into the background of everyday working life in common and the collective international experience.

Regardless of their cultural baggage, there is no denying that international judges are able to find the 'common language' for solving a dispute between States in the sole light of the norms of international law. However, it may sometimes happen that the choice between the resources offered by the techniques of international law may in part be conditioned by the diffuse notions that those judges possess of what is considered 'just' according to the standards of the society to which they once belonged and which they have interiorized or memorized. But it will also be seen that, in their intellectual activity, they constantly come up against the 'feeling of justice' held by their colleagues and that, in the professional setting, judges actually perform two roles: that of 'rule applier' and that of 'rule adjuster', which creates a latent conflict in them.

What greatly limits the element not of 'subjectivity', even in the best sense, but of 'particularity' acquired from the judges' origins and education, is the attentive and critical gaze of the 'rule transmitters':[8] professional colleagues first, then the States parties to the proceedings, and lastly the entire international legal profession. They also remain under the gaze of the legal elites of their countries of origin, who vaguely expect them to be the promoters of their own national legal culture; but this also blends and intermingles with the gaze of the other jurists in the world, with whom they rub shoulders at international fora and in whose eyes they are keen to maintain their reputation. They are also attentive to the views of learned academies, international organizations, senior international civil servants, and members of the diplomatic corps, particularly those at the headquarters of the Court and at the headquarters of the United Nations.

In short, and in many respects, there is nothing here to distinguish international judges from domestic ones: both are influenced by background and professional experience, by what they bring with them and what they receive from the professional community to which they now belong. The 'function of adjudicating',[9] in other words the exercise of discretionary and decision-making power throughout the entire judicial process, is largely the same for both: all that changes is the setting, which here is international. All of this seems to me to give the international judge a demanding international public spirit, so conscious is he of the importance of the duties entrusted to him and of the evident necessity to banish all subjectivity from his task and any approach that smacks of mere convenience. That nationally 'situated' individual, the international

[8] L. Prott, 'The Role of the Judge of the International Court of Justice', op. cit. above (n. 6), p. 481.

[9] M. Boulanger, *La pratique des jugements et des arrêts* (Paris, Libraries techniques, 1965), p. 205.

judge, is constantly 're-situated' internationally. He is braced by the constant desire to bring to the exercise of his international duties the professionalism which he acquired during his national training, and by the concern automatically to censure in himself any, as it were, particularistic approach inherited from that earlier education.

Any analysis or incursion beyond these markers would be venturesome in my view. It would be perilous, fruitless, and unfair to attempt it. This would, for example, be the case of the 'standard profile' which people seek to sketch of the international judge who, in a specific case, is a national or citizen of one of the States parties, whether or not that party has appeared in the proceedings. This would also be the case of the 'standard profile' of the judge *ad hoc* sitting in a particular case. And yet these judges *ad hoc*, chosen by a State party to proceedings in which the bench does not include any national of that State, would at first seem to be more vulnerable than the other judges, who for their part are elected by the United Nations. However, the statistics which could be compiled in these cases provide ample proof of their independence of mind.[10]

Yet it is clear that the international judge is neither more nor less vulnerable than the domestic judge, by virtue of their shared condition as human beings. Modern psychology would seem to have clearly established now that the *judgment* of the human being precedes the *concept*. As a human being, the judge has a general conceptual framework. A fact is intelligible for the judge, whether national or international, by reference to this framework. This involves what the specialists term 'a-priori categories of the mind'.[11]

It will be recalled that the 'function of adjudicating', or the act of judging, ends in a sentence (from the Latin *sententia*, derived from *sentire* (to judge)). The same Latin term gives us the origin of the term 'sentiment' which, moreover, as one author observes, also means 'opinion' or 'judgment' (above all in its archaic sense, as in the expression: 'sentiment of right' or 'national sentiment'). The same author writes that 'the sentiment (of the judge) (in the sense of *sentir* "to feel"—to judge) is a typically personal tool (for him) for discovering value and psychological mechanisms therefore have to be used for evaluating, with all the risks of distortion that any psychologization entails'.[12]

[10] Complete personal statistics since the birth of the ICJ, obviously without taking account of cases pending, where it is not yet known what the judgment will be. Prott makes an undue generalization on the attitude of judges *ad hoc* Van Wyk, chosen by South Africa in the *South West Africa* case, Riphagen, chosen by Belgium in the *Barcelona Traction* case, and Chagla, appointed by India in the case concerning *Right of Passage over Indian Territory* ('The Role of the Judge of the International Court of Justice', loc. cit. above (n. 6), pp. 482 ff.).

[11] G. Bachelard, *Essai sur la connaissance rapprochée*, p. 12, quoted by T. Ivainer, *L'interprétation des faits en droit. Essai de mise en perspective cybernétique des 'lumières du magistrat'* (Paris, LGDJ, 1988).

[12] C. Grzegorczyk, 'Le jugement juridique en tant que jugement pratique (Implications théoriques)', in *Archives de philosophie du droit* (Paris, Sirey, 1983), vol. 28, pp. 326 and 337.

The same author breaks down the inner forces of the judge as follows:

Subjectivity is (therefore) a necessary stage—only man can appraise, machines are incapable of it . . . As no absolute certainty can be achieved in legal judgment and, furthermore, as practical, social certainty is indispensable, *jurists have the impression of working in imperfect conditions, using rough tools and uncertain methods, in which legal reason is sometimes far removed from scientific reason.*[13]

There are also other limitations stemming from courts themselves, but which in this instance are imposed upon them by their task of organizing the smooth running of cases. These are the limitations stemming from the organization of the proceedings.

B. *Limitations stemming from the organization of the proceedings by the Court*

By this I mean that the International Court of Justice, in the context of its ordinary function of adjudicating, enjoys a natural discretion as regards taking the steps which seem to it the most appropriate for organizing the proceedings. Every court, no matter what it is, exercises a sovereign power of this order. Does an element of expediency surface in this instance? In a way, yes. But, in so doing, the International Court is applying a legal norm charging it to exercise all its discretion. It is a norm conferring an option.

The Statute and the Rules of the Court are full of this discretion conferred upon the Court to create and maintain throughout the proceedings optimum conditions for the sound administration of justice and the due process of law. Semantically, this freedom of appraisal is expressed in the usc of the verb 'may': the Court '*may*' form a chamber (Statute, Article 26, paragraph 2); sit elsewhere than in The Hague (Statute, Article 22); request of international organizations information relevant to cases before it (Statute, Article 34); indicate provisional measures (Statute, Article 41, paragraph 1); give an advisory opinion on any legal question at the request of an authorized body (Statute, Article 65); call upon the agents of the parties to produce any document or to supply any explanations (Statute, Article 49); entrust any individual or organization that it may select with the task of carrying out an enquiry or giving an expert opinion (Statute, Article 50); refuse to accept any further oral or written evidence (Statute, Article 52); appoint assessors (Rules, Article 9); direct that the proceedings in two or more cases be joined (Rules, Article 47); call upon the parties to produce such evidence as the Court may consider to be necessary (Rules, Article 62); admit a belated declaration of intervention (Rules, Article 82); extend any time-limit, or decide that any step taken after the expiration of the time-limit fixed therefore shall be considered as valid (Rules, Article 44, paragraph

[13] Ibid., p. 324.

3); direct or authorize a further exchange of written pleadings between the parties (Rules, Article 45, paragraph 2), etc.

Admittedly, in the exercise of these various powers or options conferred upon the Court, the latter is bound by rules of procedure that it cannot disregard. But it is perfectly clear that it has a certain margin of choice here. And of course, the desire to attain the optimum conditions for the sound administration of justice is not codified *ne varietur*. Their attainment is a matter of circumstances. Expediency appears in them. Although the Court, on 5 July 1968, and then on 12 April 1976, laid down the essential rules codifying its internal practice, it nevertheless made sure to add the caveat that it 'remains entirely free to depart from the present Resolution, or any part of it, in a given case, if it considers that the circumstances justify that course'.

In general, the Court is here guided by the rules which it sovereignly assigns itself, but also by the exceptional circumstances of a specific case, which it appraises no less sovereignly. Thus, in order to fix the order in which it may deal with cases ready for hearing, the Court has a rule, that of Article 54 of the Rules, which it has assigned to itself and which calls upon it to have regard to the order of priority required by Article 74 of the Rules, but also 'any other special circumstances, including the urgency of a particular case', which it is totally free to decide. Matters of expediency therefore arise when political events indicate, for example, to the Court that a political settlement in the making should be patiently awaited, and allowed to mature without forcing the pace and upsetting it with possibly disastrous consequences. To this end, the contacts which the President is authorized to maintain with the parties keep the Court well informed of the circumstances surrounding a case and enable the Court to do its work keeping in mind expediency without risk of damage.

The Court has never viewed its function as a disembodied work of justice, delivered by a court in an ivory tower, deaf to all information from outside and entrenched behind the barricades of international law. Its discretion is exercised in the light of all the elements of a case and of its whole context. Here I am not, of course, speaking of the merits, which must be judged through the application of the rules of international law alone, but the 'organization' of the proceedings in the most general sense. This organization is the very opposite of the definitive programme or something that is inviolably laid down in advance. The Court remains attentive to the concerns of the parties and in touch with the international community.

2. *The Limitations Stemming from the International Legislator*

If the essential function of an international court is to apply international law, for it to be able to do so, the appropriate norm must exist in that law, and must be clear and not difficult to apply.

A. *Cases of a loophole or legal vacuum*

In general, the domestic law of States regulates cases involving a stay of proceedings or refusal to rule on a case. To keep to the latter instance, many States prohibit courts from declining to rule, concerned as they are to avoid a denial of justice.

In international law the situation might appear more fluid owing to the silence of the texts governing the International Court of Justice in this respect. But neither international law in general nor the United Nations Charter, which makes the Court a principal organ, nor the Statute of the Court expressly provides that the Court may decline to rule on a contentious case. And the Court itself never loses sight of its *raison d'être*, namely to settle disputes between States. Its mission imposes upon it the duty to assist States in strengthening a peace-loving international community founded on the rule of law. The Court's jurisdiction is admittedly subject to States' consent, but once that consent has been given, the Court is under a duty to fulfil its entire judicial function and nothing but its judicial function. This is precisely why it could be justifiably concluded that the Court is not free to refuse to settle a legal dispute whatever its nature, unless, it should be added, a gap in international law forces it to make a finding of *non liquet*. Yet it is true that one may have considered whether there were gaps in international law and, on the assumption that there were, one may also have wondered whether the Court's peacemaking role should not encourage it to claim a residual rule-making power to fill in any such gaps.

Whatever the case may be, one thing is certain: the International Court of Justice acts at all times out of a concern to safeguard the integrity of its judicial function and not to venture beyond the bounds of that function. But it will be seen below how the Court actually assesses and protects that integrity and whether and how considerations of expediency surface on those occasions in the context of both its advisory function and its contentious powers. It should be noted that this is a question not of jurisdiction but of declining to rule.

B. *Limitations stemming from the indeterminate and fluid nature of certain concepts of varying content introduced by the international legislator*

Here the legal rule exists. It is applicable and applied by international courts. But its content is imprecise and variable from one case to another. When an international court is faced with a concept whose content varies according to circumstances and when it finds itself confronted by a choice offered by this concept between two or more actions, its margin of discretion is obviously broader. Moreover, the increase in its discretionary power is on a par with that of States whose conduct is also governed by this highly plastic concept. 'The source of discretionality', one author writes, is the absence of any rigorously mandatory, strict determination of the action. As soon as, on any point, in any connection whatever, the action to be performed by the subject is not absolutely determined, [there is] a certain discretionary power [which] appears . . . All it needs is for any one of the concepts to which the regulation appeals to be indeterminate in itself for the discretionary power to appear.[14]

In other words, the discretionary power feeds on the vagueness of a legal norm. Once the rule gives a State, just as much as an international court for that matter, freedom of choice and a multiform capacity for freely determining its will, discretionality immediately surfaces. Two discretionalities clash, that of the State wishing to give the vague norm a content which corresponds to its own interests and that of the court which monitors it, giving that norm a content which may be different and which, in the particular case concerned, it considers more in line with a standard, or with equity, or with reasonable conduct. Hence, the lack of determination of the legal norm, or rather its indeterminability, as Stéphane Rials notes, quite clearly confers an area of discretion and a possible margin of expediency on the international court when that court seeks to apply the norm concerned.

In the nineteenth century, when international life was not as complex, nor, therefore, its law, the school of exegesis flourished, which under the leadership of a certain Mourlon favoured stripping courts of all discretion and expediency, demanding their total submission to the letter of the law. Since that school doomed itself by leading the way to what Roscoe Pound called 'mechanical jurisprudence',[15] there is even less justification for it now that international life and the law governing it have become more complex and of necessity have given off many norms with indeterminate content. The international legislator can hardly require an international court to apply strictly a norm whose content it has not rigorously determined for that court.

Doctrine has begun to systematize the problems posed by concepts with an indeterminate or fluctuating content.[16] For example, legal concepts may vary in their content in public international law depending on various factors: owing to the 'spatial factor', in other words, the diversity of legal systems each in their own way characterizing the concept

[14] C. Eisemann, *Cours de droit administratif* (DES, 1949–1950, Les Cours de droit, Paris, 1950), pp. 429 and 451, quoted by S. Rials, 'Les standards, notions critiques du droit', in C. Perelman and R. Vander Elst, *Les notions à contenu variable en droit*, op. cit. above (n. 2), p. 46.

[15] Cf. C. Perelman, 'Jugement, règle et logique juridique', communication to the Colloquium on Legal Judgment at the Paris Faculty of Law on 18 June 1982, and published in *Archives de philosophie du droit*, 28 (1983) (pp. 315–22), pp. 319 and 321.

[16] Cf. J. J. Salmon, 'Les notions à contenu variable en droit international public', in *Les notions à contenu variable en droit international public*, op. cit. above (n. 2), pp. 252–68; and, by the same author (from whom I have borrowed the above classification of factors here), 'Le concept de raisonnable en droit international public', *Mélanges Paul Reuter*, pp. 447–78. See also C. Perelman, 'Le raisonnable et le déraisonnable en droit', *Archives de philosophie du droit*, 23 (1978), pp. 35–42.

concerned in their domestic systems; owing to the 'linguistic factor', in other words, the diversity of meaning of a single word according to the languages concerned, all deemed authentic in a single treaty; owing to the 'material factor', in other words, the diversity of meanings given to the same concept from one international convention to another; owing to the 'temporal factor', in other words, the development and the 'transformation' of a concept over time (problem of inter-temporal law); owing to the 'extension factor' or dispersion factor, in other words, the diversity of factual situations which one single concept may cover; owing to the 'comprehension factor', in other words, the ambiguity or doubts surrounding the constituent elements of the concept, etc. Among these vague, ambiguous, imprecise, undefined or indefinable, indeterminate or indeterminable concepts, one might instance international *ordre public*, good faith, due diligence, urgency, what is just, equitable, reasonable, etc.

3. *Limitations Stemming from the Nature of the Case (the Problem of Political Disputes and Legal Disputes)*

I shall refer to this problem here, though it may not be wholly appropriate, and without dwelling at any length on this 'old chestnut'.

From time to time it has happened that a respondent State has raised before the Court the question of the 'non-justiciability' of the dispute submitted to it by way of an application. The respondent State argues, for example, that the proceedings touch upon matters relating to its political and military defence needs, to the requirements of its 'national security' or to its 'vital interests', or more generally, or more simply, that the case does not lend itself to legal appraisal. There is no need to labour this problem. As early as the 1930s, Hersch Lauterpacht wrote that the distinction between legal disputes and political disputes had lost its national usefulness and now constituted an obstacle to the progress of law.[17]

According to its Statute, the Court only hears disputes of a legal nature, as otherwise it will lack jurisdiction. Yet there is no certain, reliable criterion for making this distinction. Moreover, even if this criterion did exist, it would be of no use, since the facts of the dispute merely have to be put to the Court in legal terms, regardless of how political it is. In truth, all legal disputes of which the Court may rightfully be seised have political implications with which, in principle, it must not concern itself, and every political dispute has legal aspects which may be brought before the International Court.

Yet if this question is raised here, it is less in order to rehearse it again than to seek to verify whether, through decisions turning on the

[17] H. Lauterpacht, *The Function of Law in the International Community* (1933), p. 43.

distinction between the categories of dispute, appraisals of expediency have not slipped in. It should first be noted that the development of international jurisprudence shows that the Court has strengthened its jurisdiction in legal disputes with politically explosive connotations, even if international political bodies were also seised at the same time as the Court. As the basic texts concerning the jurisdiction of the Court have not changed, the conclusion must be that the Court's discretionary power has gradually asserted itself.

Secondly, it will be noted that, in this field, the Court, which in principle is indifferent to the political implications of its decisions, nevertheless increasingly seeks to concern itself with the political capital which could be made out of its decisions. It therefore engages in appraisals of expediency, which are expressed in a certain jurisprudential policy.

What is this policy? This is the subject of the second part.

II. Opening the Judicial Function to the Field of Expediency; Discretionary but not Arbitrary Power

The International Court enjoys a discretionary power of appraisal, which is sometimes extended, in its case, by a certain deference to expediency, and which can be detected through the following:

1. agreeing to rule, despite the existence of the norm;
2. declining, directly or indirectly, to rule, despite the existence of the norm;
3. the Court's function of individualizing the norm;
4. the Court's function of correcting the norm;
5. the Court's function of creating the norm;

Let us take these five points in turn, among many others which might have been mentioned.

1. *The Decision to Rule, despite the Existence of the Norm*

I shall here consider one single decision from the case law: the case concerning the *Frontier Dispute (Burkina Faso/Republic of Mali)*. The Chamber of the Court over which I had the honour to preside and which had the task of ruling on this dispute had, under the Special Agreement, to make a ruling in law and refrain from deciding the case *ex aequo et bono*. The parties had invited the Chamber to apply the legal principle of *uti possidetis juris*, thanks to which the newly-independent States were to be confirmed in the frontiers inherited from the colonial period. And the Chamber gallantly applied this principle, endeavouring, through colonial law texts, geographical maps, and *effectivités*, to identify precisely the colonial course of the frontier which, in places, was undetermined. It acquitted itself of its task, not without a number of difficulties, as the applicable law sometimes proved to be vague, inconsistent, and even disconcerting owing to the existence (existence is not exactly the word) of what I termed 'phantom pools' and 'phantom villages'. In short, in *uti possidetis juris* the Court had a clear principle, one undisputed by the parties, yet a principle impotent when faced with an uncertain colonial frontier legacy in several places.

Neither *uti possidetis*, nor colonial law, nor cartography, nor the *effectivités*, nor the evidence, were of any help. Since the applicable law had proved powerless as regards permitting the identification of a few points on the frontier, in particular a pool called Kétiouaire, a veritable nightmare to locate, the International Court could have opted for declaring a comprehensive *non liquet*, to avoid having to present a fragmented frontier. That was not its decision; on the contrary, it granted itself the power to locate this pool itself and one or two segments of frontier, by appealing to equity. It therefore decided to complete the fragmented frontier course by adopting the solutions which seemed to it the most reasonable and equitable for this frontier dispute. In this case, the Chamber incontestably made use of its discretion and of its desire to act with all due prudence in order to adopt the most expedient and acceptable courses of certain segments which otherwise would have thwarted all attempts at determination. The Chamber was especially anxious not to offend the parties but at the same time to see that equity and justice prevailed. In so doing, the Chamber did nothing different from what other tribunals have done in sensitive cases such as the *Frontiers of the Andes* or the *Rann of Kutch*.[18] It can only be concluded that discretion and expediency were successful in the particular case referred to, as the international press welcomed the judgment as a 'judgment of Solomon' and as the two parties publicly expressed their satisfaction and proceeded with the demarcation and marking out of the frontier on the basis of the course decided upon by the Chamber. In this respect, and bearing in mind in particular these elements of expedient

[18] Dutheil de la Rochère, 'Les procédures de règlement des différends frontaliers', in *La Frontière*, Colloquium of the Société française de droit international, Poitiers, 1979 (Paris, Pedone, 1980), p. 149.

discretion, the judicial settlement arrived at was akin to an arbitral settlement.

2. *The Expediency in Declining, Directly or Indirectly, to Rule, despite the Existence of the Norm*

A distinction must be drawn between the jurisdiction of the Court in contentious cases and its advisory function.

A. *Jurisdiction in contentious cases*

Here too there is only one legal case I could consider. In fact, the Court has never, to my knowledge, had to decline to rule and frontally make a finding of *non liquet*. The course of events was more subtle and the dispute on which the Court had to rule, in the *South West Africa* case in 1966, with potentially explosive political implications, was transposed to another domain than that of lack of jurisdiction or *non liquet*. The application was rejected on other grounds.

The Court had previously declared that it had jurisdiction to rule on the application filed by Ethiopia and Liberia against South Africa for its handling of the mandate over South West Africa—present-day Namibia. But by its judgment of 18 July 1966, the Court eventually opted in favour of rejecting that application on the ground, which caused surprise, that these two African States, already independent at the time of the League of Nations, which had granted the mandate, did not have a 'legal interest to act'. Most of the authors who analysed the judgment clearly considered that the Court had taken refuge in this unexpected solution to avoid upsetting certain States and a certain public opinion. It was as though the Court, afraid of facing their criticisms, had as it were censored itself in advance.[19]

Yet if this is so, the conclusion is that the Court, in so doing, had jumped out of the frying-pan into the fire, as it did not escape the far more vociferous displeasure of the other States and the rest of international opinion. If expediency did play a role in this case, its role would seem to have been disastrous. This extremely unpopular decision had deep and lasting negative repercussions, notably in the United Nations, where it precipitated the loss by South Africa of its mandate over Namibia.[20]

Over and above this case, one must understand how legitimate the

[19] Cf. R. Higgins, 'The International Court and South West Africa: The Implications of the Judgment', *International Affairs*, 42 (1966), p. 573, at p. 589. L. Prott wrote that 'the Court has been unduly influenced by the anticipated criticism' ('The Role of the Judge of the International Court of Justice', loc. cit. above (n. 6), p. 432).

[20] The debates in the United Nations General Assembly following the delivery of the judgment of 18 July 1996 were full of singular indignation at that half of the Court which, as the Australian President Spender had the casting vote, took this disparaged decision.

Court's concern is when showing an interest in the reception of its decisions by the parties or by public opinion. For example, in his dissenting opinion, the American Judge Philip Jessup wrote that international law must not be treated like an antiquated collection of dead letters harking back to a remote period in the history of the world. He added that '[The] standard to be applied by the Court *must be one which takes account of the views and attitudes of the contemporary international community*'.[21] Another author wrote:

> The case in question demonstrated [that] law is not something that is apart from reality, apart from politics . . . The case highlights the delicate line the Court must tread. It generally attempts in its judgment to include some statements that make the decisions at least *partly acceptable to the losers*; it is never highly critical or abusive. The trick, indeed, is to try to make the decision carry *as little pain for the loser* as possible, *to try to avoid making the Court itself unpopular* with any part of the International Community.[22]

It would be wrong to think that all this is exclusive to the International Court. The same problem of the rejection of judicial decisions by public opinion also exists within States and sometimes assumes worrying proportions ranging from popular outcry to acts of violence. Whether national or international, justice cannot avoid concerning itself with earning acceptance through decisions which, while expressing the state of the law, do not completely neglect the current standards of morality. It is this approach which is also called expediency. One author has noted that 'Judges do not live in isolation. Their opinions are subject to criticism, and they are, and should be, influenced by popular reaction. The process often works in subtle ways . . . .'[23]

In the *South West Africa* case, the Court did not act outside the bounds of international legality. Yet, apparently sensitive to political expediency, it opted for an approach which, while legal, was outmoded; what was all the more surprising about it was that, precisely, it enabled the Court to avoid making a ruling on the merits, such a ruling having been particularly anticipated since the Court had already declared that it had jurisdiction and had ruled that the application was admissible.

This case shows the exactness of the comment by Chaïm Perelman that: 'It is very rare for legal reasoning to lead, like . . . mathematical proofs, to a binding conclusion'. Thus, the problem of 'the social acceptability' of its decision arises in sharp relief just as easily for the domestic or international court.[24] 'In fact', Stéphane Rials adds, 'despite the majesty surrounding its decisions, the court cannot dispense with

[21] *ICJ Reports*, 1966, p. 441 (emphasis added).

[22] G. Sturgess and P. Chubb, *Judging the World — Law and Politics in the World's Leading Courts* (Butterworths, 1988), ch. 7, 'The Courts in Collision', p. 213 (emphasis added).

[23] N. Redlich, 'Judges as Instruments of Democracy', in *The Role of the Courts in Society*, ed. Shimon Shetreet (Nijhoff Publishers, 1988), ch. 11, pp. 149–56.

[24] C. Perelman, *Logique juridique, nouvelle rhétorique* (Paris, 1976), pp. 7 and 9.

techniques which will make its handiwork more persuasive and legitimate'.[25]

This is all the more true as regards an international court which is excessively dependent, where the matter of its seisin and jurisdiction are concerned, on the consent of States. In the *South West Africa* case, the International Court had sterilized in advance the scope of the technical solution it put forward and which could but strike the public as a derisory expedient, since the Court had already confirmed that it had jurisdiction and that the application was admissible. Opinion and the expectations of the 'public' are not a negligible element, constituting what certain authors term 'infra-law'.[26]

B. *The advisory function*

In this context, the Court has clear discretionary power regarding the expediency even of giving an advisory opinion. It has stated that 'Article 65, paragraph 1, of the Statute, which establishes the power of the Court to give an advisory opinion, is *permissive* and, under it, *that power* is of a *discretionary* character'.[27] It has on several occasions reverted to this interpretation, which it considers as 'of course well established'.[28] In the *Western Sahara* case, it firmly laid down the principle that it was under no obligation to rule and that it was free to decline to reply to a request for an opinion.

It derives this freedom to rule first and foremost from the fact that no obligation can be imposed on it in this field if it risks prejudicing the integrity of its judicial function. For example, the United Nations sought, by a laborious and inappropriate procedure, to make the Court, which, however, rules on disputes between States, into a sort of appeals body against the rulings of UNAT and ILOAT concerning international civil servants. The Court, which has firmly indicated its lack of enthusiasm for requests for advisory opinions on rulings by UNAT, has not failed on several occasions to detail a 'number of criticisms of this procedure', which scarcely complies with the due process of law to which it is accustomed in the context of the integrity of its judicial function. On the basis of this, it has always indicated its power to decline to give its

[25] S. Rials, 'Les standards, notions critiques du droit', loc. cit. above (n. 14), p. 52.

[26] A.-J. Arnaud, *Critique de la raison juridique. Où va la sociologie du droit?* (Paris, LGDJ, 1981) and especially his observations entitled 'Repères pour une exploration méthodique de l'infra-droit', pp. 325 ff. 'The pre-judgment situation' ('l'avant-dire-droit'), as the author calls it, is made up of a number of factors, both objective and subjective, which, in the popular imagination, really create the contours of a legal decision before it is delivered and which feed the public's expectation: levels of awareness and legal education, in other words, conformist or revolutionary behaviour on the part of the public, associated with more subjective factors consisting of attitudes, opinions, behaviours, beliefs, images.

[27] *ICJ Reports*, 1975, p. 21, para. 23 (emphasis added).

[28] Ibid., 1987, p. 31, para. 25.

opinion. But there then appeared, in that freedom to do well, an opportunity to do better. It then set out the reasons which, while not taking it outside its own particular legal framework, made it regard giving an opinion nevertheless as a good opportunity (all these reasons coming down to the expediency of protecting the international civil servant and the expediency of serving the international organization by taking part in its action and advising it in this action). In the case of UNAT, the General Assembly decided, by a resolution adopted in 1995, to put an end to this procedure in view of its shortcomings, which the Court had helped to highlight.

For the other category of advisory opinions given by the Court to a competent United Nations body or authorized international institution, the Court always seeks to establish whether it has a 'compelling reason', derived from the circumstances of the case, for declining to reply to the request for an opinion.

Even when a State concerned in one way or another by the advisory opinion requested by a United Nations body opposes this request for an opinion, this does not mean that the Court, by this fact alone, is automatically obliged to decline to give the opinion. The fact that a State, such as Spain in the *Western Sahara* case, or Romania in the *Mazilu* case, 'does not consent, it says, to the exercise of the advisory jurisdiction of the Court, does not concern that jurisdiction, but the *expediency* of its exercise'.[29] It therefore measures what it terms the *expediency* of delivering its opinion as follows: '[w]hen the circumstances disclose that to give a reply [to a request for an opinion when a State is opposed to it] would have the effect of circumventing the principle that a State is not obliged to allow its disputes to be submitted to judicial settlement without its consent', the Court would then prohibit itself from engaging in such an abuse of procedure. In the discretionary appraisal of expediency, the Court cannot lend itself to a manoeuvre making it possible, through the advisory procedure, to circumvent the failure of a State to agree to submit to contentious proceedings. It should be noted that the Court, by its decision of 8 July 1996 delivered on the request for an opinion submitted to it by the WHO concerning the *Legality of the Use by a State of Nuclear Weapons in Armed Conflict*, for the first time declined to give an advisory opinion, for lack of an essential condition of its jurisdiction. It did not therefore have to consider the arguments set out before it concerning the exercise of its discretionary power to give an opinion.

[29] ICJ, advisory opinion, *Mazilu* case (*Applicability of Article VI, Section 22, of the Convention on the Privilege and Immunities of the United Nations*), *ICJ Reports* (1989), pp. 177 ff. (paras. 29–39).

3. *Expediency in the Court's Function of Individualizing the Law (or the Process of Choosing a Solution Perfectly Suited to a Specific Case)*

We must take care to understand the message. A discreet dose of expediency is not only inevitable and inescapable but is also indispensable and salutary. We know the Faustian power of computing and robotics, but we also know that it cannot eliminate the Court, performing as it does a function whose very stuff is nuance and prudence.

Between the legislator and the court there is a relationship characterized by what I would term 'the pendulum law'. The way a legal norm is produced is different from the way physical or mathematical laws are produced. The law of the jurist is not the law of the scientist. The latter discovers laws only by taking care never to become divorced from reality and by always analysing and experimenting with that reality. The jurist on the contrary, where the observation of that reality is concerned, must necessarily distance himself from it in order to conceptualize it and give his law the degree of generality and abstraction he wants it to have and to assign to it certain purposes that he expects of it. In relation to reality, the law is thus a construct, subjecting international or domestic relations to a certain chosen order. That is the first swing of the pendulum, or the first movement away from the point of equilibrium represented by reality.

When the Court's turn to intervene comes, it reverses the movement of the pendulum, bringing it towards that reality which it is the Court's task to take into account through a particular case. A latent conflict then develops between the legislator, divorced from international reality through his necessary effort of conceptualization and abstraction, and the Court, whose efforts to adapt and adjust prompt it to take such a reality into account in concrete terms.

Hence the latent conflict between the legislator, who sees reality as it ought to be, and the Court, which views it as it is presented, is quite simply necessary and beneficial, as it is the agent of legal progress. In this unending process, the discreet dose of expediency sometimes left to the Court is like a little leaven giving rise to legal progress. In this to-and-fro movement of the pendulum we are well aware that the abstract legal norm is destined to keep international society in a certain order, but in no way to tyrannize it, overtly at least, otherwise there will be rejection. In the application of the law, an international court helps to preserve the desired order, while taking on the tasks of maintenance, cleaning and restoration and sometimes remodelling.

Whatever the case, it is not the law which makes and remakes international society, but international society which makes and remakes the law. Courts contribute to this, their day-to-day tasks revealing as they do the degree to which the law is or is not adapted to the contemporary world the law seeks to govern.

4. *Expediency in the Function of Adding to or Clarifying a Norm with Indeterminate Content*

When the international norm is sufficiently precise and complete, this means that it provides an international court with the necessary and sufficient guidelines for enabling it without difficulty to make a ruling in a particular case, and thus to remain within its particular function, which is to apply a given norm to a specific case within the limits of its jurisdiction. Yet this is not always so:

Bearing in mind the variety of circumstances, the fact that it is not capable of foreseeing everything and regulating everything with precision, since rigid rules can only be applied with difficulty to changing situations, the legislator can intentionally introduce into the text of the law concepts with varying, vague, indeterminate content, such as equity, what is reasonable, [due diligence, etc.], leaving to the court the task of clarifying them in each particular case.[30]

In international law, the concepts of what is reasonable, equitable, just, urgent, of due diligence, good faith, international *ordre public*, all have variable content. In European Community law, there is even a small explosion of indeterminate concepts: so-called 'normal' possibilities of remuneration, so-called 'normal' conditions of competition, so-called 'fair' limits on prices, so-called 'rational' exploitation of resources, so-called 'comparable' conditions of production, the so-called 'equalization' principle in progress, etc. One author, an expert in this context, has written:

Lack of normative determination in a legal system is a means *of delegation* or reservation of power. It is necessary to *the legislator* who cannot or will not concern himself with the detail, and necessary to the administrator and *the court*, in that it leaves them a freedom of *action*.

It is therefore the changing search for normality as it apprehends it at a given moment that permits a court 'to justify (its) decision by an effort to achieve coherence and generalization founded on the (direct or indirect) reference to normal conduct'.[31]

We are aware of what the international arbitrator made of the concept of 'due diligence' in the *Alabama* case, by recourse to discretion. The extent of the concept, bearing in mind the territorial and personal jurisdiction of the State, the degree of vigilance which it requires depending on the situations, the *risks* incurred and the degree to which they are foreseeable depending on the means available to the State, on the capacity of the person to be protected, etc. must be freely appraised by an international court, which may undertake an assessment of the circumstances and expediency which may dictate diligent conduct in a concrete

[30] C. Perelman, *Les notions à contenu variable en droit*, op. cit. above (n. 2) p. 365.

[31] H. Bauer-Bernet, 'Notions indéterminées en droit communautaire', in *Les notions à contenu variable en droit*, op. cit. above (n. 2) (pp. 269–87), p. 269.

situation. This is what is termed 'review of discretion', which certain domestic courts decline to exercise against their administration, but which the International Court in no way declines to exercise.

The concept of what is 'reasonable' appears in many conventions and treaties whose aim it is to contain the freedom of action of the contracting States within acceptable proportions: reference is made to reasonable time-limits or notice, reasonable quantities or prices etc. International jurisprudence has to weigh up the circumstances in order to determine what, in an appraisal where the degree of expediency is hard to measure, and bearing these circumstances in mind, seems to it to merit the label of reasonable, at the moment when it takes its decision.

However, it is, of course, the concept of 'equitable principles' which can easily reveal the small areas of expediency available to an international court. Let us first note three points:

— First, the concept of 'equitable principles' is essentially a judge-made creation. It is the International Court which, in its judgment of 1969 on the *North Sea Continental Shelf*, truly established the pedigree of this concept.
— Second, this concept, which has experienced the fleeting favours of treaty law, and the more robust ones today of customary law, constitutes a positive norm.
— The difficulty with it is that its content is still imprecise and elusive, even though this flexibility, which confers on the International Court a certain freedom of appraisal, does not thereby deprive it of all its normativity.

Equity has made enormous inroads in the field of law, to begin with in the formation and elaboration of the legal norm, whose very substance is equity, and also in the application of the rule of law, in which equity serves to temper the disproportion between the legal rule, which is slow to evolve, and changing social needs, thus making it possible to humanize the law, to relax its rigidity, make it less rigorous, in short, to adapt it to the case concerned. In the hands of an international court, equity *infra legem* appears to be a technique for the interpretation of the law, distinguishing itself from the decision *ex aequo et bono* by virtue of the fact that it intervenes within the strict limits of positive law in order to adjust it to the case and not to usurp its function. In it, an international court enjoys discretion whose scope is a function of the margin separating the legal rule from the concrete situation. The second role which can be attributed to equity, still in the context of the application of the rule of law, consists in complementing positive law, either in cases where the law is silent or in cases where the law is inadequate or obscure. The choices of expediency, or the court's discretion, are there exercised in the context and on the occasion of a loophole or shortcoming in the legal norm. It is equity *praeter legem* which here plays a complementary role.

Yet in all cases, recourse to equity is 'an operation which is all nuance and finesse'[32] and it is 'impossible to contain in any formula whatever the infinitely supple and diverse mental operations which guide the court towards what it envisages as a just solution'.[33]

These observations provide an appropriate introduction to the question of the law of the sea, where equity assumes considerable importance as a substantive rule. It has been said that the law of the sea is still at a rudimentary stage and that its degree of normativity remains weak. And yet the contemporary law of maritime delimitations is awash with equity, present both in the norm of which it constitutes the entire substance and in the application of the norm. The difficulty is that, in its way, the concept of equity has a variable, indeterminate content. What is essentially required is to increase the degree of normativity of this law by making the content of equity ever more precise.

But where is the court's discretion, or choice of circumstance or expediency in this sphere? It must be noted that it is the international legislator who, in the Montego Bay Convention of 1982, conferred on the court a high degree of discretion, in giving it as a tool this norm which ill deserved to be baptized a 'fundamental' norm especially as it appeared virtually empty of content. In the words of one author, 'the discretion enjoyed by courts very faithfully reflects the situation of a law whose tensions and contradictory movements criss-crossing it result in compromises where flexibility sometimes verges on vacuity'.[34]

However, through the ebb and flow of jurisprudence it was ultimately realized that the concept of 'equitable principles', having vanished from the positive norm—which now refers only to an 'equitable result'—and then having been reintroduced as customary law, was in danger of not being able to perform its function if it did not have the qualities of security which a rule of law procures and if its application remained uncertain and, moreover, given over to institutionalized unpredictability.

So in the end the Court reacted positively, by conferring upon equity and equitable principles a normative, security-inducing, predictable dimension, general in its application. That was the *Libya/Malta* judgment of 1985. However, the power of the Court which is a real one, with

[32] C. de Visscher, *De l'équité dans le règlement arbitral et judiciaire des litiges de droit international public* (Paris, Pedone, 1972), p. 12.

[33] Id., *Théories et réalités en droit international* (Paris, Pedone, 4th edn., 1970), p. 422.

[34] E. David, 'La sentence arbitrale du 14 février 1985 sur la délimitation de la frontière Guinée-Guinée-Bissau', *Annuaire français de droit international* (1985), p. 365.

a few choices of expediency still detectable, is not so great as to make maritime delimitation a 'lottery', as Prosper Weil says:[35]

The 1985 Judgment restored the normative function to the law of delimitation. Equity ceases to fluctuate on the whim of judicial subjectivities.[36]

However, this must not be regarded as an absolute certainty. Despite great progress in the conquest of normativity, it is not possible to get rid, radically and totally, of all trace of personal discretion from these operations. Furthermore, the analytical tool (equitable principles) is not rigorously precise, indeed anything but. The appraisal of the relevant circumstances, in every case by means of these equitable principles, cannot therefore be like an operation of mathematical precision, governed by rigid rules which provide an instantaneous reading of the exact and invariable weight to be attributed to each element in the case. It could even be said that the quality of this intellectual operation and the equity of the final result depend on the existence of a minimum of flexibility in the discretion left to the International Court.

The 'equitable principles' ultimately have the appearance of being a legal arsenal from which the Court selects the tools making it possible to identify, evaluate, understand, and satisfy circumstances recognized as being legally relevant by reference to an equitable principle taken by the Court as a postulate and involved in the appraisal of this relevant circumstance. Equitable principles are full of 'individualizing action', as Charles de Visscher put it, in other words, charged with the function of adapting the law to a concrete case.

The normative enrichment which has gradually been achieved in the law of maritime delimitations, thanks today to the juridicity of equitable 'principles' and tomorrow to the normativity of the applicable 'methods'—an enrichment which is the product of victories which were neither easy nor irreversible—should not make one lose sight of the fact that equity, even that equity which is the most firmly tied to the law, by its very essence conceals an element of subjectivity. Equity is a fundamentally contingent concept, which varies according to individuals, prejudices, morals, society and also time. The three signatories, one of them myself, of the joint separate opinion in the *Libya/Malta* case were thus able to write, legitimately it seems to me, that:

The entire process of maritime delimitation law is dominated by a 'fundamental norm', that of the equitable result, which is as uninstructive as it is all-embracing. That being so, a judge can but anxiously, humbly, gauge and compare his crushing responsibility and the modest means at his disposal for assuming it. He undergoes what Verlaine called 'l'extase et la terreur de celui qui a été choisi'. He cannot see how to escape from the frustrating tyranny of a

[35] P. Weil, *Perspectives du droit de la délimitation maritime* (Paris, Pedone, 1988) (319 p.), p. 147.

[36] Ibid.

certain 'praetorian subjectivism' when the very margin of indeterminacy responsible for it originated in a law still young and permeated with equity—which, though a highly respectable legal concept, is inevitably measured with a 'human' yardstick. The finest legal dissertations on equity will never succeed in completely eliminating what is perhaps an irreducible core of the judicial subjectivism mentioned above. The utmost, in all honour, that a judge can then do is modest: to summon up all his resources with a view to reducing its scope and effects to a minimum.[37]

5. *Expediency in the Function of Supplementing the Norm with a Well-Defined Content for the Purpose of Resolving All Aspects of a Dispute Submitted to the Court*

Even when the legislator has elaborated a norm with a well-defined content, the necessity may still arise, when this appears to be the intention of the parties to a case before the Court, to resort to a certain form of expediency when the mechanical application of the norm does not make it possible to arrive at a satisfactory result. This was so in the case concerning the *Gabcíkovo-Nagymaros Project (Hungary/Slovakia)*, in which the Court, after declaring that the 1977 Treaty concerning that project was still in force, contrary to the assertions of Hungary, stated the following:

> The Court, however, cannot disregard the fact that the Treaty has not been fully implemented by either party for years, and indeed that their acts of commission and omission have contributed to creating the factual situation that now exists . . .
>
> What is essential . . . is that the factual situation as it has developed since 1989 shall be placed within the context of the preserved and developing treaty relationship, in order to achieve its object and purpose in so far as that is feasible. For it is only then that the irregular state of affairs which exists as the result of the failure of both Parties to comply with their treaty obligations can be remedied.
>
> . . . What might have been a correct application of the law in 1989 or 1992, if the case had been before the Court then, could be a miscarriage of justice if prescribed in 1997.[38]

Whence a number of legal consequences which the Court was called upon to determine, in accordance with the Special Agreement concluded between the parties, and which the Court managed to do by thus enabling considerations of expediency to play a not negligible role.

[37] Joint separate opinion by J.-M. Ruda, M. Bedjaoui and E. Jimenez de Aréchaga, ICJ *Reports* (1985), p. 90, para. 37.

[38] *ICJ Reports* (1997), p. 76, paras. 133–4.

Conclusion

Expediency is a subject which it is difficult, if not impossible, to study. Resisting all attempts to clarify and systematize it, it has the air of a challenge. The discretion of shadow suits it better than the glare of the footlights.

It is the basic function of the International Court to apply the law almost exclusively in its task of 'stating the law', as the precise expression has it. In so doing, it dispenses legal security, the role for which it was created. Yet the particular circumstances of the case being considered remind it of its subsidiary role, which is to extinguish the dispute, to help to pacify and normalize relations between States. Its decision to 'state the law' must not be counterproductive and exacerbate emotions. The circumstances of the case will therefore prompt it to add a more or less discreet note of expediency whenever legality so permits.

The manifestations of this expediency are varied, as much as the circumstances of the cases. They may range from simply the manner of presenting or formulating a passage with a view to giving it the most acceptable style, to the act of supplementing a deficient norm, of giving it content if, in the abstract, it is indeterminate, or of adjusting this norm to the concrete case. These various operations, and others too in the 'function of adjudicating', are far from all connected with or amounting to matters of expediency. Let us be wary of giving the impression that expediency envelops them completely in its cloak, and say more modestly that 'nuggets' of expediency appear here and there.

The discretionary power of the International Court, and its fitting episodic corollary—expediency—necessarily belong to the judicial function as inseparably as a man and his shadow. Their use from a desire for the smooth administration of justice adds to legal security a quality of justice and equity liable to extinguish disputes and harmonize relations. Depending on the density of intervention of the discretionary power, should one think of ebbs and flows of normativity with a hint of disquiet or regret? I do not think so. One may well feel that the legal security provided by the law deserves to be invigorated and consolidated from time to time, when necessary, by a discreet legal impressionism of the Court, in order to achieve a sound dialectic of progress.

There are of course also various cases in which, despite the Court's efforts, the principle of legal security, composed of a guarantee of equality, uniformity, impartiality, predictability, is impossible to adhere to when the Court is faced with legal concepts with indeterminate or indeterminable content. But this does not mean that, in agreeing to rule and, in so doing, using a certain discretionary power, the International Court makes a triumphant legal impressionism prevail over a sacrificed legal security. These are not uncertain ebbs and flows of normativity. It is normativity giving itself a spiritual boost, and enhancing its life force, in itself organizing, in the legal context which it clearly signposts, the conditions for its fertilization by the International Court.

THE *PINOCHET* CASE: INTERNATIONAL HUMAN RIGHTS LAW ON TRIAL*

By ROSANNE VAN ALEBEEK[1]

Whenever a change is made, someone some time has to make the first move. One country alone may start the process. Others may follow. At first a trickle, then a stream, last a flood.

Lord Denning MR[2]

1. Introduction

On 17 October 1998 the Chilean General Augusto Pinochet Ugarte was arrested in the United Kingdom (UK) while ill in a London hospital. More than twenty-five years after Pinochet commanded the violent military coup that evicted the government of President Allende on 11 September 1973, the Spanish judge Garzon decided that it was time to end the impunity of the man often held responsible for the acts of systematic and widespread human rights violations that characterized the military regime in Chile. A Spanish international warrant of arrest had been issued on 16 October and was eventually followed by a second international warrant and an official extradition request by the Spanish Government pursuant to the 1957 European Convention on Extradition.[3] On the basis of these international warrants, UK Metropolitan Magistrates issued two provisional warrants for Pinochet's arrest under section 8(1) of the Extradition Act 1989. The first warrant alleged the murder of Spanish citizens in Chile, while the second warrant included allegations of torture, hostage-taking and murder. Applications were made on behalf of Pinochet for judicial review and habeas corpus in respect of the two warrants.[4]

[1] Law Degree Leiden University, M. Jur. (Oxon), M. St. (Oxon). Doctoral Research Fellow, E. M. Meijers Institute for Legal Research, Leiden University. Research for this article was completed in August 2000.

[2] *Trendtex Trading Corp.* v. *Central Bank of Nigeria*, [1977] QB 529, at p. 556.

[3] Incorporated in UK law by the European Convention on Extradition Order 1990 as amended by the Extradition Act 1989. The Spanish request was followed by an extradition request from the French, the Belgian, and the Swiss Governments.

[4] See for a comprehensive overview of the facts of the case *R* v. *Bow Street Metropolitan Stipendiary Magistrate and others, ex parte Pinochet Ugarte*, [1999] 2 All ER 97, at pp. 101–4 *per* Lord Browne-Wilkinson. This article is not concerned with the truth of the allegations. As Lord Browne-Wilkinson held at p. 101, '[t]here is no real dispute that during the period of the . . . Pinochet regime appalling acts of barbarism were committed in Chile and elsewhere in the world:

Two pivotal questions dominated the proceedings before the British courts. The first question was whether the alleged acts of torture could qualify as extradition crimes under the UK Extradition Act 1989. Was torture committed outside UK territory already a crime punishable under UK law—through the concept of universal jurisdiction—before a statutory basis of jurisdiction was available? The second question was whether Pinochet, head of State when he allegedly committed these crimes, could invoke the concept of ex-head of State immunity as a shield against the allegations. Both questions are essentially questions of international law. However, the UK State Immunity Act 1978 and UK law in general played a significant role in the proceedings. This warrants the question whether the *Pinochet* decision reflects the position of the immunity rule in international law and the influence of international human rights law correctly.

Pinochet had his fate decided in a veritable courtroom-drama consisting of four acts. After a judgment of the Divisional Court,[5] appeal was made to the House of Lords. The learned Lords had to decide the case twice. The first decision of 25 November 1998[6] was set aside by a House of Lords Committee on 17 December 1998 because the Appellate Committee had been improperly constituted.[7] A final judgment was given on 24 March 1999. A 6–1 majority decided that there could be no immunity for a former head of State for the torture allegations under consideration.[8] On 2 March 2000 the UK Home Secretary Jack Straw decided that General Pinochet's ill-health made him unfit to stand trial

torture, murder and the unexplained disappearance of individuals, all on a large scale'. The events that took place in Chile during the military regime have been the subject of thorough investigation, both in Chile (e.g. *Report of the Chilean National Commission on Truth and Reconciliation* (the Rettig Report) (translation P.E. Berryman, 1993)) as well as on the international level (e.g. Amnesty International, United Nations). See for more information International Commission of Jurists, *Crimes Against Humanity: Pinochet Faces Justice* (1999); R. J. Wilson, 'Prosecuting Pinochet: International Crimes in Spanish Domestic Law', *Human Rights Quarterly*, 21 (1999), pp. 927–79.

[5] The Divisional Court of the Queen's Bench Division [1998] All ER (D) 509 delivered on 28 October 1998 (Divisional Court). Lord Bingham of Cornhill CJ, Collins and Richards JJ unanimously quashed both warrants.

[6] *R* v. *Bow Street Metropolitan Stipendiary Magistrate and others, ex parte Pinochet Ugarte* (*Amnesty International and others intervening*), [1998] 4 All ER 897 ([1998] 3 WLR 1456, HL) delivered on 25 November 1998 (*Pinochet No. 1*). The majority allowed the appeal (Lords Nicholls of Birkenhead, Steyn and Hoffmann; Lords Slynn of Hadley and Lloyd of Berwick dissenting).

[7] Lord Hoffmann had failed to disclose his close links with Amnesty International, an intervener in the case: *R* v. *Bow Street Metropolitan Stipendiary Magistrate and others, ex parte Pinochet Ugarte*, [1999] 1 All ER 577 ([1999] 2 WLR 272), oral judgment on 17 December 1998, reasons delivered on 15 January 1999 (*Pinochet No. 2*). See on this T. H. Jones, 'Judicial Bias and Disqualification in the Pinochet Case', *Public Law*, 1999, pp. 391–9.

[8] *R* v. *Bow Street Metropolitan Stipendiary Magistrate and others, ex parte Pinochet Ugarte* (*Amnesty International and others intervening*), [1999] 2 All ER 97 [1999] 2 WLR 827, HL delivered on 24 March 1999 (*Pinochet No. 3*). The majority allowed the appeal but did significantly reduce the number of extradition crimes (Lords Browne-Wilkinson, Hope of Craighead, Hutton, Saville of Newdigate, Millett and Phillips of Worth Matravers; Lord Goff of Chieveley dissenting).

before an English court and that he was allowed to return to Chile.[9] Although this decision was a blow in the face for the victims of the military regime in Chile it did not in any way detract from the judicial decision of the Law Lords in the *Pinochet* case. Moreover, the events in Chile following the return of the former General to his homeland indicate that the decision of the Home Secretary did not necessarily entail impunity. The August 2000 decision of the Chilean Supreme Court to lift any immunity Pinochet might have enjoyed under Chilean law has brought the possibility of conviction in Chile one important step closer.[10] This article will analyse the *Pinochet* case from an international law perspective. The focus of this analysis will primarily be on the issue of universal jurisdiction and head of State immunity with regard to the torture allegations in the final House of Lords judgment.[11]

2. Extradition Crimes: The Issue of Universal Jurisdiction over Torture

2.1. *The Court's Decision*

For a person to be extraditable under the UK Extradition Act 1989 he or she must be accused of an 'extradition crime' as defined in that Act. One of the prerequisites is the double criminality rule: the relevant act—in this case, the torture of persons in Chile—must be a crime punishable under the law of the requesting country as well as under UK law (section 2(1)(*b*) in conjunction with section 2(2), Extradition Act). This issue was not fully explored until the final House of Lords proceedings. In *Pinochet No. 3* the Lords unanimously decided that for an act to qualify as an extradition crime under the Extradition Act it is necessary that it constituted a crime under UK law at the date it was committed and not merely at the time of the extradition request.[12]

[9] On the basis of a medical report the Home Secretary decided that Pinochet would not be extradited to Spain. See on this Straw's Letter to the Spanish Ambassador, http://www.parliament.the-stationery-office.co.uk/pa/cm199900/cmhansrd/v000302/text/00302w09.htm. Straw stated that: 'The principle that an accused person should be mentally capable of following the proceedings, instructing his lawyers and giving coherent evidence is fundamental to the idea of a fair trial', ibid., para. 20.

[10] 8 August 2000. See *The Times*, 9 August 2000.

[11] The appeal before the House of Lords only concerned the second warrant. The issue of non-justiciability and the other allegations in the second warrant will be left aside.

[12] *Pinochet No. 3*, at pp. 104–7 *per* Lord Browne-Wilkinson. The issue had been raised before but had not been conclusively decided. The relevant considerations in the first two decisions contrast with the findings in *Pinochet No. 3*: Lord Bingham had held that 'the conduct alleged against the subject of the request need not in my judgment have been criminal here at the time the alleged crime was committed abroad': Divisional Court, para. 44. Lord Lloyd of Berwick, the only Lord to consider this issue in the first House of Lords judgment, endorsed that view, holding that the alleged acts must 'constitute an offence in the United Kingdom now': *Pinochet No. 1*, at p. 921.

The majority subsequently concluded that torture outside UK territory was not a crime punishable under UK law until the provisions of the Convention against Torture and Other Cruel, Inhuman or Degrading Treatment or Punishment 1984 (Torture Convention)[13] were implemented by section 134 of the Criminal Justice Act (CJA). The Torture Convention imposes a duty on State parties either to extradite or to prosecute persons alleged to have committed acts of torture when found in their territory.[14] The provisions of the Convention did not take effect in the UK until the entry into force of the CJA on 29 September 1988. Six Lords held that torture only became an extra-territorial offence against the law of the United Kingdom from that date onwards. Consequently, charges of torture and conspiracy to torture relating to conduct before that date were considered not to be extradition crimes. The majority decision on this issue left the Lords with only a handful of torture charges allegedly committed after 29 September 1988.[15]

Lord Millett wrote the only dissent. He held that the systematic use of torture on a large scale and as an instrument of State policy was an international crime attracting universal jurisdiction under customary international law by 1973. He continued:

> The jurisdiction of the English criminal courts is usually statutory, but it is supplemented by the common law. Customary international law is part of the common law, and accordingly I consider that the English courts have and always have had extra-territorial criminal jurisdiction in respect of crimes of universal jurisdiction under customary international law.[16]

He concluded therefore that all torture charges against Pinochet qualified as extradition crimes under the Extradition Act.

Some scholars have argued that the question whether the alleged acts qualified as extradition crimes should have been avoided in *Pinochet No. 3* and should rather have been decided in the subsequent extradition proceedings.[17] Moreover, it has been suggested that the analysis that conduct should have been criminal under UK law at the date of commission in order to satisfy the requirements of the double criminality

[13] 10 December 1984, *UN Treaty Series*, vol. 1465, p. 85.

[14] The *aut dedere, aut judicare* principle, Art. 5 and Art. 7 Torture Convention.

[15] See *Pinochet No. 3*, at pp. 141–5 *per* Lord Hope of Craighead, for an overview of the remaining charges.

[16] Ibid., at p. 177.

[17] e.g. H. Fox, 'The Pinochet Case No. 3', *International and Comparative Law Quarterly*, 48 (1999), p. 687, at p. 690; International Commission of Jurists, *Crimes Against Humanity, Pinochet Faces Justice* (1999), pp. 70–1; M. Cosnard, 'Quelques observations sur les décisions de la chambre des Lords du 25 novembre 1998 et du 24 mars 1999 dans l'affaire Pinochet', *Revue générale de droit international public*, 103 (1999), p. 309, at p. 324.

rule 'is contestable'.[18] More fundamentally, the majority decision on the qualification of the alleged crimes as extradition crimes under the Act has been heavily criticized because of the failure to find jurisdiction before 29 September 1988 on the basis of the universality principle.[19] The remainder of this section will assess both the minority and the majority opinion on the issue of (universal) jurisdiction over extra-territorial torture in light of relevant international law principles.

2.2. *Universal Jurisdiction: An International Law Perspective*

The principle of universal jurisdiction allows every State to exercise jurisdiction over a limited category of offences of universal concern, irrespective of the *situs* of the offence and the nationalities of the offender and the offended. The principle dates back to at least the seventeenth century, when pirates were considered to be '*hostes humani generis*', enemies of all mankind and therefore subject to universal jurisdiction.[20] After World War II several international conventions have been concluded that oblige parties to either extradite or prosecute those who commit offences prohibited by the conventions, irrespective of any direct connection between the prosecuting State and the offence. Examples are the Geneva Conventions,[21] the Hijacking Convention,[22] the Hostage Convention,[23] and the Torture Convention. It is, however, widely accepted that the permissive principle of universal jurisdiction reflected

[18] C. Warbrick, 'Extradition Law Aspects of *Pinochet 3*', *International and Comparative Law Quarterly*, 48 (1999), p. 958, at p. 964.

[19] e.g. M. Cosnard, 'Quelques observations sur les décisions de la chambre des Lords du 25 novembre 1998 et du 24 mars 1999 dans l'affaire Pinochet', *Revue générale de droit international public*, 103 (1999), p. 309, at p. 328; R. Bank, 'Der Fall Pinochet: Aufbruch zu neuen Ufern bei der Verfolgung von Menschenrechtsverletzungen?', *Zeitschrift für ausländisches öffentliches Recht und Völkerrecht*, 59 (1999), p. 677, at pp. 685–8.

[20] K. C. Randall, 'Universal Jurisdiction under International Law', *Texas Law Review*, 66 (1988), p. 785, at pp. 791–8. W. B. Cowles, 'Universality of Jurisdiction over War Crimes', *California Law Review*, 33 (1945), p. 177, at p. 189, claims that the principle dates back to the sixteenth century. It is now codified in Article 105 of the 1982 United Nations Convention on the Law of the Sea. Another offence that has been subject to universal jurisdiction from a very early stage onwards is slave trading: E. D. Dickinson, 'Is the Crime of Piracy Obsolete?', *Harvard Law Review*, 38 (1925), p. 334, at pp. 335–9.

[21] 12 August 1949: Convention for the Amelioration of the Condition of the Wounded and Sick in Armed Forces in the Field (I), *UN Treaty Series*, vol. 75, p. 31; Convention for the Amelioration of the Condition of the Wounded, Sick and Shipwrecked Members of Armed Forces at Sea (II), ibid., p. 85; Convention Relative to the Treatment of Prisoners of War (III), ibid., p. 135; Convention Relative to the Protection of Civilian Persons in Time of War (IV), ibid., p. 287.

[22] 23 September 1971, Convention for the Suppression of Unlawful Acts Against the Safety of Civil Aviation, *UN Treaty Series*, vol. 974, p. 177; 16 December 1970, Convention for the Unlawful Seizure of Aircraft, ibid., vol. 860, p. 105.

[23] 17 December 1979, International Convention Against the Taking of Hostages, *International Legal Materials*, 18 (1979), p. 1456.

in conventions that codify *jus cogens* norms is part of customary international law.[24] Customary international law is held to grant jurisdictional authority over violations of *jus cogens* norms to all States.[25]

Usually, the principle of universal jurisdiction is rationalized by reference to the egregious nature of acts that 'shake the international community to its very foundations'.[26] The principle is also often linked to the concept of crimes against international law. This concept, although crucial for the possibility of individual criminal responsibility under international law, does, however, not legitimize the principle of universal jurisdiction. It is suggested that the universality principle should now be seen as having its theoretical basis in the concept of *erga omnes* obligations. Although the International Court of Justice in the 1970 *Barcelona Traction* case focused on 'the obligations of a State towards the international community as a whole', rather than the category of norms they are derived from, it is obvious that it had the most fundamental norms of international law in mind when it held that 'all States . . . have a legal interest in their protection'.[27] The reasoning of the Court has been interpreted to imply a link between *erga omnes* obligations and *jus cogens* norms.[28] It is often maintained that *jus cogens* norms and obligations *erga omnes* are two sides of the same coin. Bassiouni put the relation as follows: 'Jus cogens refers to the legal status that certain international crimes reach, and obligations erga omnes pertains to the legal implica-

[24] F. A. Mann, 'The Doctrine of Jurisdiction in International Law', *Recueil des cours*, 111 (1964–I), p. 1, at p. 95; T. Meron, 'International Criminalization of Internal Atrocities', *American Journal of International Law*, 89 (1995), p. 554, at p. 569. Some scholars even hold universal jurisdiction to be mandatory and argue in favour of a customary duty to prosecute human rights violators: e.g. D. F. Orentlicher, 'Settling Accounts: The Duty to Prosecute Human Rights Violations of a Prior Regime', *Yale Law Journal*, 100 (1991), pp. 2537–615; M. C. Bassiouni and E. M. Wise, *Aut Dedere Aut Judicare: The Duty to Extradite or Prosecute in International Law* (1995), pp. 20–68; J. J. Paust, 'Federal Jurisdiction Over Extraterritorial Acts of Terrorism and Nonimmunity for Foreign Violators of International Law under the FSIA and the Act of State Doctrine', *Virginia Journal of International Law*, 23 (1983), p. 191, at p. 226. The exercise of universal jurisdiction is subject to normal jurisdictional requirements: compare for the US situation: *Filartiga* v. *Pena-Irala*, 630 F 2d 876 (2d Cir. 1980), at p. 890; V. A. Carter, 'God Save The King: Unconstitutional Assertions of Personal Jurisdiction over Foreign States in US Courts', *Virginia Law Review*, 82 (1996), pp. 357–84.

[25] Which does not necessarily mean that all States can exercise criminal jurisdiction, since the concept of *jus cogens* norms is not intrinsically linked with the concept of individual accountability for crimes against international law.

[26] *Attorney General of the Government of Israel* v. *Eichmann*, Supreme Court Israel 1962, 36 ILR 277, at p. 299. (See also *Attorney General of the Government of Israel* v. *Eichmann*, District Court of Jerusalem 1961, 36 ILR 18.)

[27] *Barcelona Traction Power and Light Co.* case, *ICJ Reports*, 1970, p. 3, paras. 33–34. See also *Genocide Convention* case *(Preliminary Objections)*, *ICJ Reports*, 1969, p. 616. The ICTY has held that 'the violation of [an *erga omnes*] obligation . . . constitutes a breach of the correlative right of all members of the international community . . . ': *Prosecutor* v. *Furundžija* (ICTY 1998), Case No. IT–95–17/1, T.Ch.II, para. 151.

[28] A. de Hoogh, *Obligations Erga Omnes and International Crimes, A Theoretical Inquiry into the Implementation and Enforcement of the International Responsibility of States* (1996), p. 55 and the literature under n. 245.

tions arising out of a certain crime's characterization as jus cogens . . .'.[29] Some scholars, however, assert that *erga omnes* rules could exist which are not of a *jus cogens* character.[30] For present purposes it suffices to conclude that *jus cogens* norms necessarily apply *erga omnes* and that all States have a legal interest in their protection. The principle of universal jurisdiction can be said to follow from this legal interest in the protection of *jus cogens* norms.[31]

Although controversy exists as to exactly which norms qualify as *jus cogens*, it is widely accepted that the prohibition of torture has acquired the status of a *jus cogens* norm[32] and that universal jurisdiction arises when this norm is violated. Universal criminal jurisdiction under customary international law can be said to arise when acts of torture moreover amount to a crime against international law. The Torture Convention codified this rule and imposed the duty of *aut dedere aut judicare* on the States party to it. Although Burgers and Danelius explain that 'the principal aim of the Convention is to *strengthen* the existing prohibition of [torture] by a number of supportive measures',[33] the Convention did establish mandatory universal jurisdiction over single, isolated, acts of torture although such acts are not thought to qualify as crimes against international law.[34] Finally, it is important to realize that the Convention is limited to torture committed by public officials.[35]

[29] M. C. Bassiouni, 'International Crimes: Jus Cogens and Obligatio Erga Omnes', *Law and Contemporary Problems*, 25 (1996), p. 63, at p. 68. See also B. Simma, 'Bilateralism and Community Interest in the Law of State Responsibility', in Y. Dinstein (ed.), *International Law at a Time of Perplexity: Essays in Honour of Shabtai Rosenne* (1989), p. 821, at p. 825.

[30] T. Meron, *Human Rights Law-Making in the United Nations* (1987), p. 187; M. Byers, 'Conceptualising the Relationship between Jus Cogens and Erga Omnes Rules', *Nordic Journal of International Law*, 66 (1997); p. 211, at p. 237.

[31] Of course, the relationship between these concepts is actually more complex than this. Moreover, it should be noted that universal jurisdiction over piracy was also based on more practical considerations since this crime is by definition committed on the high seas and thereby outside the territorial jurisdiction of any State.

[32] e.g. *Prosecutor* v. *Furundžija* (ICTY 1998), Case No. IT–95–17/1, T.Ch.II, para. 153, where the tribunal held that '[b]ecause of the importance of the values it protects, [the prohibition of torture] has evolved into a peremptory norm or jus cogens.'

[33] J. H. Burgers and H. Danelius, *The United Nations Convention against Torture: A Handbook on the Convention against Torture and Other Cruel, Inhuman or Degrading Treatment or Punishment* (1988), p. 1.

[34] With the, somewhat ironic, qualification that a single act of torture during armed conflict would violate the laws of war and common Article 3 of the Geneva Conventions, in which case it would amount to a crime against international law. An isolated act of torture does violate the *jus cogens* prohibition of torture. Universal jurisdiction over such acts has occasionally been exercised in civil suits, compare *Filartiga* v. *Pena-Irala,* 630 F 2d 876 (2d Cir. 1980).

[35] More precisely, the qualification of the perpetrator as 'public official or other person acting in an official capacity' is one of the constitutive elements of the definition of torture under the Convention (Art. 1). See on this, J. H. Burgers and H. Danelius, *The United Nations Convention against Torture: A Handbook on the Convention against Torture and Other Cruel, Inhuman or Degrading Treatment or Punishment* (1988), pp. 45–6 and p. 120. It is unclear whether this limitation is inherent in the definition of torture under customary international law as well. Although the ICTY Statute does not explicitly include this element, the ICTY has held that the definition of torture in the Torture Convention is now part of customary international law, e.g. *Čelebići* (ICTY 1998), Case No. IT–96–21, T.Ch.II, paras. 452–9. The Tribunal did however hold that '[i]n the

Hence, acts of torture committed by persons acting in a purely individual capacity are not subject to the duty to prosecute under the Convention.

2.3. *Universal Jurisdiction: Lord Millett's Conclusion on its Reception in UK Law*

Lord Millett argued that since 'customary international law is part of the common law', and since the systematic use of torture on a large scale attracted universal jurisdiction under customary international law by 1973, English courts already had jurisdiction over acts of torture committed outside UK territory before the codification of the jurisdictional provision of the Torture Convention. Oppenheim formulates the famous maxim on which Lord Millett based his conclusion as follows: 'As regards the United Kingdom all rules of customary international law as are either universally recognised or have at any rate received the assent of this country are *per se* the law of the land. To that extent there is still valid in England the common law doctrine, to which Blackstone gave expression in a striking passage, that the law of nations is part of the law of the land. It has been repeatedly acted upon by the courts and can be regarded as an established rule of English law.'[36] Higgins adds to this: 'There have in the past occasionally been suggestions that . . . general international law requires some form of incorporation before it has effect in English law. But this is clearly wrong . . . '.[37]

On the face of it, Lord Millett's approach thus seems sensible. Several commentators have endorsed this approach and criticized the majority for refusing to find a basis for jurisdiction before 1988.[38] Cosnard, for example, states that 'Le principe de double incrimination doit donc être interprété et appliqué à la lumière des règles coutumières du droit international pénal. . . . Nous ne pouvons que constater, et déplorer, que les principes coutumiers du droit international pénal ont été écartés, voire ignorés, au profit de l'application de la loi anglaise, consacrant ainsi

context of international humanitarian law, this requirement must be interpreted to include officials of non-State parties to the conflict': ibid., para. 473. In the ICC Statute and the Report of the Preparatory Commission for the International Criminal Court on the Elements of Crimes (PCNICC/2000/INF/3/Add.2) there is again no mention of the status-requirement.

[36] R. Jennings and A. Watts (eds.), *Oppenheim's International Law*, vol. 1 (9th edn., 1992), pp. 56–7.

[37] R. Higgins, 'The Role of Domestic Courts in the Enforcement of International Human Rights: The United Kingdom', in B. Conforti and F. Francioni (eds.), *Enforcing International Human Rights in Domestic Courts* (1997), p. 37, at p. 51

[38] e.g. M. Cosnard, 'Quelques observations sur les décisions de la chambre des Lords du 25 Novembre 1998 et du 24 Mars 1999 dans l'Affaire Pinochet', *Revue générale de droit international public*, 103 (1999), p. 309, at pp. 325–8; R. Bank, 'Der Fall Pinochet: Aufbruch zu neuen Ufern bei der Verfolgung von Menschenrechtsverletzungen?', *Zeitschrift für ausländisches öffentliches Recht und Völkerrecht*, 59 (1999) , p. 677, at pp. 685–8.

une primauté du droit interne par rapport au droit international.'[39] He argues that the only relevant date for the double criminality rule 'est donc celle de l'apparition de la qualification, en droit international, d'un acte comme criminel'.[40] In this article, however, it is argued that the majority approach—although poorly articulated—is to be preferred. Two arguments—one factual and one theoretical—warrant this conclusion.

2.4. *Universal Jurisdiction: In Defence of the Majority Conclusion*

First, it is important to note that it is not unusual for domestic courts to refuse to exercise universal jurisdiction over crimes against international law without national legislation to that effect. Of the many examples available in State practice, only a few need be recalled here.

In Switzerland universal jurisdiction over violations of the Geneva Conventions is codified in the Military Penal Code.[41] Moreover, Article 6*bis* of the Penal Code provides for universal jurisdiction over extraterritorial crimes which Switzerland is obliged to prosecute under a treaty. In April 1999 a Swiss military tribunal convicted a Rwandan national suspected of committing serious crimes during the 1994 Rwandan genocide, for murder, attempted murder, incitement to murder, and war crimes. The tribunal refused, however, to consider the charges of genocide and crimes against humanity because it could not find a basis for jurisdiction in Swiss law.[42] Thus, without such a basis the possible existence of universal jurisdiction over these crimes under customary international law was irrelevant.

The Dutch Supreme Court decided in the 1997 *Darko Knezevic* case that the Dutch War Crimes Act[43] did provide a basis for the exercise of universal jurisdiction.[44] The decision proceeded from the proposition that if the Act could not be interpreted as providing a jurisdictional basis, Dutch courts would have no jurisdiction to try war criminals from the former Yugoslavia, Rwanda, or any other foreign war zone.

In France, the legislator has recently enacted legislation enabling the prosecution of Yugoslav and Rwandan war criminals before French courts.[45] The immediate cause of this legislation was the establishment of

[39] Cosnard, loc. cit. above (n. 38), at p. 328.

[40] Ibid., at p. 326.

[41] Arts. 108 ff., Code Pénal Militaire.

[42] Tribunal Militaire de Division 2 (Lausanne), 30 April 1999, *Fulgence Niyonteze.*

[43] Wet Oorlogsstrafrecht, 10 July 1952, Stb. 408.

[44] Hoge Raad der Nederlanden 11 November 1997, *Nederlandse Jurisprudentie,* 1998, nr. 463. Reproduced in *Yearbook of International Humanitarian Law,* 1 (1998), p. 604.

[45] Loi no. 95–1 of 2 January 1995, *Journal officiel,* 3 January 1995; Loi no. 96–432 of 22 May 1996, *Journal officiel,* 23 May 1996.

the International Criminal Tribunal for the Former Yugoslavia (ICTY) and the International Criminal Tribunal for Rwanda (ICTR) by the United Nations Security Council.[46] Before this legislation was enacted, however, French courts were confronted with the quandary of finding jurisdiction in a few cases initiated by Bosnian and Rwandan refugees in France. In 1993 Bosnian victims of gross human rights violations in the former Yugoslavia filed a criminal complaint against X, the alleged perpetrator, in a French court. X was accused of torture, war crimes, crimes against humanity and genocide, based on several international documents providing for universal jurisdiction over these crimes. French statute law only provided for universal jurisdiction when France has ratified a convention that contains a self-executing provision on universal jurisdiction (Article 689 Code de procédure pénale) or in case of exhaustively numerated conventions (Articles 689–2 to 7). Jurisdiction could therefore only be based on Article 689–2 that implements the jurisdictional provision of the 1984 Torture Convention.[47] The court refused to consider the possibility of universal jurisdiction over crimes against humanity under customary international law. This was reaffirmed in a 1996 decision. Rwandan refugees of Tutsi origin, victims of the 1994 genocide in Rwanda, had filed a complaint against a Rwandan Hutu priest residing in France.[48] When this case finally came before the Cour de Cassation in 1998, the new legislation was in force, which *ipso facto* resolved the question of jurisdiction.[49]

The position of French courts with regard to the requirement of a domestic basis for the exercise of universal jurisdiction was—implicitly—at the basis of the French extradition request in the *Pinochet* case. Before the French Government could request extradition, the Tribunal de Grande Instance of Paris had to decide whether French courts could exercise jurisdiction over the acts alleged in the request. The earlier finding that there is no universal jurisdiction for crimes against humanity in the French legal system and the requirement that for the exercise of such jurisdiction in cases of torture, the accused be present in France,[50] forced the Tribunal to rely on the passive personality principle.[51] Hence,

[46] Resolution 827 (1993) and Resolution 955 (1994). See B. Stern, 'La competence universelle en France: le cas des crimes commis en ex-Yougoslavie et au Rwanda', *German Yearbook of International Law*, 40 (1997), p. 280, at pp. 296–9.

[47] *Affaire Javor et autres*: Tribunal de Grande Instance de Paris, 6 May 1994; Cour d'appel de Paris, 24 October 1994; Cour de Cassation, 26 March 1994.

[48] The Tribunal de Grande Instance de Paris, *Dupaquier, Kalinda et autres* v. *Wenceslas Munyeshyaka*, 9 January 1996.

[49] Cour de Cassation, 6 January 1998.

[50] Article 689–1, Code de procédure pénale.

[51] B. Stern, '*In re* Pinochet, French Tribunal de Grande Instance', *American Journal of International Law*, 93 (1999), p. 696, at p. 697.

the French extradition request was based on crimes allegedly committed by Pinochet against French victims only.[52]

In this respect, it is interesting to note the decision of the Belgian court involved in the Belgian request for extradition of General Pinochet. The court in that case did not feel restrained by the limited domestic basis of jurisdiction available.[53] Although at the time the Belgian law only provided universal jurisdiction over war crimes committed in international and non-international armed conflicts,[54] it was explicitly held that the extradition request could be based on universal jurisdiction over crimes against humanity under customary international law. The court reasoned as follows:

> . . . we find that, before being codified in a treaty or statute, the prohibition on crimes against humanity was part of customary international law and of international *jus cogens*, and this norm imposes itself imperatively and *erga omnes* on our domestic legal order. . . . Customary international law is equivalent to conventional international law and is directly applicable in the Belgian legal order. . . . Hence, it follows that even in the absence of a treaty, national authorities have the right—and in some circumstances the obligation—to prosecute the perpetrators independently of where they hide. . . . For these reasons we find that, as a matter of customary international law, or even more strongly, as a matter of *jus cogens*, universal jurisdiction over crimes against humanity exists, authorizing national judicial authorities to prosecute and punish the perpetrators in all circumstances.[55]

In many ways, this Belgian decision seems the exception that proves the rule. In general, domestic courts require an explicit basis in a domestic statute for the exercise of universal criminal jurisdiction.

More important even—and this is the second argument—is the rationale vindicating this accepted State practice. In the administration of criminal justice, some basic principles—common to criminal law systems all over the world—should always be complied with. One of the most important principles of criminal law is the legality principle, expressed in the maxim *nullum crimen, nulla poena sine lege*; no crime, no

[52] The Spanish decision on whether or not Spanish courts would have jurisdiction to try Pinochet is quite obviously influenced by similar jurisdictional concerns. See M. del Carmen Márquez Carrasco and J. Alcaide Fernández, '*In re* Pinochet, Spanish National Court', *American Journal of International Law*, 93 (1999), p. 690, at pp. 694–6.

[53] Tribunal de Première Instance de Bruxelles, (Investigating Magistrate Vandermeersch), 8 November 1998.

[54] Loi relative à la répression des infractions graves aux Conventions internationales de Genève du 12 août 1949 et aux Protocols I and II du 8 juin 1977, additionnels à ces Conventions, 16 June 1993, *Moniteur Belge*, 5 August 1993. In 1999 this law was amended to enable courts to exercise jurisdiction over perpetrators of genocide and crimes against humanity, as defined in the Statute of the ICC: Loi relative à la répression des violations graves de droit international humanitaire, 10 February 1999, *Moniteur Belge*, 23 March 1999, reproduced in *International Legal Materials*, 38 (1999), p. 918.

[55] Translated by L. Reydams, '*In re* Pinochet, Belgian Tribunal of First Instance of Brussels', *American Journal of International Law*, 93 (1999), p. 700, at pp. 702–3.

punishment without law.[56] Some authors have argued that in international criminal law:

> perfect justice, totally detached and objective, and fulfilling all requirements of legality is unachievable; to leave these crimes, the gravest and most heinous crimes, unpunished is such a grave injustice that it fully justifies the imperfect justice which is attainable.[57]

As a basic assumption, that proposition is rejected here. The rights of the accused are central to the concept of justice. It is asserted that the legality principle applies even to the most serious crimes, 'reaffirming the very sense of "humanity" which those crimes damaged'.[58]

Although it falls outside the scope of this article to discuss the many aspects of this principle or its exact contours, it is important to consider certain aspects of its application in the field of international criminal law. The legality principle in fact comprises several, interrelated, principles: the non-retroactivity principle, the *lex certa* principle, and the prohibition of establishing new criminal offences on the basis of analogy. Much has been written on the application of these three elements of the legality principle in international criminal law. The prohibition of analogy does not have any bearing on the topic involved and will not be discussed further. It is important, however, briefly to set out the prevailing discussion on the non-retroactivity principle and the *lex certa* principle in international criminal law, in order sharply to distinguish those discussions from the question under consideration.

The prohibition of retroactive criminalization in international criminal law has been the subject of ample debate since the Nuremberg Trials in 1945. Many scholars argued that individual criminal responsibility for crimes against international law did not exist before the enactment of the Nuremberg Charter[59] and that the prosecution of war criminals on this basis violated the non-retroactivity principle.[60] Whatever the merit of

[56] e.g. M. Catenacci, 'Nullum Crimen Sine Lege', in F. Lattanzi (ed.), *The International Criminal Court, Comments on the Draft Statute* (1998), p. 159, at p. 159. This maxim was introduced by P. J. A. von Feuerbach, *Lehrbuch des gemeinen in Deutschland gültigen peinlichen Rechts* (1801), paras. 12 ff. The principle is laid down in several international documents, e.g. Article 11(2), Universal Declaration of Human Rights; Article 7, European Convention of Human Rights (ECHR); Article 15, International Covenant of Civil and Political Rights; Article 7(2), African Charter of Human and People Rights.

[57] M. Kremnitzer, 'The World Community as an International Legislator in Competition with National Legislators', in A. Eser and O. Lagodny (eds.), *Principles and Procedures for a New Transnational Criminal Law* (1992), p. 337, at p. 341.

[58] M. Catenacci, 'Nullum Crimen Sine Lege', in F. Lattanzi (ed.), *The International Criminal Court, Comments on the Draft Statute* (1998), p. 159, at p. 161.

[59] 8 August 1945, *UN Treaty Series*, vol. 82, p. 279.

[60] e.g. S. R. Ratner and J. S. Abrams, *Accountability for Human Rights Atrocities in International Law: Beyond the Nuremberg Legacy* (1997), p. 20; G. A. Finch, 'The Nuremberg Trial and International Law', *American Journal of International Law*, 41 (1947), pp. 20–37; F. B. Schick, 'The Nuremberg Trial and the International Law of the Future', *American Journal of International Law*, 41 (1947), pp. 770–94; H. Kelsen, 'Will the Judgment in the Nuremberg Trial Constitute a Precedent in International Law?', *International Law Quarterly*, 1 (1947), pp. 153–71.

this argument, since then the concept of individual criminal responsibility under international law has been firmly established.[61] In this respect, it is widely acknowledged that legislation in this field—e.g. the statutes for the ICTY and ICTR or domestic criminal statutes—authorizing prosecution for conduct that precedes the legislation does not violate the non-retroactivity principle provided that the conduct involved constituted a crime under international law or was criminal according to the general principles of law recognized by the community of nations.[62] Admittedly, the UK legislator could have given section 134 CJA retroactive force without violating the *nullum crimen* principle. But that is not what was at issue in *Pinochet No. 3*. The question was not whether legislation prohibiting extra-territorial torture could be applied retroactively and whether courts at present have jurisdiction to prosecute acts of extra-territorial torture committed before 1988. Rather the question was whether courts before 1988 had jurisdiction to do so without any legislation to that effect. The decision is confined to a determination of a situation in the past.[63]

The *lex certa* requirement proscribes vague definitions of crimes and compels legislators to draft criminal legislation in as clear and detailed terms as possible. Commentators have argued that the definitions of crimes in the Statutes of the ICTY and ICTR are too vague and hence that the *nullum crimen* principle is violated. It is moreover noted that many domestic statutes also incorporate international criminal law by reference to rather vague notions such as 'crimes against humanity' and 'war crimes'.[64] This issue must, again, be sharply distinguished from *Pinochet No. 3* although the discussion is relevant in one respect: if the vagueness of definitions in criminal statutes is reason for concern, surely this applies *a fortiori* to the absence of any criminal statute whatever?

The issue under consideration does concern the *lex certa* principle, but on a fundamentally different level. Does international criminal law in its present, unwritten, form satisfy the requirements flowing from this

[61] e.g. GA Res. 177 (II), 21 November 1947; 1950 ILC Report on the Formulation of the Nürnberg Principles, UN Doc. A/1316 (A/5/12) (1950); 1954 ILC Draft Code of Offences against the Peace and Security of Mankind, UN Doc. A/2693 (A/9/9) (1954), as revised by the 1996 ILC Draft Code of Crimes against the Peace and Security of Mankind, UN Doc. A/51/10. The establishment of the ICTY, ICTR and ICC are recent manifestations of this theory in practice.

[62] Compare Report of the Secretary-General pursuant to paragraph 2 of Security Council Resolution 808 (1993), UN Doc. S/25704 (3 May 1993), paras. 33–4; J.M. Wagner, 'U.S. Prosecution of Past and Future War Criminals and Criminals Against Humanity: Proposals for Reform Based on the Canadian and Australian Experience', *Virginia Journal of International Law*, 29 (1989), p. 887, at pp. 921–2 and 930–1; *Extradition of Demjanjuk*, 612 F Supp. 544 (DC Ohio 1985), at p. 567; *Demjanjuk* v. *Petrovsky*, 776 F 2d 571 (6th Cir. 1985), at pp. 581–3. See also Art. 7(2), ECHR.

[63] Hence, even if the UK legislator had given retrospective force to section 134 CJA this would not have made a difference to the facts of this case.

[64] See J. J. Paust, 'Nullum Crimen and Related Claims', *Denver Journal of International Law and Policy*, 25 (1997), pp. 321–32; J. J. Paust 'It's no Defense: Nullum Crimen, International Crime and the Gingerbread Man', *Albany Law Review*, 60 (1997), p. 657, at pp. 671–9, for examples in domestic statutes.

principle? Civil law countries have traditionally held the *lex certa* principle to imply a *lex scripta* requirement. Accordingly, it is agreed that no one can be punished without a written law to that effect. Common law countries have extensively relied on unwritten law, including in the administration of criminal justice. There are still in many common law countries purely common law crimes.[65] Over the past few decades, however, the call for the codification of crimes and for an enhanced legality of the criminal law in the common law system has grown stronger. After the enactment of the Model Penal Code in the US, most States have renounced the concept of common law crimes.[66] In the UK the concept has yielded to a growing body of criminal statute law, although there is still no comprehensive statute.[67] It is accepted that unwritten criminal law does not necessarily violate the legality principle, although indisputably, the codification of crimes does further the legality principle and therewith enhances the legitimacy of a criminal law system.[68] It is, however, asserted that customary international criminal law, at its present stage of development, cannot possibly satisfy the minimum requirements of the legality principle.

In the first place, there is no general agreement as to which norms actually qualify as crimes against international law.[69] Moreover, there are no uniform and accepted definitions of the individual crimes against international law.[70] Apart from these deficiencies in the scope and definition of the material norms, it should be realized that criminal law entails more than norm setting. It should normally also contain jurisdictional provisions and provisions on time limits, statutory limitations, and other information important to a suspect in order to determine his legal

[65] See examples: J. R. Spencer, 'Nulla Poena sine Lege in English Criminal Law', in B. S. Markesinis and J. H. M. Willems (eds.), *The Cambridge-Tilburg Law Lectures*, Third Series 1980 (1983), pp. 33–57.

[66] See *Model Penal Code and Commentaries* (1985), para. 1.05, 75 ff. for an enumeration of States that have not denounced common law crimes. Compare M. Conant, 'Federal Common-Law Crimes and Non-Statutory Crimes against the Law of Nations', *Anglo-American Law Review*, 24 (1995), pp. 456–92.

[67] J. Smith and B. Hogan, *Criminal Law: Cases and Materials* (6th edn., 1996), pp. 1–2.

[68] Compare A. Ashworth, *Principles of Criminal Law* (1991), pp. 64–6. It should be noted that the European Court of Human Rights has held with regard to the word 'law' in Article 10(2), ECHR, that it means 'not only statute but also unwritten law'. It is generally accepted that the word 'law' in the different provisions of the Convention should be interpreted consistently. With regard to Article 7, ECHR, the Court has held that this 'cannot be read as outlawing the gradual clarification of the rules of criminal liability through judicial interpretation from case to case, provided that the resultant development is consistent with the essence of the offence and could reasonably be foreseen': European Court of Human Rights, 22 November 1995, *CR* v. *The United Kingdom*, Series A, No. 335–C. However, this latter consideration does not relate to a common law crime but rather to the flexibility of interpretation of a statutory crime.

[69] e.g. M. C. Bassiouni, *Crimes Against Humanity in International Criminal Law* (2nd edn., 1999), pp. 282–369.

[70] Although it is widely expected that the definitions used in the Statute of the ICC may develop to become authoritative. Compare, e.g. the Belgian Loi relative à la répression des infractions graves de droit international humanitaire, 10 February 1999, *Moniteur Belge*, 23 March 1999, reproduced in *International Legal Materials*, 38 (1999), p. 918.

position like the (maximum) punishment available for the alleged crime and provisions on liability and defence.

In this respect, it is noted that the jurisdiction of the ICTY and the ICTR is strictly limited to the crimes enumerated in the ICTY Statute and the ICTR Statute.[71] Also the 1996 Report of the Preparatory Committee of the Establishment of an International Criminal Court (PrepCom) does not leave room for doubt on this point.[72] The PrepCom indicated that the Court's jurisdiction would be limited to 'the most serious crimes of concern to the international community as a whole'.[73] It was stated that:

> the crimes within the jurisdiction of the Court should be defined with the clarity, precision and specificity required for criminal law in accordance with the principle of legality . . . The definition of war crimes should clearly indicate in what circumstances, by which perpetrators and against which victims certain acts would constitute such crimes.[74]

Hence, customary international law was not considered to give sufficient guidance with respect to the definition of the crimes and, crucially, the ICC does not have jurisdiction over crimes not covered by the Statute even though customary international law may recognize universal jurisdiction in respect of these crimes. It was also noted that 'the principle of legality . . . required that penalties be defined . . . as precisely as possible'.[75] Moreover:

> there was broad agreement that the fundamental principles of criminal law to be applied to the crimes punishable under the Statute should be clearly laid down in the Statute in accordance with the principle of legality. . . . It was noted that conventions defining international crimes provided only one aspect of the substantive criminal law; they usually did not contain principles of liability and defence and other general rules of criminal law to be used to apply the definitions of crimes. It was considered important, therefore, that all general elements of crimes and the basic principles of liability and defence should be elaborated . . . and laid down in the Statute . . . The articulation of fundamental principles of criminal law in the Statute . . . would ensure predictability and certainty in the application of law, which would be essential for the protection of the rights of the accused.[76]

[71] Confirmed in *Prosecutor* v. *Tadić* (ICTY 1998), Case No. IT–94–1, T.Ch.II, para. 558.

[72] Report of the Preparatory Committee on the Establishment of an International Criminal Court, Volume I (Proceedings of the Preparatory Committee during March-April 1996), *General Assembly Official Records*, 51st Session, Supplement Nr. 22 (A/51/22) 1996.

[73] Ibid., para. 51.

[74] Ibid., paras. 52–3.

[75] Ibid., para. 303.

[76] Ibid., paras. 180–1.

These considerations apply with equal force to the prosecution of individuals for crimes against international law before domestic courts. There is, as yet, no such thing as a comprehensive, fully-fledged system of international criminal law under customary international law. Customary international criminal law does not in any way satisfy the minimum requirements of the legality principle.

It is important to realize that the majority decision in *Pinochet No. 3* did not deny that the prohibition of torture was part of the common law before 1988. It was moreover not denied that torture qualified as a crime against international law entailing universal jurisdiction before that date. However, where Lord Millett derived from these propositions jurisdiction of the English criminal courts under the common law, the majority decision did not consider this to be sufficient to find criminal jurisdiction under UK law.

In light of the legality considerations outlined above, Lord Millett is too enthusiastic in applying the theory of incorporation of customary international law in the common law. The concept of crime under international law cannot in this way be transposed into the domestic criminal law system. Moreover, even if international criminal law should develop into a system satisfying the requirements flowing from the legality principle, a basis for the exercise of jurisdiction would still be lacking. The principle of universal jurisdiction under customary international law over certain crimes cannot itself form the basis for the exercise of such jurisdiction but is rather an authorization of the formulation of a jurisdictional basis. In this respect the principle of universal jurisdiction is not different from, for example, the passive personality principle of jurisdiction. As explained above, universal jurisdiction under customary international law is a permissive, not a mandatory principle. Hence, States can always choose not to have certain crimes against international law prosecuted before their courts. In order not to violate the *lex certa* requirement encompassed in the legality principle it needs to be clear that a State has made use of the jurisdictional authority granted to it under international law.

Jurisdictional principles crucially distinguish themselves from other rules of international law. The theory of reception of international law as relied upon by Lord Millett does not mean that the relevant authority is automatically transposed into a jurisdictional basis. A clear act of acceptance of that authority is required. A reference to conventional international criminal law is instructive here. It is even doubtful whether the jurisdictional provisions in international conventions satisfy the requirements for such a basis for jurisdiction. A French court has held, for example, that the provision on universal jurisdiction in the Geneva Conventions was not self-executing because: '. . . ces dispositions revêtent un caractère trop général pour créer directement des règles de compétence en matière pénale . . . '.[77] It is suggested that Lord Millett has confused the possibility of the formulation of universal jurisdiction over torture by a legislator—a principle of customary international law which admittedly directly influences the reach of the jurisdictional powers of the UK legislator—with a clear basis for jurisdiction for the courts as required in criminal procedure.

Apart from the precedents cited above, Lord Millett could have found support for the majority opinion closer to home in the 1876 decision of a UK court in *R* v. *Keyn*.[78] This case, although not concerned with universal jurisdiction, can be seen to lend support to the existence of a distinction between the authority of a court to exercise criminal jurisdiction in a specific case without explicit legislation to that effect and the jurisdiction of Parliament, according to international law, to enact a statute to cover the facts of that specific case.[79]

Many commentators have criticized the majority decision for requiring a conventional basis before universal jurisdiction can be exercised.[80] This is, however, a misreading of the decision. The majority opinion seems to be confined to the view that a statutory basis is required before UK courts can exercise universal jurisdiction.[81] This proclaimed necessity of national legislation is not synonymous with the necessity of a treaty. The French statutes granting jurisdiction for the prosecution of war criminals responsible for the genocide in the former Yugoslavia and Rwanda, which are based on customary law rather than treaty law, confirm that.[82]

It has been asserted that 'the universality principle remains underutilized in the struggle to eliminate the most heinous crimes of the modern world'[83] and that 'the international community is in need of more

[77] *Javor et autres*, Cour d'appel de Paris, 24 October 1994. See for a different view B. Stern, 'La compétence universelle en France: le cas des crimes commis en ex-Yougoslavie et au Rwanda', *German Yearbook of International Law*, 40 (1997), p. 280, at pp. 285–6; B. Stern, 'Universal Jurisdiction over Crimes Against Humanity under French Law—Grave Breaches of the Geneva Conventions of 1949—Genocide—Torture—Human Rights Violations in Bosnia and Rwanda', *American Journal of International Law*, 93 (1999), p. 525, at p. 529.

[78] (1876) 2 Ex. D 63.

[79] See J. Crawford, 'The Contribution of Professor D. P. O'Connell to the Discipline of International Law', this *Year Book*, 51 (1980), p. 1, at pp. 48–61, for an overview of the facts and the legal doctrine pertaining to this case.

[80] e.g. R. Wedgwood, 'International Criminal Law and Augusto Pinochet', *Virginia Journal of International Law*, 40 (2000), p. 829, at p. 841; J. Horowitz, 'Regina v. Bartle and the Commissioner of Police for the Metropolis and Others Ex Parte Pinochet: Universal Jurisdiction and Sovereign Immunity for Jus Cogens Violations', *Fordham International Law Journal*, 23 (1999), p. 489, at pp. 525–6.

[81] *Pinochet No. 3*, at pp. 142–3.

[82] Loi no. 95–1, 2 janvier 1995, published in *Journal officiel*, 3 janvier 1995; Loi no. 96–432, 22 mai 1996, published in *Journal officiel*, 23 mai 1995. The French Cour de Cassation has confirmed this universal jurisdiction over crimes of genocide in *Dupaquier et autres* v. *Wenceslas Munyeshyaka*, 6 January 1998, still emphasizing 'la necessaité d'un "filtre de la loi" française'.

[83] K. C. Randall, 'Universal Jurisdiction under International Law', *Texas Law Review*, 66 (1988), p. 785, at p. 791.

aggressive utilization of universal jurisdiction'.[84] This may be true. However, utilization of the authority granted by the principle of universal jurisdiction requires the formulation of an explicit basis of universal jurisdiction and fulfilment of the other demands of the legality principle as outlined above. Therefore, the majority conclusion that UK courts could not exercise criminal jurisdiction over acts of extra-territorial torture before section 134 of the CJA was enacted is in line with international practice and legal theory and is to be preferred.[85] Admittedly, the majority opinions on this point are underdeveloped. The conclusion would have benefited from the drawing of a distinction between jurisdictional principles as formulated by international law and jurisdictional bases as required for the exercise of domestic criminal jurisdiction. Although the existence of the principle of universal jurisdiction under customary international law was not denied, the failure to elucidate the issues involved did cast doubt on the concept.

3. The Immunity Issue

3.1. *Introduction*

The *Pinochet* case can be said to epitomize the tension between two areas of international law: State immunity on the one hand and human rights law on the other. The principal question in the proceedings before the Divisional Court as well as before both the Appellate Committees of the House of Lords was whether Pinochet could invoke the concept of ex-head of State immunity as a shield against the torture allegations. Before the decisions of the respective courts on the immunity question are analysed, something should first be said about two preliminary issues: first, the theory of head of State immunity, and secondly, State practice with regard to immunity for human rights violations.

3.2. *Head of State Immunity*

Historically, the immunity of the State and that of the head of State were considered indistinguishable since the State and its ruler were considered to be one:[86] in the words of Louis XIV, 'L'Etat, c'est moi'. Today, two distinct concepts exist. On the one hand heads of State in

[84] B. Stern, 'Universal Jurisdiction over Crimes Against Humanity under French Law—Grave Breaches of the Geneva Conventions of 1949—Genocide—Torture—Human Rights Violations in Bosnia and Rwanda', *American Journal of International Law*, 93 (1999), p. 525, at p. 529.

[85] With the qualification that the premiss it proceeded from may be contested, see nn. 12 and 18 above.

[86] J. L. Mallory, 'Resolving the Confusion over Head of State Immunity: The Defined Rights of Kings', *Columbia Law Review*, 86 (1986), p. 169, at p. 170; K. Highet *et al.*, 'Lafontant v. Aristide', *American Journal of International Law*, 88 (1994), p. 528, at pp. 529–30.

office are granted at least the same immunity that the State itself would be entitled to, since they can be considered to be the personal manifestation of the State they represent.[87] It is now generally accepted that international law does not require an absolute immunity to be granted to States. The theory of restrictive immunity prevails. State immunity is often held to be an immunity *ratione materiae*, dependent on the subject-matter of the act involved. Although there is no uniform State practice on the question which acts still attract immunity and which acts do not, a very general distinction is usually made between public, sovereign acts—*acta jure imperii*—and private acts—*acta jure gestionis*—to distinguish between immune and non-immune acts.[88] However, heads of State are often accorded a form of diplomatic immunity *ratione personae* as well, conferring a wider immunity on heads of State than on the State itself. It has been held that 'State practice casts an uneven light' on the law of head of State immunity and the rule has been held to be 'unsettled',[89] 'uncertain',[90] 'problematic and ambiguous',[91] and 'lacking coherence'.[92] One US commentator held head of State immunity to be 'at best [an] amorphous legal doctrine whose very existence is not entirely settled in U.S. law and whose reach is almost completely uncertain'.[93]

There is consensus that heads of State are entitled to immunity in respect of their sovereign acts, exercised under their public authority. This rule can be traced back to the case of *Duke of Brunswick* v. *King of Hanover*,[94] and has been consistently applied since.[95] There also seems to

[87] A. Watts, 'The Legal Position in International Law of Heads of State, Heads of Government and Foreign Ministers', *Recueil des cours*, 247 (1994–III), p. 13, at p. 36.

[88] Apart from the fact that there is no consensus on which acts qualify as public and which acts qualify as private, this theory suffers from oversimplification. Exceptions to immunity are made that cannot be explained by this distinction, like the exception many States recognize for torts committed within the territory of the forum State causing death or personal injury or the US exception for acts of expropriation. See on this J. Crawford, 'International Law and Foreign Sovereigns: Distinguishing Immune Transactions', this *Year Book*, 54 (1983), pp. 75–118.

[89] A. Watts, 'The Legal Position in International Law of Heads of State, Heads of Government and Foreign Ministers', *Recueil des cours*, 247 (1994–III), p. 13, at p. 52.

[90] R. Jennings and A. Watts (eds.), *Oppenheim's International Law*, vol. 1 (9th edn., 1992), p. 1041.

[91] J. L. Mallory, 'Resolving the Confusion over Head of State Immunity: The Defined Rights of Kings', *Columbia Law Review*, 86 (1986), p. 169, at p. 171.

[92] P. E. Bass, 'Ex-Head of State Immunity: A Proposed Statutory Tool of Foreign Policy', *Yale Law Journal*, 97 (1987), p. 299, at p. 303.

[93] K. Highet *et al.*, 'Lafontant v. Aristide', *American Journal of International Law*, 88 (1994), p. 528, at p. 531. Compare *In re Grand Jury Proceedings*, 817 F 2d 1108 (4th Cir. 1987), at p. 1110; *Doe* v. *United States*, 860 F 2d 40 (2d Cir. 1988), at p. 44.

[94] (1848) 2 HLC 1.

[95] For example *De Haber* v. *The Queen of Portugal* (1851) 17 QB 171; *Ministère Public* v. *Dlle Masset* (1870), in A.-C. Kiss, *Répertoire de la pratique française en matière de droit international public*, vol. 3 (1965), pp. 269–70; *L'Empereur d'Autriche* v. *Lemaître* (1872), ibid., p. 269; *Bey of Tunis* v. *Mahmoud Ben Aïad* (1893), ibid., p. 272; *Ben Aïad* v. *Bey of Tunis* (1914), ibid., p. 271.

be a certain level of consensus that heads of State enjoy absolute immunity from the criminal jurisdiction of foreign domestic courts,[96] although there is some support for the proposition that this immunity should be qualified in respect of certain crimes against international law.[97] This is where the controversy starts. The developments in the law of State immunity suggest a restrictive approach. However, the often-professed analogy with diplomatic immunity implies an almost absolute immunity from civil jurisdiction for a head of State in office.[98] Hence, unlike the concept of State immunity, there is little agreement as to the scope and rationale of head of State immunity.

A head of State who leaves office remains protected by immunity with regard to official acts performed in the exercise of his or her functions as head of State. The consensus on this residual immunity for official acts is somewhat deceptive, since the question of which acts qualify as such is controversial.[99] Immunity for a former head of State extends beyond those acts that qualify for State immunity *ratione materiae*, since an 'official act performed in the exercise of his functions' is a wider notion than 'sovereign act'. For example, a commercial contract concluded by a head of State on behalf of the State is not a 'sovereign' act in the sense that it is *jure imperii*, but it would qualify as an official act performed in the exercise of the functions of the head of State.[100]

[96] A. Watts, 'The Legal Position in International Law of Heads of State, Heads of Government and Foreign Ministers', *Recueil des cours*, 247 (1994–III), p. 13, at p. 54. See for support J. L. Mallory, 'Resolving the Confusion over Head of State Immunity: The Defined Rights of Kings', *Columbia Law Review*, 86 (1986), p. 169, at pp. 194–5.

[97] A. Watts, 'The Legal Position in International Law of Heads of State, Heads of Government and Foreign Ministers', *Recueil des cours*, 247 (1994–III), p. 13, at pp. 81–4.

[98] A. Watts, 'The Legal Position in International Law of Heads of State, Heads of Government and Foreign Ministers', *Recueil des cours*, 247 (1994–III), p. 13, at p. 55. See for proponents of a more restrictive theory K. Highet *et al.*, 'Lafontant v. Aristide', *American Journal of International Law*, 88 (1994), pp. 528–32; S. Varughese George, 'Head of State Immunity in the United States Courts: Still Confused After All These Years', *Fordham Law Review*, 64 (1995), p. 1051, at p. 1077 ff.; J.L. Mallory, 'Resolving the Confusion over Head of State Immunity: The Defined Rights of Kings', *Columbia Law Review*, 86 (1986), p. 169, at p. 187 ff. International documents on State immunity are not helpful in the quest for State practice on the issue. Although the Draft Articles of the ILC do mention heads of State, the referral to their position under international law begs the question. Heads of State are within the definition of State in Article 3, and thereby in principle subject to the distinction between *acts jure imperii* and *jure gestionis*. However, Article 4.2 stipulates that the Draft Articles are without prejudice to the privileges and immunities accorded under international law to heads of State *ratione personae*: ILC Report (41st Session, 1989), paras. 418, 443.

[99] The discussion with regard to residual immunity for diplomats illustrates this. See, e.g., Y. Dinstein, 'Diplomatic Immunity from Jurisdiction *Ratione Materiae*', *International and Comparative Law Quarterly*, 15 (1966), pp. 76–89; J. Salmon, 'Immunités et actes de la fonction', *Annuaire français de droit international*, 38 (1992), pp. 314–57.

[100] This former head of State immunity concept seems troubled by theoretical confusion. The concept is a hybrid of the immunity rule and the rules on internal attribution. It falls outside the scope of this article to discuss this further.

3.3. *State Immunity and Human Rights Violations: State Practice*

The tension between State immunity and developments in international human rights law has been the subject of ample debate in recent international law doctrine.[101] In general, the theory starts from the idea that the international law rule of State immunity should be considered a right contingent on compliance with at least the most fundamental rules that the international community has set for itself: the *jus cogens* norms. With respect to immunity *ratione materiae* this would appear to follow from the limits put on the concept of sovereignty by international law.[102] Moreover, a coherent interpretation of the immunity rule with respect to the international legal system to which it belongs suggests that neither immunity *ratione materiae* nor immunity *ratione personae* should extend to acts that violate the public order of the international community.[103] This article does not seek to contribute to the general theory. Rather it analyses the immunity decision in the *Pinochet* case against the background of this theory and relevant State practice.

State practice, however, does not fully reflect the theory. In large part this is due to the constraints put on courts by domestic codifications of the immunity rule. When the restrictive theory of State immunity rapidly gained acceptance from the 1950s onwards, several common law

[101] Usually, scholars conclude in favour of a denial of immunity when gross human rights violations are at issue. However, most of them focus on the peculiarities of the US legal system rather than analysing the issue from an international law perspective, e.g. A. C. Belsky *et al.*, 'Implied Waiver under the FSIA: A Proposed Exception to Immunity for Violations of Peremptory Norms of International Law', *California Law Review*, 77 (1989), pp. 365–425; M. Reimann, 'A Human Rights Exception to Sovereign Immunity: Some Thoughts on Princz v. Federal Republic of Germany', *Michigan Journal of International Law*, 16 (1995), pp. 403–32; D. J. Bederman, 'Dead Man's Hand: Reshuffling Foreign Sovereign Immunities in U.S. Human Rights Litigation', *Georgia Journal of International and Comparative Law*, 25 (1996), pp. 255–85; J. A. Gergen, 'Human Rights and the Foreign Sovereign Immunities Act', *Virginia Journal of International Law*, 36 (1996), pp. 765–99; H. M. Osofsky, 'Foreign Sovereign Immunity from Severe Human Rights Violations: New Directions for Common Law Based Approaches', *New York International Law Review*, 11 (1998), pp. 35–69. Exceptions: A. Bianchi, 'Denying State Immunity to Violators of Human Rights', *Austrian Journal of Public and International Law*, 46 (1994), pp. 195–229; J. Bröhmer, *State Immunity and the Violations of Human Rights* (1997). See for a different conclusion A. Zimmerman, 'Sovereign Immunity and Violations of International *Jus Cogens*—Some Critical Remarks', *Michigan Journal of International Law*, 16 (1995), pp. 433–40; R. Garnett, 'The Defence of State Immunity for Acts of Torture', *Australian Yearbook of International Law*, 18 (1997), pp. 97–126. Moreover, until the *Pinochet* case, the discussion was concentrated on the position of the State immunity defence in civil human rights law suits.

[102] See for some general comments on State sovereignty and human rights, e.g., W. M. Reisman, 'Sovereignty and Human Rights in Contemporary International Law', *American Journal of International Law*, 84 (1990), pp. 866–76; L. Henkin, Sibley Lecture, March 1994, 'Human Rights and State Sovereignty', *Georgia Journal of International and Comparative Law*, 25 (1996), pp. 31–45.

[103] Often scholars fail to sustain their assertions in this field with adequate arguments. A prominent exception is Bianchi. He has made a substantial contribution to the development of the theory underlying denial of immunity for serious human rights violations: A. Bianchi, 'Denying State Immunity to Violators of Human Rights', *Austrian Journal of Public and International Law*, 46 (1994), pp. 195–229; A. Bianchi, 'Immunity versus Human Rights: The Pinochet Case', *European Journal of International Law*, 10 (1999), pp. 237–77.

countries decided to codify the rule in a domestic statute. The United States set the trend with the enactment of the Foreign Sovereign Immunities Act in 1976.[104] The United Kingdom followed in 1978 with the State Immunity Act.[105] But such domestic codification, at least partially, severs the link between the international law concept of State immunity and the domestic application of that concept as defined in the statute. In the first place, the national legislation may confer a wider immunity on foreign states than required by international law for political or economic reasons or in the hope of receiving reciprocal courtesies when the roles are reversed.[106] An additional problem may stem from the inflexible terms used to codify the restrictive theory. National legislation exhaustively enumerates what qualifies as private, non-sovereign acts, denying the flexible nature of the immunity concept. Whether an act qualifies as public or private should ideally be based on a uniform distinction derived from international law.[107] The parameters of the international law concept of State immunity should not be defined exclusively according to domestic law conceptions. Static definitions of non-sovereign acts as found in domestic codifications also disregard this principle. This may result in a domestic immunity concept divergent from the gradually evolving international law concept. Thus, the requirements for an exception to immunity in domestic legislation do not necessarily reflect international law requirements. Although courts usually undertake to interpret domestic legislation in accordance with international law,[108] this is only relevant in the case of ambiguous or flexible statutory provisions.

In the United States courts proceed from the proposition that the FSIA provides the 'sole basis for obtaining jurisdiction over a foreign state in a federal court'.[109] Hence, claims against States based on the most egregious human rights violations have to be 'squeezed into the poorly

[104] *International Legal Materials*, 15 (1976), p. 1388.

[105] Ibid., 17 (1978),.p. 1123. Canada, Australia, Argentina, Singapore, South Africa, and Pakistan have also codified the immunity rule in a domestic statute. The restrictive rule has also been codified in several international law documents: see, e.g., the European Convention on State Immunity; the International Law Commission's Draft on the Jurisdictional Immunity of States and their Property; the International Law Association's Draft Articles for a Convention on State Immunity.

[106] C. H. Schreuer, *State Immunity: Some Recent Developments* (1988), p. 6.

[107] *Dralle* v. *Republic of Czechoslovakia*, Supreme Court Austria (1950), 17 ILR 155; *Floridi* v. *Sovexportfilm* (Italy, 1951), *Annali* X (1952), pp. 115–18. However, in practice domestic conceptions of public and private acts often prevail, D. P. O'Connell, *International Law* (2nd edn., 1970), p. 845. Compare *Claim against the Empire of Iran* case, Federal Constitutional Court Germany 1963, 45 ILR 57, at p. 80.

[108] The US case *Alexander Murray* v. *Schooner Charming Betsy*, 6 US 62 (1804), is an example of the common law approach on international law and statutory interpretation. See also the *Restatement (Third) of Foreign Relations Law of the United States*, para. 114. See on this R. G. Steinhardt, 'The Role of International Law as Canon of Domestic Statutory Construction', *Vanderbilt Law Review*, 43 (1990), pp. 1103–97.

[109] *Argentine Republic* v. *Amerada Hess Shipping Corp.*, 488 US 428 (1989), at p. 438.

fitting garments of the FSIA'.[110] Human rights victims have attempted to fit their arguments in the exceptions of the FSIA. Courts, however, have interpreted these exceptions strictly, denying redress for victims of human rights violations that occurred outside the US.[111] In *Siderman de Blake* v. *Republic of Argentina* a victim of severe torture by the Argentinian police sued for damages in a US court.[112] The court agreed that a set of peremptory norms of customary international law to which no derogation is permitted exists, being *jus cogens* principles. The court also agreed that the prohibition of torture is one of these norms.[113] However, the US Foreign Sovereign Immunities Act does not create an exception to sovereign immunity for violations of *jus cogens* norms, although the court noted that 'as a matter of international law [it] carries much force'.[114] The court held that:

international law does not recognize an act that violates *jus cogens* as a sovereign act. A state's violation of the *jus cogens* norm prohibiting official torture therefore would not be entitled to the immunity afforded by international law.

However, the court continued:

unfortunately, we do not write on a clean slate. We deal not only with customary international law, but with . . . the FSIA . . . we conclude that if violations of *jus cogens* committed outside the United States are to be exceptions to immunity, Congress must make them so.[115]

Hence, US courts have indicated that the constraints of the FSIA are not in conformity with international law requirements. Decisions of Greek and New Zealand courts—both States without immunity legislation—also indicate that under international law immunity may not be available

[110] J. Fitzpatrick in B. S. Thornton, 'International Human Rights in American Courts: The Case of Nelson v. Saudi Arabia', *American Society of International Law Proceedings*, 86 (1992), p. 324, at p. 341.

[111] Until the *Pinochet* case the State immunity defence had only been at issue in civil human rights law suits. Compare *Martin* v. *Republic of South Africa,* 836 F 2d 91 (2d Cir. 1987); *Denegri* v. *Republic of Chile,* No. 86–3085, 1992 WL 91914 (DDC 6 April 1992); *Saudi Arabia* v. *Nelson,* 507 US 349 (1993); *Princz* v. *Federal Republic of Germany,* 26 F 3d 1166 (DCCir. 1994) (see however the forceful dissenting opinion of Judge Wald: at pp. 1176–84); *Smith* v. *Socialist People's Libyan Arab Jamahirya,* 101 F 3d 239 (2d Cir. 1996); *Hirsh* v. *Israel,* 962 F Supp. 377 (SDNY 1997). In 1996 the US Congress amended the FSIA to include a new exception to State immunity on human rights grounds: Antiterrorism and Effective Death Penalty Act, Public Law No. 104–132, 110 Stat. 1214 (1996). It provides redress for US nationals who suffered personal injury or death that was caused by an act of torture, extrajudicial killing, aircraft sabotage, hostage taking, or the provision of material resources. However, the amendment only applies to countries designated 'State sponsor of terrorism'. Currently seven States are so designated: Cuba, Iran, Iraq, Libya, North Korea, Sudan, and Syria: 61 Fed. Reg. 43, 462 (1996). Compare *Flatow* v. *Islamic Republic of Iran,* 999 F Supp. 1 (DDC 1998); *Alejandre* v. *Republic of Cuba,* 996 F Supp. 1239 (SD Fla. 1997).

[112] 965 F 2d 699 (9th Cir. 1992).

[113] Ibid., at p. 714 and p. 717.

[114] Ibid., at p. 718.

[115] Ibid., at pp. 718–19.

for violations of *jus cogens* norms.[116] Belgian criminal legislation has been enacted which explicitly denies immunity to defendants suspected of committing war crimes, crimes against humanity, and genocide.[117]

However, State practice on the matter is still very limited. It is too early to conclude that under international law there can never be immunity for human rights violations. Arguably, State practice alone is even too limited to warrant the conclusion that under international law State immunity can be denied when human rights have been violated. However, a close examination of State practice in this area of law together with international legal theory should lead to the conclusion that the development of international human rights law is undeniably affecting the traditional notion of State immunity, although domestic immunity legislation is often too inflexible to allow courts to respond to these developments.

In the UK the issue of State immunity for serious human rights violations came before the courts for the first time in 1996 in a civil law suit of a torture victim against the government of Kuwait. In 1990 Al-Adsani, both a British and Kuwaiti national, was kidnapped, tortured and severely burned, allegedly by government forces. After his release he fled to the UK and started civil proceedings against Kuwait in a UK court.[118] The Court of Appeal decided that Kuwait was protected by State immunity since torture outside UK territory did not fit any of the exhaustively enumerated exceptions to the rule of State immunity laid down in section 1 of the SIA. Stuart-Smith LJ held that the SIA . . .

> is a comprehensive code and not subject to overriding considerations. At common law, a sovereign state could not be sued at all against its will in the courts of this country. The 1978 Act, by the exceptions therein set out, marks substantial inroads into this principle. It is inconceivable it seems to me, that the draughtsman, who must have been well aware of the various agreements about torture, intended section 1 to be subject to an overriding qualification.[119]

The judge relied heavily on US cases like *Siderman de Blake* to come to the conclusion that Kuwait was entitled to immunity under the SIA. Ward LJ, coming to the same conclusion, held that in case of an unambiguous statutory provision, it is irrelevant for the purposes of

[116] Greece: *Prefecture of Voiotia* v. *Federal Republic of Germany*, Case No. 137/1997, Court of First Instance of Leivadia, 30 October 1997. See on this case I. Bantekas, 'State Responsibility in Private Civil Action: Sovereign Immunity for *Jus Cogens* Violations', *American Journal of International Law*, 92 (1998), pp. 765–8. This decision has been confirmed by the Greek Supreme Court in April 2000; New Zealand: *Controller & Auditor General* v. *Davison*, [1996] 2 NZLR 278, Richardson J., 23, Cook J., ibid., 14–15, See M. Byers, case note, this *Year Book*, 67 (1996), p. 537, at pp. 540–1.

[117] Article 5, para. 3, Loi relative à la répression des infractions graves de droit international humanitaire, 10 February 1999, *Moniteur Belge*, 23 March 1999, reproduced in *International Legal Materials*, 38 (1999), p. 918.

[118] *Al-Adsani* v. *Government of Kuwait* (1996), 107 ILR 536.

[119] Ibid., at p. 542.

English law whether that provision is inconsistent with customary international law.[120]

In the case of General Pinochet, it was however not section 1 SIA but section 20 that controlled the proceedings. This proved to make a crucial difference to the outcome of the case. Section 20 (1) provides that:

> subject to the provisions of this section and to any necessary modifications, the Diplomatic Privileges Act 1964 shall apply to
> (*a*) a sovereign or other Head of State;
> (*b*) members of his family forming part of his household; and
> (*c*) his private servants,
> as it applies to the head of a diplomatic mission, to members of his family forming part of his household and to his private servants.

The Diplomatic Privileges Act 1964 (DPA) gives effect to the 1961 Vienna Convention on Diplomatic Relations in English law. The relevant provision in the Pinochet trial was Article 39(2) of the Convention, which provides as follows:

> When the functions of a person enjoying privileges and immunities have come to an end, such privileges and immunities shall normally cease at the moment when he leaves the country, or on expiry of a reasonable period in which to do so, but shall subsist until that time, even in case of armed conflict. However, with respect to acts performed by such a person in the exercise of his functions as a member of the mission, immunity shall continue to subsist.

Lord Steyn commented that 'the technique of applying article 39(2) to a former head of state is somewhat confusing',[121] and Lord Browne-Wilkinson described section 20 as 'baffling'.[122] The suggestions that immunity would extend only to acts performed by a visiting head of State while within the UK or that immunity only applies to acts of heads of State in the exercise of their external functions, that is to say, in the conduct of international relations and foreign affairs generally, were

[120] Ibid., at pp. 549–50. It is interesting to note that Mr Al-Adsani has brought a complaint to the European Court of Human Rights where his case is now pending before a Grand Chamber. It has been argued before that State immunity might violate Article 6 or 13 of the European Convention of Human Rights. It falls outside the pale of this article to elaborate on this argument; for more information, see W. P. Pahr, 'Die Staatenimmunität und Artikel 6 Absatz 1 der Europäischen Menschenrechtkonvention', in *Mélanges offerts à Polys Modinos, Problèmes des droits de l'homme et de l'unification européenne* (1968), p. 222, at p. 231; J. Bröhmer, *State Immunity and the Violations of Human Rights* (1997), pp. 163–71; H. G. Schermers, 'Diplomatic Immunity in Modern International Law', in: E. Denters and N. Schrijver (eds.), *Reflections on International Law from the Low Countries* (1998), pp. 156–64.

[121] *Pinochet No. 1*, at p. 944.

[122] *Pinochet No. 3*, at p. 113. Lord Browne-Wilkinson finds the origin of this dubious construction in the parliamentary history of the section. The original s. 20(1)(*a*) read: '. . . a sovereign or other head of State *who is in the United Kingdom at the invitation or with the consent of the Government of the United Kingdom*.': ibid., at p. 113.

resolutely rejected.[123] The parties to the case did eventually acquiesce in the proper interpretation of the provisions. It was held that for the purposes of English law, a former head of State continues to enjoy immunity from the criminal jurisdiction of UK courts with respect to official acts performed by him in the exercise of his functions as a head of State.[124] The controversy was therefore confined to the qualification of the acts involved. The principal question to be answered by the courts was whether the alleged acts of torture would qualify as official acts performed in the exercise of the functions of a head of State entitled to immunity.

Which acts qualify as official acts performed in the exercise of his functions as head of State under section 20 is thus not exhaustively enumerated but is left to the courts to decide independently. In principle, the SIA left the Lords the freedom to decide in accordance with international law principles and to take all relevant developments in international human rights law into account. The Lords agreed that their decision on whether or not the alleged acts of torture satisfy the requirements of section 20 SIA must depend on the rules of international law.[125]

3.4. *The Court Decisions: An Analysis*

The Divisional Court unanimously decided that Pinochet was protected by immunity from the jurisdiction of the English courts. The judges held that there could be no limitation to immunity based on the nature of the crimes committed. Lord Bingham rationalized his decision with the following question: 'If the former sovereign is immune from process in respect of some crimes where does one draw the line?'[126]

However, the answer to this question is not as clear as Lord Bingham evidently assumed it was. The first House of Lords panel decided by a 3–2 majority that Pinochet was not protected by ex-head of State immunity for the acts involved.[127] Lord Nicholls held that:

[123] See *Pinochet No. 1*, at pp. 932–3 *per* Lord Lloyd of Berwick. Only Lord Phillips held: 'I do not consider that s 20 of the 1978 Act has any application to conduct of a head of state outside the United Kingdom. Such conduct remains governed by the rules of public international law': *Pinochet No. 3*, at p. 192.

[124] *Pinochet No. 1*, at p. 933. See pp. 943–4 *per* Lord Steyn on the rationale for this formulation. Although in *Pinochet No. 3* the phrase 'acts performed by him in the exercise of his functions as a head of state' is used, there appears to be no difference in substance between the two formulations: see E. Denza, *Diplomatic Law, A Commentary on the Vienna Convention on Diplomatic Relations* (2nd edn., 1998), p. 363.

[125] The Lords emphasized this several times. Compare, *inter alia*, *Pinochet No. 3*, at p. 111 *per* Lord Browne-Wilkinson, at p. 119 *per* Lord Goff, at p. 146 *per* Lord Hope, at p. 165 *per* Lord Hutton, at p. 168 *per* Lord Saville, at p. 171 *per* Lord Millett, at p. 181 *per* Lord Phillips.

[126] Divisional Court, para. 63.

[127] See H. Fox, 'The First *Pinochet* Case: Immunity of a Former Head of State', *International and Comparative Law Quarterly*, 48 (1999), pp. 207–16.

torture of his own subjects, or of aliens, would not be regarded by international law as a function of a head of state. . . . International law has made plain that certain types of conduct, including torture and hostage-taking, are not acceptable conduct on the part of anyone. This applies as much to heads of state, or even more so, as it does to everyone else; the contrary conclusion would make a mockery of international law.[128]

Lord Steyn articulated the nucleus of his argument as follows:

the development of international law since the 1939–45 war justifies the conclusion that by the time of the 1973 coup d'état, and certainly ever since, international law condemned genocide, torture, hostage taking and crimes against humanity (during an armed conflict or in peace time) as international crimes deserving of punishment. . . . it seems to me difficult to maintain that the commission of such high crimes may amount to acts performed in the exercise of the functions of a head of state.[129]

The majority opinion in *Pinochet No. 1* was acclaimed by many. Jubilant commentators commended the decision as 'a birthday gift for international human rights'.[130] But it also encountered criticism.[131] Even some scholars who agreed with the outcome of the case criticized the reasoning of the House of Lords. It was regretted that it was 'le sentiment que certains crimes ne sauraient rester impunis qui justifie l'absence d'immunité', rather than an actual criterion for distinction.[132] Admittedly, the majority argument is underdeveloped, although Lord Steyn did allude to the concept of international crimes to support his conclusion. A convincing rebuttal of the quandary of distinction as advanced by Lord Bingham requires further elaboration of the relevant concepts of international law.

On 24 March 1999 the second House of Lords chamber delivered its judgment on the merits. A 6–1 majority denied Pinochet immunity *ratione materiae* with respect to the torture allegations involved. The decision was lauded as providing 'le critère qui permet de distinguer parmi les actes d'un gouvernant'.[133] Another commentator summarized the decision as follows: 'l'ancien Chef d'Etat, en principe au bénéfice de l'immunité de juridiction pénale pour ses actes de fonction, n'est cependant pas à l'abri des poursuites lorsque ces actes revêtent le

[128] *Pinochet No. 1*, at pp. 939–40.

[129] Ibid., at p. 945.

[130] M. Byers, 'A Safer Place for All', *The World Today*, January 1999, p. 4, at p. 4.

[131] e.g. J. Klabbers, 'The General, The Lords, and the Possible End of State Immunity', *Nordic Journal of International Law*, 68 (1999), pp. 85–95.

[132] M. Cosnard, 'Quelques observations sur les décisions de la chambre des Lords du 25 novembre 1998 et du 24 mars 1999 dans l'affaire Pinochet', *Revue générale de droit international public*, 103 (1999), p. 309, at p. 315.

[133] Ibid., at p. 319.

caractère de crimes de droit international'.[134] Alas, this is exactly the conclusion that *cannot* be drawn from *Pinochet No. 3*.

All seven members of the House of Lords delivered individual opinions. Although the majority concluded that Pinochet was not protected by immunity for the acts under consideration, it is impossible to derive a common *ratio decidendi* from these six majority opinions. The individual majority opinions on the immunity question are divided on several critical issues. Apart from Lord Hutton's opinion, all opinions rely to a different degree on the specific terms of the Torture Convention for the denial of immunity. Moreover, only Lords Browne-Wilkinson and Hutton (and Phillips in an *obiter dictum*) actually concluded that acts of torture do not qualify as official acts performed in the exercise of the functions of a head of State; the others construed the denial of immunity differently. These variations are also manifested in the dates that were considered to be decisive for the immunity issue.

This section will review all seven opinions. Although their opacity makes it a precarious business to attempt classification, an attempt will be made to set out the most important elements of each separate opinion.

Lord Saville of Newdigate based his conclusion exclusively on the specific terms of the Torture Convention. He considered that before the coming into existence of the Torture Convention there was no exception to immunity for acts of torture.[135] Subsequently, he reiterated that the Convention only applies to acts of torture 'inflicted by or at the instigation of or with consent or acquiescence of a public official or other person acting in an official capacity' and concluded:

> So far as the states that are parties to the convention are concerned, I cannot see how, as far as torture is concerned, this immunity can exist consistently with the terms of that convention. Each state party has agreed that the other state parties can exercise jurisdiction over alleged official torturers found within their territories . . . and thus, to my mind, can hardly simultaneously claim an immunity from extradition or prosecution that is necessarily based on the official nature of the alleged torture.[136]

He held that the immunity defence was no longer available after 8 December 1988, the day the United Kingdom ratified the Torture Convention. From that date onwards Spain, Chile, and the UK were all parties to the Convention. Although acts of torture would normally qualify for protection under section 20 SIA, he considered the 'unequivocal terms of the Torture Convention' to qualify as an express waiver.[137]

Only Lord Hutton can be said to actually have based the denial of

[134] C. Dominicé, 'Quelques observations sur l'immunité de juridiction pénale de l'ancien chef d'etat', *Revue générale de droit international public*, 103 (1999), p. 297, at p. 307.

[135] *Pinochet No. 3*, at p. 168.

[136] Ibid., at p. 169.

[137] Ibid., at p. 170.

immunity on the qualification of torture as a crime against international law. After a comprehensive review of relevant developments in international law, he concluded that:

> since the end of the 1939–45 war there has been a clear recognition by the international community that certain crimes are so grave and so inhuman that they constitute crimes against international law and that the international community is under a duty to bring to justice a person who commits such crimes. Torture has been recognised as such a crime.[138]

Subsequently he held that since there is no jurisdiction to try Pinochet for acts of torture prior to 29 September 1988:

> it is unnecessary to decide when torture became a crime against international law prior to that date, but I am of opinion that acts of torture were clearly crimes against international law and that the prohibition of torture had required the status of ius cogens by that date.[139]

Lord Hutton did allude to the Torture Convention in his final conclusion[140] but this does not seem to be relevant to his conclusion in any way.[141] This is confirmed by the fact that he adopted the date of 29 September 1988 for the immunity issues; not because that date is relevant with regard to immunity but only because there was no jurisdiction prior to that date. On 29 September 1988 the Torture Convention had not been ratified by the United Kingdom nor Chile. Customary international law considerations alone must therefore have been sufficient for Lord Hutton to deny immunity for the torture allegations. Finally, Lord Hutton disputed the relevance of the concept of waiver. He concluded:

> In my opinion there has been no waiver of the immunity of a former head of state in respect of his functions as head of state. My conclusion . . . is based on the view that the commission of acts of torture is not a function of a head of state . . . [142]

The basis of the remaining four majority opinions is ambiguous. They consist of elements derived from both the specific construction of the Torture Convention as well as the more general argument based on the concept of crimes against international law.

Although Lord Millett did argue that crimes under international law attract universal jurisdiction and that all alleged crimes qualify as extradition crimes under the Extradition Act, he did not come to the general conclusion that the notion of crimes under international law

[138] Ibid., at p. 163.
[139] Ibid., at p. 164.
[140] Ibid.
[141] See, for a different view, H. Fox, 'The Pinochet Case No. 3', *International and Comparative Law Quarterly*, 48 (1999), p. 687, at p. 697.
[142] *Pinochet No. 3*, at p. 166.

influences the immunity rule. His progressive observations on the issue of universal jurisdiction have confused commentators since many have interpreted Lord Millett's opinion as denying immunity for international crimes in general.[143] This is certainly not correct. Lord Millett's conclusion on immunity is, as will be seen below, strictly limited to the specific characteristics pertaining to the crime of torture.

Lord Millett allowed the appeal in respect of all the torture charges against General Pinochet.[144] He held:

> The definition of torture . . . is in my opinion entirely inconsistent with the existence of a plea of immunity ratione materiae. The offence can be committed *only* by or at the instigation of, or with the consent or acquiescence of, a public official or other person acting in an official capacity. The official or governmental nature of the act, which forms the basis of the immunity, is an essential ingredient of the offence. No rational system of criminal justice can allow an immunity which is co-extensive with the offence.[145]

He continued:

> If the respondent's arguments were accepted, s 134 would be a dead letter. Either the accused was acting in a private capacity, in which case he cannot be charged with an offence under the section; or he was acting in an official capacity, in which case he would enjoy immunity from prosecution.[146]

Hence, Lord Millett's opinion is obviously limited to the international crime of torture and does not have immediate implications for the more general concept of crimes against international law. Moreover, although formally Lord Millett did not rely on the entry into force of the Torture Convention, in fact his conclusion relies entirely on the explicit provisions of the Torture Convention. It is unclear whether the status of the perpetrator is inherent in the definition of torture or whether it is a limitation specific to the Torture Convention.[147] This means that, at least materially, the Torture Convention is of crucial importance to Lord Millett's conclusion on immunity.

The above observations already denote that Lord Millett qualified acts of torture as acts in essence protected by section 20 of the SIA. He also stressed that the acts involved 'were official and governmental or sovereign acts by any standard'.[148] The Torture Convention did not,

[143] e.g. R. Wedgwood, 'International Criminal Law and Augusto Pinochet', *Virginia Journal of International Law*, 40 (2000), p. 829, at p. 841; C. M. Chinkin, 'Regina v. Bow Street Stipendiary Magistrate, Ex parte Pinochet Ugarte (No. 3)', *American Journal of International Law*, 93 (1999), p. 703, at p. 705 n. 15; N. Bhuta, 'Justice Without Borders? Prosecuting General Pinochet', *Melbourne University Law Review*, 23 (1999), p. 499, at pp. 524–5.

[144] *Pinochet No. 3*, at p. 180.

[145] Ibid., at pp. 178–9.

[146] Ibid., at p. 179.

[147] See n. 35, above. With the statement of the ICTY in the *Čelebići* case in mind, it can at least be argued that the immunity is not co-extensive with the offence when officials of non-State parties to a conflict can commit acts of torture as well.

[148] *Pinochet No. 3*, at p. 172.

therefore, affect the possible qualification of acts of torture under section 20 SIA as such. Moreover, he did not regard the ratification of the Torture Convention to entail a waiver of immunity since 'there was no immunity to be waived'.[149] Rather he concluded that 'international law cannot be supposed to have established a crime having the character of a jus cogens and at the same time to have provided an immunity which is co-extensive with the obligation it seeks to impose'.[150]

The opinion of Lord Phillips of Worth Matravers has also generally been interpreted as denying former head of State immunity with respect to all international crimes, not just torture.[151] Although at first sight this interpretation seems reasonable, it is suggested that it needs qualification. Lord Philips began with the premiss that:

> There are some categories of crime of such gravity that they shock the consciousness of mankind and cannot be tolerated by the international community. Any individual who commits such a crime offends against international law.[152]

Subsequently, he held that:

> no established rule of international law requires state immunity ratione materiae to be accorded in respect of prosecution for an international crime. International crimes and extra-territorial jurisdiction in relation to them are both new arrivals in the field of public international law. I do not believe that state immunity ratione materiae can co-exist with them. The exercise of extra-territorial jurisdiction overrides the principle that one state will not intervene in the internal affairs of another. It does so because, where international crime is concerned, that principle cannot prevail. An international crime is as offensive, if not more offensive, to the international community when committed under colour of office. Once extra-territorial jurisdiction is established, it makes no sense to exclude from it acts done in an official capacity.[153]

On close consideration it is questionable whether Lord Phillips' opinion can be read as denying immunity *ratione materiae* for all crimes against international law. On the one hand he considered the possibility of extra-territorial jurisdiction to be decisive. In combination with his, seemingly passing, assertion that it is not clear whether international

[149] Ibid., at p. 179.

[150] Ibid.

[151] e.g. C. M. Chinkin, 'Regina v. Bow Street Stipendiary Magistrate, Ex parte Pinochet Ugarte (No. 3)', *American Journal of International Law*, 93 (1999), p. 703, at p. 705 n. 15; A. Bianchi, 'Immunity versus Human Rights: The Pinochet Case', *European Journal of International Law*, 10 (1999), p. 237, at p. 249; N. Bhuta, 'Justice Without Borders? Prosecuting General Pinochet', *Melbourne University Law Review*, 23 (1999), p. 499, at pp. 524–6. Although less explicit, a similar interpretation can be found in R. Bank, 'Der Fall Pinochet: Aufbruch zu neuen Ufern bei der Verfolgung von Menschenrechtsverletzungen?', *Zeitschrift für ausländisches öffentliches Recht und Völkerrecht*, 59 (1999), p. 677, at pp. 698–9.

[152] *Pinochet No. 3*, at p. 188.

[153] Ibid., at p. 189–90.

customary law recognises universal jurisdiction in respect of international crimes,[154] it could well be argued that the Torture Convention is indispensable for his conclusion on immunity. Lord Phillips' opinion should then be read in the light of his limited view on universal jurisdiction. Moreover, Lord Phillips then turned to the Torture Convention and considered:

> The only conduct covered by this convention, is conduct which would be subject to immunity ratione materiae, if such immunity were applicable. The convention is thus incompatible with the applicability of immunity ratione materiae. . . . the state parties to the convention proceeded on the premise that no immunity could exist ratione materiae in respect of torture, a crime contrary to international law.[155]

On the other hand, however, his *dictum* that no immunity *ratione materiae* is available for acts of genocide either[156] introduces uncertainty since the Genocide Convention does not provide for universal jurisdiction.[157] This would seem to contradict the finding that he requires a conventional basis for the exercise of jurisdiction. Lord Phillips omitted to pinpoint a date as from which immunity is no longer available and leaves us to guess which of the above considerations he himself considered to be decisive.

Finally, it should be noted that Lord Phillips did 'not consider that s 20 of the 1978 Act has any application to conduct of a head of State outside the United Kingdom'. He held this conduct to be 'governed by the rules of public international law'.[158] Since he argued that international law does not require State immunity *ratione materiae* to be accorded in respect of prosecution for an international crime, the possible qualification of the acts under consideration under section 20 SIA was not relevant for his conclusion. However, he also held that:

> In so far as Pt III of the 1978 Act entitles a former head of state to immunity in respect of the performance of his official functions, I do not believe that those functions can, as a matter of statutory interpretation, extend to actions that are prohibited as criminal under international law.[159]

Lord Browne-Wilkinson asserted that State torture was 'an international crime in the highest sense' long before the Torture Convention. He admitted that torture qualified as *jus cogens* long before the Torture Convention and cited the exercise of universal jurisdiction in the *Eichmann* and *Demjanjuk* cases approvingly.[160] Later on, however, he

[154] Ibid., at pp. 188–9.
[155] Ibid., at p. 190.
[156] Ibid., at pp. 189–90.
[157] 9 December 1948, Convention on the Prevention and Punishment of the Crime of Genocide, *UN Treaty Series*, vol. 78, p. 277.
[158] *Pinochet No. 3*, at p. 192.
[159] Ibid.
[160] Ibid., at p. 109.

held that torture could not be described as 'a fully constituted international crime' until the Convention provided States with universal jurisdiction to try torturers.[161] This internal contradiction epitomizes the difficulty with Lord Browne-Wilkinson's opinion. On the one hand he wished to confirm the importance of international human rights law while on the other hand he felt the need to limit the judgment to the specific features of the Torture Convention.

He considered that it cannot . . .

be for international law purposes an official function to do something which international law itself prohibits and criminalises.[162]

The acts of torture under consideration did not therefore qualify for protection under section 20 SIA: Pinochet had not been 'acting in any capacity which gives rise to immunity *ratione materiae*'.[163] However, this conclusion was made dependent on the Torture Convention. Lord Browne-Wilkinson concluded that given the definition of torture in the Torture Convention, the elaborate structure of universal jurisdiction over torture committed by officials would be rendered abortive when immunity *ratione materiae* was available. This he considered to be a decisive argument against Pinochet's immunity claim. Therefore, he held that immunity is not available for acts of torture after 8 December 1988,[164] according a decisive voice to the Torture Convention.

Lord Hope of Craighead began his opinion by rejecting the argument that former head of State immunity cannot protect perpetrators of crimes against international law.[165] He then turned to the Torture Convention, maintaining that immunity *ratione materiae* has not by necessary implication been removed from a former head of State in regard to every act of torture of any kind which might be alleged against him.[166] However, Lord Hope returned to considerations of customary international law to come to a conclusion on the immunity issue:

Nevertheless there remains the question whether the immunity can survive Chile's agreement to the Torture Convention if the torture which is alleged was of such a kind or on such a scale as to amount to an international crime.[167]

He considered that there was already widespread agreement that the prohibition against official torture had achieved the status of a *jus cogens* norm by 29 September 1988.[168] He continued with regard to the Torture Convention:

[161] Ibid., at p. 114.
[162] Ibid.
[163] Ibid., at p. 115.
[164] Ibid., at pp. 114–15.
[165] Ibid., at p. 147.
[166] Ibid., at pp. 148–51, esp. p. 150.
[167] Ibid., at p. 151.
[168] Ibid., at p. 152.

In my opinion, once the machinery which it provides was put in place to enable jurisdiction over such crimes to be exercised in the courts of a foreign state, it was no longer open to any state which was a signatory to the convention to invoke immunity ratione materiae in the event of allegations of systematic or widespread torture committed after that date being made in the courts of that state against its officials or any other person acting in an official capacity.[169]

This is not a waiver and not an implied term in the Torture Convention, and is also not based on the conclusion that acts of torture can no longer qualify as 'official acts':

It is just that the obligations which were recognised by customary international law in the case of such serious international crimes by the date when Chile ratified the convention are so strong as to override any objection by it on the ground of immunity ratione materiae to the exercise of the jurisdiction over crimes committed after that date which the United Kingdom had made available.[170]

Lord Hope's conclusion seems to rely on an interaction between the Torture Convention and the concept of crimes against international law. He considered that the date as from which immunity *ratione materiae* was lost was 30 October 1988, which was the date that Chile's ratification of the Torture Convention took effect.[171]

Lord Goff of Chieveley delivered the only dissent on the immunity issue. He proceeded from the proposition that the mere fact that the crime involved is torture does not exclude State immunity.[172] He continued:

There can . . . be no doubt that, before the Torture Convention, torture by public officials could be the subject of state immunity. Since therefore exclusion of immunity is said to result from the Torture Convention and there is no express term of the convention to this effect, the argument has, in my opinion, to be formulated as dependent upon an implied term in the convention.[173]

In the first place, Lord Goff rejected the assumption that the continued availability of State immunity is inconsistent with the obligations of States party to the convention:

in the majority of cases which may arise under the convention, no question of state immunity will arise at all, because the public official concerned is likely to be present in his own country. Even when such a question does arise, there is no reason to assume that state immunity will be asserted by the state of which the alleged torturer is a public official; on the contrary it is only in unusual cases . . . that this is likely to be done.[174]

[169] Ibid.
[170] Ibid.
[171] Ibid.
[172] Ibid., at p. 119. He here endorses the line of reasoning of Lord Slynn of Hadley in *Pinochet No. 1*: ibid., at p. 117.
[173] Ibid., at p. 122.
[174] Ibid., at p. 127.

Moreover, he asserted that waiver can only be achieved by express agreement[175] and concluded that the reliance on an implied term in the convention would create the unacceptable possibility that 'state immunity could be waived in a treaty sub silentio'.[176]

All majority opinions ended with the suggestion that the Home Secretary should reconsider his decision to give authority to proceed with the extradition process in light of the exclusion of a very large number of the charges and the resulting 'substantial change in the circumstances'.[177] The Home Secretary did reconsider his decision, but nevertheless renewed his authority to proceed.[178] In March 2000 the extradition proceedings before the British Courts came to an end when the Home Secretary decided to allow Pinochet to return to Chile because his ill-health made him unfit to stand trial.

3.5. *The Immunity Decision in* Pinochet No. 3*: A Victory for Human Rights Law?*

The grant of immunity to General Pinochet would have seriously undermined the credibility of human rights theory as developed over the past half-century. The 6–1 majority in favour of denial of immunity *ratione materiae* for the international crime of torture thus suggests a victory for international human rights law. Close reading commands a more balanced conclusion.

It should be realized that the annulment of *Pinochet No. 1* and the unprecedented circumstances of the rehearing put the Lords in a precarious position: both the denial of immunity as well as the granting of immunity, and effectively overruling *Pinochet No. 1*, would be a bold decision with major implications.[179] In this light, one could see the final House of Lords decision as an attempt to control damage. Although *Pinochet No. 1* was not overruled, immunity was denied on such limited grounds that the precedential value of the final decision is limited. This section discusses the principal reasons why the majority decision in *Pinochet No. 3* is a weak precedent for immunity decisions in future human rights cases.

In the first place, all the Lords apart from Lord Hutton based the denial of immunity, in varying degree, on the specific provisions of the

175 Ibid., at pp. 123–5.

176 Ibid., at pp. 126–30, quotation at p. 130.

177 Ibid., at p. 115 *per* Lord Browne-Wilkinson.

178 HL Debates, vol. 329, col. 311 (15 April 1999).

179 It is instructive to recall that until a few decades ago the House of Lords could not even overturn its earlier decisions in later, unrelated, cases. The strict application of the *stare decisis* rule was denounced in the 1966 Practice Statement on Precedent: Practice Direction (Judicial Precedent), [1966] 1 WLR 1234 (HL).

Torture Convention and not on customary international law considerations. This seriously limits the significance of the decision. Lord Saville relied exclusively on the specific provisions of the Torture Convention while Lords Millett, Phillips, Browne-Wilkinson, and Hope used a mixture of customary international law and conventional law arguments, with the latter two positively according a decisive voice to the Torture Convention.[180] Only Lord Hutton unequivocally relied on customary international law in his conclusion on denial of immunity. Clearly, two distinct questions are at issue. Lord Browne-Wilkinson did indicate the correct order in which these questions should be considered by the court:

the issue is whether international law grants state immunity in relation to the international crime of torture and, if so, whether the Republic of Chile is entitled to claim such immunity even though Chile, Spain and the United Kingdom are all party to the Torture Convention.[181]

It is submitted that the first of these questions should already have been answered in the negative on the basis of customary international law considerations, as Lord Hutton did. Crimes against international law qualifying as *jus cogens* norms cannot be protected by immunity *ratione materiae*. In view of the critical weight accorded to the specific provisions of the Torture Convention by the majority of Lords, *Pinochet No. 3* does not reflect this argument.

It has been asserted that the mechanisms of the Torture Convention would have sufficed for the demonstration that no immunity is available.[182] This is of course true. An unequivocal reliance on the definition of torture in the Convention would undoubtedly have rendered the judgment less opaque, although this would disregard the logical order of the questions involved. The fact that a plurality of the members of the House of Lords discussed the customary international law arguments against immunity for crimes against international law but did not base their conclusion on these considerations has unnecessarily cast doubt on the general theory.

As stated above, reliance on the specific provisions of the Convention seriously limits the significance of the decision. First, not all crimes against international law are supported by a convention. Moreover, the explicit limitation to State officials in the definition of torture is a peculiarity not applicable to other crimes against international law. Does

[180] Admittedly Lord Millett's conclusion allows for a different interpretation: purely formally he only relied on the definition of torture and allowed the appeal for all the torture charges involved. However, his argument relied entirely on the definition of torture provided for in the Torture Convention. See p. 58 above.

[181] *Pinochet No. 3*, at p. 111.

[182] M. Cosnard, 'Quelques observations sur les décisions de la chambre des Lords du 25 novembre 1998 et du 24 mars 1999 dans l'affaire Pinochet', *Revue générale de droit international public*, 103 (1999), p. 309, at p. 319.

the fact that non-State actors can, for example, commit genocide mean that Pinochet would have been able to invoke immunity for acts of genocide? Finally, the ratification of the Convention by Chile and even Spain played a role in the considerations of some Lords. Not all States are party to the Torture Convention.[183] Would Iraqi or Zimbabwean nationality have protected General Pinochet from extradition?

One cannot but conclude that the common denominator of the majority judgment is confined to the outcome of the case. This lack of a common *ratio decidendi* was also manifested in the disagreement on the qualification of acts of torture as official acts protected by the SIA. A majority of Lords explicitly held acts of torture in principle protected by immunity *ratione materiae*. Only Lords Browne-Wilkinson and Hutton—and Lord Phillips *obiter*—decided to deny immunity because the acts of torture under consideration did not qualify for protection under section 20 SIA.

This latter—minority—approach has been criticized. It has been held that '[t]o deny the official character of such offences is to fly in the face of reality'.[184] Commentators have also argued that Lords Browne-Wilkinson and Hutton relied on an artificial distinction between the official nature of the act of torture as defined in the Torture Convention and the official nature required for qualification of the acts under section 20 SIA.[185] It was stated that '[I]t does seem rather odd to rely on the official nature of an offence in order to assert jurisdiction and then to deny that official nature in order to avoid the plea of head of state immunity'.[186]

This criticism is not convincing. Critically, the Torture Convention does not rely on the official nature of the act involved. Rather, the official capacity of the offender and commitment of the act in the performance or purported performance of official duties is decisive. US practice establishes that an imperative distinction should be made between the requirements for the exercise of jurisdiction and the requirements for the application of immunity. In *Hilao* v. *Marcos* a US court addressed the tension between the jurisdictional requirements of the US Alien Tort Claims Act and the ominous applicability of the Foreign Sovereign Immunity Act by holding that:

[183] See, for an up-to-date overview of States party to the Torture Convention, the Treaty Bodies Database of the United Nations High Commissioner for Human Rights, http://www.unhchr.ch/tbs/doc.nsf.

[184] J. C. Barker, 'The Future of Former Head of State Immunity after *Ex Parte Pinochet*', *International and Comparative Law Quarterly*, 48 (1999), p. 937, at p. 943.

[185] R. Bank, 'Der Fall Pinochet: Aufbruch zu neuen Ufern bei der Verfolgung von Menschenrechtsverletzungen?', *Zeitschrift für ausländisches öffentliches Recht und Völkerrecht*, 59 (1999), p. 677, at p. 693. See also J. Bröhmer, 'Diplomatic Immunity, Head of State Immunity, State Immunity: Misconceptions of a Notorious Human Rights Violator', *Leiden Journal of International Law*, 12 (1999), p. 361, at p. 370.

[186] J. C. Barker, 'The Future of Former Head of State Immunity after *Ex Parte Pinochet*', *International and Comparative Law Quarterly*, 48 (1999), p. 937, at p. 948.

An official acting under color of authority, but not within an official mandate, can violate international law and not be entitled to immunity under the FSIA.[187]

This approach convincingly rebuts the criticism referred to. A State official can in the—purported—exercise of his official functions commit acts that do not fall within an official mandate and that do not qualify for protection by immunity *ratione materiae*.[188]

A second reason why the majority decision is of limited precedential value is its limitation to former heads of State. All Lords explicitly considered that serving heads of State enjoy absolute immunity from jurisdiction and would therefore be immune with regard to torture allegations. Lord Goff commented in his dissenting opinion that:

it is not suggested that it is inconsistent with the convention that immunity ratione personae should be asserted; if so, I find it difficult to see why it should be inconsistent to assert immunity ratione materiae.[189]

This observation raises a critical question. Is the basis of the majority decision consistent with the argument that serving heads of State continue to enjoy immunity for acts of torture? Do the relevant provisions of the Torture Convention warrant a different conclusion for serving heads of State than for former heads of State? It depends on the construction for denial of immunity used whether a distinction is tenable. Fox has argued in this respect that 'there is nothing in article 1 [Torture Convention] to confine its scope to a former head of State; the retention of immunity in favour of a serving head of State then becomes equally inconsistent with the *aut dedere aut punire* scheme of the convention'.[190] Admittedly, the Torture Convention itself does not provide a justification for the distinction. However, if immunity is denied because '[t]he official or governmental nature of the act, which forms the basis of the immunity, is an essential ingredient of the offence' and '[n]o rational system of criminal justice can allow an immunity which is co-extensive with the offence',[191] a justification for the distinction is implicitly stated. However, those majority opinions invoking *jus cogens* arguments cannot similarly defend the limitation. It has been asserted that reliance on *jus cogens* for denial of immunity necessarily implicates the rule of immunity *ratione personae* unless it is proposed that that rule

[187] *Hilao* v. *Marcos*, 25 F 3d 1467 (9th Cir. 1994), at p. 1472. See also *Filartiga* v. *Pena-Irala*, 630 F 2d 876 (2d Cir. 1980).

[188] See on this T. Lininger, 'Overcoming Immunity Defenses to Human Rights Suits in U.S. Courts', *Harvard Human Rights Journal*, 7 (1994), p. 177, at p. 186.

[189] *Pinochet No. 3*, at p. 127.

[190] H. Fox, 'The Pinochet Case No. 3', *International and Comparative Law Quarterly*, 48 (1999), p. 687, at p. 700.

[191] *Pinochet No. 3*, at pp. 178–9.

itself qualifies as *jus cogens*.[192] Although, it has to be noted that the *jus cogens* arguments against immunity *ratione personae* are not as strong as those against immunity *ratione materiae*, a crucial difference between the two concepts for the purpose of immunity from acts of torture was not elucidated in *Pinochet No. 3*.

It seems the Lords were eager to limit the scope of their judgment to former rulers to make it politically more acceptable. Undoubtedly a serving head of State would have been held immune from the jurisdiction of UK courts in similar circumstances. This is imperatively laid down in the SIA. However, parliamentary history demonstrates that 'the reading of SIA 20 as an accurate statement of the position of a head of state under customary international law is misleading'.[193] It has to be observed that the various arguments advanced in the majority decision do, at least theoretically, have implications for serving heads of State as well.[194]

In this respect it is interesting to note that immunity *ratione personae* was not available before the Nuremberg Tribunal, is not available before the ICTY and ICTR, and will not be available before the International Criminal Court. Likewise, the already mentioned Belgian legislation provides that immunity *ratione personae* is not available for acts of genocide, crimes against humanity, and war crimes.[195] The UN Committee against Torture has recommended '[t]he reform of the State Immunity Act 1978, to ensure that its provisions conform to the obligations contained in the [Torture] Convention'.[196]

Finally, *Pinochet No. 3* is limited to criminal proceedings against a former State official and does not overrule the 1996 *Al-Adsani* case.[197] In civil proceedings against States and State officials, State immunity is still the rule, only subject to those exceptions explicitly enumerated in the SIA. This imperative statutory limitation of the scope of the *Pinochet* ruling is however compounded by the arguments of Lords Hutton and Millett. Lord Hutton held that under international law Chile could claim immunity if sued in civil proceedings with respect to the acts involved. Moreover, he held that Pinochet could also claim immunity if sued in

[192] M. Cosnard, 'Quelques observations sur les décisions de la chambre des Lords du 25 novembre 1998 et du 24 mars 1999 dans l'affaire Pinochet', *Revue générale de droit international public*, 103 (1999), p. 309, at p. 321. Compare *Pinochet No. 3*, at p. 149 *per* Lord Hope.

[193] See H. Fox, 'The Pinochet Case No. 3', *International and Comparative Law Quarterly*, 48 (1999), p. 687, at pp. 693–4.

[194] A critical commentator held with regard to this issue: '[t]he Pinochet decision [might be] little more than a pyrrhic victory for human rights, providing dictators with the strongest possible incentive to keep on dictating': J. Klabbers, 'The General, The Lords and the Possible End of State Immunity', *Nordic Journal of International Law*, 68 (1999), p. 85, at p. 89.

[195] Article 5, para. 3, Loi relative à la répression des infractions graves de droit international humanitaire, 10 February 1999, *Moniteur Belge*, 23 March 1999, reproduced in *International Law Materials*, 38 (1999), p. 918.

[196] Concluding observations of the Committee against Torture: United Kingdom of Great Britain and Northern Ireland, 17 November 1998, A/54/44, para. 72–77, 77.

[197] *Al-Adsani* v. *Government of Kuwait* (1996), 107 ILR 536.

civil proceedings for damages in a court in the UK.[198] Hence, Lord Hutton declared the constraints of the SIA to be in conformity with international law requirements.[199] This view is disputable. The immunity rule in international law has developed beyond the inflexibly worded codification of the rule in domestic statutes and international documents. Fox asks in this regard why the obligation to provide 'fair and adequate compensation to the victim' (Article 14, Torture Convention) is not equally inconsistent with the retention of a plea of State immunity.[200] Notably, the Lords did not, and did not have to on the basis of the facts of the case before them, find that their conclusion has implications for the discussion on State immunity under international law. However, it is regrettable that some Lords felt it necessary explicitly to confirm the 1996 *Al-Adsani* decision and moreover declare Pinochet immune from civil jurisdiction. Alternatively, they should have limited their *obiter dictum* statements to the compulsive reality of the SIA.[201]

4. Conclusion

The *Pinochet* case is an important step towards a more effective protection of human rights through national court proceedings. The case illustrates that domestic courts can, subject to the legality principle, exercise criminal jurisdiction over certain human rights violations committed on foreign territory. Moreover, it is the first time that a foreign domestic court has decided that an abdicated head of State cannot escape criminal responsibility for certain human rights violations committed under his command by invoking former head of State immunity.

However, the case also illustrates that there are still obstacles to overcome before a real victory for international human rights law can be proclaimed. The *Pinochet* decision does reflect a growing sensitivity to the notion of *jus cogens* norms and crimes against international law in national courts.[202] However, the decision also displays an ambiguous

[198] *Pinochet No. 3*, at p. 167. He refers to the principle stated in *Jaffe* v. *Miller (No. 2)* (1993), 95 ILR 446.

[199] See also *Pinochet No. 3*, at p. 179 *per* Lord Millett.

[200] H. Fox, 'The Pinochet Case No. 3', *International and Comparative Law Quarterly*, 48 (1999), p. 687, at p. 700.

[201] Compare *Al-Adsani* v. *Government of Kuwait* (1996), 107 ILR 536, at pp. 549–50 *per* Ward LJ. See C. A. Bradley and J. L. Goldsmith, 'Pinochet and International Human Rights Litigation', *Michigan Law Review*, 97 (1999), pp. 2129–84, for support to distinguish civil (US) litigation from the *Pinochet* case.

[202] Almost all Lords held that the prohibition of torture is a *jus cogens* norm and that violation amounts to a crime against international law. This acceptance of the notion of *jus cogens* by a traditionally conservative judicial body may be called remarkable and promising. It is good to remember that the International Court of Justice has until now treated the concept with great caution: compare G. A. Christenson, 'The World Court and *Jus Cogens*', *American Journal of International Law*, 81 (1987), pp. 93–101; J. Sztucki, *Jus Cogens and the Vienna Convention on the Law of Treaties: A Critical Appraisal* (1974), pp. 12–22.

attitude towards customary international law and was explicitly qualified with regard to serving heads of State and civil proceedings.

When Pinochet visited the Netherlands in 1994, the Dutch Public Prosecutor did not act on the requests for arrest of the General. After Pinochet had safely left the country, a claim was brought against the Public Prosecutor for this failure to prosecute the ex-dictator. The court dismissed the claim, stating that 'it was evident that prosecution of Pinochet . . . could encounter so many legal and practical problems that the Public Prosecutor was perfectly within his rights not to prosecute'.[203] Recently, several domestic courts have shown a greater willingness to overcome the 'legal and practical problems' that are undoubtedly involved in the prosecution of (former) foreign State officials for human rights violations abroad. A Senegalese prosecutor started a judicial investigation into the alleged human rights violations of Hissein Habre, the exiled dictator of Chad living in Senegal, and Belgium has announced that it is investigating the alleged human rights abuses of the former President of Iran, Rafsanjani. In the Netherlands, a court is considering whether it would have jurisdiction to try the former President of Suriname for the cruel killings of twelve opposition leaders in Suriname in 1982.[204] The court's suggestion that the former leader may be prosecuted for torture might mean that the Netherlands is now prepared to take its obligations under the Torture Convention more seriously.[205]

The 'Pinochet precedent' is, apart from the theoretical considerations set out above, likely to be restricted by practical considerations, and the 'Pinochet effect' should therefore not be overrated. One commentator pessimistically argued that 'the decision will presumably only lead to more sophisticated travel plans by those who have reason to fear foreign prosecutors'.[206] More importantly, as a rule, States are likely to remain apprehensive of adjudicating claims that have no direct bearing on their

[203] Gerechtshof Amsterdam, *Chili Komitee Nederland* v. *Public Prosecutor* (1995), reproduced in *Netherlands Yearbook of International Law*, 28 (1997), pp. 363–5; C. Ingelse and H. van der Wilt, 'De Zaak Pinochet, Over Universele Rechtsmacht en Hollandse Benepenheid', *Nederlands Juristen Blad*, 71 (1996), pp. 280–5; M. Kamminga and M. Tijssen, 'Pinochet, Nederland en het VN-Verdrag tegen Foltering', *NJCM-Bulletin*, 20 (1995), pp. 986–95.

[204] Gerechtshof Amsterdam, Beschikking 3 March 2000 (rekestnr. R 97/163/12Sv & R 97/176/12Sv).

[205] Ibid., para. 5.5.3. A report on the possibility of establishing jurisdiction over these crimes under customary international law, produced on request of the court, concluded that the relevant acts probably qualify as crimes against humanity as well as torture and are subject to universal jurisdiction under customary international law (C. J. R. Dugard, *In re Bouterse* (7 July 2000), on file with author). However, there is no basis in Dutch legislation to prosecute crimes against humanity, while the Dutch torture legislation was enacted in 1988 and does not have retroactive effect. Moreover, it should be noted that with regard to any immunity questions, the Pinochet precedent could not be relied upon since Suriname is not a party to the Torture Convention and the prohibition on crimes against humanity is not codified in a convention comparable to the Torture Convention.

[206] J. Bröhmer, 'Diplomatic Immunity, Head of State Immunity, State Immunity: Misconceptions of a Notorious Human Rights Violator', *Leiden Journal of International Law*, 12 (1999), p. 361, at p. 370.

internal affairs.[207] The investigation into the acts of Habre was abandoned shortly and when the former Ethiopian dictator Mengistu visited South Africa in November 1999 for medical treatment, the Pinochet precedent did not convince the South African authorities to exercise their judicial powers over him. On 6 January 1999 three complaints were filed in French courts by two Cuban nationals and one French national against Fidel Castro for, *inter alia*, crimes against humanity. On 26 February 1999 the court issued an 'Ordonnance de non-informer', declining to proceed. The recent activity in domestic courts should probably be seen as exceptions to the prevailing reluctance of States to exercise extra-territorial jurisdiction, especially when (former) foreign heads of State are involved. The *Pinochet* case and the subsequent interest in the possibility of prosecution for crimes against international law before foreign domestic courts is promising. A world in which there is no safe haven for perpetrators of heinous crimes is, however, still some distance away.

[207] See the Redress Report on Universal Jurisdiction in Europe, http://www.redress.org/unijeur.html for an overview of State practice of ten European States with respect to universal jurisdiction.

THE LAW AND PROCEDURE OF THE INTERNATIONAL COURT OF JUSTICE 1960–1989*

(PART ELEVEN)

By HUGH THIRLWAY*

IV. Questions of Jurisdiction and Competence, 1954–1989 (*concluded*)

 Professor of International Law, Graduate Institute of International Studies Geneva; Visiting Professor, Meijers Institute, University of Leiden; sometime Principal Legal Secretary, International Court of Justice.

V. Questions of Procedure, 1954–1989

IV. Questions of Jurisdiction and Competence, 1954–1989 (*concluded*)

CHAPTER I: JURISDICTION IN CONTENTIOUS CASES (*concluded*)

11. *Jurisdiction and admissibility*

The distinction between these two concepts is material exclusively in a procedural context, in particular as regards the treatment of preliminary objections, and might therefore be discussed in the section of these articles devoted to questions of procedure; but Fitzmaurice chose to discuss the matter under the general heading of jurisdiction,[1] and it seems more convenient to follow his example.[2] At this point, however, no attempt will be made to survey the various objections which have been presented before the Court, as jurisdictional or admissibility questions or otherwise, and to comment on such specific classification, since such a discussion would be better placed in a discussion of preliminary objections. The present purpose is merely to comment on the disputed question of the nature of the distinction between the two categories—if indeed such a distinction exists or can be usefully employed—, and the question of the relative priority to be accorded to the two categories in the consideration of objections presented in a given case. Both are to be distinguished from the 'merits'—though, as noted in a previous article,[3] that distinction is not always as sharp as might be expected.

In passing, it may be noted that it is also uncertain whether the two categories together cover all the possible objections which may be made to prevent the Court examining the merits of the case: the contrary is suggested by the extensive wording of Article 79 of the 1978 Rules of Court: 'Any objection by the respondent to the jurisdiction of the Court or to the admissibility of the application, or other objection the decision upon which is requested before any further proceedings on the merits . . . '.[4] The previous (1946) Rules, and those of the Permanent Court, did not define a 'preliminary objection', and most, though not all, of

[1] This *Year Book*, 34 (1958), pp. 11–13; G. Fitzmaurice, *The Law and Procedure of the International Court of Justice* (1986) (hereinafter referred to as the *Collected Edition*), Vol. II, pp. 438–40.

[2] Furthermore, while categorization of objections as relating to jurisdiction or admissibility is a practical issue for purely procedural purposes, the underlying distinction is linked with considerations of principle going to the nature of jurisdiction.

[3] This *Year Book*, 69 (1998), p.13.

[4] Article 97 of the Rules of the International Tribunal for the Law of the Sea, which follows the wording of Art. 79 of the ICJ Rules, was the subject of an interesting interpretation in the case of the *M/V Saiga (Nr. 2)*; see para. 52 of the Judgment of 1 July 1999.

those presented to the Permanent Court, and treated by it as such, were objections to jurisdiction. The logic of suspending the proceedings on the merits, pending settlement of questions of jurisdiction, is clear, on the basis that a respondent State should not be called upon to defend itself before a tribunal whose jurisdiction is not yet established. However, the same logic does not extend to an objection to admissibility; an alleged ground of inadmissibility may very well be such that it is logically *appropriate* (or merely convenient) to settle it before turning to the merits, but to assert inadmissibility does not imply, as does an objection to jurisdiction, that the Court has *no power* to examine the merits. It has even been argued (and denied) that there may be a 'merits preliminary objection'.[5]

In his 1958 article, dealing with decisions of the Court given from 1951 to 1954, Fitzmaurice expressed the view that 'there is a clear jurisprudential distinction between an objection to the jurisdiction of the tribunal, and an objection to the substantive admissibility of the claim', and that this distinction 'ought to be maintained, both on account of its jurisprudential importance and because it may involve considerable differences of treatment and procedure in particular cases'.[6] He defined the distinction as follows:

> The latter [admissibility] is a plea that the tribunal should rule the claim to be inadmissible on some ground other than its ultimate merits: the former [jurisdiction] is a plea that the tribunal itself is incompetent to give any ruling at all whether as to the merits or as to the admissibility of the claim.[7]

The procedural differences to which Fitzmaurice referred were exemplified in the *Ambatielos* case, which he was discussing, and which presented special features; but broadly, the point of the distinction may be taken to be that a Court must be satisfied that it has jurisdiction before it examines questions of admissibility.

Consistently with this approach, in the *Norwegian Loans* case in 1957 the Court disposed of the application by upholding a Norwegian objection to jurisdiction, and left undetermined an objection to admissibility based on alleged failure to exhaust local remedies. However, in the *Interhandel* decision in 1959, the Court took a different course, which attracted doctrinal comment and disapproval. It was in this context that

[5] See Morelli, 'Eccezioni preliminari di merito?', *Rivista di diritto internazionale*, LVIII (1975), p. 5; Sperduti, 'Ancora sulle eccezioni preliminari di merito', ibid., p. 657.

[6] This *Year Book* 34 (1958), pp. 11, 12; *Collected Edition*, Vol. I, pp. 438, 439.

[7] Loc. cit., footnote omitted. Cf. the definition of the distinction made by Grisel (*Les exceptions d'incompétence et d'irrecevabilité dans la procédure de la CIJ*, Berne, 1968, pp. 74–5): 'l'exception d'incompétence conteste toujours la réalité, la validité ou l'étendue du *consentement* donné par les parties aux pouvoirs de la Cour; si celle-ci accueille un tel moyen dans une affaire donnée, elle se déclare ainsi sans pouvoir pour trancher aucun élément de ce litige. Au contraire, l'exception d'irrecevabilité s'appuie sur toutes les règles de procédure qui ne sont pas relatives au problème du consentement; quand elle est admise par la Cour, cela ne signifie pas que celle-ci est privée de tout pouvoir en l'occurrence, mais seulement que la requête est entachée d'un vice de procédure.'

Fitzmaurice returned to the question of the order of examination of objections to jurisdiction and objections to admissibility, after his election as a Member of the Court, but in an academic capacity. In one of his articles on 'Hersch Lauterpacht—the Scholar as Judge', he discussed the Court's handling of the objections presented by Switzerland in the *Interhandel* case, and approved the position taken by Lauterpacht in his dissenting opinion. The Court in the *Interhandel* case rejected two of the three jurisdictional objections, and left aside the third (relating to the validity and effect of the 'Connally reservation' in the United States acceptance of the optional clause), to uphold the objection based on non-exhaustion of local remedies. For Lauterpacht and Fitzmaurice, '*all* the *jurisdictional* objections raised in a case must be heard and rejected first, before the Court can deal with anything else, since only then will it be competent to deal with anything else'.[8]

The essence of Fitzmaurice's argument was that 'until a Court has decided that it has jurisdiction, in a case where its jurisdiction is the subject of challenge, it cannot properly decide, or even consider anything else at all—for in the absence of jurisdiction, it lacks all competence of any kind';[9] he reserved of course the exercise of ancillary jurisdiction, not dependent on the existence of substantive jurisdiction, e.g. the jurisdiction to indicate provisional measures.[10] The logic of this position is unassailable; but it would mean that if the Court were faced with a number of unconvincing objections to jurisdiction, and a convincing objection to admissibility, it would have to work through all the objections to jurisdiction before rejecting the application as inadmissible, a course involving some lack of judicial economy. This would be particularly inappropriate if the objection to admissibility were of a kind which, if upheld, would put an end to the case irrevocably. In the *Interhandel* case, the essential justification of the strictures of Lauterpacht lay in the circumstance that the objection upheld by the Court, that of non-exhaustion of local remedies, was one which could be cured. For Lauterpacht,

> A judgment of this Court, based on the fact of the non-exhaustion of local remedies, implies the assurance to the applicant State that, once it has done its best to exhaust local remedies, the Court will proceed to the adjudication of the case on the merits—unhampered by any other objections to the jurisdiction. There would otherwise be no point in requiring the injured party to exhaust local remedies—only, once it had done so, to see its claim defeated on account of some other preliminary objection.[11]

[8] This *Year Book*, 38 (1962), p. 57; *Collected Edition*, Vol. II, p. 761 (emphasis original).

[9] This *Year Book*, 38 (1962), p. 54; *Collected Edition*, Vol. II, p. 758.

[10] See a previous article in this series, this *Year Book*, 69 (1998), pp. 17 ff.

[11] *ICJ Reports*, 1959, p. 100; quoted in this *Year Book*, 38 (1962), p. 56, and *Collected Edition*, Vol. II., p. 760, with the omission of the word 'other' in the first sentence; Fitzmaurice pointed out that the local remedies objection was not itself a jurisdictional one.

But can the Court give such an assurance? The acceptance of an objection based on the non-exhaustion of local remedies puts an end to the proceedings currently before the Court; the applicant may then exhaust the available remedies and present a new application, but although the *claim* remains the same, the *case* or the *proceedings* are different.[12] By the time the new case is presented, the title of jurisdiction relied on in the original proceedings may have expired or been withdrawn. The respondent may also present, in the second set of proceedings, a valid jurisdictional objection that it simply had not thought of when defending the first proceedings.[13] At least, Lauterpacht's dictum must be limited to an assurance relating to jurisdictional objections presented in the proceedings in which the dismissal for non-exhaustion of local remedies occurs. But in that case, the argument becomes circular: if all jurisdictional objections have in fact been disposed of, the decision may be taken as an assurance that they have been disposed of,[14] if one has been specifically left open, as in the *Interhandel* decision, then the assurance does not extend to that objection.

A much stronger argument is therefore that the Court simply has no power to rule on a question of admissibility unless it has first established its jurisdiction over the merits, however inconvenient the practical result of applying this principle may be. Given that all jurisdiction rests on consent, an argument could however possibly be made for a sort of jurisdiction by acquiescence or *forum prorogatum*, to the effect that, unless indicated otherwise, the respondent will be leaving to the Court the choice of which objection it upholds, provided the result is to dismiss the claim. The applicant, however, in the scenario envisaged by Lauterpacht of dismissal for non-exhaustion of local remedies, might well want to know what the ultimate fate of the jurisdictional objections might be, in order to know whether there was any point in exhausting them.

In his judicial capacity in the *Northern Cameroons* case, Fitzmaurice reiterated the distinction he had made in the 1958 *Year Book* article, but gave a somewhat different definition of the distinguishing criterion:

> [T]he real distinction and test would seem to be whether or not the objection is based on, or arises from, the jurisdictional clause or clauses under which the jurisdiction of the tribunal is said to exist. If so, the objection is basically one of jurisdiction.[15]

[12] In the *Barcelona Traction* case, Spain contended that the discontinuance of the earlier proceedings brought by Belgium, relative to the same events in Spain, 'disentitled the Applicant Government from bringing the present proceedings' (*ICJ Reports*, 1964, p. 16); see below, text and n. 26.

[13] In such circumstances, the applicant would no doubt argue that the failure to raise the objection earlier involved some estoppel or *forum prorogatum*, but it is suggested that these arguments would not be sound.

[14] Technically, even that may be doubted: the effect of *res judicata* under Article 59 is limited to 'that particular case', and the new proceedings will be a new 'case' even if the claim is identical.

[15] Separate opinion, *ICJ Reports*, 1963, pp. 102–3.

He went on to recall that, as he had observed in 1958, the classification into jurisdictional questions and admissibility questions is oversimplified, and to discuss, in the context of the *Northern Cameroons* decision the distinction between substantive jurisdiction and preliminary or incidental jurisdiction, already examined in the previous article in this series.[16]

In the same case Judge Koretsky followed and applied Fitzmaurice's distinction, and was thus led to dissent from the Court's decision (which Fitzmaurice himself had supported); this was because the question on which the judgment turned—whether the claim had become without object, and adjudication therefore devoid of purpose—was classified by Fitzmaurice, and by implication, by the majority of the Court, as a pre-preliminary jurisdictional question, whereas for Judge Koretsky it was a question of admissibility. In his view therefore the Court had departed from the 'broadly accepted rule' that 'the Court should first decide on its jurisdiction and subsequently consider the plea of inadmissibility'.[17]

In his opinion in the *Northern Cameroons* case Fitzmaurice also modified his view as to the relationship between objections to admissibility and objections to jurisdiction. Repeating an earlier observation[18] that the classification of preliminary objections into these two categories was oversimplified, he suggested that

> in the field of admissibility or receivability, some objections clearly cannot, or ought not to, be gone into or decided until after the competence of the tribunal is fully established; whereas others can, and must, be taken in advance, and irrespective of any determination of competence.[19]

As an example of an objection of the latter category, he suggested

> a plea that the Application did not disclose the existence, properly speaking, of any legal dispute between the parties, [which] must precede competence, for if there is no dispute, there is nothing in relation to which the Court can consider whether it is competent or not. It is for this reason that such a plea would be rather one of admissibility or receivability than of competence.[20]

Again, the conclusion does not seem to be logically inescapable: it is possible for the Court to examine its jurisdiction on the assumption that there is, as asserted by the applicant State, a legal dispute between the parties; and having established that it has jurisdiction on that basis, to turn, in the exercise of the jurisdiction so established, to the question whether that dispute really exists. This may or may not be an economical

[16] This *Year Book*, 69 (1998), pp. 17–22.

[17] Declaration of Judge Koretsky, *ICJ Reports*, 1963, p. 39.

[18] In this *Year Book*, (1958), pp. 56–60; *Collected Edition*, pp. 482–6.

[19] *ICJ Reports*, 1963, p. 104. The French translation has not retained the distinction 'admissibility or receivability', referring simply to 'la recevabilité'; this is understandable, but it probably blurs a distinction that Fitzmaurice considered it useful to make.

[20] Ibid., p. 105.

method of proceeding, depending on how convincing or otherwise the arguments are in favour of the existence of the dispute: but there is no inherent logical reason to proceed otherwise. To reserve the question of merits jurisdiction for a later stage necessarily involves exercising the 'pre-preliminary' jurisdiction discerned by Fitzmaurice, and employed in *Northern Cameroons* and *Nuclear Tests*; the existence of such jurisdiction may be conceded, but it is surely exceptional in nature, and to be carefully kept within bounds, in view of the over-riding sanctity of the principle of jurisdiction as based on consent.

This approach may be compared with the view taken by Judge Morelli in his dissenting opinion in the first phase of the *South West Africa* case. He there observed that the terms 'admissibility' and 'inadmissibility' had sometimes been used to indicate the presence or absence of jurisdiction;[21] or even to refer to questions of merits, though this usage he considered incorrect. He continued:

> Admissibility can relate only to conditions lack of fulfilment of which prevents a decision on the merits. Within these limits, however, it is quite possible to give the term a very wide meaning so as to refer to all the conditions having that character, including jurisdiction.[22]

Judge Morelli thought the question of terminology 'of only secondary importance', but emphasized that, in his view, among the conditions of admissibility other than those relating to jurisdiction,

> there are some which must be considered before the question of jurisdiction is considered. One of these, for example, is the condition of validity of the application, because a Court which is not validly seised cannot adjudicate even on its jurisdiction. Another such is the condition of the existence of a dispute, since it is only in relation to a genuinely existing dispute that it is possible to decide whether such a dispute is subject or not to the jurisdiction of the Court to which it has been referred.[23]

The second difficulty, at least, can be got round by applying the principle noted above, that, in determining the existence of jurisdiction, the Court is entitled to proceed on the hypothesis that the contentions (other than as to jurisdiction) of the applicant State are correct: i.e. to express the question in the form: assuming that a dispute of the kind alleged by the Applicant exists, does it fall within the jurisdictional title asserted?

Furthermore, a question which is prompted by Judge Morelli's analysis is this: if the Court, when dealing with the problem of the existence of a dispute, has *ex hypothesi* not yet determined whether or not it has jurisdiction, from what source does it derive jurisdiction to determine the existence of a dispute? Article 36, paragraph 6, of the

[21] *ICJ Reports*, 1962, pp. 573–4, referring to the *Phosphates in Morocco* case.
[22] *ICJ Reports*, 1962, p. 574.
[23] Ibid.

Statute resolves this dilemma in the context of problems of jurisdiction, so that to examine an objection to jurisdiction before turning to questions of admissibility cannot, *pace* Judge Morelli, be faulted on jurisdictional grounds; but can the *compétence de la compétence* be extended so as to be also a *compétence de la recevabilité*? Presumably one answer to this conundrum is Fitzmaurice's theory of 'pre-preliminary jurisdiction'; this was in effect the answer given by the Court 12 years later in the *Nuclear Tests* cases (examined below), where, before ascertaining whether or not it had jurisdiction, the Court rejected the applications on the ground that 'the dispute having disappeared, the claim . . . no longer has any object';[24] to do so it claimed to be exercising

> an inherent jurisdiction enabling it to take such action as may be required, on the one hand to ensure that the exercise of its jurisdiction over the merits, if and when established, shall not be frustrated, and on the other, to provide for the orderly settlement of all matters in dispute . . . [25]

In its 1964 Judgment on preliminary objections in the *Barcelona Traction* case, the Court dealt first with an objection which might have been regarded as one addressed to admissibility, before turning to a clearly jurisdictional objection based on an alleged lack of a 'jurisdictional nexus'. The first objection was to the effect that a discontinuance of previous proceedings relative to the same events in Spain 'disentitled the Applicant Government from bringing the present proceedings' (the wording is that of the Court).[26] However, this objection had been presented by the Spanish Government itself in its submissions in the form of asking the Court 'to adjudge and declare that the Application . . . and the final Submissions [of Belgium] . . . are definitely inadmissible', on the ground (*inter alia*) that

> any jurisdiction of the Court to decide issues relating to the claim formulated in the new Belgian Application of 1962, either to competence, to admissibility or to the merits, came to an end as a result of [the discontinuance].[27]

The objection was thus presented as an objection to admissibility based on lack of jurisdiction; or possibly as a sort of 'pre-preliminary' objection as identified by Fitzmaurice in his opinion in the *Northern Cameroons* case.[28] The Court did not enter into the question of the procedural nature of the objection, but this question was closely examined by Judge Morelli in a dissenting opinion; his conclusion was that the question raised by the objection was not a preliminary one at all, but part of the merits, and the

[24] *ICJ Reports,* 1974, p. 271, para. 56; ibid., p. 476, para. 59.
[25] Ibid., 1974, p. 259, para. 23; ibid., p. 463, para. 23.
[26] Ibid., 1964, p. 16.
[27] Ibid., p. 15.
[28] Ibid., 1963, p. 103; see also a previous article in this series, this *Year Book*, 69 (1998), pp. 17 ff.

objection should therefore have been declared inadmissible as a preliminary objection.[29]

In the second phase of the *South West Africa* case, in 1966, the question of categorization of matters of jurisdiction and admissibility took on an unexpected importance. Having in 1962 rejected four preliminary objections and found that it had 'jurisdiction to adjudicate upon the merits', the Court in 1966 found that

> the Applicants cannot be considered to have established any legal right or interest appertaining to them in the subject-matter of the present claims, and that, accordingly, the Court must decline to give effect to them.[30]

The Court took note in its decision that it had been suggested that this question 'is really one of the admissibility of the claim, and . . . as such it was disposed of by the Court's 1962 Judgment'.[31] Its response to this was simply to deny that any question of the admissibility of the claim had been raised at the preliminary objection stage, the Respondent's preliminary objections being addressed solely to jurisdiction; and that 'If therefore any question of admissibility were involved, it would fall to be decided now'.[32] This categorization was strongly rejected by dissenting Judges such as Judge Koretsky[33] and Judge Jessup.[34]

In the *Nuclear Tests* cases the Court declined to treat the concept of 'questions of admissibility' as an overall category, as presented in the philosophy of Judge Morelli, and comprising all 'preliminary questions'; since, after referring to issues of jurisdiction and admissibility that had been raised in the case, it found that

> while examining these questions of a preliminary character, the Court is entitled, and in some circumstances may be required, to go into other questions which may not be strictly capable of classification as matters of jurisdiction or admissibility but are of such a nature as to require examination in priority to those matters.[35]

Judge Gros, in that case, considered that when grounds had been invoked in support of a contention that a case be not judged on the

[29] *ICJ Reports,* 1964, p. 107, para. 9. Judge Morelli pointed out that 'the only possible subject of a declaration of inadmissibility would be the application instituting the proceedings in which the declaration of inadmissibility is made', and that what Belgium was really asking for was a judgment on the merits, that Belgium, by abandoning the earlier proceedings, had renounced its claim: see ibid., pp. 107–8.

[30] *ICJ Reports,* 1966, p. 51, para. 99.

[31] Ibid., 1966, p. 42, para. 74.

[32] Ibid., p. 43, para. 75.

[33] Ibid., p. 239; Judge Koretsky considered that 'The question of an applicant's "interest" (as a question of a "*qualité*") even in national-law systems is considered as a jurisdictional question'.

[34] Ibid., p.336; Judge Jessup asserted that 'as explained in the 1962 Judgment and as emphasized in the dissenting opinion of Judge Morelli, they include objections to the *admissibility* of the claim'. No references are given; and it is suggested that there is here a confusion between what the Court decided and the decision that Judge Morelli would have preferred, the latter being, indeed, that 'the claims should be held inadmissible' (*ICJ Reports,* 1962, p. 573).

[35] *ICJ Reports,* 1974, p. 259, para. 22.

merits, the Court had always 'taken the greatest possible care not to commit itself either to any sort of classification of these various grounds . . . or to any sort of ranking them in order'.[36] In his view,

the principle which the Court applies is a common-sense one: if a finding is sufficient in itself to settle the question of the Court's competence, in the widest sense of the word, that is to say to lead to the conclusion that it is impossible to give judgment in a case, then there is no need to proceed to examine other grounds.[37]

However, the ground on which Judge Gros would have put an end to the case was not one on which his colleagues were agreed, namely that there never had been a legal dispute between Australia and New Zealand and France. A similar view was taken by Judge Petrén.[38] These two judges were therefore presumably adopting the approach of Morelli in *South West Africa*, quoted above,[39] that the question of the existence of a dispute logically precedes, or at least may be allowed to precede, the question of the existence of jurisdiction.

The joint dissenting opinion of Judges Onyeama, Dillard, Jiménez de Aréchaga and Waldock in the *Nuclear Tests* cases drew attention to a further source of confusion between matters of jurisdiction and matters of admissibility. In their view, the Court had jurisdiction under the 1928 General Act for the Pacific Settlement of International Disputes; Article 17 of that Act referred to disputes 'with regard to which the parties are in conflict as to their respective rights', thus excluding political or non-legal disputes. The question whether the dispute before the Court was a political one had been raised; and the four dissenting judges pointed out that:

The matters raised by the issues of 'legal or political dispute' and 'legal interest', although intrinsically matters of admissibility, are at the same time matters which, under the terms of Article 17 of the 1928 Act, also go to the Court's jurisdiction in the present case. Accordingly, it would be pointless for us to characterize any particular issue as one of jurisdiction or of admissibility, more especially as the practice neither of the Permanent Court nor of this Court supports the drawing of a sharp distinction between preliminary objections to jurisdiction and admissibility.[40]

There is no reason why an instrument conferring jurisdiction should not, presumably *ex abundante cautela*, specify as conditions of jurisdiction requirements which would in any event be treated as matters of admissibility—for example by excluding disputes which had become 'moot'. Anything which is a condition of the consent given to the

[36] Separate opinion, *ICJ Reports*, 1974, p. 277, para. 3.
[37] Op. cit., p. 278, para. 3.
[38] *ICJ Reports*, 1974, p. 306.
[39] Above, text and n. 23.
[40] *ICJ Reports*, 1974, p. 363, para. 105.

jurisdiction of the Court has to be treated as a jurisdictional matter, whether or not it would have been otherwise characterized had it not been mentioned in the title of jurisdiction.[41]

More recent cases on the whole support the general rule of priority advanced by Lauterpacht and Fitzmaurice, inasmuch as the Court, when faced with challenges both to jurisdiction and the admissibility of the claim, has chosen to take the jurisdictional issues first.[42] This was the course adopted in *Military and Paramilitary Activities in and against Nicaragua*,[43] and *Border and Transborder Armed Actions*,[44] *Maritime Delimitation and Territorial Questions between Qatar and Bahrain*,[45] and in the two cases concerning *Questions of Interpretation and Application of the 1971 Montreal Convention arising from the Aerial Incident at Lockerbie*.[46] In *Elettronica Sicula*, the Court noted that it was common ground between the parties that the Court had jurisdiction in the case before turning to an objection of the United States to the admissibility of the application.[47]

In the case of *Certain Phosphate Lands in Nauru*, one of the preliminary objections of Australia was classifiable, from one aspect, as a matter of jurisdiction, and from another aspect, as a matter of admissibility. Nauru's claim, in proceedings brought against Australia, was for reparation for injury suffered at the hands of the Administering Authority for Nauru during the period that Nauru was a trust territory under Chapter XII of the UN Charter. Australia based an objection (among others) on the absence of the proceedings from the other two States which had, with Australia, made up that Administering Authority (United Kingdom and New Zealand). So far as this objection was based on an assertion that a claim for breach of the Trusteeship could only be brought against all three States jointly, this was treated as a matter of admissibility.[48]

[41] Contrariwise, Fitzmaurice observed in *Northern Cameroons* that 'since the validity of admissibility objections normally depends on considerations lying outside the jurisdictional clause as such, it is obviously immaterial that the latter has not specifically made the absence of any such grounds of objection a condition of the Court being able to proceed to the ultimate merits'; *ICJ Reports*, 1963, p. 128.

[42] Rosenne offers a different and more sophisticated analysis: 'the general rule is that objections to the receivability of the case (whether on the ground that the title of jurisdiction invoked is not in force or on the ground that the seisin of the Court or the document issuing proceedings is formally or substantially invalid), including objections *ratione personae*, have priority over objections to the jurisdiction *ratione materiae*; and objections to the jurisdiction *ratione materiae* have priority over objections to the admissibility of the claim *ratione materiae* (when there is no question of the validity of the seisin, or of jurisdiction)': Rosenne, *The Law and Practice of the International Court, 1920–1996*, 3rd edn., (1997) Vol. II, p. 904.

[43] *ICJ Reports*, 1984, p. 392.

[44] Ibid., 1988, p. 69.

[45] Ibid., 1995, p. 6, in which the Court observed halfway through its decision that 'Having thus established its jurisdiction, the Court still has to deal with certain problems of admissibility'; loc. cit., p. 24, para. 44.

[46] *ICJ Reports*, 1998, pp. 9 and 115.

[47] Ibid., 1989, pp. 41–2, paras. 48, 49.

[48] Ibid., 1992, pp. 258–9, para. 48.

However, Australia also invoked the principle laid down in the *Monetary Gold* case to assert that the case could not be decided without passing on the legal position of the other two States, and this is a jurisdictional question (though not one of the *existence* of jurisdiction so much as of the propriety of its exercise), since the Court was asked to decline to exercise its jurisdiction—which it refused to do.[49]

In the recent case of the *Land and Maritime Boundary between Cameroon and Nigeria*,[50] the Court proceeded methodically to dispose of the eight Nigerian preliminary objections in the order in which they had been presented; however, those objections which were clearly matters of jurisdiction were presented first, and the precise qualification of some of those appearing later might have been subject to debate, so that the Court's approach seems fully justified.

12. *Jurisdiction and intervention*[51]

The institution of intervention, provided for in Articles 62 and 63 of the Statute,[52] permits a State to become involved in contentious proceedings already set in motion by one State against another. It is necessary to

[49] Ibid., pp. 261–2, para. 55. Australia also objected to one particular Nauruan claim (that relating to the assets of the British Phosphate Commissioners) on the ground that it was a 'new claim' submitted after the institution of proceedings; it was asserted that this claim 'is inadmissible and . . . the Court has no jurisdiction in relation to that claim' (ibid., p. 264, para. 62). The Court devoted the last part of its judgment to dismissing this Nauruan claim as 'inadmissible' (ibid., p. 267, para. 70), without commenting on the jurisdictional aspect. In the operative clause, the Court upheld this particular preliminary objection, as a unit (ibid., p. 268, para. 72 (1) (*g*)).

[50] *ICJ Reports*, 1998, p. 275. In the recent arbitral award in the *Southern Bluefin Tuna* case the arbitrators took the objection based on 'mootness' before questions of jurisdiction (p. 83, para. 45 of the Award); having rejected it, they turned to 'the fundamental and multifaceted issues of jurisdiction', and found that the Tribunal was without jurisdiction (p. 105, para. 65). The Tribunal presumably reasoned that if the ICJ could deal with an issue of 'mootness' without first confirming jurisdiction, in the *Nuclear Tests* cases, then the same power belonged to the Tribunal, even though, unlike the Court, it rejected mootness, and then found it was without jurisdiction. The Tribunal then went on to say that, since it lacked jurisdiction, it 'does not find it necessary to pass upon questions of the admissibility of the dispute', with the curious implication that it could have done so, despite having no jurisdiction.

[51] This question might have been reserved for a subsequent article, under the heading of Procedure, dealing with the conditions and procedure of intervention generally; but as in the case of provisional measures (dealt with in this *Year Book*, 69 (1998) at pp. 22–3), it has seemed more appropriate to give some account here of the special problems of jurisdiction, even if they may have to be discussed further later. If a reader wonders why jurisdiction in relation to intervention was not dealt with under incidental jurisdiction, along with provisional measures, I can only recall what was said at the outset of the series as to the difficulty of advance planning and the need for the occasional afterthought: this *Year Book* 60 (1989), p. 6.

[52] Article 62: 1. Should a State consider that it has an interest of a legal nature which may be affected by the decision in the case, it may submit a request to be permitted to intervene. 2. It shall be for the Court to decide upon this request.
Article 63: 1. Whenever the construction of a convention to which States other than those concerned in the case are parties is in question, the Registrar shall notify all such States forthwith. 2. Every State so notified has the right to intervene in the proceedings; but if it uses this right, the construction given by the judgment will be equally binding upon it.

use the loose term 'to become involved in' because one of the most controverted questions in relation to intervention has been whether or not an intervening State can be said to become a party to the proceedings. Even if the intervening State is not a party (and *a fortiori* if it is), its involvement poses the question of consent in relation to jurisdiction: the consent of the respondent State is essential for the Court to exercise jurisdiction over it, but that consent will generally be limited *ratione personae*, and the applicant State will have to show that there is what has come to be called a 'jurisdictional link' between itself and the respondent. This is particularly evident in the context of proceedings brought on the basis of acceptances of jurisdiction under the 'optional clause' of Article 36, paragraph 2, of the Statute,[53] but is a universal requirement for jurisdiction to exist.

The consent of the intervening State, like that of the applicant State, may be taken to be entailed in its decision to enter the proceedings; but the intervention may not be welcomed by the original parties, and the question therefore arises whether there must exist also a 'jurisdictional link' between those States and the intervener. There is in any event a 'consent to Statute': all States parties to the Statute have agreed, by becoming parties, that intervention in proceedings to which they are parties may take place according to Articles 62 and 63, just as they have agreed that the Court may indicate provisional measures in such proceedings according to Article 41. In the latter case, as noted in a previous article,[54] the jurisdiction to indicate measures is an independent jurisdiction, derived solely from consent to Statute, with the consequence that the Court can validly indicate measures without first establishing its jurisdiction over the merits, and even if it proves subsequently to have had no merits jurisdiction (as occurred in the *Anglo-Iranian Oil Co.* case). Similarly, the consent to Article 62 and 63 might be taken to be sufficient to enable the Court to proceed with a case involving an intervener even without the immediate consent of the original parties.[55] Alternatively, it might be thought that since an intervener can take the side of, for example, the applicant (as Fiji sought to do in the *Nuclear Tests* case), it would be unjust (and therefore cannot be the correct interpretation of the Statute) for it to do so unless there exists a title of jurisdiction which would have permitted it to bring independent proceedings against the respondent for the same cause of action. It is probable that the draftsmen of the Statute did not have a clear view one

[53] See section 10 of the present Chapter, in the previous article in this series: this *Year Book*, 70 (1999), pp. 29 ff.

[54] This *Year Book*, 69 (1998), pp. 22–3.

[55] This was the view of Fitzmaurice, writing at a time when the question had not yet been raised in a case before the Court: this *Year Book*, 34 (1958), p. 125; *Collected Edition*, Vol. II, p. 550.

way or the other on this point;[56] at all events the text gives no particular handle for either interpretation.

The problem had not arisen in practice when Fitzmaurice discussed intervention in his articles, and he then appears to have had no doubts on the point: but during the period now under review the matter became one of practical importance and fairly fierce controversy. In two successive cases an attempt was made by a third State to intervene in circumstances where the original parties might be expected to be unenthusiastic at the prospect: first, because the cases concerned maritime delimitation, and in each of them neither State party was likely to be anxious to see their bilateral delimitation complicated by being made trilateral;[57] and because the cases were brought by special agreement, which, on the political level, made them more the 'property' of the original parties, and on the legal level made it impossible for any intervening State to assert the *same* title of jurisdiction as that linking the parties.

The question had however already arisen, but remained unsettled, in the *Nuclear Tests* cases, when Fiji sought to intervene in the proceedings brought against France by Australia and by New Zealand. That application lapsed when the Court decided that the main proceedings no longer had any object;[58] but four Members of the Court and the judge *ad hoc* indicated, in declarations attached to the Order recording the lapse, that it would have been necessary to enquire into the question whether 'there existed a sufficient jurisdictional link between Fiji and France to justify the former's intervention'.[59]

The question was then raised in a different context: that of the drafting of the Rules of Court. In the revised Rules adopted in 1978, the provision as to the content of a request for permission to intervene[60] included a new requirement, corresponding to nothing in Article 62 of the Statute:

> The application . . . shall set out:
> . . .
> (*c*) any basis of jurisdiction which is claimed to exist as between the State applying to intervene and the parties to the case.

[56] In this sense Rosenne, *The Law and Practice of the International Court*, 3rd edn. (1997) Vol. III, p. 1485; it should not be forgotten that the Statute was originally drafted on the basis that the Court would have universal compulsory jurisdiction, and if this had been maintained the question would never have arisen.

[57] Even though one of the 'relevant circumstances' to be taken into account in a delimitation has been stated to be 'the effects, actual or prospective, of any other continental shelf delimitations between adjacent States in the same region' (*North Sea Continental Shelf, ICJ Reports,* 1969, p. 54, para. 101 (D) (3)).

[58] Judgments of 20 December 1974, *ICJ Reports,* 1974, pp. 253, 457.

[59] Joint declaration of Judges Dillard and Waldock, ibid., 1974, p. 532; see also the declaration of Judge Onyeama, ibid., p. 531, and that of Judge *ad hoc* Barwick, ibid., p. 533.

[60] Article 82, paragraph 2, of the 1978 Rules, replacing Article 64, paragraph 2, of the 1946 Rules.

This text was to puzzle commentators and counsel: did it imply that the existence of such a basis of jurisdiction was a condition for the grant of permission to intervene? Was it open to the Court to add a new condition of intervention, not provided for in the Statute? And if that were the intention, one would have expected the words '*the* basis of jurisdiction which . . . ';[61] the word 'any' seemed to recognize that there might be no such basis, and that that would not necessarily be a bar to the admission of the intervention. But if a basis of jurisdiction was not a requirement, why mention it at all?[62]

An answer was given to this question when in 1981 Malta applied to intervene in the *Continental Shelf* case between Tunisia and Libya. Malta conceded that there was no jurisdictional link between itself and those two States. Its application for permission to intervene was rejected, but not directly on that ground; it had not sought to become a full party to the case, but merely to inform the Court, and the Court held that this 'direct yet limited form of participation in the subject-matter of the proceedings' could not 'properly be admitted as falling within the terms of . . . intervention' under Article 62.[63] The Court carefully kept open the jurisdictional question, indicating that it was

> unnecessary to decide in the present case the question whether the existence of a valid link of jurisdiction with the parties to the case is an essential condition for the granting of permission to intervene under Article 62 of the Statute.[64]

Surprisingly, in view of this reservation, the Court went out of its way to explain its action in 1978 in including the reference to jurisdiction in the Rules. After recalling the fate of Fiji's application in 1974, and the comments in judges' declarations, it mentioned the inclusion by the Court of sub-paragraph (*c*) in Article 82, the purpose of which, it explained, had been

> to ensure that, when the question did arise in a concrete case, [the Court] would be in possession of all the elements which might be necessary for its decision. At the same time the Court left any question with which it might in future be confronted in regard to intervention to be decided on the basis of the Statute and in the light of the particular circumstances of each case.[65]

As this case showed, and as the subsequent case between Libya and Malta was to show still more dramatically, it was not possible to resolve

[61] The French text points to the same interpretation: 'La requête indique . . . *toute* base de compétence qui, selon l'État demandant à intervenir, existerait . . . '

[62] The declarations made by some judges in 1974 in the *Nuclear Tests* case suggest that, when drafting the new Rules, the Court was divided on the point, and adopted a compromise text which, like most compromises, is somewhat unsatisfactory.

[63] *ICJ Reports*, 1981, p. 19, para. 34.

[64] Ibid., p. 20, para. 36.

[65] Ibid., p. 16, para. 27. A slightly different account was given by Judge Schwebel in his separate opinion: the 'intention was merely to draw attention to the point and to ensure that a State which could indicate such a title of jurisdiction should so inform the Court': ibid., p. 40.

the problem of the jurisdictional link without first making up one's mind what an intervention under Article 62 really consists of, or involves; and whether there is only one kind of intervention, or two or more. Judge Oda did not fail to observe this: while voting for the decision, he disagreed with the finding that the kind of intervention—'non-party intervention'—sought by Malta did not fall under Article 62, and pointed out that this question was 'closely interrelated with two further questions': first, whether or not a jurisdictional link is required, and secondly whether the judgment would be binding on the intervening State.[66]

In 1984 the Court had to rule on a request by Italy for permission to intervene in the *Continental Shelf* case between Libya and Malta. Italy had studied the previous case, and endeavoured to draft its application so as not to encounter the obstacles on which Malta's application had come to grief. On the jurisdictional point, the Court was able to assert that, in order to arrive at its decision, it

> does not have to rule on the question whether, in general, any intervention based on Article 62 must, as a condition for its admission, show the existence of a valid jurisdictional link.[67]

At an earlier stage of the decision, the Court had stated two different arguments, either of which in its view would suffice to justify refusing Italy's application to intervene; 'and the Court accordingly does not have to decide between them'.[68] One of those arguments was that if the Court were to accept that, as urged by Italy, Article 62 by itself sufficed to create the necessary basis of jurisdiction, and to apply that finding to an intervention of the particular kind presented by Italy,

> it would be admitting that the procedure of intervention under Article 62 would constitute an exception to the fundamental principles underlying its jurisdiction: primarily the principle of consent, but also the principles of reciprocity and equality of States. The Court considers that an exception of this kind could not be admitted unless it were very clearly expressed . . . Article 62 of the Statute contains no such express derogation . . . [A]ppeal to that article should thus, if it is to justify an intervention in a case such as that of the Italian application, be backed by a basis of jurisdiction.[69]

The 1984 judgment on the Italian application was obviously the product of a very divided Court, and in view of subsequent developments, too much time should not be spent in analysing its tortured reasoning.[70] For Judge Mbaye, the 'true reason' for the rejection of Italy's application was

[66] *ICJ Reports*, 1981, p. 24, para. 4. This is not the place to study Judge Oda's very thorough analysis of the historical and legal aspects of the question, which will very much repay reading.

[67] Ibid., 1984, p. 24, para. 38.

[68] Ibid.

[69] Ibid., 1984, p. 22, para. 35.

[70] Cf. the criticisms of Abi-Saab, 'De l'évolution de la Cour internationale: réflexions sur quelques tendances récentes', *Revue générale*, 1992, pp. 289–290.

the absence of a jurisdictional link, and that 'unavowed reason makes its presence felt, in spite of the careful language used by the Court . . . '.[71] He took the view, following Judge Oda's approach in the previous case, that it would be consistent with Article 62 to recognize two kinds of intervention: intervention as a party, for which a jurisdictional link would be required; and intervention as a non-party, for which no such link would be required.[72] Judge Jiménez de Aréchaga stated bluntly at the outset of his opinion that he had voted against the Italian application 'because of the absence of a jurisdictional link between Italy and each of the original Parties to the case'.[73] Judge Sette-Camara did not consider that intervention under Article 62 required a jurisdictional link, and pointed out that if that were so in all cases, intervention would only be possible where it was unnecessary, since the intervener could bring direct proceedings against the other parties.[74] However, Judge Oda conceded that even in those circumstances intervention might well be useful 'because it will serve to decrease the number of similar litigations'.[75]

It must have seemed at this point that no intervention under Article 62 of the Statute would ever be permitted, in view of the failure both of the Maltese application, held to ask too much, and the Italian application, held to ask too little. In 1990 however an application for permission to intervene was at last accepted, by a judgment of a Chamber—a detail that may have been significant in view of the divisions of view within the full Court. The Chamber formed to deal with the case of the *Land, Island and Maritime Frontier Dispute* between El Salvador and Honduras decided by a judgment of 13 September 1990 to admit the intervention of Nicaragua. On the vexed question of the 'jurisdictional link', the Chamber was categorical:

> It follows from the juridical nature and from the purposes of intervention that the existence of a valid link of jurisdiction between the would-be intervener and the parties is not a requirement for the success of the application. On the contrary, the procedure of intervention is to ensure that a State with possibly affected interests may be permitted to intervene even though there is no jurisdictional link and it therefore cannot become a party.[76]

This finding has to be read in conjunction with the Chamber's earlier finding that, while intervention under Article 62 does not automatically constitute the intervener a party to the case, this result can follow if the original parties are agreeable: in other words, there are two kinds of intervention, as a party or as a non-party. The necessary consent creative of jurisdiction to admit and entertain the intervention is given by consent

71 Separate opinion of Judge Mbaye, ibid., p. 35.
72 *ICJ Reports,* 1984, p. 43.
73 Ibid., p. 55.
74 Ibid., p. 89.
75 Ibid., p. 92, para. 6.
76 Ibid., 1990, p. 135, para. 100.

to Statute, but this does not extend to admission of the intervener as a party:

> Intervention cannot have been intended to be employed as a substitute for contentious proceedings. Acceptance of the Statute by a State does not of itself create jurisdiction to entertain a particular case; the specific consent of the parties is necessary for that. If an intervener were held to become a party to a case merely as a consequence of being permitted to intervene in it, this would be a very considerable departure from this principle of consensual jurisdiction.[77]

The necessary consent of the parties must, it seems be given *ad hoc*: though the question apparently remains open whether it would be possible for a State which could point to a jurisdictional link with each of the original parties, to intervene as a party even without such *ad hoc* consent, in lieu of commencing separate proceedings and (presumably) asking for them to be joined to the original proceedings.

The Chamber's solution to the puzzle has much to commend it, particularly on the practical level. At first sight, however, it creates a juridical oddity: the Court (or Chamber) is exercising jurisdiction in relation to (it seems difficult to say 'over') the intervener, yet the intervener is not a party, and, as the Chamber itself made clear, therefore 'does not acquire the rights, or become subject to the obligations, which attach to the status of a party, under the Statute and Rules of Court, or the general principles of procedural law'.[78] One such obligation is that of complying with, as being bound by, the eventual judgment in the case. This question arose when the Chamber was preparing its decision, and appears to have come as a surprise, since the 1990 decision to admit the non-party intervention, containing the sentence just quoted, was adopted unanimously, but Vice-President Oda and Judge *ad hoc* Torres Bernardez disagreed with the finding in the 1992 judgment on the merits that 'a State permitted to intervene under Article 62 of the Statute, but which does not acquire the status of party to the case, is not bound by the Judgment given in the proceedings in which it has intervened'.[79] Judge Torres Bernardez based his disagreement on 'the fact that I cannot, as a general proposition, conceive of rights without obligations'[80]—i.e. he was looking to the reciprocity of the relations between the parties and the intervener, rather than those between the intervener and the Court. This was however one of the considerations which the majority of the Chamber had taken into account in deciding that Nicaragua as intervener

[77] Ibid., 1990, p. 134, para. 99.

[78] Ibid., 1990, p. 135, para. 102. What these are, is obscure. See also Rosenne, *The Law and Practice of the International Court, 1920–1996*, 3rd edn., (1997) Vol. III, p. 1544.

[79] *ICJ Reports*, 1992, p. 609, para. 423.

[80] Separate opinion of Judge Torres Bernardez, p. 730, ibid., para. 208.

was not bound. The reason why, in the Chamber's view, an intervener cannot become a party in the absence of a jurisdictional link, or the *ad hoc* consent of the parties, was

> because the force of *res judicata* does not operate in one direction only: if an intervener becomes a party, and is thus bound by the judgment, it becomes entitled equally to assert the binding force of the judgment against the other parties.[81]

Nicaragua had at one stage announced that it intended to 'submit itself to the binding effect of the decision to be given'. The Chamber did not consider that this modified the position:

> A non-party to a case before the Court, whether or not admitted to intervene, cannot by its own unilateral act place itself in the position of a party, and claim to be entitled to rely on the judgment against the original parties.[82]

Judge Oda had in fact foreseen the problem: in his separate opinion in the *Tunisia/Libya* case, he had taken the view later espoused by the Chamber in 1990, that non-party intervention was possible without a jurisdictional link, but even in that case, '[t]he intervening State cannot, of course, escape the binding force of the judgment, which naturally applies to it to the extent that its intervention has been allowed'.[83] In his view, 'to the extent that the Court gives a judgment positively recognizing rights of either of the litigant States, the intervening State will certainly lose all present or future claim in conflict with those rights'.[84] For Judge Oda also, therefore, the matter is one of the relations between the parties and the intervener.

One may thus ask: what is the meaning of 'jurisdiction' in relation to a State which is not bound by any ruling the Court may give?[85] If jurisdiction means the power, conferred by the consent of States, to hear and determine with binding force a dispute between those States, then it becomes apparent that the Court is not in fact exercising any jurisdiction vis-à-vis the intervening State; it simply has jurisdiction, conferred by the original parties through their consent to the Statute, to authorise a third State to make certain presentations to it, and to take them into account in deciding the issues between the parties.

[81] *ICJ Reports*, 1992, p. 610, para. 424.

[82] Ibid.

[83] Separate opinion of Judge Oda, *Continental Shelf (Tunisia/Libya), ICJ Reports*, 1981, p. 27, para. 9.

[84] Ibid.

[85] Is a State which is not a party, and will not be bound by the eventual decision on the merits, bound by any interlocutory decision the Court may take, for example as to time-limits? The intervening State is hardly likely to disregard such decisions, but that does not resolve the issue.

CHAPTER 2: JURISDICTION AND ITS EXERCISE IN ADVISORY PROCEEDINGS

1. *Introduction*

(1) *Jurisdiction, competence, and admissibility in advisory proceedings*

In the present discussion, no distinction will be made between the terms 'jurisdiction' and 'competence', essentially for the same reasons as explained in a previous article[86] in the context of the contentious jurisdiction of the Court. Rosenne suggests that 'in the advisory practice, the same distinction exists between 'jurisdiction' and 'competence', based respectively on an objective and on a subjective element, as is found in the contentious practice';[87] but he does not elaborate, and the distinction seems to serve even less of a useful purpose in the advisory context than in that of contentious proceedings.[88] Another writer has suggested that the distinction is inappropriate in the advisory context since the Court's advisory functions derive directly from the Charter and Statute, and not from the consent of States;[89] however, it is a general axiom that judicial jurisdiction depends upon, and its extent is determined by, the consent of the States concerned. Those instruments thus apply by virtue of an act of consent on the part of States embodied in the act of becoming parties to them; there remains the question whether any other subjective element underlies, or conditions, the Court's power to give opinions.

The distinction between matters of jurisdiction and matters of admissibility is also little used in advisory proceedings, though the author just quoted would make the same distinction as was made by Judge Fitzmaurice in the *Northern Cameroons* case, already quoted above,[90] namely that an objection to the Court entertaining a case is a jurisdictional objection if it 'is based on, or arises from, the jurisdictional clause or clauses under which the jurisdiction of the tribunal is said to exist'[91]—i.e. the Charter or the Statute—and is otherwise one of admissibility, while conceding that attributing a particular contention to the one category or the other may be a matter of considerable difficulty.[92]

[86] This *Year Book*, 69 (1998), p. 4.

[87] *The Law and Practice of the International Court*, 3rd edn., p. 987.

[88] Ibid., p. 535.

[89] Radicati di Brozolo, 'Sulle questioni preliminari nella procedura consultativa', *Rivista di diritto internazionale*, 59 (1976), p. 677. This author also suggests that questions of seisin may be raised in an advisory case, so that Rosenne's tripartite categorization of objections (*The Law and Practice of the International Court*, 2nd edn. (1961) p. 442; see also 3rd edn. (1997) Vol. II, pp. 904–5) could be transferred as a whole to advisory proceedings: op. cit., n. 1.

[90] Text and n. 15 above.

[91] *ICJ Reports*, 1963, pp. 102–3.

[92] Radicati di Brozolo, 'Sulle questioni preliminari nella procedura consultativa, *Rivista di diritto internazionale*, 59 (1976), pp. 681–2.

One reason why the distinction has not taken on any particular importance in practice is because the Court does not, in advisory cases, devote a separate phase of the proceedings to preliminary issues;[93] at most, it may record in the advisory opinion a separate vote on the question whether it should give the opinion at all, before recording the voting on the merits.[94] A procedure of this kind was apparently at one time suggested by Rosenne; but Fitzmaurice appears to have considered that it would cause unacceptable delay in giving the opinion to the organization requesting it.[95] In the *Namibia* case South Africa specifically requested that 'the question of the Court's jurisdiction and the propriety of its furnishing the opinion requested of it be dealt with as preliminary points', and that 'only after these have been determined should arrangements be made for any further proceedings that may be necessary'.[96] The Court, however, did not accept this request. The need for some division of the procedure on these lines was also urged by Judge Petrén in the *Western Sahara* case;[97] and one State participating in the proceedings in the case of the *Legality of the Use by a State of Nuclear Weapons in Armed Conflict* urged the need for two successive sets of hearings, the one for jurisdiction and propriety questions and the second for the merits; but again, the Court did not see fit to adopt this suggestion.[98]

The advantages of such a division in terms of convenience and judicial economy, in any case where there appears to be serious doubt as to the existence of jurisdiction or the propriety of exercising it, are clear; there is also frequently the complication of a claim to appoint a judge *ad hoc*, which is also a matter that has to be resolved at an early stage. However, there is no legally or logically compelling reason to adopt such a

[93] There is, as a result, some risk of losing sight of them: cf. the failure of the Court to respond to one of Mauritania's contentions in the *Western Sahara* case, mentioned below, p. 178. Rosenne (*The Law and Practice of the International Court*, 3rd edn., (1997) Vol. II, p. 1050) even argues that in the *Legal Status of South West Africa* case the Court ignored an objection to jurisdiction presented by Poland (*Pleadings*, pp. 152–3); but it is questionable whether Poland was challenging the Court's jurisdiction, as distinct from arguing that the request should not have been made.

[94] See for example *Application for Review of UNAT Judgment No. 158, ICJ Reports,* 1973, p. 213; *Interpretation of the Agreement of 25 March 1951 between the WHO and Egypt, ICJ Reports,* 1980, p. 96; *Application for Review of UNAT Judgment No. 273, ICJ Reports,* 1982, p. 366. For the difficulties faced by individual judges when this is not done, cf. separate opinion of Judge Azevedo in *Interpretation of Peace Treaties, ICJ Reports,* 1950, p. 79. In the case concerning *Legality of the Use by States of Nuclear Weapons in Armed Conflict*, this lack of a separate preliminary phase meant that a considerable part of the oral and written proceedings was devoted to issues which the Court never came to consider at all, at least in the context of that case, though the material to some extent duplicated that considered by the Court in the parallel case of *Legality of the Threat or Use of Nuclear Weapons*.

[95] This *Year Book*, 34 (1958), p. 140; *Collected Edition*, Vol. II, p. 565.

[96] Letter to the Court dated 14 January 1971, *Legal Consequences for States, Pleadings,* Vol. II, p. 659.

[97] Separate opinion, *ICJ Reports,* 1975, p. 107.

[98] On this see Griffith and Staker, 'The Jurisdiction and Merits Phases Distinguished', in Boisson de Chazournes and Sands (eds.), *International Law, the International Court of Justice and Nuclear Weapons*, (1999) pp. 60–1.

procedure, in view of the extent to which preliminary questions tend, as explained below, to resolve themselves into matters of discretion for the Court: in the contentious context, the Court *cannot* proceed to examine the merits, or any other question, before establishing jurisdiction, but in advisory proceedings there is no reason why it should not enquire fully into the merits before deciding, perhaps in the light of that examination, that it should exercise its discretion to go no further, and decline to give an opinion.[99]

(2) *The* compétence de la compétence

In contentious proceedings, it is clear that it is for the Court to decide whether it is competent to entertain a case, in application of the principle of the *compétence de la compétence*, and of Article 36, paragraph 6, of the Statute. The same principle must apply in advisory proceedings;[100] and indeed, while the Court had, until the case of the *Legality of the Use by a State of Nuclear Weapons in Armed Conflict*, never found a lack of competence, it has, as we shall see, regularly examined the question of its own competence. What is the basis of the *compétence de la compétence* in the advisory sphere? In the previous article in this series the views of Judge Shahabuddeen were quoted, from his separate opinion in the case of the *Arbitral Award of 31 July 1989*, as to the basis of the principle in judicial (contentious) and arbitral proceedings. He there expressed the view that such competence is not based on a general principle applicable to tribunals, but is 'ultimately derived from a grant presumed by law to have been made to the tribunal by the parties'.[101] The existence of the power in advisory proceedings lends support to this view; for it is questionable whether a principle which was developed for tribunals settling disputes by binding judicial decisions, and derives its force from the need for such a principle in order to enable them to achieve this end, can automatically be extended to a body merely engaged in giving non-binding legal advice.

In the exercise of this competence, the Court has in particular had to consider whether the request made to it may be invalid as having been *ultra vires* the requesting organ, in view of the limitation of Article 96, paragraph 2, of the Charter to matters arising within the scope of the

[99] Contra, Judge Moreno Quintana in the *Certain Expenses* case: for him the possible refusal of an opinion was 'a question of procedure which, connected with the much more important problem of the Court's competence in the matter, must be solved at the outset': *ICJ Reports*, 1962, p. 250.

[100] It was in an advisory opinion (*Interpretation of the Greco-Turkish Agreement of December 1 (1926)*) that the Permanent Court observed that 'as a general rule, any body possessing jurisdictional powers has the right in the first place itself to determine the extent of its jurisdiction' (*PCIJ Series B, No. 16*, p. 20); it was however not referring to itself. The principle has the consequence, as Judge Onyeama pointed out in the *Fasla* case, that Members of the Court are bound by the decision on jurisdiction, and 'obliged to approach the rest of the case on the footing that the Court's decision on jurisdiction is the right one': *Application for Review of UNAT Judgment No. 158, ICJ Reports*, 1973, p. 223.

[101] *ICJ Reports*, 1991, p. 109, quoted in this *Year Book*, 70 (1989), p. 4.

activities of that organ. Where the problem is whether or not a question submitted for opinion does or not arise within those activities, the Court's competence in effect depends on whether that body made a correct assessment of its own competence. The correctness of that assessment cannot be presumed, since this would be to render meaningless the limitation contained in Article 96, paragraph 2.[102] In the *WHO* case the Court recalled its earlier dictum that 'each organ must, in the first place at least, determine its own jurisdiction',[103] so that it was a matter for the World Health Assembly to decide on its own competence and that of the Organization; but, as the Court went on to say,

> it is incumbent on the Court to satisfy itself that the conditions governing its own competence to give the opinion requested are met; through the reference made, respectively, by Article 96, paragraph 2, of the Charter to the 'scope of [the] activities' of the Organization and by Article X, paragraph 2, of the Agreement of 10 July 1948 to its 'competence', the Court also finds itself obliged, in the present case, to interpret the Constitution of the WHO.
> The exercise of the functions entrusted to the Court under Article 65, paragraph 1, of its Statute requires it to furnish such an interpretation . . . ; and in so doing the Court arrives at different conclusions from those reached by the World Health Assembly when it adopted [the resolution requesting the opinion].[104]

The contrary argument has some affinity with that addressed to the Court in the *Appeal Relating to the Jurisdiction of the ICAO Council*, and the Court's rejection of it:

> Also pleaded [by Pakistan] is the principle of the '*compétence de la compétence*' as making the Council's jurisdictional decisions conclusive and unappealable. But this prejudges the question, for if on other grounds it appears that these decisions must be held appealable, this principle could not be permitted to prevail without defeating *a priori* all possibility of appeal.[105]

(3) *The role of consent of States*

The role of consent of States in advisory proceedings was initially obscure. In one pre-war case, that of *Eastern Carelia*, the Permanent Court declined to give an advisory opinion in a matter related to a dispute involving Soviet Russia, not a Member of the League; but the terms of its decision were such as to permit of varying interpretations, and indeed to leave unsettled whether the determining factor had been a matter of jurisdiction or rather of judicial propriety. A key sentence in the decision, frequently quoted since, was: 'The Court, being a Court of Justice,

[102] Which, in the view of Judge Ferrari Bravo, was included 'to prevent those political functions that the logic of the system has entrusted *only* to the United Nations from being usurped by other organizations which, to say the least, have neither the competence nor the structure to assume them'; declaration of Judge Ferrari Bravo, *ICJ Reports*, 1996, Vol. I, p. 87.

[103] *Certain Expenses of the United Nations*, *ICJ Reports*, 1962, p. 168. This dictum of course refers to organs of the UN, not to specialized agencies, but the same principle is presumably applicable.

[104] *ICJ Reports*, 1996, Vol. I, p. 83, para. 29.

[105] Ibid., 1972, p. 53, para. 15.

cannot, even in giving an advisory opinion, depart from the essential rules governing their activity as a Court';[106] and this seems more directed to propriety than to questions of jurisdiction properly so-called.

The present Court has on occasion mentioned the *Eastern Carelia* decision in the course of examination, not of its jurisdiction to render an opinion, but of the question whether as a matter of discretion it should exercise that jurisdiction, with the implication that that was the basis of the PCIJ decision.[107] In the *Western Sahara* case, it indicated the considerations which, in its view, had been those 'considered by the Permanent Court, for reasons of judicial propriety, to prevent it from giving an opinion'.[108] In a more recent advisory opinion, it summed up the *Eastern Carelia* case as follows:

> The Permanent Court of International Justice took the view on only one occasion that it could not reply to a question put to it, having regard to the very particular circumstances of the case, among which were that the question directly concerned an already existing dispute, one of the States parties to which was neither a party to the Statute of the Permanent Court nor a Member of the League of Nations, objected to the proceedings, and refused to take part in any way.[109]

This was to stress an element of that case which the Court in *Western Sahara* had regarded as having been secondary, in comparison with the doubt as to the feasibility of establishing the facts of the dispute without the co-operation of the objecting State.

There therefore continued to be some doctrinal dispute as to the role of consent of interested States in the context of advisory proceedings. The experience of the *Eastern Carelia* case, however, had led[110] to the inclusion in the texts governing advisory proceedings[111] of a provision to the effect that the Court, in the exercise of its advisory functions, was to be guided by the provisions of the Statute which apply in contentious cases to the extent to which it recognized them to be applicable.

It was in implementation of this principle that the Permanent Court found it necessary to make a distinction, when dealing with requests for advisory opinions: one that is necessary and clear in principle, even if it may sometimes be difficult to draw in relation to specific cases. This was the distinction between a request for advisory opinion on a question which is of interest to the requesting body, but is not related to any actual

[106] *Status of Eastern Carelia, PCIJ Series B, No.* 5, p. 29.

[107] Contra, Judge Oda in *Legality of the Threat or Use of Nuclear Weapons, ICJ Reports,* 1996, p. 370: 'The Permanent Court once declined to give an opinion [sc., in the *Eastern Carelia* case], but not because it exercised its discretion to do so'.

[108] *ICJ Reports,* 1975, p. 28, para. 46.

[109] *Legality of the Threat or Use of Nuclear Weapons, ICJ Reports,* 1996, pp. 235–6, referring to *Status of Eastern Carelia, PCIJ Series B, No.* 5.

[110] See Rosenne, *The Law and Practice of the International Court,* 2nd edn. (1961) p. 652, text and n. 2.

[111] See 1922 Rules, Article 74, now Article 68 of the Statute of the present Court.

dispute between two or more States, and a request on what is to be classified, in the words of what is now Article 102, paragraph 2, of the present Rules of Court, as 'a legal question actually pending between two or more States'. The distinction was however initially not relevant so much to the problem of consent, as rather to the justification for procedural arrangements designed to put the States interested in the question to some extent in the position of parties to a contentious case, in particular by recognizing their entitlement, where appropriate, to the appointment of judges *ad hoc*.

The distinction is however illuminating in relation to the question of consent and jurisdiction. Clearly, there is no reason why the consent of any particular State should have any role to play in determining the existence of jurisdiction to give an opinion in the first class of case. It follows that, if all jurisdiction is based ultimately on the consent of States, the consent creative of jurisdiction to give advisory opinions *in general* must be that conferred by the consent of States given by accession to the Statute;[112] it was not however until the *Western Sahara* case in 1975 (discussed below) that this was clearly stated by the Court.[113] Accordingly, if consent has any special role to play in the determination of jurisdiction in the second class of cases, it must both be a different consent, a more immediate one, and one limited to certain States, and can only be required as a *condition* for the exercise of the principal, general, jurisdiction. In other words, all States parties to the Statute have consented to the giving of advisory opinions by the Court; but it might be argued that they have done so on the condition that no such opinion may be given on a 'legal question actually pending between two or more States' without the direct consent of those States. It goes without saying that no such condition is expressly stated in the Statute, and could therefore only result from general principles governing the judicial process.

An argument on these lines was in fact presented to the Court by Spain in the *Western Sahara* case. Spain conceded that jurisdiction in advisory cases rested on the consent of States, given by becoming parties to the Statute, to the Court's power to render advisory opinions, but sought to

[112] What is more, the jurisdiction so created empowers the Court to give an advisory opinion even where the question submitted relates to the acts or omissions of a State not a party to the Statute. In the *Interpretation of Peace Treaties* case, Bulgaria and Romania, non-Members of the United Nations, drew attention to this point in support of their contention as to lack of jurisdiction: *Pleadings*, pp. 197, 202–3. See the argument in reply of Mr. Cohen (United States), ibid., pp. 274–6, and Mr. Fitzmaurice (United Kingdom), ibid., pp. 304–6. The Court's only comment on the point was to observe that 'no State, whether a Member of the United Nations or not, can prevent the giving of an Advisory Opinion' (*ICJ Reports*, 1950, p. 71); it would have been more precise to say 'whether or not a party to the Statute'.

[113] By becoming a Member of the United Nations, Spain had 'accepted the provisions of the Charter and Statute; it has thereby in general given its consent to the exercise by the Court of its advisory jurisdiction': ibid., 1975, p. 24, para. 30.

limit this to matters falling within the competence *ratione materiae* of the requesting organ:

Ce serait, certes, une interprétation extensive de la volonté des États de soutenir qu'une fois le consentement donné pour des questions propres au cadre de l'activité de l'Organisation, ces États sont censés avoir consenti par rapport à toute question qu'un organe venait à connaître. Ce qui importe donc, c'est la compétence de l'organe requérant *ratione materiae*.[114]

As regards organs other than the General Assembly and the Security Council, this point is met by the limitation of requests to matters 'arising within the scope of their activities'. Spain endeavoured to show that questions emanating from the Assembly or Council had similarly to be limited, where a dispute between States was concerned:

le Conseil de sécurité et l'Assemblée générale ont des compétences en matière de reglement pacifique des différends, mais cette compétence ne peut pas passer outre au consentement des États, parties à un différend, sur une question qui doit être résolue par application du droit international général et qui est, par conséquent, étrangère au cadre de compétence matérielle de l'Organisation.[115]

Presented as an objection to *jurisdiction*, and with the emphasis on State consent, this must be interpreted as the assertion of an implied condition of that consent. The Court however rejected this contention: it appears that the consent given by accession to the Statute extends to the giving of advisory opinions even on questions which are the subject of dispute between States, and which those States do not, or one of them does not, wish to see dealt with by advisory opinion. States in such a situation are, as we shall see, protected by the policy proclaimed by the Court that, as a matter of its discretion, it will not permit the principle of consent as essential to dispute-settlement to be evaded by use of the advisory procedure. This, being a *trouvaille* of the Court's own, can hardly be supposed to have as theoretical basis an implied condition attached to States' consent to Statute.

The question of the relevance of the consent of interested States had in fact been clarified by the decision in the case of *Interpretation of Peace Treaties with Bulgaria, Hungary and Romania*[116] in 1950. That decision established the principle that, as expressed by Fitzmaurice,

The consent of individual states who may be affected by a request for an opinion, or who may be invoked in a dispute to which that request relates, is not necessary in order to enable the Court to give the opinion. The opinion is given not to states but to the organ requesting it.[117]

[114] *Western Sahara, Pleadings*, Vol. V, p. 36 (M. Lacleta).
[115] Ibid.
[116] *First Phase, Advisory Opinion, ICJ Reports 1950*, p. 65.
[117] This *Year Book*, 29 (1952), p. 46; *Collected Edition*, Vol. 1, p. 117.

The Court was thus in effect rejecting the view that the general consent to the exercise of jurisdiction might be subject to a tacit condition requiring specific consent of interested States when the question submitted was one with which they were directly concerned, a condition the consequence of which would be that the absence of consent signified absence of jurisdiction.

No implied condition can therefore be read into acceptance of the jurisdiction conferred by the Statute; but what of an express reservation? No State has purported to attach reservations to its acceptance of the Statute, and since that instrument is part of the UN Charter, it is clear that no reservation would be accepted. An argument analogous to that based on a reservation to the Statute was however addressed to the Court in the case of *Applicability of Article VI, Section 22, of the Convention on the Privileges and Immunities of the United Nations* (the *Mazilu* case).

The Privileges and Immunities Convention, upon the applicability of which the Court was asked to advise, contained a provision (Section 30)[118] for the settlement of disputes between the United Nations and States parties to the Convention by means of an advisory opinion which the parties to the Convention agreed to accept as binding. The request for advisory opinion was not made in implementation of Section 30; on the basis of the decision in the case of *Reservations to the Genocide Convention*, the mere presence of the disputes settlement clause did not prevent the Court giving an advisory opinion independently of that clause.[119] However, Romania, when acceding to the Convention, had entered a reservation stating that it did not consider itself bound by Section 30:

> with respect to the competence of the International Court in . . . differences [arising out of the interpretation or application of the Convention], the Romanian People's Republic takes the view that, for the purpose of the submission of any dispute whatsoever to the Court for a ruling, the consent of all the parties to the dispute is required in every individual case. This reservation is equally applicable to the provisions contained in the said section which stipulate that the advisory opinion of the International Court is to be accepted as decisive.[120]

Romania argued that the reservation debarred the United Nations from seeking any advisory opinion at all in respect of its difference with Romania concerning the Privileges and Immunities Convention, or

[118] 'If a difference arises between the United Nations on the one hand and a Member on the other hand, a request shall be made for an advisory opinion on any legal question involved in accordance with Article 96 of the Charter and Article 65 of the Statute of the Court. The opinion given by the Court shall be accepted as decisive by the parties.'

[119] *ICJ Reports*, 1951, p. 20; and see Fitzmaurice, this *Year Book*, 34 (1958), p. 146; *Collected Edition*, Vol. II, p. 571.

[120] Quoted at *ICJ Reports*, 1989, p. 188, para. 29.

indeed, it would appear, any difference whatever between the United Nations and Romania without the latter's consent.[121]

Since the request for opinion was not made under Section 30, it would not be binding on Romania; the reservation could only be effective as a matter of jurisdiction if it could be treated as a reservation *to the Statute*, putting Romania in the exceptional position of having attached an express condition to its consent to Statute, requiring its consent to any request for advisory opinion concerning a dispute to which it was party and relating to the Privileges and Immunities Convention.[122]

The Court would have none of this: Section 30 of the Convention 'operates on a different plane and in a different context from that of Article 96 of the Charter'.[123] The Court recognized that 'In the case of a request for an advisory opinion made under Section 30, the Court would of course have to consider any reservation which a party to the dispute had made to that Section'; but 'The request is not made under that Section, and the Court does not therefore need to determine the effect of the Romanian reservation to that provision.'[124]

Judge Shahabuddeen interpreted Romania's contention as logically equivalent to the position

> that its reservation to Article 30 of the General Convention is applicable to the Charter so as to impose a requirement for consent as a pre-condition to recourse to [the advisory] jurisdiction [under Article 96 of the Charter],[125]

a contention that he rejected inasmuch as it could not be accepted that a reservation to one treaty could also operate as a reservation to another. There was also the difficulty, to which Judge Shahabuddeen alluded, whether the Charter admits of reservations; but if such reservations were acceptable, would a reservation on the lines of Romania's reservation to the General Convention have the effect sought? As we have seen, for the consent of interested States to be a precondition to the existence of jurisdiction to give an advisory opinion on a 'legal question actually

[121] The terms of the Memorandum submitted to the Court by Romania are sweeping: 'en ce qui concerne la compétence d'examiner *tout différend* surgi entre les Nations Unies et la Roumanie, y compris dans le cadre de la compétence consultative, la Cour ne saura se déclarer compétente que s'il existe le consentement de toutes les parties au différend, la Roumanie comprise': *Pleadings*, p. 202, emphasis added.

[122] The idea that a reservation to one instrument may be treated as a reservation to a different instrument may appear bizarre; but something rather like it was argued by France in the *Nuclear Tests* cases, namely that France's reservations to its acceptance of jurisdiction under the optional clause should be read as qualifying also its acceptance of jurisdiction under the 1928 General Act for the Pacific Settlement of International Disputes; see the annexe to the letter from the French Ambassador of 16 May 1973, *Nuclear Tests, Pleadings*, Vol. II, at pp. 356–7. Cf. also the argument of Honduras in *Border and Transborder Armed Actions*, linking the reservations in its acceptance of jurisdiction under the optional clause with its acceptance of jurisdiction under the Pact of Bogotá: *ICJ Reports*, 1988, pp. 82–3, paras. 28–31.

[123] Ibid., 1989, p. 189, para. 32.

[124] Ibid., 1989, p. 190, para. 34.

[125] Separate opinion, ibid., 1989, p. 214.

pending', it would be necessary to interpret the consent of States to Article 96 of the Charter to be subject to an implied condition; a reservation of the Romanian type would simply make this condition express. The condition would not relate to the future specific consent of the reserving State, but to the future specific consent of whatever State might prove to be an 'interested State'.[126] This is consistent with the fact that in the *Peace Treaties* case the States who were refusing consent were not themselves parties to the Charter and Statute, and had therefore given no consent to Article 96. Since in that case and the *Western Sahara* case the Court may be taken to have rejected the idea that the consent of interested States became relevant to jurisdiction by way of an implied condition on States' consent to the Charter and Statute, presumably an argument based on an express condition, in the form of a reservation to the Charter, would suffer the same fate.

What then would have been the position if the request *had* been made under Section 30? Would the Romanian reservation, plus the lack of Romanian consent, have signified that the Court had no jurisdiction to give the opinion? The Court was careful to leave this matter open: if it had had to 'consider' the Romanian reservation in the context of a request under Section 30,

> the Court would have to consider whether the effect of its reservation could be to act as a bar to the operation of the procedure of request for advisory opinion, or merely to deprive any opinion given of the decisive effect attributed to such opinions by Section 30.[127]

The second effect would, it is suggested, be unavoidable: Romania had, when becoming party to the Convention, clearly entered a reservation to, at the very least, the binding effect of an opinion under Section 30. But could it be said that the very request for such an opinion would be vitiated by conflict with the Romanian reservation? The problem is that, *pace* the Court, Section 30 does *not* operate on a different plane from Article 96 of the Charter. In adopting a resolution asking for an opinion under Section 30, the requesting organ would be acting simultaneously in exercise of its general powers under Article 96, and its specific powers under Section 30. It could be argued that the sentence in Article 30 beginning 'If a difference arises between the United Nations on the one hand and a Member on the other hand, a request shall be made for an advisory opinion . . . ' is inoperative if the Member concerned has

[126] The hypothetical situation bears some resemblance to the effect of the 'Vandenberg reservation' in the United States' acceptance of jurisdiction under the optional clause: in a case to which the reservation applied, the absence of any of the convention parties *other* than the United States would be a bar to jurisdiction (though of course the United States could presumably waive the reservation).

[127] Ibid. In the view of Judge Ago, 'the reply to at least one of these two questions would have had to have been in the affirmative': ' "Binding" Advisory Opinions of the International Court of Justice', 85 *AJIL* (1991), p. 447.

excluded Section 30, so that, for the purposes of that Section only, the State concerned is not a 'Member'. There would thus be no 'difference' between the United Nations and a 'Member' to bring the Section into operation. On that basis, the requesting organ would be acting in reliance on an inapplicable text; whether from this it would follow that the resolution would have to be treated as a nullity is another matter.

In the instant case, the question of Romania's consent remained relevant, on the lines of the dicta in the *Western Sahara* case, for the problem of the propriety of giving the opinion; this aspect is discussed below.

The rejection by the Court of any idea of an implied or express reservation to the provisions of the Statute concerning advisory opinions did not however signify that, all States parties to the Statute having thus given unconditional consent to the exercise of advisory jurisdiction, no question of jurisdiction could ever arise, nor did it mean that the attitude of interested States was wholly irrelevant. States have consented to the exercise of advisory jurisdiction within the limits, and subject to the conditions, laid down in the Charter and Statute, and non-compliance with these texts results in absence of jurisdiction; this was exemplified in the *Fasla*[128] and *Mortished*[129] cases, in which the Court found that it had jurisdiction, but examined a number of reasons why it could be suggested that it had not, and most recently in the case of *Legality of the Use by a State of Nuclear Weapons in Armed Conflict*,[130] in which it found that it had no jurisdiction. This may be regarded as a constitutional question, inasmuch as the Court may not function otherwise than in accordance with its Statute; but it may also be seen as a jurisdictional question, the consent of States to the Court's operation being on the implied condition that such operation will be in accordance with the Statute. Even where jurisdiction is established, on the other hand, the Court enjoys a discretion, under the terms of article 65, paragraph 1, of the Statute, whether or not to give the opinion requested, and the consent of States directly concerned in the question submitted for opinion remains material to the question of the exercise by the Court of this discretion, as was made very clear in the *Western Sahara* case.

In many of the cases to be examined, both questions—that of jurisdiction and that of the propriety of giving an opinion in the exercise of discretion—have been considered; and indeed, it is not clear that, particularly in the earlier cases, the Court itself has clearly distinguished between them. However, in view of the conceptual difference between

[128] *Application for Review of Judgment No. 158 of the United Nations Administrative Tribunal, ICJ Reports*, 1973, p. 166.

[129] *Application for Review of Judgment No. 273 of the United Nations Administrative Tribunal, ICJ Reports*, 1982, p. 325.

[130] *ICJ Reports*, 1996, Vol. I, p. 66

these questions, the case-law will be reviewed in the light first of the one and then of the other.

2. *The conditions of jurisdiction to give an advisory opinion*

Until the request by the WHO in 1996 for an opinion on the *Legality of the Use of Nuclear Weapons in Armed Conflict,* the Court had never found itself obliged to decline to give an advisory opinion for lack of compliance with jurisdictional requirements.[131] However, in a number of cases matters have fallen to be considered which were relevant to the problem of the existence of jurisdiction as distinct from that of the propriety of its exercise, even though in those cases they were not found to justify a finding of lack of jurisdiction.

(1) *Is the question submitted a 'legal question'?*

Both Article 96 of the Charter and Article 65 of the Statute of the Court provide that the appropriate organs and agencies may request, and the Court may give, an advisory opinion on 'any legal question'. It therefore requires no particularly subtle techniques of treaty-interpretation to deduce that if the question put is not a legal one, it should not have been put, and the Court may not answer it. In the case of *Certain Expenses of the United Nations* in 1962, the Court spelled this out; after recalling the dictum of the Permanent Court in the *Eastern Carelia* case, that 'The Court, being a Court of Justice, cannot, even in giving advisory opinions, depart from the essential rules guiding its activity as a Court',[132] it explained:

> Therefore, and in accordance with Article 65 of its Statute, the Court can give an advisory opinion only on a legal question. If a question is not a legal one, the Court has no discretion in the matter; it must decline to give the opinion requested. But even if the question is a legal one, which the Court is undoubtedly competent to answer, it may nevertheless decline to do so.[133]

Non-legal questions, which the Court might thus have to refuse to answer, could conceivably be of two kinds: factual questions and political questions.

[131] The PCIJ also never had to refuse an opinion on that ground; as already noted, the *Eastern Carelia* case, while subjected to varying interpretations, is normally regarded as an example of the operation of the Court's discretion to refuse an opinion for reasons of judicial propriety.

[132] *PCIJ Series B, No. 5*, p. 29.

[133] *ICJ Reports,* 1962, p. 155. Note that the Court cited only Article 65 and not Article 96 when discussing the requirement that the question be a legal one. Rosenne (*The Law and Practice of the International Court*, 3rd edn. (1997) Vol.II, p. 1000) suggests that this implies that 'the concept of "legal question" applicable for a political organ is not necessarily the same as the concept of "legal question" applicable for the Court'. It is not clear what would follow: the Court, whether applying Article 96 or Article 65, would employ its own definition of the concept; it is hardly conceivable that an opinion may be validly *requested* as a legal question under Article 96, but no opinion could be *given* because the question was not a legal one under Article 65.

(*a*) Legal questions and the ascertainment of facts

One of the elements of the *Eastern Carelia* case which contributed to the decision of the Permanent Court to decline to give an opinion was that the controversy between Finland and Russia 'can only be decided by an investigation into the facts underlying the case',[134] and that 'the Court would, of course, be at a very great disadvantage in such an enquiry, owing to the fact that Russia refuses to take part in it.' As a matter of principle, the Court declined to say

> that there is an absolute rule that the request for an advisory opinion may not involve some enquiry into facts, but, under ordinary circumstances, it is certainly expedient that the facts upon which the opinion of the Court is desired should not be in controversy, and that it should not be left to the Court to ascertain what they are.[135]

In the *Namibia* case, South Africa invoked this precedent, and drew attention to the complex factual issues which, in its contention, the Court would have to resolve in order to give the opinion requested. On this basis, it made a twofold submission:

> Since the Court may only give an advisory opinion on a *legal* question, it may consequently be doubted whether it is entitled to furnish an opinion if, in order to do so, it has also to make findings as to primary facts. On the assumption, however, that the Court is indeed entitled to do so, it is submitted that the Court, in the exercise of its discretion, should refuse to give an advisory opinion if has to establish controverted primary facts, which do not fall within a limited compass admitting of easy and speedy ascertainment.[136]

The Court recognized that there were two aspects to this submission, since it quoted South Africa in its opinion as having 'expressed doubts whether the Court is competent to, *or should*, give an opinion, if, in order to do so, it should have to make findings as to extensive factual issues'.[137] However, the Court's actual response to the submission was limited to the first aspect:

> In the view of the Court, the contingency that there may be factual issues underlying the question posed does not alter its character as a 'legal question' as envisaged in Article 96 of the Charter. The reference in this provision to legal questions cannot be interpreted as opposing legal to factual issues. Normally, to enable a court to pronounce on legal questions, it must also be acquainted with, take into account and, if necessary, make findings as to the relevant factual issues. The limitation of the powers of the Court contended for by the Government of South Africa has no basis in the Charter or the Statute.[138]

[134] *PCIJ Series B, No.* 5, pp. 28–9.

[135] Ibid., p. 28.

[136] *Legal Consequences for States, Pleadings*, Vol. I, p. 448 (Written Statement of South Africa); see also argument of Mr Grosskopf, ibid., Vol. II, pp. 188–190.

[137] *ICJ Reports*, 1971, p. 27, para. 40.

[138] Ibid.

While the South African contentions in the specific case should perhaps not have been upheld, on the level of principle this is not a very satisfactory ruling. In the first place, the word 'legal' as defining the type of question that may be put to the Court must be taken to have excluded *some* class of questions as being 'non-legal'; and one would have thought that factual questions would fall into this category. The Court seems to be implying that an advisory opinion could be requested on a question of pure fact; to take an example from a contentious case, the question whether the mines encountered by British warships in the Corfu Channel were laid by Albania or by someone else. While the answer to the question would carry legal consequences, can it in itself be regarded as a 'legal question' for the purposes of the Charter? Secondly, the reference to what 'a court' must do 'normally' completely ignores the distinction pointed out in the South African argument[139] between the powers and practices of the Court in contentious cases and in advisory proceedings. To suggest that, *in order to give an advisory opinion*, the Court can and does, normally, make findings as to the relevant factual issues, is both question-begging and of dubious accuracy.

It has not subsequently been submitted to the Court that the presence of a strong factual element in the issues submitted to the Court might render the question not a 'legal question' within the meaning of Article 96 of the Charter, with the consequence that the Court would lack competence to give an opinion, although the presence of factual issues has been urged[140] as a reason why the Court should, in the exercise of its discretion, decline to give an opinion. The view has however been taken by Judge de Castro in the *Western Sahara* case that

> Today it would seem certain that, when the fact on the existence of which an advisory opinion is requested is disputed or in controversy, the Court has *no competence* to decide upon its existence.[141]

As the starting point of his argument, Judge de Castro took the dictum in the *Certain Expenses* case that the Court can give an advisory opinion only on a legal question, and that 'If a question is not a legal one, the Court has no discretion in the matter; it must decline to give the opinion requested'.[142] For Judge de Castro, this dictum is not merely an interpretation *a contrario* of the text of the Charter, but is 'binding, because it flows from the nature of the advisory [procedure], which is very different from that of contentious proceedings'.[143]

It is not a question, in Judge de Castro's thinking, of degree, as the

[139] *Pleadings*, Vol. I, pp. 448–9, paras. 46–7.

[140] In the *Western Sahara* case: see below.

[141] *ICJ Reports*, 1975, p. 138, emphasis added.

[142] *ICJ Reports*, 1962, p. 155, quoted in the separate opinion of Judge de Castro, *loc. cit.*

[143] Ibid.; 'procedure' has been substituted for 'proceedings', the term used in the English translation of Judge de Castro's opinion to correspond to the French *procédure*.

majority of the Court held: the problem for him is not whether there is sufficient factual evidence available.

> [T]he Court cannot content itself with the evidence, which may be biased, supplied by the States interested or concerned; the effect of an advisory opinion is not confined to the parties as though it were a matter of a judgment; the opinion is authoritative *erga omnes* . . .

Whatever the merits of this extreme view, it has not been accepted in the jurisprudence of the Court. It may, however, be relevant as sounding a warning note: the Court probably should, in deciding whether or not to give an opinion in a case involving factual issues, be attentive not merely to the quantity of evidential material availability, but also to its reliability in the light of the possibility of bias in its source or sources. Thus in the *Namibia* case, South Africa was able to draw attention at least to certain examples of charges which had repeatedly been made against it, and which, it alleged, underlay the controversy leading to the request for opinion, that could be shown to be demonstrably false.[144]

We are not here concerned with the second part of the South African submission quoted above, that the Court as a matter of discretion should decline to give an opinion because of the need to enquire into facts, but may note in passing that on this aspect the Court gives no response at all.

(*b*) Political questions

In a number of cases, to be reviewed in Section 3 (3) below, it has been argued before the Court that the question put to it for advisory opinion was 'intertwined with political questions',[145] or that the request was 'nothing but a political manoeuvre',[146] but this was asserted as grounds for the Court to decline, in the exercise of its discretion, to give an opinion. It is conceivable, though highly unlikely, that a resolution might be adopted in a political organ submitting to the Court a question which, while having some cosmetic legal component, was in effect a purely political question.[147] In such circumstances, it may be doubted whether the Court would have the jurisdiction to answer it; but for reasons of

[144] See for example, *Namibia, Pleadings*, Vol. II, pp. 597–9. It might appear inconsistent in Judge de Castro to have voted in favour of the *Namibia* opinion (as he indicated in his separate opinion that he had), but in that separate opinion he indicated how it was that the factual issues challenged by South Africa were, legally speaking, not pertinent to the request made of the Court. Some explanation of this kind would have strengthened the advisory opinion itself in that case.

[145] *Certain Expenses of the United Nations, ICJ Reports*, 1962, p. 155.

[146] *Interpretation of the Agreement of 15 March 1951 between the WHO and Egypt, ICJ Reports*, 1980, p. 87, para. 33.

[147] It is assumed here that the distinction legal/political is meaningful at the international level; contra, Rosenne, *The Law and Practice of the International Court*, 2nd edn. (1961) pp. 2–3; 3rd edn. (1997) Vol. I, p. 4. In the domain of contentious proceedings, the Court has not gone further than rejecting the view that 'because a legal dispute submitted to the Court is only one aspect of a political dispute, the Court should decline to resolve for the parties the legal questions at issue between them': *United States Diplomatic and Consular Staff in Tehran, ICJ Reports*, 1980, p. 20, para. 37.

judicial tact it might well prefer to gloss over this question and simply exercise its discretion to decline.

In the more recent case (outside the period nominally covered by the present series of article) of the *Legality of the Threat or Use of Nuclear Weapons*, the Court did deal with the matter in the context of jurisdiction rather than discretion. It described the question submitted for opinion as 'indeed a legal one, since the Court is asked to rule on the compatibility of the threat or use of nuclear weapons with the relevant principles and rules of international law', and observed that

> The fact that this question also has political aspects, as, in the nature of things, is the case with so many questions which arise in international life, does not suffice to deprive it of its character as a 'legal question' and 'to deprive the Court of a competence conferred on it by its Statute'.[148]

The Court did not, curiously enough, go on to add that the political aspects of the question were also not such as to lead it to exercise its discretion to refuse an opinion, though this was clearly the view that it took on the point.

(*c*) Legal questions and *non liquet*

There remains a further issue for consideration in respect of the limitation of advisory opinions to 'legal questions': that of the possible role of *non liquet* in this domain. Can a question be regarded as a legal question if positive law provides no answer to it? In the first article of the present series, the possibility of a court declaring a *non liquet* was discussed in connection with the related problem of the existence, or otherwise, of lacunae in international law;[149] and if one starts from the premise of the completeness of international law, there is perhaps no more to be said. Such completeness may however be itself something of a legal fiction or even an illusion; and it is in the advisory context that this could become particularly apparent. At the time when satellites were beginning to invade the stratosphere, and the prospects of space travel were beginning to look like something more than idle speculation, a concrete dispute between States over a question of what is now called space law still remained virtually impossible, so that the Court could not, in the exercise of its contentious jurisdiction, be called upon to determine such a question. But if the General Assembly, instead of adopting its Declarations on matters of the law of outer space,[150] had asked the Court for an advisory opinion in such a matter—for example, the possibility of

[148] *ICJ Reports,* 1996, p. 234, para. 13, quoting *Application for Review of Judgment No 158 of UNAT, ICJ Reports,* 1973, p. 172, para. 14.

[149] This *Year Book*, 60 (1989), pp. 77 ff.

[150] See GA res. 1348 (XIII); GA res. 1472 (XIV); GA Res. 1721 (XVI); and in particular Declaration of Legal Principles Governing the Activities of States in the Exploration and Use of Outer Space, GA res. 1962 (XVII). On the law of space at this period, see Lachs, 'The International law of Outer Space', 113 *Recueil des Cours*, (1964–III), p. 7.

legal appropriation of heavenly bodies— on what basis could it have replied? If not on the basis of positive law, would such a question be a legal one? The matter may thus be seen as a jurisdictional one, but also as one going to the exercise of the Court's discretion: in what circumstances may a court decline to exercise jurisdiction on the ground that to do so is impossible for lack of an applicable legal rule?

Given the difference of function involved in the Court's exercise of its advisory jurisdiction, the question arises whether the principles and rules, whatever they may be, governing *non liquet* in contentious proceedings, are also applicable in advisory proceedings. The opportunity should perhaps be taken, in this connection, to take brief note of a recent case (and therefore one not strictly within the period covered) in which the issue was examined, with results that have given rise to a certain amount of doctrinal dispute.

When the Court was asked by the General Assembly to give an advisory opinion on the *Legality of the Threat or Use of Nuclear Weapons*, the opinion it gave was seen by many as containing a *non liquet*, specifically because of the presence in the operative part of the decision of a finding that, while 'the threat or use of nuclear weapons would generally be contrary to the rules of international law applicable in armed conflict', yet

> in view of the current state of international law, and of the elements of fact at its disposal, the Court cannot conclude definitively whether the threat or use of nuclear weapons would be lawful or unlawful in an extreme circumstance of self-defence in which the very survival of a State would be at stake.[151]

For the purposes of discussion, we may accept that this is tantamount to a *non liquet*: that it is a finding that, at least on one aspect of the problem, international law does not supply an answer.[152] On that basis, does the finding offend against a canon of law or of judicial duty excluding recourse to *non liquet*? Judge Vereshchetin, in a declaration appended to the advisory opinion, drew what is, it is suggested, a correct and vital distinction:

> In critically assessing the importance for our case of the doctrinal debate on the issue of *non liquet*, one cannot lose sight of the fact that the debate has concerned predominantly, if not exclusively, the admissibility or otherwise of *non liquet* in a contentious procedure in which the Court is called upon to pronounce a binding, definite decision settling the dispute between the parties.
>
> In the present case, however, the Court is engaged in advisory procedure. It is requested not to resolve an actual dispute between actual parties, but to state the law as it finds it at the present stage of its development . . .

[151] *ICJ Reports*, 1996, p. 266, para. 105(2)(E).

[152] An alternative reading, referred to in Section 3(4) below, is that it is merely a finding that the Court had not been supplied with sufficient factual material to draw the appropriate legal conclusion.

In advisory procedure, where the Court finds a lacuna in the law or finds the law to be imperfect, it ought merely to state this without trying to fill the lacuna or improve the law by way of judicial legislation. The Court cannot be blamed for indecisiveness or evasiveness where the law, upon which it is called to pronounce, is itself inconclusive.[153]

This distinction has been approved by legal authors;[154] and the present writer maintains his view, advanced at a time when the Court was still seised of the case but had not handed down its decision, that:

In the field of the Court's advisory function, where the prohibition of *non liquet*, if it exists, must be greatly attenuated, the decision to refrain from giving an opinion must . . . be at least an option when the law on the question submitted is insufficient, undeveloped, or simply non-existent; and the making of such a decision may even be 'ineluctable'.[155]

For the authors referred to, however, the matter is seen as one of the exercise of the Court's discretion to refuse to give an opinion, and this was also the approach of the present writer in the paper quoted. On reflection, however, it does appear that the matter could be viewed, and is perhaps better viewed, as one of jurisdiction, at least if (as was not the case in the *Nuclear Weapons* proceedings) the whole question put to the Court is one to which positive international law affords no answer.[156]

(2) *Requests made* ultra vires

The competence of the Court to render an advisory opinion obviously depends primarily on the validity of the request made to it: if, for whatever reason, that request is not validly made, or goes beyond the limits authorised by Article 96 of the Charter, the only competence of the Court is to find that it has no competence, and cannot therefore

[153] *ICJ Reports,* 1996, pp. 279–280.

[154] See in particular the penetrating discussion by Weil, ' "The Court cannot conclude definitively . . . ": *non liquet* revisited', 36 *Columbia Journal of Transnational Law,* (1997), p. 109; also Bodansky, '*Non liquet* and the incompleteness of international law', in Boisson de Chazournes and Sands (eds.), *International Law, the International Court of Justice and Nuclear Weapons* (1999). Judge Vereshchetin has elaborated on his thinking in a recent article: 'Is "deceptive clarity" better than "apparent indecision" in an advisory opinion?', Yakpo and Boumedra (eds.), *Liber Amicorum Mohamed Bedjaoui* (1999), p. 531.

[155] 'The Advisory Function of the International Court of Justice, 1946–1996: Achievements and Prospects', paper delivered at a conference in New Delhi in 1996, and published in *Essays on International Law, 40th Anniversary Commemorative Volume, Asian-African Legal Consultative Committee,* (1997). The term 'ineluctable' alludes to the dictum in the *Northern Cameroons* case that the decision not to adjudicate 'ineluctably must be made': *ICJ Reports,* 1963, p. 38.

[156] This appears to be implied in the interesting approach taken by Marcelo Kohen, who argues that, having accepted to give the opinion, the Court thereby recognized that the question submitted was a legal one, and could not thereafter back down on the ground that the law was insufficient or imperfect: 'L'avis consultatif de la CIJ sur la *Licéité de la menace ou de l'emploi d'armes nucléaires* et la fonction judiciaire', 2 EJIL (1997), 336, at p. 349.

give the opinion requested.[157] The request must emanate from a body authorized by, or under, Article 96 of the Charter; and save in the case of the UN General Assembly and Security Council,[158] the question submitted must be one 'arising within the scope of [the] activities' of the requesting body. In a number of cases, particularly those concerning requests made by the UN Committee on Applications for Review of Administrative Tribunal Judgments, circumstances surrounding the adoption of the request, or the nature and operation of the requesting body, have been discussed; but the Court has maintained the distinction between arguments going to the *validity* of a request, and thus to the Court's jurisdiction, and those tending to induce the Court to exercise its discretion to decline to give an opinion, thus what might be called the *admissibility* of the request.

(*a*) Interpretation of Peace Treaties with Bulgaria, Hungary and Romania

One of the contentions put forward in the *Peace Treaties* case demonstrates clearly how the competence of the Court is dependent on the competence of the requesting body, since if this latter competence is lacking, the conditions of Article 96 of the Charter are not fulfilled. It was argued in that case that

> the Request for an Opinion was an action *ultra vires* on the part of the General Assembly because, in dealing with the question of the observance of human rights in the three States . . . , it was 'interfering' or 'intervening' in matters essentially within the domestic jurisdiction of States. This contention against the exercise by the Court of its advisory function seems thus to be based on the alleged incompetence of the General Assembly itself, an incompetence deduced from Article 2, paragraph 7, of the Charter.[159]

The Court did not accept this argument, since it was not concerned with the allegations of human rights violations themselves, but simply with the interpretation of the treaty provisions for dispute settlement; it did however, correctly, treat the argument as one going to its jurisdiction rather than its discretion.[160]

[157] As is evident from the decision in *Legality of the Use by States of Nuclear Weapons in Armed Conflict*, it does so by means of an instrument entitled, paradoxically, 'advisory opinion'; see Queneudec, 'E.T. à la CIJ: méditations d'un extra-terrestre sur deux avis consultatifs', in Boisson de Chazournes and Sands (eds.), *International Law, the International Court of Justice and Nuclear Weapons* (1999) p. 53.

[158] For the contention that even these organs may not submit *any* legal question whatever for advisory opinion, see the *Nuclear Weapons* case, referred to in section (*f*) below.

[159] *ICJ Reports*, 1950, p. 70.

[160] Although the passage quoted refers to the 'exercise' by the Court of its advisory function, it is introduced by a statement that 'the power of the Court' to exercise that function had been challenged, and its conclusion on the point was that the considerations it set out had 'dispose[d] of the objection based on the principle of domestic jurisdiction and directed specifically against the *competence* of the Court': loc. cit., p. 71, emphasis added.

(*b*) Legal consequences for States of the continued presence of South Africa in Namibia (South West Africa)

In the *Namibia* case South Africa did not dispute the entitlement of the Security Council to request an opinion on 'any legal question', but asserted that for constitutional reasons the Council resolution actually adopted, requesting the opinion, was invalid, from which it would have followed, as the Court noted, that 'the Court is not competent to deliver the opinion'.[161] The grounds put forward by South Africa were: that the resolution was adopted over the abstention of a permanent member of the Council, and was not therefore validly adopted under Article 27, paragraph 3, of the Charter; that the question related to a dispute between South Africa and other UN Members, and that therefore South Africa should have been invited to participate in the Council's discussion under Article 32 of the Charter; and that the proviso to Article 27, paragraph, 3, requiring abstention from voting by parties to a dispute, should have been complied with.[162] The merits of these contentions are not here our concern;[163] they were all rejected, but it is clear that had any of them been held to invalidate the resolution, the Court would have lacked jurisdiction in the case.

(*c*) Application for Review of UNAT Judgment No. 158 (the *Fasla* case)

The request for an opinion was made to the Court by the Committee on Applications for Review of Administrative Tribunal Judgments, a committee established by the General Assembly in 1955.[164] The General Assembly had at the same time, in the exercise of its powers under Article 96, paragraph 2, of the Charter, authorized the Committee to request advisory opinions, on a specified range of issues which might arise in relation to a judgment of the Administrative Tribunal.[165] Prima facie, therefore, there was no jurisdictional problem: the requirements of the Charter and Statute for the submission of the request to the Court were satisfied. However the Court, in examining *proprio motu* the

[161] *ICJ Reports,* 1971, p. 22, para. 20.

[162] Ibid., paras. 21–26.

[163] The question of the interpretation or application of Article 27, paragraph 3, was discussed in an earlier article in this series, in connection with the question of the significance for customary law of practice within an international organization: this *Year Book*, 61 (1990), pp. 75–80).

[164] GA resolution 957 (X), 8 November 1955, adding a new article 11 to the Statute of UNAT: text reproduced in *ICJ Reports,* 1973, pp. 170–1.

[165] An interesting question is: what would be the position if the Committee requested an opinion on a Tribunal judgment which was found to be a nullity? If there was no judgment to be reviewed, could the Committee's request to review it be a valid one, and if not, would that signify that the Court had no jurisdiction? In the *Mortished* case (examined below) there was an irregularity in the judgment (4 judges sitting where the Statute provided for only 3 to sit), but this had not affected the result, and the Court noted that the same had happened in a number of previous cases, without protest. Since there did not appear to be any 'failure of justice', the Court did not pursue the matter: *Application for Review of Judgment No. 273 of the United Nations Administrative Tribunal, ICJ Reports,* 1982, pp. 341–2, para. 35.

question of its competence, noted that there were three arguments which cast doubt on this aspect of the case. In the first place it was questioned whether the Court's advisory jurisdiction might be used 'for the judicial review of contentious proceedings which have taken place before other tribunals and to which individuals were parties'. Secondly, it was suggested that the Committee was not, despite the General Assembly's action, an 'organ' of the United Nations within the meaning of Article 96, and could not therefore be the beneficiary of an authorization under that text. Thirdly, it was questioned whether the Committee had any 'activities' of its own; if it had none, no legal question could qualify as one 'arising within the scope of the activities' of the requesting organ.

The Court found that in the circumstances none of these arguments were valid so as to invalidate the jurisdiction which the texts and the decision of the Committee conferred upon it prima facie; so far as the second and third contentions are concerned, its reasoning on these points concerns rather questions of United Nations constitutional law, and will not be dwelt on here. All three arguments were dealt with, not as going to the exercise of the Court's discretion, but to the existence of its jurisdiction. So far as the second and third arguments are concerned, this seems to be fully justified: if the Committee was not an 'organ', or if the legal question submitted was not one 'arising within the scope of its activities', then the terms of Article 96 of the Charter were not satisfied, and there was no jurisdiction to give an opinion; and on the basis of a finding to that effect, no question of the propriety of the exercise of that jurisdiction would have arisen. In the case of the first argument, however, it may be doubted whether the matter is really one of jurisdiction. It is true that, as the Court found,

> The mere fact that it is not the rights of States which are in issue in the proceedings cannot suffice to deprive the Court of a competence expressly conferred on it by its Statute,[166]

but the real question may be whether it is right, as a matter of judicial propriety, to exercise that jurisdiction in the circumstances. In its opinion, the Court in fact went on to examine certain other circumstances (discussed in section 2 (*b*) below) in the light of which the propriety of the exercise of its jurisdiction might be called in question; it is therefore clear that the choice to treat the issue of the interests of non-State parties as one of jurisdiction was deliberate.

In its examination of the question, the Court referred to the *Unesco* case,[167] observing that in that case 'the Court upheld its competence to entertain a request for advisory opinion for the purpose of reviewing

[166] *ICJ Reports*, 1973, p. 172, para. 14.

[167] *Judgments of the Administrative Tribunal of the ILO upon Complaints Made against Unesco, ICJ Reports*, 1956, p. 77.

judicial proceedings involving individuals'.[168] The opinion in that case, however, does not appear to treat that question as a matter of jurisdiction; after noting that the Executive Board of Unesco had exercised a power conferred on it by the General Assembly, it then continued: 'The Court will consider at the outset *whether it should comply* with the Request for an Opinion',[169] a form of words which seems clearly directed to the question of the propriety of exercise of the jurisdiction. Furthermore, the Court in the *Unesco* case stated later in its discussion:

> The Court . . . must consider only the question whether its Statute and its judicial character do or do not stand in the way of its participating in this procedure by complying with the Request for an Advisory Opinion.[170]

In the passage of its opinion in the *Fasla* case, referred to above, dealing with the first argument against jurisdiction, the Court appears to be replying to the dissenting opinions of two of its Members: Judges Gros and Morozov. The opinion of the latter judge is so sparsely reasoned that it is not of great assistance; he contends that the procedure for review of UNAT judgments amounts to permitting individuals to become parties before the Court, contrary to Article 34 of the Statute, an argument which had in effect already been rejected in the *Effect of Awards* and *Unesco* cases, even though those cases did not concern the procedure of Article 11 of the UNAT Statute. Judge Gros quoted from the *Unesco* decision: 'The Court . . . is bound to remain faithful to the requirements of its judicial character. Is that possible in the present case?', and observed 'This question has also to be raised in the present proceedings, and I feel compelled to answer it in the negative.'[171] He also referred extensively to the separate and dissenting opinions in the *Unesco* case, and in particular to that of Judge Klaestad who had

> declared that the Court, although jurisdiction had regularly been conferred upon it by the terms of Article XII of the Statute of the ILO Administrative Tribunal, ought to have abstained from exercising that jurisdiction.[172]

The Court in the *Fasla* case may therefore be criticized for treating as an argument directed to the existence of jurisdiction in the case one which, properly understood, was addressed rather to the propriety of exercising that jurisdiction.

[168] *ICJ Reports*, 1973, pp. 171–2, para. 14.

[169] Ibid., 1956, p. 84.

[170] Ibid., p. 85.

[171] Ibid., 1973, p. 254, para. 6, quoting from ibid., 1956, p. 84.

[172] Ibid., 1973, pp. 254–5, para. 8; the reference is to Judge Klaestad's separate opinion at ibid., 1956, pp. 112–13.

(*d*) Application for Review of UNAT Judgment No. 273 (the *Mortished* case)

The competence of the Court to give an advisory opinion in response to a request from the Committee on Applications for Review of Administrative Tribunal Judgments depended on, *inter alia*, the validity of the request. Any such request necessarily related to a particular judgment given by the Administrative Tribunal. What then would be the position if the request were otherwise perfectly in order, but the judgment to which it referred were invalid? If such invalidity meant that the judgment was void, the request would be based on something which had no legal existence and would therefore itself be a nullity; and the Court, not being seised of a valid request, would have no competence to give an opinion.

In the *Mortished* case in 1982, the judgment which was the subject of the proceedings had been given by the Tribunal with a stated composition of four judges, three members and one alternate member. According to Article 3, paragraph 1, of the Statute of the Tribunal, only three of its members could sit in any particular case. The President of the Tribunal was authorized to designate the three members to constitute the Tribunal for any case or group of cases, and the President might, in addition, 'designate one or more members of the Tribunal to serve as alternates'. The judgment contained no explanation of the composition of the Tribunal; as the Court therefore commented,

> The silence of the Tribunal's Judgment on the issue leads to speculation as to whether an alternate member is expected to be designated by the President normally in the absence of one of the regular three members or when such alternate member possesses exceptional expertise or qualifications not to be found in the three ordinary members of the Tribunal.[173]

In the light of the practice of the Tribunal, the Court did not find that in the instant case it had not been legally constituted, 'nor does the matter appear on the face of it to disclose any failure of justice'.[174]

Had the Court come to a different conclusion, what would have been the consequence for its own competence? It began its examination of the point by noting that 'it might be suggested' that the composition of the Tribunal 'was irregular', and that 'if the irregularity were found to be such as to vitiate the decision of the Tribunal, further examination of the question put to the Court would be *unnecessary*'.[175] This wording suggests an analogy with contentious cases such as *Northern Cameroons*

[173] Ibid., 1982, p. 341, para. 34. The Court tactfully omits to mention that the alternate member was of United States nationality, and it was the US that had taken a particularly strong line on the question which was the essence of the case before the Tribunal; outvoted, the US member had attached a dissenting opinion (an example which was followed by the Member of the Court of US nationality).

[174] Ibid., pp. 341–2, para. 35.

[175] Ibid., 1982, p. 340, para. 33 (emphasis added).

and *Nuclear Tests*, in which the application made to the Court had become, or was *ab initio*, without object: certainly there would be no point in discussing the possible imperfections of a Judgment which was, for other reasons, a nullity. It is however suggested that, as observed above, the matter is more fundamental than that: the nullity of the judgment would result in the nullity of the request, and hence to a finding of lack of competence for non-compliance with Article 96.[176]

(*e*) Legality of the Use by a State of Nuclear Weapons in Armed Conflict[177]

In the case concerning *Legality of the Use by a State of Nuclear Weapons in Armed Conflict*, the Court for the first time found itself unable to give an advisory opinion on the grounds that it was not competent, inasmuch as the requirements of Article 96, paragraph 2, of the Charter were not satisfied: although the World Health Organization had been duly authorized by the General Assembly to request advisory opinions, the question put, as the Court found, did not relate to a question arising 'within the scope of the activities' of the requesting organization. The merits of this question, i.e. the arguments that the question did or did not fall within the scope of those activities, concern the constitution and functions of the WHO, and are thus not here to the purpose; what is of interest is the fact that the Court clearly—and correctly—maintained the distinction between the discretion to give or refuse an opinion, and the prior question whether it had or had not competence to respond to the request.

The distinction was however somewhat blurred in, for example, the dissenting opinion of Judge Weeramantry, who referred consistently to the Court's 'refusal to grant an opinion', referring to the dictum in the *Peace Treaties* case that the Court's reply to a request, being its participation in the activities of the organization, 'in principle, should not be refused'.[178] In the *Legality of Nuclear Weapons* case, however, the decision of the Court from which Judge Weeramantry dissented was not to *refuse* an opinion—in the exercise of the discretion conferred by Article 65 of the Statute—, but a finding that the Court *had no competence*

[176] The Court would, however, presumably have had to give a decision to this effect, so that the request would have been effective to set advisory proceedings in motion. There is a difference between this situation and that in the case of *Legality of the Use of Nuclear Weapons by States in Armed Conflict*, in which, as noted above, the Court issued an 'advisory opinion' refusing an advisory opinion; in that case the request was valid as an act of the requesting organ, but failed to comply with the conditions of Article 96; but is the difference between the two cases a difference of quality or merely of degree?

[177] At the present stage of the progress of these articles, it has become superfluous to apologize for including in them reference to decisions of the Court rendered since the end of the period to which the articles are, *nominatim*, devoted.

[178] *ICJ Reports*, 1950, p. 71. It should be conceded that this expression is used in a paragraph of the 1950 opinion which initially concerns jurisdiction, and leads up to the reference made by the Court to the discretion under Article 65.

to give (or indeed to refuse) an opinion. The word 'refusal' implies an act of will or choice, and therefore a discretion; it is inappropriate to a finding of lack of competence.[179]

The question whether the Court has jurisdiction is, whether in advisory or contentious proceedings, a preliminary question. Judge Shahabuddeen, in his dissenting opinion, examined the distinction between preliminary questions and questions of 'merits' in advisory proceedings, as he considered that the Court had failed properly to make that distinction. He found a 'general criterion for identifying the merits' in a dictum of Judge Read in a dissenting opinion in the *Anglo-Iranian Oil Co.* case:

> the merits of a dispute consist of the issues of fact and law which give rise to a cause of action, and which an applicant State must establish in order to be entitled to the relief claimed.[180]

For Judge Shahabuddeen,

> The case at bar is, of course, a case within the Court's advisory jurisdiction, and caution is appropriate; but that basic approach appears transposable.[181]

However, the essence of his argument is that the WHO, by referring in the question submitted to its own constitution, had made it impossible for the Court to find that the question was not one 'arising within the scope of the activities' of the organization without *ipso ictu* deciding what were the obligations of members States under that constitution, and thus giving a (negative) answer on the merits. He therefore does not enter into what would have constituted a preliminary question, according to the definition borrowed from Judge Read, since for him there could not be one, in view of the framing of the question submitted.

Another argument presented in support of the Court's competence is somewhat reminiscent of the concept of *forum prorogatum*.[182] It was contended that, even assuming the question did not otherwise fall within the category of those arising in the scope of the activities of the WHO,

> the General Assembly of the United Nations, as the source from which the WHO derives its power to request advisory opinions has, in its resolution 49/75K, confirmed the competence of that organization to request an opinion on the question submitted to the Court . . .

[179] Judge Weeramantry himself recognized that 'The Court is of course entitled to refuse a request for an advisory opinion for cogent reasons—and indeed should so refuse if cogent reasons be present' (*ICJ Reports*, 1996, p. 108), which is a paraphrase (using the word 'cogent' in place of 'compelling') of what the Court has repeatedly said about the exercise of its discretion.

[180] Ibid., 1952, p. 148.

[181] Ibid., 1996, Vol. I, p. 99.

[182] This concept as such has little, if any, role to play in the advisory context, since it is difficult to imagine circumstances in which there would be a need to supplement the consent given by States by becoming parties to the Statute. Judge de Castro stated categorically in 1973 that 'no *forum prorogatum* can apply in regard to advisory opinions': separate opinion in *Application for Review of UNAT Judgment No. 158, ICJ Reports*, 1973, p. 274.

The tendentious reference to the General Assembly as the 'source' of the power will be noted, as will the implication that if the General Assembly was satisfied, the Court should not second-guess it. The Court quoted the terms of the resolution, by which the Assembly 'welcomed' the WHO request to the Court, and continued:

However, the Court does not consider that [by expressing this opinion] the General Assembly mean to pass upon the competence of the WHO to request an opinion on the question raised. Moreover, the General Assembly could evidently not have intended to disregard the limits within which Article 96, paragraph 2, of the Charter allows it to authorize the specialized agencies to request opinions from the Court . . . [183]

It is perhaps a matter of tact that the Court does not go a step further and point out that, even if that had been the intention of the Assembly, it would have been acting *ultra vires*. The Assembly could neither give a special authorization to a body to request an opinion not falling within the scope of its activities, since this would be contrary to the Charter,[184] nor redefine its activities so as to include the pertinent question within them, since those activities were defined by the constitution of the specialized agency. This latter aspect differentiates the case from that of, for example, the Committee on Applications for Review of Administrative Tribunal Judgments, which was an organ created by the Assembly; the Assembly in such case was sovereign in defining the scope of the activities of the organ.[185]

(*f*) Legality of the Threat or Use of Nuclear Weapons

The question of the powers of the General Assembly was raised in a more direct way in the other case of 1996 concerning nuclear weapons. The General Assembly had asked for an opinion on the question:

Is the threat or use of nuclear weapons in any circumstance permitted under international law?[186]

Inasmuch as Article 96 of the Charter empowers the Assembly and the Security Council to ask for an opinion on 'any legal question', without the added limitation applicable to other authorized bodies, that the question must be one 'arising within the scope of their activities', it might have been thought that no question of the relationship of the

[183] *ICJ Reports*, 1996, Vol. I, pp. 83–4, para. 30.

[184] It might be argued that the Assembly could *delegate* its own power to request an opinion, but it would probably remain the case that the 'activities' of the body concerned would remain defined by its own constitution, so that the request would still be *ultra vires*.

[185] Cf. the discussion of the Committee's activities in the *Fasla* case, *ICJ Reports*, 1973, pp. 173–5, paras. 19–23.

[186] General Assembly resolution 49/75K of 15 December 1994, quoted in ibid., 1996, Vol. I, pp. 227–8.

question to the activities of the Assembly could be raised. Nevertheless,

Some States which oppose the giving of an opinion by the Court argued that the General Assembly and Security Council are not entitled to ask for opinions on matters totally unrelated to their work. They suggested that, as in the case of organs and agencies acting under Article 96, paragraph 2, of the Charter, and notwithstanding the difference in wording between that provision and paragraph 1 of the same Article, the General Assembly and Security Council may ask for an advisory opinion on a legal question only within the scope of their activities.[187]

This was a bold argument in the context of jurisdiction, since it involved an interpretation of a treaty which flew in the face of the text; a stronger contention would have been that if the Court were faced with a request for an opinion on a subject which did not fall within the functions and activities of the Assembly or the Council, it might consider that it should exercise its discretion to decline to give an opinion.[188] The Court however dealt with the matter as one of jurisdiction, and did not reject the contention out of hand. It held that the Assembly 'has a long-standing interest' in such matters as the threat or use of force, disarmament, and progressive development of international law, 'and in their relation to nuclear weapons'.[189] It therefore said that 'In the view of the Court, it matters little whether this interpretation of Article 96, paragraph 1, is or is not correct.'[190] Thus the question remains open[191] whether it be the case that even the General Assembly and the Security Council do not have a totally unlimited power of requesting advisory opinions on any question on which a majority in one of these bodies would like to see a ruling by the Court.

(3) *Requests otherwise in conflict with the Statute*

One other case should be mentioned as having raised (and settled) a doubt as to the Court's jurisdiction: the first of the series of cases brought under Article 11 of the Statute of the United Nations Administrative Tribunal, the so-called *Fasla* case.[192] The Court stated in its opinion that 'doubts have been raised regarding the legality of the use of the advisory

[187] *ICJ Reports,* 1996, Vol. I, pp. 232–3, para. 12.

[188] This was in fact suggested by Fitzmaurice in 1952: he thought that the Court might regard it as inconsistent with its judicial role to give an opinion (*inter alia*) 'if the request related to something which had nothing to do with the work of the organ requesting it, and appeared directed to some ulterior purpose': this *Year Book,* 29 (1952), p. 53; *Collected Edition,* Vol. I, p. 122.

[189] In this connection it rejected the argument that 'the Assembly [can] request an opinion only in those circumstances in which it can take binding decisions': *ICJ Reports,* 1996, p. 233, para. 12.

[190] Ibid., 1996, Vol. I, p. 233, para. 11.

[191] In this sense, Rosenne, *The Law and Practice of the International Court of Justice,* 3rd edn. (1997) Vol. II, p. 998.

[192] *Application for Review of Judgment No. 158 of UNAT, ICJ Reports,* 1973, p. 166.

jurisdiction for the review of judgments of the Administrative Tribunal'.[193] As was pointed out by Judge de Castro, the question had not been raised by the interested parties;[194] he referred to a duty of the Court to examine *proprio motu* its own jurisdiction, but also relevant was the dissenting opinion of Judge Morozov, who stated flatly (and in italics) that '*the Court has no competence* to give the advisory opinion',[195] but did not indicate clearly what the basis of this view was, except that the procedure was not '*really judicial*'.

The Court treated the point on the basis that the gravamen of the criticism was that 'the existence, in the background, of a dispute the parties to which may be affected as a consequence of the Court's opinion', coupled with the fact that those parties were individuals,[196] affected the legality of the process. Having observed that if the request emanates from a body authorized under the Charter to make it, 'the Court is competent . . . to give such opinion', the Court concluded that

> The mere fact that it is not the rights of States which are in issue in the proceedings cannot suffice to deprive the Court of a competence expressly conferred on it by its Statute.[197]

The wording used is curious, with its suggestion that competence could be given with one hand and taken away with the other.[198] Presumably the argument has to be analysed on the basis that Judge Morozov's objection was that it was a *condition* of the advisory competence that it be exercised in a judicial manner in relation to the rights of States, not those of individuals; and that if that condition were not satisfied, then there was no competence at all. The Court's rejection of the objection may therefore be taken to mean that there is no condition of this kind impliedly attached to the advisory competence. The existence of the discretion to refuse an opinion enables the Court to read the terms of the Statute literally, without any implied reservations: if the Court had felt that it was improper or inappropriate for the advisory jurisdiction to be used for review of UNAT judgments, it could have employed that discretion to reject the request.[199]

[193] Ibid., p. 171, para.14.

[194] Ibid., dissenting opinion of Judge de Castro, p. 274, para. 1.

[195] Ibid., dissenting opinion of Judge Morozov, p. 296.

[196] Query whether the Secretary-General, party to the dispute merely *ès-qualités* as an institution, could properly be regarded as an individual? But the staff-member of course fell in that category.

[197] *ICJ Reports*, 1973, p. 172, para. 14.

[198] Cf. the wording of the finding as to the relevance of political aspects in the case of *Legality of the Threat or Use of Nuclear Weapons* quoted at p. 106 (n. 148) above.

[199] In fact, the Court in the *Fasla* case did not return to the point in the later part of the introduction to its opinion, dealing with possible reasons why it should decline to give the opinion; it presumably considered that it had already sufficiently dealt with the matter.

3. *Conditions pertinent to the exercise of the discretion to give or refuse an opinion*

The present Court has never yet exercised the discretion claimed under Article 65 of the Statute to decline to give the opinion requested. It has on occasion reformulated the question; this, however, has been avowedly in the interests of replying to the true intention of the requesting organ,[200] rather than excluding or avoiding some aspect of the question that it considers inappropriate, as an alternative to refusing an opinion altogether. In most cases submitted to it there have however been elements which, in the view of States appearing in the case, or individual Members of the Court, have been such as to justify a refusal; it is therefore useful to survey the practice to see what circumstances the Court has regarded as capable, if only potentially, of leading to such a refusal.

(1) *Existing disputes and the consent of States concerned*

As noted above, a logical deduction from the idea that an advisory opinion is given to the organ requesting it, and thus is not a dispute-settlement mechanism, is that the consent of States has no role to play in determining the existence of jurisdiction in the Court to give the opinion. Even where the question submitted for opinion does relate to, or overlap with, a dispute between States, that does not imply that the consent of the States parties to it is necessary for the Court to have competence to give an opinion upon it. On the other hand, as the Court was to explain with particular clarity in the *Western Sahara* case (examined below), consent of interested States remains pertinent, not for the existence of jurisdiction, but as a matter of judicial propriety, as an element affecting the Court's exercise of its discretion to give or to refuse an advisory opinion. The matter has been examined in a number of decisions.

(*a*) *Legal consequences for States of the continued presence of South Africa in Namibia (South West Africa) notwithstanding Security Council resolution 276 (1970)*

In 1971 it was argued by South Africa in the *Namibia* case[201] that 'even if the Court had competence to give the opinion requested,[202] it should nevertheless, as a matter of judicial propriety, refuse to exercise its

[200] A striking example is the opinion on *Interpretation of the Agreement of 25 March 1951 between the WHO and Egypt*, in which the Court re-wrote the terms of the question, and stated that its reformulation 'in the Court's opinion must . . . be considered to be the legal question submitted to it by the request': *ICJ Reports*, 1980, p. 88, para. 35. It must be doubtful whether the Court could 'cure' a request submitting a question which was not a legal one, by rewriting the question so as to transform it into such a question.

[201] *Legal Consequences for States of the Continued Presence of South Africa in Namibia (South West Africa) notwithstanding Security Council resolution 276 (1970)*, *ICJ Reports*, 1971, p. 16.

[202] Which South Africa disputed on other grounds, noted above.

competence',[203] and one of the grounds for this was that 'the relevant legal question relates to an existing dispute between South Africa and other States'.[204] The Court's discussion of this contention does not refer to the element of consent; and indeed it was not entirely clear from South Africa's argument whether it was the mere existence of the dispute, as distinct from the existence of the dispute coupled with the lack of South Africa's consent to the judicial settlement of it, that should lead the Court to decline to exercise jurisdiction.[205] The matter was complicated by the fact that the existence or otherwise of a dispute was relevant to other questions, and specifically to the question whether South Africa was entitled to appoint a judge *ad hoc* to sit in the case; the right to do so would depend, according to the Statute and Rules of Court, on whether the request for an opinion related to a 'legal question actually pending' between South Africa and one or more other States, whether or not South Africa consented to the Court's giving an opinion on that legal question. It does not, however, appear that the Court would consider itself debarred from giving an opinion on a question related to an existing dispute if it was clear that it was the desire of the parties to the dispute that it should do so;[206] this was later to become clear from the *Headquarters Agreement* case (examined below).

The Court rejected South Africa's contentions (both as to appointment of a judge *ad hoc* and as to its duty to refuse to give an opinion) on the basis of a finding that the Security Council's request did not relate to a legal question actually pending between two or more States.[207] In this connection, it emphasized that

> It is not the purpose of the request to obtain the assistance of the Court in the exercise of the Security Council's functions relating to the pacific settlement of a dispute pending before it between two or more States,[208]

with the implication that if this had been the case, the Court would have been likely to decline to give the opinion. However, it does not indicate whether such a decision would be based on the basis of lack of consent of the State principally concerned. One reading of the South African contention would be that the *mere existence of a dispute* underlying the request for opinion would be sufficient to justify a refusal of the opinion; and the Court's decision can be taken as a rejection of this on the basis that there was no such underlying dispute; nothing in the decision

[203] *ICJ Reports,* 1971, p. 23, para. 27.

[204] Ibid., para. 30.

[205] See *Namibia, Pleadings,* Vol. 1, pp. 442–447, Vol. II, pp. 185–8.

[206] The reservation should be made that the Court might find that, for practical reasons (e.g. problems of fact-finding), it would be inappropriate for it to give an opinion in such circumstances.

[207] *ICJ Reports,* 1971, p. 24, para. 32.

[208] Ibid.

suggests that a refusal would have to be based on the existence of a dispute coupled with *the lack of consent* of an interested State.

(*b*) *Western Sahara*

As noted above, in the *Western Sahara* case, Spain endeavoured to convince the Court that the lack of its consent to the giving of an opinion on what amounted to the subject of a dispute between itself and other States was a reason why the Court lacked jurisdiction in the case. The Court rejected this contention, referring to the *Peace Treaties* case, but continued:

The Court, it is true, affirmed [in that case] . . . that its competence to give an opinion did not depend on the consent of the interested States, even when the case concerned a legal question actually pending between them. However, the Court proceeded not merely to stress its judicial character and the permissive nature of Article 65, paragraph 1, of the Statute but to examine, specifically in relation to the opposition of some of the interested States, the question of the judicial propriety of giving the opinion. Moreover, the Court emphasized the circumstances differentiating the case then under consideration from the *Status of Eastern Carelia* case and explained the particular grounds which led it to conclude that there was no reason to refuse to reply to the request. Thus the Court recognized that lack of consent might constitute a ground for declining to give the opinion requested if, in the circumstances of a given case, considerations of judicial propriety should oblige the Court to refuse an opinion. In short, the consent of an interested State continues to be relevant, not for the Court's competence, but for the appreciation of the propriety of giving an opinion.[209]

In its decision the Court made a number of references to the *Namibia* opinion, but none of these concern the question of the existence of a dispute; the emphasis in *Western Sahara* is laid entirely on the question of consent. Thus the Court continues in the next following paragraph:

In certain circumstances, therefore, the lack of consent of an interested State may render the giving of an advisory opinion incompatible with the Court's judicial character. An instance of this would be when the circumstances disclose that to give a reply would have the effect of circumventing the principle that a State is not obliged to allow its disputes to be submitted to judicial settlement without its consent.[210]

The Court did not think that that was the situation in the case before it: it was able to find that

the legal questions of which the Court has been seised are located in a broader frame of reference than the settlement of a particular dispute and embrace other elements.[211]

[209] Ibid., 1975, pp. 24–25, para. 32.
[210] Ibid., 1975, p. 25, para. 33.
[211] Ibid., p. 26, para. 38.

It stressed that the legal controversy had arisen 'during the proceedings of the General Assembly and in relation to matters with which it was dealing', and that 'It did not arise independently in bilateral relations.'[212] It concluded that

The object of the General Assembly has not been to bring before the Court, by way of a request for advisory opinion, a dispute or legal controversy, in order that it may later, on the basis of the Court's opinion, exercise its powers and functions for the peaceful settlement of that dispute or controversy. The object of the request is an entirely different one: to obtain from the Court an opinion which the General Assembly deems of assistance to it for the proper exercise of its functions concerning the decolonization of the territory.[213]

The interrelation of these arguments is unclear: is difference between the dispute and the question submitted for opinion relevant as illustrating the object of the General Assembly, or as an argument in itself? Or is the Court saying that an opinion might be refused if *either* the question submitted was identical with a 'legal question actually pending' between two States, *or* it was the intention of the Assembly to prepare for the exercise of its powers in the field of dispute-settlement, even if the question put was expressed differently from the terms of the dispute?[214]

The Court continued with an additional point:

Furthermore, the origin and scope of the dispute, as above described, are important in appreciating, from the point of view of the exercise of the Court's discretion, the real significance in this case of the lack of Spain's consent.[215] The issue between Morocco and Spain regarding Western Sahara is not one as to the legal status of the territory today, but one as to the rights of Morocco over it at the time of colonization. The settlement of this issue will not affect the rights of Spain today as the administering Power, but will assist the General Assembly in deciding on the policy to be followed in order to accelerate the decolonization process in the territory. It follows that the legal position of the State which has refused its consent to the present proceedings is not 'in any way compromised by the answers that the Court may give to the questions put to it' (*Interpretation of Peace Treaties with Bulgaria, Hungary and Romania, First Phase, ICJ Reports 1950*, p. 72).[216]

[212] Ibid., para. 34.

[213] Ibid., pp. 26–7, para. 39.

[214] There is also the question whether a request not made with a view to dispute settlement, but also not related to the functions of the requesting body, would be given effect to: as noted above (n. 188), Fitzmaurice suggested in 1952 that it would not be in accordance with the judicial functions of the Court to give an opinion 'if the request related to something which had nothing to do with the work of the organ requesting it, and appeared to be directed to some ulterior purpose'.

[215] This is a curious wording: the meaning would appear to be rather 'the real reason why the lack of Spain's consent is not of [legal] significance in this case'. The French text of the Opinion was authoritative, but it is similarly constructed: 'il s'agit d'apprécier, du point de vue de l'exercise par la Cour de son pouvoir discrétionnaire, les conséquences en l'espèce du défaut de consentement de l'Espagne.'

[216] *ICJ Reports*, 1975, p. 27, para. 42.

The problem raised by this dictum is that, in view of the non-binding character of advisory opinions, it is not clear in what way the position of such a State *could* be compromised, as a matter of law, by the answers given by the Court. Nothing in an advisory opinion, whatever its terms, could 'affect the *rights* of Spain'. Clearly if the only possible interpretation of the Court's opinion amounted to finding that the contention of the non-consenting State in relation to the 'legal question actually pending' was utterly unfounded in law, the position of that State would be seriously compromised at least in political terms; but its rights would be unaffected, and there would be no finding, having the status of *res judicata*, that its contentions were legally unsound.

It would of course be somewhat specious to contend that the position of a State party to a 'legal question actually pending' is unaffected by an advisory opinion given on that question in order to reject any assimilation, for this purpose, of advisory to contentious proceedings. As Judge Gros pointed out in *Western Sahara*:

> The advisory opinion determines the law applicable to the question put; it is possible for the body which sought the opinion not to follow it in its action, but that body [and, it may be added, an interested State] is aware that no position adopted contrary to the Court's pronouncement will have any effectiveness whatsoever in the legal sphere.[217]

An advisory opinion can to some extent be assimilated to a declaratory judgment; the legal rule stated in either decision applies in any event of its own force to the State whose conduct or position is in question, and it is not easy to define what is the precise element added by the formal status as *res judicata* of the judgment as compared with the opinion.[218]

The decision in the *Western Sahara* case suffers from an excess of reasoning, which blurs the finding of the Court on the relationship between the consent of an interested State and the Court's discretion to give or to refuse an opinion. One statement of principle does however emerge, which had already been adumbrated in the *Peace Treaties* case: this is that lack of consent would (or at least 'may') render the giving of an opinion incompatible with the Court's judicial character if

[217] *Western Sahara, declaration of Judge Gros, ICJ Reports,* 1975, p. 73, para. 6. Judge Gros in fact differed from the Court in holding that there was no 'legal question actually pending', and that the interlocutory decision on the question of judges *ad hoc* had been mistaken, and had committed the Court prematurely to an incorrect holding. Cf. also Judge de Castro in the same case: 'the effect of an advisory opinion is not confined to the parties as though it were a matter of a judgment; the opinion is authoritative *erga omnes* . . . ': loc. cit., p. 138.

[218] For Benvenuti (*L'accertamento del diritto mediante pareri consultativi della Corte internazionale di giustizia,* 1984), a declaratory judgment is binding as the natural and necessary consequence of the fact that its content corresponds to the content of positive law; *contra*, Morelli, 'Sulla nozione di sentenza internazionale dichiarativa', in *International Law at the Time of its Codification (Mélanges Ago)*, Vol. III, p. 210.

the circumstances disclose that to give a reply would have the effect of circumventing the principle that a State is not obliged to allow its disputes to be submitted to judicial settlement without its consent.[219]

This was a question which arose with more force in the so-called '*Mazilu*' case, now to be considered.

(c) *Applicability of Article VI, Section 22, of the Convention on the Privileges and Immunities of the United Nations* (*the* 'Mazilu' *case*).

This case faced the Court directly with the problem of an allegation that recourse to the advisory procedure was being had in order to get round the principle that a State is not obliged to accept judicial settlement of a dispute without its consent. There was no doubt that there was a dispute between the Government of Romania and the United Nations over the former's treatment of Mr Mazilu, a Romanian national who had been appointed a member of the Sub-Commission of the UN Economic and Social Council dealing with Prevention of Discrimination and Protection of Minorities. The legal question put to the Court was that of the 'applicability' of Section 22 of the Privileges and Immunities Convention (referred to by the Court as 'the General Convention') 'in the case of Mr Dumitri Mazilu as Special Rapporteur of the Sub-Commission'; that section provides for certain privileges and immunities for 'experts on mission', which, it was alleged, had not been respected by Romania in Mr Mazilu's case.

Two special features of the legal situation, already adverted to above in connection with the question of jurisdiction to give advisory opinions, were, first, that the General Convention contained a disputes settlement clause (Section 30) which provided (*inter alia*) that

If a difference arises between the United Nations on the one hand and a Member on the other hand, a request shall be made for an advisory opinion on any legal question involved in accordance with Article 96 of the Charter and Article 65 of the Statute of the Court. The opinion given by the Court shall be accepted as decisive by the parties;

and secondly that, when acceding to the General Convention Romania attached a reservation excluding the application of this section, expressing the view that

for the purpose of the submission of any dispute whatsoever to the Court for a ruling, the consent of all the parties to the dispute is required in every individual case. This reservation is equally applicable to the provisions contained in the said section which stipulate that the advisory opinion of the International Court is to be accepted as decisive.[220]

As noted above, it was not disputed that the reservation was effective

[219] *ICJ Reports*, 1975, p. 25, para. 33.
[220] Quoted at ibid., 1989, p. 188, para. 29.

according to its terms, though the Court left open the question whether it would prevent an opinion being requested under Article 30 in a dispute with Romania, or whether an opinion could be obtained, but would not be binding.[221]

The Court, having re-stated the principle enunciated in the *Peace Treaties* case as to the difference between contentious and advisory proceedings, ruled, for reasons already discussed, that Romania's reservation did not affect the Court's jurisdiction to entertain the request for opinion.[222] The Court, however, continued, consistently with its jurisprudence, that

While, however, the absence of the consent of Romania to the present proceedings can have no effect on the jurisdiction of the Court, it is a matter to be considered when examining the propriety of the Court giving an opinion.[223]

It quoted the passage from the *Western Sahara* opinion, already set out above, to the effect that

In certain circumstances, . . . the lack of consent of an interested State may render the giving of an advisory opinion incompatible with the Court's judicial character. An instance of this would be when the circumstances disclose that to give a reply would have the effect of circumventing the principle that a State is not obliged to allow its disputes to be submitted to judicial settlement without its consent.[224]

In view of the existence of Romania's reservation to Section 30 of the General Convention, and its express objection to the request being made to the Court,[225] this was clearly a possibility to be considered; Romania itself had not presented any argument on propriety, but much of what it had submitted on the question of jurisdiction was equally relevant to the other question.

The Court's treatment of the problem was brief: after stating that it must consider whether in the current case to give a reply would have the effect of circumventing the consent principle, it stated:

The Court considers that in the present case to give a reply would have no such effect. Certainly the [Economic and Social] Council, in its resolution requesting the opinion, did conclude that a difference had arisen between the United Nations and the Government of Romania as to the *applicability* of the Convention to Mr. Dumitri Mazilu. But this difference, and the question put to the Court in the light of it, are not to be confused with the dispute between the

[221] See above, pp. 98–101.

[222] *ICJ Reports,* 1989, p. 190, para. 36.

[223] Ibid., 1989, pp. 190–1, para. 37.

[224] Ibid., 1975, p. 25, para. 33, quoted in ibid., 1989, p. 191, para. 37.

[225] In the form of a memorandum to the United Nations Legal Counsel dated 6 January 1989, referred to in its Memorandum to the Court, *Pleadings*, p. 202.

United Nations and Romania with respect to the *application* of the General Convention in the case of Mr. Mazilu.[226]

The distinction between 'application' and 'applicability' in the circumstances of the case is so fine as to be barely perceptible to the naked eye.[227] For the purposes of the present discussion, it is difficult to escape the conclusion that the Court was concerned to restrict the scope of the limitation on its powers involved in the requirement that it should not permit circumvention of the principle of consent; it may have felt that a pronouncement on the treatment of Mr Mazilu was needed,[228] or that reservations to such texts as Section 30 of the General Convention were undesirable and should not be permitted anything more than minimal application (or—should one say?—applicability).

There has in fact always been a latent tension between two dicta of the Court as to the role of individual interested States in relation to a request for advisory opinion. On the one hand, the Court has asserted that 'no State . . . can prevent the giving of an advisory opinion which the United Nations[229] considers to be desirable in order to obtain enlightenment as to the course of action it should take';[230] on the other hand, the Court has recognized that, in principle, an opinion will not be given if it is shown that the request is made to circumvent the principle that States are not obliged to submit disputes to judicial settlement against their will. If an interested State can demonstrate that this is the case, then it is hard to see in what way it is not 'preventing the giving' of the opinion. However, the first dictum is probably to be understood as meaning simply that no State can block an opinion merely by showing lack of consent; the circumstances must, independently of the attitude of the interested State, also be such that to override that lack of consent would be to circumvent the consent principle.

[226] *ICJ Reports,* 1989, p. 191, para. 38.

[227] Cf. the recent decision in the *Difference relating to Immunity from Legal Process of a Special Rapporteur of the Commission on Human Rights*, given on the basis of Section 30 of the General Convention, in which the question put to the Court, that of the 'applicability' of Section 22 of the General Convention was found to have been intended to pertain not only to the question whether the individual involved was or was not an 'expert on mission', but, in the event of an affirmative answer to that question, 'to the consequences of that finding in the circumstances of the case', i.e. to the application of the text: *ICJ Reports,* 1999, p. 62, para. 39.

[228] The writer has pointed out elsewhere the impropriety of allowing considerations of the desirability of a ruling on the merits of a case to influence the decision on jurisdiction and admissibility questions, to which such considerations should be entirely foreign: 'The Contribution of the International Court of Justice to the Development of Law: the *South West Africa* Experience', *African Society of International and Comparative Law, Proceedings of the 7th Annual Conference,* Johannesburg, 1995, pp. 132–5.

[229] As Rosenne has pointed out, the reference to the UN, rather than to the requesting organ, is unexpected: *The Law and Practice of the International Court*, 2nd edn. (1961) p. 710, footnote 1; 3rd edn. (1997) p. 1015, n. 61.

[230] *Interpretation of Peace Treaties, ICJ Reports,* 1950, p. 71.

(*d*) *Applicability of the obligation to arbitrate under Section 21 of the United Nations Headquarters Agreement of 26 June 1947*

In the *Western Sahara* case, a distinction was drawn between two sets of circumstances in which the General Assembly might submit a request for advisory opinion. In the one instance, the Assembly might bring a 'dispute or legal controversy' before the Court, 'in order that it may later, on the basis of the Court's opinion, examine its powers and functions for the peaceful settlement of the controversy'; in the other, the Assembly would seek to obtain from the Court an opinion deemed of assistance for the proper exercise of functions other than dispute-settlement functions (*in casu* decolonization functions).[231] It was because the *Western Sahara* case fell into the latter category that the Court did not consider the objections of Spain, as a State concerned in an alleged dispute, should weigh with it so as to lead to a refusal of an opinion: only in a case of the former category might the lack of consent of an interested State have that effect.

These were the circumstances of the *Headquarters Agreement* case,[232] with one important qualification: the State party to the existing dispute (there was only one such State, the other party being the United Nations itself) made no objection whatsoever to the Court being asked for, and giving, an advisory opinion.[233] The question submitted to the Court was whether 'in the light of the facts reflected in the reports of the Secretary-General', the United States was 'under an obligation to enter into arbitration' under the terms of the 1947 Headquarters Agreement;[234] the Secretary-General's reports showed how the USA had passed legislation providing for the closing of the PLO Observer Mission's office in New York, thus, it was suggested, interfering with the relations between that mission and the UN.

There was in effect a dispute as to whether there was a dispute between the parties: the Court began its reasoning by stating that it 'has to determine whether there exists a dispute between the United Nations and the United States' to which the Headquarters Agreement would apply.[235] It noted the assertion of the Secretary-General that there was such a dispute, and the laconic response of the United States that arbitration would not be 'appropriate or timely'.[236] The purpose of the Assembly in asking for the opinion was to clear the way for the submission of the principal dispute to arbitration; it was therefore acting in the exercise of its functions related to the peaceful settlement of

[231] *ICJ Reports*, 1975, pp. 26–7, quoted at p. 122 (n. 213) above.

[232] *Applicability of the Obligation to Arbitrate under Section 21 of the United Nations Headquarters Agreement of 26 June 1947, ICJ Reports*, 1988, p. 12.

[233] That State—the USA—also by coincidence had a Judge of its nationality on the Bench, so no problem of appointment of a judge *ad hoc* presented itself.

[234] Quoted from GA resolution 42/229B, set out at *ICJ Reports*, 1988, p. 13.

[235] Ibid., 1988, p. 27, para. 34.

[236] Written statement of the USA, quoted at ibid., 1988, p. 29, para. 39.

disputes. Had the US therefore objected to the request for the opinion, it would have been difficult to deny that the case fell within the second category identified in the *Western Sahara* case, and that the Court should decline to give an opinion.

The advisory opinion given makes no reference either to any question of jurisdiction (no-one questioned that the request was regular under Article 96 of the Statute) or to any question of the exercise of the Court's discretion to give or refuse an opinion. Clearly the presence and participation of the United States[237] made it quite obvious that no question of lack of consent arose, but one may consider that the Court could and perhaps should have put the matter to itself *proprio motu* and responded,[238] and perhaps have given some indication in the opinion of having done so. On the basis that a US objection would have made it necessary to refuse an opinion, the case also demonstrates that, to a limited extent, the existence of something analogous to *forum prorogatum* in the advisory context—analogous, because the fact remains that jurisdiction in that context is not created by consent (except in the sense, already noted, of consent to the Statute), but the lack of consent may be a bar to the *exercise* of jurisdiction.

(2) *Equality of parties to judicial proceedings*

(*a*) *Judgments of the Administrative Tribunal of the ILO upon complaints made against Unesco*

In the cases, already discussed, in which the advisory procedure has been used as a means of verifying the legality of decisions of administrative tribunals, a problem which has attracted much discussion is that of the equality of parties in the context of such a procedure. In the first of these cases,[239] that of *Judgments of the ILO Administrative Tribunal upon complaints made against Unesco*, the Court stated the principle that

> According to generally accepted practice, legal remedies against a judgment are equally open to either party. In this respect each possesses equal rights for the submission of its case to the tribunal called upon to examine the matter.[240]

[237] That participation was in fact minimal: having been invited to 'furnish information' under Article 66 of the Statute, the United States responded with a brief letter from its Ambassador (*Pleadings*, p. 187) which was treated by the Court as a written statement under that provision; and the US was not represented at the oral proceedings.

[238] In this sense Judge de Castro in *Application for Review of UNAT Judgment No. 158*, dissenting opinion, *ICJ Reports*, 1973, p.274.

[239] The case of *Effect of Awards of Compensation made by the United Nations Administrative Tribunal* (*ICJ Reports*, 1954, p. 47) was addressed to a different problem, and did not raise the question of equality. Given in 1954, that decision falls within the period covered by the last of Fitzmaurice's articles on Jurisdiction, Competence and Procedure (this *Year Book*, 34 (1958), pp. 1–161; *Collected Edition*, Vol. II., pp. 428–586), but he does not comment on the case.

[240] *ICJ Reports*, 1956, p. 85.

The procedure by which the Court had been seised, by the Executive Board of Unesco, was provided for in Article XII of the Statute of the ILO Administrative Tribunal, and enabled Unesco, but not the other party to an Administrative Tribunal Judgment, to challenge the decision by way of a request for advisory opinion. The Court, while not considering itself called upon to consider the merits of this procedure, did consider

the question whether its Statute and judicial character do or do not stand in the way of its participating in this procedure by complying with the Request for an Advisory Opinion.[241]

So far as the remedy against the decisions of the Tribunal was concerned, the inequality, in the view of the Court,

does not in fact constitute an inequality before the Court. It is antecedent to the examination of the question by the Court. It does not affect the manner in which the Court undertakes that examination.[242]

However, the question of inequality also arose in connection with the proceedings before the Court: since the Statute makes no provision for the participation of individuals in advisory proceedings, the Court could only hear directly the requesting organization and any States that chose to 'furnish information on the question' under Article 66 of the Statute. The difficulty was met by an arrangement, consented to by all those concerned, whereby a written statement on behalf of the staff-members was submitted through Unesco; and no oral proceedings (in which, it was then thought, the staff-members could not by any procedural device make an appearance)[243] were held. By this means, the Court was 'satisfied that adequate information has been made available to it'. Its conclusion was thus that

In view of this there would appear to be no compelling reason why the Court should not lend its assistance in the solution of a problem confronting a specialized agency of the United Nations authorized to ask for an advisory opinion of the Court.[244]

In short, the Court found that it might be a reason for declining to give an opinion if the circumstances were such that the procedure *before the Court* involved a breach of the principle of equality of parties; but that in assessing this, the Court will in each case look at the actual practical

[241] Ibid.

[242] Ibid. The Court also observed that the inequality in the current case was 'somewhat nominal', since the staff-members concerned had won their cases before the Tribunal, and had therefore no complaint (*ICJ Reports*, 1956, p. 85). This is a rather startling argument, since the Court was, in effect being asked to overturn the judgments favouring the officials, but they would not have been able to ask the Court to overturn a judgment in favour of the administration.

[243] But see the suggestion of the Secretary-General in 1987 referred to by Judge Schwebel in the *Yakimetz* case: *ICJ Reports*, 1987, p. 18 and p. 134 below.

[244] Ibid., 1956, p. 86.

arrangements made to remedy any potential inequality, rather than to the mere interpretation of the background texts, or any 'worst-case' scenario.[245] Inequality in the procedure by which the matter is brought before the Court is apparently unimportant in this respect.[246]

(*b*) *Application for Review of UNAT Judgment No. 158* (*the* Fasla *case*)

No further requests have been brought before the Court for opinions arising out of the decisions of the ILO Administrative Tribunals, but a number were brought under a similar procedure laid down in Article 11 of the Statute of the UN Administrative Tribunal,[247] until that procedure was abolished in 1995. The first of these was the case known as the *Fasla* case[248] in 1973.

So far as equality before the Court was concerned, a similar procedure was adopted to that employed in the *Unesco* case; but the Court nevertheless found it appropriate to re-examine the question of inequality in relation to oral proceedings before the Court. Dissenting judges in the previous case had questioned whether the mere fact that it had been possible to avoid holding oral proceedings was sufficient to meet the criticism that the parties to the original judgment would necessarily be in a position of inequality before the Court. Judge Zafulla Khan pointed out that any member State could have asked the Court to hold oral proceedings, which would have confronted the Court with a dilemma.[249] The General Assembly, when adopting Article 11 of the UNAT Statute, had endeavoured to meet this difficulty, by including in its resolution a recommendation that Member States and the Secretary-General should not make any oral statements in proceedings under that Article. The Court in its opinion emphasized that the holding of oral proceedings was a matter for the discretion of the Court.

> In exercising that discretion, the Court will have regard both to the provisions of its Statute and to the requirements of its judicial character. But it does not appear to the Court that there is any general principle of law which requires that in review proceedings the interested parties should necessarily have an opportunity to submit oral statements of their case to the review tribunal. General principles of law and the judicial character of the Court do require that, even in advisory proceedings, the interested parties should each have an opportunity,

[245] This emphasis on the actual rather than the hypothetical is also observable in the comment that the pre-ICJ inequality was 'somewhat nominal': see n. 242 above.

[246] Judge Klaestad dissented on this point among others; for him, the Court should not 'appear to acquiesce in a review procedure which fails to observe generally recognized principles by according to only one of the parties to the judgments of the Administrative Tribunal the right to challenge these judgments'; *ICJ Reports*, 1956, p. 112.

[247] For the text of Article 11, see ibid., 1973, pp. 170–1.

[248] *Application for Review of Judgment No. 158 of the United Nations Administrative Tribunal, ICJ Reports*, 1973, p. 166. All the cases of this type have a title in this form, but they are more conveniently referred to by the name of the staff-member concerned, in this case Mr Mohamed Fasla.

[249] *ICJ Reports*, 1956, pp. 114–15.

and on the basis of equality, to submit all the elements relevant to the questions which have been referred to the review tribunal. But that condition is fulfilled by the submission of written statements.[250]

As to equality in the prior proceedings, leading up to the seisin of the Court, the UNAT Statute procedure was superior to that of Article XII of the ILOAT Statute inasmuch as the initiative to challenge a Tribunal decision could come from the staff-member as well as from the Secretary-General. Either could make an application to a General Assembly Committee specially established for the purpose, which might, if so minded, then ask the Court for an advisory opinion. A curious feature of the procedure was, however, that any member State could also make an application to the Committee for the review of a Tribunal Judgment; such State would clearly not be a party to the original proceedings, and would not normally have any special interest in the decision, except to the extent that, via its contribution to the budget of the Organization, it might bear some share of any compensation or other financial benefit awarded the staff-member. The Court took note of this aspect, and of the suggestion[251] that to allow a member State to initiate proceedings for review would 'be contrary to the general principles governing judicial review'.[252] The Court reserved the point, inasmuch as the review actually brought before it had been initiated by the staff-member. This was consistent with the pragmatic approach adopted in the *Unesco* case, of seeing how the procedure had actually operated in the current case; but it appears to represent a departure from the previous view of the Court that inequality—and presumably other departures from judicial principle—in the proceedings leading up to the matter being brought before the Court, were irrelevant.

(*c*) *Application for Review of UNAT Judgment No. 273* (*the* Mortished *case*)

This view was definitively abandoned in the case of *Application for Review of UNAT Judgment No. 273*, concerning the staff-member Mortished. The established procedure of communication of the staff-member's contentions by the Secretary-General, and the omission of oral proceedings, was followed, and the Court was satisfied that

> the problem of the implementation of the principle of equality does not give rise to any particular difficulty as regards the proceedings before the Court itself,[253]

though the Court added a caveat that the omission of oral proceedings was justified 'on the basis that the task of the Court in relation to the

[250] Ibid., 1973, p. 181, para. 36.
[251] Made in discussion at the time of adoption of Article 11.
[252] *ICJ Reports*, 1973, p. 178, para. 31.
[253] Ibid., 1982, p. 339, para. 30.

judgment of the Tribunal is not fundamentally different from the task it performed in the 1973 [*Fasla*] opinion'. However, the Court continued:

> But the problem is not merely that of equality before the Court . . . comparison of the review procedure with the requirements governing the judicial process, and thus in particular with the principle of the equality of the parties, must also be made with regard to that stage of the review procedure which involves the intervention of the Committee.[254]

On the other hand, the Court continued to adopt the approach whereby what counted was effective equality in the procedure actually followed in the case, rather than the possibility of inequality in the abstract. For reasons to be noted in a moment, the Court examined the existence of a particular 'cause of inequality between the parties concerned in the review procedure':

> Since the Court, maintaining the approach it adopted on this point when it gave its 1973 Opinion, proposes to assess whether inequality exists at both the theoretical level and the practical level, it can conclude at once that on the theoretical level inequality exists. To ascertain whether it exists on the practical level, the Court must examine what the Committee actually did.[255]

The theoretical inequality identified appears to be twofold: in the first place, the Committee, being an organ of the General Assembly, is an organ of 'the party which was unsuccessful before the Tribunal, that is to say the United Nations', so that 'one of the parties . . . has the right to decide the fate of the application for review made by the other party, the staff member'.[256] Secondly, each member State is entitled to apply to the Committee to review a particular judgment, and that State may be serving on the Committee when it considers the application (which was, in fact, what had happened in the *Mortished* case, in which the review procedure had been initiated by the United States).[257] These two elements made it necessary for the Court to make 'a particularly careful examination of the rules governing the composition and functioning of the Committee',[258] and to

> endeavour to establish whether the Committee duly respected the elementary principle governing the judicial process, that an organ which intervenes in a

[254] Ibid., 1982, p. 339, para. 31.
[255] Ibid., p. 340, para. 32.
[256] Ibid., pp. 339–40, para. 31.
[257] A point which weighed particularly with Judge Ruda was the fact that the United States representative was thus able to vote on the proposal in the Committee to request an advisory opinion; the representative of the staff-member was not permitted to participate in the discussion, let alone to vote: see *ICJ Reports*, 1982, pp. 345–6, para. 41–42, and separate opinion of Judge Ruda, ibid., p. 375.
[258] Ibid., p. 340, para. 31 *in fine*.

procedure which, taken as a whole, is judicial in nature, must observe the rules governing its composition and functioning.[259]

The Court apparently saw no further need to examine whether those rules in themselves were appropriate, since it had already observed that they entailed an inequality on the theoretical level. Presumably therefore it pressed its pragmatic approach to the extent that a theoretical inequality could be regarded as cured by a sufficiently fair and balanced procedure in the specific case; though to achieve this, one might have expected that something more than a mere observance of the rules would be needed.

The proceedings before the Committee turned out to have involved a whole series of irregularities, which the Court found added up to a 'failure of the Committee to show the concern for equality appropriate to a body discharging quasi-judicial functions'; so much so that the irregularities 'could well be regarded as constituting 'compelling reasons' for a refusal by the Court to entertain the request'.[260] Nevertheless, in the name of 'the stability and efficiency of the international organizations', the Court considered that it should not, by refusing an opinion, 'fail to assist a subsidiary body of the United Nations General Assembly in putting its operation upon a firm and secure foundation.' With some logical inconsistency, the Court appears to have identified two levels of 'compelling reasons'; having noted that the irregularities in themselves 'could well be regarded' as such, it went on to say:

While it could have been a compelling reason, making it inappropriate for the Court to entertain a request, that its judicial role would be endangered or discredited, that is not so in the present case, and the Court thus does not find that considerations of judicial restraint should prevent it from rendering the advisory opinion requested.[261]

While the wording of this part of the decision may thus be open to criticism, what the Court was in fact doing exemplifies the use of a discretion as distinct from the application, even the flexible application, of a set of rules. The Court was balancing the requirements of its judicial character, which would point to a refusal to appear to endorse a thoroughly flawed quasi-judicial procedure underlying the request, against its role as principal judicial organ of the United Nations, which would point to co-operation in the review procedure, the opportunity to call the Committee to order for its slovenly procedure,[262] and (in the

[259] Ibid., p. 340, para. 32 *in fine*.

[260] Ibid., 1982, p. 347, para. 45.

[261] Ibid. The expression 'judicial restraint' is unexpected; it seems to suggest care not to go too far, rather than a finding that, for compelling reasons, it should not go as far as it would have power to do.

[262] Though this could of course have been done, and perhaps done more effectively, in a decision refusing an opinion, as was pointed out by Judge Ruda in his separate opinion: *ICJ Reports*, 1982, p. 378.

special circumstances of the case) avoiding a refusal which 'would leave in suspense a very serious allegation against the Administrative Tribunal, that it had in effect challenged the authority of the General Assembly'.[263]

(d) Application for Review of UNAT Judgment No. 333 (the Yakimetz *case)*

Only one further request for an advisory opinion was made by the Committee on Applications for Review of Administrative Tribunal Judgments before it, and the procedure set up under Article 11, were abolished. This was the *Application for Review of UNAT Judgment No. 333*, relating to the staff-member Mr Yakimetz. The same procedure was followed by the Court as in the two previous cases, and the procedure before the Committee (to which application had been made by the staff-member) was free of irregularities. The only point of interest for present purposes was an observation made by the Secretary-General in a report on the feasibility of establishing a single administrative tribunal, which was quoted with approval in the dissenting opinion of Judge Schwebel.

The Secretary-General referred to the problem of equality in oral proceedings, and to the recommendation of the General Assembly that no-one concerned in a case of this type should upset the apple-cart by pressing for oral proceedings to be held. This recommendation had so far been complied with, but

> unease has been expressed that this does violence to the judicial procedures of the Court, that in some cases a hearing may be necessary for the proper presentation of a case and that the entire procedure is at the mercy of any State that might insist on its right to make an oral statement under article 66 (2) of the ICJ Statute (which would result in the type of inequality of arms *vis-à-vis* the applicant that would almost surely cause the Court to abort the proceeding).[264]

The suggestion of the Secretary-General was that, if oral proceedings were held, 'counsel selected by the applicant (and acceptable to the Court) could be introduced as the Secretary-General's special representative to express the applicant's views'.

From this survey of the exercise of the impact of the principle of equality of the parties on the Court's discretion to give or decline to give an opinion, in the context of the procedure of review of administrative

[263] This is not the place to go into details of this aspect, which involves complicated questions of the relations between various texts governing the rights of UN staff: briefly, it was argued (principally by the United States) that the Tribunal had deliberately failed to apply a modification made by the Assembly of the Staff Regulations governing what was known as the 'repatriation grant'. The Court did not consider that the Tribunal was guilty of this charge: see in particular ibid., p. 363, para. 75 *in fine*.

[264] UN doc. A/C.5/397, paras. 88–90, quoted in *ICJ Reports*, 1987, pp. 132–3.

tribunal judgments, it may be concluded that when the advisory opinion procedure is used as a means of scrutinising decisions of another judicial, or quasi-judicial, body, the Court will require to be satisfied that both the procedure adopted to bring the matter to the Court, and any special procedure before the Court required for the review to be effected, are in harmony with the principles governing judicial activity, particularly the principle of equality of the parties. At the same time, the matter is one of the exercise of discretion, and the Court's duty, as an organ of the United Nations, to contribute positively to the activity of the organisation and the specialised agencies, will weigh heavily in favour of giving the opinion requested, unless the insufficiencies of the procedure are such that, as the Court put it in the *Mortished* case, the Court's 'judicial role would be endangered or discredited'.[265]

(3) *The political background*

In the nature of things, requests addressed to the Court for advisory opinions, particularly those emanating from the political organs, the General Assembly and the Security Council, are likely to be made in the context of some controversy which has a political as well as a legal component, and the former may in fact dominate the latter. The Court has therefore frequently been urged to decline to give an opinion on the grounds, broadly expressed, that the matter is a political rather than a legal one;[266] but it has never found it appropriate to do so.

In its 1960 opinion on the *Constitution of the Maritime Safety Committee of IMCO*, the Court observed rather cryptically that

> The Statements submitted to the Court have shown that linked with the question put to it there are others of a political character. The Court as a judicial body is however bound, in the exercise of its advisory function, to remain faithful to the requirements of its judicial character.[267]

In that case, however, none of the participating States suggested that the Court should not reply to the question, though in the IMCO Assembly some delegations had suggested that it was unnecessary or inappropriate to ask for an opinion.[268]

In the case of *Certain Expenses of the United Nations*, the Court was asked by the General Assembly to interpret article 17, paragraph 2, of the Charter, and it was perfectly satisfied that this in itself was a 'legal question' for the purposes of Article 96, paragraph 1, of the Charter and

265 *ICJ Reports*, 1982, p. 347, para. 45.

266 In a contentious case, the Court has indicated that it cannot make for the parties a choice based 'on considerations of practicability or of political expediency': *Haya de la Torre*, *ICJ Reports*, 1951, p. 79.

267 *ICJ Reports*, 1960, p. 153; the last sentence has become a sort of mantra, repeated or referred to with regular insistence: it follows the lines of a dictum of the Permanent Court in the *Eastern Carelia* case quoted *supra*, text and n. 106.

268 See for example the Written Statement of the Netherlands, *Pleadings*, p. 247.

Article 65, paragraph 1, of the Statute. However, it was contended before it

> that the question put to the Court is intertwined with political questions, and that for that reason the Court should refuse to give an opinion. It is true that most interpretations of the Charter of the United Nations will have political significance, great or small. In the nature of things it could not be otherwise. The Court, however, cannot attribute a political character to a request which invites it to undertake an essentially judicial task, namely the interpretation of a treaty provision.[269]

This reasoning was introduced by the words 'The Court finds no "compelling reason" why it should not give the advisory opinion . . . ', which place the matter squarely within the domain of discretion. Thus the meaning is apparently not that the 'intertwining' has the effect of altering the character of the question put—that question remains legal; the legal character of the question is a matter affecting the existence or otherwise of jurisdiction. For the purpose of the exercise of the Court's discretion, the problem was rather whether the intertwining with political questions made it in some way inappropriate or undesirable that the Court should give an opinion. The answer given seems to be that if the question is clearly legal (or perhaps, sufficiently legal), then political considerations become irrelevant. The reasoning in the *Expenses* case is therefore not entirely satisfying.

The political aspect was given a rather different slant in the *Namibia* case, in which South Africa urged a 'disability' of the Court to give the opinion 'because of political pressure to which the Court, according to the Government of South Africa, has been or might be subjected'. The Court rejected this suggestion as a matter of principle:

> It would not be proper for the Court to entertain these observations, bearing as they do on the very nature of the Court as the principal judicial organ of the United Nations, an organ which, in that capacity, acts only on the basis of the law, independently of all outside influence or interventions whatsoever, in the exercise of the judicial function entrusted to it alone by the Charter and its Statute. A court functioning as a court of law can act in no other way.[270]

This passage reproduces a decision announced by the President of the Court at the opening of the oral proceedings.[271]

In the case of *Interpretation of the Agreement of 25 March 1951 between the WHO and Egypt*, the situation was similar to that in the *Maritime Safety Committee* case: no State had suggested that the Court should decline to respond to the request 'by reason of its allegedly political character', but the proposal to request an opinion had been opposed as

[269] *ICJ Reports*, 1962, p. 155

[270] Ibid., 1971, p. 23, para. 29.

[271] *Pleadings*, Vol. II, p. 27. For the contentions of South Africa thus rejected, see ibid., Vol. I, pp. 426–42 and Vol. II, pp. 659–63.

'nothing but a political manoeuvre' designed to postpone a decision on removing the WHO Regional Office from Alexandria. The Court however raised the point *proprio motu*, while at the same time observing that any such contention 'would have run counter to the settled jurisprudence of the Court'. That jurisprudence established that

if . . . a question submitted in a request is one that otherwise falls within the normal exercise of its judicial process, the Court has not to deal with the motives which may have inspired the request . . . . Indeed, in situations in which political considerations are prominent it may be particularly necessary for an international organization to obtain an advisory opinion from the Court as to the legal principles applicable with respect to the matter under debate, especially when these may include the interpretation of its constitution.[272]

(4) *Questions involving complex issues of fact*

Mention has been made above of the contention of South Africa in the *Namibia* case that, even on the basis that the question before the Court was a legal question, it should exercise its discretion to refuse an opinion since it would have to 'establish controverted primary facts'; and of the fact that the Court did not accept this contention but did not give any explanation in its advisory opinion as to why it did so, as distinct from its explanation that the question remained a 'legal' one so that it had jurisdiction.[273]

The matter was raised again in the *Western Sahara* case, in which Spain asserted that

in this case the Court cannot fulfil the requirements of good administration of justice as regards the determination of the facts . . . . In advisory proceedings there are properly speaking no parties obliged to furnish the necessary evidence, and the ordinary rules concerning the burden of proof can hardly be applied. That being so, according to Spain, the Court should refrain from replying in the absence of facts that are undisputed, since it would not be in possession of sufficient information such as would be available in adversary proceedings.[274]

The Court referred to the *Eastern Carelia* precedent, and in effect conceded that the Spanish contention was correct in law, so that

the issue is whether the Court has before it sufficient information and evidence to enable it to arrive at a judicial conclusion upon any disputed questions of fact the determination of which is necessary for it to give an opinion in conditions compatible with its judicial character.[275]

The Court however found, partly on the basis of the material supplied to it by Spain itself, that 'the information and evidence before it are

[272] *ICJ Reports*, 1980, p. 87, para. 33.
[273] Section 2(1)(*a*) above.
[274] *ICJ Reports*, 1975, p. 28, para. 44.
[275] Ibid., pp. 28–9, para. 46.

sufficient to enable it to arrive at a judicial conclusion concerning the facts',[276] and therefore proceeded to give the opinion requested.

On the basis of the *Eastern Carelia* and *Western Sahara* precedents, it is thus open to the Court to find that the opinion requested could not be given without a more extensive enquiry into factual issues than would be appropriate or possible in advisory proceedings, particularly if, as in the former case, one of the States concerned, and in a position to assist in establishing the facts, were declining to co-operate.[277] For what is the alternative? If the Court proceeds in such a case, and is eventually not satisfied that it has a clear picture of the facts, based on satisfactory evidence, it must either base its opinion on such inadequate material—hardly a judicial proceeding[278]—or leave the relevant issues undetermined, with the consequence of giving no, or an incomplete, opinion.

According to one view, this is in effect what happened in the case of *Legality of the Threat or Use of Nuclear Weapons*. Having come to the conclusion that 'the threat or use of nuclear weapons would generally be contrary to the rules of international law applicable in armed conflict, and in particular the principles and rules of humanitarian law', the Court nevertheless found itself unable to 'conclude definitively whether the threat or use of nuclear weapons would be lawful or unlawful in extreme circumstances of self-defence, in which the very survival of a State would be at stake'.[279] Exactly what this means is controversial: but it seems to be based at least in part on the observation made earlier in the opinion that

> The Court considers that it does not have sufficient elements to enable it to conclude with certainty that the use of nuclear weapons would necessarily be at variance with the principles and rules of law applicable in armed conflict in any circumstance.[280]

This appears to respond to the contentions of some of the nuclear-weapon States that there could be circumstances—factual circumstances—in which a nuclear weapon, despite its fundamental inaptitude

[276] Ibid., 1975, p. 29, para. 47.

[277] As noted above, Spain had, as it were, sawn off the branch it was sitting on by supplying factual material to the Court while contending that the Court could not decide without such material. Similarly in the *Namibia* case South Africa's co-operative attitude may have made it more difficult to press this argument; Judge Dillard, at least, was ready to distinguish the *Eastern Carelia* case on the ground that 'In the present case, while South Africa registered objections, she was yet a vigorous advocate and offered the Court optimum co-operation' (*ICJ Reports,* 1971, p. 156), a plaudit that South Africa must have received with some bitterness.

[278] As South Africa had in fact pointed out in *Namibia*, the Court cannot in advisory proceedings fall back on the solution of finding that the onus of proof has not been discharged, since there are no parties and no onus of proof in advisory proceedings: *Pleadings*, Vol. I, p. 449.

[279] *ICJ Reports,* 1996, p. 266, para. 105(2)(E).

[280] Ibid., pp. 262–3, para. 95.

to discriminate between military and civilian targets, might be used without breach of humanitarian law. To this extent therefore, the qualification placed by the Court on its finding, which has been interpreted as a sort of *non liquet*,[281] is an escape from the dilemma indicated above, and, in effect, a refusal in part to give the opinion requested.

(5) *Abstract or concrete questions*

As Fitzmaurice noted in his 1952 article in this series, the Court decided as long ago as the *Admissions* cases that '[t]he Court may advise on abstract questions'; he cited the brusque rejection by the Court in those cases of the opposite view:

> It has also been contended that the Court should not deal with a question couched in abstract terms. That is a mere affirmation devoid of any justification. According to Article 96 of the Charter, the Court may give an opinion on any legal question, abstract or otherwise.[282]

The matter was thus settled 'once and for all'; but as Fitzmaurice also noted, 'there are ambiguities about the term "abstract" '.[283]

In the *Western Sahara* case, Judge Petrén referred to the fact that the Court was asked to define the status of the territory at a period in the past, and was 'not asked to draw from its historical research any legal conclusion relating to the Western Sahara of today or tomorrow'. Had the Court not redefined the questions, Judge Petrén would not, he indicates, have found 'that they had the legal character required by Article 65, paragraph 1, of the Statute, for they would not call for any answer bearing on the solution of a legal problem at the present time'.[284] Even allowing for the difference of purpose between the advisory and contentious functions of the Court, is it appropriate for the Court to give an opinion on a question which is so abstract that the opinion is incapable of having any 'forward reach', to use the terminology of the *Northern Cameroons* case, in the sense that it 'can affect existing legal rights or obligations'?[285]

[281] See above, Section 2(1)(*c*); and cf. for example Weil, ' "The Court cannot conclude definitively . . . ": *Non Liquet* Revisited', in *Essays in International Law in honour of Professor Louis Henkin, Columbia Journal of Transnational Law*, Vol. 36 (1997), p. 109. For the view, taken above, that the problem was rather one of incomplete facts, see Bodansky, '*Non Liquet* and the Incompleteness of International Law', in Boisson de Chazournes and Sands (eds.), *International Law, the International Court of Justice and Nuclear Weapons* (1999).

[282] *Conditions of Admission of a State to Membership in the United Nations, ICJ Reports*, 1947–48, p. 61, quoted in this *Year Book*, 29 (1952), p. 48; *Collected Edition*, Vol. I, p.117.

[283] Fitzmaurice in this *Year Book*, 34 (1958), p. 147; *Collected Edition*, Vol. II, p. 574.

[284] Ibid., 1975, p. 111.

[285] Ibid., 1963, pp. 37, 34.

In the case concerning *Legality of the Threat or Use of Nuclear Weapons*, one of the reasons adduced by States appearing before the Court as justifying the Court in using its discretion to decline to give an opinion was the 'The question presented is vague and abstract'.[286] The Court's view on this contention was that:

In contending that the question put to the Court is vague and abstract, some States appeared to mean by this that there exists no specific dispute on the subject-matter of the question. In order to respond to this argument, it is necessary to distinguish between requirements governing contentious procedure and those applicable to advisory opinions. The purpose of the advisory function is not to settle—at least directly—disputes between States, but to offer legal advice to the organs and institutions requesting the opinion . . . . The fact that the question put to the Court does not relate to a specific dispute should consequently not lead the Court to decline to give the opinion requested.[287]

Only after giving this explanation did the Court go on to cite its dictum in the *Admissions* case.[288]

This is perhaps an over-restrictive interpretation of the term 'abstract'. If the Court were unable to give an opinion whenever 'there exists no specific dispute', and were also bound, whenever there was such a dispute, to refrain from giving an opinion if it appeared that the principle of State consent to dispute-settlement was being evaded, then its power to give opinions would be very considerably reduced. Questions not related to an existing dispute may be of varying degrees of abstractness, and an issue sufficiently removed from concrete reality might, for that reason, be considered not to be truly a 'legal question', or at least one not suitable for examination by a judicial body.

Judge Oda, in a powerful dissent, argued that this was a new and different sort of 'abstract question', inasmuch as 'no request for an advisory opinion concerning a legal question of a general nature, where that question is unrelated either to a concrete dispute or to a concrete problem awaiting a practical solution, has ever been submitted to the Court'.[289] He considered that the case was eminently one for the use of the discretion to decline to give an opinion.

[286] Written Statement of the USA, quoted in ibid., 1996, p. 236, para. 15.

[287] Ibid., 1996, p. 236, para. 15.

[288] It also cited the *Effect of Awards* case, in which the Court referred in passing to 'the general and abstract question' put to it (*ICJ Reports*, 1954, p. 51), and, more mysteriously, the *Namibia* case, *ICJ Reports*, 1971, p. 27, para. 40, a paragraph dealing with the argument (discussed in Section 2(1)(*a*) above) that the Court should not give an opinion involving findings on extensive factual issues.

[289] *ICJ Reports*, 1996, p. 371, para. 51. Judge Oda distinguished the *Reservations to the Genocide Convention* case, in view of the circumstances of 'practical necessity' in that case (ibid., para. 50).

(6) *Advisory opinions given binding effect*[290]

In discussing the *Mazilu* and *Headquarters Agreement* cases we have already encountered the phenomenon of provision being made in a treaty or convention for disputed questions to be referred to the Court for advisory opinion, the opinion given being accepted in advance by the parties to the treaty as a binding settlement of the dispute. As those cases show, this is a particularly useful device where one of the parties to the treaty is the United Nations itself, inasmuch as Article 34 of the Court's Statute prevents the organization from being a party to a contentious case.

The first case in which an arrangement of this kind came before the Court was the *Unesco* case, though the binding effect of the opinion in that case was, under Article XII of the Statute of the ILO Administrative Tribunal, merely effective in the relations between the requesting organization and the staff-member concerned. The Court took note of this factor, and observed that 'Such effect of the Opinion [to be given] goes beyond the scope attributed by the Charter and by the Statute of the Court to an Advisory Opinion'; however, the provision was 'nothing but a rule of conduct for' the requesting body:

> It in no wise affects the way in which the Court functions; that continues to be determined by its Statute and its Rules. Nor does it affect the reasoning by which the Court forms its Opinion or the content of the Opinion itself. Accordingly, the fact that the Opinion of the Court is accepted as binding provides no reason why the Request for an Opinion should not be complied with.[291]

Only one Member of the Court appears to have had doubts on this point: in his dissenting opinion Judge Córdova mentioned, as one of the arguments which had convinced him that the Court lacked jurisdiction to act as a sort of appellate Court, that

> the jurisdiction of the Court derives entirely and exclusively from its Statute and no other international instrument, including the Statutes of Administrative Tribunals or the resolutions of any Organ of the United Nations, can introduce any modification with regard to the jurisdiction of the Court; they cannot, in particular, either enlarge or diminish the competence of the Court, as defined by the Statute, with regard to its two legal activities, the judicial and the advisory functions.[292]

In contrast to this, the Court saw clearly that it was not a question of any 'modification' of the Court's jurisdiction, but rather a totally separate

[290] On this, see in particular Bacot, 'Réflexions sur les clauses qui rendent obligatoires les avis consultatifs de la CIJ', 84 *Revue générale* (1980), p. 1027; Ago, 'I pareri consultivi "vincolanti" della Corte internazionale di giustizia: problemi di ieri e di oggi'. 73 *Rivista di diritto internazionale* (1990), p. 5, and ' "Binding" advisory opinions of the International Court of Justice', 85 *AJIL* (1991), p. 439.

[291] *ICJ Reports*, 1956, p. 84.

[292] *ICJ Reports*, 1956, p. 156.

international transaction which took the advisory opinion as it emerged from the normal processes of the Court, and employed it as part of a treaty arrangement.

In the three cases brought by the Committee on Applications for Review of Administrative Tribunal Judgments, the Court consistently followed its ruling in the *Unesco* case:

> the special effect to be attributed to the Court's opinion by Article 11 of the Statute of the United Nations Administrative Tribunal furnishes no reason for refusing to comply with the request for an opinion in the present instance.[293]

These cases concerned, in effect, international administrative law, governing the relations between international officials and their employing organizations. The Court has never been asked to settle a dispute by an opinion binding upon *States* by virtue of a treaty provision. In the *Mazilu* case, such a provision (Section 30) existed in the Convention on the Privileges and Immunities of the United Nations, the text the applicability of which was the disputed question before the Court; but the request for opinion was not framed under that provision, so that the opinion given would not be binding.[294] In the *Headquarters Agreement* case, the Agreement in question provided for settlement of disputes, not through an advisory opinion of the Court, but by binding arbitration; the Court was asked merely whether the arbitration clause had become applicable. There seems no reason to doubt, however, that the Court would apply the same reasoning to a request for an opinion binding upon States under a treaty as it did to requests for opinions binding under the Statutes of the administrative tribunals.

While the jurisprudence of the Court is thus clear in the sense that the mere fact that the opinion to be given is, by virtue of a treaty provision, to be binding, is not a ground for refusal of the opinion, requests of this nature should, it is suggested, be treated with caution. There is a certain procedural inequality involved, inasmuch as, of the two parties to the dispute, only the international organization can take the initiative of asking for the opinion. Furthermore, the request for opinion is unlikely to be the product of an open-minded desire for advice from the Court; if the request is made, it is frequently because the political organ is already convinced of the soundness of its case, and simply seeks the endorsement of the Court.[295] Hence there is a certain tension between the consent of

[293] *Application for Review of UNAT Judgment No. 158, ICJ Reports,* 1973, p. 183; in the same sense, the decisions concerning UNAT Judgments Nos. 273 (*ICJ Reports,* 1982, p. 336, para. 25) and 333 (ibid., 1987, p. 32, para. 26).

[294] See the discussion above of the implications of the existence of Section 30 for the question of State consent, and the propriety of giving the opinion (*supra*, p. 124).

[295] See Dominice, 'Le règlement juridictionnel du contentieux des organisations internationales', in *L'ordre juridique international entre tradition et innovation*, IUHEI Geneva, 1997, p. 159. Outside the context of the settlement of disputes, this was also alleged to be the case of the General Assembly's request for an opinion on *Legality of the Threat or Use of Nuclear Weapons*: see in particular the dissenting opinion of Judge Oda, *ICJ Reports,* 1996, p. 367, para. 43.

the State concerned to the possibility of binding reference to the Court, and the unilateral, non-reciprocal, right of seising it.[296]

4. *Provisional measures in advisory proceedings?*[297]

As was noted in an earlier article in this series,[298] the jurisdiction to indicate provisional measures under Article 41 of the Statute is independent of the jurisdiction to entertain the merits of the case in which measures are requested; it is a form of incidental jurisdiction, and the necessary consent of States to its existence derives from the consent expressed by becoming a party to the Statute containing Article 41. It may be asked whether in advisory proceedings, in which the consent to the Court's dealing with the merits (i.e. giving the opinion) is also a matter of consent to Statute, the jurisdiction to indicate provisional measures exists similarly alongside that jurisdiction. In most case, of course, the question is purely academic, in the sense that an advisory opinion is not normally asked for in circumstances in which there is an imminent threat to the rights or interests of a party to a dispute.

However, in the *Headquarters Agreement* case in 1988, the General Assembly asked for an advisory opinion in connection with a law adopted by the Government of the United States directed to closing down the New York office of the Palestine Liberation Organization; the Court was asked to say whether the US was bound, under the Headquarters Agreement, to go to arbitration with the UN. In its resolution requesting the opinion the Assembly referred to Article 41 of the Statute,[299] and indicated that its decision was taken 'taking into account the time constraint'. This was a clear hint to the Court that, in view of the threat to the PLO office, and thus to the observer status of that organization with the UN, the Court might consider indicating as a provisional measure a directive to the United States to stay its hand. In its first Order in the case, regulating the procedure, the Court recited that the resolution, while containing the reference to the Articles mentioned, 'does not constitute a formal request for the indication of provisional measures', and continued:

[296] It is of course perfectly possible for States to agree that a future dispute may be referred to the Court by the unilateral act of one of them, the other having no initiative in the matter; this was the case of the Anglo-Icelandic and Germano-Icelandic exchange of notes in the *Fisheries Jurisdiction* cases.

[297] See also the present writer's paper on 'The Advisory Function of the International Court of Justice, 1946–1996: Achievements and Prospects', in *Essays on International Law, 40th Anniversary Volume of the Asian-African Legal Consultative Committee* (1997).

[298] This *Year Book*, 69 (1998), pp. 22–3.

[299] Along with Article 65, whereby the Court in advisory proceedings is to be 'guided by the provisions of the present Statute which apply in contentious cases to the extent to which it recognizes them to be applicable'.

Whereas it is not appropriate, in the circumstances of the case, for the Court to consider whether or not provisional measures may be indicated in proceedings on a request for advisory opinion.[300]

It is suggested that, had the Court pursued the matter, it could not properly have concluded that measures could be indicated. The purpose of provisional measures, as was indicated, for example, in the case of the *Arbitral Award of 31 July 1989*, is to protect 'rights which are the subject of dispute in judicial proceedings'; measures, according to the same decision, are indicated 'pending the final decision', and

therefore they are measures such that they will no longer be required as such once the dispute over those rights has been resolved by the Court's judgment on the merits of the case.[301]

Assuming that there was in the *Headquarters Agreement* case a dispute over the respective rights of the United States and the United Nations, the advisory opinion would not resolve it, as though it were a judgment.[302] Even if the Court had been asked for an opinion whether the US legislation closing the PLO office would be a breach of the Headquarters Agreement, an advisory opinion to that effect would not 'resolve the dispute', in view of the non-binding effect of advisory opinions.

Chapter 3: Jurisdiction and its Non-Exercise: 'General Admissibility' in Contentious and Advisory Proceedings

'Is there any other point to which you would wish to draw my attention?'
'To the curious incident of the dog in the night-time.'
'The dog did nothing in the night-time.'
'That was the curious incident,' remarked Sherlock Holmes.
A. Conan Doyle, *Silver Blaze*.

During and immediately following the period under review, in four contentious cases the Court has, without examining the question of the existence of jurisdiction, declined in advance to exercise any jurisdiction which it might have.[303] It has also, during the same period, in a number of cases examined considerations which might lead to its declining

[300] *Applicability of the Obligation to Arbitrate under Section 21 of the United Nations Headquarters Agreement of 26 June 1947, Order of 9 March 1988, ICJ Reports*, 1988, p. 4.

[301] *Order of 2 March 1990, ICJ Reports*, 1990, p. 69, para. 24.

[302] The parallel with the case of the *Arbitral Award of 31 July 1989* is striking: in that case Guinea-Bissau was asking for measures to protect the rights it claimed as part of the merits of the dispute referred to the Arbitral Tribunal, but the proceedings before the Court were only concerned with the validity of the Decision of the Tribunal. In the *Headquarters Agreement* case, the Court was not asked whether the United States would be in breach of the Agreement if it closed the PLO office, but only if the US was bound to proceed to arbitration on that issue.

[303] *Northern Cameroons, ICJ Reports*, 1963, p. 15; *Nuclear Tests (Australia* v. *France), ICJ Reports*, 1974, p. 253; *Nuclear Tests*, ibid., p. 457; *East Timor, ICJ Reports*, 1995, p. 90.

similarly to exercise its jurisdiction to give an advisory opinion, the legal possibility of such a refusal being well recognized. These examples of actual or potential non-exercise of jurisdiction merit examination for the light they may throw on the nature of the international judicial process; something has been said in an earlier article of the phenomenon in contentious cases, and the Court's examination of its discretion to refuse an advisory opinion has been considered above, but at this point an attempt will be made at synthesis on the basis of the case-law.

It is well established, on the basis of the wording in Article 65, paragraph 1, of the Statute ('The Court *may* give an advisory opinion on any legal question . . .') that the Court has a discretion to give an advisory opinion, or to decline to do so.[304] This discretion is, as we have seen, unrelated to the question of jurisdiction: the Court may have to examine whether it has jurisdiction to give a particular opinion requested, and may in fact find that it does not, but this involves the application of a clear procedural principle, and not the exercise of any discretion. It is on the basis that the Court does possess jurisdiction to give the opinion that it may still, basing itself on Article 65, indicate that as a matter of discretion it will decline to give it.

This situation is often contrasted, if only implicitly, with that in contentious cases. The Statute defines the function of the Court as being to 'decide in accordance with international law such cases as are submitted to it',[305] but it does not in so many words say that the Court *shall* give judgment in any case in which it is regularly seised and possessed of jurisdiction. That however is the implication of the text, and the general understanding of the role of an international judicial body.[306] Jurisdiction, at least in contentious cases, entails at once the power to decide a given dispute with binding force, and a duty to exercise that power.[307] In his separate opinion in the *Northern Cameroons* case, Sir

[304] Abi-Saab has shown, in a recent article, that it is doubtful whether the use of the words 'may give' in the original PCIJ Statute was intended to convey the idea of discretion ('On discretion: Reflections on the nature of the consultative function of the International Court of Justice', in Boisson de Chazournes and Sands (eds.), *International Law, the International Court and Nuclear Weapons* (1999) p. 38); but the jurisprudential interpretation of the English text, and the later modification to the French text to align it with the English, now permit of no other interpretation.

[305] Quoted in support of a general duty to decide, in *Nuclear Tests, ICJ Reports,* 1974, p. 271, para. 57.

[306] Judge Oda, in a recent dissenting opinion, has suggested that the discretion to refuse an advisory opinion is to be explained by the fact that the Court's advisory function is something 'parallel with its contentious function, but continuing to be regarded as an exception and to be seen as an incidental function of the Court'; *Legality of the Threat or Use of Nuclear Weapons, ICJ Reports,* 1996, pp. 379–80, para. 47.

[307] In this sense, Weil, ' "The Court cannot conclude definitively . . . ": *Non liquet* revisited', 36 *Columbia Journal of Transnational Law,* (1997), p. 115. It is on this basis that the Guinea-Bissau arbitral award was attacked for failure to exercise jurisdiction (paradoxically classified as a form of *excès de pouvoir*); while the Court in its decision did not uphold this contention, it recognized, at least by implication, the duty of an arbitral tribunal to exercise its jurisdiction to the full: *Arbitral Award of 31 July 1989, ICJ Reports,* 1991, pp. 66–7.

Gerald Fitzmaurice observed that, in contentious cases, 'it may be argued that if a court is competent in relation to a given case, it must exercise that competence', and that 'it is in a general way evident that courts exist in order to go into and decide the cases they are both duly seised of, and have jurisdiction to entertain, without picking and choosing which they will pronounce upon and which not'.[308] Similarly in the *Nuclear Tests* case, the Court disavowed any idea that 'the Court may select from the cases those it feels suitable for judgment while refusing to give judgment in others'.[309] Thus, the pattern might appear to be that, once jurisdiction is established in a particular contentious case, the Court has no choice but to give judgment upon it; whereas on receipt of a request for an opinion duly made by a body authorized to make such request, and within the limits of the authorization, the Court has jurisdiction to give an opinion but may nevertheless decline to do so—may, in fact 'pick and choose' which opinions it will give and which not.

The true position is of course less simple. Paradoxically enough, the discretion asserted in advisory cases has never yet been exercised by the post-war Court in the sense of refusing to give an advisory opinion; while the Court, though lacking any textually recognized discretion in contentious cases has declined in four cases to give judgment. In a previous article in this series,[310] these cases were discussed; as was there observed, the case-law supports two propositions:

> first, that in certain circumstances the Court may be validly seised of a case and have (or appear to have) jurisdiction to entertain it, but nevertheless be debarred from exercising that jurisdiction; secondly, that the Court has, in certain circumstances, a discretion to decline to exercise jurisdiction in a concrete case . . . [311]

It was also there observed that it was not entirely clear whether these are 'independent propositions or two facets of the same principle'.[312] What is clear is that, as the Court put it in the *Northern Cameroons* case, 'even if the Court, when seised [of a contentious case], finds that it has jurisdiction, the Court is not compelled in every case to exercise that jurisdiction'.[313]

Nor, on the other hand, is the Court as free to choose whether or not to give an advisory opinion as the sacred verb 'may' in the Statute might

[308] *ICJ Reports,* 1963, p. 101.

[309] Ibid., 1974, p. 271, para. 57.

[310] This *Year Book*, 69 (1998), pp. 34 ff.

[311] Ibid., 69 (1998), p. 34.

[312] loc. cit., p. 35.

[313] *ICJ Reports,* 1963, p. 29. It may be added, to avoid misunderstanding, that to declare a *non liquet*—assuming that to be possible for the Court—in the present writer's view does constitute an exercise of jurisdiction, since the Court is not declining to rule as to the law applicable to the case, but indicating that there is no such applicable law: cf. the discussion at pp. 106–8 above, and in this *Year Book*, 60 (1989), pp. 77–84.

suggest. The Court has repeatedly emphasized that, despite the terms of the Statute, it has a duty to respond affirmatively to a request for advisory opinion, unless there are 'compelling reasons' for not doing so.[314] This is a principle that has been developed on the basis of the status of the Court as an organ of the United Nations: 'the reply of the Court' to a request for opinion 'represents its participation in the activities of the Organization, and, in principle, should not be refused'.[315] The principle was originally defined in order to refute the contention that the lack of consent of States directly interested in the legal question submitted for opinion should be a bar to the giving of the opinion; it has subsequently been advanced in response to all the various arguments, discussed above in Chapter 2, Section 3, adduced in favour of a refusal to give an opinion. None of these have yet been found, *in casu*, to constitute a 'compelling reason'.

Some of these suggested grounds for refusal have been rejected in principle as incapable of constituting 'compelling reasons', but for others the door perhaps remains open. Furthermore, there is at least one situation which the Court has defined so precisely as one in which it would have to refuse in order to protect its judicial integrity, that we may say that such refusal could only formally be described as a matter of discretion; it would in effect be the performance of a duty. This is indeed the implication of the term 'compelling reasons' employed to refer to the situation in which the Court, supposedly in the exercise of a discretion, declines to give an opinion: if the reasons are compelling, presumably no further choice is presented: the Court *must* decline.[316]

The situation which the Court has defined as having this effect has already been referred to; it was expressed in the opinion given in the *Western Sahara* case in 1975:

> In certain circumstances, . . . the lack of consent of an interested State may render the giving of an advisory opinion incompatible with the Court's judicial character. An instance of this would be when the circumstances disclose that to give a reply would have the effect of circumventing the principle that a State is not obliged to allow its disputes to be submitted to judicial settlement without its consent.[317]

This may be linked with the references made in other cases to the relevance of the object of the proceedings: if the intention was to implement a disputes-settlement procedure, and the consent of one of

[314] A statement to this effect has appeared in almost every advisory opinion given by the post-war Court: for a convenient list of references, see the opinion in the case of the *Legality of the Threat or Use of Nuclear Weapons, ICJ Reports,* 1996, Vol. I, p. 235, para. 14.

[315] *Interpretation of Peace Treaties with Bulgaria, Hungary and Romania, ICJ Reports,* 1950, p. 71.

[316] In the *Western Sahara* case, the Court contemplated the possibility that 'considerations of judicial propriety should *oblige* the Court to refuse an opinion': *ICJ Reports,* 1975, p. 25, para. 32, emphasis added.

[317] Ibid., 1975, p. 25, para. 33, quoted in ibid., 1989, p. 191, para. 37.

the States involved in the dispute is lacking, this would be a compelling reason for refusal.

As has recently been pointed out by Abi-Saab, there is at least an apparent contradiction between a statement that the Court has a discretion to give or to refuse an advisory opinion, and a statement that it should only refuse if there are 'compelling reasons' to do so.[318] His conclusion is that the discretion in question is very far from being an unfettered one:

> It is in fact reduced to a special duty of vigilance for the Court lest in any advisory proceedings (but also in any contentious proceedings) be trespassed those 'inherent limitations' of the judicial function 'which are none the less imperative because they may be difficult to catalogue'. In other words, the discretionary power of the Court comes down to no more than a wider margin of appreciation of the general conditions of admissibility ('recevabilité générale' in French) of requests for advisory opinions, considerations whose default would mean that answering the question would be incompatible with the judicial function and not merely 'inopportune' or 'inconvenient' for the Court . . . , and would thus constitute one of those 'compelling reasons' which alone 'should lead [the Court] to refuse to give the requested opinion'.[319]

The discretion claimed in advisory cases is in fact well on the way to becoming ossified, in the sense that, as Abi-Saab observes, the 'compelling reasons' for refusing an opinion, in theory an open-ended category,

> have been refined and reduce to a relatively small number of considerations which are invoked from case to case, . . . and which phenomenologically correspond to a set of 'conditions of admissibility' whose contours are by now well defined through the cumulative and 'consistent jurisprudence' of the Court.[320]

The situation in the contentious context and that in the advisory context are thus more similar to each other than might at first appear; and as long ago as 1967 Abi-Saab had suggested a theory—referred to in the passage quoted above—apt to cover both: that of 'general admissibility' (*recevabilité générale*). In his classification, objections to the admissibility of a claim may be formal (non-compliance with the procedural requirements for bringing the action), or substantive (lack of *locus standi*, failure to exhaust local remedies, etc.). In either case, the inadmissibility is directly related to the claim itself. The category of general admissibility or inadmissibility however, while connected with the specific claim made, derives from considerations of judicial propriety. As Abi-Saab put it:

[318] 'On discretion: Reflections on the consultative function of the International Court of Justice', in Boisson de Chazournes and Sands, *International Law, the International Court of Justice and Nuclear Weapons* (1999), p. 36.

[319] Abi-Saab, op. cit., p. 45, citing a passage from *Northern Cameroons, ICJ Reports*, 1963, p. 30.

[320] Abi-Saab, op. cit., p. 49.

De même que l'on a distingué, dans le cadre de la compétence, entre la compétence spéciale et la compétence générale, il est possible de distinguer, dans le cadre de la recevabilité matérielle, entre les conditions spécifiques de recevabilité constituant les conditions d'existence ou d'exercise du droit d'action et les considérations de recevabilité générale qui tracent les limites de la fonction judiciaire.[321]

It was in the advisory field, Abi-Saab suggested, that the question had first arisen, with the *Eastern Carelia* decision. In contentious cases, he identified as examples of general inadmissibility the case of the absence from the proceedings of an essential party (*Monetary Gold*, to which he would no doubt have added *East Timor*), and the case of incompatibility of the object of the claim with the Court's judicial function (*Free Zones, Haya de la Torre, Northern Cameroons*, with, one may suppose, the addition of *Nuclear Tests*).

A more recent study of the question (Giuffrida, *La ricevibilità generale nella giurisprudenza della Corte internazionale di Giustizia*, Milan, 1995) has found it more appropriate to confine the concept of general inadmissibility to contentious proceedings, inasmuch as the Statute itself provides for the discretion of the Court to decline to give an advisory opinion.[322] In the context of contentious proceedings, Giuffrida also includes cases in which the Court has declined to rule on some *part* of the claim: *Continental Shelf (Libya/Malta)*—the limitation of the area covered by the decision to that not included in the untested claims of Italy;[323] *Right of Passage over Indian Territory*—the refusal of the Court to order India to end the measures opposing the Portuguese right of passage;[324] *Military and Paramilitary Activities*—refusal of the Court in its judgment on the merits to accept Nicaragua's request for an interim award of reparation.[325]

Abi-Saab himself however continues to hold that the concept constitutes a unifying factor for the two types of jurisdiction, as will be clear from the passage quoted above.[326] By way of general theory underlying inadmissibility of this type, in 1967 he indicated simply that the limits of the judicial function referred to were those which

s'imposent lorsque la Cour est appelée à agir d'une manière qui dépasse ou qui est incompatible avec ses pouvoirs tels qu'ils sont tracés par le Statut et le Règlement et par la notion même de fonction judiciaire.[327]

[321] *Les exceptions préliminaires*, pp. 146–7.
[322] Giuffrida, op. cit., p. 17, para. 8.
[323] *ICJ Reports*, 1985, pp. 24–8, paras. 20–3.
[324] See the submissions of Portugal, ibid., 1960, p. 19, and cf. the operative part of the Judgment, ibid., pp. 45–6.
[325] Ibid., 1986, p. 143, para. 285.
[326] Text and notes 319, 320.
[327] *Les exceptions préliminaires*, pp. 146–7.

Does the case-law of the Court indicate a sufficient identity or parallelism between the grounds invoked by the Court for declining to exercise contentious jurisdiction and those discussed by the Court as—potentially—justifying a refusal to give an advisory opinion, for it to be possible to regard the two categories as part of a general concept of 'general inadmissibility'? There does seem to be a common thread running through the decisions on what is often called 'judicial propriety': there are circumstances in which the Court must (or should) refrain from giving a decision or opinion in order to 'safeguard the judicial function', as the Court put it in *Northern Cameroons*.[328] It is, in short, sometimes the essential role of a judge not to decide—a sort of *lucus a non lucendo*. The Court says to the parties, or to the requesting organ in the case of an advisory opinion: 'you are asking for something which in the normal course of events would be an appropriate judicial act, a proper exercise of the judicial function; but in view of the particular circumstances this would not in fact be so'.

The source of this principle is somewhat obscure. The judicial function is conferred on the Court, and its modalities and limits defined, by the Statute, which is an international treaty. The treaty itself contains no text which would justify the Court in asserting a power to refuse to exercise jurisdiction in contentious cases; such a power has, by one means or another to be read into the Statute, perhaps as a matter of implied powers. It is however difficult to bring within the definition of the *Reparation for Injuries* case[329] a power to refrain from exercising the powers expressly conferred. A more promising approach, particularly in the light of the Court's repeated emphasis on its judicial character is to suppose that, in establishing a 'court', the States parties to the Statute meant to create a body which would (so far as not inconsistent with the governing texts) have the positive and negative attributes of bodies designated 'courts' in the municipal sphere.[330] This would thus be, not the direct application of a 'general principle of law', but its incorporation by implied intention into a treaty regime.

Whether such a general characteristic of courts as they exist at the domestic level can in fact be shown, is more doubtful. The International Court of Justice plays the role of a court in a legal order which differs markedly from municipal orders, as is evidenced by, for example, the principle of jurisdiction deriving from consent—a principle underlying a major aspect of general admissibility in the context of cases of the *Monetary Gold* and *East Timor* type. Giuffrida sees the underlying

[328] *ICJ Reports*, 1963, p. 38.

[329] '. . . those powers which, though not expressly provided in the Charter, are conferred upon it [the Organization] by necessary implication as being essential to the performance of its duties': ibid., 1949, p. 82. There is also the question whether the doctrine of implied powers is applicable to an *organ* of an organization.

[330] On the dangers of this approach, see a previous article in this series, this *Year Book*, 69 (1998), p. 4.

motivation, and apparently the legal justification, for decisions not to decide, in a political conception of the role of the Court whereby it does not, or should not, confine itself to a rigorously and exclusively juridical approach, but should exercise an international function of pacification and *détente* in accordance with the principles of the Charter.[331] This is too wide a question to be gone into here.

Comparison of the Court's treatment of general admissibility in the contentious and advisory spheres may be made under the following headings.

(1) *The interests of States not before the Court*

In the first place, the case-law suggests that it is not judicial to decide on the lawfulness of the conduct of a State which has not consented to such a decision being taken, and is not a party to the proceedings (*Monetary Gold, East Timor*), and this notwithstanding the fact that under Article 59 of the Statute, the decision has no force of *res judicata* in relation to that State; nor to give an advisory opinion which would in effect constitute such a decision without the consent of the State concerned (*Western Sahara, Mazilu*), To adjudicate on (for example) the international responsibility of the third State in its absence

> would run counter to a well-established principle of international law embodied in the Court's Statute, namely, that the Court can only exercise jurisdiction over a State with its consent.[332]

Similarly, the Court has indicated that it should not give an advisory opinion

> when the circumstances disclose that to give a reply would have the effect of circumventing the principle that a State is not obliged to allow its disputes to be submitted to judicial settlement without its consent.[333]

For the purpose of the advisory proceedings, the States concerned are thus assimilated to the position of Albania in the *Monetary Gold* case, or Indonesia in the *East Timor* case; to give the advisory opinion will involve a judicial determination in which the rights or interests of those States will 'form the very subject-matter of the decision'. If this is so, notwithstanding the fact that technically the States concerned are not 'parties', and the opinion has no binding force for them (or anyone else), there will be a 'compelling reason' for refusing an opinion.

[331] Giuffrida, op. cit., p. 170. He observes, correctly it is submitted, that a number of aspects of the Court's activity in recent years may be interpreted as indicating, at the least, a sensitivity in this direction; ibid., pp. 171–2, citing inter alia Abi-Saab, 'De l'évolution de la Cour internationale: Réflexions sur quelques tendances récentes', *Revue générale*, 1992, p. 290.

[332] *Monetary Gold Removed from Rome in 1943, ICJ Reports,* 1954, p. 32.

[333] *Western Sahara, ICJ Reports,* 1975, p. 25, para. 33.

There is a certain apparent inconsistency in the application of this touchstone of judicial propriety in the advisory context: the Court insists on the fact that, even when giving advisory opinions, it remains a court;[334] yet the most important—perhaps indeed the only—situation in which it is prepared to contemplate declining to give an opinion because of a conflict with its judicial character is when the requesting organ is seeking its participation in a dispute-settlement exercise, that is to say when it is *really* acting as a court. The discrepancy is however only apparent: if it is not fitting for a court to *decide* on the rights or obligations of a State without that State's consent, it is equally not fitting that it should do so by way of advisory opinion; but if the giving of the opinion is not tantamount to making such a decision, to 'circumventing the principle that a State is not obliged to allow its disputes to be submitted to judicial settlement without its consent', but merely involves giving advice to an international body in order that that body may exercise its own—non dispute-settling—functions, then the Court is not being asked to act as a *judging* court, and the propriety test does not fall to be applied.

(2) *The purpose for which the decision is requested and its potential usefulness*

There would seem to be at least one exception to the unity of the conditions of 'general admissibility' in contentious and advisory cases. In contentious proceedings, the Court will sometimes refuse to exercise its jurisdiction because of considerations related to the future use or usefulness of the judgment it is asked to give: it may refuse a judgment which is incapable of any 'forward reach',[335] or find that no decision can be given because the claim 'no longer has any object'.[336] But in advisory proceedings the Court does not permit itself to look ahead to the use which may be made of the opinion requested, or the motives underlying the request. In the case of *Legality of the Threat or Use of Nuclear Weapons*,

Certain States . . . observed that the General Assembly has not explained to the Court for what precise purposes it seeks the advisory opinion. Nevertheless, it is not for the Court itself to purport to decide whether or not an advisory opinion is needed by the Assembly for the performance of its functions. The General Assembly has the right to decide for itself on the usefulness of an opinion in the light of its own needs.

Equally, once the Assembly has asked, by adopting a resolution, for an advisory opinion on a legal question, the Court, in determining whether there are any compelling reasons for it to refuse to give such an opinion, will not have regard

[334] Cf. *Eastern Carelia, PCIJ Series B, No.* 5, p. 29.
[335] *Northern Cameroons, ICJ Reports,* 1963, p. 37.
[336] *Nuclear Tests, ICJ Reports,* 1974, p. 272, para. 62.

to the origins or to the political history of the request, or to the distribution of votes in respect of the adopted resolution.[337]

In this respect, the Court's 'discretion' is therefore more fettered in advisory proceedings than in contentious procedure; it has not hesitated to 'purport to decide' whether or not the judgment asked for by Cameroon, Australia or New Zealand was needed by those States.[338] It seems that if two (or more) States have agreed to ask the Court for judgment on a dispute between them, the Court will not necessarily respect their will and judgment in the matter, and may refuse to exercise jurisdiction; but that the Court does not reserve the right to 'second-guess' a body requesting an advisory opinion, and to say to it, in effect, 'You are entitled to ask for this opinion, but we do not think you ought to have it, for this and this reason.' This suggests that, contrary to the suggestion of Abi-Saab,[339] the Court has in advisory proceedings a *narrower* appreciation of the 'general conditions of admissibility'.

This greater deference to the judgment of the requesting organ may be contrasted with the attitude shown by the Court in cases in which one and the same dispute has been brought before the Court and the Security Council.[340] The fact that the Court is an organ of the United Nations, and the 'primary responsibility' of the Security Council in matters of international peace and security, have not so far been regarded as justifying the Court in disseising itself, or finding that it should not exercise jurisdiction, in such a situation. However, the giving of advisory opinions by the Court is not the only form of its 'participation in the activities of the Organization';[341] in exercising its jurisdiction in contentious cases, it is also acting as the 'principal judicial organ' of the United Nations. A situation which has not so far arisen which would test the compatibility of the Court's approaches in this field would be if an advisory opinion were requested on an issue which was also the subject of contentious proceedings before the Court. In the *Military and Paramilitary Activities* case, the Court considered that proceedings on the same matter could properly be pursued *pari passu* before the Court and the Security Council;[342] but what if the Security Council, in order to

[337] *ICJ Reports,* 1996, p. 237, para. 16; cf. also, on the irrelevance of motive, *Interpretation of the Agreement of 25 March 1951 between the WHO and Egypt, ICJ Reports,* 1980, p. 87, para. 33.

[338] Giuffrida (op. cit., p. 170) even argues that refusals to give a judgment on grounds of judicial propriety are in many cases influenced or motivated by an assessment of what might be the consequences of the decision as regards their usefulness or appropriateness, and this includes not merely cases in which the decision would have no practical effect, but also cases in which the Court wished to avoid the practical consequences which the decision would have.

[339] Above, text quoted and note 320.

[340] Discussed in a previous article in this series: this *Year Book,* 69 (1998), pp. 52–6.

[341] See *Interpretation of Peace Treaties, ICJ Reports,* 1950, p. 72, and *Certain Expenses of the United Nations, ICJ Reports,* 1962, p. 155.

[342] *ICJ Reports,* 1984, p. 433, para. 93; see this *Year Book,* 69 (1998), p. 55.

continue to deal with the question, found it appropriate or even necessary to seek an advisory opinion of the Court?

Yet in advisory proceedings there seems to be one exception to this self-denying ordinance: if the opinion is asked for in the context of dispute settlement, the question of consent will arise, as the Court made clear in *Western Sahara*, and the Court has therefore to look to the future (and perhaps also to the history of the resolution requesting the opinion) in order to see whether this is the case. The Court indicated in that case that it will consider 'the object of the General Assembly' and the question whether that body 'may later, on the basis of the Court's opinion, exercise its powers and functions for the peaceful settlement of disputes'.[343]

This difference of treatment between contentious and advisory cases may to some extent be justified by the difference in nature between a judgment and an advisory opinion. In the *Northern Cameroons* case, the Court seemed to be espousing the theory of rules of general admissibility[344] applicable to both contentious and advisory proceedings:

> Both Courts have had occasion to make pronouncements concerning requests for advisory opinions, which are equally applicable to the proper role of the Court in disposing of contested cases; in both situations the Court is exercising a judicial function. That function is circumscribed by inherent limitations which are none the less imperative because they may be difficult to catalogue, and may not frequently present themselves as a conclusive bar to adjudication in a concrete case. Nevertheless, it is always a matter for the determination of the Court whether its judicial functions are involved.[345]

However, this passage is introduced by the words 'The Court may, of course, give advisory opinions, not at the request of a State, but at the request of a duly authorized organ or agency . . .', which suggests that what Cameroon was asking for would have posed no problem, or less of a problem, had it been the subject of an authorized request for advisory opinion. In the same vein, the Court laid emphasis on the possibility of compliance with the judgment it was being asked to give, and its duty to consider 'whether the judgment, if rendered, would be susceptible of any compliance or execution whatever, at any time in the future'.[346] It regarded as an essential element of judicial intervention in a dispute that

> Whenever the Court adjudicates on the merits of a dispute, one or the other party, or both parties, as a factual matter, are in a position to take some

[343] *ICJ Reports*, 1975, pp. 26–7, para. 39.

[344] Sir Gerald Fitzmaurice in his separate opinion considered that the Court had 'in effect (to make use of the French term *recevabilité*) treated it as non-receivable or unexaminable . . . ', and he himself thought that the claim was such that it had to be regarded as inadmissible; *ICJ Reports*, 1963, p. 101.

[345] Ibid., p. 30.

[346] Ibid., p. 37.

retroactive or prospective action or avoidance of action, which would constitute a compliance with the Court's judgment or a defiance thereof.[347]

If the criterion of 'forward reach' were the possibility of compliance, then an advisory opinion, requiring *ex definitione* no compliance, would not have fallen foul of the test of general admissibility.

However, other aspects of the Court's argument in the *Northern Cameroons* decision are less closely related to the compliance aspect of a contentious judgment. It declined to render a declaratory judgment, not because it had no power to do so, but because its judgment would have no continuing applicability: the dispute was one about

the interpretation and application of a treaty—the Trusteeship Agreement—which has now been terminated, is no longer in force, and there can be no opportunity for a further act of interpretation or application of that treaty in accordance with any judgment the Court might render.[348]

Do 'interpretation and application' necessarily involve 'compliance or execution' or 'action or avoidance of action'?

If then the Court had in 1963 been asked by the General Assembly for an advisory opinion on the conduct of the United Kingdom which had been impugned by Cameroon, there would have been no question of compliance with the opinion; would the Court would have seen a 'compelling reason' to refuse?[349] The theory of general admissibility would suppose an identity of approach in contentious and advisory cases, and thus point to a refusal; but the reluctance of the Court in other cases to find the existence of such a reason suggests otherwise.

(3) *Abstract questions*

The 1974 decisions in the *Nuclear Tests* cases based the refusal of exercise of jurisdiction on a ground similar to, but not identical with, the reasoning in the *Northern Cameroons* case: briefly expressed that 'the dispute having disappeared' as a result of the unilateral French announcements of the cessation of tests, 'the claim advanced by Australia [and New Zealand] no longer has any object. It follows that any further finding would have no *raison d'être*'.[350] By way of more general statement of principle, the Court observed that

[347] Ibid., pp. 37–8.

[348] Ibid., p. 37.

[349] The Court noted that the termination of the Trusteeship by GA resolution 1608 (XV) had 'definitive legal effect' even if the Assembly had acted on an incorrect interpretation of the Trusteeship Agreement (*ICJ Reports,* 1963, p. 32), and that the Assembly was, as a result of the resolution, 'no longer competent' in relation to the Territory (ibid., p. 35). Even so, on the basis of the Court's dicta as to the exclusive right of the requesting organ to determine the usefulness of the opinion, the Court would not have refused an opinion.

[350] *ICJ Reports*, 1974, p. 271, para. 56.

It does not enter into the adjudicatory functions of the Court to deal with issues *in abstracto*, once it has reached the conclusion that the merits of the case no longer fall to be determined. The object of the claim having disappeared, there is nothing on which to give judgment.[351]

This may be contrasted with the Court's attitude to requests for advisory opinion on abstract questions, examined in Chapter 2, Section 3(5), above: the Court has had no doubt that it could give opinions on abstract questions, equated, in the *Legality of the Threat or Use of Nuclear Weapons* case, with questions on which 'there exists no specific dispute'.[352] In view of the difference between the advisory and contentious functions of the Court, this disparity is hardly surprising; but it weakens the case for an overall conception of 'general admissibility' common to both.

(4) *Other considerations*

It is noteworthy that the Court has refused, in both contentious and advisory proceedings, to recognize as a ground of general inadmissibility any political implications of the case before it. In the advisory context this is shown by the cases, discussed above, of the *Maritime Safety Committee of IMCO, Certain Expenses of the United Nations, Interpretation of the WHO/Egypt Agreement, Namibia* and *Legality of the Threat or Use of Nuclear Weapons*. In the contentious context one may cite the *Military and Paramilitary Activities* case:

It must also be remembered that, as the *Corfu Channel* case . . . shows, the Court has never shied away from a case brought before it merely because it had political implications . . . [353]

This may be true according to its terms, but the *Haya de la Torre* case has been mentioned as one in which the Court refused to give a decision requested of it because to do so involved making choices determined by political expediency rather than law.[354]

With regard to problems of the establishment of facts, we have seen that it is not impossible that the Court might decline to give an opinion on a pure question of fact, or if the answer to a legal question depended upon the establishment of controverted facts, which would be difficult to achieve, for lack of co-operation of a key State, or for some other reason. This does not find a parallel in contentious proceedings, for the reason already mentioned that the procedural principle of the burden of proof makes it possible to reach a judicial finding whether facts alleged are proved or unproved.

[351] Ibid., pp. 271–2, para. 59.
[352] Ibid., 1996, p. 236, para. 15.
[353] Ibid., 1984, p. 435, para. 96.
[354] Ibid., 1951, p. 81.

(5) *Conclusion*

In both advisory and contentious cases, it seems, the rule is that the Court is under an obligation to give a decision, whether judgment or advisory opinion; the exception to the rule is that in certain circumstances it may or must refrain from doing so. What those circumstances are can be defined at least to this extent: if to give the decision would involve the Court in action inappropriate to the exercise of the judicial function, then it must refuse. Furthermore, despite the absence of any rule of binding precedent, and the use of the term 'discretion' in the advisory context, it seems that there is no turning back; once the Court has decided that a certain factor justifies non-exercise of jurisdiction, then the presence of that factor in further cases will lead—inexorably, even if expressed as a matter of 'discretion'—to a non-exercise in those cases.[355]

Nevertheless, the exercise of the judicial function is not identical in the contentious and advisory proceedings, so that the circumstances pointing to a refusal do not necessarily fall into exactly the same categories for an advisory opinion as for a judgment. The overall conception of 'general admissibility', applicable to both classes of cases, is not without usefulness, but may need too much adaptation to the one category or the other to prove a really useful analytical tool.

One element common to contentious and advisory cases is that the Court regards it as its duty to raise *proprio motu* the possibility that considerations of judicial propriety should lead it to decline to exercise jurisdiction. In the *Monetary Gold* case, the matter had been raised by Italy, and in the *East Timor* case by Australia; yet in the *Northern Cameroons* and *Nuclear Tests* cases, in which the interests of no third State were at stake—and thus the reasons for not giving judgment were, to use the expression employed in advisory proceedings, less 'compelling'—, the Court decided it should not give judgment even though the parties were desirous that it should. Similarly, while the question of the consent of States involved in a dispute was clearly raised by Spain in the *Western Sahara* case and Romania in the *Mazilu* case, and adverted to by South Africa in *Namibia*, in the cases brought by way of review of judgments of the United Nations Administrative Tribunal, the Court addressed itself to a whole series of considerations which *might* have led it to the conclusion that it should decline to give an opinion. Where the question is one of the consent of a State or States, this initiative of the Court might be influenced by considerations of *forum prorogatum*, in the sense that if that consent could be discerned through actions—or conceivably inaction—on the part of the State concerned

[355] In this sense Abi-Saab, quoted above (text and note 320).

which revealed such consent,[356] the fact that it did not take part in the proceedings would not justify the Court in refusing a decision.

V. Questions of Procedure, 1954–1989

1. *Introduction*

The present section of this series of articles poses particular problems. In the first place, Sir Gerald Fitzmaurice's election to the Court caused him to leave unfinished the series he was then engaged on, dealing with the period 1954–1959—hence the dates in the section title above. However, in addition, the nature of these articles as a contribution to legal literature is not the same when matters of ICJ procedure are under examination as in the earlier articles dealing with substantive law. Those articles, while dealing successively with many major fields of international law—State responsibility, law of the sea, treaty-law, etc.—were not offered as mini-treatises on those subjects, but merely as a survey of the contribution made to them by the decisions of the Court in the period considered, a contribution which might well be very limited in scope. Those fields of law are much wider, and contain material from sources other, than the decisions of the Court. The same cannot be said of the procedural law and practice of the Court itself: in the material sense it is derived solely from the Court's decisions (including decisions not embodied in judgments or even orders, but emerging from statements in Court and correspondence from the Registrar).[357] Furthermore, some decisions of the Court have very little to contribute to general substantive law; but there have been few cases which have not involved some problem of procedural law, and the period now to be examined has seen very extensive development of practice in such fields as, for example, chambers of the Court, intervention, and counter-claims. Thus to discuss the decisions of the Court in the field of procedure during the period considered is, if those decisions are examined in as close detail as

[356] In both the *Namibia* and *Western Sahara* cases the Court took into account the co-operation in the advisory procedure of the States which objected to the Court giving an opinion, though this was rather in connection with the question whether the Court could establish the facts of the case (in contradistinction to the *Eastern Carelia* decision); see above, pp. 137–8 and n. 277.

[357] The Court has not so far found it necessary to consider the sources of the law governing its procedure, since the Statute and Rules have proved adequate to the needs of the Court's work. Presumably the procedural law of the Court, being part of international law, must derive from the same sources as substantive law (in this sense, for example, Coussirat and Eisemann, 'La procédure devant les juridictions internationales permanentes', in *La juridiction internationale permanente*, Société française pour le droit international, 1987, p. 108, and Rosenne, *The Law and Practice of the International Court, 1920–1996*, 3rd edn. (1997) Vol. I, p. 254). The Chamber in the *Land, Island and Maritime Frontier Dispute* referred to the obligations of a party before the Court 'under the Statute and Rules of Court, or *the general principles of procedural law*': *ICJ Reports*, 1990, p. 136, para. 102, emphasis added. This is an unusual observation, if not unique, in the Court's jurisprudence: see Rosenne, op. cit. Vol. III, p. 1065.

those dealing with substantive law, in effect to compile a treatise on procedural law.[358] The prospect is daunting for author and reader alike, as bidding fair to involve as much text as has already been devoted to substantive law, unbalancing the series—a case of the tail wagging the dog. If the field were comparatively unexplored, such a body of writing might be very valuable; but on many of the procedural questions that have arisen in recent years, there is already an abundant mass of commentary,[359] and the recent publication of the revised and expanded version of the magisterial work of Shabtai Rosenne[360] more than adequately fills any gap there might be in the literature of the subject.

The conclusion that appears to follow from this observation is that the part of the present series devoted to procedural matters may be, and probably should be, less ambitious than the substantive-law part. Not every point that has arisen on the application of the Court's Statute and Rules will be expounded; and those issues that are treated will, in general, be dealt with less extensively than the reader of the previous articles may have come to expect. However, procedural law, though limited in scope, is law, and may involve the application of principles of profound importance: where any of these may be discerned, the reader's indulgence is asked for a more detailed discussion.

2. *The governing texts: the ICJ Statute and Rules of Court*

The primary source of the procedural law of the International Court is of course the Statute; and that text provides, in article 30, for the secondary source constituted by the Rules of Court:

> The Court shall frame rules for carrying out its functions. In particular, it shall lay down rules of procedure.

It is evident that the power to make rules has to be exercised consistently with the Statute, so that any purported rule which conflicted with the Statute would be void. However, there is no authority other than the Court which could declare the existence of such a conflict; and no party before the Court has attempted to challenge a provision of the Rules on this ground.

The Statute is, of course, a treaty,[361] and therefore to be interpreted according to the general rules of treaty interpretation. Attention may

[358] The same is of course true of the question of jurisdiction, already dealt with; and the fact that two-and-a-half articles have had to be devoted to that question is perhaps something of a warning.

[359] For a striking example, consider the super-abundant material on the question of intervention, listed for example in recent editions of the Court's own *Bibliography*.

[360] Rosenne, *The Law and Practice of the International Court, 1920–1996*, 3rd edn. (1997).

[361] Since it is declared by Article 92 of the Charter to form 'an integral part of the present Charter'.

therefore be drawn to what is, at the least, a curiosity, in the Rules of Court adopted in 1978. Article 13, paragraph 3, of the Statute provides that Members of the Court who have been 'replaced' at the end of their term of office 'shall finish any cases which they may have begun'. At what point may a Member of the Court be said to have 'begun' a case? Is it sufficient if proceedings have been instituted during his term of office; or must he have participated in some actual handling of the case by the Court, and if so what? The answer arrived at in the practice of the Court, and incorporated into Article 33 of the 1978 Rules, was that Members of the Court should 'discharge the duty imposed upon them' by Article 13, paragraph 3,

by continuing to sit until the completion of any phase of a case in respect of which the Court convenes for the oral proceedings prior to the date of such replacement.

Since this is an implementation of a provision of the Statute, it is at the same time an interpretation of what the Statute means by 'finishing' a case which a judge has 'begun'.

However, Article 33 contains the proviso: 'Except as provided in Article 17 of these Rules . . . ', and article 17, which deals with Chambers formed to deal with a particular case, lays down in paragraph 4 that

Members of a Chamber formed under this Article who have been replaced, in accordance with Article 13 of the Statute following the expiration of their term of office, shall continue to sit in all phases of the case, whatever the stage it has then reached.

The underlying idea is that, since the members of a Chamber formed to deal with a particular case may well have been chosen *intuitu personae*,[362] it would be at the least inappropriate for them not to sit until the case has been finally determined. The problem is that Articles 17 and 33 of the Rules of Court thus give two quite different interpretations of the meaning of Article 13 of the Statute. That article makes no distinction between Chamber cases and cases before the full Court; however desirable the object in view, is it permissible to adopt two conflicting interpretations of a single treaty-text?

It was doubly unfortunate, therefore, that the first time Article 17 came to be applied, the circumstances were such as to involve a 'stretching' of its terms leading to something approaching an *abus de droit*. When the Court decided to form a Chamber to deal with the *Gulf of Maine* case, the election of the judges to sit in the Chamber was held

[362] The text was drafted before any such Chamber had been established; but it was probably foreseen that, as became clear in the *Gulf of Maine* case, the parties to a case submitted to a Chamber of this kind would assert their control over its composition, going beyond the mere consent to the number of its members provided for in Article 26, paragraph 2, of the Statute.

on 15 January 1982.[363] One of the Members of the Court elected to the Chamber was Judge Gros, whose term of office was due to expire on 5 February 1982; and prior to that date nothing had been done by the Chamber in relation to the case.[364] On the interpretation of Article 13 of the Statute embodied in the general provision of Article 33 of the Rules, Judge Gros had not 'begun' the case; indeed, he could not have been said to have 'begun' the case, as a member of the Chamber, in any meaningful sense whatever. The effect of Article 17 was, however, that he continued to sit until October 1984, more than two years after he had been 'replaced' by the election of Judge de Lacharriere.[365] On the other hand, it was no secret that the parties to the case (the United States and Canada) had insisted on a particular composition of the Chamber, presumably including Judge Gros, and indicated that if they were not indulged in this desire, the case would be withdrawn and the dispute taken to arbitration.[366] Assuming that it was a good thing that the case should be heard by a Chamber of the Court,[367] the object in view was meritorious; but the question of principle, of two different interpretations of a single text, remains, and was emphasized by the *ad absurdum* interpretation needed to achieve the desired composition of the Chamber.

A subsequent case threw into still higher relief the conflict between the two interpretations of the Statute embodied in Articles 17 and 33 of the 1978 Rules. The question arose in the *Land, Island and Maritime Frontier Dispute* whether a particular issue (admission or refusal of an application for permission to intervene) should be determined by the full Court or by the Chamber which had been formed for the purposes of the case. The term of office, as a Member of the Court, of the judge elected President of the Chamber (Judge Sette-Camara) had expired since the Chamber was formed. He continued to sit as member and President of the Chamber by virtue of Article 17 of the Rules, but could not sit when the full Court considered the matter, presumably because Article 17 was treated as inapplicable for that purpose, so that Article 33 necessarily

363 Two Members of the Court pressed for the election to be postponed until after the date of replacement of outgoing Members, and when this was refused, voted against the Order forming the Chamber: Order of 20 January 1982, *ICJ Reports*, 1982, p. 3.

364 Even the fixing of the initial time-limits was effected by an Order of the full Court dated 1 February 1982: ibid., 1982, p. 15.

365 In view of the convention that France, as one of the permanent members of the Security Council, always has a judge of its nationality, one French judge may be regarded as 'succeeding' to the seat of another. Strictly, however, the Statute uses the word 'replace' in relation to the groups of five judges who go out of office every three years, and it is not possible to say that any individual judge is the 'replacement' of any other individual judge.

366 It should not be overlooked that this occurred in a period when very few cases were being brought before the Court, and its reputation had suffered, and was suffering, as a result.

367 It is generally thought that the *Gulf of Maine* case was something of a breakthrough, since a number of subsequent cases were referred to Chambers (the *Frontier Dispute* and *Elettronica Sicula* cases, and the *Land Island and Maritime Delimitation* case), after the provision in the Statute for such Chambers had been more or less a dead letter since 1920.

applied.[368] This anomaly is however not so shocking as might first appear, since the full Court was not sitting as composed for the case, but in 'administrative composition'—without judges *ad hoc*—to deal with a general question of procedure, as explained below.[369] The Court decided that the application for permission to intervene should be heard by the Chamber; had it decided that it should be heard by the full Court—the solution favoured by a number of judges[370]—a very strange situation would have arisen: either the President of the Chamber would have been unable to take part in that decision, in the case for which the Chamber had been formed, or the Court would have been composed (in addition to the judges *ad hoc*) of sixteen elected judges in lieu of fifteen. When Article 17 of the Rules was drafted, it was presumably thought that such a situation could not arise, since it was not foreseen that any 'phase' of a case allocated to a Chamber could ever, once the Chamber had been formed, come before the full Court for decision.

Chapter 1: The Composition of the Court for Particular Cases

1. *Judges* ad hoc

This is a topic which was not discussed at all in the series of articles by Sir Gerald Fitzmaurice to which the present articles form a pendant; the reason may be taken to be that no particular controversial points arose in this respect which would have warranted inclusion in those articles. During the period now under review, however, a number of somewhat unexpected problems have arisen which require to be examined.

One general issue which should be mentioned at the outset arises out of the terms of Article 31, paragraph 6, of the Statute, whereby judges *ad hoc* are to 'take part in the decision on terms of complete equality with their colleagues'. The decision referred to is of course primarily the judgment in the case, including of course any preliminary judgment on jurisdiction or on preliminary objections. The judges *ad hoc* are however in practice treated as entitled to participate in all decisions in the case, including those of a procedural or interlocutory nature,[371] and this is surely the correct interpretation of paragraph 6. It may however not always be clear what is a decision *in the case* in which the judges *ad hoc*

[368] The relationship between the two texts is that Article 33 applies, according to its terms, 'except as provided in Article 17', and Article 17 refers to the case of 'Members of a Chamber' and to 'all phases of the case', *sc*., the case being heard by the Chamber.

[369] Chapter 1, Section 1, below.

[370] See in particular the powerful dissent of Judge Shahabuddeen attached to the Order of 28 February 1990, *Land, Island and Maritime Frontier Dispute, ICJ Reports*, 1990, pp. 18–62.

[371] In fact, routine procedural decisions (e.g. fixing of time-limits) have frequently been adopted without the participation of the judges *ad hoc* simply for practical reasons: it would have been impractical to bring the judges *ad hoc* to The Hague merely to approve a routine decision.

have been appointed; a judge *ad hoc* is of course not entitled to participate in a decision in any case other than that in which he is sitting, nor in general administrative sessions of the Court. Two special situations may arise: first, the phenomenon of parallel cases, brought between different parties but relating to the same issues (*South West Africa* and *North Sea Continental Shelf* (before joinder), *Fisheries Jurisdiction, Nuclear Tests, Lockerbie*, etc.) may result in two Courts of slightly different composition dealing with the same matters, because of the presence on the Bench of a national of a State which is a party to the one case but not to the other. Apart from the problem of parties 'in the same interest', discussed below, this may mean that, on a strict interpretation of the Statute, a judge *ad hoc* in one case may lack information which is available to all his colleagues, elected judges, through their participation in the parallel case: this occurred in the El Al *Aerial Incident* cases.[372] The problem is however a minor one, and easily solved by administrative action.

More delicate is the distinction between decisions in the specific case and decisions which, although of a procedural nature, are general in scope, and therefore appropriate for decision in its 'administrative' composition, i.e. without the participation of any judges *ad hoc*. An example of this was the decision in the *Continental Shelf (Tunisia/Libya)* case on the possibility of appointment of a judge *ad hoc* by a State seeking permission to intervene, examined below.

(1) *Judges* ad hoc *and parties 'in the same interest'*

Article 31 of the Statute, providing for the appointment of judges *ad hoc* by parties to cases in which there is no national of theirs on the Bench, provides in paragraph 5 that 'Should there be several parties in the same interest, they shall, for the purposes of the preceding provisions, be reckoned as one party only. Any doubt upon this point shall be settled by the decision of the Court'. During the period on which Fitzmaurice commented in this *Year Book*, no problem arose with regard to the implementation of Article 31; but in the *South West Africa* cases, before his election to the Court, this provision fell to be interpreted, and in the *Fisheries Jurisdiction* cases Fitzmaurice's own presence on the bench was a contributing factor to a problem concerning paragraph 5 of the Article.

The *South West Africa* cases were instituted as two separate proceedings, one by Ethiopia against South Africa, and one by Liberia against

[372] The judge *ad hoc* appointed by Israel had the right to receive all documentation in the proceedings instituted by Israel, but would not automatically receive the documentation in the cases instituted by the US and the UK. The judges of those nationalities, being elected Members of the Court would see all the documentation in all three cases. It is understood that for the sake of equality the President directed that the Israeli judge *ad hoc* should also see the papers in all three cases. In the *Nuclear Tests* cases, the same person was appointed judge *ad hoc* in the proceedings brought by Australia and by New Zealand. For the problem of the *Fisheries Jurisdiction* cases, see subsection (1) below.

South Africa. Once the Memorials had been filed, it became evident that, as already suggested by the applications, the contentions of the two applicants were substantially identical. By an Order of 20 May 1961, the Court therefore 'join[ed] the proceedings instituted by the Applications of the Government of Ethiopia and the Government of Liberia'; at the time the Rules contained no provision for joinder of cases,[373] but it was well established in the practice of the Permanent Court that such an order could be made under the general power contained in Article 48 of the Statute.[374] The 1961 Order continued with a finding that the two Governments 'are in the same interest', and fixed a time-limit within which they might, 'acting in concert', choose 'a single judge *ad hoc*'.[375]

Prior to the joinder, there were two separate cases, in each of which the applicant State did not have a judge of its nationality 'on the Bench' for that case; after the joinder, the presence of a judge of the nationality of either Applicant would have rendered the provision for appointment of a judge *ad hoc* inapplicable, and, according to the specific words of the Rules, the two Applicants, being one party, could only appoint one judge *ad hoc*. This they duly did, and it was the bench so constituted that gave the two Judgments of 1962 and 1966.[376]

The two *Fisheries Jurisdiction* cases were also brought separately, by the United Kingdom against Iceland and by the Federal Republic of Germany against Iceland; but at no stage of the proceedings were they joined, and the Court gave two separate judgments, one for each case, both at the jurisdiction stage and the merits stage. No judge of Icelandic nationality was present on the bench, but since Iceland was boycotting the proceedings, it did not seek to exercise its undoubted right to appoint a judge *ad hoc*. The United Kingdom had a judge of its nationality on the bench, in the person of Sir Gerald Fitzmaurice, but the Federal Republic did not, and it purported to exercise the right to appoint a judge *ad hoc* to sit in the proceedings instituted by the Federal Republic (not, of course, in the parallel proceedings instituted by the United Kingdom). No objection was made by Iceland (though this of course is not of great significance, in view of Iceland's attitude to the proceedings).

> However, the Court, taking into account the proceedings instituted against Iceland by the United Kingdom on 14 April 1972 in the case concerning *Fisheries Jurisdiction* and the composition of the Court in this case, which includes a judge of United Kingdom nationality, decided by eight votes to five that there was in the present phase, concerning the jurisdiction of the Court, a

[373] See now article 47 of the 1978 Rules of Court.

[374] 'The Court shall make orders for the conduct of the case . . . '

[375] *ICJ Reports*, 1961, pp. 14–15.

[376] The nomination as judge *ad hoc* of a person who was subsequently elected a Member of the Court gave rise to bitter controversy when that judge was, apparently, obliged to refrain from sitting in the case purely because of the earlier nomination; but this is a matter of interpretation or application of the Rules relating to disqualification, unrelated to the appointment of judges *ad hoc*.

common interest in the sense of Article 31, paragraph 5, of the Statute which justified the refusal of the request of the Federal Republic of Germany for the appointment of a judge *ad hoc*.[377]

No Member of the Court commented on this decision in a declaration or opinion, and at the time the Rules of Court did not, as they do now,[378] provide for the names of judges voting on each side to be recorded in the judgment.[379] One may regret that Sir Gerald himself did not comment on what must have been, in the light of the voting figures, a controverted question. The matter was not reverted to at the merits stage of the proceedings, as the Federal Republic, probably making a virtue of necessity, announced that, taking account of the fact that Iceland was not participating in the proceedings and not availing itself of its right to a judge *ad hoc*, it 'did not feel it necessary to insist on the appointment of a judge *ad hoc*' so long as that situation persisted.[380]

Doubt may however be felt whether the decision not to permit appointment of a judge *ad hoc* can be legally justified. When the Statute refers to 'several parties in the same interest', it must surely be referring to parties *to one and the same case*, not to parties to different cases. If the two Applicants in the *Fisheries Jurisdiction* cases had, like Ethiopia and Liberia in the *South West Africa* cases, both been States without regular judges on the bench, there could have been no possible reason for permitting the appointment of a judge *ad hoc* in one case and not in the other; it was the joinder of the two cases which justified treating the two African States as in the same interest. What must have weighed with the Court in the *Fisheries Jurisdiction* cases was, as the decision quoted above reveals, the fact that a British judge would be sitting in both cases. In the one case his presence would debar the applicant State from appointing a judge *ad hoc*;[381] given the quasi-identity of the claims in the two cases,[382] it was presumably thought that the British judge would in effect play the

[377] *Fisheries Jurisdiction (Federal Republic of Germany* v. *Iceland), Jurisdiction of the Court, ICJ Reports,* 1973, p. 51, para. 7. The decision was taken four days before the opening of the oral proceedings on jurisdiction; no Order was made, but the decision was announced to the parties by letter from the Registrar (*Pleadings,* Vol. II, p. 421, no. 77). That letter uses a slightly different formula: 'the Court . . . is unable to find that the appointment of a judge *ad hoc* by the Federal Republic of Germany in this phase of the case would be admissible.'

[378] See Article 95, paragraph 1, of the 1978 Rules of Court.

[379] It is doubtful whether this requirement extends to the voting on an interlocutory matter, the decision on which is recorded in the judgment; or even to the voting on such a matter recorded in an Order.

[380] *Fisheries Jurisdiction (Federal Republic of Germany* v. *Iceland), Merits, Judgment, ICJ Reports,* 1974, p. 178, para. 10.

[381] Article 37, paragraph 1, of the 1978 Rules of Court (not in force at the time of the *Fisheries Jurisdiction* cases) now provides that 'If a Member of the Court having the nationality of one of the parties is or becomes unable to sit in any phase of a case, that party shall thereupon become entitled to choose a judge *ad hoc* . . . '

[382] There was in fact rather more difference between the UK and FRG contentions than there had been between the contentions of Ethiopia and Liberia, which had been drafted by the same team of counsel.

role of a judge *ad hoc*, not only in the case brought by the United Kingdom, but also in that brought by the Federal Republic. But what was that role? The cynical view is that a judge *ad hoc* can be counted upon to vote in favour of the case of the appointing party, but that is not the justification advanced for the existence of the institution of judges *ad hoc*. The underlying idea is that of equality of the parties; but it is not an equality of presumed voting strength; and if the idea of equality is pushed too far, the results become strange indeed, as will appear below in connection with the case concerning *Legality of the Use of Force*. As Rosenne has observed, the Informal Inter-Allied Committee fairly summarised the position in its Report:

> Countries will not in fact feel full confidence in the decision of the Court in a case in which they are concerned if the Court includes no Judge of their own nationality, particularly if it includes a Judge of the nationality of the other party. Moreover, while national Judges are not, or should not be, representatives in the Court of the case of their own country, they fulfil a useful function in supplying local knowledge and a national point of view.[383]

It is not clear how a British judge could fulfil these functions in relation to the Federal Republic of Germany.

In a pair of cases, and subsequently in a set of cases, all arising well outside the period covered by the present articles, the point arose in a still more acute and controversial form, so much so as to justify a further excursion outside the defined chronological limits of this survey. In 1992 Libya brought proceedings, in two separate cases, against the United Kingdom and against the United States, cases which were each given the title of case concerning *Questions of Interpretation and Application of the 1971 Montreal Convention arising from the Aerial Incident at Lockerbie*. For the sake of the present discussion, it may be taken that the contentions of the two respondent States, at least on the questions of jurisdiction and admissibility, were effectively identical, though this was disputed by the United Kingdom. When the Court came to consider those preliminary questions, it included a judge of US nationality (Judge Schwebel) and a judge of British nationality (Judge Higgins); but Judge Higgins had acted as counsel at an earlier stage of the case, and therefore felt bound to withdraw from sitting, in accordance with article 17, paragraph 2, of the Statute. The United Kingdom therefore, in reliance on article 37, paragraph 1, of the 1978 Rules of Court (quoted in note 381 above), claimed the right to appoint a judge *ad hoc*, and the Court accepted this, but only by a majority decision, taken after hearing the

[383] *Report of the Informal Inter-Allied Committee on the Future of the Permanent Court of International Justice*, 10 February 1944, British Parliamentary Paper, Misc. No. 2 (1944), Cmd. 6531, para. 39, quoted in Rosenne, *The Law and Practice of the International Court*, 3rd edn. (1997) Vol. III, p. 1126. Cf. also the remarks on the role of a judge *ad hoc* made by Judge *ad hoc* Palmer in *Request for an Examination of the Situation in Accordance with Paragraph 63 of the Court's Judgment of 20 December 1974, ICJ Reports*, 1995, pp. 420–1.

parties.[384] When the Court rendered its decision on jurisdiction and admissibility, the three judges who had voted against permitting the appointment filed a joint declaration explaining why they had done so.[385] For them, the United Kingdom and the United States were 'in the same interest', and the presence of Judge Schwebel on the Bench in the *Libya v. United Kingdom* case therefore debarred the United Kingdom from appointing a judge *ad hoc*. The point of interest in the present context is that these judges did not accept the view outlined above, that parties could be found to be 'in the same interest' *only* if they were parties to one and the same case, whether as a result of joinder or otherwise. The three judges relied on the decision in the *Fisheries Jurisdiction* cases to conclude that

> for two States to be 'in the same interest' they indeed have to present the same submissions to the Court, whether in a single application or in two separate applications, and whether or not the latter are joined. This procedural detail is of little importance.[386]

While this conclusion is indeed suggested by the *Fisheries Jurisdiction* decision, that decision, for the reasons given above, is strange and unconvincing. It is suggested that both the United Kingdom in its submissions on the question, and the three judges, missed the point: the United Kingdom argued, it is submitted correctly, that

> Article 31, which uses a form of wording in the singular, 'applies separately to each case on the Court's List'. 'In the presence of two separate cases between two sets of parties (even if one party is common to both cases), Article 31, paragraph 5, has no application'.[387]

The reason why the article has no application is however simply that in the case brought by the United Kingdom, the United States *is not a party*, and accordingly, in the context of that case, cannot be a party in the same interest. The word 'party' in the Statute and procedure of the Court only has meaning in relation to a particular case; a State is not a 'party before the Court' in some abstract or general sense. All procedural provisions have to be looked at within the four walls of the individual case as it stands at the time of the procedural decision to be taken. Another way of putting the point is thus that when the Statute and Rules refer to the presence of a judge 'on the Bench', they mean the presence of that judge among those sitting in a particular case; this indeed is the

[384] Judgment of 27 February 1998, ibid., 1998, p. 13, para. 9.

[385] Declaration of Judges Bedjaoui, Guillaume and Ranjeva, *ICJ Reports*, 1998, p. 32. It is tempting to assume that, since all three are primarily French-speaking, their difference of opinion from their colleagues may turn on the French text of the Statute rather than the English; but there is no trace of this in their reasoning—except insofar as to say that parties 'font cause commune' may have different implications from being 'in the same interest', a point not here pertinent.

[386] *ICJ Reports*, 1998, p. 38.

[387] Ibid., p. 40, emphasis deleted.

justification for permitting, as does article 37 of the Rules, the appointment of a judge *ad hoc* when there is a national judge who is a Member of the Court, but is not sitting in the case—the position of Judge Higgins.[388] The underlying principle is that equality of parties means exactly that—parties to a case.

This may be tested by considering the situation if, for example, the United Kingdom had delayed making its application in the *Fisheries Jurisdiction* case, or the United States had similarly delayed in the *Lockerbie* case, until the parallel proceedings (brought by the Federal Republic or the United Kingdom) were practically terminated. By then the judge *ad hoc* appointed in the prior case would have sat, even though the contentions to be advanced before the Court by the relevant party in the later case were identical. In such circumstances, if one takes the view that the national judge (Judge Fitzmaurice in 1973; Judge Schwebel in 1998) would necessarily take the same view as the judge *ad hoc*, there would indeed be an inequality; but that is totally the wrong assumption to make. Another possibility would be that two States might each bring proceedings in respect of the same claim, but before two tribunals—for example, the Court and the International Tribunal for the Law of the Sea (by no means an unlikely scenario, in view of the terms of article 287 of the Law of the Sea Convention). If the two cases proceeded *pari passu*, and the same submissions were made by each applicant, could it be said that they were 'parties in the same interest', and therefore the party which had chosen the ICJ should not be permitted a judge *ad hoc* if there were on the bench a judge of the nationality of the party which had chosen ITLOS?

In short, it is suggested that the *Fisheries Jurisdiction* decision should be treated as taken *per incuriam*, and that the majority of the Court were correct in declining to follow it in the *Lockerbie* cases.

The question attained a sort of *reductio ad absurdum* in the multiple cases brought by Yugoslavia in 1999 against the States members of NATO, concerning the *Legality of the Use of Force*. Judge Kreća, the judge *ad hoc* appointed by Yugoslavia, in his dissenting opinion attached to the Order on the Yugoslavian request for provisional measures in the case brought against Belgium, argued that none of the respondent States who did not already have a judge of their nationality on the Court (Belgium, Canada, Italy, Portugal[389] and Spain) were entitled to appoint a judge *ad hoc*, since they were in the same interest as the five States

[388] Since Judge Higgins had acted as counsel only in the case brought against the United Kingdom, on a narrow construction of the Statute she could have continued to sit in the case brought against the United States. Very properly, however, she stood down in that case also; but it is interesting to consider what the position would have been if she had not. She would have been 'on the Bench' in the sense of being a Member of the Court; and she would have been 'on the Bench' in the *Libya* v. *United States* case; would the United Kingdom have been entitled to a judge *ad hoc* in its own case, or would it be held to have a national 'on the Bench'?

[389] Portugal, alone of this group, did not exercise the right to appoint a judge *ad hoc*.

whose nationals were sitting as elected Members of the Court (France, Germany, Netherlands, United Kingdom, United States). On the basis of the *Fisheries Jurisdiction* decision and the declaration of the three judges in the *Lockerbie* case, this would have been difficult to refute; but the Court did not accept this view, and permitted the appointments of four judges *ad hoc*—one, of course, for each case. Had the cases been joined, it may be assumed that all the Respondents would have been parties in the same interest, and no judge *ad hoc* (except of course Judge Kreća himself) would have been appointed. This would still have left an inequality of sorts, since, on that assumption, there would have been five judges whose national States were parties in the same interest; but it has always been clear that no consideration of this kind justifies the withdrawal—let alone the exclusion—of an elected Member of the Court.

Judge Kreća was however prepared to contend that in that event—and, indeed, even in the actual circumstances of the case, i.e. in the absence of joinder—the principle of equality implied the right of Yugoslavia to choose *five* judges *ad hoc*, to balance the French, Dutch, German, British and United States judges. It is needless to say that the Court was not ready to accept this bold proposal.

2. *Judges* ad hoc *and intervention*

The right to choose a judge *ad hoc* belongs, in the terms of Article 31 of the Statute, to the 'parties' to the case. There is normally no difficulty in ascertaining whether or not a State is a party to a case;[390] but as we have already seen in connection with problems of jurisdiction, the status of a State permitted to intervene under Article 62 of the Statute remained for long undetermined, to a large extent because the nature and purpose of such intervention were also unclear.[391] States wishing to make use of the procedure of Article 62 have naturally seen advantage in endeavouring to have a judge *ad hoc* chosen by them included on the Bench, and that at an early stage; and this has presented the Court with some delicate problems.

In the *Continental Shelf (Tunisia/Libya)* case, Malta applied for permission to intervene under Article 62, and subsequently notified the Court that it was nominating a judge *ad hoc* 'for the purpose of the intervention proceedings'.[392] The Court decided, within a few days of the

[390] A respondent State which declines to participate in the proceedings brought against it is nevertheless a 'party' to those proceedings, and bound by the judgment given in them: see the present writer's *Non-Appearance before the International Court of Justice*, Chapter 4 *passim*, and cf. *Military and Paramilitary Activities in and against Nicaragua, ICJ Reports*, 1986, pp. 23–4, para. 27.

[391] See above, Ch. 1, section 12.

[392] It also asserted that Tunisia and Libya should be treated as parties 'in the same interest' for the purpose of those proceedings, and accordingly should only be entitled to a single judge *ad hoc* between them; see Section 1 above.

receipt of the Maltese communication, and without any further hearing,

> that, on their face, the matters which were the subject of [the Maltese letter] did not at that time fall within the ambit of Article 31 of the Statute of the Court; that a State which seeks to intervene under Article 62 of the Statute has no other right than to submit a request to be permitted to intervene, and has yet to establish any status in relation to the case; that pending consideration of and decision on a request for permission to intervene, the conditions under which Article 31 of the Statute may become applicable do not exist; and therefore that the letter . . . being in the circumstances premature, the matters to which it referred could not be taken under consideration by the Court at that stage of the proceedings.[393]

The Court took care to mention, when communicating this decision, that it had been taken 'without the participation of the two judges *ad hoc*' already nominated by Tunisia and Libya.

This observation makes it clear that the decision that a State asking for permission to intervene is not entitled to choose a judge *ad hoc* was treated by the Court as a general procedural decision, an interpretation of the Statute and Rules analogous to the exercise of its rule-making power under Article 30 of the Statute, and therefore to be adopted by the Court in its 'administrative' composition, rather than in the 'contentious' composition (including judges *ad hoc*) appropriate for a procedural decision taken within the framework of a pending case.[394] Under Article 31, paragraph 6, of the Statute, judges *ad hoc* are to 'take part in the decision on terms of complete equality with their colleagues', including decisions on interlocutory and procedural matters within the case for which they have been appointed; but the decision referred to above was not, despite appearances, a decision within the case. Another way of putting the point is that the Court without judges *ad hoc* decides on the *applicability* of any particular rule or process to a pending case, but must sit with the judges *ad hoc* to rule on the actual *application* of that rule or process in the case.[395]

The decision emphasizes the status of an intended intervention as a mere incident in a current case;[396] the more so inasmuch as when hearing and ruling on the actual application of Malta, the Court sat with the

[393] *Continental Shelf (Tunisia/Libya) Application by Malta for Permission to Intervene, Judgment, ICJ Reports,* 1981, pp. 6–7, para. 8.

[394] If this were not so, could it be argued that Malta should be able to choose a judge *ad hoc* to take part in the decision whether Malta could choose a judge *ad hoc* for the hearing of its application for permission to intervene?

[395] The writer has commented unenthusiastically on this distinction as used by the Court in the *Mazilu* case (above, Ch. 2, section 3(1)(*c*)), but considers that it is correct and defensible in the present context.

[396] '[E]very intervention is incidental to the proceedings in a case': *Haya de la Torre, ICJ Reports,* 1951, p. 76; this was a reference to an intervention under Article 63, but, as the Court explained in the *Land, Island and Maritime Frontier Dispute*, this finding applies equally in a case under Article 62 (*ICJ Reports,* 1990, p. 4).

judges *ad hoc* appointed by Tunisia and Libya. This produced the spectacle of three States pleading their individual causes before the Court on the same level, if not with the same status, while the Bench included judges *ad hoc* appointed by only two of them. Malta had, as the Court had observed, 'yet to establish any status in relation to the case', if by 'the case' is meant the proceedings instituted by Tunisia and Libya; but if the proceedings on the application of Malta had been seen as a separate 'case-within-a-case', it would have been appropriate for the Bench to include also a judge chosen by Malta. This latter view is defensible, bearing in mind that the phase of the proceedings devoted to Malta's application is so distinct as to be closed by a judgment,[397] not a mere Order or informal decision. Furthermore, the decision given is presumably binding on the State that sought to intervene, even if permission is refused: yet Article 59 of the Statute limits the *res judicata* of a 'decision' to the parties. That said, the Court's ruling is nevertheless sensible and practical, and a reasonable interpretation of the Statute.

Since permission was refused for Malta to intervene, the question whether an intervener may appoint a judge *ad hoc* (left open by the wording of the decision quoted above) did not fall to be settled; and a similar course of events followed in the *Libya/Malta* case on the application of Italy for permission to intervene. In the latter case, the fortuitous presence on the Bench of a regular judge of Italian nationality placed the parties and the would-be intervener on a footing somewhat nearer equality, thereby emphasising the anomaly in the previous case.[398]

A still more complicated situation arose in the *Land, Island and Maritime Frontier Dispute*, which the parties, El Salvador and Honduras, had agreed should be referred to a Chamber specially formed for the purpose, of five judges including judges *ad hoc* chosen by each of them. Nicaragua applied for permission to intervene under Article 62; if the intervention were admitted, and if Nicaragua as intervener were authorized to choose a judge *ad hoc*, the whole structure of the Chamber would be altered, in a manner clearly unwelcome to the original parties. Furthermore, if the decision on whether or not to permit the intervention were to be taken by the Chamber, the judges *ad hoc* (who for the purposes of discussion could be taken as likely to favour the views of the

[397] Neither the Statute nor the Rules provide for this in terms, and the Maltese application was the first to be made under Article 62 before the present Court. The Statute says that 'it shall be for the Court to *decide*', and it may have been thought that a judgment is the appropriate form for a decision; but note that Article 48 also states that the Court is to 'decide the form and time in which each party must conclude its arguments', a decision normally made informally or, at most, by Order.

[398] An interesting conundrum would have been posed if the Italian judge had been disqualified from sitting for some reason: could Italy then have claimed the right to appoint a judge *ad hoc*? Probably not: Article 37 of the Rules, which provides for such a substitution, refers to judges 'having the nationality of one of the *parties*', and Italy was not a party.

States appointing them) would cast two votes out of five, as against two out of 17 if the decision were to be taken by the full Court.[399] It is therefore hardly surprising that Nicaragua, when applying for permission to intervene, contended that the decision on its application was 'a matter exclusively within the procedural mandate of the full Court', and should thus not be decided by the Chamber. The first decision to be taken, therefore, was whether it should be the full Court or the Chamber that ruled on the application to intervene; and this decision was taken by the full Court, without the participation of judges *ad hoc*.[400] This, it is suggested, was correct: the question was one of principle, not limited to the particular case, and was therefore one for the Court in 'administrative' composition.

The Court however held (by majority, over the powerful dissent of Judge Shahabuddeen, among others) that the decision whether or not to permit the intervention was one to be taken by the Chamber; the reasoning on this point will be examined later. The Chamber for its part decided to permit the intervention, though to a limited extent; and, as explained above,[401] treated the intervention as being on a non-party basis.[402] It accordingly declared that 'the intervening State does not become party to the proceedings, and does not acquire the rights, or become subject to the obligations, which attach to the status of a party, under the Statute and Rules of Court';[403] no specific reference was made to the question of appointment of a judge *ad hoc*, but the right to make such appointment, being clearly 'attached to the status of a party', was obviously excluded.

3. *Judges* ad hoc *in advisory proceedings*

During the period covered by Fitzmaurice's articles, the Court did not have to face a problem which had exercised the Permanent Court on a number of occasions: that of the application of article 68 of the Statute, and specifically the question of the appointment of judges *ad hoc* in advisory proceedings. That article provides that

> In the exercise of its advisory functions the Court shall further be guided by the provisions of the present Statute which apply in contentious cases to the extent to which it recognizes them to be applicable.

The special application of the principle here stated to the question of the

[399] Judge Shahabuddeen was to go further: he observed that 'the selection of all the members of a five-member chamber was substantially, if not decisively influenced or determined by the existing Parties', so that it would be unjust to expect Nicaragua to bring its application before the Chamber: dissenting opinion appended to the *Order of 28 February 1990, ICJ Reports*, 1990, p. 58.

[400] Ibid., p. 3.

[401] Above, Ch. 1, Section 12.

[402] *Application to Intervene, Judgment, ICJ Reports*, 1990, p. 92.

[403] *ICJ Reports*, 1990, pp. 135–6, para. 102.

composition of the Court was reflected in article 83 of the 1936 Rules of the PCIJ, taken over in a slightly modified form[404] in 1946:

> If the advisory opinion is requested upon a legal question actually pending between two or more States, Article 31 of the Statute shall apply, as also the provisions of these Rules concerning the application of that Article.

In the *Interpretation of Peace Treaties* case, it might well have been said that the opinion requested related to such a 'legal question actually pending',[405] but the States which objected to the giving of the opinions in that case did not make any claim to appoint judges *ad hoc*, since such a claim might have appeared inconsistent with the stand they were taking regarding the Court's jurisdiction.[406]

A point which was not entirely clear from the practice of the Permanent Court was whether article 83 defined exhaustively the circumstances in which a judge *ad hoc* might be appointed for the purposes of a request for advisory opinion, or whether article 68 of the Statute, with its broad reference to 'the extent to which the Court recognizes' provisions relating to contentious cases 'to be applicable', would justify permitting such appointment even in the absence of a 'legal question actually pending'. This was one of the points which arose in the *Namibia* case.[407] South Africa contended in that case that

> the question on which the Court is now asked to advise, forms the subject of disagreement and controversy between the South African Government and certain other States Members of the United Nations, including States nationals of which are Members of this Court. It is accordingly submitted that the question upon which the Court is now asked to advise should be regarded as 'a legal question actually pending between two or more States' within the meaning of Article 83 of the Rules of Court, and that the South African Government is therefore entitled to choose a judge *ad hoc* in the terms of Article 31, paragraph 2, of the Statute.[408]

The Court heard argument on the point (in an unprecedented closed hearing), and rejected the contention by an Order[409] which gave no reasons, reserving them (as it turned out) for statement in the eventual advisory opinion. In view of the close connection between the arguments

[404] The 1936 text referred to questions relating to an existing dispute between two or more Members of the League of Nations or States; the 1946 text substituted the (presumably) wider term 'legal question actually pending'.

[405] But see below, discussion of the *Namibia* case, on the distinction between a dispute between States and a dispute between a State and the United Nations.

[406] At one time the PCIJ practice was to draw the attention of States which might be thought to be entitled to appoint a judge *ad hoc* to this possibility, but that practice was discontinued: see Hudson, *The Permanent Court of International Justice* (1934), p. 335.

[407] *Legal Consequences for States of the Continued Presence of South Africa in Namibia (South West Africa) notwithstanding Security Council resolution 276 (1970), ICJ Reports*, 1971, p. 16.

[408] Letter of 13 November 1970 from the South African Government, *Pleadings*, Vol. II, p. 641, no. 26.

[409] *Order of 29 January 1971, ICJ Reports*, 1971, p. 12.

on the claim to appoint a judge *ad hoc* and those relating to other issues, this was probably a justified procedure; this consideration was specifically mentioned by three dissenting judges as a reason for not indicating at once their grounds of dissent.[410]

The opinion was however fairly laconic on the reasons for the rejection of the South African claim. In the relevant paragraph (35) of the opinion it referred back to an earlier passage in which it had refuted the argument that the Court should refuse an opinion, on the basis of the *Eastern Carelia* precedent, because the question related to an existing legal dispute. It had there indicated that the Court did not find 'that the Security Council's request relates to a legal *dispute* actually pending between two or more States', since 'It is not the purpose of the request to obtain the assistance of the Court in the exercise of the Security Council's functions relating to the pacific settlement of a dispute pending before it between two or more States.'[411] With regard to the question of the judge *ad hoc*, the Court considered that 'the circumstances in which [the request] had been submitted', as well as the considerations as to the absence of a dispute, 'were such as to preclude the interpretation that an opinion had been "requested upon a legal question actually pending between two or more States" '.[412] There is here something of a slide from the idea that there was no *dispute* to the idea that there was no *pending legal question*.

There was also the possibility that the legal question might be pending between South Africa and the United Nations as an entity, but on this aspect of the contention that it should refuse an opinion the Court did not find 'that in this case the advisory opinion concerns a *dispute* between South Africa and the United Nations'.[413] The reference is again to a 'dispute', and the Court does not, either here or in the later paragraph dealing with the claim to a judge *ad hoc*, directly answer the question whether there was a 'legal question actually pending' between South Africa and the United Nations, and if so whether this would justify appointment of a judge *ad hoc*.

An interesting comment on the difficulties of applying the provisions of the Statute and Rules in a controversy of the kind involved in the *Namibia* case, was made by Judge Ammoun.

> To justify the appointment of a judge *ad hoc*, not only would a dispute [*sic*: legal question actually pending] have had to be present but there would have had to be on the Bench no judge of the nationality of one of the parties while the Bench

[410] Declaration of Judges Fitzmaurice, Gros and Petrén, ibid., pp. 13–14.
[411] *ICJ Reports*, 1971, p. 24, para. 32, emphasis added.
[412] Ibid., 1971, p. 25, para. 35.
[413] Ibid., para. 33, emphasis added.

did include a judge of the nationality of the opposing party.[414] But what, in the present proceedings, would have been the identity of that opposing party? The States which voted against South Africa? But in that case those which voted for South Africa are *in the same interest* as it, within the meaning of Article 31 of the Statute, and as such are already represented.

Of the judges who had voted in favour of permitting South Africa to appoint a judge *ad hoc*, only Judge Petrén considered it clearly established that there was a 'legal question actually pending' justifying that appointment.[415] Judge Fitzmaurice thought it unnecessary to determine the point, since in his view the Court had, and should have exercised, a discretion to authorize the appointment; Judges Dillard and Onyeama also based their position on the view that such a discretion should have been exercised, since they '[did] not think that under Article 83 of the Rules of Court the Republic of South Africa has established the right to designate a judge *ad hoc*'.[416]

The question of a discretion to authorise an appointment was of course also dealt with in the advisory opinion:

> The view has also been expressed that even if South Africa is not entitled to a judge *ad hoc* as a matter of right, the Court should, in the exercise of the discretion granted by Article 68 of the Statute, have allowed such an appointment, in recognition of the fact that South Africa's interests are specially affected in the present case. In this connection the Court wishes to recall a decision taken by the Permanent Court at a time when the Statute did not include any provision concerning advisory opinions, the entire regulation of the procedure in the matter being thus left to the Court (*PCIJ, Series E, No. 4*, p. 76). Confronted with a request for the appointment of a judge *ad hoc* in a case in which it found that there was no dispute, the Court, in rejecting the request, stated that 'the decision of the Court must be in accordance with its Statute and with the Rules duly framed by it in pursuance of Article 30 of the Statute' (Order of 31 October 1935, *PCIJ, Series A/B, No. 65*, Annex 1, p. 69 at p. 70). It found further that the 'exception cannot be given a wider application than is provided for by the Rules' (ibid., p. 71). In the present case the Court, having regard to the Rules of Court adopted under Article 30 of the Statute, came to the conclusion that it was unable to exercise discretion in this respect.[417]

Despite the final words of this passage, it seems that the Court was finding that it *had no* discretion, rather than that it had a discretion but did not feel that it should exercise it.

[414] This of course is not quite correct, since paragraph 3 of Article 31 permits the appointment of a judge *ad hoc* by one party even where there is no judge of the nationality of the opposing party on the Bench; and in practice this means also even if the other party refrains from appointing a judge *ad hoc*.

[415] See his separate opinion at *ICJ Reports*, 1971, pp. 129–130.

[416] Joint declaration attached to the Order of 29 January 1971, ibid., 1971, p. 14, quoted in the separate opinion of Judge Dillard appended to the advisory opinion, ibid., 1971, p. 152.

[417] Ibid., pp. 26–7, para. 39.

The fullest statement of the contrary argument is to be found in the dissenting opinion of Judge Sir Gerald Fitzmaurice.[418] The essence of the divergence of views is the relationship between Article 68 of the Statute and Article 83 of the Rules. Sir Gerald saw no conflict between them:

They deal with different aspects of the matter . . . Article 68 . . . , despite its quasi-mandatory form, confers what is in effect a power or discretion on the Court to assimilate requests for advisory opinions to contentious cases, either in whole or in part. Rule 83 on the other hand contains what amounts to a direction by the Court to itself as to how it is to exercise this discretion in certain specified circumstances. If these circumstances are found to obtain, then the Rule obliges the Court to allow the appointment of a judge *ad hoc*. But this in no way means, nor was ever intended to mean, that by making Rule 83 the Court parted with the residual discretion it has under Article 68 of the Statute, and that in *no other* circumstances that those specified in Rule 83 could the Court allow such appointment.[419]

It is submitted that, purely as a question of textual interpretation, Sir Gerald's view is to be preferred to that of the majority of the Court. The latter view involves some rigidity, and implies that it is essential to establish definitively the existence or not of a 'legal question actually pending' at a very early stage, in order to settle the very preliminary question (if the expression may be permitted) of the composition of the Court to determine all other questions. This was a practical problem that arose in the *Namibia* case itself, and again in the *Western Sahara* case.

For the first time since the establishment of the post-war Court, a finding was made in the *Western Sahara* case in 1975 that the opinion did relate to a 'legal question actually pending', and one of the States concerned was therefore authorised to choose a judge *ad hoc*. It was contended both by Morocco and by Mauritania that the question put to the Court related to a legal question actually pending between each of those two States and Spain; and the Court included upon the Bench a judge (Judge de Castro) of Spanish nationality. After hearing the interested States, the Court decided, by an Order dated 22 May 1975,[420] that when the resolution requesting the opinion was adopted, there 'appeared to be' a legal dispute between Morocco and Spain regarding the Territory of Western Sahara, and that therefore the opinion requested 'appears to be' one upon a legal question actually pending between those States. It accordingly found that 'Morocco is entitled under Articles 31 and 68 of the Statute of the Court and Article 89 [corresponding to the old Article 83] of the Rules of Court to choose a

[418] See also, however, Judge Petrén at ibid., pp. 128–130, Judge Onyeama at ibid., pp. 139–141, Judge Dillard at ibid., pp. 152–3, and Judge Gros at ibid., pp. 330–1.

[419] Dissenting opinion, *ICJ Reports*, 1971, p. 310, para. 21.

[420] Ibid., 1975, p. 6.

person to sit as judge *ad hoc*'.[421] As regards Mauritania, it found that 'there appeared to be no legal dispute' between that State and Spain, and accordingly 'the conditions for the application of' the texts cited 'are not satisfied in the present proceedings'.[422]

The two parts of the decision were each adopted by majority, of 10 votes to 5 and 8 to 7 respectively, and in the opinions attached to the advisory opinion much criticism was attached to the notion that it was sufficient that there had 'appeared to be' a legal question actually pending. In a declaration attached to the opinion Judge Gros referred to the 'effective disappearance of the bilateral dispute in the Court's train of reasoning in its Opinion, and the veil drawn over the existence of a legal question pending between States'; yet the Court had been unwilling to modify what it had said in its earlier Order, 'although the reason for the appointment of a judge *ad hoc* does not stand'.[423] For Judge Petrén, a dispute between Spain and Morocco had 'perhaps existed on 13 December 1974', the date on which the resolution requesting the opinion had been adopted, but the Court had not examined the question whether that dispute had perhaps disappeared by the time the Court came to decide the question of a judge *ad hoc*.

> Further, it should be observed that Article 89 of the Rules only calls for application of Article 31 of the Statute if a legal question pending between two or more States is a matter of current reality. It does not refer to a dispute which *appears* to exist . . . The appointment of a judge *ad hoc* is definitive, and operates for the whole of the proceedings. To accept such an appointment on the supposition that a dispute exists, but to leave in suspense any definitive decision as to the existence of that dispute, involves serious risks. First of all, if the ultimate decision is negative, and contrary to the provisional assessment made by the Court, this will imply that there should not have been any judge *ad hoc*. In addition, the judge *ad hoc* will be permitted to take part in the final vote on the question upon which the Court has made the legality of his presence depend; it could even happen that his own vote tipped the scale on that point.[424]

The difficulty was the same as that which had arisen in the *Namibia* case: that the question of appointment of a judge *ad hoc* in advisory proceedings 'possesses . . . absolute logical priority',[425] but has for that reason to be taken before the Court has been able fully to examine the circumstances of the case, including those material to the decision whether or not a judge *ad hoc* may be appointed. By deciding in *Namibia* that the question was one for the strict application of Article 83 (later Article 89) of the Rules, the Court had painted itself into a corner; the logical

421 Ibid., 1975, pp. 7–8.
422 Ibid., p. 8.
423 Ibid., 1975, pp. 73–4, para. 7.
424 Ibid., 1975, pp. 106–7.
425 Ibid., 1971, p. 25.

dilemma to which Judge Petrén mercilessly drew attention was inescapable. Had the Court considered that Article 68 of the Statute gave it a wider discretion, the situation would be different: the Court could exercise that discretion on the basis that there 'appeared' to be circumstances justifying it. The later discovery that those circumstances were not as first contemplated need not then disturb: the exercise of a discretion can contemplate a future re-assessment, where the strict application of limitative conditions cannot.

What then of the question of the exercise of discretion in the *Western Sahara* case? Here the Court's two decisions (the Order and the Opinion) contain a lacuna so great as to be regarded as a possible failure of justice on the grounds of *infra petita*. Counsel for Mauritania (Professor Jean Salmon) had argued very forcibly that Mauritania was entitled to appoint a judge *ad hoc* on the basis of a 'legal question actually pending' between itself and Spain; but he had also formally submitted, on the basis of equally penetrating arguments, that

> à titre subsidiaire, la République islamique de Mauritanie demande respectueusement à la Cour de bien vouloir, en tenant compte des circonstances particulières de l'espèce, user des pouvoirs que lui donne l'article 68 de son Statut pour fair jouer au bénéfice de la Mauritanie l'article 31 du Statut.[426]

The Court made no response whatsoever to this submission;[427] and, what is perhaps even more surprising, none of the judges who attached declarations or opinions referred to it, not even Judge Petrén, who had taken such a firm line on the question in the *Namibia* case.

The question whether or not the Court enjoys a discretion to authorize the appointment of a judge *ad hoc* in appropriate cases even where the specific conditions of Article 89 [83] of the Rules are not satisfied must apparently be regarded as unsettled; the decision in the *Namibia* case appears inimical to the assumption of such a discretion, and has been so interpreted by an eminent author who was himself a member of the Court in that case.[428] The powerful argument of Professor Salmon, urging a contrary interpretation of the *Namibia* decision has already been referred to. It is possible, as he urges, to read that decision as a refusal to exercise a discretion, supposing it to exist, rather than a denial of the existence of the discretion at all; the drafting of the opinion on this point

[426] *Western Sahara, Pleadings,* Vol. IV, p. 57.

[427] Whether technically this was a failure to dispose of a *petitum* is unclear, since the matter was a procedural and interlocutory one, though one of great practical importance. The Court might be excused for ignoring an argument addressed to it which was clearly in conflict with an unambiguous previous decision, despite the limitations on *res judicata* declared in Article 59 of the Statute; but in fact Professor Salmon was able to show that it was by no means clear that the *Namibia* decision had constituted a firm ruling that Article 68 confers no discretion outside the limits of Article 83 [89] of the Rules. It is unfortunate that space does not permit a full treatment of Professor Salmon's argument, which should be read as the best account of the problem to be found in the literature.

[428] See Jiménez de Aréchaga, 'Judges *ad hoc* in Advisory Proceedings', 31 *Zeitschrift fur auslandisches offentliches Recht und Volkerrecht,* 1971, p. 697.

(as on others) is less than perfectly lucid. It is material to ask how the decision was understood by the judges who voted against it;[429] but here too the indications are not univocal. Each dissenting judge indicates that he would have wished the Court to have exercised the discretion he believed to exist, but only Judge Petrén spells out whether the error of the advisory opinion was to deny the discretion or to fail to employ it. He reads the decision as stating 'as the grounds for the Order of 29 January [refusing the appointment of a judge *ad hoc*] that the Rules of Court would not have permitted it to exercise any discretionary power with regard to South Africa's application'.[430]

In no subsequent advisory case has any State urged the appointment of a judge *ad hoc*, whether because the circumstances seemed inappropriate or because the general pattern of the Court's jurisprudence on the question was seen as restrictive. In the case of *Interpretation of the Agreement of 25 March 1951 between the WHO and Egypt*,[431] the background to the request clearly involved a difference or dispute between Egypt on the one hand and other Arab States on the other: the case sprang from an attempt by the other Arab States members of Sub-Committee A of the WHO Regional Committee for the Middle East to have the WHO regional office transferred from Alexandria, as a political sanction on Egypt related to its stance toward Israel. It was the 'differing views' in the World Health Assembly[432] over the legal feasibility of this transfer which led to the request to the Court. As it happened, moreover, the Court included upon the Bench a judge of Egyptian nationality (Judge El-Erian), so that an application for joint appointment of a judge *ad hoc* by the other Arab States that participated in the proceedings (Iraq, Jordan, Kuwait, Syrian Arab Republic, Tunisia, United Arab Emirates) would have been prima facie justifiable; yet no such application is recorded.

The cases of *Applicability of the Obligation to Arbitrate under Section 21 of the United Nations Headquarters Agreement of 26 June 1947*,[433] *Applicability of Article VI, Section 22, of the Convention on Privileges and Immunities of the United Nations*,[434] and most recently *Difference relating to the Immunity from Legal Process of a Special Rapporteur of the Commission on Human Rights*,[435] each involved a dispute between an individual State and the United Nations as an organization; furthermore, these were what one might call 'domestic' disputes, concerning the

429 Indications from such a source are, it is suggested, a sounder guide than expressions of view outside the Court by judges concerned, such as the article referred to in the previous note, which were not made in the collegiate context.

430 *ICJ Reports*, 1971, p. 128.

431 Ibid., 1980, p. 73.

432 Ibid., 1980, p. 88, para. 34.

433 Ibid., 1988, p. 12.

434 The '*Mazilu*' case, ibid., 1989, p. 177.

435 Ibid., 1999, p. 62.

interests of the organization as a whole, and not involving the particular interests or political position of any member State other than the one in conflict with the organization. It would therefore have been difficult to assert the existence of a 'legal question actually pending between two or more *States*'; and no request for appointment of a judge *ad hoc* was made.[436]

The cases of *Legality of the Use by a State of Nuclear Weapons in Armed Conflict* and *Legality of the Threat or Use of Nuclear Weapons* might be said to represent the other extreme, since they concerned a question on which the member States of the United Nations were divided sharply into two camps, the one (the nuclear weapon States) asserting the lawfulness of the retention of such weapons, and the other denying it. This very universality of participation in the legal controversy however rendered superfluous any appointment of judges *ad hoc*; China, France, Russia, the United Kingdom and the United States all had judges of their nationality on the Bench, as did the Federal Republic of Germany, Italy, and Japan among the non-nuclear States participating in the proceedings.[437]

[436] In the former case, there was in any event a judge of the nationality of the State involved in the conflict (the United States) upon the Bench (Judge Schwebel).

[437] Whether this situation could be said to respect the principle of equality is another matter: cf. the suggestion of Judge Kreća in the *Legality of Use of Force (Yugoslavia* v. *Belgium) case* that Yugoslavia should have been permitted to appoint several judges *ad hoc*: above, this Chapter, Section 1(1) *in fine*.

THE CONFLICT OF LAW AND POLICY ON RESERVATIONS TO HUMAN RIGHTS TREATIES

By YOGESH TYAGI*

I. Introduction

Normative treaties have overtaken customary rules as the main sources of international law in recent decades. This is true in a variety of fields, including human rights. Human rights treaties have contributed to the development of customary rules and general principles of international law. These treaties create obligations not only among parties but also between parties and individuals; they attract the application of special rules of succession; and their denunciation is regarded as, at least, a retrograde act. More important, these treaties have become a source of inspiration to many judges and lawyers in their interpretation of domestic legislation. Because of the intensity of the human rights movement, States may find it difficult to justify their non-ratification of a human rights treaty. Some international organizations grant their membership only to those States which ratify certain human rights treaties. The ratification of a human rights treaty demonstrates the ratifying State's adherence to civilized standards. As a result, a State's credentials in international society depend in part at least on the acceptance of and compliance with its obligations under human rights treaties. On the other hand, State bureaucracies generally remain apprehensive of international accountability and maintain their customary caution as to the acceptance of treaty obligations. Determined to avoid isolation in human rights diplomacy, States resort to the practice of ratifying human rights treaties with reservations.[1] Such reservations give rise to a range of

 Professor of International Law, School of International Studies, Jawaharlal Nehru University, New Delhi, India. This article is a revised version of a lecture delivered at the Faculty of Law, University of Tokyo, Japan, on 4 February 2000. The author is grateful to Professors James Crawford, Vaughan Lowe, Detlev Vagts, Yasuaki Onuma, Yozo Yokota, Yuji Iwasawa, Kazuhiro Nakatani, Koichiro Nakamura, Rangachari Narayanan, Susan Marks, and V. S. Mani for their invaluable comments and suggestions on an earlier draft of this article. He would like to thank Librarians Anne Burnett, Pramod Singh, and Werner Simon for their prompt supply of useful information and materials. He would also like to thank Ms Kalpalata Iyer and Mr Ravindra Pratap for their assistance.

[1] Unless otherwise specified, the term 'reservations' includes 'declarations' and 'understandings' within the scope of the present study. This is justifiable for several reasons. First, the possibility of abuse is inherent in the distinction between reservations and interpretative declarations. Secondly, most of the interpretative declarations purport to exclude, limit or modify the State's obligations, thus having the effect of a reservation and proving that the distinction between the two concepts is elusive and can be manipulated easily. Thirdly, even an interpretative declaration in the proper sense

questions as to their legal basis, the limits within which reservations can be made and the consequences of overstepping those limits. They also give rise to questions of policy. Are available institutional mechanisms suitable to address the prevailing inadequacies? How best to meet the challenge of reservations?

The present study seeks to address these issues in the context of reservations to seven human rights treaties of the United Nations system: the International Convention on the Elimination of All Forms of Racial Discrimination (CERD); the International Covenant on Civil and Political Rights (CCPR); the International Covenant on Economic, Social and Cultural Rights (CESCR); the Convention against Torture and Other Cruel, Inhuman or Degrading Treatment or Punishment (CAT); the Convention on the Elimination of All Forms of Discrimination Against Women (CEDAW); the Convention on the Rights of the Child (CRC); and the Optional Protocol to the International Covenant on Civil and Political Rights (CCPR Protocol). These treaties have been selected according to the importance of their subject matter[2] and also to the existence of monitoring bodies[3] which are independent but integral parts of the United Nations system.

The identification of the legal bases of reservations is the first concern of the present study. The study takes stock of various reservations, compares them from different angles, and enquires whether the end of the Cold War has influenced the corpus of reservations. It gives various reasons for the formulation of reservations with illustrations. It examines the most far-reaching consequences of reservations in light of the substance of the UN human rights treaties and the experience of their monitoring bodies. Since human rights are action-oriented norms, one can notice a number of responses to the problems of reservations. It seems appropriate to assess those responses, especially in view of current conflicts involving reservations. Finally, the study seeks to emphasize

may assume the character of a reservation as soon as it becomes a target of objections or contrary interpretation. Finally, there is no fundamental difference between the law of reservations and the law of declarations. In support of this viewpoint, see, among others, *Restatement (Third) of the Foreign Relations Law of the United States*, vol. 1 (St. Paul, 1987), section 313, pp. 182–3. Also, an overview of a study entitled *Impact of the United Nations Human Rights Treaties in Twenty UN Member States*, p. 16 (hereinafter referred to as '*UN Human Rights Treaties Impact Study*'), which is in the process of publication. Anne Bayefsky and Christof Heyns coordinated the study that was conducted by twenty country correspondents, including the author, from Asia, Africa, Europe and the Americas; Christof Heyns and Frans Viljoen prepared the overview; and both the study and the overview were submitted to the Office of United Nations High Commissioner for Human Rights in July 2000. A copy of the study, along with its overview, is available with the author.

[2] The seven treaties under discussion figure in the UN Secretary-General's list of twenty-five treaties that deserve universal participation. See the Secretary-General's letter of 15 June 2000 to Heads of State and Government, in United Nations, *Millennium Summit Multilateral Treaty Framework: An Invitation to Universal Participation* (New York, 2000), or visit http://www.un.org/millennium/law/treaties.htm.

[3] For a study of these treaty bodies, see Philip Alston (ed.), *The United Nations and Human Rights: A Critical Appraisal* (Oxford, 1992); Philip Alston and James Crawford (eds.), *The Future of UN Human Rights Treaty Monitoring* (Cambridge, 2000).

that, since the first line of defence against human rights violations is generally available at the domestic level, the main battles against apparently unreasonable reservations ought to be fought at that level. Thus, in order to develop a new policy perspective, it provides an analysis of various bases, causes, consequences, responses, inadequacies, conflicts, and remedies concerning reservations to a selected group of human rights treaties.

II. Legal Bases of Reservations

In general, the right to make reservations is a manifestation of the sovereignty of States and of the principle of consent. At the same time, it is an indication of the necessity of promoting international cooperation among States with differing social systems. A German commentator observed that 'despite partially diverging interests of the States it would be possible by way of making reservations to secure wide participation in multilateral treaties and thus to expand international relations'.[4] In other words, reservations are a price for creating a wide network of treaty arrangements.

The legal basis of reservations to a treaty depends on the content of the treaty, particularly its final clauses. In this context, human rights treaties may be broadly divided into four categories: treaties permitting reservations;[5] treaties prohibiting reservations;[6] treaties permitting specified

[4] Peter Werchan, 'Reservations and Declarations to International Human Rights Instruments', *Bulletin of the GDR Committee for Human Rights*, 2/83 (1983), p. 51.

[5] None of the major human rights treaties expressly authorizes States to exercise absolute freedom to make reservations to its provisions.

[6] See, e.g., the UN Supplementary Convention against Slavery, the Slave Trade, and Institutions and Practices Similar to Slavery [Article 9; see *Human Rights: A Compilation of International Instruments*, vol. I (New York, 1993), UN Doc. ST/HR/1/Rev.4, p. 213 (hereinafter '*Human Rights Instruments I*')]; the European Convention for the Prevention of Torture and Inhuman or Degrading Treatment or Punishment [Article 21; see *Human Rights: A Compilation of International Instruments*, vol. II (New York, 1997), UN Doc. ST/HR/1/Rev.5, p. 271 (hereinafter '*Human Rights Instruments II*')]; the European Convention on the Exercise of Children's Rights [Article 24; see ibid., p. 305]; the Hague Convention on Protection of Children and Cooperation in Respect of Intercountry Adoption [Article 40; see *International Legal Materials*, 32 (1993), p. 1144]; the Rome Statute of the International Criminal Court [Article 120; see *International Legal Materials*, 37 (1998), p. 1066]; the Optional Protocol to the Convention on the Elimination of All Forms of Discrimination against Women [Article 17; see UN Doc. E/1999/27 (1999), p. 6]. Second Optional Protocol to the International Covenant on Civil and Political Rights, aiming at the abolition of the death penalty, prohibits reservations with the sole exception relating to the application of the death penalty in time of war for serious crimes during wartime [Article 2; see *Human Rights Instruments I*, p. 46]. The position of the Protocol to the American Convention on Human Rights to Abolish the Death Penalty is similar [Article 2; see *Human Rights Instruments II*, p. 48].

reservations;[7] and treaties maintaining silence on the issue of reservations.[8] Barring some isolated instances,[9] there is no serious problem regarding the authority of a State to make or not to make reservations to

[7] See, e.g., the Convention on Human Rights and Fundamental Freedoms of the Commonwealth of Independent States [Article 36; see Francisco Forrest Martin *et al.* (eds.), *International Human Rights Law and Practice: Documentary Supplement* (The Hague, 1997), p. 597]; the European Charter for Regional or Minority Languages [Article 21; visit http://www.coe.fr/eng/legaltxt/148e.htm]; the European Convention for the Protection of Human Rights and Fundamental Freedoms (the European Convention) [Article 57 of the present text (visit http://www.coe.fr/eng/legaltxt/5e.htm) and Article 64 of the former text (see *Human Rights Instruments II*, p. 90)]; the American Convention on Human Rights (the American Convention) [Article 75; see ibid., p. 34] and the Additional Protocol thereto [Article 20; see ibid., p. 45]; the American Convention to Prevent and Punish Torture [Article 21; see ibid., p. 54]; the American Convention on the Forced Disappearance of Persons [Article 19; see ibid., p. 60]; the American Convention on the Prevention, Punishment and Eradication of Violence against Women [Article 18; see ibid., p. 68]; the European Convention on Human Rights and Biomedicine [Article 36; see ibid., p. 318]; the Convention relating to the Status of Refugees [Article 42; see *Human Rights Instruments I*, p. 649] and the Protocol thereto [Article 7; see ibid., p. 653]; the Convention relating to the Status of Stateless Persons [Article 38; see ibid., p. 632]; the Convention on the Reduction of Statelessness [Article 17; see ibid., p. 619]; the Convention on the Political Rights of Women [Article 7; see ibid., p. 165]; the Convention on the Nationality of Married Women [Article 8; see ibid., pp. 609–10]; the Convention on the Elimination of Racial Discrimination [Article 20; see ibid., p. 78]; the Convention on the Elimination of Discrimination against Women [Article 28; see ibid., p. 162]; the Convention against Torture and Other Cruel, Inhuman or Degrading Treatment or Punishment [Article 28; see ibid., p. 305]; the Convention on the Rights of the Child [Article 51; see ibid., p. 194]; the Convention on the Rights of All Migrant Workers and Members of Their Families [Articles 88 and 91; see ibid., pp. 587 and 588].

[8] See, e.g., the CCPR [see *Human Rights Instruments I*, pp. 20–40]; the CESCR [see ibid., pp. 8–19]; the Convention on the Prevention and Punishment of the Crime of Genocide (the Genocide Convention) [see ibid., pp. 669–73]; the Convention on Consent to Marriage, Minimum Age for Marriage and Registration of Marriage [see ibid., pp. 487–90]; the Convention on the Non-Applicability of Statutory Limitations to War Crimes and Crimes against Humanity [see ibid., pp. 674–7]; the Convention on the Suppression and Punishment of the Crime of Apartheid [see ibid., pp. 80–6]; the African Charter on Human and Peoples' Rights (the African Charter) [see *Human Rights Instruments II*, pp. 330–46]; the African Charter on the Rights and Welfare of the Child [see ibid., pp. 347–65]; the OAU Convention Governing the Specific Aspects of Refugee Problems in Africa [ibid., pp. 323–9]; the European Framework Convention for the Protection of National Minorities [ibid., pp. 286–95]; the Arab Charter on Human Rights [visit http://ecolu-info.unige.ch/FormaConti/Droits-Homme/A27.html]; the Protocol to the African Charter on Human and Peoples' Rights on the establishment of the African Court on Human and Peoples' Rights [visit http://www.up.ac.za/chr/ahrdb/afcourt.htm]; the Optional Protocol to the Convention on the Rights of the Child on the Involvement of Children in Armed Conflict [see UN Doc. A/RES/54/263 (26 June 2000), pp. 2–7]; the Optional Protocol to the Convention on the Rights of the Child on the Sale of Children, Child Prostitution and Child Pornography [see ibid., pp. 7–15].

[9] There have been attempts to make reservations to some of those treaties which prohibit reservations, sometimes under names such as 'understandings' or 'declarations' and sometimes with the help of a supplementary protocol or resolution. For example, while Article 310 of the 1982 United Nations Convention on the Law of the Sea prohibits reservations, the Philippines made a statement in respect of the Convention. According to the statement, the concept of archipelagic waters is similar to the concept of internal waters under the Constitution of the Philippines, and removes straits connecting these waters with the economic zone or high sea from the rights of foreign vessels to transit passage for international navigation. This statement seems to have the effects of a reservation, and a reservation of that kind is ineffective without actual acceptance by all other parties to the treaty. It has been the target of objections by several States (e.g., Australia, Belarus, Bulgaria, Slovakia, the Russian Federation, Ukraine). For instance, Slovakia has asked the UN Secretary-General to deal with the statement in his capacity as depositary of the Convention, implying a plea for declaring it inadmissible. The Secretary-General has yet to respond to the problem arising out of the statement and the objections. For details, visit http://untreaty.un.org/ENGLISH/bible/

the first three categories of treaties. It is in relation to the last category that problems mostly arise. These problems have a direct bearing on three constituents of the International Bill of Rights: the CCPR, the CESCR, and the CCPR Protocol. The *travaux préparatoires* of the CCPR reveal acute controversy over the issue of reservations. Neither the UN Commission on Human Rights (the Commission), which drafted the two Covenants,[10] nor the Third Committee of the UN General Assembly, which finalized these instruments along with the CCPR Protocol,[11] made any progress on the issue. Because of the indecisiveness of the Third Committee, in particular, the CCPR was adopted without any provision on reservations. For this reason, reservations to these instruments are neither permitted nor prohibited in explicit terms.

Since the CCPR, the CESCR, and the CCPR Protocol do not prohibit reservations, States have exercised the inherent right to make reservations to them. The absence of an express provision means that the issue is governed by general rules of international law. The advisory opinion of the International Court of Justice in the *Reservations to the Convention on the Prevention and Punishment of the Crime of Genocide* case (the *Reservations to the Genocide Convention* case) provides the most authoritative expression of the rules relating to reservations.[12] Even if a convention contains no article on reservations, it does not follow that they are prohibited; the character of the convention, its purposes, and its provisions must be taken into account; and it is the compatibility of the reservation with the purpose of the convention which furnishes the criterion of the attitude of the State making the reservation, and of the State which objected to it. Reservations are not unconditionally permissible. Although the ICJ addressed only the Genocide Convention, its advisory opinion came to be widely accepted as a statement on the question of reservations in general. The UN General Assembly approved

englishinternetbible/partI/chapterXXI/treaty6.asp#N14. For an analysis in a larger context, see Sam K.N. Blay, R.W. Piotrowicz and B.M. Tsamenyi, 'Problems with the Implementation of the Third United Nations Law of the Sea Convention: The Question of Reservations and Declarations', *Australian Yearbook of International Law*, 11 (1984–87), pp. 67–107.

[10] In 1954 the Commission discussed the question of reservations. Having failed to reach an agreement, it referred the question to the UN General Assembly along with the summary records of the discussion and various proposals. Therefore, the Draft CCPR did not contain any article on reservations; all proposals and amendments were put in *Commission on Human Rights: Report of the Tenth Session (23 February to 16 April 1954)*, ESCOR, eighteenth session, supplement no. 7, UN Doc. E/2573, Annex II, paras. 262–305 and pp. 72–3.

[11] In the Third Committee, the United Kingdom submitted a proposal on reservations (UN Doc. A/C.3/L.1353/Rev.1) but later withdrew it. For details, see *Report of the Third Committee*, GAOR, twenty-first session (1966), *Annexes*, vol. II, agenda item 62, UN Doc. A/6546 (13 December 1966), paras. 139–46; and *Summary Records of Meetings of the Third Committee*, GAOR, twenty-first session (1966), UN Doc. A/C.3/SR.1375–1464, agenda item 62, mtg. 1437, paras. 8, 18, 27, and 31.

[12] *ICJ Reports* 1951, pp. 19 *et seq.* Although the ICJ made it clear that its opinion was necessarily and strictly limited to the Genocide Convention, there is consensus that the same considerations would be applicable to the CCPR and the CCPR Protocol. See David Weissbrodt, 'United States Ratification of the Human Rights Covenants', *Minnesota Law Review*, 63 (1978), p. 58.

the opinion[13] and the International Law Commission 'codified' it in what became Article 19 of the 1969 Vienna Convention on the Law of Treaties (the Vienna Convention).[14] Pursuant to Article 19, a State may, when signing, ratifying, accepting, approving, or acceding to a treaty, formulate a reservation unless (*a*) the reservation is prohibited by the treaty; (*b*) the treaty provides that only specified reservations, which do not include the reservation in question, may be made; or (*c*) the reservation is incompatible with the object and purpose of the treaty.[15] This formulation is repeated almost verbatim in Article 20 of the 1978 Vienna Convention on Succession of States in Respect of Treaties[16] and Article 19 of the 1986 Vienna Convention on the Law of Treaties between States and International Organizations or between International Organizations.[17]

Although the Vienna regime as such is not binding on those States which are not parties to the relevant instruments, the ensuing State practice has elevated most of its provisions to the status of customary international law. Following the widespread acceptance of the Vienna regime, there should not have been any difficulty about the legal basis of reservations. But that is not the case. The difficulty is, essentially, that the concept of human rights is not based on the idea of reciprocity. There is a feeling that human rights treaties are different from other treaties and that reservations thereto must be justified on a different legal basis. At present, such a basis is found either in the final clauses of human rights treaties or in the Vienna regime-driven customary international law. The final clauses will be analyzed in a subsequent section on practice under particular treaties. Their application in State practice can be seen from an examination of the corpus of reservations.

III. The Corpus of Reservations

All the human rights treaties under discussion have been subjected to reservations. The CCPR is the target of the largest number of reserva-

[13] General Assembly Resolution 598 (VI), 12 January 1952; and General Assembly Resolution 1452 (XIV), 7 December 1959.

[14] The Vienna Convention of 23 May 1969 came into force on 27 January 1980. As of 12 October 2000, ninety States had become parties to the Convention, implying that it enjoys widespread support. For the latest status of the Convention, including declarations and reservations thereto, visit http://untreaty.un.org/ENGLISH/bible/englishinternetbible/partI/chapterXXIII/treaty1.asp.

[15] *International Legal Materials*, 8 (1969), pp. 686–7.

[16] *International Legal Materials*, 17 (1978), p. 1499. The Convention of 23 August 1978 is in force since 6 November 1996. As of 12 October 2000, only seventeen States had become parties to the Convention. For the latest status of the Convention, including declarations and reservations thereto, visit http://untreaty.un.org/ENGLISH/bible/englishinternetbible/partI/chapterXXIII/treaty2.asp.

[17] *International Legal Materials*, 25 (1986), p. 556. The Convention of 21 March 1986 is not yet in force. As of 12 October 2000, it had been ratified by only thirty-one States. For the latest status of the Convention, including declarations and reservations thereto, visit http://untreaty.un.org/ENGLISH/bible/englishinternetbible/partI/chapterXXIII/treaty3.asp.

tions,[18] followed by the CEDAW,[19] the CRC,[20] the CAT,[21] the CESCR,[22] the CERD,[23] and the CCPR Protocol.[24] It is true that a

[18] As of 12 October 2000, there are 147 parties to the CCPR, and 55 of these have accepted it with reservations. Except for the right to recognition before the law (Article 16), all other rights or their corollaries have been subjected to reservations. It is on account of the right to a fair trial (Article 14) and the rights of accused persons (Article 10) that the largest number of States have made reservations. For the text of reservations, see Note by the UN Secretary-General, *Reservations, Declarations, Notifications and Objections Relating to the International Covenant on Civil and Political Rights and the Optional Protocols Thereto*, UN Doc. CCPR/C/2/Rev.4 (24 August 1994) [hereinafter '*Note on Reservations*'], or visit http://untreaty.un.org/ENGLISH/bible/englishinternetbible/partI/chapterIV/treaty5.asp.

[19] As of 12 October 2000, there are 166 parties to the CEDAW, and 68 of these have accepted it with reservations. Article 29 of the CEDAW, which contains a dispute settlement clause, is the target of the highest number of reservations. As for the substantive provisions of the CEDAW, Article 9(2), which grants women equal rights with men with respect to the nationality of their children, is burdened with the largest number of reservations. For the text of reservations, see *Declarations, Reservations, Objections and Notifications of Withdrawal of Reservations Relating to the Convention on the Elimination of All Forms of Discrimination against Women*, UN Doc. CEDAW/SP/1998/2 (6 February 1998), or visit http://untreaty.un.org/ENGLISH/bible/englishinternetbible/partI/chapterIV/treaty9.asp.

[20] As of 12 October 2000, there are 191 parties to the CRC, and 73 of these have accepted it with reservations. The highest number of reservations are attached to Article 14 of the CRC, which enshrines (*a*) the right of the child to freedom of thought, conscience and religion; (*b*) the rights and duties of parents to provide direction to the child; and (*c*) freedom to manifest one's religion or belief. For the text of reservations, see Note by the UN Secretary-General, *Reservations, Declarations and Objections Relating to the Convention on the Rights of the Child*, UN Doc. CRC/C/2/Rev.8 (7 December 1999), or visit http://untreaty.un.org/ENGLISH/bible/englishinternetbible/partI/chapterIV/treaty15.asp.

[21] As of 12 October 2000, there are 123 parties to the CAT, and 38 of these have accepted it with reservations. Article 1 of the CAT, which defines the term 'torture', is the target of the largest number of reservations. For the text of reservations, see Note by the UN Secretary-General, *Status of the Convention against Torture and Other Cruel, Inhuman or Degrading Treatment or Punishment, and Reservations, Declarations and Objections under the Convention*, UN Doc. CAT/C/2/Rev.5 (22 January 1998), or visit http://untreaty.un.org/ENGLISH/bible/englishinternetbible/partI/chapterIV/treaty12.asp.

[22] As of 12 October 2000, there are 143 parties to the CESCR, and 43 of these have accepted it with reservations. Article 26(1) of the CESCR, which deals with the eligibility of States to become parties to this instrument, is the target of the highest number of reservations. As for the substantive provisions of the CESCR, Article 8, which enshrines the right to form and join trade unions, is subjected to the largest number of reservations. For the text of reservations, see Note by the UN Secretary-General, *Status of the International Covenant on Economic, Social and Cultural Rights and Reservations, Withdrawals, Declarations and Objections under the Covenant*, UN Doc. E/C.12/1993/3/Rev.4 (5 August 1998), or visit http://untreaty.un.org/ENGLISH/bible/englishinternetbible/partI/chapterIV/treaty4.asp.

[23] As of 12 October 2000, there are 156 parties to the CERD, and 53 of these have accepted it with reservations. The highest number of reservations are attached to Article 4 of the CERD, which condemns and prohibits all propaganda and all organizations that are based on racial prejudices. For the text of reservations, see Note by the UN Secretary-General, *Declarations, Reservations, Withdrawal of Reservations, Objections to Reservations and Declarations Relating to the International Convention on the Elimination of All Forms of Racial Discrimination*, UN Doc. CERD/C/60/Rev.3 (12 February 1999), or visit http://untreaty.un.org/ENGLISH/bible/englishinternetbible/partI/chapterIV/treaty2.asp.

[24] As of 12 October 2000, there are 97 parties to the CCPR Protocol, and 24 of these have accepted it with reservations. The largest number of reservations target Article 5(2) of the Protocol, which provides that the HRC will not consider an individual case if the same matter is being examined by another procedure of international investigation or settlement. For the text of reservations, see *Note on Reservations*, above (n. 18), pp. 123–9, or visit http://untreaty.un.org/ENGLISH/bible/englishinternetbible/partI/chapterIV/treaty6.asp.

working paper of the UN Sub-Commission on the Promotion and Protection of Human Rights (formerly the Sub-Commission on Prevention of Discrimination and Protection of Minorities) gives the impression that the CRC is the victim of the largest number of reservations, followed by the CCPR, the CEDAW, the CERD, the CESCR, the CAT, and the CCPR Protocol.[25] It indicates that there are about 700 reservations to the seven treaties under discussion, whereas my estimate is that these treaties carry nearly 900 reservations.[26] Following this game of numbers, one can try to fathom the depth and breadth of reservations by noting that almost 40 per cent of all the States parties to the CCPR have made more than 250 reservations of varying significance to the obligations under the instrument. By contrast, only about 24 per cent of all the States parties to the CCPR Protocol have made about 26 reservations to this instrument, and only four of these (those made by Germany, Guyana, Trinidad and Tobago, and Venezuela) affect their substantive obligations. Unlike the reservations to the CCPR, therefore, there is almost complete absence of distinct reservations to the Protocol.[27]

The United States has entered the largest number of reservations to the CAT, the CCPR, and the CERD. The United Kingdom has made the highest number of reservations to the CEDAW and the CESCR. Singapore has made the largest number of reservations to the CRC; Germany the highest number of reservations to the CCPR Protocol. Among developed countries overall, the United Kingdom has made the largest number of reservations, whereas Japan has made the smallest. Japan has not made any reservation to the CAT and the CEDAW. It entered a tiny reservation to the CCPR, enlarging the definition of the term 'police' by including fire service personnel within the scope of Article 22(2). It made a reservation to Article 4(*a*) and (*b*) of the CERD, in order to maintain the status quo with respect to the rights to freedom of assembly, association, and expression and other rights under the Constitution of Japan. Its reservations to the CRC are modest, except for giving the impression that children of aliens/immigrants do not enjoy the equal protection of law in Japan. But Japan's reservations to the CESCR are quite substantial, implying that the second richest country in the world is not yet prepared to guarantee all economic, social, and cultural

[25] See *Reservations to Human Rights Treaties: Working Paper Submitted by Ms. Françoise Hampson Pursuant to Sub-Commission Decision 1998/113*, UN Doc. E/CN.4/Sub.2/1999/28 (28 June 1999), Annex.

[26] Unlike the large number of reservations to human rights treaties, the corpus of reservations to multilateral treaties as a whole is very small. There were no reservations at all to 85 per cent of multilateral treaties until 1971 [John King Gamble, Jr, 'Reservations to Multilateral Treaties: A Macroscopic View of State Practice', *American Journal of International Law*, 74 (1980), p. 379], but that percentage has gone down by virtue of adoption and ratification of a number of human rights treaties since then.

[27] For an appreciation of this aspect of reservations, see below n. 181, para. 24.

rights to its subjects. This perhaps casts doubt on the view that economic prosperity necessarily leads to human rights security.

Many developing countries have made reservations to the UN human rights treaties. Among them, Islamic States have entered the largest number of reservations to the CEDAW, the CERD, and the CRC. India and Trinidad and Tobago have made the largest number of reservations to the CCPR. The highest number of reservations to the CESCR have come from Algeria and Guinea. Chile entered the largest number of reservations to the CAT. Trinidad and Tobago has made the most extensive reservation to the CCPR Protocol. Nonetheless, in total the reservations of developing countries are much less than those of developed countries. This statistical imbalance does not necessarily signify, however, that the human rights commitment of the developing world is stronger than that of the developed world.

The former socialist countries have exercised the greatest restraint in making reservations. They withdrew certain reservations after the end of the Cold War; and their successors have followed suit in this regard.[28] On the other hand, as noted earlier, Western countries entered the largest number of reservations. The United States ratified a few human rights treaties only after the end of the Cold War, and then with many reservations. It is apparent that, in spite of assuming the leadership of the human rights movement, the West remains unwilling to accept international human rights law wholeheartedly. However, this comparison does not reveal everything. Despite making only a few reservations to the human rights treaties, the socialist countries did not match their Western counterparts in the implementation of those treaties. Further, the Helsinki process exposed the socialist countries as sceptical about international arrangements for the promotion and protection of human rights. The speed of ratification of a human rights treaty and the quantity of reservations thereto can be misleading.

Besides their reservations to substantive provisions, certain States have made reservations to some of the general provisions of the UN human rights treaties, including preambles and final clauses. Comparatively, however, reservations to substantive provisions outnumber those to other provisions. Indeed, there is no reservation to the main implementation provisions which enact the reporting procedures. Overall, most of the substantive provisions of the human rights treaties under discussion are subjected to reservations. Although no single provision is reserved by a majority of States, overall the reserving States outnumber those which have not made any reservations. The fact of reservations and

[28] See, among others, Theodor Schweisfurth, 'The Acceptance by the Soviet Union of the Compulsory Jurisdiction of the ICJ for Six Human Rights Conventions', *European Journal of International Law*, 2 (1991), pp. 110–17.

their scope indicate that, in spite of the extensive human rights movement, States are not yet fully committed to international human rights.

IV. Causes of Reservations

The making of reservations is essentially a discretionary function of the government of the ratifying State. Nonetheless, official information may not disclose the policy underlying reservations actually made, unless the ratification process is carried out through an open legislative route. There are not many States where the ratification of a human rights treaty is debated and discussed by the legislature. As a result, the causes for reservations by many States are not well known. The opaqueness of some reservations raises questions about their causes. Answering these questions becomes a necessity if one is to develop an effective strategy to deal with the issue of reservations. The rationale of reservations is multidimensional, ranging from jurisprudential sophistication to diplomatic confrontation. A brief analysis of major causes, along with suitable illustrations, is in order.

1. *Domestic Law Constraints*

States may lack the legislative infrastructure needed to carry out their obligations under human rights treaties, and they may make reservations in cases where they cannot conceal a conflict between domestic legal rules considered sacrosanct and the provisions of the treaties. Reservations may clarify the legal situation where there is an obvious discrepancy between the treaties and existing domestic legislation.[29] Giving a positive dimension to the matter, the Human Rights Committee (HRC) states: 'Reservations may serve a useful function to enable States to adapt specific elements in their laws to the inherent rights of each person as articulated in the Covenant [CCPR].'[30] According to this view, reservations can enrich the content of human rights without affecting the integrity of a multicultural society. But not many reserving States have exhibited this kind of sophistication.

A former legal adviser to the US Department of State gives a different justification: 'The rationale behind the reservations is, rather, that we take our international legal obligations seriously, and therefore will

[29] *Report of the Human Rights Committee*, GAOR, thirty-second session (1977), supplement no. 44, UN Doc. A/32/44, para. 126.

[30] General Comment 24 (52), adopted by the HRC on 2 November 1994, in *Compilation of General Comments and General Recommendations by Human Rights Treaty Bodies*, UN Doc. HRI/GEN/1/Rev.3 (15 August 1997), p. 43, para. 4 [hereinafter '*Compilation of General Comments*'].

commit ourselves to do by treaty only that which is constitutionally and legally permissible within our domestic law.'[31] In this scheme, however, US sincerity to comply with human rights treaty obligations helps sustain the rigidity of US domestic law and the dominant interest groups do not accept certain important human rights standards. The truth of the matter is that US practice regarding ratification of human rights treaties is still influenced by insularity and unwillingness to accept new obligations.[32] In US practice, reservations are generally necessary to satisfy diverse interests and pressure groups. Otherwise, Senate approval of the treaty concerned would not be possible. In such cases, reservations are not so much a legal as a legislative necessity. This kind of 'political legalism' explains the mass of US reservations to the CCPR,[33] the CERD,[34] and the CAT.[35] The same factors help explain why the United States failed to ratify the CESCR: the Carter administration could not develop an adequate set of reservations to satisfy the conservative forces in the Senate[36] and successive administrations did not care or dare to reopen the issue.[37]

Trinidad and Tobago's reservation to Article 1 of the CCPR Protocol is the most striking instance of domestic law constraints shaping a reservation. Under this reservation, the HRC is denied competence to receive and consider communications concerning any prisoner who is under sentence of death in respect of any matter relating to the prosecution, detention, trial, conviction, sentence or method of execution of that person and any matter connected therewith.[38] The Government of Trinidad and Tobago has stated that, in order to comply with the constitutional time frames laid down by the Judicial Committee of the Privy Council in *Pratt* v. *Attorney-General for Jamaica*,[39] it had to

[31] Davis R. Robinson, in *International Human Rights Treaties: Hearings before the Committee on Foreign Relations, United States Senate, Ninety-sixth Congress, First Session on November 14, 15, 16 and 19, 1979* (Washington, 1980), p. 31 [hereinafter '*US Senate Hearings* (1979)'].

[32] For an excellent exposure of this mindset, see Louis Henkin, 'U.S. Ratification of Human Rights Conventions: The Ghost of Senator Bricker', *American Journal of International Law*, 89 (1995), pp. 341–50.

[33] US ratification of the CCPR (8 June 1992) is subject to five reservations, five understandings, three declarations, and one proviso. However, the proviso is not part of the US instrument of ratification submitted to the UN Secretary-General. For details, above n. 18.

[34] For details, above n. 23.

[35] For details, above n. 21.

[36] For instance, Senator Jesse Helms opposed the ratification because the Carter administration had failed to formulate convincing reservations to the effect that the CESCR did not endanger the rights guaranteed under the US Constitution. See *US Senate Hearings* (1979), above n. 31.

[37] In 1991 the Bush administration recommended only the CCPR for ratification by the Senate. The Clinton administration never felt the need to recommend the CESCR for ratification.

[38] Trinidad and Tobago had initially acceded to the CCPR Protocol on 14 November 1980. On 26 May 1998 the Government of Trinidad and Tobago informed the UN Secretary-General of its decision to denounce the Protocol with effect from 26 August 1998. On that same date, the Government reacceded to the Protocol with a heavy reservation. For the text of the reservation and the explanation thereto, above n. 24.

[39] *Weekly Law Reports*, 3 December 1993, p. 995.

institute a number of measures to ensure the completion of appeals in capital cases within the shortest possible time, consistent with due process of law; that it had little success in reducing delays before the international human rights bodies; and that these bodies had employed protracted procedures in the processing of petitions.[40] Since the resulting delays were incompatible with the time frames imposed by the Privy Council, the Government entered reservation to the Protocol. However, it concealed the fact that the State itself was responsible for delays in the disposal of a majority of the capital cases and that the HRC had drawn the State's attention to that lapse well before *Pratt*.[41] The discriminatory nature and damaging impact of the reservation were bound to provoke many. Certain Western States,[42] jurists,[43] law firms,[44] and NGOs[45] questioned the validity of the reservation and the HRC found it invalid.[46] This result shows that the reserving States may often make a poor choice of means to overcome perceived domestic law constraints on the acceptance of treaty obligations.

2. *Higher National Standards*

Some States have very high standards of civil and political rights. Such standards do not find universal acceptance and human rights treaties do not recognize them to the fullest extent. Evidently, no State in becoming a party to a human rights treaty wishes to reduce the entitlements of its people. In this regard, Article 5(2) of the CCPR provides the clearest solution: 'There shall be no restriction upon or derogation from any of the fundamental human rights recognized in any State Party to the present Covenant pursuant to law, conventions, regulations or customs on the pretext that the present Covenant does not recognize such rights or that it recognizes them to a lesser extent.' This provision leaves no doubt about the continuing validity of higher domestic standards of human rights even after the ratification of the CCPR. Yet, certain States have nonetheless made reservations to the relevant provisions. For

[40] UN Doc. CCPR/C/TTO/99/3 (22 February 2000), paras. 100–2.

[41] At the time of the consideration of the initial report of Trinidad and Tobago, in October 1984, HRC members noted that 'at times long delays occurred between a person's arrest and trial, which was not consistent with article 9 of the Covenant and which could give rise to serious miscarriage of justice'. See *Report of the Human Rights Committee*, GAOR, fortieth session (1985), supplement no. 40, UN Doc. A/40/40, p. 22, para. 115.

[42] See the objections made by Denmark, France, Germany, Ireland, Italy, the Netherlands, Norway, Spain, and Sweden. Above n. 24.

[43] See the joint opinion of Professors James Crawford, Bruno Simma, and Alberto Szekely, below n. 181.

[44] Among others, Ashurst Morris Crisp, Simons Muirhead & Burton, and Simmons & Simons have challenged Trinidad and Tobago's reservation.

[45] A coalition of NGOs, including Amnesty International and INTERIGHTS, opposed Trinidad's reservation.

[46] See below n. 182.

example, the United States grants greater guarantees of freedom of speech and expression than are provided under Article 19 of the CCPR. In order to maintain its constitutional supremacy, as well as the higher standards of protection for the freedom of speech and expression, the United States declared that it would continue to adhere to those standards. As a result, for the benefit of Americans, the First Amendment protection overcomes the CCPR Article 19 restrictions. While the United States wants to maintain higher standards in certain fields domestically, some other States want to promote certain human rights by rewriting a lower standard internationally. For instance, Colombia ratified the CRC with a reservation providing that the minimum age of 15 years for recruitment into the armed forces under Article 38 of the treaty is 'understood to be 18 years', in conformity with Colombian legislation. In these instances 'reservations' elevate the level of protection provided for under the treaty in question, but earmarking such instances as 'reservations' in the ordinary sense of the word is a misnomer.[47] There are not many instances of this kind; none of them in Africa or Asia; and the process of elevating the level of human rights protection through reservations has little support among jurists.

3. *Ideological Dissent*

At times, States make reservations to record their dissent on certain provisions of human rights treaties that are not acceptable to them. For instance, all the former socialist States, along with some others, made reservations to Article 48(1) and (3) of the CCPR[48] on the grounds that the criterion for joining the treaty regime was of a 'discriminatory nature', 'contrary to the basic principles of international law', and 'incompatible with the object and purpose of the Covenant'. They believed that the CCPR should have been open for signature/accession by all States, instead of excluding some by the implications underlying paragraphs 1 and 3 of Article 48. They made similar reservations to the comparable provisions of other human rights treaties as well. The legal

[47] Heyns and Viljoen, above (n. 1), p. 16 n. 9.

[48] Article 48 reads as follows:

1. The present Covenant is open for signature by any State Member of the United Nations or member of any of its specialized agencies, by any State Party to the Statute of the International Court of Justice, and by any other State which has been invited by the General Assembly of the United Nations to become a Party to the present Covenant.

2. The present Covenant is subject to ratification. Instruments of ratification shall be deposited with the Secretary-General of the United Nations.

3. The present Covenant shall be open to accession by any State referred to in paragraph 1 of this article.

4. Accession shall be effected by the deposit of an instrument of accession with the Secretary-General of the United Nations.

5. The Secretary-General of the United Nations shall inform all States which have signed this Covenant or acceded to it of the deposit of each instrument of ratification or accession.

and practical significance of these reservations is very limited. No State has so far been denied an opportunity to ratify any human rights treaties of the United Nations system. Taiwan is the only instance of an entity losing the right to remain a party to those treaties, on account of the lack of the separate status accorded to Taiwan within that system.[49]

4. *Political Objectives*

Sometimes a reservation involves the conduct of diplomacy by other means. Some States make reservations in pursuit of their foreign policy goals. Some seek to settle their political scores with the help of reservations. For example, most of the Arab States parties to the UN human rights treaties made a reservation whereby they refused to recognize Israel's participation in those treaties. Israel made a fitting reply:

> [The Government of Israel] has noted the political character of the declaration[s] made by the Government[s] of . . . [the Arab States] on signing the above Convention [on the Elimination of Racial Discrimination]. In the view of the Government of Israel, the Convention [or any other human rights treaty] is not the proper place for making such political pronouncements. The Government of Israel will, in so far as concerns the substance of the matter, adopt towards the Government[s] of . . . [the Arab States] an attitude of complete reciprocity. Moreover, it is the view of the Government of Israel that no legal relevance can be attached to those . . . statements [of the Arab States] which purport to represent the views of the other States.[50]

As a consequence of the Camp David agreements of 1978, Egypt withdrew its Israel-specific reservation to the CERD in 1980. Most of the Arab States maintain their reservation against Israel's participation in the UN human rights treaties, although it has become obsolete in view of State practice following the Middle East peace process since the Oslo accords of 1993.

5. *Vital Interests*

In some cases, States attach reservations to human rights treaties to safeguard perceived vital interests. That is what India tried to do at the time of its accession to the CCPR and the CESCR in 1979. India made a declaration with regard to the right of self-determination. The declaration clarifies that the words 'the right of self-determination' appearing in common Article 1 of both the Covenants 'apply only to the peoples under

[49] Taiwan signed the CCPR, the CCPR Protocol, the CESCR, and the CERD soon after their adoption by the UN General Assembly during 1965–66. However, those signatures lost their value as soon as China replaced Taiwan in the United Nations with effect from 25 October 1971.

[50] Above n. 23.

foreign domination and that these words do not apply to sovereign independent States or to a section of a people or nation which is the essence of national integrity'.[51] Considering the continuing problem of secessionism in Kashmir, Nagaland, and elsewhere, India maintains this declaration. Its restrictive interpretation of the right of self-determination is the bulwark of State policy on national integrity and international law. Despite the fact that France, Germany, and the Netherlands have raised objections to this interpretation,[52] India maintains its position and finds its reaffirmation in the 1993 Vienna Declaration and Programme of Action (the Vienna Declaration)[53] and also in the writings of some jurists.[54] One can infer that States will not allow human rights norms to affect their perceived vital interests and that a human rights treaty might not be ratified by many States if reservations thereto cannot be made. The legitimate right of States to qualify their human rights treaty obligations with national security safeguards testifies that human rights law does not undermine the basic structure of the nation State system. This aspect should help reassure those politicians who cry wolf at the first sight of a human rights treaty.

6. *Harmonization of Parallel Obligations*

In certain cases, States make reservations to reconcile various treaty obligations. For instance, in line with its reservation to Article 10(2)(*a*) of the CCPR (the obligation to segregate young people from other prison inmates), Australia entered a reservation to Article 37(*c*) of the CRC in respect of the imprisonment of children.[55] Similarly, Austria made a reservation to CRC Articles 13 (the child's right to freedom of expression) and 15 (the rights of the child to freedom of association) in order to harmonize them with Articles 10 and 11 of the European Convention.[56] A majority of the European States ratified the CCPR Protocol with the

[51] See India's instrument of accession to the CCPR and the CESCR (27 March 1979), in *Note on Reservations*, above (n. 18), p. 24.

[52] While France and Germany argued that India's reservation to the right of self-determination was inconsistent with both Article 1 of the two Covenants and Article 1 of the UN Charter, the Netherlands argued that the reservation was inconsistent with the UN Declaration on Friendly Relations as well. Contrary to the reservation, therefore, the objections emphasized that the right of self-determination was applicable to all peoples. Ibid., pp. 50–3.

[53] UN Doc. A/CONF.157/23 (12 July 1993), part I, para. 2. In view of the increasing international attention to the violent secessionist movement in Kashmir in the early 1990s, the Indian delegation to the Vienna Conference was happy over its success in securing a restrictive articulation of the right of self-determination in the Vienna Declaration.

[54] See, for example, Crawford, 'State Practice and International Law in Relation to Secession', this *Year Book*, 69 (1998), pp. 85–117.

[55] Similarly, the Government of Finland proposed a reservation to Article 37(*c*) of the CRC, in order to bring it in line with a similar reservation to Article 10 of the CCPR, but the Parliament of Finland did not accept this and Finland ratified the CRC without any reservations. Cf. Eero J. Aarnio, 'Finland', in *UN Human Rights Treaties Impact Study*, above (n. 1), p. 276.

[56] Above n. 20.

reservation that the HRC may consider a case only when it has determined that the 'same matter' has not been examined under other procedures of international investigation or settlement within the terms of Article 5(2)(*a*) of this Protocol. The European States did so in view of their older and stronger commitments under the European Convention. Though apparently repetitive of Article 5(2)(*a*), the European reservations are justified as a common policy to achieve coordination between the European system and the UN human rights treaty system. Since the bureaucracies of the European States already had a heavy workload owing to an increasingly large number of cases against them before the European Convention institutions, they felt it necessary to limit their UN human rights treaty burden by entering a reservation to the 'same matter' clause. A number of the Latin American States have made similar reservations to harmonize their obligations under the American Convention and the UN human rights treaties. By contrast, none of the African States have resorted to reservations in order to harmonize their obligations under the African Charter and the UN human rights treaties, implying perhaps that harmonization of parallel obligations is possible even without reservations.

7. *Precautionary Measures*

Some reservations are a precautionary response to adverse experience perceived by certain States. According to Sir Vincent Evans, the experience of the dynamic mode of interpretation applied by the European Convention institutions was one of the reasons why European States made so many reservations to the CCPR.[57] Similarly, the HRC's liberal interpretation of some of the general provisions of the CCPR, particularly Article 26 in the *Dutch Social Security* cases,[58] made Germany enter a reservation to Article 5(2) of the CCPR Protocol. Accordingly, Germany precluded the HRC from considering communications alleging a violation of the CCPR if the violation refers to rights other than those guaranteed under that instrument.[59] The fact that Germany made the reservation, despite the moderation of the HRC's

[57] Cf. Iain Cameron, 'Turkey and Article 25 of the European Convention on Human Rights', *International and Comparative Law Quarterly*, 37 (1988), p. 905 n. 82.

[58] See, e.g., *S.W.M. Broeks* v. *Netherlands* (Communication No. 172/1984), *L.G. Danning* v. *Netherlands* (Communication No. 180/1984) and *F.H. Zwaan-de Vries* v. *Netherlands* (Communication No. 182/1984), *Report of the Human Rights Committee*, GAOR, forty-second session (1987), supplement no. 40, UN Doc. A/42/40, Annex VIII B to D, pp. 139–69. In these cases, certain nationals of the Netherlands challenged the social security laws of their State mainly on the ground of alleged discrimination within the terms of Article 26 of the CCPR. The Netherlands initially contested the admissibility of all those claims on the ground that their subject matter was covered by the CESCR, not the CCPR. But the HRC did not accept that position and went on to examine the merits of those cases and found a violation of Article 26 in a majority of them.

[59] For the text of the reservation, above n. 24.

Article 26 jurisprudence, shows the caution often displayed by States in accepting human rights treaty obligations.

8. *Balancing Acts*

Sometimes States make reservations so as to balance binding obligations with non-binding exhortations, legal considerations with moral compulsions, or domestic public pressure with world public opinion. For instance, as noted earlier, Trinidad and Tobago reacceded to the CCPR Protocol with a reservation excluding capital cases from jurisdiction under the Protocol.[60] The main purpose of this reservation was to satisfy that section of Trinidadian society that favoured the death penalty to curb increasing criminality but felt insecure from the human rights lobby of the international community. The reservation was a legally dubious measure. In effect, it was an attempt to claim impunity for violations of Articles 6, 7, 9, 10, and 14 of the CCPR. As a consequence, it sought to preclude the HRC from considering the communications of the victims of the most serious violations of human rights in Trinidad and Tobago. Following this precedent, Guyana reacceded to the CCPR Protocol with a reservation that is similar to the reservation of Trinidad and Tobago.[61] As noted earlier,[62] questions have been raised as to the validity of the Trinidadian reservation and the HRC has declared the reservation invalid. Guyana's reservation is likely to meet the same fate.

9. *Economic Constraints*

A majority of members of the United Nations and many other international organizations consist of developing States. Lack of financial resources for their development has been a perennial problem. The same problem has left its imprint on the human rights policies of these States. Some developing States have entered reservations to those provisions of the UN human rights treaties which require mobilization of additional economic resources. For example, Zambia entered a reservation to Article 13(2)(*a*) of the CESCR, which recognizes the right of free universal primary education. The main reason behind this reservation is the lack of financial resources to implement the provision fully. Bangladesh made a reservation to Article 14(1) of the CAT, which incorporates the right of compensation to the victims of torture. This reservation

[60] Above n. 38.

[61] The Government of Guyana had initially acceded to the CCPR Protocol on 10 May 1993. On 5 January 1999 the Government notified the UN Secretary-General that it had decided to denounce the Protocol with effect from 5 April 1999. On that same date, the Government reacceded to the Protocol with a heavy reservation. For the text of the reservation and the explanation thereto, above n. 24.

[62] See above nn. 42–5.

enunciates that State authorities would only ensure redress and compensation for victims of torture when this is in consonance with existing laws and legislation. Although the official motivation for the reservation was the need to respect the applicable domestic law, the weak economy of the State remains the real reason. Bangladesh was less subtle at the time of its accession to the CCPR. It made the declaration that, 'So far as the first part of paragraph 3 of Article 10 relating to reformation and social rehabilitation of prisoners is concerned, Bangladesh does not have any facility to this effect on account of financial constraints and for lack of proper logistics support.'[63] Similarly, India made a reservation to Article 9 of the CCPR, which guarantees a right of compensation on account of unlawful arrest or detention. This reservation seeks to establish that, under the Indian legal system, there is no enforceable right to compensation for persons claiming to be victims of unlawful arrest or detention. The main reason behind the reservation is the poor condition of the State exchequer. India also made a reservation concerning Article 32 of the CRC, which prohibits child labour. The main motivation for the reservation is that India has nearly fifteen million child workers; that its 'realist' domestic law does not completely prohibit child labour; that the prevailing socio-economic conditions do not allow the complete abolition of child labour; and that, in this regard, the applicable domestic law and practice are incompatible with international human rights law. If that is the case with one of the most developed States in the developing world, the situation of others is not difficult to imagine. That is why developing States often speak in one voice against social clauses in the proposed international agreements under the auspices of the World Trade Organization.

Like many developing States, a few developed States seem to have economic constraints in the implementation of some human rights and seek to moderate their obligations with the help of reservations. For example, Australia entered a reservation to the right to paid maternity leave on the ground that it was not in a position to take the measures required by Article 11(2)(*b*) of the CEDAW to introduce maternity leave with pay or with comparable social benefits throughout the country. Unlike their counterparts from the developing world, the reserving States from the developed world do not defend their economic constraints as a matter of common policy and rather present them as temporary obstacles in the implementation of human rights.

10. *Religious Fundamentalism*

In the human rights field, many problems arise from interpretations or adaptations of local customs or traditions. In certain contexts (especially

[63] Above n. 18.

in the field of family law and personal status) such customs and traditions may take precedence over national legislation. According to a general assessment of State practice, 'Deference to tradition is often responsible for debilitating reservations that limit the impact of [human rights] treaties . . . '[64] In case of their conflict with religious laws (even if these are not codified), domestic legislation and human rights treaties find themselves in a vulnerable position. Except for Turkey, which has modernized or Westernized its legal system since the 1920s, all Islamic States follow Shariah in one form or the other. Armed with the conservative interpretations of the precepts of Shariah, well-organized fundamentalist forces in the Islamic States seek to enforce the implementation of their traditional practices. These forces do not allow their States to become parties to human rights treaties without adjusting them to Shariah.[65] All these factors prompted the Islamic States parties to the UN human rights treaties to attach reservations to those provisions of the treaties which clash with religious laws and practices, or to the treaties in general.[66] For example, under Saudi Arabia's reservations to the CEDAW, the CERD, and the CRC, it will not implement those provisions of the Conventions which may be in conflict with the precepts of Shariah. A more specific example, from a different religious tradition, is the Holy See's reservation to Article 24(2) of the CRC, by which it interprets the phrase 'family planning education and services' to mean only those methods of family planning which it considers morally acceptable, that is, natural methods of family planning.[67] The reason

[64] Heyns and Viljoen, above (n. 1), p. 35.

[65] For example, while the Kingdom of Iran did not attach any reservations to its ratification of the CERD, the CESCR, and the CCPR before the Islamic Revolution of 1979, the Islamic Republic of Iran found itself unable to ratify any human rights treaty without reservations. When the President of Iran requested the Islamic Consultative Assembly to ratify the CRC in 1994, the Assembly's Commission on Judicial Matters studied the provisions of the Convention for possible inconsistencies with Shariah. At that time, attention was drawn to the Guardian Council's opinion that Articles 12–16 and 32 of the CRC were inconsistent with Islamic law and that the Convention could not be approved without reservations. Thereafter, both the houses of the Iranian parliament—the Islamic Consultative Assembly and the Guardian Council—approved the CRC with the following reservation: 'The Government of the Islamic Republic of Iran reserves the right not to apply any provisions or articles of the Convention that are incompatible with Islamic laws and the internal legislation in effect.' Conversely, the High Council on Cultural Revolution, a body composed of a number of high-ranking officials with policymaking responsibility on cultural affairs in Iran, decided that Iran should not accede to the CEDAW. The main reason behind this decision is that Articles 2(*g*), 9, 10, 15(1), 15(2), 15(4), and 16 of the CEDAW are incompatible with Islamic laws and domestic law. The Iranian authorities feel that a detailed reservation specifying those provisions which are incompatible with Islamic laws may be entered upon accession to the CEDAW, but they have apprehension that a very negative international reaction will follow if the Convention is ratified with the intended reservation. Hence, the policy of no accession without reservation is in place. Cf. Mehrdad Rezaeian, 'Iran', in *UN Human Rights Treaties Impact Study*, above (n. 1), pp. 338–40, including footnotes.

[66] With respect to the CRC, for example, see reservations of Bangladesh, Brunei Darussalam, Egypt, Iran, Iraq, Jordan, Kuwait, the Maldives, Morocco, Oman, Pakistan, Qatar, Saudi Arabia, Syria, and the United Arab Emirates. Above n. 20.

[67] Above n. 20.

behind this reservation is the Vatican's opposition to abortion and artificial contraception.[68]

Even a secular State like India has not been able to overcome the influence of religious fundamentalism. That is why India made two declarations in respect of the CEDAW. The first relates to the Convention's Articles 5(*a*) (the duty to modify the social and cultural patterns in order to achieve the elimination of prejudices against women) and 16(1) (the duty to eliminate discrimination against women in matters relating to marriage and family relations). By making a declaration that it will abide by these provisions in conformity with its policy of non-interference in the personal affairs of any community, India reaffirmed the autonomy of its personal law of minorities. This declaration reflects the reality that no government in the world's largest democracy wants to displease the Muslim community by applying secular laws and practices to everybody. It became particularly necessary in the aftermath of the Indian Supreme Court's judgment in the *Shah Bano* case,[69] which provoked the dominant section of the Muslim community to pressure the

[68] See Addendum to the Initial Report by the Holy See under Article 44 of the CRC, UN Doc. CRC/C/3/Add.27 (28 March 1994), paras. 8 and 16.

[69] *Mohd. Ahmed Khan* v. *Shah Bano Begum*, AIR 1985 SC 945. This case originated from a maintenance suit filed by Shah Bano Begum, a 68-year-old Muslim woman, against her husband, Mohd. Ahmed Khan, a rich practicing lawyer. In response to the suit, Khan dissolved his 43-year-old marriage by pronouncing *talak* (an irrevocable proclamation of divorce resulting from repudiation by the husband). Shah Bano claimed that she was entitled to payments on account of *matta* (a provision for the welfare of divorced women that is binding upon the pious and god fearing Muslim men in order to ward off evil), *mahr* (a sum of money or other property which the wife is entitled to receive from the husband in consideration of the marriage) and *iddat* (a period of chastity imposed on a Muslim woman on the dissolution of her marriage in the interest of certainty of paternity). Khan countered that he had already paid maintenance—two hundred rupees ($13.35) per month for two years and a dower of three thousand rupees ($200.00) during *iddat*—in accordance with Muslim personal law and that he was under no obligation to provide further maintenance. He also argued that *matta* did not apply in his case. The lower court directed Khan to pay twenty-five rupees ($1.70 at the exchange rate of that time) per month to his ex-wife. Shah Bano appealed this decision to the High Court in the State of Madhya Pradesh. She was partially successful in her suit: the High Court increased her maintenance rate to 179.20 rupees ($11.90 at the exchange rate of that time) per month. Khan appealed this decision to the Supreme Court of India. On 23 April 1985 the Supreme Court upheld Shah Bano's right to continued maintenance payments. In the process, it made at least three important observations. First, Section 125(1)(*b*) of the Code of Criminal Procedure (CrPC), which defines the term 'wife', includes a divorced Muslim woman who has not remarried. In case of a conflict between the Muslim personal law in this regard and Section 125, the latter shall prevail. Secondly, a Muslim husband is liable to provide maintenance for his divorced wife under Section 125, which deals with cases in which a person who is possessed of sufficient means neglects or refuses to maintain, among others, his wife who is unable to maintain herself. In this regard, there is no conflict between the Muslim personal law and Section 125. Thirdly, Section 127(3)(*b*) of the CrPC, which deals with alterations in maintenance allowances under Section 125, cannot be used to defeat the purpose of the right to maintenance. In brief, this judgment was a victory of modern secular law over medieval personal law. For an appreciation of the judgment, see V.R. Krishna Iyer, 'The Shah Bano Case, the Constitution and the Court', *Indian Bar Review*, 13 (1986), pp. 1–21. For a critique of the judgment, see a collection of articles and statements in M. Sanaulla Khan (ed.), *How Wrong the Supreme Court in Shah Bano's Case?* (Mysore, 1986). The *Shah Bano* case is still popular in the secular press. See, for instance, an editorial comment entitled 'Trial by Talaq', *Times of India*, 23 September 2000, p. 10, which refers to the case in the context of reforms in Muslim personal law.

Government of India to pilot the adoption of the Muslim Women (Protection of Rights on Divorce) Act[70] at the expense of the Code of Criminal Procedure,[71] the Directive Principles of State Policy,[72] and CEDAW.[73] The second declaration, concerning CEDAW Article 16(2), allows India not to comply strictly with the obligation to register all marriages. It is mainly based on socio-religious realities. According to Indian traditions, marriage is a religious act, not a contract. In India, a person can get married in various ways, including *saptapadi* (i.e. taking seven steps at a religious ceremony). Most marriages in India are performed in traditional ways, without registration, and many people cannot afford the registration fee. If India had not made the said declaration, the validity of the non-registered marriages of a great many Indians would have become questionable. This would have hurt the feelings of some religious groups as well.

A comparative study suggests that the compulsion to harmonize domestic law with international law has been the most compelling factor in the making of reservations. Because of their attachment to well-established domestic laws, States may not recognize or accept that their laws are deficient. Even if they do, conservative forces do not allow them to amend their laws. Even if a consensus may be emerging on the need for amendment, the time factor may get in the way. In such situations, a quick solution is found in the form of reservations. In the process, reserving States more or less ignore that ratification of international treaties entailed obligations to adopt new legislation and to amend laws contradicting international instruments.

V. Consequences of Reservations

The effect of reservations is noticeable at various levels. At the domestic level, a human rights treaty provision which has been subject to

70 Act No. XXV of 1986 (19 May 1986). Among other things, this legislation seeks to exclude the issue of maintenance of a divorced Muslim woman from the scope of Sections 125 and 127(3)(*b*) of the CrPC. [For an appreciation of the Act, see Tahir Mahmood, 'The Muslim Women (Protection of Rights on Divorce) Act, 1986: Perspectives and Prospects', *Indian Bar Review*, 13 (1986), pp. 221–42. For a critique of the Act, see Lucy Carroll, 'The Muslim Women (Protection of Rights on Divorce) Act 1986: A Retrogressive Precedent of Dubious Constitutionality', *Journal of the Indian Law Institute*, 28 (1986), pp. 364–76.] As a result, while all Indian women can apply for maintenance under Section 125 of the CrPC, Muslim women cannot.

71 Act No. II of 1974 (25 January 1974).

72 Article 44 of the Constitution of India obligates the State to endeavour to secure for the citizens a uniform civil code throughout the territory of India. Agitated over the *Shah Bano* case, certain conservative Muslims asked for the deletion of Article 44. For instance, on 29 March 1985, G.M. Banatwala (General Secretary of the Muslim League) introduced a Bill to that effect in Lok Sabha (lower house of Parliament). For Banatwala's statement in favour of the Bill, see Sanaulla Khan, above (n. 69), pp. 32–42.

73 For further comments, see Anika Rahman, 'Religious Rights Versus Women's Rights in India: A Test Case for International Human Rights Law', *Columbia Journal of Transnational Law*, 28 (1990), pp. 473–98.

reservations by the forum State is likely to receive an unfavourable treatment from national institutions in general and judicial bodies in particular. However, the most striking effect is seen at the international level. Considering the gravity of the problem, the present section focuses on the main consequences of reservations: lowering human rights standards, diluting the principle of universality, and avoiding international accountability. An illustrative analysis of these consequences may promote a better understanding of the subject.

1. *Lowering Human Rights Standards*

Restrictions upon the applicable human rights treaty, which cannot be found in the instrument either expressly or implicitly, may be imposed by way of subjecting the scope of that treaty to the domain of less liberal human rights regimes. Although this amounts to a de facto amendment to the treaty concerned, States may exploit the absence of a *de jure* prohibition of such restrictions.

Since permissible restrictions are less broadly based in the CCPR,[74] some of the European States have relied on the European Convention.[75] When explaining Belgium's reservations to Articles 19, 21 and 22 of the CCPR, its representative admitted that Articles 10 and 11 of the European Convention accorded greater rights of exception than those permitted in the CCPR and that Belgium had therefore decided to refer to the more explicit rights of exception in the Convention.[76] The French declaration upon ratification of the CCPR exemplifies this situation more clearly:

> The Government of the Republic [of France] declares that articles 19, 21 and 22 of the Covenant [on Civil and Political Rights of 16 December 1966] will be implemented in accordance with articles 10, 11 and 16 of the European Convention for the Protection of Human Rights and Fundamental Freedoms of 4 November 1950.[77]

In a statement before the HRC, the French representative described the purpose of this declaration: 'France was eager to ensure that the two [the CCPR and the European Convention] were legally consistent and that their provisions were applied uniformly.'[78] However, a comparison of the corresponding provisions of the two instruments reveals another

[74] *Report of the Human Rights Committee*, GAOR, fifty-second session (1997), supplement no. 40, UN Doc. A/52/40, vol. I, para. 65 [hereinafter '*HRC 1997 Report I*'].

[75] See, for example, reservations of Austria, Belgium, France, Germany and Malta, in *Note on Reservations*, above (n. 18), pp. 14, 15–16, 20, and 29.

[76] *Report of the Human Rights Committee*, GAOR, forty-seventh session (1992), supplement no. 40, UN Doc. A/47/40, para. 403 [hereinafter '*HRC 1992 Report*'].

[77] *Note on Reservations*, above (n. 18), p. 20.

[78] *Report of the Human Rights Committee*, GAOR, forty-third session (1988), supplement no. 40, UN Doc. A/43/40, para. 400 [hereinafter '*HRC 1988 Report*'].

possible purpose, namely, adherence to lower human rights standards. For instance, in comparison to Article 10 of the European Convention, Article 19 of the CCPR provides a broader right to freedom of speech and expression and imposes fewer restrictions. Also, Article 16 of the European Convention permits additional restrictions on the right to freedom of speech and expression of aliens, but the CCPR does not do so. What is true for the right to freedom of speech and expression is also true for the right to freedom of assembly (Article 21 of the CCPR and Article 11 *juncto* Article 16 of the European Convention), the right to freedom of association (Article 22 of the CCPR and Article 11 *juncto* Article 16 of the European Convention), and the right to equality and freedom from discrimination (Article 2 *juncto* Article 26 of the CCPR and Article 14 *juncto* Article 16 of the European Convention).

In some respects, the UN human rights treaties are an improvement over the European Convention in respect of substantive human rights law. The States that accord primacy to the European Convention thereby deny the higher standards of human rights, as well as restricting the role of the UN human rights treaty bodies.

The Congo has made a declaration that 'it does not consider itself bound by the provisions of article 11' of the CCPR,[79] which enshrines the non-derogable right to freedom from imprisonment in cases of breach of contract. This reservation remains applicable despite the Belgian objection,[80] because the significance of such objections is not clear and the HRC has not yet pronounced the reservation incompatible with Article 4(2) of the CCPR. Similarly, by entering a reservation, Trinidad and Tobago has arrogated to itself 'the right not to apply in full the provision of paragraph 2 of article 4 of the Covenant [CCPR],'[81] which seeks to protect the minimum attributes of human dignity in time of emergency. Although Germany and the Netherlands consider Trinidad's reservation 'incompatible with the object and purpose of the Covenant',[82] the lack of follow-up action has allowed the reservation to remain a threat to the entire range of non-derogable rights during a state of emergency.

The most controversial instance of entering a reservation for the purpose of lowering human rights standards is the US reservation to Article 6(5) of the CCPR, which prohibits the imposition of the death penalty against juvenile offenders. Equally striking is the US reservation

[79] *Note on Reservations*, above (n. 18), pp. 16–17.

[80] The Belgian objection is based on the grounds that the Congolese reservation is unnecessary; that there is no contradiction between the Congolese legislation and the letter and the spirit of Article 11 of the CCPR; that the reservation is in contradiction with the letter and the spirit of the CCPR in general and its Article 4 in particular; and that the reservation may, by reason of its very principle, constitute a precedent which might have considerable effects at the international level. Ibid., pp. 47–8.

[81] Ibid., p. 36.

[82] Ibid., pp. 51 and 52.

against Article 7 of the CCPR, which reaffirms the right to freedom from torture. Both the reservations target the articles that belong to the category of non-derogable provisions. It is well known that there are an increasing number of death sentences and executions in the United States.[83] Although the CCPR grants strong protection to juveniles, it is a matter of concern that the United States is one of a few countries where juvenile offenders have been executed;[84] that many juvenile offenders are awaiting executions in the United States;[85] and that some of them are on death row for more than ten years.[86] By reason of its reservation to Article 6(5), the United States retains the right to execute persons aged less than eighteen. Some commentators[87] and many governments[88] consider that this reservation is incompatible with the object and purpose of the CCPR and also violates international law; certain human rights bodies, both governmental[89] and nongovernmental,[90] seek to stop those executions which seem to enjoy impunity by virtue of the reservation; and the

[83] The US States executed nearly 100 death row inmates during 1999, a significant increase over the preceding year and far more than any annual total since the US Supreme Court allowed capital punishment to resume in 1976. See Paul Duggan, 'More U.S. Executions and More Debate on Death Penalty', *International Herald Tribune,* 15 December 1999, p. 2.

[84] In terms of the total number of executions of juvenile offenders between January 1990 and July 2000, the United States is the leader, followed by Iran, Pakistan, Saudi Arabia, Nigeria, Yemen, and the Democratic Republic of the Congo.

[85] In mid-2000, eighty child offenders were awaiting executions in the United States.

[86] For instance, Alexander Edmund Williams, who was convicted of the abduction, rape, and murder of Aleta Carol Bunch in the State of Georgia in 1986 when he was only 17 years old, has been on death row since August 1986.

[87] Edward F. Sherman, Jr, 'The U.S. Death Penalty Reservation to the International Covenant on Civil and Political Rights: Exposing the Limitations of the Flexible System Governing Treaty Formation', *Texas International Law Journal*, 29 (1994), pp. 76 and 92; William A. Schabas, 'Invalid Reservations to the International Covenant on Civil and Political Rights: Is the United States Still a Party?', *Brooklyn Journal of International Law*, 21 (1995), pp. 277–325.

[88] Belgium, Denmark, Finland, France, Germany, Italy, the Netherlands, Norway, Portugal, Spain, and Sweden have made objections to the reservation [above n. 18] because they abolished the death penalty within their own jurisdiction and many of their nationals accused of capital crimes in the United States were denied their right to consular access after arrest by the US authorities. For details, see *USA: Worlds Apart—Violations of the Rights of Foreign Nationals on Death Row—Cases of Europeans* (London, 2000), AI Doc. AMR 51/101/00, July 2000. The case of Walter LaGrand, a German national convicted of murder in the State of Arizona, demonstrates the European dissatisfaction with the US law and practice on the subject. Even the ICJ's intervention proved to be futile there. See *Germany* v. *United States of America, ICJ Reports*, 1999, p. 16; and ICJ Press Communiqué 9/12, 8 March 1999.

[89] For instance, on 13 June 2000, the UN Special Rapporteur on Summary or Arbitrary Executions requested the US Secretary of State to take steps to ensure the right to life and physical integrity of Gary Graham, who had been arrested as a juvenile offender in Texas and was sentenced to death. When the United States failed to comply with her request, the Special Rapporteur said that Graham's execution was evidence of disregard for the growing international movement for abolition of the death penalty. Similarly, on 22 August 2000, the UN Special Rapporteur on the Independence of Judges and Lawyers expressed his grave concern over the scheduled execution of Alex Williams on 24 August 2000, who was convicted of crimes committed in 1986 when he was only 17 years old. On 17 August 2000 the UN Sub-Commission on the Promotion and Protection of Human Rights stated that executions of child offenders violated international law.

[90] For instance, in August 2000, Amnesty International released a report on the execution of Alex Williams, who was scheduled to die in Georgia's electric chair on 24 August 2000 for a murder he

reservation perhaps obstructs the ratification of the CRC by the United States.[91] Although the CCPR does not prohibit the death penalty in general, it prohibits cruel, inhuman, or degrading treatment or punishment without any exception. The fact that the United States is not a party to the Second Optional Protocol to the CCPR, aiming at the abolition of the death penalty, does not mean that it has the unfettered right to impose the death penalty. The US reservation to Article 7 enables the United States to defend the death row phenomenon, which amounts to inhuman treatment within the terms of the *Soering* judgment by the European Court of Human Rights (the European Court).[92] This situation is perhaps unavoidable because all 50 States of the United States have their own criminal laws; 37 of them retain the death penalty; and more than three thousand convicts are on death row in the United States. Although the Western objections to the reservation have raised doubts about its validity and the HRC has declared it incompatible with the CCPR, these international attempts have been allowed to stop neither the death penalty for juvenile offenders nor the death row phenomenon in the United States. It has been claimed that the death row phenomenon partly arises out of the due process of law guarantees under the US Constitution. Neither Amnesty International[93] nor the American Bar Association (ABA)[94] can change this reality, despite persistent campaigns.

2. *Diluting the Principle of Universality*

Reservations fly in the face of the principle of the universality of human rights. If all human beings do not have the equal protection of the

had committed when he was aged 17. It stressed: 'The USA must act now to stop this execution and uphold the rule of law . . . To do otherwise would confirm its reputation as the world's chief rogue nation on this aspect of the death penalty'. *USA: Abandoning Justice: The Imminent Execution of Alexander Williams, Mentally Ill Child Offender* (London, 2000), AI Doc. AMR 51/121/00. Following the submission of his application to the Georgia Board of Pardons and Paroles, Williams received a stay of execution on 22 August. Amnesty International continues to appeal for his sentence to be commuted. For details, visit http://www.amnesty.org.

[91] For different reasons, only two States (Somalia and the United States) are not parties to the CRC.

[92] In *Soering* v. *United Kingdom*, the European Court unanimously held that if the petitioner, a German national detained in the United Kingdom, was extradited to the United States to stand trial for the crime of murder, there would be a violation of Article 3 of the European Convention. European Court of Human Rights, *Judgments and Decisions*, series A, 161 (1989), p. 50. Following an assurance that Jens Soering will not be subjected to the death penalty, however, the United Kingdom extradited him to the United States.

[93] The abolition of the death penalty is one of the main objectives of Amnesty International. Amnesty International's concerns about the ongoing use of the death penalty in the United States include the execution of juvenile offenders (prisoners who were under 18 at the time of the crime) and the disproportionate numbers of poor, black and other ethnic minorities who are executed there. For details, visit http://www.amnesty.org. In addition to its own campaign, Amnesty International supports Benetton's worldwide campaign against the death penalty in the United States. Visit http://www.amnesty.org/news/2000/A5000300.htm.

[94] The ABA has opposed (*a*) capital punishment for any offence committed while under the age of eighteen, (*b*) discrimination in capital sentencing on the basis of the race of either the victim or the

law, what is the use of celebrating the notion of 'a common standard of achievement'?[95] Reservations to multilateral treaties create difficult problems. On the one hand, by making reservations, the reserving State seeks special treatment for itself.[96] On the other, entering reservations encourages other States, directly or through reciprocal effects, to feel free to do likewise and to interpret the treaty to suit their interests. In this way, reservations tend to fragment a single treaty into a number of smaller multilateral or even bilateral regimes.[97] Wilfred Jenks observed that 'the effect on the obligations resulting from the Covenants [the CCPR and the CESCR] of any reservation or objection thereto remains somewhat indeterminate; there is therefore a real danger that the Covenants may disintegrate into series of bilateral agreements expressed in two common instruments but binding in different degrees between different parties'.[98] The developments since the adoption of the Covenants bear out Jenks' concern. Moreover, some sophisticated procedures have been evolved to undermine the principle of universality. For instance, the Committee of Experts of the Committee of Ministers of the Council of Europe declared in its Resolution (70) 17 that . . .

defendant, and (*c*) the death penalty for any mentally retarded person. It has supported the adoption of the 'Guidelines for the Appointment and Performance of Counsel in Death Penalty Cases' and legislative measures to prevent or minimize disproportionate effects of federal death penalty legislation on Native Americans subject to federal jurisdiction. It has recommended that each jurisdiction imposing capital punishment not carry out the death penalty until it implements policies and procedures that are consistent with ABA policies intended to (*a*) ensure the fair and impartial administration of the death penalty, and (*b*) minimize the risk that innocent persons may be executed. See American Bar Association, *Legislative Issues: Current Through February 2000*, p. 26, which is also available at http://www.abanet.org/poladv/lgpolicy.html.

[95] The last preambular paragraph of the Universal Declaration of Human Rights (UDHR) contains this phrase.

[96] In his study of the law and practice on reservations to the constitutions of the League of Nations, the United Nations and the specialized agencies of the United Nations, M. H. Mendelson argues, among other things, that reservations contradict the principle of sovereign equality. Mendelson, 'Reservations to the Constitutions of International Organizations', this *Year Book*, 43 (1971), pp. 146–7. Since the functioning of these organizations would have been adversely affected by reservations to their respective constitutions, the drafters of those constitutions generally prohibited reservations and the organizations have always detested those reservations. In that sense, the sovereign equality argument against reservations goes along with the institutional effectiveness argument. A similar alliance of arguments is applicable to the UN human rights treaties to a lesser extent because these treaties have created mini-organizations, which are also worried about their effectiveness. Yet, the sovereign equality argument is less forceful against reservations to the human rights treaties; the guiding principles of the human rights treaty bodies with limited membership rarely match the fundamental principles of universal organizations like the United Nations; and the treaty bodies mainly rely on the 'object and purpose' test, not the institutional effectiveness or sovereign equality argument, for the purpose of questioning the compatibility of any reservations against their respective constituent instruments.

[97] *Restatement (Third) of the Foreign Relations Law of the United States*, above (n. 1), p. 181.

[98] Jenks, 'Human Rights, Social Justice and Peace: The Broader Significance of the ILO Experience', in Asbjörn Eide and August Schou (eds.), *International Protection of Human Rights: Proceedings of the Seventh Nobel Symposium, Oslo, September 25–27, 1967* (Stockholm, 1968), p. 246.

as long as the problem of interpretation of [former] Article 62 of the European Convention is not resolved, States Parties to the Convention which ratify or accede to the UN Covenant on Civil and Political Rights and make a declaration under Article 41 of that Covenant should normally utilise only the procedure established by the European Convention in respect of complaints against another Contracting Party to the European Convention relating to an alleged violation of a right which in substance is covered both by the European Convention (or its protocols) and by the UN Covenant on Civil and Political Rights, it being understood that the UN procedure may be invoked in relation to rights not guaranteed in the European Convention (or its protocols) or in relation to States which are not Parties to the European Convention.[99]

On the same lines, the Committee of Ministers transmitted to the member States of the Council of Europe a text drafted by the Committee of Experts, so that governments may use it, either as a declaration of interpretation or as a reservation, when ratifying the CCPR Protocol.[100] Following this recommendation, most European States ratified the CCPR Protocol with almost identical reservations,[101] which present a difficult choice to the applicants who wish to seek redress for their human rights grievances. In effect, the reservations attempt to dilute universal human rights law.

A number of explanations have been given in favour of the precedence of the European procedure over the universal procedure. It has been pointed out that Article 33 of the UN Charter approves the principle of regional settlement of disputes between States. The European Convention procedure results in a judicial decision, which the universal instruments do not. There is a belief that it would be undesirable that States which had brought a case before the European Convention institutions unsuccessfully should refer the same matter subsequently to some other international body, since this might create the impression of an 'appeal' from the former to the latter and undermine, or at least weaken, the authority of the European institutions. Moreover, the possibility of such an 'appeal' would be contrary to Articles 44 and 46 (former Articles 32

[99] Cf. *Yearbook of the European Convention on Human Rights, 1970* (The Hague, 1972), p. 74, hereinafter '*European Yearbook (1970)*'. Former Article 62 is now Article 55 of the European Convention, reading as follows: 'The High Contracting Parties agree that, except by special agreement, they will not avail themselves of treaties, conventions or declarations in force between them for the purpose of submitting, by way of petition, a dispute arising out of the interpretation or application of this Convention to a means of settlement other than those provided for in this Convention.'

[100] See *European Yearbook (1970)*, p. 76. See also Torkel Opsahl, 'The Coexistence between Geneva and Strasbourg: Inter-Relationship of the International Covenant on Civil and Political Rights and the European Convention on Human Rights and Their Respective Organs of Implementation', *Canadian Human Rights Yearbook* (1991–2), p. 160.

[101] Above n. 24.

and 52) of the European Convention, which provide that the decisions of the Committee of Ministers and the European Court will be final.[102]

Whatever the justifications for giving preference to the European Convention institutions, the UN human rights treaty bodies only receive a small number of communications from European nationals. And the HRC in particular is unlikely to have an opportunity to consider inter-State communications from the European States parties to the CCPR Article 41 procedure owing to the application of reservations inspired by Resolution (70) 17 of the Committee of Ministers of the Council of Europe. The Netherlands is worried that the European practice 'could be followed in other regional contexts, undermining the world-wide system for the protection of human rights'.[103] But Resolution (70) 17 has been in existence for more than thirty years and there is no initiative to amend it. The continuing existence of the resolution indicates that there is no keenness to resolve the problem of interpretation of Article 55 (former Article 62) of the European Convention, and that most of the European States are happy with the status quo because they prefer the more exclusive approach of the European Convention, in contrast with the thrust of the UN human rights treaties.

Though 'eager to ensure that the two [universal and regional regimes] were legally consistent and that their provisions were applied uniformly',[104] the European States have expressed their intentions through reservations in such a manner that one gets the impression of the European attempt to prefer regional jurisprudence over universal jurisprudence. The HRC has expressed 'its concern over the apparent preference accorded, in domestic law as well as in legal doctrine and jurisprudence, to the European Convention . . . as against the International Covenant [CCPR] . . . '[105] In that regard, it is pertinent to point out that the UN human rights treaties guarantee a number of rights not protected under the European Convention[106] and that permissible

[102] Memorandum by the Directorate of Human Rights, *Effects of the Various International Human Rights Instruments Providing a Mechanism for Individual Communications on the Machinery of Protection Established under the European Convention on Human Rights*, Council of Europe Doc. H (85) 3 (1 February 1985), p. 8.

[103] The Government of the Netherlands took this position in an explanatory memorandum to the Second Chamber of the States-General of the Kingdom of the Netherlands (1975–76, No. 13932, 42). Ibid., p. 10.

[104] *HRC 1988 Report*, para. 400.

[105] See, e.g., *Report of the Human Rights Committee*, GAOR, forty-ninth session (1994), supplement no. 40, UN Doc. A/49/40, vol. I, paras. 76 and 123 [hereinafter '*HRC 1994 Report I*']; *HRC 1997 Report I*, para. 65.

[106] In comparison to the CCPR alone, the European Convention does not recognize the right to self-determination, the right to seek pardon or commutation of the sentence, the right to have access to public services, the prohibition of war propaganda, the rights of the child, the rights of aliens, and minority rights. However, most of these rights are covered by the additional Protocols and Conventions.

restrictions are less broad-based in those universal instruments.[107] For obvious reasons, the HRC has recommended that the European States should consider amending their respective Constitutions in order to reflect the provisions of the CCPR.[108] The European States can ignore these concerns and recommendations only at the risk of their credibility, thus implying the need for the reconsideration of their reservations sooner than later. Questioning the wisdom of using reservations to harmonize parallel obligations, Antonio Cançado Trindade states that,

> With the expansion of the law on the international protection of human rights and the accumulation of experience of international supervisory organs in this area in the last four decades, there seems to be a lesser ground or reason for resorting to co-ordination *via* the expedient of reservations or interpretative declarations, which may prove to be incompatible with the object and purpose of human rights treaties. As States display, in growing number, their preparedness to embark with more determination on common endeavours to foster international implementation of human rights, the individualistic and voluntarist method of co-ordination *via* reservations appears more clearly not strictly in keeping with the basic notion of a collective guarantee underlying human rights treaties.[109]

In spite of its soundness, however, this statement has not been able to persuade the reserving States to reconsider their policies on the subject.

3. *Avoiding International Accountability*

Many States, developed and developing, have deployed reservations with the result that they escape accountability under the UN human rights treaties. For instance, the French reservation substitutes a less stringent test of compliance with the CCPR for what is prescribed in Article 4, which deals with derogation in time of emergency; it establishes the supremacy of French law over the CCPR; and it excludes the HRC from assessing the objective necessity for, or proportionality of, the emergency measures taken by France.[110] The irony is that while a similar reservation to Article 15 of the European Convention has been a bone of contention and even considered invalid because incompatible with the object and purpose of the Convention, the reservation to Article 4 of the CCPR has so far escaped the critical attention of the other States. Indeed

[107] See the discussion on the French declaration in respect of Articles 19, 21 and 22 of the CCPR. Above nn. 77–8 and the accompanying text.

[108] See, e.g., *HRC 1994 Report I*, paras. 80 and 128; *Report of the Human Rights Committee*, GAOR, fifty-fourth session (1999), supplement no. 40, UN Doc. A/54/40, vol. I, paras. 61 and 184 [hereinafter '*HRC 1999 Report I*'].

[109] Cançado Trindade, 'Co-existence and Co-ordination of Mechanisms of International Protection of Human Rights (At Global and Regional Levels)', *Recueil des cours*, 202 (1987–II), p. 405.

[110] *Note on Reservations*, above (n. 18), p. 19.

a few members of the HRC consider it a 'correct interpretation of the Covenant [CCPR]'.[111]

The influence of the reservation-based approach to escape international accountability is apparent from the application of the reservations made by a majority of the European States parties to the CCPR Protocol.[112] According to these reservations, as noted earlier, the HRC is not competent to examine a communication submitted by an individual if the same matter has already been examined under any other procedure of international investigation or settlement. The reservation of Spain precludes consideration by the HRC even if the matter was only submitted to, although not actually examined by, another international institution.[113] As a result, an aggrieved individual's options are restricted to just one international procedure. The complainant has to decide at the outset whether his or her case can be examined by the HRC or by the European Convention institutions or by any other expert body. The HRC has viewed such reservations as not violating the object and purpose of the CCPR Protocol.[114] This seems to ignore the fact that even apparently reasonable reservations may deprive complainants of their freedom to seek benefits arising out of differences in the jurisprudence of different human rights regimes. The protection of such benefits may be a reasonable favour to complainants.

The debilitating effect of the European reservations is clear from a survey of the CCPR Protocol procedure, where many individual communications have been dismissed at the admissibility stage. In the *Danish Pakistani Prisoner* case,[115] for instance, the HRC was barred from considering the case because the same matter had previously been referred to the European Commission of Human Rights (ECHR). Although the ECHR had declared the petition inadmissible without examining the merits, the HRC declined to consider the case owing to the application of the Danish reservation. Similarly, it pronounced the *Spanish Military Officer* case inadmissible because the same matter had earlier been submitted to and summarily dismissed by the ECHR without considering the merits.[116] The HRC found itself precluded from

[111] See the statements of Bernhard Graefrath and Leonte Herdocia Ortega during the consideration of the second periodic report of France in July 1983. UN Docs. CCPR/C/SR.441 (15 July 1983), para. 35, and CCPR/C/SR.440 (14 July 1983), para. 23, respectively.

[112] Austria, Croatia, Denmark, France, Germany, Iceland, Ireland, Italy, Luxembourg, Malta, Norway, Poland, Romania, the Russian Federation, Slovenia, Spain, and Sweden made those reservations. For the text of reservations, above n. 24.

[113] See *Note on Reservations*, above (n. 18), p. 128.

[114] General Comment 24, above (n. 30), p. 46, para. 14.

[115] *A.M.* v. *Denmark*, Communication No. 121/1982, *Human Rights Committee: Selected Decisions under the Optional Protocol (Second to Sixteenth Sessions)* (New York, 1985), UN Doc. CCPR/C/OP/1, p. 33.

[116] *V.E.M.* v. *Spain*, Communication No. 467/1991, *Report of the Human Rights Committee*, GAOR, forty-eighth session (1993), supplement no. 40, UN Doc. A/48/40, vol. II, Annex XIII J, p. 216, para. 5.2 [hereinafter '*HRC 1993 Report II*'].

considering the *Croatian Hotel Expropriation* case, because the ECHR had earlier rejected an application concerning the same parties, the same facts and the same issues as were before the HRC.[117] These decisions have emboldened reserving States to such an extent that they feel free to argue for the inadmissibility of individual communications on the slightest grounds. In the *Austrian Murder* case, for instance, Austria recalled its reservation under Article 5(2)(*a*) of the CCPR Protocol, submitted that the complainant had already had correspondence with the Secretary to the ECHR with regard to the same matter, and argued that the HRC was thus precluded from examining the instant case.[118] The issue was whether mere correspondence with the ECHR precluded the jurisdiction of the HRC. The HRC answered in the negative, as it ascertained that the complainant's petition was not being examined and had not been formally examined by the ECHR.[119]

The application of the European reservations to the CCPR Protocol has not merely constrained the HRC from considering a number of human rights complaints but it has also created a split in this body.[120] For an institution like the HRC, which strives to adopt decisions by consensus, a majority-minority divide is not a happy development. Many victims continue to invoke the CCPR Protocol procedure, though unsuccessfully, and the HRC continues to feel helpless in the face of these reservations. A leading expert holds the view that 'the well-recognized necessity of co-ordination of distinct mechanisms of human rights protection at global and regional levels cannot prevail over, in the sense of being made to operate to the detriment of, the protection of the individuals concerned, which is the *raison d'être* and ultimate purpose of those mechanisms'.[121] This view raises doubts about the propriety of the European reservations.

Reservations to the substantive provisions of the UN human rights treaties adversely affect not only human rights but also their monitoring process. The HRC finds that reservations made by a State ratifying the CCPR and consequent non-reporting on many issues related to such reservations, which may bear directly or indirectly on the enjoyment of CCPR rights, make it difficult to assess fully and comprehensively the situation in regard to human rights in the State.[122] No less serious is the impact on the individual communication procedure. In the *Italian Lockheed Scandal* case, for instance, the HRC managed to overcome the

[117] *Mme Dagmar Urbanetz Linderholm* v. *Croatia*, Communication No. 744/1997, UN Doc. CCPR/C/66/D/744/1997 (27 July 1999), para. 4.2.

[118] *Salah Abdoh Darwish Mohamed* v. *Austria*, Communication No. 679/1996, UN Doc. CCPR/C/60/D/679/1996 (14 August 1997), para. 4.4.

[119] Ibid., para. 6.2.

[120] See the individual opinion of Graefrath in the *Danish Pakistani Prisoner* case, above (n. 115), pp. 33–4.

[121] Cançado Trindade, above (n. 109), p. 176.

[122] *HRC 1997 Report I*, para. 390.

Italian reservation to the implementation provisions of the CCPR Protocol, but it could not get around the reservation to the substantive provisions of the CCPR.[123] Similarly, in the *Finnish Drug Dealer* case, Finland successfully invoked its reservation to Article 14 of the CCPR and the HRC quickly declared the complaint inadmissible.[124] In fact, the HRC did not even question the application of the reservation. From the perspective of the reserving States, therefore, the *Finnish Drug Dealer* decision was an 'improvement' over the *Italian Lockheed Scandal* decision.

The *Breton* cases highlight how decisive reservations are in creating escape routes for States. There, several Breton-speaking French nationals alleged that the French courts' refusal to register their petitions drafted in the Breton language, not in French, and the denial to provide them with the services of an interpreter constituted a language-based discrimination in contravention of Article 27 of the CCPR (rights of minorities). France contended that upon ratification of the CCPR it had entered a 'declaration' with respect to Article 27, which in effect made that article inapplicable to France, and that there was no concept of minority rights in France. Despite the fact that the French instrument of ratification speaks of a 'declaration', not a 'reservation', concerning Article 27, the HRC ignored the formal designation, took note of the State's clear intent, construed the declaration as a reservation within the meaning of Article 2(1)(*d*) of the Vienna Convention, and concluded that, because of this reservation, it was not competent to consider complaints directed against France concerning alleged violations of Article 27.[125]

All these cases demonstrate that States exercise considerable discretion in entering reservations to the provisions of the UN human rights treaties, and that their monitoring bodies do not have comparable competence regarding the interpretation and application of those reservations. How can a UN human rights treaty body, then, pronounce upon the ultimate question as to whether a reservation is incompatible with the object and purpose of the treaty?

[123] *Duilio Fanali* v. *Italy*, Communication No. 75/1980, *Report of the Human Rights Committee*, GAOR, thirty-eighth session (1983), supplement no. 40, UN Doc. A/38/40, Annex XIII, pp. 160–5.

[124] *R.M.* v. *Finland*, Communication No. 301/1988, *Report of the Human Rights Committee*, GAOR, forty-fourth session (1989), supplement no. 40, UN Doc. A/44/40, Annex XI. I, p. 302, para. 6.4 [hereinafter '*HRC 1989 Report*'].

[125] See, e.g., *T.K.* v. *France* (Communication No. 220/1987) and *M.K.* v. *France* (Communication No. 222/1987), *Report of the Human Rights Committee*, GAOR, forty-fifth session (1990), supplement no. 40, UN Doc. A/45/40, vol. II, Annex X, pp. 122–3 (para. 8.6) and 130–1 (para. 8.6) respectively [hereinafter '*HRC 1990 Report II*']; *S.G.* v. *France*, Communication No. 347/1988, *HRC 1992 Report*, Annex X, p. 348, para. 5.3; *G.B.* v. *France*, Communication No. 348/1989, ibid., p. 353, para. 5.3; *Dominique Guesdon* v. *France*, Communication No. 219/1986, *HRC 1990 Report II*, Annex IX G, p. 65, para. 7.3. See also below n. 174.

VI. Responses to Reservations

Starting from the UN General Assembly's request to the ICJ for an advisory opinion in the *Reservations to the Genocide Convention* case, several international institutions and a few national forums have tried to respond to the challenge of reservations. In view of their origins and status, various responses may be divided into four categories: *lex generalis*, practice under particular treaties, practice in municipal courts, and emerging law.

1. *Lex generalis*

Even after the ICJ's advisory opinion in the *Reservations to the Genocide Convention* case, some human rights experts were dissatisfied with the modestly modernized reservations regime. Reacting to the rule that acceptance by even a single State party of a reservation makes the reserving State a party to the treaty in relation to that State, Egon Schwelb expressed doubts whether it could fit into the scheme of human rights treaties. In 1967 he gave an extreme illustration: if South Africa were to decide to ratify the two Covenants (the CCPR and the CESCR) subject to reservation that it did not accept those of their provisions which prohibited discrimination and if one single other State party were to accept that reservation, South Africa would become a party to the Covenants with all the prestige and status this might imply.[126] In other words, Schwelb sought to emphasize that the ICJ had answered a few questions while leaving many unanswered. Subsequently, the ILC has attempted to answer those questions, but essentially focused on the main elements of the advisory opinion. At present, the Vienna Convention constitutes the *lex generalis* on reservations. A few other instruments supplement it. Accordingly, a reservation may be subjected to (*a*) objections, (*b*) a demand for the settlement of a dispute relating to the reservation, and (*c*) a request for a review. A brief analysis of this set of responses may facilitate a detailed enquiry.

(*a*) *Objections*

According to Article 20(5) of the Vienna Convention, a State party to a treaty may raise an objection to the reservation of another State party within twelve months after it was notified of the reservation or by the date on which it expressed its consent to be bound by the treaty, whichever is later. Many States have made use of this provision against selective reservations to the UN human rights treaties, but only a few

[126] Schwelb, 'Some Aspects of the International Covenants on Human Rights of December 1966', in Eide and Schou, above (n. 98), p. 114.

follow a consistent policy on the subject.[127] Most of the objections have been raised by West European States. Among them, the Netherlands has made the largest number of objections,[128] closely followed by Finland, Germany, and Sweden. The reservations of developing States are the targets of most of the objections. The Islamic States' reservations to the CEDAW, the CERD, and the CRC received the largest number of objections in the context of these instruments. With respect to the CCPR, the largest number of objections came against the reservations of the United States.[129] In the case of reservations to the CESCR, the reservations of Kuwait carried this dubious distinction.[130] Regarding the reservations to the CAT, Chile's reservations attracted the largest number of objections.[131] As for the CCPR Protocol, the reservation of Trinidad and Tobago became the target of the largest number of objections[132] and Guyana's reservation is expected to attract as many objections.[133] A majority of the leading reserving States (Australia, India, Singapore, and the United States) have not objected to the reservations of any other States parties to the treaties under discussion. Also, the three most powerful States in the world (China, Russia, and the United States) have not entered objections to reservations by other States parties regarding any of the treaties within the scope of the present study. There are a few States (for example, Estonia, the Philippines, Senegal, South

[127] For example, Finland has a policy to object especially to reservations which mean that international law will be submitted to national law: see Aarnio, above (n. 55), p. 277. It has made objections to the reservations of a number of States. The name(s) of the target State(s) follow the name of the treaty concerned. The CERD: Saudi Arabia [above n. 23]. The CCPR: the United States [above n. 18]. The CESCR: Kuwait [above n. 22]. The CAT: the United States [above n. 21]. The CEDAW: Kuwait, Lesotho, Libya, Malaysia, the Maldives, Singapore, and Pakistan [above n. 19]. The CRC: Brunei Darussalam, Indonesia, Iran, Malaysia, Oman, Pakistan, Qatar, Saudi Arabia, Singapore, and Syria [above n. 20].

[128] Here, the name(s) of the target State(s) follow the name of the treaty concerned. The CERD: Saudi Arabia and Yemen [above n. 23]. The CCPR: Algeria, Australia, India, Kuwait, the Republic of Korea, Thailand, Trinidad and Tobago, and the United States [above n. 18]. The CESCR: Algeria, India and Kuwait [above n. 22]. The CAT: the United States [above n. 21]. The CEDAW: Bangladesh, Egypt, Brazil, India, Iraq, Jamaica, Kuwait, Lesotho, Libya, Malawi, Malaysia, the Maldives, Mauritius, Morocco, the Republic of Korea, Thailand, Tunisia, and Turkey [above n. 19]. The CRC: Andorra, Botswana, Brunei Darussalam, Djibouti, Indonesia, Iran, Kiribati, Liechtenstein, Malaysia, Oman, Pakistan, Qatar, Saudi Arabia, Singapore, Syria, and the United Arab Emirates [above n. 20]. And the CCPR Protocol: Guyana, and Trinidad and Tobago [above n. 24].

[129] The objecting States are: Belgium, Denmark, Finland, France, Germany, Italy, the Netherlands, Norway, Portugal, Spain, and Sweden. Above n. 18.

[130] The objecting States are: Finland, Germany, Italy, the Netherlands, Norway, and Sweden. Above n. 22.

[131] The objecting States are: Australia, Bulgaria, Canada, Denmark, Finland, France, Greece, Italy, Luxembourg, the Netherlands, New Zealand, Norway, Portugal, Spain, Sweden, Switzerland, and Turkey. Above n. 21.

[132] The objecting States are: Denmark, France, Germany, Ireland, Italy, the Netherlands, Norway, Spain, and Sweden. The timing and wording of the objections indicate a common stand of these States. For details, see above n. 24.

[133] This presumption is based on the fact that both the Caribbean States made similar reservations to the CCPR Protocol.

Africa) that have neither made any reservations nor objected to any reservations entered by other States parties to any of the treaties under discussion. Except for certain politically motivated objections to a few reservations to the CERD,[134] Asian and African States have never made any objection to any reservation to any human rights treaties under discussion.

This practice indicates the relative activism or passivity of the executive branch of different governments. It also indicates the different perceptions of States about their obligations under the UN human rights treaties. Most important, the common elements of objections indicate certain trends. First, the objecting States generally rely on the 'object and purpose' test to challenge the validity of reservations. Secondly, they hardly get the opportunity to reaffirm their objections. Thirdly, they rarely withdraw their objections. Fourthly, they want the reserving State to remain a party to the treaty despite their objections to reservations. Fifthly, they also want the reserving State to reconsider its reservations in due course. Finally, they expect the treaty monitoring body to formulate its opinion on reservations in the light of their objections. In sum, the objecting States expect some action against their targets.

Barring limited instances of objections, States usually accept, acquiesce in, or tolerate reservations. There are several reasons for this practice. First of all, States intend to encourage greater participation of their peers in the UN human rights treaty system. Then, they want to receive the benefits of reciprocal restraints. From the procedural angle, Article 20(5) of the Vienna Convention gives States a relatively short twelve-month period during which they may file objections to reservations. Because the operation of the classic rules on reservations is so inadequate for the UN human rights treaties, States generally do not see any legal interest in or need to object to reservations.[135] In fact, most State bureaucracies simply do not consider the matter to be important enough to respond. Finally, they know that an intolerant approach towards reservations may give rise to legal and political complications.[136] Hence the reluctance of States to raise objections to reservations is not

[134] Ethiopia, Mongolia, Pakistan, and Vietnam made those objections. See above n. 23.

[135] General Comment 24, above (n. 30), p. 47, para. 17. The first and foremost among all the classic rules relating to reservations is the unanimity rule. The emergence of the Communist States, the decolonization of Asia, Africa, and Latin America, the expansion of international society, the establishment and strengthening of regional human rights regimes, and growing economic and technological disparities have dealt a death blow to the unanimity rule. Secondly, States generally disagree about the rules of international law on reservations. Thirdly, the tradition of designating a person to act as depository has not ensured the uniformity of law and practice on reservations. Fourthly, the compatibility test of reservations is too subjective, uncertain and ineffective. Finally, the majority rule to determine the validity of reservations is hopelessly mechanical.

[136] A striking instance of the absence of protest to a reservation came to light when the HRC noticed that the French declaration relating to Article 27 of the CCPR amounted to stating that there was no notion of minority rights in France, and that no State party had objected to that declaration. Only Germany interprets the declaration as meaning that the Constitution of France already fully guarantees the individual rights protected by Article 27.

considered unreasonable. In any case, the pattern of objections and also that of their absence are not clear.

Whatever the reasons for the reluctance of States to object to reservations, the HRC believes that '[t]he absence of protest by States cannot imply that a reservation is either compatible or incompatible with the object and purpose of the Covenant [CCPR].'[137] On the other hand, States continue to recognize and emphasize the role of objections as regards the applicability of reservations.[138] As a matter of fact, protest remains the most powerful tool to challenge the validity of a reservation; at least, it raises doubts about the legitimacy of the impugned reservation; it helps the treaty body to focus its attention on the matter whenever the opportunity arises; and it prepares the ground for an inter-State communication if the procedure is applicable to the States parties concerned. The effect of objections to a reservation depends on a set of factors: the number of the objections; the substance of arguments in the objections; the coherence of the objections; the importance of the subject matter of the reservation/objections; the gravity of human rights restrictions arising out of the reservation; the willingness of the objecting States to reaffirm their objections on all available occasions; the credibility of the objecting States; the influence of the objections on civil society, international jurists, and human rights NGOs; and the competence of the treaty body to examine the incompatibility of the reservation. Western European States' objections to the reservations made by Trinidad and Tobago in respect of the CCPR Protocol demonstrate this point. Some reserving States themselves recognize the impact of objections.[139] Unwilling to attach any importance to objections, however, the HRC holds the view that 'it is open to question what effect objections have between States *inter se*'.[140] The other treaty bodies do not have a different opinion on this point.

The very fact that the ILC is seized of the issue of reservations once

[137] General Comment 24, above (n. 30), p. 47, para. 17.

[138] See, for example, statements of the United States, *Report of the Human Rights Committee*, GAOR, fiftieth session (1995), supplement no. 40, UN Doc. A/50/40, vol. I, p. 127 [hereinafter '*HRC 1995 Report I*'], the United Kingdom, ibid., p. 132 and France, *Report of the Human Rights Committee*, GAOR, fifty-first session (1996), supplement no. 40, UN Doc. A/51/40, vol. I, pp. 105–6 [hereinafter '*HRC 1996 Report I*'].

[139] For example, while replying to the questions asked about China's reservations to the CAT, the State representative said that several government departments were currently undertaking a comprehensive review of the issue, with particular attention to the views of the other States parties concerning reservations and the impact of reservations on the CAT Committee's work. UN Doc. CAT/C/SR.252/Add.1 (8 May 1996), para. 12. Similarly, in response to the objections regarding Iran's reservation to the CRC, there have been expert meetings in the Office for Women's Affairs of the Judiciary to compare the provisions of the Convention with domestic law. Also, the legal department of the Ministry of Foreign Affairs prepared a report, proposing that the reservation be amended and those articles of the CRC which are not going to be applied be specified. Although the reservation has so far not been withdrawn, the objections have forced the Government of Iran not to take the liberty of making a similar reservation to the CEDAW. See above n. 65.

[140] General Comment 24, above (n. 30), p. 47, para. 17.

the Vienna Declaration is certainly more than a declaration. If one reads the Convention in conjunction with the Declaration, it becomes clear that State objections are no longer considered the main tools of checking reservations; obligatory reassessment of reservations by the reserving States themselves is the new focus of attention. This goes well with the basic thrust of the concept of human rights that primary responsibility for the promotion and protection of human rights rests with the State concerned. Obviously, other States and international bodies can play a supportive role.

2. *Practice under Particular Treaties*

As soon as a human rights treaty body is faced with a reservation to its constituent instrument, its normal response is more or less negative. Generally, the response remains mute. Occasionally, however, the treaty body airs its views and worries. In this regard, the most opportune moment comes when the treaty body considers a matter involving a questionable reservation. At an advanced stage of the treaty practice, the treaty body may consolidate its views and concerns, reflecting important aspects of the treaty-related reservations in the form of a general comment on the subject. Since each treaty body has its own rules of procedure and practice, each one has developed its own body of law to deal with the reservations to its constituent instrument. Let us look at the practice of each body of law and then proceed towards a comparative evaluation.

(*a*) *CERD*

The CERD lays down three important rules on reservations. First, Article 20(2) gives expression to the advisory opinion of the ICJ in the *Reservations to the Genocide Convention* case and, accordingly, provides that a reservation should be compatible with the object and purpose of the CERD. Secondly, it improves upon the advisory opinion and, consequently, prohibits a reservation the effect of which would inhibit the operation of any of the bodies established by the Convention. Thirdly, it enunciates the implementation of these two rules with the help of a uniform procedure and, therefore, prescribes that a reservation shall be considered incompatible or inhibitive if at least two thirds of the States parties to the Convention object to it within ninety days. While the incompatibility of a reservation may be determined in view of the substantive obligations of the reserving State, the inhibitive character of a reservation may be ascertained if the reserving State intended to obstruct the functioning of the CERD bodies, namely, the Committee on the Elimination of Racial Discrimination (the CERD Committee) and the Ad hoc Conciliation Commission.[145] In this way, Article 20 seeks to preserve the integrity of both substantive and procedural obligations. The Convention does not mention anything about the role of its monitoring body in this regard. In other words, not the CERD Committee but the collegiate system of the States parties to the Convention controls the supervisory mechanism regarding reservations.

Being the first UN human rights treaty body, the CERD Committee confronted the question of reservations and attempted to check them. Once, it declared a reservation incompatible with the object and purpose of the CERD. This was an unprecedented decision, but the States parties to the CERD and the United Nations establishment were unable to approve it. Therefore, they raised questions about the legal effect of the decision. They asked the United Nations Secretariat to answer a set of questions regarding the role of the States parties and the competence of the Committee in reservation matters. The Secretariat prepared a Memorandum, containing answers to those questions, for use by all those who were involved in the matter. The Memorandum magnified the role of the States parties and restrained the Committee's freedom of action in reservation matters. It pointed out that the Committee was not a representative organ of the States parties; that the States parties alone had general competence with regard to the implementation of the Convention in general and the acceptance/rejection of reservations in particular; and that the Committee should take account of not only reservations but also the reserving State's statements of interpretation in considering the reports submitted by that State.[146] On the basis of the Memorandum, the Director of the UN Human Rights Division told the Committee that its decision in question had no legal effect. In fact, the Director was rather blunt: 'The Committee must take the reservations made by States parties at the time of ratification or accession into account: it has no authority to do otherwise. A decision—even a unanimous one—by the Committee that a reservation is unacceptable could not have any legal effect.'[147] Committee members took 'special note' of this clarification, and some of them expressed dissent on subsidiary issues.[148] But this retreat reopened an old issue: What can the Committee do with an unreasonable reservation? Nobody sought the ICJ's help in this regard. On the other hand, it attracted conflicting opinions. For instance, while José D. Inglés argued that the 'State party

[145] Antonio Cassese, 'A New Reservations Clause (Article 20 of the United Nations Convention on the Elimination of All Forms of Racial Discrimination)', in *Recueil d'etudes de droit international: en hommage a Paul Guggenheim* (Geneva, 1968), p. 269; Nathan Lerner, *The UN Convention on the Elimination of All Forms of Racial Discrimination* (The Hague, 1980), p. 96.

[146] See *United Nations Juridical Yearbook, 1976* (New York, 1978), p. 221.

[147] See *Report of the Committee on the Elimination of Racial Discrimination*, GAOR, thirty-third session (1978), supplement no. 18, UN Doc. A/33/18, p. 85.

[148] Ibid., pp. 85–6.

might be asked to withdraw its reservation,'[149] Theodor Meron argued that the Committee could make only an 'appeal'.[150] Little attention was paid to a number of options within the terms of the Memorandum. First, the Committee could study and discuss a reservation at the time of consideration of a report of the reserving State. At the end of this exercise, it could make some suggestions and incorporate them in its annual report to the UN General Assembly. Secondly, States parties could draw the attention of the Committee to the fact that the reserving State was not giving effect to the provisions of the Convention. During the course of its conciliation proceedings, the Committee could consider the ways and means to neutralize the negative effects of the reservation in question. In case of its failure to resolve the matter through an agreement between the States parties concerned, the Committee could prepare a report, including suggestions, and submit it to all the States parties. The result of ignoring these options was that the Committee focused on its limitation in reservation matters and, in the process, lost its enthusiasm to explore unconventional solutions.

However, a lot has happened since then. The Memorandum of 1976 has lost ground over the years and the CERD Committee has become active in reservation matters. In the course of the consideration of State reports, the Committee enquires about reservations and requests States to review, reduce and withdraw their reservations, irrespective of their compatibility with the object and purpose of the CERD.[151] Partly in response to the Committee's requests, as well as a consequence of State objections and self-correcting processes, some States have reviewed, reduced or even withdrawn their reservations.[152] Since the individual and inter-State complaints procedures of the Committee have played no

[149] See Note by the UN Secretary-General, *Study on the Implementation of Article 4 of the International Convention on the Elimination of All Forms of Racial Discrimination*, UN Doc. A/CONF.119/10 (18 May 1983), para. 224.

[150] Meron, *Human Rights Law-Making in the United Nations: A Critique of Instruments and Process* (Oxford, 1986), p. 49.

[151] For instance, in the course of the consideration of Italy's eighth and ninth periodic reports, the representatives of Italy said that a procedure for the withdrawal of Italy's reservations had been set in motion. *Report of the Committee on the Elimination of Racial Discrimination*, GAOR, fiftieth session (1995), supplement no. 18, UN Doc. A/50/18, para. 86. During the consideration of the ninth, tenth, and eleventh periodic reports of Romania, CERD Committee members asked whether the Government of Romania was considering withdrawing its reservations to Articles 17, 18 and 22 of the Convention. Ibid., para. 254. In its concluding observations on the initial report of Switzerland, the CERD Committee urged the State to reconsider the reservation made to Article 2(1)(*a*) of the Convention. *Report of the Committee on the Elimination of Racial Discrimination*, GAOR, fifty-third session (1998), supplement no. 18, UN Doc. A/53/18, para. 62. It repeatedly asked Nepal to avail itself of the possibility, under Article 20(3) of the Convention, to withdraw its reservations in order to ensure the full applicability of the provisions of Articles 4 and 6. Ibid., para. 435.

[152] See, e.g., Bulgaria, Byelorussia SSR, Czechoslovakia, Denmark, Egypt, Hungary, Mongolia, Tonga, Ukrainian SSR, USSR. Above n. 23.

role in reservation matters, the expert body has relied on the reporting procedure in such matters. Although there are many objections to certain reservations, particularly South Yemen's reservation concerning Article 5(*c*) and Article 5(*d*)(iv), (vi) and (vii) of the CERD,[153] the 'two-thirds' rule has never allowed any such reservation to be declared incompatible with the object and purpose of the Convention. Its ninety-day limit for States to raise objections makes it less useful than the Vienna Convention's provision that allows States to do so within one year. In spite of this disadvantage, States parties still enjoy the privilege to determine the compatibility of reservations with the object and purpose of the Convention. As a result, while 'the CERD [Committee] remains in the hands of the States parties',[154] reservations remain out of their effective control.

In her assessment of reservations, Liesbeth Lijnzaad points out that although the 'two-thirds' rule has been the most important element of the law on reservations in the CERD, it creates pseudo-objectivity, as all States parties to the Convention decide themselves about the compatibility of reservations and the final determination is mere arithmetic. She doubts the utility of the 'object and purpose' test on the ground that the obligations contained in the Convention are so diverse that it is difficult to establish which rules do or do not constitute the object and purpose of the Convention. She is disappointed with the role of the CERD Committee in reservation matters, because the expert body lacks institutional memory and its members maintain conflicting views on certain vital questions of reservations.[155] One could see conflicts coming out in the open when the Chairperson of the CERD Committee joined hands with his counterparts representing other UN human rights treaty bodies

[153] The People's Democratic Republic of Yemen (South Yemen) made the reservation to exclude its fundamental obligation to prohibit and eliminate racial discrimination in respect of the following rights: the right to participate in elections on the basis of universal and equal suffrage; the right to participate in the government as well as in the conduct of public affairs; the right to have equal access to public service; the right to marriage and choice of spouse; the right to inherit; and the right to freedom of opinion and expression. The objecting States (Australia, Belgium, Canada, Czechoslovakia, Denmark, Finland, France, Germany, Mexico, the Netherlands, New Zealand, Norway, Sweden, and the United Kingdom) considered the reservation incompatible with the object and purpose of the CERD and impermissible under its Article 20(2). Interestingly, the reservation has disappeared by virtue of the application of the 1990 unification agreement between North Yemen and South Yemen. The agreement lays down that, as concerns the treaties concluded prior to their union by two Yemens, the unified State is to be considered as a party to those treaties as from the date when one of these States first became a party to the treaties. Since North Yemen had acceded to the CERD without an Article 5 reservation and prior to accession by South Yemen, the reservation is no longer applicable. See *Multilateral Treaties Deposited with the Secretary-General: Status as at 31 December 1999* (New York, 2000), UN Doc. ST/LEG/SER.E/18, vol. I, pp. 11, 109–13 and 117.

[154] Susan Marks, 'Reservations Unhinged: The *Belilos* Case before the European Court of Human Rights', *International and Comparative Law Quarterly*, 39 (1990), p. 322 n. 59.

[155] Lijnzaad, *Reservations to UN-Human Rights Treaties: Ratify and Ruin?* (Dordrecht, 1995), pp. 174–84.

in their bold response to the challenge of reservations[156] while two members of the Committee pleaded for a restrained position on the subject.[157] Obviously, the Committee appears to be a divided house in crucial matters concerning reservations.

In a nutshell, the CERD *lex specialis* was extraordinary at its inception, in the sense that the Convention was the first human rights instrument to incorporate the essence of the *Reservations to the Genocide Convention* opinion and the CERD Committee was the first human rights body to declare a reservation incompatible with the object and purpose of the Convention. It became quite ordinary within a decade, as States entered unrestrained reservations that underlined their traditional timidity in accepting treaty obligations and the UN Legal Counsel expressed an opinion that restrained the CERD Committee's role in reservation matters. Ever since the Committee has joined the process of regular and greater interaction with its sister bodies,[158] which have been playing an increasingly assertive role in reservation matters, it has made some improvement in its practice relating to reservations. On the whole, however, the practice does not exhibit any significant innovation. Certainly, it is not commensurate with the importance of the obligation to eliminate racial discrimination in all its forms.

(*b*) *CCPR*

Unlike the CERD, the CCPR does not contain any provision on reservations. The development of a *lex specialis* to deal with reservations to the CCPR is an interesting example of modernity joining tradition, and the principal credit for this goes to the HRC, which is considered 'the universalist counterpart to regional organs' such as the European Court of Human Rights and the Inter-American Court of Human

[156] With reference to the seventh meeting of the chairpersons of the treaty bodies, held in September 1996, CERD Committee Chairperson Michael Banton wrote a letter to the Chairperson of the Sub-Commission on Prevention of Discrimination and Protection of Minorities (now the Sub-Commission on the Promotion and Protection of Human Rights) containing a proposal that a study be undertaken on reservations to treaties. UN Doc. E/CN.4/Sub.2/1997/31 (27 May 1997). The CERD Committee Chairperson emphasized that the Vienna regime did not concern itself specifically with problems associated with reservations to a human rights treaty. Besides other initiatives, his letter prompted the Sub-Commission to adopt a decision to undertake a study on reservations. See below n. 235.

[157] See Ion Diaconu and Yuri Rechtov, *Reservations to the International Convention on the Elimination of Racial Discrimination: The Role of the CERD*, UN Doc. CERD/C/53/Misc.23 (10 August 1998).

[158] The treaty bodies have an institutionalized form of interaction with the help of periodic meetings of their chairpersons. The chairpersons had met for the first time in 1984 and biennially from 1988 until 1994. As of 1995, they meet annually; in 1998, they met twice. These meetings were initiated primarily to exchange thoughts on the functioning of the treaty bodies, especially their reporting procedures. However, the scope of these meetings has gradually expanded. Now these meetings have assumed the form of a common policy forum of the treaty bodies, covering a wide range of issues, including reservations to human rights treaties and strategy to obtain sufficient resources and services to enable the treaty bodies to carry out their respective mandates efficiently.

Rights.[159] Since the HRC was conscious of its limited authority in reservation matters, it rarely went beyond a 'constructive dialogue' on the issue of reservations and avoided evaluation of the admissibility, compatibility or validity of reservations with the CCPR. It even turned down an Austrian request for an opinion or comments on the reservations made by that State.[160] It also decided against seeking an advisory opinion of the ICJ on the question of reservations.[161] A turning point came on 2 November 1994, when the HRC adopted General Comment 24 on issues relating to reservations to the CCPR and the Optional Protocols.[162] Among other things, the General Comment affirms the competence of the HRC in determining the compatibility of reservations with the object and purpose of the CCPR, customary rules and peremptory norms of international law. Within six months of the adoption of the General Comment, the HRC seized an opportunity to apply its guidelines to a specific set of reservations. At the end of the consideration of the initial report of the United States in the spring of 1995, the HRC declared that the US reservations to Articles 6(5) and 7 of the CCPR were incompatible with the object and purpose of the treaty.[163] This was nothing less than a revolution. It took a clear view on the power of a treaty body in reservation matters. It set a precedent for other treaty bodies.

Since then the HRC has continued to expand its role in reservation matters. As a result, it has developed a systematic procedure with regard to reservations. Its consolidated guidelines for State reports under Article 40 of the CCPR require that '[a]ny reservation to or declaration as to any article of the Covenant [CCPR] by the State party should be explained and its continued maintenance justified.'[164] Conversely, in case of withdrawal of a reservation, the HRC expects the State party to explain the reasons and effect of the withdrawal.[165] The lists of issues for the consideration of State reports, which constitute the bases of the HRC's discussions with State representatives, invariably include questions relating to reservations. During the consideration of State reports, members of the HRC may ask questions concerning the bases, causes,

[159] Editorial Preface by Ian Brownlie to Dominic McGoldrick, *The Human Rights Committee: Its Role in the Development of the International Covenant on Civil and Political Rights* (Oxford, 1991).

[160] The HRC forty-fifth session's Working Group on Article 40, headed by Vojin Dimitrijević, examined the issue and prepared a draft text for possible use by the treaty body. Eventually, however, the HRC decided not to provide any abstract opinion on the Austrian reservations. See UN Doc. CCPR/C/SR.1149 (5 August 1992), para. 22.

[161] UN Doc. CCPR/C/SR.1228 (12 May 1993), paras. 33, 38, 57 and 60.

[162] Above n. 30.

[163] *HRC 1995 Report I*, para. 279.

[164] UN Doc. CCPR/C/66/GUI/Rev.1 (1 November 1999), para. C.2.

[165] For instance, while welcoming the withdrawal by Austria of some of its reservations to the CCPR, the HRC observed that it would have been appreciated if the reasons for these withdrawals and the precise nature of their effect, as well as the reasons for the maintenance of the remaining reservations, had been more clearly explained. See *HRC 1999 Report I*, para. 181.

and implications of reservations. In its concluding comments on a report of the reserving State, the HRC may express concern or regret about the objectionable reservations; may treat the continued presence of those reservations as an impediment to the effective implementation of the CCPR, and may urge the reserving State to reconsider, reduce, or withdraw certain reservations.[166] Generally, however, the HRC refrains from declaring a reservation incompatible with the object and purpose of the CCPR. Its response to the French declaration concerning Article 27 of the CCPR,[167] which denies the existence of minorities in that country, illustrates this policy.[168] For example, the HRC merely asked France to review its Article 27 declaration, while it had already gone to the extent of pronouncing the US reservations to Articles 6(5) and 7 incompatible with the object and purpose of the CCPR. Evidently it invokes this ultimate power in exceptional cases only.

The catalytic effect of the movement against reservations is evident from the HRC's approach towards the Italian declaration with regard to Article 14(3)(*d*) of the CCPR, which entitles an accused person to have fair trial guarantees such as the right to be present at the time of his or her trial and to defend himself or herself through an effective legal representation. Italy, upon becoming a party to the CCPR, had made a declaration that '[t]he provisions of article 14, paragraph 3(*d*), are deemed to be compatible with existing Italian provisions governing trial of the accused in his presence and determining the cases in which the accused may present his own defence and those in which legal assistance is required.'[169] The scope of the declaration was a bone of contention in the *Iranian–Italian Truck Driver* case.[170] An Iranian citizen, who was tried *in absentia* in Italy and was not granted a retrial after his arrest, complained to the HRC that he was a victim of a violation of due process of law guarantees under Article 14. The HRC considered that the Italian

[166] For instance, the HRC urged Austria, Belgium, Denmark, France, Iceland, India, Italy, the Republic of Korea, Luxembourg, Malta, New Zealand, Norway, Sweden, Switzerland, the United Kingdom, and the United States to reconsider their reservations so as to withdraw as many as possible. See *HRC 1992 Report*, paras. 121, 430 and 518; *HRC 1993 Report I*, para. 145; *HRC 1994 Report I*, paras. 81, 96, 129 and 282; *HRC 1995 Report I*, paras. 190, 292 and 428; *HRC 1996 Report I*, para. 93; *HRC 1997 Report I*, paras. 66, 106, 414 and 429; *HRC 1998 Report I*, para. 339; *HRC 1999 Report I*, paras. 61 and 82.

[167] The French declaration reads as follows: 'In the light of article 2 of the Constitution of the French Republic, the French Government declares that article 27 is not applicable so far as the Republic is concerned.' See *Note on Reservations*, above (n. 18), p. 20.

[168] In the course of the consideration of the third periodic report of France in July 1997, the HRC found itself unable to agree that France was a country without minorities. It recalled that the mere fact that equal rights were granted to all individuals and all individuals were equal before the law did not exclude the existence in fact of minorities in a country and their entitlement to the enjoyment of their culture, the practice of their religion, or the use of their language in community with other members of their group. In the fitness of things, it recommended reconsideration of the said declaration. See *HRC 1997 Report I*, para. 411.

[169] *Note on Reservations*, above n. 18.

[170] *Sr Ali Maleki* v. *Italy*, Communication No. 699/1996, UN Doc. CCPR/C/66/D/699/1996 (27 July 1999), para. 6.5.

declaration only dealt with paragraph 3(*d*) of Article 14, and that the basic requirements of fair trial under paragraph 1 of this article must be maintained, even when a trial *in absentia* is not in itself in violation of the State party's undertakings. It recalled that a trial *in absentia* is compatible with Article 14 only when the accused was summoned in a timely manner and informed of the proceedings against him. It found that there was no evidence that this had happened in the instant case, and accordingly held that a violation of Article 14(1) had occurred.[171] This approach underlines the HRC's competence to circumvent a reservation even without determining its compatibility with the object and purpose of the CCPR.

Although the individual communication procedure under the CCPR Protocol makes considerable contribution to the development of jurisprudence on reservations, the reporting procedure under Article 40 of the CCPR remains the main vehicle for going into the details of reservation matters. The HRC does not attach much significance to State objections to reservations, turns down State requests for advisory opinions on reservations, and carries out constructive discussions with State representatives on various aspects of reservations. Invariably, it tries to convince States to review, reduce and withdraw their reservations, irrespective of their compatibility with the object and purpose of the CCPR. And it has succeeded in some cases.[172] Undoubtedly, reservations to the CCPR are governed by the most progressive body of law, much to the discomfort of States.

(*c*) *CCPR Protocol*

Like the CCPR, the CCPR Protocol contains no provision on reservations. Quite a few reservations to the Protocol have been challenged, tested and applied in the course of the consideration of a number of individual communications. Also, many cases under the Protocol have raised the issue of the validity of certain reservations to the CCPR. For a long time, the HRC evaded the issue and did not declare any of those reservations incompatible with the object and purpose of the CCPR or the Protocol. In fact, the jurisprudence of several cases restrained the HRC from addressing the issue of incompatibility. In the context of the French declaration concerning Article 27 of the CCPR, for instance, it did not evade the issue; it simply treated the declaration as a reservation by invoking Article 2(1)(*a*) of the Vienna Convention and merely admitted its incompetence to determine the incompatibility of the reservation-like declaration.[173] In her individual opinions, however,

[171] Ibid., paras. 9.4–10.

[172] The following States have withdrawn some of their reservations to the CCPR: Australia, Austria, Belarus, Belgium, Finland, France, Iceland, Ireland, Liechtenstein, the Netherlands, Norway, the Republic of Korea, Switzerland, and the United Kingdom. Above n. 18.

[173] Above n. 125.

Professor Rosalyn Higgins expressed the view that, although the CCPR did not itself make the distinction between reservations and declarations, the distinction between these concepts existed for the purpose of the treaty. She pointed out that the French instrument of ratification contained (*a*) reservations in relation to Articles 4(1), 9, 14 and 19 of the CCPR, and (*b*) a declaration concerning certain CCPR terms, such as 'minorities'. She argued that a declaration should not be transformed into a reservation. She therefore advocated a role for the HRC in determining whether an interpretation of a provision of the CCPR as given by a State party in its 'declaration' was compatible with the interpretation of that provision by the treaty body.[174] Matching the creativity of European jurisprudence,[175] this was an intelligent move to secure the rights of minorities through an international procedure and to carve out a role for the HRC in reservation matters. Yet, the HRC could not translate it into practice. In fact, in all the subsequent cases arising out of the French–Breton controversy, it deemed France's 'declaration' concerning Article 27 'tantamount to a reservation' and declined to address the scope of the 'declaration'.[176] In *Hervé Barzhig* v. *France*, in particular, it paid no attention to the complainant's argument that the French refusal to recognize the linguistic identity of the Breton minority and not to apply Article 27 violated both the UDHR (which is a part of customary international law) and the spirit of a resolution adopted by the European Parliament on 30 October 1987 (which emphasizes the need to protect European regional and minority languages and cultures).[177] In these cases Professor Higgins did not reaffirm her individual opinions, expressed earlier in the *Breton* cases. No doubt she felt that there was no point in expressing an individual opinion each time on the same issue.[178]

The case law of the HRC during its first twenty years demonstrated the extent of its reluctance to address the issue of incompatibility of reservations. In *Christopher Bethel* v. *Trinidad and Tobago*, for instance, the HRC refused to examine the complainant's allegation concerning the

[174] See *T.K.* v. *France*, above (n. 125), Appendix II, pp. 125–6; *M.K.* v. *France*, above (n. 125), Appendix II, pp. 133–4; *S.G.* v. *France*, above (n. 125), Appendix, p. 358; and *G.B.* v. *France*, above (n. 125), Appendix, p. 362.

[175] In *Belilos* v. *Switzerland,* the European Court reflected on a distinction between a 'reservation' and an 'interpretative declaration'. Also, the Court exercised its authority to determine the validity of a Swiss interpretative declaration, which was in fact construed as a reservation. See European Court of Human Rights, *Judgments and Decisions*, series A, 132 (1988), paras. 41–9 and 60.

[176] See, e.g., *Yves Cadoret and Hervé Le Bihan* v. *France*, Communication Nos. 221/1987 and 323/1988, *Report of the Human Rights Committee*, GAOR, forty-sixth session (1991), supplement no. 40, UN Doc. A/46/40, Annex XI A, p. 224, para. 5.3, including footnote [hereinafter '*HRC 1991 Report*']; *C.L.D.* v. *France*, Communication No. 439/1990, *HRC 1992 Report*, Annex X.X, p. 425, para. 4.3; *R.L.M.* v. *France*, Communication No. 363/1989, *HRC 1992 Report*, Annex X J, p. 370, para. 5.3.

[177] Communication No. 327/1988, *HRC 1991 Report*, Annex XI F, p. 263, para. 3.2.

[178] Professor Higgins expressed these views in an informal discussion with the author at the Palais des Nations, Geneva, in November 1992, when she was a member of the HRC.

legal effect of Trinidad and Tobago's denunciation of the CCPR Protocol and the State party's reaccession with a heavy reservation against the body's competence to deal with death penalty cases.[179] Even the joint individual opinion of Professors Fausto Pocar and Martin Scheinin concurred with the majority and merely reiterated the HRC's desire to deal with the issue of incompatibility and legal effect of the reservation 'in due course',[180] implying a 'wait and see' attitude. While the HRC and its members were extremely economical in their response to the issue of the incompatibility of Trinidad's reservation, certain international lawyers conducted an in-depth analysis of the reservation in order to check its adverse effects. In their joint opinion, Professors Crawford, Simma, and Szekely argued that a reservation may be considered impermissible (*a*) if it significantly impairs the competence of the HRC under the Protocol, (*b*) if it relates to fundamental, non-derogable rights under the CCPR, (*c*) if it curtails those rights which have the status of *jus cogens*, (*d*) if its breadth is too wide, and (*e*) if it constitutes an abuse of power by the reserving State.[181] Following these criteria, they expressed the opinion that Trinidad's reservation was incompatible not only with the object and purpose of the Protocol (as inferred from its preamble) but also Articles 1 and 2 (which establish a direct link between the CCPR and the Protocol). This opinion had little impact on the reserving State, but may have influenced the HRC. Barely a year later, the HRC changed its attitude and, in *Rawle Kennedy* v. *Trinidad and Tobago*, declared that the reservation in question was incompatible with the object and purpose of the Protocol.[182]

Apparently, the gravity of the subject matter heavily weighed against the incompatibility of the reservation. Unable to respect the HRC's verdict, Trinidad and Tobago decided to denounce the Protocol for the second time.[183] Paradoxically, the HRC could invalidate the reservation but not the denunciation. Its attempt to stress that the reservation/denunciation were not healthy signs prompted the Attorney-General of Trinidad and Tobago to state that the HRC should respect the decisions and the policies of his Government to maintain capital punishment and that, if the Committee was to criticize the country's Constitution, it

[179] Communication No. 830/1998, UN Doc. CCPR/C/65/D/830/1998 (30 April 1999), para. 8.2.

[180] Ibid.

[181] The Opinion, titled 'Trinidad and Tobago: Legal Effect of Denunciation of the Optional Protocol', was delivered on 5 December 1998 at the request of INTERIGHTS, a London-based nongovernmental organization. A copy is available with the author.

[182] Communication No. 845/1999, UN Doc. CCPR/C/67/D/845/1999 (31 December 1999).

[183] On 27 March 2000 the Government of Trinidad and Tobago notified the UN Secretary-General that it had decided to denounce the Optional Protocol for the second time with effect from 27 June 2000. For details, visit http://untreaty.un.org/ENGLISH/bible/englishinternetbible/partI/chapterIV/treaty6.asp.

should make a report which would be discussed by the Government.[184] This illustrates the need to address the root causes of the reservation/ denunciation. Also there is scope for diplomacy in support of the *lex specialis*.

In spite of its hostile reception on the part of Trinidad and Tobago, the decision in the *Kennedy* case underscores the HRC's bold response to grossly unreasonable reservations. It provides an impetus to the development of an increasingly assertive jurisprudence on reservations. Even where the HRC as a collective body does not use its individual communication procedure to pronounce on the incompatibility of a reservation with the object and purpose of the CCPR or the Protocol (and it only does so in extreme cases), its members may question the validity of a reservation through their individual opinions. These have the potential to become majority opinions of the treaty body itself; and, at least, they can initiate debate on an objectionable reservation. One may refer to the individual opinions of Bernhard Graefrath, Cecilia Médina Quiroga, Elizabeth Evatt, Fausto Pocar, Martin Scheinin, Maxwell Yalden, and Rosalyn Higgins in a range of cases.

The CCPR Protocol's *lex specialis* carries the distinction of being the only body of law concerning reservations that has been developed at the initiative of individuals. At the same time, the HRC seeks to maintain a judicious balance in functioning under its different procedures. If it generally acts like a judicial body under the Protocol, on the one side, it seeks to play a dynamic role under the CCPR, on the other, involving interaction and dialogue. In this way, it makes use of the CCPR Article 40 procedure to reinforce the CCPR Protocol procedure. There is no inhibition in extending this dynamic relationship to cover reservation matters as well. As a result, the HRC may adopt its concluding comments on the reserving State's report under Article 40, including a pronouncement that the reservation in question is not compatible with the object and purpose of the Protocol. In the process, the *lex specialis* may be strengthened.

(*d*) *CEDAW*

Article 28 of the CEDAW permits reservations which are compatible with the object and purpose of the instrument. However, there is no provision to help determine the object and purpose. Also, unlike the CERD, the CEDAW does not authorize its States parties to determine the compatibility of a reservation through a collegiate system of decision making. The UN Secretary-General, who acts as the depository of the instruments of accession to or ratification of the Convention, has the

[184] See the statement of Ramesh Lawrence Maharaj, the head of the delegation at the time of consideration of the third and fourth periodic reports of Trinidad and Tobago in the autumn of 2000, UN Press Release of 17 October 2000. Visit http://www.unhchr.ch/huricane/huricane.nsf/newsroom.

resources to perform the task of examining the compatibility but has no legal mandate to declare a reservation incompatible.[185] In case of a dispute between States regarding the interpretation and application of the Convention, including the question as to what constitutes its object and purpose, the matter may be referred to a dispute settlement mechanism under Article 29 of the Convention. However, this mechanism is itself not free from reservations and has not been used so far. Although a majority of States parties to the Convention made no reservation to the Convention, the reservations of others, especially those of the Islamic States, have been very controversial. The reservations relating to the legal status of women under religious law and religious practices concerning marriage and the family have captured the attention of critics.[186] Many Western countries objected to those reservations, and States parties to the Convention dealt with the matter in a rather controversial manner.

The Committee on the Elimination of Discrimination against Women (the CEDAW Committee) has been very uncomfortable with reservations to the CEDAW. Although the Office of Legal Affairs of the United Nations expressed the opinion that the functions of the Committee 'do not appear to include a determination of the incompatibility of reservations,'[187] that opinion has lost its influence after the emergence of the HRC-led jurisprudence on reservations. The CEDAW Committee has tried to search for, seize and maximize opportunities to address the issue of reservations. In its General Recommendation No. 4, adopted on 10 April 1987, the Committee expressed concern over the significant number of reservations that appeared to be incompatible with the object and purpose of the Convention. It supported the States parties in their move to consider reservations at their meeting in 1988, and to that end suggested that all States parties concerned should reconsider such reservations with a view to withdrawing them.[188] This recommendation and the following meeting of the States parties had little impact on the reserving States. Therefore, the Committee adopted another general comment on reservations in 1992, recommending that, in connection with preparations for the 1993 Vienna World Conference on Human Rights, States parties should:

(*a*) Raise the question of the validity and the legal effect of reservations

[185] By Resolution 598 (VI) of 12 January 1952, which approved the ICJ advisory opinion in the *Reservations to the Genocide Convention* case, the UN General Assembly directed the Secretary-General (*a*) to continue to act as depository of documents containing reservations or objections, without passing any judgment upon the legal effect of such documents, and (*b*) to communicate the text of such documents to all States concerned, leaving it to each State to draw legal consequences from such communications.

[186] See, for instance, Meron, above (n. 150), pp. 78–80.

[187] See *Report of the Committee on the Elimination of Discrimination against Women*, GAOR, thirty-ninth session (1984), supplement no. 45, UN Doc. A/39/45, vol. II, Annex III, pp. 55–6.

[188] *Compilation of General Comments*, above (n. 30), p. 118.

to the Convention in the context of reservations to other human rights treaties;

(*b*) Reconsider such reservations with a view to strengthening the implementation of all human rights treaties;

(*c*) Consider introducing a procedure on reservations to the Convention comparable with that of other human rights treaties.[189]

As noted earlier, the issue of reservations was successfully raised at the Vienna Conference and eventually culminated in the adoption of a set of recommendations.[190] Both States and human rights bodies are expected to follow the recommendations contained in the Vienna Declaration. In other words, the CEDAW Committee's initiative and its support by other human rights treaty bodies led to the further development of law relating to reservations.

Since the CEDAW does not envisage any complaints procedure, the CEDAW Committee seeks to monitor reservations and their impact on women's rights through its reporting procedure. According to the Committee's reporting guidelines, States parties that have entered general reservations which do not refer to a specific article of the Convention or reservations to Article 2 (the State party's duty to condemn and eliminate discrimination against women) and Article 3 (the State party's duty to take all appropriate measures to ensure the full development and advancement of women) should make a particular effort to report on the effect and the interpretation of those reservations. The Committee considers such reservations to be incompatible with the object and purpose of the Convention.[191] Like other UN human rights treaty bodies, the Committee conducts constructive dialogue with States parties regarding various aspects of their reservations. It commends those States which ratify the Convention without reservations.[192] It expresses its concern about reservations to the Convention, singles out those reservations which obstruct the full implementation of the Convention and urges States to reconsider, reduce, and withdraw their reservations.[193] In particular, it routinely expresses concern at the entry of reservations to Articles 2 and 16 (the State party's duty to eliminate discrimination against women in matters relating to marriage and family relations), because these two are considered the core of the Convention.

[189] General Recommendation No. 20, adopted on 30 January 1992, ibid., p. 134.

[190] Above n. 142 and the accompanying text.

[191] UN Doc. CEDAW/C/7/Rev.3 (26 July 1996).

[192] For example, the Committee commended the Government of South Africa for ratifying the Convention without reservations. See *Report of the Committee on the Elimination of Discrimination against Women (Eighteenth and Nineteenth Sessions)*, GAOR, fifty-third session (1998), supplement no. 38, UN Doc. A/53/38/Rev.1, para. 109 [hereinafter '*CEDAW 1998 Report*'].

[193] See, for instance, *Report of the Committee on the Elimination of Discrimination against Women*, GAOR, fiftieth session (1995), supplement no. 38, UN Doc. A/50/38, para. 596; *Report of the Committee on the Elimination of Discrimination against Women*, GAOR, fifty-fourth session (1999), supplement no. 38, UN Doc. A/54/38, paras. 67 and 69.

Since 1998, it has tried to ensure that the reserving States should withdraw or modify their reservations.[194] Most important, it maintains the view that cultural and religious values cannot be allowed to undermine the universality of women's rights. As a result of various efforts, including those led by the Committee, a number of States have withdrawn their reservations to the Convention[195] and the Optional Protocol to the Convention on the Elimination of All Forms of Discrimination against Women has been adopted with an express provision prohibiting reservations.[196] It shows growing intolerance towards reservations.

The CEDAW Committee clearly outshines the CERD Committee as concerns their comparative performance in reservation matters, but its law and practice on the subject is not as developed as that of the HRC. Of course, States parties to the CEDAW have been more active in reservation matters than their CCPR counterparts. The Optional Protocol to the Convention strengthens the anti-reservation posture of the CEDAW Committee, whereas the CCPR Protocol's silence on reservations reminds the HRC of its limitations in the matter.

(*e*) *CRC*

The most important statement of law regarding reservations to the CRC is found in its Article 51(2): 'A reservation incompatible with the object and purpose of the present Convention shall not be permitted.' This is merely a truncated version of Article 19 of the Vienna Convention. The CRC does not specify who will apply the 'object and purpose' test: whether States parties to the Convention, the Committee on the Rights of the Child (the CRC Committee), or both. Nor does it contain a dispute settlement clause. It is the most widely ratified treaty in the field of human rights, but has also been the target of almost 200 reservations. Many States have raised objections to those reservations, mostly on the ground of incompatibility with the object and purpose of

[194] This is the result of a report dated 28 June 1998, prepared by the Committee's working group concerning reservations to the CEDAW. See *CEDAW 1998 Report*, pp. 47–50.

[195] These States are: Bangladesh, Belarus, Brazil, Bulgaria, Canada, France, Hungary, Ireland, Jamaica, Liechtenstein, Malawi, Mongolia, New Zealand, Poland, the Republic of Korea, and Romania. Above n. 19.

[196] In support of the inclusion of Article 17 in the Optional Protocol, which prohibits reservations, a number of delegations noted that the Vienna Convention permitted such an article; that the inclusion of the article was consistent with existing international practice; and that the article would be appropriate for a modern international instrument designed for the twenty-first century. United Nations, *The Convention on the Elimination of All Forms of Racial Discrimination against Women: The Optional Protocol: Text and Materials* (New York, 2000), pp. 57–8. The UN General Assembly adopted the Protocol on 6 October 1999 and opened it for signature on Human Rights Day 1999. For the text of the Protocol, see Annex to General Assembly Resolution 54/4 of 6 October 1999. As of 12 October 2000, the Protocol had been signed by 62 States and ratified by eleven. For details, visit http://untreaty.un.org/ENGLISH/bible/englishinternetbible/partI/chapterIV/treaty11.asp. Pursuant to its Article 16(1), the Protocol came into force on 22 December 2000, i.e. three months after the deposit of the tenth instrument of ratification or accession. Now, the CEDAW Committee is able to entertain individual complainants, including those relating to the applicability of reservations to the provisions of the Convention.

the Convention. A few States, such as Kuwait and Myanmar, have withdrawn their reservations partly in response to those objections.

It is not easy for the CRC Committee to apply the 'object and purpose' test. With the help of its dynamic interpretation of the CRC, however, the Committee attempts to check reservations to the provisions of the instrument. According to the Committee, it has 'a decisive role to play in the assessment of the validity and impact of reservations made by States parties, and will continue to systematically raise this issue with States parties'.[197] The Committee has resolved (*a*) that it will continue to encourage the review of reservations by States parties, as well as their withdrawal with a view to achieving the highest level of implementation of the Convention, and (*b*) that it will consider adopting a general comment on the subject of reservations. It has stated that it will raise with States parties the compatibility of reservations with the object and purpose of the Convention, clarify the situations where a lack of compatibility exists and reservations may be invalid, and suggest specific steps to reverse such situations.[198] The Committee encourages the provision of technical assistance to help States parties in their effort to review reservations with a view to their withdrawal. It suggests that a detailed study be carried out on existing reservations, including on the experience of the Committee, follow up given to its recommendations for withdrawal, comparison with reservations entered by the same States parties to other human rights treaties, and potential implications of the alternative approaches the expert body could adopt.[199]

In sum, while the text of the CRC is barely concerned with reservations to its provisions, its monitoring body has a comprehensive plan to develop its law on the subject. The importance of the plan is not in doubt, as a leading expert emphasizes that 'the issue of reservations to the Convention on the Rights of the Child has wider ramifications than the Convention regime itself'.[200] At present, it seems premature to assess whether the CRC Committee will be able to develop its work effectively to meet the challenge of reservations.

(*f*) *CAT*

Although the right to freedom from torture is a non-derogable right, as well as a peremptory norm of general international law, the CAT has two permissive provisions on reservations. First, according to Article 28 of the Convention, States may make a reservation to Article 20 of the

[197] See Office of the High Commissioner for Human Rights/Committee on the Rights of the Child, 'Tenth Anniversary of the Convention on the Rights of the Child Commemorative Meeting: Achievements and Challenges', Palais des Nations, Geneva, 30 September–1 October 1999. For the electronic version of this report, visit http://www.unhchr.ch/html/menu2/6/10than.htm.

[198] Ibid.

[199] Ibid.

[200] Geraldine Van Bueren, *The International Law on the Rights of the Child* (Dordrecht, 1995), p. 397.

Convention, which embodies the confidential inquiry procedure of the Committee against Torture (the CAT Committee). Secondly, States may enter a reservation to Article 30(1) of the Convention, which embodies the dispute settlement mechanism, consisting of an alternative method, namely, a court of arbitration or the ICJ. Since the Convention does not state that its remaining provisions are free from reservations, a number of States exploited this ambiguity and entered reservations to the substantive provisions of the instrument. Under the Pinochet regime, for instance, Chile became a party to the Convention with reservations to Articles 1 (definition of the term 'torture') and 2(3) (non-applicability of the 'superior order' defence).[201] This was an attempt to secure impunity for the perpetrators of torture in Chile. Obviously, the Article 2(3) reservation was rigorously opposed by a number of States, closely examined by the Committee and eventually withdrawn by the post-Pinochet regime.

One can draw some useful inferences from the law and practice concerning reservations to the CAT. First, the Convention is ambiguous about the scope of reservations. The practice of the CAT Committee does not help achieve any clarity in this regard. No State has so far invoked the dispute settlement clause to clarify the scope of reservations. State practice follows a maximalist approach, whereby no provision of the Convention is immune from reservations. Neither the individual communication procedure nor the inter-State communication procedure of the Committee has been used to challenge the validity of any reservation. The Committee has made use of its reporting procedure to scrutinize reservations, to seek information on the implications of reservations, and to impress upon States to reconsider, reduce or withdraw reservations.[202] Yet, its impact has been minimal. Although a number of States have withdrawn their reservations,[203] the Committee can hardly claim credit for that; arguably, the credit goes to State objections and change of hearts by the reserving States themselves. As a result, the CAT *lex specialis* on reservations does not match the importance of the subject matter. There is a slow but steady improvement in the Committee's procedures, which may eventually reflect on the body's competence to deal with reservation matters. As a result, one may expect improvement in the *lex specialis* as well.

[201] For the text of reservations, above n. 21.

[202] See, for instance, the CAT Committee's comments on the reports of the Republic of Korea [*Report of the Committee against Torture*, GAOR, fifty-second session (1997), supplement no. 44, UN Doc. A/52/44, para. 69], Ukraine [ibid., para. 148], Israel [*Report of the Committee against Torture*, GAOR, fifty-third session (1998), supplement no. 44, UN Doc. A/53/44, para. 240] and Kuwait [ibid., para. 228].

[203] The following States have withdrawn their reservations: Belarus, Bulgaria, Chile, the Czech Republic, Guatemala, Hungary, the Russian Federation, Slovakia, Tunisia, and Ukraine. Above n. 21.

(*g*) *CESCR*

Like the CCPR and the CCPR Protocol, the CESCR is silent on the question of reservations. Unlike most of the human rights treaties of the United Nations system, however, the CESCR is constructed on a unique philosophy: it is expected to be implemented progressively, not immediately. In that sense, some measure of reservation is inherent in the CESCR's provisions, since States can take the measures best suited to their domestic conditions. This flexibility reflects on the applicable *lex specialis*. Unlike other human rights monitoring bodies of the United Nations system, the Committee on Economic, Social and Cultural Rights (the CESCR Committee) has not been very active in reservation matters. The main reason is that the foundations of the Committee are not as strong as those of its sister bodies.[204] The Committee is conscious that the implementation of the CESCR is a progressive phenomenon, implying considerable scope for both declared and undeclared reservations. As a result, it has not gone beyond (*a*) appreciating those States which have not attached any reservations to the CESCR,[205] (*b*) expressing hope that the reserving States will withdraw their reservations,[206] and (*c*) giving moral support to its sister bodies in their struggle against reservations.[207] The Committee is conspicuous by its economy of expression on the question of reservations. Members of the Committee have paid 'little attention to the complexities of the issues involved',[208] implying that reservations are not a matter of serious concern there. During the process of drafting an optional protocol to the CESCR, Committee members discussed various aspects of reservations without any agreement on the crucial aspects of the subject.[209]

(*h*) *Overview*

It is clear from the preceding analysis that there is much variation in law and practice from one human rights treaty to another. Although the

[204] In strict legal terms, the CESCR Committee is not a monitoring body of the CESCR. In 1987 ECOSOC created the Committee, implying that the latter is a subsidiary organ of the former. Since its inception, however, the Committee generally acts as an independent body. Like other UN human rights expert bodies, the Committee provides in its rules of procedure that, before assuming his or her duties, each member of the Committee shall make the solemn declaration to discharge his or her duties as a member of the body impartially and conscientiously. See UN Doc. E/C.12/1990/4/Rev.1 (1 September 1993).

[205] See, for instance, the Committee's concluding observations on the initial report of Zimbabwe on Articles 1 to 15 of the CESCR, in *Committee on Economic, Social and Cultural Rights: Report on the Sixteenth and Seventeenth Sessions (28 April–16 May 1997, 17 November–5 December 1997)*, ESCOR, 1998, supplement no. 2, UN Doc. E/1998/22, para. 67.

[206] See, for example, the Committee's concluding observations on the initial report of New Zealand, Tokelau and Niue on Articles 1 to 15 of the CESCR, in UN Doc. E/C.12/1993/13 (4 January 1994), para. 22.

[207] See below n. 245.

[208] Matthew C.R. Craven, *The International Covenant on Economic, Social, and Cultural Rights: A Perspective on its Development* (Oxford, 1995), p. 214.

[209] UN Doc. E/C.12/1996/SR.49 (13 December 1996).

UN human rights treaty bodies have not yet gone to the extent of the HRC, most are increasingly assertive in reservation matters. Despite the autonomy of the law and practice of each one of the treaty bodies, there is at least one common feature of the laws developed by them: constructive discussions with the reserving States regarding reservations, irrespective of their compatibility with the object and purpose of the respective treaties. In the course of the consideration of State reports, the treaty bodies discuss with the representatives of the reserving States a variety of questions and seek additional information on the reservations entered by them. Invariably, States respond to the questions and requests by providing explanations and information. This exercise enables the treaty bodies to have a better understanding of the causes and consequences of reservations. Finally, in their concluding comments on State reports, the treaty bodies draw attention to objectionable reservations and recommend their review, reduction, or withdrawal. In this way, the treaty bodies use a series of tools and techniques to tackle the problem of reservations and the thrust of their efforts is to introduce flexibility in their mandates.

Not all the UN human rights treaty bodies have been equally effective in persuading States to review, reduce, or withdraw their reservations. Apparently, the CEDAW Committee and the HRC have a reasonable record in this regard. The CAT Committee and the CRC Committee are far behind. The CERD Committee lacks the confidence to claim any credit for the withdrawal of any reservation. And the CESCR Committee has little in its docket. Overall, while their cumulative effect on reservations as such may have been limited, the treaty bodies have had a considerable impact on the debate on the subject.

3. *Practice in Municipal Courts*

The question of interpretation, application, and implementation of UN human rights treaties is increasingly raised in the municipal courts of many States. Although the question of reservations has not been frequently raised before municipal courts, one can see the possibility of these courts confronting such questions on some occasions. For instance, a US reservation to a human rights treaty is expected to be compatible not only with the object and purpose of that treaty but also with US domestic law in general and the US Constitution in particular. Since customary international law is part of US domestic law, it is arguable that the reservation must be compatible with the applicable customary law as well. Whether the reservation is compatible with the applicable law, domestic or international, may thus be justiciable before US courts, at least where the treaty provision is self-executing. Unhappy with the US practice of attaching excessive reservations to human rights treaties, Henkin makes a passionate plea: 'Lawyers in the United States should take arms against the anticonstitutional practice of declaring human rights conventions non-self-executing.'[210] Although there is no case questioning the validity of a reservation before US courts so far,[211] the possibility of such challenges remains, both in the United States and elsewhere.

The importance of the involvement of municipal courts in reservation matters becomes clear from decisions in a few cases. In *Elisabeth* v. *Council of State of Thurgao Canton*,[212] for example, the Federal Court of Switzerland had to decide on the validity of the revised 'interpretative declaration',[213] which had been made by the Swiss Government in the aftermath of the European Court's decision in the *Belilos* case.[214] On 17 December 1992 the Federal Court held that the revised declaration was invalid because it was a new reservation that was incompatible with Article 64(1) of the European Convention,[215] which was itself part of Swiss domestic law.[216] Eventually the Government withdrew its reservations/declarations with regard to Article 6 of the European Convention and notified the Council of Europe of this decision on 24 August 2000.[217] This was a late but appropriate response to the *Elisabeth* case. In his fifth report on reservations to treaties, the ILC Special Rapporteur on the subject advanced the view that 'the judgement of the Swiss Federal Court should certainly be regarded as a reaffirmation of the prohibition in principle on reservations formulated following the definitive expression of consent to be bound and also, perhaps, of the impossibility of formulating a new reservation in the guise of an interpretation of an existing reservation.'[218] More important, he tacitly acknowledged the legitimacy and significance of domestic remedies against questionable reservations.

[210] Above n. 32, p. 349.

[211] The author gratefully acknowledges the help of Professor Henkin on this point.

[212] 118 Ia 473 (1992). For a German summary, see *Europäische Grundrecht Zeitschrift*, 20 (1993), p. 72.

[213] The 1988 declaration concerning Article 6(1) of the European Convention, which recognized the right to public hearings in proceedings relating to the determination of civil rights and obligations or of any criminal charge, added a number of clarifications to the 1974 declaration. For their texts, visit http://conventions.coe.int.

[214] The *Belilos* case concerned only the criminal law aspect of the 1974 Swiss declaration, which was declared invalid by the European Court because the Swiss Government had not given any details of the laws in question. Above n. 175. Afterwards, in 1988, the Government sent the Council of Europe a long list of all the relevant laws in order to 'revive' the interpretative declaration. It seems that this way of proceeding was not considered to be correct by the Federal Court in the *Elisabeth* case. See above n. 212.

[215] Following the entry into force of Protocol 11 to the European Convention on 1 October 1994, former Article 64(1) has become Article 57(1), reading as follows: 'Any State may, when signing this Convention or when depositing its instrument of ratification, make a reservation in respect of any particular provision of the Convention to the extent that any law then in force in its territory is not in conformity with the provision. Reservations of a general character shall not be permitted under this article.' Visit http://www.coe.fr/eng/legaltxt/5e.htm.

[216] See above n. 212.

[217] Visit http://conventions.coe.int.

[218] UN Doc. A/CN.4/508/Add.3 (23 June 2000), para. 282.

The jurisprudence of the Supreme Court of India also highlights the importance of the 'domestic law' test of reservations. It admits the possibility of using domestic legal procedures to test the validity of reservations which affect fundamental rights under the Constitution of India. In *D.K. Basu* v. *State of West Bengal*, for instance, the Supreme Court observed on 18 December 1996: 'Of course, the Government of India at the time of its ratification (of ICCPR) in 1979 had made a specific reservation to the effect that the Indian legal system does not recognize a right to compensation for victims of unlawful arrest or detention and thus did not become a party to the Covenant [in that respect]. That reservation, however, has lost its relevance in view of the law laid down by this Court in a number of cases awarding compensation for the infringement of the fundamental right to life of a citizen.'[219] Thus, the Supreme Court found the reservation redundant at the domestic level. Also, it upheld the validity of certain remedial measures, which it would probably not have done if it were guided by the policy underlying the reservation. Since then, a number of judicial and quasi-judicial bodies in India have awarded compensation in cases of custodial death and torture.

On the other hand there have been few attempts to test the validity of reservations at the domestic level, and municipal courts are generally reluctant to examine such matters. In most democratic States, the relationship between domestic law and international law is still governed by the classic rules; the doctrine of the separation of powers is well entrenched; and judicial restraint in the face of executive decisions in the field of treaty-making is considered a virtue. As a Japanese commentator points out, 'Even if a treaty has been ratified, if it is accompanied by a reservation it cannot be used before the courts.'[220] The Tokyo High Court's judgment of 15 November 1998 illustrates this limitation.[221] Even in a country like the United States, where the judiciary is the ultimate arbiter in legal disputes, judicial enforcement of human rights has not flourished and judicial scrutiny of unconstitutional reservations has not taken place.[222] Perhaps it is the result of a benign neglect of international law by domestic lawyers, as well as a tendency to adopt a convenient litigation strategy by relying on the US Constitution and its legislative superstructure. Also, there is an intense culture of rights in the

[219] AIR 1997 SC 610, at p. 624. In respect of the right to compensation under Article 9(5) of the CCPR, the Supreme Court cited the *Basu* case with approval in *People's Union for Civil Liberties* v. *Union of India*, AIR 1997 SC 1203, at p. 1206.

[220] Yuji Iwasawa, *International Law, Human Rights and Japanese Law: The Impact of International Law on Japanese Law* (Oxford, 1998), p. 37.

[221] The Court confirmed that the right to strike provided in Article 8(1) of the CESCR does not apply to workers in Japan because Japan has made a reservation to that clause. Ibid.

[222] Henkin, 'International Human Rights Standards in National Law: The Jurisprudence of the United States', in Benedetto Conforti and Francesco Francioni (eds.), *Enforcing International Human Rights in Domestic Courts* (The Hague, 1997), p. 192.

United States though it is almost entirely a domestic one. The US Courts consider that there is no room for the application of international human rights, and they are supported in this by reservations of various kinds especially as to the non-self-executing character of the treaties. In any case, however, it is not an unbreakable trend.

As a matter of principle, domestic procedures may be utilized to challenge the validity of objectionable reservations at least in those States which have healthy traditions of judicial activism, public interest litigation, open debate and discussion, and readiness to rely on the UN human rights treaties. Even if one gets around the technical problems of this proposition,[223] these conditions do not exist in the majority of the leading reserving States; the States having those conditions generally review, reconsider, or withdraw their reservations without any judicial intervention; and a municipal court's decision against a reservation may not result in the withdrawal of the impugned reservation.[224] Still, the main advantage of the domestic approach is that various forums are available for the scrutiny of reservations in view of their nexus with domestic conditions. On the other hand, the chief disadvantage is that the active domestic procedures may create an uneven pattern of accountability in respect of treaty obligations in general and reservations in particular, and that different decisions of different forums may produce confusion on some occasions. At best, the domestic approach may supplement the international approach in some cases.

4. *Emerging Law*

In a sense, all the responses to reservations beyond the provisions of the Vienna Convention and the UN human rights treaties are no more than fragmented elements of *lex ferenda*. Certain practices of the leading bodies of the UN human rights treaty system, which have become part of their *lex specialis*, are still *lex ferenda* for the remaining bodies. Even if the increasing assertiveness of the treaty bodies goes unchallenged, mainly because of the indifference of a majority of States, the controversial elements of *lex specialis* remain part of *lex ferenda*. The main elements may be summarized here. First, the treaty bodies have the competence to

[223] There is however a problem: if the State concerned has made a reservation, even if arguably impermissible, how is the broader treaty rule (the subject of the reservation) part of the local law so as to be justiciable? Municipal courts do not normally consider it their function to criticise the foreign policy of the forum. One possibility would be to argue that national ratification operated, as it were, to bring the whole treaty into national law if the reservation was internationally impermissible. However, even in respect of internationally permissible reservations, the tenability of this argument would depend on the nature of a particular national legal system in view.

[224] For instance, while the Swiss Federal Court's decision of 17 December 1992 in the *Elisabeth* case led to the withdrawal of Switzerland's reservation to Article 6 of the European Convention only on 3 July 2000, the Indian Supreme Court's decision in the *Basu* case has not yet led to the withdrawal of India's reservation to Article 9 of the CCPR.

determine the incompatibility of a reservation with the object and purpose of their respective constituent instruments. Secondly, while the compatibility of a reservation with the object and purpose of the treaty concerned is the minimum requirement of its legitimacy, the validity of that reservation may be tested on the larger anvil of law and policy. Thirdly, the treaty bodies have a right to ask the reserving States to modify or withdraw their reservations. Finally, the treaty bodies can take follow-up action to monitor implementation of their recommendations regarding reservations. These elements are part of *lex ferenda*, not because their merits are debatable in terms of the underlying human values, but because of their fragile legal basis. As for the legal recognition of these elements, a drawback is that the States parties to the human rights treaties under discussion have so far had inadequate opportunities to exchange views on the merits and demerits of *lex ferenda*.

The most constructive and provocative aspect of *lex ferenda* is that, in effect, it seeks to expand the compatibility/validity test of reservations. It is based on the premise that the normal 'object and purpose' test is not adequate or clear. It has gained currency in the field of human rights by virtue of some thought-provoking expert opinions, judicial pronouncements, and treaty practices. Accordingly, the validity of a reservation depends on its conformity with (*a*) the object, purpose, and crucial provisions of the treaty concerned, (*b*) customary international law, (*c*) peremptory norms of international law, (*d*) the institutional effectiveness of the treaty body, and (*e*) the applicable domestic law. It is appropriate to deal with each in turn.

First, it has not always been easy to identify the object and purpose of a treaty. But even if it were, the object and purpose alone cannot always help determine the validity of a reservation. In such circumstances, a teleological interpretation of the treaty becomes necessary. For example in their joint opinion, noted earlier, Crawford, Simma, and Szekely seek to emphasize that the validity of Trinidad and Tobago's reservation to the CCPR Protocol should be determined with reference to the preambular paragraph (which states the object and purpose) and Articles 1 and 2 of the Protocol (which state the scope of protection) and the target provisions of the CCPR (which guarantee the human rights at stake).[225]

Secondly, it is possible that a reservation may not defeat the object and purpose of a treaty as such but may still threaten some norms of customary international law. The reserving State is not entitled to violate customary international law by making a reservation to a treaty; the truncated treaty obligations of the reserving State cannot undo its obligations under customary international law; and the reserving State should not do indirectly what it cannot do directly. That is why the

[225] Above n. 181, p. 1.

reservation must meet both the compatibility test and the customary law test. The HRC, among others, presents this vision in its general comment on reservations.[226]

Thirdly, no State is free under any circumstances to play with peremptory norms of international law. This is necessary to maintain the minimum morality of international law. Some human rights have become peremptory norms of international law,[227] and any reservation against them cannot be justified even if it conforms to the compatibility test. The HRC general comment on reservations[228] reaffirms the significance of *jus cogens* in this respect.[229]

Fourthly, if a treaty contains both substantive and procedural obligations and also creates a body to monitor their implementation, a reservation to one set of obligations cannot be evaluated in isolation from its effect on the other. At stake are not only the state of compliance with the obligations but also the fate of the treaty body: no reservation should be allowed radically to impair the functioning and effectiveness of the treaty body. Accordingly, the validity of a reservation to a treaty depends on the following: whether the treaty monitoring body remains in charge of its authority to decide upon the proper interpretation of the reservation; whether the reservation leads to a sweeping curtailment of the obligations of the reserving State; and whether a coherent and plausible explanation for the reservation is possible.[230] The effectiveness test signifies the restrictive interpretation of reservations, the liberal application of the authority of the treaty body and the exhibition of good faith on the part of the reserving State.

Finally, since human rights treaty provisions are generally incorporated into domestic law and implemented at the domestic level, it is necessary to be sensitive to the applicable domestic law and practice in respect of reservations. As has been seen, a large number of States base their reservations on their domestic law constraints. If those constraints

[226] According to the HRC, a State may not reserve the right to engage in slavery, to torture, to subject persons to cruel, inhuman or degrading treatment or punishment, to arbitrarily deprive persons of their lives, to arbitrarily arrest and detain persons, to deny freedom of thought, conscience, and religion, to presume a person guilty unless he proves his innocence, to execute pregnant women or children, to permit the advocacy of national, racial, or religious hatred, to deny to persons of marriageable age the right to marry, or to deny to minorities the right to enjoy their own culture, profess their own religion, or use their own language. And while reservations to particular clauses of Article 14 of the CCPR may be acceptable, a general reservation to the right to a fair trial would not be. See above n. 30, p. 44, para. 8.

[227] Crawford, Simma and Szekely assert that the hard-core of non-derogable human rights have the status of *jus cogens*. See above n. 181, para. 17. See also above n. 226.

[228] Above n. 226.

[229] Several experts argue on the same lines. See, for example, Note by the UN Secretary-General, *Effective Implementation of International Instruments on Human Rights,* UN Doc. A/44/668 (8 November 1989), p. 35, para. 82; the joint opinion of Crawford, Simma and Szekely, above n. 181, para. 17.

[230] On the basis of this test, Crawford, Simma, and Szekely doubt the validity of Trinidad's reservation to Article 1 of the CCPR Protocol. See above n. 181, para. 16.

no longer exist, the reserving States may be expected to withdraw their reservations; their continuation in such circumstances would contradict the principle of good faith.

The UN human rights treaty bodies assume that they have implied powers in reservation matters as well. On the basis of this assumption, they are seeking to expand the *lex ferenda*. In this regard, they are guided by their strong commitment to the cause of human rights, a liberal understanding of their mandates and by far-reaching recommendations of the meetings of their chairpersons.[231] The chairpersons have suggested, among other things, that if reservations give rise to significant questions in terms of their apparent incompatibility with the object and purpose of a treaty, the treaty body may consider requesting ECOSOC or the UN General Assembly to seek an advisory opinion on the issue from the ICJ.[232] The joint policy statements of persons chairing the treaty bodies generally ignore the distinction between what their law is and what it ought to be. This benign neglect is considered a sign of progress in the direction of the *lex ferenda*. The General Assembly has never questioned the wisdom of recommendations made by the chairpersons,[233] the ILC Special Rapporteur on the issue of reservations has taken cognizance of them,[234] and the Sub-Commission on the Promotion and Protection of Human Rights has appointed a special rapporteur with the task of preparing a comprehensive study (presumably including suggestions and recommendations) on reservations to human rights treaties.[235] All these developments may accelerate the growth of *lex ferenda* on the subject. Also, taking a clue from the HRC, some other treaty bodies (particularly the CAT Committee, the CEDAW Committee, and the CRC Committee) may attempt to question the validity of the most objectionable reservations to their respective constituent instruments. The treaty bodies may argue that, irrespective of their mandates to determine the compatibility of a reservation, they have an inherent right (*a*) to assess the impact of that reservation on the rights recognized

[231] For the background of the chairpersons' meetings, see above n. 158.

[232] *Report of the Fourth Meeting of Persons Chairing the Human Rights Treaty Bodies*, in Note by the UN Secretary-General, *Human Rights Questions: Implementation of Human Rights Instruments*, UN Doc. A/47/628 (10 November 1992), pp. 17–18, paras. 61–64.

[233] See, for example, General Assembly Resolution 52/116 of 12 December 1997, paras. 8 and 9.

[234] *Second Report on Reservations to Treaties by Alain Pellet, Special Rapporteur*, UN Doc. A/CN.4/477/Add.1 (13 June 1996), pp. 6, 27, 63–4, 67, 73, 79 and 83.

[235] By its decision 1998/113 of 26 August 1998, the Sub-Commission had requested Françoise Jane Hampson (an expert from the United Kingdom) to prepare a working paper on reservations to human rights treaties. In 1999 Hampson submitted the working paper (above n. 25). The Sub-Commission endorsed the conclusions contained in the paper, including one with regard to the importance of undertaking a full study on reservations to human rights treaties, and requested Hampson to submit a preliminary report to the Sub-Commission at its fifty-second session (2000), a progress report at its fifty-third session (2001) and a final report at its fifty-fourth session (2002). In its resolution (E/CN.4/Sub.2/RES/2000/26), the Sub-Commission decided to appoint Hampson as Special Rapporteur with the task of preparing the proposed study.

in their respective constituent instruments and (*b*) to express their views as to whether the reservation affects their functioning and effectiveness. This line of argument may help reduce the depth of disagreement on the competence of the treaty bodies in reservation matters.

In their pursuit of *lex ferenda*, the UN human rights treaty bodies have received considerable support from various activists, NGOs, and commentators on the subject. Some of them have suggested the urgent reassessment not only of the Vienna regime but also of the treaty regimes.[236] A constant questioning and constructive criticism of a reservation can make it controversial, thus raising doubts about its political legitimacy at least. This process may lead to the use of the inter-State communication procedure on the ground that the reservation in question was incompatible with the object and purpose of the treaty concerned. However, not all the human rights treaties under discussion have the inter-State communication procedure; no State has invoked it so far; and the optional nature of the procedure remains an impediment.

Most proposals for reassessment of the UN human rights treaty regimes on reservations relate to the CCPR and the CEDAW.[237] According to a British commentator, for instance, 'Amendment of the Covenant [CCPR] to enshrine severance as the inevitable legal consequence of formulating an incompatible reservation, and the competence of the Committee [HRC] to determine compatibility, would provide welcome certainty.'[238] Recognizing that 'the Covenant provides a fairly typical—and cumbersome—amendment procedure', the commentator floats the idea of 'circumventing these procedures' through a separate agreement supplementing the CCPR, a new collegiate system of States parties, residual rules of the Vienna Convention on the question of reservations, and extended functions of the UN Secretary-General who acts as the depository of the instruments of accession or ratification of the CCPR.[239] This scheme, inspired by European jurisprudence, seeks to introduce changes in several directions. Like other reform proposals,[240] it is too ambitious and has no chance of adoption.

[236] For instance, an American commentator argues that the time has come to rethink the flexible system that governs treaty formation. In order to preserve the integrity of human rights treaties, in particular, he proposes that the most effective approach would be to replace the tacit consent rule with a procedure that would require every State party to a treaty to respond in a set fashion to each of a ratifying party's reservations. He suggests a voting system whereby a reservation will be deemed incompatible with the treaty's object and purpose if two thirds of the States so vote. Sherman, above (n. 87), pp. 92–3. This suggestion seems wildly implausible, but its objective is laudable. By forcing States parties to react to reservations, it is less likely that incompatible reservations will be overlooked.

[237] Catherine J. Redgwell, 'Reservations to Treaties and Human Rights Committee General Comment No. 24 (52)', *International and Comparative Law Quarterly*, 46 (1997), p. 409.

[238] Ibid.

[239] Ibid., pp. 409–11.

[240] See above n. 236.

Most of the attempts to create *lex ferenda* underestimate the depth of disagreement on issues relating to reservations. Governments believe that, instead of introducing any major change in reservation regimes, the UN human rights treaty bodies should try to deal with the problem of reservations through their traditional procedures.[241] In essence, therefore, States like the *lex generalis* on reservations. On the other hand, the treaty bodies prefer their independent practices under their respective regimes and few favour municipal law analogies. These competing preferences for different responses to reservations ensure a lack of coordination, implying a slim chance of success in developing a common, acceptable and effective regime of reservations. The lack of coordination is not merely a matter of administrative inefficiency in the international legal system; it is a result of international conflicts, old and new.

VII. Layers of Conflict

Reservations reflect differences. They represent diverse socio-economic conditions, multiple moral standards, complex legal notions, competing national interests, and other anomalies at both domestic and international levels. Invariably, it is difficult to develop consensus among nearly two hundred States in respect of sensitive matters, quite apart from problems of internal dissensus in the political organs of each ratifying State. Each legal system is built and sustained on the basis of accommodation of common and many conflicting interests. Reservations underline difficulties while accommodating some conflicting interests. Even contemporary responses to reservations have created conflicts in the process of resolving others. Hence, one can detect several layers of conflict, involving States, human rights bodies and other institutions. It is useful to focus on the most important layers, ranging from the conflict among States to the conflict between reservations and globalization, in order to point out their impact on the contemporary debate on reservations to the UN human rights treaties.

1. *Conflict among States*

Reservations to the Genocide Convention in its early years demonstrated their potential to create conflicts among parties to the Conven-

[241] Besides the leading Western powers (above n. 138), Asian and African States also are unwilling to equip the UN human rights treaty bodies with a larger mandate in reservation matters. This impression is drawn from the special meeting of the Asian-African Legal Consultative Committee on reservations to normative treaties, held at New Delhi on 14 April 1998. It is strengthened by China's reply to the ILC questionnaire on the topic of reservations. See UN Doc. A/CN.4/508 (29 March 2000), p. 9, para. 16.

tion. In response to the East–West crisis compounded by those reservations, as noted earlier, the UN General Assembly sought an advisory opinion of the ICJ, which substantially affirmed the capacity to make reservations. Later, the Islamic States parties to the CEDAW had a bitter conflict with their Western counterparts on the question of reservations to the Convention. In recent years, the US reservations to the CCPR have been a source of conflicts among ideological allies within the Western world; Trinidad and Tobago's reservation to the CCPR Protocol has given rise to conflicts between the Caribbean State and several European States; and other reservations have the potential to do likewise. These conflicts have surfaced in the form of strong objections by some States. For instance, while the United States has no doubts about the validity of its reservations to Articles 2, 4, 6, 7, 15, and 26 of the CCPR, Sweden holds otherwise: 'A reservation by which a State modifies or excludes the application of the most fundamental provisions of the Covenant, or limits its responsibilities under that treaty by invoking general principles of national law, may cast doubts upon the commitment of the reserving State to the object and purpose of the Covenant. The reservations made by the United States of America include both reservations to essential and non-derogable provisions, and general references to national legislation. Reservations of this nature contribute to undermining the basis of international treaty law.'[242] Likewise, Denmark, France, Germany, Ireland, Italy, the Netherlands, Norway, Spain, and Sweden contend that Trinidad and Tobago's reservation to the CCPR Protocol contravenes the rules of treaty law in general and the principle of good faith in particular; that the reservation weakens the position of individuals; and that it is incompatible with the object and purpose of the Protocol.[243] No doubt these conflicts arise at the diplomatic level, and may be considered particular if not isolated. But they are real enough.

2. *Conflict between States and Human Rights Bodies*

While UN human rights treaty bodies claim a role in establishing the accountability of the reserving States and even in judging the validity of reservations, leading Western powers rebut this claim. As noted earlier, HRC General Comment 24 deals with this matter in the following manner: 'It necessarily falls to the Committee to determine whether a specific reservation is compatible with the object and purpose of the Covenant. This is in part because . . . it is a task that the Committee cannot avoid in the performance of its functions.'[244] The competence of

[242] For the text of the objection, above n. 18.
[243] For the text of objections, above n. 24.
[244] Above n. 30, p. 48, para. 18.

the HRC to determine the compatibility of a reservation with the object and purpose of the CCPR has been endorsed by its sister bodies[245] and also by the Sub-Commission on the Promotion and Protection of Human Rights.[246] In the General Comment, the HRC reflects on the possible means of checking the authority of States in entering reservations. It notes that reservations incompatible with the object and purpose of the CCPR are inadmissible. It also notes that reservations that offend customary or peremptory norms of international law would not be compatible with the CCPR. However, France, the United Kingdom, and the United States do not endorse the General Comment. According to the United States, for instance, '[t]he Committee's position . . . runs contrary to the Covenant scheme and international law'.[247] Most Asian and African States feel likewise. Still, the HRC is not dissuaded from taking bold initiatives. It took note of the concerns expressed by the United States about the General Comment,[248] clarified its position,[249] and pointed out in its concluding comments that the US reservations to Articles 6(5) and 7 of the CCPR were incompatible with the object and purpose of the treaty.[250] The concluding comments thus reaffirmed the General Comment on issues relating to reservations and, in the process, rejected the American, British, and French position that the HRC did not have the competence to determine either the compatibility of reservations with the object and purpose of the CCPR or their validity under customary international law.

Yet, the HRC's comments are not part of the hard law on reservations. The HRC cannot easily overcome the constraints upon its action. Its power is essentially recommendatory, not judicial, and it is certainly not competent to amend its constituent instrument. There is a risk that its increasing assertiveness in reservation matters will merely underline its continuing conflict with a majority of States. To the extent that the other treaty bodies have joined hands with the HRC in this matter, the conflict will be widespread.

[245] At their ninth meeting, held in February 1998, the chairpersons of the UN human rights treaty bodies expressed their support for the approach reflected in General Comment 24. See UN Doc. E/CN.4/Sub.2/1998/25 (26 June 1998), para. 4.

[246] In Sub-Commission Resolution 1999/27 of 26 August 1999, para. 2, the Sub-Commission takes note of the working paper submitted by one of its members (above n. 25) and endorses the conclusions contained therein, including the following: 'It does not appear to be disputed that enforcement/monitoring bodies have the authority to determine what comes within their competence. That must, logically, include the authority to determine the validity of a reservation which would affect the *scope* of their competence or jurisdiction. It appears to be an inherent feature of the type of authority which they are given. It should be emphasized that this refers only to the *validity* of the reservation and not to the effects of an invalid reservation.' See UN Doc. E/CN.4/Sub.2/1999/28, para. 20 (emphasis in the original).

[247] Above n. 138, p. 127.

[248] Ibid.

[249] UN Doc. CCPR/C/SR.1406 (24 April 1995).

[250] *HRC 1995 Report I*, para. 279.

3. *Conflict between the United Nations and Human Rights Bodies*

Although the UN human rights treaty bodies are part of the United Nations human rights system and receive funds and facilities from the budget of the Organization, they are independent bodies and their members serve in their individual capacities. On several occasions, the bodies have found that their position on reservations and related matters was not upheld by the Organization. In 1976 the Legal Counsel of the United Nations expressed the opinion that the CERD Committee did not have competence to determine the compatibility of a reservation to the applicable treaty.[251] As a result the Committee has been reluctant to be assertive and innovative in reservation matters. In 1984 the Office of Legal Affairs of the United Nations expressed a similar opinion that the CEDAW Committee's functions did not include a determination of the incompatibility of reservations to the applicable treaty.[252] Since then, however, the CEDAW Committee has taken a number of steps in reservation matters, asserting its mandate to promote and protect women's rights. In performing his role as the depository of multilateral treaties, the Secretary-General of the United Nations has changed his position at the expense of human rights treaties. In the context of the CERD, in particular, he stated the well-established practice in 1976 that a reservation may be formulated only at the time of signature, ratification or accession, not later.[253] Two years later, however, the Legal Counsel expressed a different opinion to accommodate the position of a permanent member of the Security Council in the context of an international trade convention.[254] Since then, as observed by the ILC Special Rapporteur on reservations, the Secretary-General appears to have adhered continuously to the practice of accepting reservations even after the entry into force of a treaty for the reserving State.[255] There is a danger of extending the same practice to human rights treaties. In 1984 the Legal Counsel gave an opinion in favour of the Secretary-General's revised practice in respect of late reservations,[256] thus threatening the certainty and continuity of human rights treaty obligations. This goes against the position of the treaty bodies, and indeed the Vienna Convention itself, which only allows reservations to be made at the time of the consent to be bound.

On the other hand, in response to the North Korean Government's decision to withdraw from the CCPR in 1997, the Secretary-General stated in effect that a State party could only withdraw from a human

[251] Above n. 146 and the accompanying text.
[252] Above n. 187 and the accompanying text.
[253] See *United Nations Juridical Yearbook, 1976* (New York, 1978), p. 221.
[254] *United Nations Juridical Yearbook, 1978* (New York, 1981), pp. 199–200.
[255] UN Doc. A/CN.4/508/Add.3 (23 June 2000), para. 298.
[256] *United Nations Juridical Yearbook, 1984* (New York, 1991), p. 183.

rights treaty if other parties agreed with such a withdrawal.[257] This was a controversial statement of law and practice, not acceptable to many and barely reconcilable with the earlier practice of the Secretariat in the matter of late reservations. In General Comment 26 of 29 October 1997, the HRC expressed the view that the CCPR does not contain any provision regarding its termination, denunciation or withdrawal; that the Covenant does not have a temporary character typical of treaties where a right of denunciation is deemed to be admitted; and that no State party has the right to withdraw from the Covenant.[258] The other treaty bodies also subscribe to this view. In the present context, the main problem with the Secretary-General's position is twofold: the discontinuity of treaty obligations, and the permissibility of new reservations at the time of reaccession or later. Obviously, it is not helpful to the cause of human rights.

4. *Conflict between the ILC and Human Rights Bodies*

It was hoped that with the adoption of the Vienna Convention on the Law of Treaties in 1969, the controversy surrounding reservations had been settled. This hope was strengthened with the reaffirmation of the Vienna Convention's formulation on reservations in Article 20 of the 1978 Vienna Convention on Succession of States in Respect of Treaties and Article 19 of the 1986 Vienna Convention on the Law of Treaties between States and International Organizations or between International Organizations. But the Vienna Convention regime was exposed by subsequent practice and by associated legal uncertainties, especially in the field of the UN human rights treaties. That is why the CEDAW Committee adopted a general recommendation on reservations on more than one occasion, sought the intervention of States parties to the CEDAW, urged them to raise the issue of reservations at the Vienna Conference, and issued a statement regarding reservations on the eve of the fiftieth anniversary of the UDHR.[259] More effectively, the HRC adopted its general comment on reservations, applied its authority against the most controversial reservations of the most powerful State, and became the most assertive body in reservation matters. Later, the CRC Committee announced its intention to follow suit. Accordingly, the treaty bodies believe that the Vienna regime is 'inappropriate to address the problem of reservations to human rights treaties' and that 'the

[257] The notification of withdrawal and the aide-mémoire containing the Secretary-General's opinion were duly circulated to all States parties to the CCPR under cover of UN Doc. C.N.1997.TREATIES–10 (12 November 1997).

[258] *Report of the Human Rights Committee*, GAOR, fifty-third session (1998), supplement no. 40, UN Doc. A/53/40, vol. I, Annex VII, p. 102 (hereinafter '*HRC 1998 Report I*').

[259] For the text of the statement, which was adopted on 10 July 1998, see *CEDAW 1998 Report*, pp. 47–50.

operation of the classic rules on reservations is . . . inadequate for the Covenant'.[260] These bodies want to apply their own yardsticks to measure the reservations to their constituent instruments. Most critics and commentators on the subject are dissatisfied with the Vienna regime even in respect of those human rights treaties that have reservation clauses.[261] In brief, the Vienna regime is under fire.

On the other hand, the ILC has not found any major fault with the Vienna regime. At the most, it is willing to try to fill in the lacunae and if feasible to remedy the ambiguities and clarify the obscurities in the regime. This objective led to the adoption of the Preliminary Conclusions of the International Law Commission on reservations to normative multilateral treaties, including human rights treaties,[262] and the preparation of a Guide to Practice, including model clauses relating to reservations which the ILC would recommend for their inclusion in future treaties.[263] The UN human rights treaty bodies have sharply reacted to the Preliminary Conclusions.[264] The conflict of interests and the conflict of perceptions place the ILC and the treaty bodies in apparently opposite camps on the following matters: the scope of the Vienna regime; the status of universal human rights bodies and regional human rights organs; the permissibility of late reservations; the criterion of validity of reservations; the competence of the treaty bodies in reservation matters; and the effect of invalid reservations. It is pertinent to point out at the outset that, unlike the treaty bodies, the ILC's position on these matters is still evolving. Not all members of the ILC subscribe to the Special Rapporteur's current positions; the Special Rapporteur's positions are themselves undergoing evolution; and the ILC project on reservations is not completed yet.

First, the basic problem is that the agenda of the ILC is different from that of the UN human rights treaty bodies: the former is concerned with reservations and interpretative declarations relating to treaties in general,

[260] General Comment 24, above (n. 30), p. 47, para. 17. See also above nn. 156 and 245.

[261] See, for example, Belinda Clark, 'The Vienna Convention Reservations Regime and the Convention on Discrimination Against Women', *American Journal of International Law*, 85 (1991), p. 283.

[262] For the text of the Preliminary Conclusions, see *Report of the International Law Commission on the Work of its Forty-ninth Session, 12 May–18 July 1997*, GAOR, fifty-second session (1997), supplement no. 10, UN Doc. A/52/10, pp. 125–7, or visit http://www.un.org/law/ilc/reports/1997/97repfra.htm.

[263] For the text of draft guidelines, see, inter alia, UN Docs. A/CN.4/508/Add.2 (1 May 2000) and A/CN.4/L.599 (9 June 2000).

[264] See, for instance, a letter dated 9 April 1998 by HRC Chairperson Christine Chanet to ILC Special Rapporteur Alain Pellet, in *HRC 1998 Report I*, Annex IX, p. 105; a letter dated 5 November 1998 by HRC Chairperson Christine Chanet to ILC Chairman Baena Soares, in *HRC 1999 Report I*, Annex VI, p. 128; a letter dated 29 July 1998 by the presiding officer of the eighth and ninth meetings of the chairpersons of the treaty bodies to the ILC Chairman, in UN Doc. A/CN.4/508, p. 7, para. 14; the CAT Committee's comments on the Preliminary Conclusions, ibid., para. 13; the CEDAW Committee's statements on reservations, in *CEDAW 1998 Report*, pp. 47–50.

both bilateral and multilateral, whereas the latter are worried about reservations and declarations concerning the UN human rights treaties only, and that too in the context of specific fact situations. The ILC looks at the Vienna regime in general terms, particularly from the perspective of States. In contrast, the treaty bodies see the same regime's ineffectiveness in respect of the human rights treaty commitments as modified by the applicable reservations. They feel that the ILC does not accord sufficient attention to the fact that human rights treaties, by virtue of their subject matter and their recognition of the role of individuals, cannot be placed on precisely the same footing as other treaties with different characteristics.

Secondly, the ILC recognizes the validity of progressive reservation regimes of regional human rights organs, endorsing their law and practice beyond the domain of the Vienna regime, but does not place the UN human rights treaty bodies in the same category. The UN human rights treaty bodies do not accept the conclusion that, while the Vienna regime remains valid and applicable to them, regional human rights organs are free to innovate and operate outside the Vienna regime. These bodies point out that, like regional organs, they also have developed their own law and practice on reservations.[265]

Thirdly, the ILC Special Rapporteur on reservations recognizes the possibility and permissibility of late reservations, which may be made after the acceptance of the treaty by the reserving State.[266] The treaty bodies are bound to oppose such freedom to States parties to the UN human rights treaties, because it may lead to an anarchical reservations regime. In fact, they seek withdrawal of even those reservations which are properly made.

Fourthly, except for its reaffirmation of the normal compatibility test, the ILC has so far been extremely economical in articulating its views on the criteria of determining the validity of reservations. In contrast, the

[265] See *HRC 1998 Report I*, Annex IX, p. 105.

[266] UN Doc. A/CN.4/508/Add.3, pp. 24–34, paras. 279–305. The Special Rapporteur supports the practice of late reservations by citing France's reservation to the 1931 Convention Providing a Uniform Law for Cheques. Ibid., para. 296. One can oppose that practice by citing Egypt's reservations to the 1989 Basel Convention on the Control of Transboundary Movements of Hazardous Wastes and Their Disposal. Article 26 of the Basel Convention prohibits reservations but permits declarations at the time of signing, ratifying, accepting, approving, formally confirming, or acceding to this treaty. *International Legal Materials*, 28 (1989), p. 677. More than two years after acceding to the Basel Convention, Egypt informed the UN Secretary-General that its instrument of accession should have been accompanied by the declarations concerning (*a*) the passage of foreign ships carrying inherently dangerous or noxious substances through its territorial sea, (*b*) a complete ban on the import of hazardous wastes to its territory, and (*c*) the need for effective control of transboundary movement of hazardous wastes and their disposal. Finland, Italy, the Netherlands, Sweden and the United Kingdom objected to these declarations on the grounds that Egypt was late in making the declarations and that the declarations appeared to be in the nature of reservations. The Secretary-General took the position that the declarations were not acceptable in view of the depository practice and the objections. For details, visit http://untreaty.un.org/ENGLISH/bible/englishinternetbible/partI/chapterXXVII/treaty16.asp.

UN human rights treaty bodies in general and the HRC in particular have given considerable thought and expression to the problem. That is why they have articulated solutions going beyond the Vienna regime. Unlike the ILC, which maintains its faith in the State-centric regulation of the reservations regime, the treaty bodies seek to promote a multi-pronged strategy against reservations.

Fifthly, being aware of the original intentions of the drafters of the human rights treaties, as well as the present mood of a majority of States, the ILC is not ready to recognize the treaty bodies' authority to declare a reservation invalid on any ground. At the maximum, it has conceded with some difficulty that the treaty bodies are competent to comment upon and make recommendations with regard to the admissibility of reservations by States, in order to carry out the functions assigned to them. The treaty bodies dislike the ILC's reluctance to accept their increasing assertiveness in reservation matters, especially when some of them have already developed and applied their *lex specialis* to the extent of declaring a few reservations incompatible with the object and purpose of the treaty concerned, customary rules and peremptory norms of international law, or a combination of all these.

Finally, the ILC notes that, in the event of inadmissibility of a reservation, it is the reserving State that has the responsibility for taking actions, such as the modification of the reservation, withdrawal of the reservation, or withdrawal from the treaty concerned.[267] The UN human rights treaty bodies do not like this proposition. They claim that the reserving State's freedom of action in respect of an inadmissible reservation is confined to the implementation of the treaty body's recommendations in that respect. As a consequence, there is a dispute about what the treaty bodies can do when they find a State maintains an objectionable reservation. While the treaty bodies may find the reserving State in breach of its treaty obligations, leading to the application of a wide range of 'sanctions' such as naming the defaulting State, the ILC's position would not allow to the treaty bodies an interpretative competence of such an extent.

In brief, the UN human rights treaty bodies feel that the ILC's approach to reservations to their constituent instruments is unduly restrictive. In order to challenge the ILC's approach, the treaty bodies have successfully urged the Sub-Commission on the Promotion and Protection of Human Rights to conduct a detailed study on reservations to human rights treaties.[268] The Sub-Commission's working paper, a prelude to the proposed study, supports the position of the treaty bodies.[269] In other words, while the ILC is keen to protect the integrity of the Vienna regime, human rights bodies want to modify the regime to

[267] Paragraph 10 of the Preliminary Conclusions, above n. 262.
[268] Above n. 235.
[269] Above n. 246.

meet their functional needs. The conflict of interests and perceptions remains unresolved.

5. *Conflict between the Legislature and the Executive*

HRC General Comment 24 on issues relating to reservations contains many powerful statements, but the most assertive one is that the HRC has the competence to determine the compatibility of a reservation with the object and purpose of the CCPR. This Comment provoked Senator Helms of the United States and on 9 June 1995 he introduced Senate Bill 9 (S.9). The Bill provided that no funds may be expended for the conduct of any activity which has the purpose of reporting to the HRC in accordance with Article 40 of the CCPR, or responding to any effort by the HRC to use the procedures of Articles 41 and 42 of the instrument, until the President of the United States submitted to Congress the certification that the HRC has revoked General Comment 24 and expressly recognized the validity of the reservations, understandings and declarations contained in the US instrument of ratification of the CCPR. This was a move to suspend compliance with US obligations under the CCPR, to clip the wings of the US administration and to humiliate the HRC. On 14 December 1995 the Senate indefinitely postponed its proceeding with the Bill. The contents of the Bill, including the language dealing with restricting use of funds for HRC-related activities, were placed in a companion bill (House of Representatives Bill 1561 (H.R.1561)). The latter was eventually passed by both the House and the Senate by 28 March 1996 but was vetoed by President Clinton on 12 April 1996. An attempt to override the veto failed on 30 April 1996. The presidential veto saved the United States from an international embarrassment, but such moves harden the feelings of those who were defeated. The echo of the veto is likely to be heard somewhere else.

The conflict between the executive and the legislature in the United States did not last long, but its fallout was damaging to the cause of human rights. It put the executive on the defensive, forced State authorities to reset priorities and diluted their willingness to ensure compliance with CCPR-based obligations. The President of the United States had an obligation to take appropriate steps as soon as the HRC had stated that the US reservations to Articles 6(5) and 7 of the CCPR were incompatible with the object and purpose of the instrument and that the United States should reconsider those reservations with the aim of withdrawing them.[270] Since the withdrawal of the impugned reservations

[270] Above n. 163.

was not possible without the advice and consent of the Senate,[271] and the Helms Bill had already revealed the hostility of the House, the President did not dare to initiate the process of withdrawal of the reservations. Thus, the conflict between the executive and the legislature compounded the conflict between the reserving State and the HRC. It raised doubts about the political legitimacy of the reservation-related comments and decisions of the UN human rights bodies in general and the HRC in particular. It exposed the unevenness of the turf where the law of reservations is applied. Most important, it undermined a logical process of evolution of human rights treaty obligations.

6. *Conflict between Judiciary and State Policy*

Sometimes international legal conflicts trickle down to the domestic level. One can see that happening with certain reservations entered by India. As noted earlier, India made a set of 'declarations' at the time of acceding to the CCPR in 1979.[272] For instance, with respect to the right of compensation on account of unlawful arrest provided for under Article 9 of the CCPR, India appended a declaration which states that, under the Indian legal system, there is no enforceable right to compensation for persons claiming to be victims of unlawful arrest or detention. Four years later, however, the Supreme Court of India ignored this reservation. In *Rudal Saha* v. *State of Bihar*, it held that a victim of unlawful detention had a right to claim compensation for the violation of his human dignity.[273] It followed *Saha* in later cases.[274] In particular, in *Basu* v. *State of West Bengal*,[275] as noted earlier, the Court observed: 'That reservation, however, has lost its relevance in view of the law laid down by this Court in a number of cases awarding compensation for the infringement of the fundamental right to life of a citizen . . . There is indeed no express provision in the Constitution of India for grant of compensation for violation of a fundamental right to life, nonetheless, this Court has judicially evolved a right to compensation in cases of established unconstitutional deprivation of personal liberty or life.'[276] Obviously, the executive is not happy with such pronouncements. Judge P. Chandrasekhara Rao, a former Law Secretary to the Government of India and currently President of the International Tribunal for the

[271] For the most authoritative account of the law and practice of the United States concerning reservations, see *Restatement (Third) of the Foreign Relations Law of the United States*, above (n. 1), section 314, pp. 186–9.

[272] Above n. 18; or *Indian Journal of International Law*, 20 (1979), pp. 118–19.

[273] AIR 1983 SC 1086.

[274] See, e.g., *Bhim Singh* v. *State of Jammu and Kashmir*, AIR 1986 SC 494; *Saheli* v. *Commissioner of Police, Delhi*, AIR 1990 SC 513; *Sebastian M. Hongrey* v. *Union of India*, AIR 1984 SC 1026.

[275] Above n. 219, pp. 624–5.

[276] On the same lines, the National Human Rights Commission of India has awarded compensation in more than 600 cases of violations of human rights during 1993–2000.

Law of the Sea, holds the view that the 'judicially created rights' represent an 'impractical approach'.[277] Judge Rao is not alone in his outcry against judicial activism. The Supreme Court's romance with human rights treaties is beyond the imaginings of legal orthodoxy. Since there is no dialogue between the judiciary and the executive on the content of human rights law, both cling to their respective positions. Accordingly, State policy against the right of compensation coexists with the judicial recognition and enforcement of that right. Although such conflicts are not yet common, the possibility of their occurrence is always present in those States where the judiciary sincerely believes that human rights policy is too serious a matter to be left to the executive alone.

7. *Conflict between Functionalism and the Rights-based Approach*

The main objectives of permitting reservations to human rights treaties are to encourage States to ratify those treaties, to expand the network of multilateral arrangements and to promote functionalism step by step. Even most striking reservations do not defeat these objectives. This traditional mode of encouraging respect for human rights is not in tune with some contemporary developments. The United Nations now claims that 'Respect for human rights, as proclaimed in the international agreements, is central to our mandate.'[278] The Organization is now committed to a rights-based approach.[279] Accordingly, all policies and programmes of the United Nations are expected to encourage the promotion and protection of human rights. This approach is institutionalized partly with the help of a Memorandum of Understanding between UNDP and the United Nations High Commissioner for Human Rights signed in March 1998. UNDP has activities spread in about 175 members of the United Nations, and it is expected to give effect to the MOU. Is it possible to qualify a general rights-based approach with certain State-specific reservations? Can the members of the United Nations family have different versions of the rights-based approach, directly proportional to the number of States with different sets of reservations to human rights treaties? Can UNDP streamline the rights-based approach by engaging itself in a legalistic exercise such as the determination of validity, compatibility, acceptability and separability of reservations of different States that happen to be the beneficiaries of its development assistance or field presence?

[277] Rao, 'Use and Abuse of the Indian Constitution', *Zeitschrift fur Ausländisches Öffentliches Recht und Völkerrecht*, 58 (1998), pp. 823–4.

[278] See *Report of the Secretary-General on the Work of the Organization*, GAOR, fifty-fourth session (1999), supplement no. 1, UN Doc. A/54/1, para. 276.

[279] See UNDP, *Integrating Human Rights with Sustainable Human Development: A UNDP Policy Document* (New York, 1998), which is available at http://magnet.undp.org/Docs/policy5.html.

8. *Conflict between Reservations and Globalization*

The process of globalization has catalysed the worldwide sharing of information, ideas and experience in almost every field. It has introduced many changes, including a new sensitivity to world community issues. What will be the impact of these changes on the equilibrium of human rights? How can States continue to live with their sovereignty-centric mindset in the field of human rights? Will reservations survive globalization? Logically, if globalization can flourish without altering national boundaries, human rights too can flourish without eliminating national identities. Conversely, if national boundaries can survive the process of globalization, reservations too can survive universal standards of human rights. This is a curious case of coexistence of two contradictory processes. It seems that reservations to human rights treaties will have their *raison d'être* as long as peoples have different group identities, as symbolized by their nationalities, religions, languages, customs, and traditions. Simultaneously, however, the momentum of a new world order will not allow reservations to remain unchallenged. While States will continue to rely on reservations for accommodating their conflicting interests, the global community will increasingly exercise its right to question the discretion of States. As a result, reservations will come under greater scrutiny. Their own architects will forget some of them, some others will be dwarfed by dynamic interpretations, and many others will continue to create tension between States and the UN human rights treaty bodies.

The foregoing analysis of the various layers of conflict, present or possible, demonstrates the complexity of law, policy, procedure, and practice pertaining to reservations to the UN human rights treaties. Some conflicts go deep into the very basis of functionalism while others are creatures of changing circumstances. There is no readily available mechanism to resolve those conflicts; ordinary dispute settlement clauses do not serve the purpose; and various alternative solutions have so far been inadequately examined. Perhaps persistent efforts to understand and appreciate the ingredients of those conflicts will enable us to address them better.

VIII. Conclusions

The principle of national sovereignty is the principal basis of reservations. All States rely on this principle in the process of formulation, recognition and implementation of treaty obligations. Reservations become a necessity for those who could not succeed to get their national assertions duly reflected in the formulation of a treaty. Reservations also become essential when new factors and forces enter the scene and bargain for new consideration in lieu of acceptance of treaty obligations. Considering the fact that no cautious policy maker would like to accept those treaty obligations which cannot be implemented, reservations assume the form of conditional acceptance of those obligations. All these aspects have been explained in rather simple terms, such as domestic law constraints, competing international obligations, diverse socio-economic conditions, and so forth. In this perspective, reservations are not only enemies but also allies of human rights treaties. To promote their universalization, human rights treaties will continue to have uncomfortable alliances with reservations; and human rights bodies will remain suspicious of reservations. This paradox does not pose any serious problem as long as human rights treaties tolerate reservations and the latter do not damage the integrity of the former. But States have not always respected the integrity of treaties; some of their reservations offend certain non-derogable rights, customary rules, or peremptory norms of international law. Invariably, reservations reduce the rights of individuals, weaken the shield available against errant State authorities and check the growth of human rights law. By their conditional acceptance of treaty obligations, the reserving States tend to develop a false sense of security at the cost of their international image and the best interests of their citizens.

Prior to the Second World War, the unanimity rule governed reservations to multilateral treaties. Since the adoption of the Genocide Convention, however, reservations are subject to a flexible body of international law. Following the ICJ's advisory opinion in the *Reservations to the Genocide Convention* case, the 'object and purpose' test has become the mainstay of the reservations regime. The ILC recognized the importance of the advisory opinion and drafted the Vienna Convention's provisions on reservations with a view to promote wider participation in multilateral treaties. Although the human rights treaties more or less follow the Vienna Convention regime on reservations, there are many shades of law in the form of the *lex specialis* of each treaty. Since the seven human rights treaties under discussion were drafted during the Cold War era, they enshrine the politically acceptable formulations on the subject without any regard to their operational aspects. Accordingly, the two most widely used options are: the Vienna Convention formulation on reservations and silence on the question of reservations. The human rights treaties that prohibit reservations are not many. Although the reservations-free treaties are considered forward-looking instruments, they have poor prospects of universal participation. A comparative study of practices under particular treaties shows that the reservations regime of a treaty depends not only on its provisions relating to reservations but also on the powers and functions of its monitoring body. On the basis of this criterion, the HRC has an impressive record. It has used the reservations-related silence of the CCPR and CCPR

Protocol to its advantage and to the advantage of individuals. As a result, it has developed a rich *lex specialis*. It has exercised its implied powers to the extent of determining the incompatibility of the most objectionable reservations of one of the developing countries (Trinidad and Tobago) and one of the developed countries (United States). Both instances have turned out to be provocative, thus underlining the need for abundant caution in reservation matters. The ILC's current agenda and approach towards the question of reservations demonstrate its keenness to achieve interpretative codification of the Vienna Convention's provisions in the light of State practice and institutional responses to reservations. This approach is closer to the position of States, and the treaty bodies are not willing to follow that line.

The proponents of *lex ferenda* are unhappy with the Vienna Convention regime on reservations and also with the related provisions of the UN human rights treaties. That is why they plead for radical changes, including amendments to the treaties that lack an effective reservations regime. Pursuant to the continuing exchange of information, ideas and experience among the treaty bodies, there is a trend towards minimizing differences between various bodies of *lex specialis*. Obviously, a majority of States do not like an assertive or unconventional reservations regime. They certainly do not want to equip the treaty bodies with the power to determine the incompatibility of reservations. Following these constraints, the treaty bodies have not yet come out with an acceptable and effective remedy to the problem of reservations. That is why we see adverse effects of reservations on the most vulnerable sections of society (particularly women, children, aliens and minorities) and also on the impartial promoters of human dignity (the human rights treaty bodies).

The issue of acceptability, compatibility, or validity of reservations cannot be settled by looking at the provisions of the applicable treaty alone. Nor can it be dealt with by relying merely on lofty notions of international law. Reservations generally originate from ground realities, and a fair approach towards reservations necessarily requires an in-depth understanding of those realities. The issue should be addressed by examining the wording of the treaty, the gravity of reservations, the text of domestic legislation, compelling conditions within the jurisdiction of the reserving State, and the capacity and willingness of the State to comply with its treaty obligations. This is particularly useful in respect of reservations of those States which are facing dangers to their integrity and expect international bodies to make less radical criticisms and more fruitful suggestions to improve the conditions at the heart of reservations. Accordingly, the integrity of a human rights treaty need not be pitted against the integrity of a reserving State. Both are important. If the UN human rights treaty regimes fail to appreciate this equilibrium, their wisdom will come into question. Moreover, in view of the limited mandates and inadequate resources of a small number of the UN human rights treaty bodies, it is unwise to have a heavy reliance on these bodies. It makes sense to supplement the efforts of the treaty bodies by activating domestic institutions in reservation matters as well.

To develop a new policy perspective on reservations, it is essential to focus on the basic premise of human rights law. Each State party to a human rights treaty has a duty to overcome difficulties in the implementation of treaty obligations and, if those difficulties have assumed the form of reservations, the reserving State is expected to take measures to minimize the effect of reservations. By characterizing reservations as capable of giving rise themselves to persistent human rights violations, even *in abstracto*, one can invoke domestic remedies or impress upon national forums the need to evolve appropriate responses. Although domestic courts may not nullify reservations, they can neutralize the effect of unconstitutional reservations and their involvement may sensitize the executive about its customary duty to reconsider, reduce or withdraw reservations. Thus, unlike some controversial responses at the international level, the domestic approach to reservations may produce rich dividends with minimum friction and maximum comfort in the long run. Indeed, it can be a useful complement to the international legal controls of reservations.

THE JURISPRUDENCE OF THE YUGOSLAV AND RWANDAN CRIMINAL TRIBUNALS ON THEIR JURISDICTION AND ON INTERNATIONAL CRIMES

By ROBERT KOLB*

I. Introduction

This article presents an overview of the case law of the Yugoslav and Rwandan International Criminal Tribunals. This overview will be limited to matters of substantive law to the exclusion of procedural points. It will deal with the crimes within the jurisdiction of the Tribunals, issues of participation in the commission of crimes, and defences. For reasons of space, only trial and appeal judgments will be considered;[1] interlocutory decisions[2] will be mentioned in passing where appropriate. For the same reasons no attempt will be made to consider closely the post-Second World War jurisprudence on which the present ad hoc criminal Tribunals rely heavily. Where a comparison seems warranted, some references will be offered. Critical comments will also be provided where necessary.

The importance of jurisprudence in the development of the law need hardly be stressed. It has a constitutive role in areas such as that of international criminal law where the law is uncertain on many points and where previous decisions were rendered on the basis of differing legislation and legal systems. Some points decided by the present ad hoc Tribunals are still unsettled, for example those subject to appeal. But the main lines of this jurisprudence do already emerge clearly. These are the pillars on which the edifice of international criminal law is being erected, and which will be the focus of this article.

* Institute of International Studies, Geneva.

[1] The following judgments will be considered. For the ICTY : (1) *Tadic* case, judgment of the Appeals Chamber on the legality of the establishment of the ICTY and on its jurisdiction, 2 October 1995 (hereafter: *Tadic* (1995)); (2) *Tadic* case, judgment of the Trial Chamber, 7 May 1997 (hereafter: *Tadic* (1997)); (3) *Tadic* case, judgment of the Appeals Chamber on the merits, 15 July 1999 (hereafter: *Tadic* (1999)); (4) *Erdemovic* case, judgment of the Appeals Chamber, 7 October 1997; (5) *Delalic and others* case (also called *Celebici*), judgment of the Trial Chamber, 16 November 1998; (6) *Furundzija* case, judgment of the Trial Chamber, 10 December 1998; (7) *Aleksovski* case, judgment of the Trial Chamber, 25 June 1999; (8) *Jelisic* case, judgment of the Trial Chamber, 14 December 1999. For the ICTR: (1) *Akayesu* case, judgment of the Trial Chamber, 2 September 1998; (2) *Kayishema and Ruzindana* case, judgment of the Trial Chamber, 21 May 1999; (3) *Rutaganda* case, judgment of the Trial Chamber, 6 December 1999. All the substantive judgments containing developments as to the law and rendered up to the end of 1999 are thus reviewed.

[2] Also those under Rule 61 of the Rules of the ICTY.

II. The Conditions for the Jurisdiction of the Tribunals

There are certain general jurisdictional conditions which must be fulfilled for both Tribunals. First, the substantive prohibition breached (the criminal offence) must be part of customary international law, or at least of treaties binding upon the State on whose territory the conflict takes place and which are adopted into its municipal law. Moreover, the breach of the rule concerned must give rise, under customary international law, to international criminal responsibility. Second, the violations of international humanitarian law have to possess a certain seriousness and to have taken place in a certain location and time-period.

Other conditions are linked to one only of the two Tribunals, or only to a particular crime. For the ICTY there is a general requirement of the existence of an armed conflict, subject only to one qualification for the application of Article 2 of the Statute (the grave breaches regime) where it must additionally be shown that the conflict was international in character. Moreover, there must be a *nexus* between the acts of the accused (i.e. the alleged offence) and the armed conflict. Roughly speaking, the situation of the ICTR is the reverse. There is no general requirement of the existence of an armed conflict, subject only to one qualification for the application of Article 4 of the Statute (violations of Common Article 3 to the Geneva Conventions of 1949 and of Protocol II of 1977) where it must be shown that a non-international armed conflict existed and that the acts of the accused were closely linked to that conflict. This difference stems from the fact that the conflict in the former Yugoslavia was considered of mixed international and internal character whereas the one in Rwanda was exclusively internal, and from the overlapping fact that the crimes to be punished in the former Yugoslavia were committed exclusively in the context of the armed conflict whereas in Rwanda most of the genocidal acts were perpetrated alongside the armed conflict and independently from it.

1. *The Requirement that the Rules of International Humanitarian Law Applied Be Part of Customary Law*

The origin of this requirement can be traced back to the *Report of the Secretary-General of the United Nations pursuant to paragraph 2 of Security Council Resolution 808 (1993)* presented on 3 May 1993.[3] It was the opinion of the Secretary-General, when asked to comment on the legal implications of the creation of an ad hoc criminal tribunal, that

[3] UN Doc., S/25704.

respect for the principle *nullum crimen sine lege* requires that the tribunal should apply rules of international humanitarian law which are beyond any doubt part of customary law. In this way the problem of adherence of some but not all States to specific Conventions would not arise.[4] This position was partly endorsed by the Security Council, which however also allowed applicable conventions to be taken into account.[5] When it first considered this question, the ICTY also widened the sources admissible to found its jurisdiction. In the *Tadic* case (1995), it held that the core of the matter was to apply sources binding upon the parties at the moment of the offence. Therefore, the Tribunal would fully comply with the stated purpose of not infringing the *nullum crimen* principle if it applied any treaty binding upon the parties at the moment of the offence.[6] The Chamber, however, also sought to establish the customary law character of the rules to be applied wherever possible. It thereby inaugurated a practice often followed in later trials.[7] In the *Tadic* case (1995), the Chamber attempted to specify what the customary rules of international humanitarian law governing internal armed conflict are, precisely in order to satisfy the requirement set forth by the Secretary-General. It found that the corpus of customary rules was composed of some rules relating to the protection of the civilian population which had hardened through State practice since the Spanish Civil War, and of a series of conventional rules, such as Common Article 3 of the Geneva Conventions of 1949, rules contained in Additional Protocol II (1977), and some rules on the methods and means of warfare, especially on the use of certain weapons.[8]

It does not seem that this requirement that the rules applied be customary in character was either necessary or beneficial. The *nullum crimen* principle does not call for such a restriction. It was developed during the period of the enlightenment as a protection against arbitrary acts and extraordinary penalties (*poenae extraordinariae*).[9] Under the principle thus developed, any criminal conviction must rest on a law prohibiting a particular conduct; this law must be in force at the time the acts were committed; and the law must be clear in describing the conduct prohibited (*Bestimmtheitsgrundsatz*).[10] In international law, the principle

[4] Ibid., para. 34.

[5] S/PV.3217 (25 May 1993), e.g., pp. 19, 23. See also, for Article 2 of the Statute, ibid., pp. 11, 15.

[6] *Tadic* (1995), paras. 143–5. This course was followed in other cases: see, e.g., *Furundzija*, para. 166, or *Kayishema*, para. 156.

[7] See, e.g. *Tadic* (1997), para. 611; *Delalic*, paras. 307 ff., 315; *Furundzija*, paras. 137, 168; *Akayesu*, para. 495.

[8] *Tadic* (1995), paras. 100 ff.

[9] The formula was coined by J. P. A. von Feuerbach (*Lehrbuch des peinlichen Rechts* (1801), p. 20). See, earlier, T. Hobbes, *De Cive*, cap. XIII, and *Leviathan*, cap. XXVIII, and S. Pufendorf, *De jure naturae et gentium*, lib. VIII, cap. III, par. VII.

[10] See ECHR, *Kokkinakis* v. *Greece* (1993), Series A, No. 260A, p. 22, para. 52.

has always been applied with more flexibility than in municipal law.[11] If one takes into consideration its essential content, it can be seen that in the case of the ad hoc tribunals it is sufficient that the contemplated conduct was punishable on the territory where the acts took place. The principle only requires a pre-established law applicable *to the accused*.[12] It is clearly not necessary (but may be a separate requirement of international law) that the law be applicable *erga omnes* on the universal plane in order also to be applicable to a particular accused. Subsidiarity and economy of means suggest the application of a general rule according to which the more specific basis of judicial action should be examined first. Therefore, it may be useful to enquire if conduct is prohibited by customary law only if no applicable treaty or equivalent internal legislation can be found relating to the territory where the acts were committed. This view is beginning to find some favour with the Tribunals. Thus, in the *Kayishema* case (1999), the ICTR held that the Geneva Conventions of 1949 and Protocol II were binding on Rwanda and the offences charged did constitute crimes under the laws of Rwanda in conformity with these instruments. Under such conditions the Chamber thought it superfluous to go into the question of the customary status of that source.[13] The customary-law requirement seems thus grounded more on political imperatives than on legal necessity.

It may be added that the broader approach, looking to the customary character of the rules, is not as beneficial to the development of the law as may be thought at first sight. The natural tendency of the Tribunals will be to postulate custom wherever possible in order to bypass the jurisdictional obstacle. The practice has already shown that these postu-

[11] It has even been suggested that the principle had no standing in the international criminal procedure: see the conclusions of the Judge Advocate in the *Peleus Trial* (British Military Court, Hamburg, 1945), *Law Reports of Trials of War Criminals, United Nations War Crimes Commission*, vol. I, (London, 1947), p. 15. What is certain is that in international criminal law the principle has never been applied to the same extent as in the continental legal tradition based on Roman law. See the synthesis of the post-Second World War case-law in: *Law Reports . . .* , op.cit., vol. XV, (London, 1949), 166 ff. For instance, the principle '*nulla poena sine lege scripta*', which operates to the exclusion of customary law, has for obvious reasons never been applied on the international stage. On the contrary, international customary law has always been the primary basis for international criminal adjudication; for the post-Second World War trials, see the *Law Reports . . .* , op.cit., vol. XV, London, 1949, p. 5 ff. Another exception which has permeated the internal legal systems also has its origin in international law and has been codified in Article 15(2) of the International Covenant on Civil and Political Rights (1966): 'Nothing in this article [codifying the principle *nullum crimen*] shall prejudice the trial and punishment of any person for any act or omission which, at the time when it was committed, was criminal according to the general principles of law recognized by the community of nations'. See to the same effect also Article 7(2) of the European Convention on Human Rights (1950). Moreover, in international law, the penalties incurred were never clearly set out. But the gravity of the acts concerned made it clear that life sentences or even the death penalty could be applied, as it was in the trials after the Second World War. Another exception was developed in the jurisprudence of municipal law: the priority of the more lenient later law (*lex mitior*).

[12] If the source is international law, especially treaty law, it may be necessary that it be adopted into municipal law through legislation.

[13] *Kayishema*, para. 156.

lates of custom largely rest on undemonstrated assertions. A real analysis of the elements of custom is in effect unimaginable within the compass of the task of the Tribunals. Weak assertions made in more than one case do not add to the authority the Tribunals may enjoy.[14] Moreover, an excessive blurring and blending of conventional and customary law tends to produce unwelcome side-effects and to weaken the proper mechanisms of treaty law.[15]

Apart from international customary and general treaty law, or internal legislation, some other sources could also provide a basis for the jurisdiction of the Tribunals. In the first place, any special agreement among the warring parties to apply a particular set of rules of international humanitarian law—for example, to apply some rules relating to an international armed conflict in an internal conflict too—must be held to extend to the provisions of criminal law enforcing the substantive provisions.[16] Such an agreement existed among the belligerents in the Bosnian war; it was concluded on 22 May 1992.[17] A unilateral declaration committing oneself to certain rules of humanitarian law has the same effect. What is essential is not the nature of the bond undertaken but the acceptance to be bound by the rules contemplated. Thus, in *Kayishema* (1999), the ICTR found that the Rwandan Patriotic Front (RPF)[18] had declared itself bound by the rules of international humanitarian law.[19] That would have been sufficient to give the Tribunal jurisdiction over violations of Common Article 3 of the Geneva Conventions (1949) or Protocol II (1977) as against the members of the RPF. In such cases some of the combatants may not have been informed of such an undertaking; it may then be necessary to consider the defence of ignorance of the law which has sometimes been allowed if the accused had in fact no knowledge of the terms in question and if he could not reasonably be expected to know of the illegality of the conduct.[20] A

[14] An example of a problematic assertion of customary law can be found in the *Delalic* case (1998), where the Chamber confronts three different definitions of torture current in international law and then simply concludes that the 'more specific definition' of torture in the Torture Convention of 1985 is representative of customary international law (para. 459). There is not even an attempt to buttress this statement.

[15] Some inconveniences have been pointed out by P. Weil in quite sharp words: P. Weil, 'Cours général de droit international public', *RCADI*, vol. 237, 1992–VI, p. 179 ff.

[16] For the legal basis of such agreements, see Article 96(2) and (3) of Protocol I (1977).

[17] *Tadic* (1995), para. 73.

[18] The RPF was the political party of the Tutsis. During the civil war it fought in Rwanda against the Hutu-controlled governmental agencies.

[19] *Kayishema*, para. 156.

[20] Cf. the *Scuttled U-Boots* Case (1946), *Law Reports . . . (supra*, n. 11), vol. I, (London, 1947), pp. 69–70; the *Von Leeb (The High Command)* case (1948), *Law Reports . . . (supra*, n. 11), vol. XII, (London, 1949), pp. 73–4 ; the *Latza* case (1947), *Law Reports . . . (supra*, n. 11), vol. XIV, (London, 1949), p. 69. See generally, *Law Reports . . . (supra*, n. 11), vol. XV, (London, 1949), pp. 182–4.

glance at the type of offences included in the Statutes of the ad hoc Tribunals shows that this will hardly ever be the case.[21]

Another source which may provide a basis of jurisdiction is the general principles of law as recognized through the various municipal legal systems. The idea that an offence must be universally held to be criminal in order to apply it to an individual, evidenced through the customary-law requirement, is found even more conspicuously in the general principles to which the Tribunals have already often turned for the determination of substantive points.[22] That the application of such principles is not at odds with the *nullum crimen* rule was suggested by Cicero[23] and has been acknowledged in various human rights instruments.[24]

2. *The Requirement that the Violation of the Rule must Entail, under Customary International Law, Individual Criminal Responsibility*

This requirement is automatically satisfied for the crimes exhaustively codified in the Statutes, such as genocide and crimes against humanity. It is precisely because it is recognized that they give rise to criminal responsibility that they were included in the Statutes. Thus, when Article 4 of the ICTY Statute confers power on the Tribunal to prosecute persons committing genocide, it is implicit that if certain acts are qualified as 'genocide' they give rise to individual criminal responsibility. The only doubt which may arise is whether a certain act can legally be described as genocide. But this is not a jurisdictional question. It goes to the substance of the criminal charge. For the jurisdiction of the Tribunals, it is sufficient that the prosecution claims that the acts or omissions must be qualified as genocide. In the context of such crimes precisely set out in the Statutes, the requirement has no place.

[21] According to the general principle *ignorantia iuris neminem excusat* the standard of proof is generally high. It was held not to be possible to be discharged for crimes that offend against the elementary bonds of human decency and which must thus be known to be illegal by anyone (*mala per se*). See the *Von Weizsäcker (The Ministries)* case, in: *Trials of War Criminals before the Nüremberg Military Tribunals under Control Council Law No. 10*, vol. XIV, (Washington, 1952), p. 339: '[The accused] cannot be heard to say that he did not know the acts in question were criminal. Measures which result in murder, ill-treatment, enslavement, and other inhumane acts perpetrated on prisoners of war, deportation, extermination, enslavement, and persecution on political, racial, and religious grounds, and plunder and spoliation of public and private property are acts which shock the conscience of every decent man. These are crimes *per se*.' The showing of the existence of a general principle of law recognized by the municipal legal systems may also invalidate such a claim.

[22] See, e.g., *Erdemovic*, Joint. Sep. Op. McDonald/Vohrah, paras. 56 ff; Sep. and Diss. Op. Cassese, paras. 11 ff; *Furundzija*, paras. 174 ff (for the definition of rape).

[23] *In Verrem*, lib. II, cap. XXXXII.

[24] Cf. Article 15(2) of the International Covenant on Civil and Political Rights (1966) or Article 7(2) of the European Convention on Human Rights. Cf. M. Novak, *U.N. Covenant on Civil and Political Rights, Commentary* (Kehl/Strasburg, 1993), p. 281. L. E. Pettiti/E. Decaux/P. H. Imbert (eds.), *La Convention européenne des droits de l'homme—Commentaire* (Paris, 1995), pp. 299 ff.

The *raison d'être* of the requirement presently discussed is that certain offences are incorporated in the Statutes only by way of a *renvoi*. Such is the case, for example, for the violation of the laws and customs of war. The ICTY Statute contains only the phrase that there shall be prosecution for such crimes, limiting itself to giving a few examples of the offences involved (Article 3). The rest of the offences covered have to be searched for in the body of customary or conventional international law. For the offences specifically listed, there is again no question that they were (and must be) considered as giving rise to criminal responsibility under customary law. But for the great number of other rules on warfare which may be breached, the inquiry into the type of responsibility to which their breach leads was delegated to the Tribunal to be handled as the cases arise.

It is doubtful if this requirement was necessary as a general and distinct condition for jurisdiction. It seems that, in order to understand it better, a distinction must be made between the rules pertaining to international armed conflicts and rules relating to non-international armed conflicts.

In the context of international armed conflicts the requirement is, it is suggested, redundant. On a proper reading of the Nüremberg and other post-Second World War trials, it appears to have been acknowledged that *all* serious violations of the laws of war give rise to criminal responsibility.[25] There was no review of any pre-existing international custom for the single offences;[26] it would have been difficult to find. The principles emerging from that jurisprudence were then eventually endorsed by States and by the main organs of the United Nations. It may be argued that since that time, criminal responsibility has been inherent in the important substantive rules on the laws of war. It is thus customary law itself which dispenses with a case-by-case analysis into State practice in the context of a prosecution for a single offence. It establishes a simpler equation: as it is a general conception of law that any breach of engagement involves an obligation to make reparation,[27] so it is a general conception of humanitarian law that any serious breach of an important rule of the laws and customs of war entails criminal responsibility. The aforementioned *Report of the Secretary-General pursuant to Resolution 808* expresses the same idea by saying that all persons who

[25] To all of them the following famous *dictum* applies: 'Crimes against international law are committed by men, not by abstract entities, and only by punishing individuals who commit such crimes can the provisions of international law be enforced' (*Judgment of the International Military Tribunal at Nüremberg*, (London, 1947), Cmd. 6964, p. 41 or in *AJIL* vol. 41 (1947), p. 220). When the Tribunal moved to the specific war crimes it considered that the various rules of the Hague Conventions or Regulation (1907) were applicable automatically also for founding a criminal responsibility (*Judgment* . . . , loc.cit., pp. 44 ff or *AJIL*, vol. 41 (1947), pp. 224 ff).

[26] The Tribunal at Nüremberg limited itself to asserting *generally* that there has been a previous practice of prosecution of war criminals (on the national level): See *Judgment* . . . , loc.cit., p. 40 or *AJIL*, vol. 41 (1947), p. 218.

[27] P.C.I.J., *Chorzów Factory (Merits)* case (1928), ser. A, no. 17, p. 29.

participate in the execution of *serious* violations of international humanitarian law are individually responsible for their acts.[28] It therefore seems that, since the Statutes limit the jurisdiction of the Tribunals to 'serious violations of international humanitarian law' (for example, Article 1, ICTY Statute), the existence of individual responsibility was already implicit. It may be added that a case-by-case analysis of the existence of a previous practice of individual accountability encounters serious obstacles. The case-law is sparse, except for classical crimes where there is anyway no difficulty. Moreover, the basis on which many of the post-World War II trials were decided is municipal law, with its specific if not idiosyncratic offences. As was to be expected, the ICTY limited itself, when confronted with the question, to asserting in general and wholly unsupported terms that the offence charged was 'clearly' recognized as giving rise to individual responsibility under customary law.[29] It may be asked if the legal construction proposed in the present article would not be clearer, simpler, more direct and intellectually more honest.

The situation is different in the case of rules belonging to the law of non-international armed conflicts. The question of whether the serious violation of the laws governing civil strife entails individual criminal responsibility was not settled by the post-World War II trials since those trials had to deal only with international armed conflict. Hence no general acceptance of the community of States as to the criminal consequences of the violation of such rules existed. The question was raised in the *Tadic* (1995) case. The appellant had maintained that prohibitions concerning internal armed conflict do not entail individual criminal responsibility. The Chamber made reference to some factors mentioned by the Nüremberg Tribunal as warranting the conclusion that there should be criminal responsibility. It summarized these criteria in a tighter way than the Nüremberg judgment had done: '[There must be a] clear and unequivocal recognition of the rules of warfare in international law and State practice indicating an intention to criminalize the prohibition, including statements by government officials and international organizations, as well as punishment of violations by national courts and military tribunals'.[30] It may be noted that an emerging *opinio juris* of the necessity of prosecution and some proceedings in municipal courts (in application of municipal law) may be considered sufficient under that holding. The material element (practice) is subordinated to the subjective element (opinion). The Chamber concludes that it has no doubt that the (serious) violations of humanitarian rules in issue also entail criminal responsibility when committed in internal armed conflicts.[31]

[28] UN. Doc. S/25704, para. 54, emphasis added.

[29] See, e.g., *Delalic*, para. 307 ff (for Common Article 3 of the Geneva Conventions of 1949); *Furundzija*, para. 140 (for torture) and para. 169 (for rape and other serious sexual assaults).

[30] *Tadic* (1995), para. 128.

[31] Ibid., para. 129.

The Chamber puts forward a number of military manuals and national legislation, some convictions arising out of the Nigerian Civil war before Nigerian courts and certain resolutions adopted unanimously by the Security Council of the United Nations.[32] Moreover, Yugoslav legislation allows a direct applicability of the two Protocols of 1977 to which Yugoslavia was a party.[33] There was thus on this point a significant assimilation of the legal regimes of international and internal armed conflict so far as the ICTY is concerned. It may in the future be possible to apply the equation previously discussed (all serious violations of international humanitarian law entail criminal responsibility) to non-international armed conflicts.

3. *The Requirement that the Violations of Humanitarian Law are Serious and Took Place at a Certain Location and during a Certain Period of Time*

The Statutes of both Tribunals restrict the jurisdiction of those bodies to 'persons responsible for *serious* violations of international humanitarian law'.[34] This criterion again applies above all to the violation of the laws of war (Art. 3 ICTY Statute; Art. 4 ICTR Statute), since the crimes of genocide or crimes against humanity are inherently grave crimes which in principle suppose the utmost seriousness when violated. In the case-law it has been held that a violation is serious if (i) the rule breached protects important values and (ii) the breach involves grave consequences for the victim.[35] The first criterion attaches to the quality of an offence in the abstract, the second to the specific consequences its breach produced in a single case. These criteria are cumulative, since there may be some violations of important rules which are so minor as not to involve grave consequences for the victim. According to the ICTY Chamber in the *Tadic* (1997) case, the prohibitions of Common Article 3 of the Geneva Conventions (1949) are rules protecting important values, as they give expression to the elementary considerations of humanity.[36] Conversely it was held in the *Delalic* case (1998) that the systematic plunder of private property of internees by the accused was of so modest monetary value that the appropriation did not involve grave consequences for the victims.[37] Thus the Chamber held it did not possess jurisdiction over that crime. It therefore seems that the seriousness of the violation of law should be denied only for rules or breaches of international humanitarian law which are manifestly not deserving of any

[32] Ibid., paras. 130–4.
[33] Ibid., para. 132.
[34] Art. 1 ICTY / ICTR Statutes, emphasis added.
[35] *Tadic* (1997), para. 610, 612.
[36] Ibid., para. 612.
[37] *Delalic*, para. 1154.

criminal consequences. The old maxim *de minimis non curat praetor* applies. The interpretation of these exceptions has to be strict.

It has already been suggested that there is a link between this element of 'seriousness' and the requirement that an offence must give rise under customary law to individual criminal responsibility.[38] The substantial overlapping of these elements covers only the first branch of the test adopted by the ICTY, i.e. that the rule breached protects in the abstract important values. It cannot extend to the considerations proper only to the single case.

There are moreover two jurisdictional conditions, *ratione loci* and *ratione temporis*. With respect to the condition *ratione loci*, Article 1 of the ICTY Statute contains the simpler rule. The violations of humanitarian law must have been committed 'in the territory of the former Yugoslavia'. The term 'territory' is a legal term of art which must be understood in the sense given to it by public international law; it includes the territorial sea, airspace, etc. According to general principles of law, it is sufficient that the effect of criminal conduct be felt on the territory of the State; the classic example is that of the shot across the boundary. But the effects principle may also apply to conspiracy or instigation committed abroad with the aim of provoking a criminal result on the territory of the third State. One may here refer to the territoriality principle as the basis for criminal prosecution.

The problem is more intricate for the ICTR. Article 1 of its Statute provides that all persons committing the incriminating acts in Rwanda shall be prosecuted, as well as Rwandan citizens responsible for such violations committed in the territory of neighbouring States. The conflict is here treated as a unity, including the neighbouring States where the conflict spilled over. Thus there is a mixed *ratione loci vel personae* criterion. The acts or omissions must have been committed (i) either in Rwanda on the basis of the already discussed territoriality-principle; or (ii) in one of the neighbouring States where the conflict in fact spilled over, if the crime is committed there by Rwandan citizens. This bond of nationality must be considered according to the rules of public international law. As can be seen the ICTR enjoys a larger jurisdiction *ratione loci*.

As for the conditions *ratione temporis*, for the ICTY the offence must have been committed between 1991 (i.e. after 31 December 1990)[39] and the conclusion of peace on 1 December 1995 (i.e. the Dayton Agreement).[40] At the ICTR the time-span is expressed even more precisely: the offence must have been committed between 1 January 1994 and 31 December 1994.[41]

[38] *Supra*.

[39] *Report of the Secretary-General*, UN.Doc. S/25704, para. 62: 'On or after 1 January 1991'.

[40] See generally *Tadic* (1995), para. 70.

[41] Article 1 ICTR Statute.

4. *The Existence of an Armed Conflict*

a) *The ICTY*

Article 1 of the ICTY Statute dealing with the competence of the Tribunal does not contain any express reference to the existence of an armed conflict, nor does the Report of the Secretary-General address this point. The conflict in Yugoslavia was considered as a mixed international and internal conflict; the question was not further elaborated, leaving it to the Tribunal to reach its own conclusions.[42] However, the requirement of an armed conflict seems implicit in the condition that international humanitarian law must have been violated, as this branch of law applies only if there is an armed conflict. Therefore the Chamber in the *Tadic* (1997) case could conclude that it must be shown that the incriminating acts were committed 'within the context of an armed conflict'.[43]

Must the conflict be an international armed conflict, or is it sufficient, subject to express exceptions, that there is an armed conflict, international or internal? This distinction has been of the greatest importance up to 1949, shaping two distinct bodies of law, one relative to situations which were classified as war between two or more States, the other relative to civil strife. States were always reluctant to admit international rules to govern internal disturbances which they considered pertained exclusively to their domestic jurisdiction. In the *Tadic* (1995) case this distinction has been wholly upset for the purposes of international criminal law. The Chamber there held that the Statute of the Tribunal referred indistinctly to international *and* to internal armed conflicts, with the exception of Article 2, the grave breaches régime, which according to Additional Protocol I and customary law applies only to international armed conflicts.[44] This finding is based mainly on a teleological and an implied powers argument: the purpose of the Security Council to prosecute all the persons responsible for serious violations of international humanitarian law could not be served otherwise than by extending the jurisdiction of the Tribunal to the entirety of the conflict, international and internal. Moreover, as the Security Council knew that the conflict was generally considered of a mixed international and internal character, it must by necessary implication have granted the Tribunal jurisdiction also for the internal part of the conflict, for otherwise only a part of the persons responsible for serious violations of

[42] The *Report of the Secretary-General*, UN.Doc. S/25704, para. 62, is at pains to stress that 'no judgment as to the international or internal character of the conflict is being exercised'.

[43] *Tadic* (1997), para. 559.

[44] *Tadic* (1995), para. 71 ff, 81–3. Judge Abi-Saab, in his Separate Opinion, was even prepared to apply the grave breaches régime equally in internal armed conflicts. He roots his argument in the growing practice going in that direction. This practice has in his view the force of a subsequent practice modificatory of the conventional provisions of Protocol I and also the strength of a new rule of customary international law.

international humanitarian law could have been prosecuted. And this is precisely what the Security Council wanted to avoid: it would have been absurd to treat differently horrific cruelties according to the fortuitous fact of having been committed before or after a specific date, or at one place rather than another on the territory of the former Yugoslavia. Now, it may be contended that the whole argument was superfluous, as the conflict in the former Yugoslavia was at all the material times an international armed conflict[45] (a position that recommends itself). But if one starts from the assumptions accepted by the Chamber, one may grasp the extent of international legislation attributed to the Security Council by the Chamber in *Tadic*. Under the influence of criminal law there is a strong tendency to a merger of the law relating to international and internal armed conflicts.[46] This extremely important evolution prompts an array of legal consequences which cannot be mentioned here.

For the purposes of this new customary law on the obligations of participants in any armed conflict, the Chamber set out the single yardstick on which it measures the existence of an armed conflict. It thus gave the following definition of armed conflict: '[An armed conflict exists] whenever there is a resort to armed force between States or protracted armed violence between governmental authorities and organized armed groups or between such groups within a State'.[47] This definition, which has been endorsed by all the later trials,[48] marks the threshold at which the Tribunal will have jurisdiction, irrespective of the intrinsic quality of the armed conflict (except for the grave breaches régime). As explained by the Trial Chamber in the *Tadic* (1997) case, this definition has two aspects: there must, first, be a certain material *intensity* of the conflict; there must, second, be a certain *organization* of the armed forces involved which distinguishes their operations from short-lived insurrections, riots or banditry. On the first aspect there must be some sustained and concerted military operations. On the second point there must be a certain military order, probably a responsible command, and such effective control over a part of the territory as to enable the groups concerned to carry on military operations and implement the laws of war.[49] On the facts, the different Chambers of the Tribunal have always found that there has been at the material times fighting of such intensity on the Bosnian territory as to qualify as armed conflict.[50] It would be difficult to contest that finding.

[45] See e.g. the Diss.Op. Rodrigues, *Aleksovski* case, paras. 22 ff.

[46] There is no evidence that the Security Council itself intended to extend the scope of existing substantive law.

[47] *Tadic* (1995), para. 70.

[48] *Delalic*, paras. 182 ff; *Furundzija*, para. 51 ff; *Aleksovski*, paras. 42 ff; *Jelisic*, paras. 29–30.

[49] For details on these criteria, see ICRC, *Commentary on the Additional Protocols of 8 June 1977 to the Geneva Conventions of 12 August 1949*, (Geneva, 1987), pp. 1347 ff.

[50] See, e.g., *Tadic* (1995), para. 70; *Delalic*, para. 192; etc.

There do not have to be actual fighting activities amounting to an armed conflict in the location where the accused is said to have committed his crimes. As was explained in the *Delalic* case (1998), it is sufficient that there existed such a conflict in the 'larger territory of which it forms part'.[51] Thus it is enough to prove that there is an armed conflict in Bosnia-Herzegovina in order to cover all acts or omissions perpetrated on its territory.

b) *The ICTR*

The conflict which afflicted Rwanda in 1994 was an internal armed conflict. This is the reason why the régime of grave breaches was not included in the ICTR Statute; the grave breaches régime was thought to be limited to international armed conflicts. On the other hand mass killings happened in Rwanda independently from the military operations by the contending factions.[52] The prosecution of genocide and crimes against humanity is thus placed on a legally autonomous basis which is not affected by any finding as to the existence of or link with an armed conflict.

To this state of affairs there is one exception which can be found in Article 4 of the Statute. This Article deals with violations of Common Article 3 of the Geneva Conventions of 1949 and of Additional Protocol II of 1977. Under customary and conventional law those provisions or instruments only apply if there is at least a non-international armed conflict. This requirement was thus read to have also been indirectly incorporated into the Statute to the extent that it refers to those provisions and instruments.[53]

If for the ICTY there must as a general rule be shown that there existed an armed conflict, for the ICTR the general rule is the reverse, subject in both cases to specific exceptions (Article 2 for the ICTY; Article 4 for the ICTR).

5. *The Existence of a Nexus between the Offences and the Armed Conflict*

As all the offences listed in the Statute of the ICTY are subjected to the competence of this Tribunal only if there is at least a non-international armed conflict, the requirement that there must be a nexus between the acts or omissions of the perpetrator and the armed conflict applies to all the offences. Conversely, for the ICTR, a similar condition applies only for Article 4 of its Statute concerning violations of Common Article 3 of the Geneva Conventions (1949) and of Protocol II (1977).

51 *Delalic*, para. 185.
52 Such killings were often perpetrated by civilians.
53 See *Akayesu*, paras. 619 ff, 622 ff.

Moreover, for the ICTR the link requirement is not a condition for the jurisdiction of the Tribunal; its absence goes to the merits of the case and leads to the acquittal of the accused.

In the *Tadic* (1997) case, the Chamber of the ICTY expanded on the notion of the nexus.[54] It found that the incriminating acts must be 'closely related'[55] to the hostilities. It is sufficient to prove that the offence was committed in the course or as a part of the hostilities in, or in occupation of, an area controlled by one of the parties. It is not necessary that the armed conflict was occurring at that place or at that exact time, since the acts do not have to be committed in actual combat. Nor is it necessary to show that the incriminating acts were endorsed by the State authorities. In the *Kayishema* case (1999), the ICTR, in the context of Article 4 of its Statute, took up this requirement and asked for a 'direct connection';[56] it added that what a direct connection requires must be appreciated on a case-by-case basis. This last point was endorsed by another Chamber of the ICTR in the *Rutaganda* case (1999).[57]

For a better understanding of the practical scope of this requirement it is useful to look at the way it was applied. In the *Tadic* (1997) case, the acts of ethnic cleansing and the acts perpetrated in a prisoners' camp were considered connected with the armed conflict, as they were endorsed by the Serb authorities; indeed, they were acts done in execution of the Serb war policy.[58] Thus, acts done in furtherance of the war policy of one party to the conflict are considered closely related to the conflict. In the *Delalic* case (1998) it was found that the incriminating acts were committed in the prison camp of Celebici, operated by the governmental authorities of Bosnia-Herzegovina. The prisoners of that camp had been arrested as a result of military operations conducted on behalf of that government. Thus there was clearly a nexus of the character required.[59] In the *Furundzija* case (1998) the existence of a link was accepted because the accused had acted as a commander of a Croat paramilitary unit.[60]

In considering this jurisprudence it can be said that the nexus condition neither requires an endorsement of the acts by a party to the conflict, nor, at the other extreme, is it sufficient that the incriminating acts are not wholly unrelated to the armed conflict. To require that they are imputable to the State is too high a standard. On the other hand, to exclude only acts performed on purely personal grounds is too low a

[54] *Tadic* (1997), paras. 572 ff.

[55] Ibid., para. 573.

[56] *Kayishema*, para. 188: 'A direct connection . . . should be established factually. No test, therefore, can be defined *in abstracto*'. See also para. 600 ('a direct link'), para. 604.

[57] *Rutaganda*, under ch. 2.4 (no paragraphed version of this judgment is available at the present time).

[58] *Tadic* (1997), paras. 574–5.

[59] *Delalic*, paras. 193 ff, 196.

[60] *Furundzija*, paras. 61 ff, 65.

standard. What must be shown is that (i) either the accused acts for the benefit of one party to the conflict or in furtherance of its war effort or policy; or (ii) that he acts on behalf of one party to the conflict.

Some interesting light is shed on the question of the link by the jurisprudence of the ICTR on Article 4 of its Statute. In all the cases adjudicated up to this moment the ICTR has acquitted the accused from the charges under Article 4 because the link between the acts committed and the armed conflict has not been established.[61] The cardinal criterion shaped by this jurisprudence is that for the nexus requirement under Article 4 to be satisfied it must be proved that the accused 'actively supported the war effort',[62] or that he acted for one party in the conflict 'in execution of their respective conflict objectives'.[63] In the cases decided by the ICTR, the accused were civilians holding local political mandates, or businessmen. The ICTR considered that it was not proved that the acts perpetrated by these accused were committed in conjunction with the armed conflict or in supporting the war effort of one party. The Tutsis were attacked by civilian authorities as part of a campaign of hatred designed to exterminate the Tutsi population in Rwanda. Neither the Government nor the RPF army were involved in these massacres.[64] Thus, as can be seen, the link requirement under Article 4 of the ICTR Statute follows substantively the findings of the ICTY under its own link condition, whereas procedurally it has another scope, not being a preliminary question of jurisdiction but a condition of criminal responsibility of the accused.

III. Article 2 of the ICTY Statute: Grave Breaches of the Geneva Conventions of 1949[65]

In order to apply Article 2 of the Statute two conditions must be met: (1) there must exist an international armed conflict; and (2) the victims must be protected persons in the sense given by the Geneva Conventions of 1949.

1. *The Requirement of an International Armed Conflict*

(*a*) As the Geneva Conventions of 1949 and Protocol I of 1977 are limited to *international armed conflicts*, the régime for the suppression of

[61] *Akayesu*, paras. 638 ff. *Kayishema*, paras. 590 ff. *Rutaganda*, under ch. 5.6.
[62] *Akayesu*, para. 642.
[63] Ibid., para. 640.
[64] See, e.g., *Kayishema*, paras. 619–23.
[65] On the régime of grave breaches, see ICRC, *Commentary on the Additional Protocols of 8 June 1977 to the Geneva Conventions of 12 August 1949*, (Geneva, 1987) pp. 973 ff.

grave breaches contained therein[66] applies only to such conflicts and not to internal conflicts. This position has been recognized also under customary international law. That is the reason why the ICTR Statute does not contain any provision dealing with grave breaches: the conflict in Rwanda was non-international. For the same reasons, the ICTY stated clearly that in order to apply Article 2 of its Statute it had first to be satisfied that there existed an international armed conflict at the time and location that the crimes were perpetrated.[67]

This limitation of the scope of Article 2 was not accepted by all the judges. In the *Tadic* (1995) case, Judge Abi-Saab invoked a growing practice of application of the grave breaches régime also in internal conflicts. According to him this practice had already attained the complexion of a new customary rule. It could alternatively (and preferably) be analysed as a subsequent practice modifying the treaty régime.[68] For Judge Abi-Saab there is thus an evolution of the law within the system of the sources containing the grave breaches régime. For Judge Rodrigues, in the *Aleksovski* case (1999), there is no requirement of an international armed conflict because Article 2 of the Statute is autonomous with respect to the conventional régime of grave breaches and does not operate any *renvoi* to these sources. The Security Council did not qualify the conflict either as internal or international, leaving that question open; this shows that the Council wanted to incorporate the grave breaches régime into the Statute independently from any specific qualification of the conflict. In fact the references to the Geneva Conventions were only made in order to have a list of the offences, not for incorporating all the other conditions linked to the application of those instruments. Article 2, Judge Rodrigues continues, makes no reference whatsoever to the internationality of the conflict. Recent practice, as Judge Abi-Saab had explained, further grants some support to such an extensive reading of the grave breaches régime and to its independence from the Geneva Conventions.[69]

Both these positions rest on the idea of some act of legislation, either by the Tribunal, by consecrating an evolution of the law which is far from achieved, or by the Security Council, which would have carved out of its ordinary context the grave breaches régime. The Tribunal avoided striking out that far. Considering that most of the grave breaches easily

[66] Cf. Articles 49–50 / 50–51 / 129–139 / 146–7 Geneva Conventions I-IV; Article 85 of Protocol I.

[67] *Tadic* (1995), para. 81–3. *Tadic* (1997), para. 569. *Tadic* (1999), paras. 83 ff. *Delalic*, paras. 199 ff, 204 ff. *Aleksovski*, para. 46.

[68] Sep.Op. Abi-Saab, *Tadic* (1995), chap. IV.

[69] Diss.Op. Rodrigues, *Aleksovski*, paras. 29 ff. It must be said that the main argument on the choice of the Security Council has no compelling force. The Council did indeed not qualify the conflict; it left that question to be performed by the Tribunal. Its incorporation of the grave breaches régime can therefore very well be read as an instruction to the Tribunal to apply that régime *to the extent that* it should find that the conflict was international in character.

qualify also as war crimes there may not be much legal loss on the balance.

(*b*) When does an international armed conflict exist? This apparently simple question has prompted the greatest problem heretofore encountered in the jurisprudence of the ICTY. It is clearly not the definition of the concept, but its application to the circumstances of the war in Bosnia, that raised the difficulties to be discussed. As to the definition, it was stated in *Tadic* (1999) that an armed conflict is international if either (i) it takes place between two or more States, (ii) a foreign State intervenes in an internal conflict through its troops, or (iii) some of the participants in an internal conflict act on behalf of a foreign State.[70]

(*aa*) The question if the armed conflict was international for the purposes of Article 2 of the Statute first arose, albeit indirectly, in the *Tadic* (1997) judgment of the Trial Chamber. The Chamber did not discuss the character of the conflict independently from the second condition necessary to the application of Article 2, i.e. the status of the victims as protected persons. It thought that it could dispose of the applicability of Article 2 exclusively on this second ground. The reasoning of the Chamber is as follows. According to Article 4 of the Geneva Convention IV of 1949, a civilian is a protected person (and thus the grave breaches régime is applicable) if he is in the hands of a party to the conflict of which he is not a national. After the withdrawal of the JNA[71] from Bosnia on 19 May 1992, the Bosnian-Serb armed forces were a legal entity distinct from the FRY. The civilians it took into custody could only be considered in the hands of a party whose nationality they did not possess if the acts of the Bosnian-Serb armed forces could be imputed to the FRY; otherwise Bosnian civilians would have been held by Bosnian (-Serb) military forces, no difference of nationality existing. According to the Chamber, the acts of the Bosnian-Serb army (VRS) could be imputed to the FRY only if they acted as *de facto* organs of that State. As has been held by the International Court of Justice in the *Nicaragua* (*Merits*, 1986) case,[72] under customary law a person or entity can be considered a *de facto* organ of a State if there is *effective control* by the State over that person or entity. There must be a great dependency on the one side and power of control on the other. The relationship between the JNA and the VRS after 19 May 1992 did not involve more than a general level of coordination of the activities consonant with their position as allied forces in the Serbian war effort. Neither the FRY nor the JNA directed the military operations of the VRS even if there was

[70] *Tadic* (1999), para. 84. For the *Dictionnaire de la terminologie du droit international* in preparation under the lead of J. Salmon, the present author had defined the international armed conflict as a term covering 'les cas de guerre déclarée, la confrontation armée entre Etats même si la condition de guerre n'est pas reconnue entre eux, les représailles ou les interventions armées sur le territoire d'Etats tiers et les conflits issus de l'exercice du droit à l'autodétermination'.

[71] The army of the FRY.

[72] ICJ, Rep. 1986, p. 64–5, para. 115.

support by equipping, maintaining and staffing it. Therefore, there was no effective control; no attribution of the acts of the VRS to the FRY is possible. Thus, in turn, the victims were not in the hands of a foreign power and could not, in consequence, be regarded as protected persons. The Chamber concludes that Article 2 of the Statute is inapplicable.[73]

This decision and reasoning were quashed on appeal, in the *Tadic* (1999) judgment. The Appeals Chamber considered the question of the attribution of the acts of the VRS to the FRY under the requirement that there exist an international armed conflict. This difference of approach is not really explained but it is of considerable relevance. According to the Appeals Chamber, the question turns on the issue whether the VRS could be considered a *de iure* or *de facto* organ of the FRY, and for that recourse must be had to the legal criteria for the imputability to a State of acts performed by individuals not having the status of State officials.[74] This legal mechanism of imputability is the same under the law of international responsibility and for the purposes of criminal international law because it is a general legal technique. However, the effective control test propounded by the International Court of Justice in the *Nicaragua* case is at variance with international law. Contrary to the holding of the Court, international law does not know an exclusive and all-embracing test of attribution for *de facto* organs; the degree of control required varies in relation to different types of situations. Several reported cases[75] show that in the context of military or paramilitary groups acting factually in the interest of a State, an *overall control* over the group is sufficient for the purposes of imputation. It has not to be shown that each activity was specifically requested or directed by the State. It is sufficient to show that the State equipped and financed the group, or coordinated and helped in the general planning of the military activity.[76] The Appeals Chamber found that in the present case the requisite measure of overall control was exercised by the FRY over the VRS.[77] Hence even after 19 May 1992 the armed conflict in Bosnia was international in character. As

[73] *Tadic* (1997), paras. 584 ff. *Contra*, Sep. and Diss. Op. McDonald, in: ILR, vol. 112, pp. 261–2, 268 ff.

[74] Such an approach was also taken by the majority in the *Aleksovski* case (1999), Joint. Sep. Op. Vohrah/Nieto-Navia, para. 27.

[75] As the *Stephens* case, the *Yaeger* case, the *Loizidou* case or the *Jorgic* case. See *Tadic* (1999), paras. 125–9.

[76] *Tadic* (1999), paras. 122–3, 131, 137: 'The control required by international law may be deemed to exist when a State (. . .) has a role in organizing, coordinating or planning the military actions of the military group . . . '. For individuals not organized into military structures the threshold for attribution is higher: there must be specific instructions or *ex post* approval; the Chamber here quotes the *Teheran Hostages* case (ICJ, Rep. (1980), p. 29–30), ibid., para. 132.

[77] Ibid., paras. 146 ff. The Chamber mentions the transfer of JNA officers to the VRS and the payment of the salaries of the members of the VRS by the FRY; the fact that military operations of the VRS were supervised by organs of the FRY; the fact that members of the FRY's armed forces took part in combats in Bosnia; and the fact that the military goals were still formulated by the FRY. The political settings of the Dayton Agreement also confirmed the control of the FRY over the Republica Srpska.

the Appeals Chamber found that the victims were also protected persons,[78] it concluded that the grave breaches régime was applicable to the case at hand.[79]

The provisionally final stage in this question was reached in the *Delalic* case (1998). As to the international character of the conflict, the Trial Chamber adopts a very flexible and generic standard, avoiding the technical point of attribution. It simply states that with regard to the involvement of outside forces (Croat, Serb) and the degree of control exercised, the conflict was clearly international in nature. This holds true even after 19 May 1992, control and support (and even direct involvement) continuing.[80] The régime of grave breaches could thus be applied if the victims were protected persons.

(*bb*) Summarizing the case-law reviewed, one discovers three different tests adopted in different contexts. In *Tadic* (1997), the test is that of *effective control* propounded in the context of the nationality criterion of the protected persons. In *Tadic* (1999), the test is that of *overall control* in the context of the internationality of the conflict. In *Delalic* (1998), the test is one of *involvement* of external forces again in the context of the internationality of the conflict. What can be said about this state of affairs?

We may ignore at this stage the *Tadic* (1997) judgment, it being concerned with the status of the victims as protected persons, a question to be discussed below. The crux of the decision in *Tadic* (1999) seems to be the pivotal place given to the notion of imputation (or attribution) which in turn calls for control tests (effective or overall control, etc.). This merger of criteria proper to the law of State responsibility and of those necessary to the determination of the international character of an armed conflict does not seem warranted. Attribution and control are necessary if an entity is legally sought to be made responsible for acts performed by third persons as if they were its own.[81] They are not required for establishing the existence of an objective state of things, i.e. the existence of an international armed conflict, where it must only be shown that there is, in fact, a substantial implication of foreign powers. Obviously, the question is not whether these foreign powers have to be responsible for the acts of the local armies as if they were their own; the question is whether their involvement is of sufficient intensity to broaden the scope of the conflict into an international armed conflict. It may be appreciated that the two tests are not at all identical. The threshold to be reached is higher for the first than for the second. These aspects were felt

[78] Ibid., paras. 163 ff.

[79] Ibid., para. 171.

[80] *Delalic*, paras. 204 ff.

[81] Attribution is in fact the legal technique by which acts performed by an individual are legally considered as acts of a moral person, be it a corporation or a State. The acts are then the acts of that entity, as—as pointed out by Windscheid in the nineteenth century—the acts of our hands and feet are considered automatically our own.

by Judge Shahabuddeen, who correctly points out that the question was whether the FRY was using force in Bosnia, not the distinct one whether the FRY was responsible for any breaches of humanitarian law committed by the VRS.[82] It may be added, albeit in passing, that the reading given to the effective control test of the ICJ in *Tadic* (1999) is at least puzzling. This test cannot by any stretch of imagination be said to be rigid and exclusive.[83] It is essentially fact intensive and related to the specific context the Court was confronted with. It may be remembered that the *contras* were not in any way acting 'for' the United States of America as the groups in the Stephens, Yaeger and other cases quoted by the Appeals Chamber did for the respective States involved. In such a situation, the effective control test (what is 'effective' depending on the circumstances, the discipline of the forces, etc.) was not inappropriate.

2. *The Status of the Victims as Protected Persons*

(*a*) The Geneva Conventions of 1949 define precisely what persons are protected against acts qualifying as grave breaches. Thus, Article 4(1) of the Geneva Convention IV on the protection of civilians in times of war subjects to the protection of the grave breaches régime all persons in the hands of a party to the conflict or an occupying power of which they are not nationals. It is this provision which has raised a number of problems in the case-law of the Tribunals. As the three main cases once more differ in the stand to be adopted, it seems appropriate to start by reviewing their content one by one.

(*b*) In the *Tadic* (1997) case, the term 'in the hands of' has been given a very broad interpretation in order to cover not only persons physically in the hands of the enemy, but all persons in the territory occupied by the enemy (i.e. a party to the conflict of which they are not nationals).[84] This broad interpretation corresponds perfectly to the legislative intent when drafting that formula, intent clearly reflected in the ICRC's Commentary to Article 4 of the Geneva Convention IV.[85] On the other hand, the Chamber has given a very narrow interpretation of the term 'of which they are not nationals'. As has already been explained,[86] it held that Muslim Bosnians held by Serb Bosnians did not satisfy this criterion because the nationality as a formal bond was the same (Bosnian). It then embarked upon the considerations devoted to the status of the VRS as *de facto* organ of the FRY. If such an organic dependency were established the Muslim Bosnians could be considered prisoners *longa manu* of the FRY; they would then have been in the hands of a party of which they

[82] Sep.Op. Shahabuddeen, *Tadic* (1999), para. 17.
[83] This point was also correctly taken by Judge Shahabuddeen, ibid., para. 19.
[84] *Tadic* (1997), paras. 579 ff. See also *Delalic*, para. 246.
[85] J. Pictet (ed.), *Commentary to Geneva Convention IV* (Geneva, 1958), pp. 45 ff.
[86] See above, 1(aa).

were not nationals. As previously seen, the Chamber found that there was no such organic dependency of the VRS because the FRY did not exercise effective control over it. Hence the victims were not protected persons in the sense of the Geneva Conventions and the grave breaches régime was inapplicable.[87]

This reasoning was reversed in the *Tadic* (1999) judgment. The Appeals Chamber adopted a teleological and finalistic approach. It started by recalling that the bond of nationality has never been crucial under Article 4 (Geneva Convention IV), since the intention of the drafters, as revealed by the *travaux préparatoires*, was to cover also refugees or stateless persons; i.e. all those who could not enjoy the diplomatic protection of a third State. In modern wars where it is often a structurally internal conflict which becomes international by the involvement of external forces, such an approach, departing from formal nationality, is warranted. In conflicts of the type described, ethnicity or other criteria become controlling in place of nationality. It would frustrate the object and purpose of the Convention if nationality was kept as the only criterion in such conflicts. Rather, the effectiveness of the system suggests allegiance as the essential criterion.[88] The Chamber adds that these considerations are strictly speaking *obiter dicta*,[89] as its finding that the VRS was a *de facto* organ of the FRY is sufficient to grant the victims the status of protected persons.[90] The same line of argument was adopted by the Trial Chamber in the *Delalic* case (1998).[91] The Chamber stresses that the aim of Article 4 (Geneva Convention IV) is the protection of persons in real combat situations, not formal requirements of nationality according to municipal law contingencies. The broader approach is also consonant with human rights law. As, in the case under consideration, the persons were arrested on the basis of their Serb identity, they must be considered protected persons under a teleological interpretation of the law.[92]

(*c*) The teleological approach adopted in the *Tadic* (1999) Appeal judgment and in the *Delalic* case (1998) is to be preferred. The Conventions of 1949 were drafted under the paradigm of inter-State wars. In such a context the criterion of nationality has its place. It is the

[87] *Tadic* (1997), paras. 584 ff. See also the Joint Sep.Op. Vohrah/Nieto-Navia, *Aleksovski*, para. 34.

[88] *Tadic* (1999), paras. 163 ff.

[89] This expression is not used by the Chamber but introduced by the present commentator.

[90] *Tadic* (1999), para. 167.

[91] *Delalic*, paras. 247 ff.

[92] The Chamber also considered the question whether the victims were prisoners of war in the sense of Article 4 of the Geneva Convention III and thus protected persons under that Convention. Article 4 of G.C. III was drafted narrowly according to the conception of war current in 1949. The conditions of Article 4(A)(2) or (6) of the G.C. III are hardly fulfilled in the present case. The victims were neither carrying arms openly, nor was there an invading force. Thus the victims were only civilians in the sense of the G.C. IV. They were all covered by the G.C. IV since there is no gap between G.C. III and IV (ibid., paras. 267 ff.).

adequate legal vehicle for protection—which is the ultimate aim—under such factual assumptions. During the 1950s and 1960s this assumption proved insufficient in the light of the outbreak of endemic civil wars and wars by proxy. The legal system adapted its requirements and *inter alia* broadened the scope of the concept of international armed conflict by extending it to civil wars with external interventions. Unfortunately the Geneva Conventions were not adapted to the new situations on all points (but could that be expected?). Nationality for the purposes of Article 4, Geneva Convention IV, is still a workable criterion for traditional armed conflict, but not for those which are structurally internal, becoming international only by a new legal qualification. In such structurally internal but now legally international conflicts, the nationality criterion leads to the almost complete ineffectiveness of the law, opening disastrous gaps in the protection it affords. As it was the protection which was always the cardinal criterion, and the nationality requirement only a technical means to that end, it must be considered that with the legal internationalization of structurally internal armed conflicts, the nationality requirement has been implicitly modified to make workable the new legal qualification of the conflict within the body of applicable law. This operation is rendered unavoidable by elementary considerations of *effet utile* and of practicability. 'Nationality' must thus be read as meaning allegiance, i.e. a civilian is protected if he is in the hands of the adverse party.

The 'legislative' effect of such a re-reading of Article 4, Geneva Convention IV, is quite limited, as that interpretation is compelled if the provision is not to become useless. Alternatively, if one wishes to avoid such a course, the finding of a relationship of *de facto* overall control between the VRS and FRY can acquire importance; it provides an autonomous basis for concluding that the victims were protected persons, since it means that being held in the hands of the VRS may legally be equated to being in the hands of the FRY.

The narrow jurisprudence of *Tadic* (1997) has thus been overcome by the later trials of the ICTY with the consequence that the grave breaches régime will find general application to the crimes perpetrated on the territory of Bosnia-Herzegovina.

IV. Article 3 of the ICTY Statute: Violations of the Laws and Customs of War

1. This provision covers the traditional heading of war crimes on which there is a rich jurisprudence since the Leipzig, and more conspicuously, since the Nüremberg Trials. Such crimes were traditionally reserved to international armed conflicts; therefore the ICTR Statute does not contain the same type of provision. Instead, its Article 4 covers

breaches of Common Article 3 of the Geneva Conventions of 1949 and of Protocol II (1977). This Article may thus be said to criminalize some war crimes committed within an internal armed conflict. There is a partial overlap between Articles 3 (ICTY) and 4 (ICTR) of the Statutes, as the former applies to international and internal armed conflicts.[93] Article 3 contains the offences criminalized by Article 4 but has a broader range, since it extends also to war crimes committed within an international conflict. We shall first turn to the ICTY Statute and then immediately revert to Article 4 of the ICTR Statute.

2. The case-law of the ICTY has often stressed that Article 3 of its Statute constitutes a *general clause* (*clause supplétive*) which is intended to cover all serious violations of international humanitarian law not falling under other specific provisions, e.g. Article 2 (grave breaches).[94] It has the function of a residual clause assuring that no one having committed a serious violation of international humanitarian law is left unpunished because of a gap in the listing of the offences.[95] In the light of that purpose, Article 3 has a very broad scope. As was said in *Furundzija* (1998), it covers any serious violation of a rule of customary international law entailing, under customary or conventional international law, individual criminal responsibility.[96] By the same token, the list of war crimes in Article 3 is not exhaustive.[97] It makes reference only to some rules of the Hague Law, but it is meant to cover also the Geneva Law (i.e. no narrow *ejusdem generis* argument is admissible). Moreover it consists only of an umbrella rule, being an open-ended reference to all rules of international humanitarian law. Not only that: it covers the rules of humanitarian law of international armed conflicts as well as those pertaining to internal armed conflicts.[98] This sort of *renvoi mobile* to the rules of humanitarian law as a basis for criminal prosecution can easily come in conflict with the *nullum crimen* principle. It is therefore accompanied by some strict conditions for the application of Article 3, which were set out in the *Tadic* (1997) case: (i) a rule of international humanitarian law must have been violated; (ii) the rule must have been of customary law (or of treaty law applicable to the acts and persons at hand); (iii) the violation must be serious, i.e. the rule breached must protect important values and the breach must involve grave consequences for the victim; and (iv) the violation of the rule must entail individual criminal responsibility.[99] Most of these conditions have already been discussed in the chapter devoted to the jurisdiction of the

[93] See *Tadic* (1995), para. 89. *Furundzija*, para. 132.
[94] *Tadic* (1995), paras. 86 ff. *Jelisic*, para. 33.
[95] Ibid., para. 91–2.
[96] *Furundzija*, paras. 131–3, 132.
[97] Ibid., para. 133. *Aleksovski*, para 48. *Delalic*, para. 278.
[98] *Tadic* (1995), para. 89. *Furundzija*, para. 132.
[99] *Tadic* (1997), para. 610. *Delalic*, para. 279.

Tribunals and it is sufficient at this point to refer to what has been explained there.[100]

3. Some offences were submitted to the test if they satisfied those requirements for the application of Article 3 of the Statute.

(*a*) In the *Tadic* (1997) judgment, it was said that Common Article 3 of the Geneva Conventions of 1949 meets these conditions.[101] As to its customary status, the Chamber invoked *inter alia* the *dictum* in the *Nicaragua* (*Merits*, 1986) case.[102] Moreover, its breach entails criminal responsibility. In the *Delalic* case (1998) this statement was further buttressed by references to the ILC Draft Code on Crimes against the Peace and Security of Mankind, the Rome Statute on an International Criminal Court, the ICTR Statute and the Criminal Code of the former SFRY.[103] The conditions for the application of Article 3 of the Statute for breaches of Common Article 3 were thus fulfilled. In the *Tadic* (1997) case, the Chamber moreover explained what is to be understood by the words 'taking no active part in hostilities' contained in Common Article 3. The criterion is negative: it is enough to show that the victim was not directly taking part in the hostilities; if he is *hors de combat* that condition is fulfilled.[104] In the *Delalic* case, the Chamber added that a violation of Common Article 3 could also be covered by Article 2 of the Statute and qualify as a grave breach. It would be sufficient to somewhat extend the notion of grave breaches. For the case at hand, the Chamber preferred to follow the more cautious approach by including violations of Common Article 3 in Article 3 of the Statute.[105]

(*b*) The question of the application of Article 3 of the Statute was also raised for acts of plunder. In the *Delalic* case (1998), it is said that there is no doubt as to the customary nature of the prohibition of plunder and as to the criminal responsibility arising from its breach. The Chamber makes reference to the Hague Regulations of 1907 and the Geneva Conventions of 1949 and also, for the criminal aspect, to the Nüremberg Trials.[106]

V. Article 4 of the ICTR Statute: Violations of Common Article 3 of the Geneva Conventions (1949) and of Additional Protocol II (1977)

1. Common Article 3 of the Geneva Conventions of 1949 represents an attempt to spell out some core aspects implicit in the famous Martens

[100] See above, II.
[101] *Tadic* (1997), paras. 611 ff. *Delalic*, paras. 281 ff.
[102] ICJ, Rep., 1986, pp. 113/4.
[103] *Delalic*, paras. 307 ff.
[104] *Tadic* (1997), para. 614/6.
[105] *Delalic*, para. 317.
[106] *Delalic*, para. 315.

Clause whereby all civilians and combatants, in whatever armed conflict, shall remain under the protection and authority of the principles of humanity.[107] Therefore Common Article 3 contains minimum guarantees of humanity which must be respected also in internal armed conflicts. It prohibits murder, mutilation, cruel treatment, torture, outrages upon personal dignity (such as humiliating and degrading treatment), the taking of hostages, and the passing of sentences without a previous fair trial. Additional Protocol II of 1977 constitutes an attempt to further develop the legal content briefly set out in Common Article 3. Article 4 of Protocol II in particular adds some specifically prohibited acts to those contained in Common Article 3, i.e. collective punishments, acts of terrorism, slavery, pillage, and the threat to commit any of the previously listed acts.

2. According to the jurisprudence of the ICTR, several conditions must be fulfilled for Article 4 of its Statute to be applicable. There are five such conditions, some of them containing more than one aspect.

(*a*) First, the offences applied must represent *customary international law* and the substantive rules from which they are derived must give rise, under customary international law, to individual criminal responsibility. It may here be recalled that the ICTR Chambers found that Common Article 3 of the Geneva Conventions (1949) and at least Article 4 of Protocol II—the only one whose application was sought—represent customary law; moreover international and national case-law shows that violations of those rules entail criminal responsibility.[108] These aspects have already been discussed when dealing with the jurisdictional issues.[109]

(*b*) Second, there must exist a *non-international armed conflict* as distinguished from simple internal disturbances or tensions, such as riots or sporadic acts of violence. The question, as already discussed,[110] turns on the intensity of the conflict and the level of organization of the (armed) forces involved. According to Article 1 of Protocol II, there must be organized armed groups, under responsible military command, exercising control over part of the territory of the State and carrying out sustained and concerted military operations putting them in a position to apply the rules of warfare.[111] These conditions have been found fulfilled for the situation in Rwanda in 1994.[112]

[107] On this clause, see H. Strebel, 'Martens Clause', *EPIL*, vol. 3, pp. 252–3.

[108] *Akayesu*, paras 601 ff. *Kayishema*, paras 155 ff. (the criminalization of these offences under the laws of Rwanda is sufficient). *Rutaganda*, under ch. 2.4.

[109] See above, II. 1. and 2.

[110] See above, II. 4.a).

[111] For the precise application of these criteria, see ICRC, *Commentary on the Additional Protocols of 8 June 1977 to the Geneva Conventions of 12 August 1949* (Geneva, 1987), pp. 1347 ff.

[112] *Akayesu*, paras. 619 ff. *Kayishema*, paras. 170 ff. *Rutaganda*, under ch. 2.4.

(*c*) Third, there are two conditions *ratione personae*. To start with, the *victims* have to be persons 'taking no active part in hostilities'[113] or persons 'who do not take a direct part or who have ceased to take part in hostilities'.[114] In the *Kayishema* case (1999), this is equated with being a civilian; but the term is given a broad interpretation in order to cover all persons who are not combatants, i.e. also prisoners of war[115] or persons *hors de combat*.[116] The Chamber in the *Rutaganda* case (1999) proposed a slightly different criterion. The victim is a civilian in the sense asked for if he falls outside the category of persons who can be perpetrators of the violations of Common Article 3 or Protocol II (see beneath). This definition is not entirely satisfactory, because it is recognized that civilians may also be accountable as perpetrators. Now it is clear that the perpetrator cannot at the same time be the victim. Apart from that, it is uncertain if the definition discussed carries the matter any further. According to the Chamber in the same *Rutaganda* case (1999), to take 'direct' part in the hostilities means taking part in acts of war which by their nature or purpose are likely to cause actual harm to the personnel and equipment of the enemy armed forces.[117]

The second aspect relates to the *perpetrators* of the violations of Common Article 3 and Protocol II. It has been pointed out that the perpetrator must be a member of the armed forces.[118] This is not limited to commanders and combatants but, in view of the protective purpose of the provisions involved, should be interpreted in the broadest possible sense.[119] Civilians may also be held accountable if they are mandated or holding *de facto* public authority in the context of the war effort.[120]

(*d*) Fourth, there is a condition *ratione loci*. The protection afforded extends to the whole territory of the State engaged in conflict, not only to the combat area.[121]

(*e*) Fifth, and last, there are two conditions *ratione materiae*. In the first place there must be a nexus between the commission of the offence and the armed conflict.[122] This aspect has been discussed previously.[123] It may be remembered that in all three cases decided up to now by the ICTR, the accused was acquitted on the count of offences relating to Article 4 of the Statute because such a link between his acts and the armed conflict was not established on the evidence. According to the

[113] Common Article 3 to the Geneva Conventions (1949).
[114] Art. 4 Protocol II (1977).
[115] *Kayishema*, para. 179.
[116] *Rutaganda*, under ch. 2.4.
[117] Ibid. See also on the whole question *Akayesu*, para. 629.
[118] *Akayesu*, paras. 630–1. *Kayishema*, paras. 173 ff., 175. *Rutaganda*, under ch. 2.4.
[119] *Rutaganda*, under ch. 2.4.
[120] *Akayesu*, para. 631. *Kayishema*, para. 175. *Rutaganda*, under ch. 2.4.
[121] *Akayesu*, paras. 635 ff. *Kayishema*, paras. 182 ff. *Rutaganda*, under ch. 2.4.
[122] *Akayesu*, paras. 638 ff. *Kayishema*, paras. 185 ff. *Rutaganda*, under ch. 2.4.
[123] See above, II. 5.

jurisprudence the existence of a direct connection to the conflict is a fact-intensive notion to be appreciated on a case-by-case basis.[124]

In the second place, the violation of the law must be serious, a criterion also already discussed.[125] The ICTR has recalled that violations of Common Article 3 of the Geneva Conventions of 1949 and of Article 4 of Protocol II (1977) are normally *per se* such serious violations.[126]

There is not much to add on these conditions. What is noteworthy is the rigorous reading of the nexus condition which has prevented up to now any conviction under Article 4 in the particular conditions of the Rwandan conflict. But in a certain sense a conviction under Article 4 was unnecessary since the accused were condemned for the graver crimes of genocide and crimes against humanity. As their acts were not related to the armed conflict, but motivated by genocidal hatred, the result reached by the Chambers of the ICTR is understandable.

VI. Article 4 ICTY Statute/Article 2 ICTR Statute: Genocide

1. The definition of genocide contained in Article 4 ICTY Statute and Article 2 ICTR Statute follows that given by the Convention on the Prevention and Punishment of the Crime of Genocide concluded in 1948.[127] According to the case-law of the ad hoc Tribunals, this definition of the offence has become customary.[128] In *Kayishema* (1999) it was even stressed that the elements of the offence thus listed are part of the international public order (*ius cogens*).[129] In this case it was also pointed out that genocide constitutes a type of crime against humanity. However, unlike crimes against humanity, genocide requires a specific intent to exterminate a protected group in whole or in part. For crimes against humanity it is sufficient to target the civilian population as part of a widespread or systematic attack.[130] The family link between genocide and crimes against humanity was already recognized in the Nüremberg subsequent proceedings, in the *Justice Trial* (US Military Tribunal, 1947).[131] It was also taken up by the United Nations Ad Hoc Committee which drew up the Genocide Convention; some of its members considered genocide to be the most typical of the crimes against humanity.[132]

[124] *Kayishema*, para. 188. *Rutaganda*, under ch. 2.4.

[125] See above, II. 3.

[126] *Kayishema*, para. 184. *Rutaganda*, under ch. 2.4.

[127] Article 2 of the Genocide Convention. See U.N.T.S., vol. 78, pp. 277 ff.

[128] *Akayesu*, para. 495. *Kayishema*, para. 88. *Rutaganda*, under ch. 2.2. *Jelisic*, para. 60.

[129] *Kayishema*, para. 88.

[130] Ibid., para. 89.

[131] *Law Reports of Trials of War Criminals*, United Nations War Crimes Commission, vol. VI (London, 1948), pp. 32, 48, 75, 99.

[132] Ad Hoc Committee on Genocide (5 April—10 May 1948), *Report of the Committee and Draft Convention drawn up by the Commission*, ECOSOC, E/794, pp. 2–3.

It seems that since that time a difference between them was made in that genocide is aimed against groups, whereas crimes against humanity do not necessarily involve offences against or persecutions of groups.[133]

Genocide, as defined by modern international law, is made up of two main elements: (1) the *actus reus* consisting of a series of acts having the effect of destroying a particular group; and (2) the *mens rea* consisting of the specific intent to destroy, in whole or in part, that particular group. These elements need some further comment.

2. *Actus reus*

The *actus reus* of genocide consists of the following types of acts on which the jurisprudence of the ad hoc Tribunals has shed some light.

(*a*) *Killing members of the group.*[134] There is a slight divergence between the English and French texts of the respective Statutes. In the English version the word 'killing' is used whereas in the French version it is the word 'meurtre'. The question was considered in the *Akayesu* case (1998) which is the first judgment handed down concerned with the offence of genocide. It was held that the English word killing is too general, since it may include both intentional and unintentional homicide. On the other hand the term murder covers only death which has been caused intentionally. Pursuant to the general principles of criminal law, the version more favorable to the accused has to be preferred. Thus the term 'killing' has to be interpreted as the intentional and unlawful infliction of death, i.e. intentional homicide.[135]

(*b*) *Causing serious bodily or mental harm to members of the group.* The harm must not be permanent or irremediable. It consists, *inter alia*, of acts of torture, inhuman or degrading treatment, and persecution.[136] 'Serious bodily harm' means harm that seriously injures the health, causes disfigurement or causes any serious injury to the external or internal organs or senses. The term is thus considered largely self-explanatory.[137] 'Serious mental harm' should be interpreted on a case-by-case basis.[138] No further indications emerge from the case-law.

(*c*) *Deliberately inflicting on the group conditions of life calculated to bring about its physical destruction in whole or in part.* These are indirect means of physical destruction, i.e., as the Chamber said in *Akayesu* (1998), 'methods of destruction by which the perpetrator does not immediately kill the members of the group, but which, ultimately, seek their physical

[133] *Law Reports* . . . , op.cit., vol. XV, London, 1949, p. 138.
[134] As to the protected groups, see *infra*, 4.
[135] *Akayesu*, para. 500–1. See also *Kayishema*, paras. 102–4. *Jelisic*, paras. 63–5.
[136] *Akayesu*, para. 502–4. On the term of persecution, see also *infra*, VII)1.b.ee.
[137] *Kayishema*, para. 109.
[138] Ibid., para. 113.

destruction'.[139] The following examples of such means are given: subjecting a group to a subsistence diet, systematic expulsion from homes, lack of housing, reduction of essential medical services below minimum requirements, lack of clothing or hygiene, excessive work or physical exertion, starvation, and rape.[140]

(*d*) *Imposing measures intended to prevent birth within the group*. In the *Akayesu* case (1998) several examples of physical measures of this category were given: sexual mutilation, sterilization, forced birth control, separation of sexes, prohibition of marriages, using rape as a means to traumatize women in order not to have them subsequently procreate or in order to impregnate them by men of another group with the result that the child will not belong to the mother's group.[141] To this, the Chamber in the *Rutaganda* case (1999) adds also mental measures with similar traumatizing effects. No examples are given.[142]

(*e*) *Forcibly transferring children of the group to another group*. The objective of the prohibition is not only to sanction a direct act of forcible physical transfer, but also to sanction the infliction of threats or traumas which would lead to the forcible transfer.[143]

3. *Mens rea: Specific Intent*

The *mens rea* of genocide is made up of a *specific intent* to destroy, in whole or in part, a national, ethnical, racial, or religious group. This specific intent must be established for any one of the acts committed, ranging from the killing of members of the group to the forcible transfer of children. The purpose of the actions or omissions of the perpetrator must always be to destroy the group as a distinct entity;[144] therefore the victim is singled out not because of his or her individual characteristics but because s/he is a member of the persecuted group. Through the victim, it is the group which is targeted. The logic is: *pars pro toto*. It is the *genus*, not the *species* which is controlling. There is thus at the basis of genocide a persecution based on discriminatory grounds.[145] The specific intent must be formed prior to the commission of genocidal acts; the individual acts need not however be premeditated, if only they are done in furtherance of the genocidal intent.[146] This is nothing other than the application of the general principle of criminal law according to which *dolus subsequens non nocet*. It is sufficient that the intention relates

[139] *Akayesu*, para. 505.
[140] *Akayesu*, para. 506. *Kayishema*, paras. 115–16.
[141] *Akayesu*, paras. 507–8.
[142] *Rutaganda*, under ch. 2.2.
[143] *Akayesu*, para. 509. *Rutaganda*, under ch. 2.2.
[144] *Akayesu*, paras. 517 ff. *Rutaganda*, under ch. 2.2. *Jelisic*, paras. 67, 78–9.
[145] *Jelisic*, paras. 67 ff, 73 ff.
[146] *Kayishema*, para. 91.

to the partial ('in part') destruction of the group. What must be achieved is the destruction of an important part of the group. This can be true quantitatively or qualitatively. Quantitatively it is necessary to have an intention to destroy a considerable number of individuals who are part of the group.[147] Qualitatively, there is destruction of an important part of the group if the attack is directed against a representative fraction of the group, e.g. its élite or its leaders.[148] Genocide may also be perpetrated in a geographically limited area.[149]

The specific intent of the perpetrator may be inferred from the facts, i.e. the words and speeches, the methodical way of planning the acts, the selection and number of the victims, the scale of atrocities committed, etc.[150] Finally, the group need not in effect be physically extinguished. Acts of sexual violence like rape may form part of the process of destruction even if they fall short of causing death.[151] Acts not intending to cause death (but intending to contribute to the destruction of the group) are thus also covered.

4. *Groups Protected*

There is, lastly, the question of what *groups* are protected by the prohibition of genocide. The Statutes make reference to national, ethnical, racial or religious groups. A 'national group' is based on common citizenship; an 'ethnic group' is based on common language or culture; a 'racial group' is based on hereditary physical traits; a 'religious group' is based on common religious beliefs or modes of worship.[152] This list of groups contained in the Statutes is not exhaustive.[153] Other stable groups of comparable nature may be added according to the *ejusdem generis* principle. On the other hand not all groups displaying a certain feeling of common interests is covered. The group must be relatively stable and permanent, membership not being challengeable by its members, who belong to it automatically, by birth or otherwise in a continuous or irremediable manner.[154] Therefore groups where the membership is voluntary and mobile, e.g. political groups, are not protected.[155] The question of who belongs to the groups cannot be answered solely on objective criteria. The perception of the members of the group as being distinct from the rest of the community (subjective

[147] Ibid., para. 97.
[148] *Jelisic*, paras. 81–2.
[149] Ibid., para. 83.
[150] *Akayesu*, para. 523. *Kayishema*, para 93. *Rutaganda*, under ch. 2.2.
[151] *Kayishema*, para. 95.
[152] *Akayesu*, paras. 512–15.
[153] Ibid., para. 516.
[154] Ibid., para. 511. *Rutaganda*, under ch. 2.2. *Jelisic*, para. 69.
[155] Ibid.

criterion) or the stigmatization by the community is also material.[156] As was added by the Chamber in the *Rutaganda* case (1999), the determination according to the aforementioned criteria must take into account the socio-cultural background in which any genocide is irremediably bedded.[157] Finally it must be added that the special intent of the perpetrator must be directed to destroying the group persecuted,[158] but his intent need not also relate to the intrinsic quality of the group as being national, ethnical, racial, or religious. He must seek to destroy the group, but he does not have to intellectually qualify it as national, ethnical, etc. In other words, the quality of the group represents an objective condition for the application of the prohibition (*objektive Strafbarkeitsvoraussetzung*) at which the *mens rea* need not be directed.

These conditions relating to the application of the offence of genocide have been considered fulfilled in the *Akayesu* (1998), *Kayishema* (1999), and *Rutaganda* (1999) cases. In the only case of the ICTY where genocide was raised, the accused has been acquitted. According to the trial Chamber in the *Jelisic* case (1999), there was not sufficient evidence as to a plan of destruction of the Muslim group. The Serb plans for the future of the region of Brcko made allowance for a certain percentage of Muslims (from 5–20 per cent) who would be able to stay in their homes. Furthermore a number of Muslim prisoners were liberated or exchanged against other (Serb) detainees. The accused, whatever his violent words of hatred, often chose his victims accidentally whereas at the same time he gave *laisser-passer* documents to others. Therefore, the Chamber concludes, the acts of the accused do not show a clear intent to destroy totally or partially a group as such.[159]

It may well be that the Chamber on the whole correctly appreciated the absence of a sufficient intent to destroy a group. But it may be asked whether it took sufficiently into account that the intent of a partial destruction of the group is enough under the law. Thus, the argument that a percentage of 5–20 per cent of Muslims would be allowed to stay may seem more in favor of than at odds with a conviction for genocide. Moreover, the exchange of prisoners may be related to practical reasons and does not automatically disprove or even weaken the special intent required. The fact that certain victims were randomly selected may also add rather than detract from an otherwise intact will of partial destruction of a group: it may merely show that in addition to genocide the accused also murdered. All these doubts remain, but it is difficult to carry the matter any further as this would depend on a careful weighing of evidence which is unavailable.

[156] *Jelisic*, para. 70.
[157] *Rutaganda*, under ch. 2.2.
[158] *Akayesu*, paras. 517 ff.
[159] *Jelisic*, paras. 88 ff., 107.

5. *Complicity in Genocide*

Under paragraph 3(e) of the respective Statutes, complicity in genocide is made punishable *per se*. The crime of genocide must have been in effect committed by the principal(s) in order for the accomplice to be punishable. Complicity may take the form of instigation or of aiding and abetting, e.g. by procuring means for the perpetration of the offence. The accomplice must furthermore act knowingly; he must know that he is assisting the commission of an offence. He need not himself possess the special intent of genocide (intent to destroy a particular group) if only he knows or could not ignore that the principal had that specific intent.[160] The point may be summarized as follows: '[A]n accused is liable as an accomplice to genocide if he knowingly aided or abetted or instigated one or more persons in the commission of genocide, while knowing that such a person or persons were committing genocide, even though the accused himself did not have the specific intent to destroy, in whole or in part, a national, ethnical, racial or religious group, as such'.[161]

The absence of the specific intent requirement for the accomplice under paragraph 3(e) distinguishes this form of complicity from the general provisions on participation in a crime (Article 7 ICTY Statute; Article 6 ICTR Statute). Moreover, complicity under paragraph 3(e) requires positive acts of participation, whereas aiding and abetting under the general provision may consist in failing to act or refraining from action.[162]

6. *Direct and Public Incitement to Commit Genocide*

This form of participation is criminalized by paragraph 3(c) of the respective Statutes. To 'incite' means to encourage or to persuade another to commit an offence. 'Public' means done in a public place, i.e. a place accessible to all, or to a public at large through mass media. 'Direct' means that the incitement must be specific, not only by vague or indirect suggestions. The cultural background has to be taken into account as has the quality of the persons to whom the message is addressed. Thus, because of the moral authority the *bourgmestre* enjoys in Rwanda, his words may more easily qualify as direct incitement than those of some obscure person. As to the *mens rea*, there must be an intent to directly prompt or provoke another to commit genocide. There must moreover exist the specific intent of genocide, i.e. the intent to destroy a particular group.[163]

It is because of the particular dangerousness and savagery of the crime

[160] *Akayesu*, paras. 525 ff.
[161] Ibid., para. 545.
[162] Ibid., paras. 547–8.
[163] Ibid., paras. 549 ff.

that such an incitement is punishable even if it remains unsuccessful, i.e. if it was not acted upon.[164]

VII. Article 5 ICTY Statute/Article 3 ICTR Statute: Crimes Against Humanity

1. Crimes against humanity have attained the status of customary law through the post-Second World War trials and especially the Nüremberg proceedings.[165] Roughly speaking these are crimes and atrocities like murder, extermination, enslavement, deportation, or other inhumane acts, or persecutions on discriminatory grounds, committed on a widespread and systematic basis against any civilian population. There are slight differences in the conditions of application of this offence between the ICTY and the ICTR. According to the ICTY Statute, the crime must be committed in armed conflict, whether internal or international; this requirement does not exist in the ICTR Statute. On the other hand, the ICTR Statute requires that the attack on the civilian population be committed on discriminatory, i.e. on national, political, ethnical, racial, or religious grounds; the ICTY Statute is silent on this point. Bearing in mind these two divergences we may comment point by point on the elements legally required to constitute a crime against humanity under the Statutes of the ad hoc Tribunals.

(*a*) *The crimes must be committed in an international or internal armed conflict (only for the ICTY Statute)*. As the Appeals Chamber in the *Tadic* (1995) case reminded us, it is by now accepted customary law that a connection to an armed conflict is not necessary in order to have a punishable crime against humanity. Therefore, this link, as required by the Statute, is narrower than is necessary under general international law.[166] By the same token there is no violation of the *nullum crimen* principle, since the liability to the crime has been restricted rather than widened. In the *Tadic* (1997) case, it was added that the acts committed must present a nexus with the armed conflict. It is enough that the act occurred in the course or duration of the armed conflict if it is geographically and temporally linked with it and if it is not done for purely personal motives.[167] It may once more be recalled that this requirement of an armed conflict does not exist under the ICTR Statute.

[164] Ibid., para. 562.

[165] On the concept and its origin, see B. B. Ferencz, 'Crimes against Humanity', *EPIL*, vol. 8 (1985), pp. 107–9.

[166] *Tadic* (1995), paras. 138 ff., 141.

[167] *Tadic* (1997), paras. 627 ff.

(*b*) *The prohibited acts.* Law No. 10 of the Allied Control Council for Germany (1945), in Article 2, paragraph 1, provided that crimes against humanity are 'atrocities and offences, including but not limited to murder, extermination, enslavement, deportation, imprisonment, torture, rape, or other inhumane acts committed against any civilian population, or persecutions on political, racial or religious grounds, whether or not in violation of the domestic laws of the countries where perpetrated'.[168] With respect to the law developed by the Nüremberg Trials, where many uncertainties persisted, some kind of homogenous body of rules seems to emerge out of the jurisprudence of the ad hoc Tribunals on this point. In particular, the Tribunals were at pains to describe the elements of the prohibited acts as precisely as possible. In that, there is a marked difference to the approach of the Nüremberg subsequent proceedings.

As was said in *Akayesu* (1998), the acts contemplated under the heading of crimes against humanity must be inhumane in nature and character, causing great suffering, or serious injury to the body or to mental or physical health.[169] Several of such acts are listed in the Statute, ranging from murder to rape, following the pattern of Control Council Law quoted. The list is closed by a reference to 'other inhumane acts' (letter i) which according to the *Rutaganda* case (1999) is a residual clause for all other types of inhumane acts not previously expressly listed. Thus, as the Chamber states, it may be said that the list of the Statute, as far as the expressly mentioned acts are concerned, is not exhaustive but merely illustrative.[170]

(*aa*) '*Murder*' means the unlawful and intentional killing of a human being.[171] The elements are thus : (1) the death of the victim; (2) resulting from an unlawful act or omission of the accused (or a subordinate for whom he is responsible); (3) with an intention to kill or inflict grievous bodily harm having known that such bodily harm is likely to cause the victim's death, and recklessness as to whether or not death ensues.[172] The Chamber in *Kayishema* (1999) departed from that view. It held that since the French version of murder in the Statute is 'assassinat', the interpretation has to stick to the narrower term (interpretation in favor of the accused). Thus the standard of *mens rea* required would be that for an 'assassinat', i.e. intentional and premeditated killing. The result is premeditated when the actor formulated his intent to kill after a cool

[168] See, e.g., in *Law Reports of Trials of War Criminals*, United Nations War Crimes Commission, vol. XV (London, 1949), p. 134. See also Article 6(c) of the Statute of the IMT contained in the London Agreement for the Establishment of an International Military Tribunal (1946), which is shorter: *U.N.T.S.*, vol. 82, pp. 279 ff., 288.

[169] *Akayesu*, para. 578.

[170] *Rutaganda*, under ch. 2.3.

[171] *Akayesu*, paras. 587–90. *Jelisic*, para. 51.

[172] *Rutaganda*, under ch. 2.3, towards the end.

moment of reflection.[173] This discrepancy may be solved on appeal. It does not, however, seem that the translation of murder into 'assassinat' sought to create a substantial difference nor that the term 'assassinat' was intended to refer exclusively to a particular French jurisprudence where it means premeditated killing. It may be recalled that in other systems of law, such as the Swiss, 'assassinat' (*Mord*) is not linked necessarily to premeditation but to the presence of circumstances denoting a particular perversity of the perpetrator ('*besonders verwerfliche Gesinnung*').[174] The interpretation given in *Akayesu* thus seems more in tune with the dominant and modern practice on this type of offence.

(*bb*) '*Extermination*' is mass killing or murder on a massive scale.[175] It also covers the creation of conditions of life leading to the destruction or killing. The act or omission may be done with intention, recklessness or, apparently, gross negligence.[176] The elements of this crime are thus: (1) the accused or a subordinate of the accused participated in the killing of certain named or described persons; and (2) the act or omission was unlawful and intentional[177] (or reckless or, according to the *Kayishema* Chamber, grossly negligent). A single killing is sufficient, where the actor is aware that his act or omission forms part of a mass killing event. In this case the killings must have close proximity in time and space.[178] Moreover, the act or omission need not directly kill, if it cumulatively with other acts or omissions causes the death of the targeted group of individuals.[179] In addition to intention one must stress that in such a case the acts must be proximate causes of the death and that foreseeably, in the ordinary course of events, they would lead to the result reached. Finally it may be added that the accused cannot be convicted for both crimes against humanity under the heading of murder *and* of extermination for the same set of acts; these two counts are mutually exclusive: one consumes the other.[180]

(*cc*) '*Torture*' means intentionally inflicting severe pain or suffering for specific purposes and under official authority or acquiescence.[181]

(*dd*) '*Rape*' is a physical invasion of a sexual nature committed on a person under circumstances which are coercive.[182]

(*ee*) '*Persecution*' in the sense of letter h of the respective Articles of the Statutes is based on some form of discrimination that is intended to be

[173] *Kayishema*, para. 139.

[174] See e.g. S. Trechsel, *Schweizerisches Strafgesetzbuch, Kurzkommentar* (Zurich, 1989), pp. 351 ff., particularly p. 353 n. 7. As to motives satisfying that criterion, see *ibid.*, pp. 354 ff. A. Panchaud/D. Ochsenbein/V. Van Ruymbeke, *Code pénal suisse annoté* (Lausanne, 1989), pp. 125–6.

[175] *Akayesu*, paras. 591–2. *Kayishema*, para. 142. *Rutaganda*, under ch. 2.3, towards the end.

[176] *Kayishema*, para. 146.

[177] *Rutaganda*, under ch. 2.3, towards the end.

[178] Ibid., para. 147.

[179] Ibid., at the end.

[180] Ibid., under ch. 5.3, second sub-paragraph 3.

[181] See for more details *Akayesu*, paras. 593–5. See also, *infra* VIII) 2.a).

[182] *Akayesu*, para. 596–8.

and results in an infringement of an individual's fundamental rights. It must be inspired by specific grounds, namely race, religion, or politics. The jurisdiction of the Tribunals is limited to these grounds. But the list of grounds given in the Statute is not exhaustive as a matter of customary international law, where the discrimination can be based also on ethnicity or culture.[183] The fact that the incriminating acts also fulfil the conditions of other crimes, e.g. war crimes, does not impede their qualification as crimes against humanity (persecution). Conversely, the persecutions may rest on acts which are not otherwise crimes in the Statute, such as the limitation on the type of professions opened to the targeted group, collective fines, creation of ghettos, etc.[184]

(*ff*) '*Other inhuman acts*': As has been said in the *Rutaganda* case (1999), this is a residual clause which completes the list of expressly mentioned prohibited acts.[185] The acts thus covered must be of comparable seriousness (*ejusdem generis*).[186] This category of acts, according to the Chamber in the *Jelisic* case (1999), corresponds to cruel treatment under Article 3 of the ICTY Statute as defined in the *Delalic* case.[187] Cruel treatment under Article 3 in turn corresponds, according to *Delalic*, to the term 'inhuman treatment' under the grave breaches régime (Article 2 of the ICTY Statute).[188] One thus ends up with the equation: 'other inhuman acts', (Article 5, ICTY Statute) = 'cruel treatment' (Article 3, ibid.) = 'inhuman treatment' (Article 2, ibid.). Some developments on the character of these 'other inhuman acts' under the crimes against humanity régime can be found in the *Kayishema* case (1999).[189] 'Other inhumane acts' are acts or omissions that deliberately cause serious mental or physical suffering or injury or constitute a serious attack on human dignity. The determination has to be made on a case-by-case basis. Serious mental harm can consist in witnessing the killing of family members or other persons. In such a case it is necessary to prove the intent or recklessness of the actor as to the causing of such suffering. Summing up, it can be said that crimes against humanity for other inhuman acts rest on: (i) the commission of an act of similar gravity and seriousness to the enumerated crimes; (ii) the intention to cause that act (or recklessness); and (iii) the knowledge that the act is perpetrated within the overall context of the attack.[190]

[183] *Tadic* (1997), para. 711.

[184] Ibid., paras. 694 ff. That persecutions must be based on discriminatory grounds was already well established under the Nüremberg Trials: see the *Justice Trial* (US Military Tribunal, 1947), *Law Reports of Trials of War Criminals*, United Nations War Crimes Commission, vol. VI, (London, 1948), pp. 79 ff.

[185] *Rutaganda*, under ch. 2.3.

[186] *Kayishema*, para. 150.

[187] *Jelisic*, para. 52.

[188] *Delalic*, para. 551. As to the content of these terms, see *infra*, VIII).2.

[189] *Kayishema*, paras. 151 ff.

[190] Ibid., para. 154. As to this criterion of the overall context of the attack, see below, (*c*) and (*d*).

It may be worthwhile to recall that the jurisprudence of the post-Second World War trials has ruled out the possibility of committing crimes against humanity by offences against property.[191]

(*c*) *Attacks directed against any civilian population.* The fact that (only) civilians but any civilians can be victims of crimes against humanity is an essential element of this crime and its whole *raison d'être*. This new type of crime was included in the London Charter for the Establishment of an International Criminal Tribunal (1946) in order to cover all atrocities of the Nazi régime which could not be reached by traditional international offences because they were committed by Germany against its own citizens on its own territory. Crimes against humanity were thus drafted in order to defeat the *domaine réservé* argument which could not be allowed for the type of crimes under consideration. Thus, the Tribunal in the *Justice Trial* (US Military Tribunal, 1947) stressed that crimes against humanity could be committed against German nationals (e.g. Jews) or any stateless person.[192] This point was taken up with approval by the Tribunals in the *Flick Trial* (US Military Tribunal, 1947)[193] and in the *Gerbsch Trial* (Special Court in Amsterdam, 1948).[194] It was stressed again in the *Tadic* (1997) case, where it is remembered that 'any' civilian population is protected and, thus, nationality is not material.[195]

The relevant sources support a broad interpretation of the term 'civilian' in the context of crimes against humanity. For the purposes of crimes against humanity any individual is a civilian if he is *hors de combat* at the moment of the perpetration of the crime,[196] or, as it is said in another case, if he does not actively take part in the hostilities.[197] There is no material difference between these two formulae. Therefore, as was said in *Tadic* (1997), involvement in a resistance movement does not disqualify an individual from the status of civilian, once captured or defenceless.[198] One exception was however made in the *Kayishema* case (1999) for all persons who have the duty to maintain public order and have legitimate means to exercise force.[199] *Quaere* if this exception is not too broad to the extent it could be applied to persons retaining some public execution powers but in contexts unrelated to the persecutions or atrocities. However, it was certainly not such cases which the Chamber

[191] Cf. the *Flick* Trial (US Military Tribunal, 1947), *Law Reports of Trials of War Criminals*, United Nations War Crimes Commission, vol. IX, (London, 1949), pp. 48–51, and the *I.G. Farben* Trial (US Military Tribunal, 1948), *Law Reports* . . . , op.cit., vol. X, (London, 1949), pp. 41–2, 64.

[192] *Law Reports* . . . , op.cit., vol. VI, (London, 1948), pp. 39–40.

[193] Ibid., vol. IX (London, 1949), pp. 51–2.

[194] Ibid., vol. XIII (London, 1949), p. 134.

[195] *Tadic* (1997), para. 635. Stateless persons are also covered (ibid.).

[196] *Jelisic*, para. 54.

[197] *Rutaganda*, under ch. 2.3, towards the middle.

[198] *Tadic* (1997), para. 643.

[199] *Kayishema*, para. 127.

had in mind, as it illustrates the exception by speaking of members of the FAR, RPF, and the police/or gendarmerie of Rwanda.

The term 'population' implies crimes of a collective nature. It thus relates to the requirement that the attacks against the population must be widespread and systematic (see below, (d)). The term purports to exclude single or isolated acts[200] (which will be only war crimes, if anything). Thus the individual must be targeted not because of his individual attributes but because of his membership in the persecuted civilian population.[201] It may be a crime against humanity to kill a single person, but only if this killing is related to the attack as a whole (see below, (d)).

Finally, the targeted population must be of a predominantly civilian nature, but the presence of some non-civilians amidst this population does not deprive it of its civilian character.[202] The precise scope of this ruling may be difficult to grasp.

(d) The attack must be widespread and systematic. That the attack must be committed on a certain scale in order to qualify as a crime against humanity has been accepted since the very notion of this offence was coined by the post-World War II instruments and trials.[203] Random acts of violence cannot be considered crimes against humanity.[204] The term 'widespread' refers to the number of victims: it implies a massive, frequent, large-scale action, carried out collectively with seriousness and against a multiplicity of victims. The term 'systematic' indicates that a pattern or methodical plan exists: it means thoroughly organized and following a regular pattern on the basis of a common policy involving substantial public or private resources.[205] This policy element is not formalized; it flows directly from the systematic and widespread nature of the acts.[206] Moreover that policy need not any longer be one of State organs;[207] but there must be some kind of pre-conceived plan or policy.[208] It is sufficient that acts are committed on behalf of entities which *de facto* control the territory or by terrorist groups;[209] businessmen

[200] This limitation was already admitted in the post-Second World War trials; see, e.g., the *Justice Trial* (US Military Tribunal, 1947), *Law Reports . . .*, op.cit., vol. VI (London, 1948), pp. 79–80; the *Flick Trial* (US Military Tribunal, 1947), *Law Reports . . .*, op.cit., vol. IX (London, 1949), p. 51.

[201] *Tadic* (1997), para. 644.

[202] *Tadic* (1997), para. 638. *Jelisic*, para. 54. *Akayesu*, para. 582. *Rutaganda*, under ch. 2.3.

[203] See, e.g., the *Justice Trial* (US Military Tribunal, 1947), *Law Reports . . .*, op.cit., vol. VI (London, 1948), p. 79.

[204] *Akayesu*, para. 579.

[205] *Tadic* (1997), para. 648. *Akayesu*, para. 580. *Rutaganda*, under ch. 2.3.

[206] *Tadic* (1997), para. 653.

[207] This was the case at the time of the Nüremberg Trials; cf. the *Justice Trial* (US Military Tribunal, 1947), *Law Reports . . .*, op.cit., vol. VI (London, 1948), pp. 79–80 and the *Flick Trial* (US Military Tribunal, 1947), *Law Reports . . .*, op.cit., vol. IX, London, 1949, p. 51.

[208] *Tadic* (1997), paras. 653 ff. *Akayesu*, para. 580. *Rutaganda*, under ch. 2.3.

[209] *Tadic* (1997), para. 654.

can also commit crimes against humanity if they act in coordination with such entities.[210] Even a single act can qualify as a crime against humanity if it be sufficiently linked to the policy of terror or persecution.[211]

The requirements of *widespread* and of *systematic* acts are not cumulative. It is sufficient that the acts be either widespread *or* systematic.[212] The acts can obviously also be widespread *and* systematic, e.g. in cases of a clear policy, of the creation of particular institutions to carry it out, of implication of high State officials, of the importance of the means or of the scale of the attacks launched.[213]

The term 'attack' refers to the acts enumerated in the Statutes under letters (a) to (i).[214] It was added in the *Rutaganda* case (1999) that an attack may also be non-violent, e.g. imposing a system of apartheid or exerting pressure on the population to act in a particular manner.[215]

(*e*) *Must the acts be committed on discriminatory grounds?* Generally speaking, discriminatory grounds or intent means that the acts must be done for specific reasons, i.e. for religious, racial, ethnic, or political grounds. The situation as to this requirement is different under the law of the ICTY and that of the ICTR.

This attribute was held by the ICTY in the *Tadic* (1997) case to be constitutive of crimes against humanity as defined under its Statute. The Chamber recognized that there is no general condition of this kind under customary international law, where a discrimination is only required for persecution as one type of offence under the heading of crimes against humanity. However, several members of the Security Council interpreted Article 5 of the Statute as limited by this requirement. The Chamber thus accepted this criterion which corresponds to the will of the Council wherefrom the jurisdiction of the ICTY stems. In the present case, the Chamber concluded, there was such a discrimination against non-Serbs.[216]

This decision was quashed on appeal in the *Tadic* (1999) judgment. Four main arguments are made by the Appeals Chamber. First, the ordinary meaning of the words used in Article 5 makes it clear that this provision does not require all crimes against humanity to have been perpetrated with a discriminatory intent. Such an intent is only made necessary for one sub-category, namely persecutions provided for in letter h. Second, there is a logical or *effet utile* argument: the mentioning of discrimination in letter h makes sense only if it is not required elsewhere. Third, the object and purpose of Article 5 is to render all

210 *Kayishema*, para. 126.
211 *Tadic* (1997), para. 649.
212 *Tadic* (1997), para. 646–7. *Rutaganda*, under ch. 2.3. *Jelisic*, para. 53.
213 *Jelisic*, para. 53.
214 *Akayesu*, para. 581. *Rutaganda*, under ch. 2.3.
215 *Rutaganda*, under ch. 2.3.
216 *Tadic* (1997), paras. 650 ff.

crimes against humanity punishable, which in turn supports the broader definition. Fourth, in cases of doubt the interpretation should be made in order to conform with customary international law; in customary international law no discriminatory intent is generally required. The clear wording of Article 5 and the conformity with customary international law must have precedence over some statements in the Security Council. Moreover, *travaux préparatoires* may not be resorted to if the wording is clear.[217] There are some questionable points in the reasoning of the Appeals Chamber. The argument on the object and purpose, for instance, may be said to beg the question, as it is precisely at issue what shall constitute a crime against humanity to be prosecuted. The marked priority of the words over the intent—notwithstanding Articles 31 and 32 of the Vienna Treaties Convention (1969)—has always seemed suspect to the present commentator, as words exist only to express an idea; moreover customary law may be derogated from by treaty, as happens more than once in the Tribunal's Statutes. But the strongest point in favour of the holding of the Appeals Chamber is that in order to overcome precise words put in the chain of a customary tradition, the derogatory intent should be clearly expressed. It may be doubtful to depart too easily from the general jurisprudence on crimes against humanity. The suggestions within the Security Council may well have been too weak to have such an effect.

On the other hand, as the ICTR Statute expressly makes reference to the requirement of discrimination (unlike the ICTY Statute), it has been held that under this system it has to be given full effect.[218] However, if inhumane acts are committed against persons not falling within one of the discriminatory categories, this may still qualify as a crime against humanity if the perpetrator's intention is to further thereby his attack on a targeted group falling within those specified by the Statute.[219] This can happen if a Belgian priest protecting the Tutsis is slaughtered in order to proceed with the killing of the Tutsis.[220] Moreover, a crime against humanity is also committed when the perpetrator believed himself to be killing members of the group, whereas in fact this was untrue.[221] This would be a criminally irrelevant *error in persona*.

The result is that for the ICTY system discriminatory grounds are only necessary for the sub-category of persecutions, whereas in the ICTR system it constitutes a general condition which must be fulfilled in any case.

[217] *Tadic* (1999), paras. 273 ff, 283 ff. The Report of the Secretary-General also adopted the discrimination requirement: UN.DOC., S/25704, para. 48.

[218] *Akayesu*, para. 583. *Rutaganda*, under ch. 2.3.

[219] *Akayesu*, para. 584. *Rutaganda*, under ch. 2.3.

[220] *Kayishema*, para. 131.

[221] Ibid., para. 132.

(f) Mens rea: Intent to commit the offence and knowledge of the broader context in which it occurs. In the first place, the perpetrator must have the intention to commit the offence.[222] In addition, he must know of the broader context in which his acts occur, i.e. he must know of the widespread and systematic attack upon a civilian population.[223] This knowledge may be constructive: knowledge is legally imputed if the perpetrator was wilfully blind or grossly negligent as to facts and circumstances surrounding his crimes.[224] The perpetrator need not have knowledge of what exactly will happen to the victims[225] if only, according to general principles of criminal law, the chain of the events that happened was reasonably foreseeable. The perpetrator is not liable for results which are completely beyond the pale of what could be expected in the light of ordinary experience of life. In accordance with these principles, denunciations may be sufficient to constitute a crime against humanity; several post-World War II judgments can be quoted to that effect.[226]

The question of whether purely personal motives, unrelated to the attack on the civilian population, may suffice is more intricate. In the *Tadic* (1997) case, it was held that while personal motives may be present, they should not be the sole motivation for the acts.[227] Thus, if the act is done for purely personal reasons unrelated to the attack on the civilian population, there would not be a crime against humanity. This course was challenged by the *Tadic* (1999) Appeals Judgment. It held (with two judges dissenting)[228] that subjective motives have no place: the only requirement is the objective nexus between the acts and the attack on the civilian population. If such a nexus exists, there is no point to further inquire if the motives were personal. Moreover, there is a jurisprudence of the post-Second World War trials which admits crimes against humanity also if committed for personal reasons, as e.g. in cases of denunciations.[229]

Looked at closely, there does not seem to be any major difference between the two holdings. In both cases, the 'unrelated to the attack'

[222] *Tadic* (1997), para. 656.

[223] *Tadic* (1997), paras. 656–7. *Jelisic*, para. 56. *Kayishema*, paras. 133–4. See also *R.* v. *Finta* (Canada, Supreme Court, 1994), *ILR*, vol. 104, pp. 284 ff, 362–3.

[224] *Tadic* (1997), paras. 657, 659. See also *R.* v. *Finta*, loc.cit.

[225] *Tadic* (1997), para. 657.

[226] Ibid.

[227] Ibid., paras. 658, 659.

[228] Judge Nieto-Navia, Declaration, para. 12 (exclusion of acts done for purely personal reasons unrelated to the attack on the civilian population and to the armed conflict); Judge Shahabuddeen, Sep.Op., paras. 33 ff (exclusion of acts done for purely personal reasons completely unrelated to the attack on the civilian population). Judge Shahabuddeen goes on to give the example of a jealous husband who kills his wife belonging to the attacked civilian population, but for reasons for which he would have killed her also if she did not belong to the targeted group (para. 35). But it is easy to see that here the acts are simply unrelated (legally) to the attack on the civilian population.

[229] *Tadic* (1999), paras. 248 ff. See also Sep.Op. Shahabuddeen, para. 34.

element is controlling. To the extent that both the subjective element (personal motives) and the objective element (attack . . .) are present, a quite exceptional hypothesis, the latter prevails. The rule here is as follows: if the perpetrator acts for purely personal motives but takes advantage of the system of persecution of which he has knowledge and which he uses to further the desired result of his deeds, there will be a crime against humanity. For that reason the formulation of the Appeals Chamber may be more appropriate: if the acts are related to the attack it will always be a crime against humanity regardless of the existence or not of personal motives. Thus it may be immaterial to inquire into motives. But it must be seen that ordinarily it is the cases where the perpetrator acts for personal reasons which are also unrelated to the attack on the civilian population.[230] And for that hypothesis both tests lead to the same result.

In conclusion, it can be added that in the *Tadic* (1997) case the Chamber held that all the conditions for the application of Article 5 of its Statute were fulfilled. In particular, one aspect of the conflict in the relevant area (Bosnia) was the commission of inhuman acts against the non-Serb population in order to create a Greater Serbia. Moreover, the policy of inhuman acts was based on a recognizable plan.[231] The ICTR also passed several convictions based on this offence (crimes against humanity).[232]

VIII. Analysis of Individual Offences

There are several particular offences, e.g. torture, which may apply under different headings, e.g. under the heading of grave breaches or of war crimes. Some of them, such as wilful killing or murder, may qualify under each count contained in the Statutes. There is no point in analysing these offences in depth in the present article. What may be useful is to outline their constitutive elements as they were shaped by the jurisprudence of the ad hoc Tribunals. Whoever has read the post-

[230] To that extent the holding of the Chamber in *Tadic* (1997), para. 659 may still hold good: '[I]f the perpetrator has knowledge, either actual or constructive, that these acts were occurring on a widespread or systematic basis and does not commit his act for purely personal motives completely unrelated to the attack on the civilian population, that is sufficient to hold him liable for crimes against humanity'.

[231] *Tadic* (1997), para. 660.

[232] *Akayesu*, paras. 645 ff. *Kayishema*, paras. 572 ff. (the elements of the crime were found to be fulfilled, but it was thought to be consumed by the conviction on genocide for the same acts; *contra*, Sep. and Diss.Op. Tafazzal Hossain Khan, para. 3). *Rutaganda*, under chs. 5.2–5.5.

Second World War trials will know how few precise indications they contain on this point.

1. *Wilful killing and murder*

The meaning of the term 'murder' (or 'assassinat') in the context of genocide[233] and of crimes against humanity[234] has already been discussed. For the purposes of Articles 2 and 3 of the ICTY Statute, it has been said in the *Delalic* case (1998) that there is no difference between wilful killing (Article 2) and murder (Article 3, by renvoi).[235] As to *mens rea*, intention and recklessness are covered: there must be demonstrated 'an intention on the part of the accused to kill, or inflict serious injury in reckless disregard of human life'.[236] If compared, the different contexts where those terms apply do not entail substantive discrepancies. Murder in all contexts means intentional and unlawful homicide, recklessness being included. Where a Chamber has departed from this view, it is submitted that it erred.[237]

2. *Mistreatments*

There are several mistreatments which must be considered separately:

(a) *Torture*. The elements of torture are the following: (i) an act or omission causing severe pain or suffering, mental or physical; (ii) inflicted intentionally; (iii) for purposes such as obtaining information, confessions, punishment, intimidation, coercion of the victim or of a third person, or for any reason based on discrimination; (iv) committed or acquiesced in or instigated by a person acting in an official capacity; and (v) for the purposes of the ICTY Statute, the acts must be linked to an armed conflict.[238] The level of severity or pain required cannot be articulated in the abstract. The practice of the human rights bodies (in particular the European Court of Human Rights) should be taken as a yardstick. This practice recognizes that this threshold depends on the circumstances, as with the related notion of inhuman treatment.[239] As to the prohibited purpose, it has been held that it must simply be part of the motivation behind the conduct; it need not be the predominating or sole

233 Above (VI)2.a).
234 Above (VII)1.b)aa).
235 *Delalic*, paras. 431–3.
236 Ibid., para. 439.
237 See above, (VII)1.b).aa).
238 *Delalic*, para. 494. *Furundzija*, para. 162.
239 *Delalic*, paras. 461 ff.

purpose. Moreover, the purpose must not be exclusively private.[240] Rape may qualify as torture if the constitutive elements of both offences are met. Guidance can again be gathered from the human rights law jurisprudence, e.g. from the *Meija* case (Inter-American Commission of Human Rights) or from the *Aydin* case (European Court of Human Rights).[241]

The prohibition of torture is customary in character. It applies to times of peace as well as to times of armed conflict. The prohibition is addressed to individuals, who are criminally accountable for its breach.[242] It is an absolute prohibition which can never be derogated from, not even in times of emergency. It has become so important that other particular attributes attach to it. They were considered in the *Furundzija* case (1998). First, the prohibition covers also *potential breaches*. It is insufficient to intervene after the infliction of torture; there is a duty of prevention. Thus, all the measures necessary for implementing the prohibition, or the abrogation of all contrary laws, have to be undertaken immediately.[243] Secondly, the prohibition imposes *obligations erga omnes*. All States have a (correlative) right and may claim in case of a violation.[244] Thirdly, the prohibition is part of the international public order (*ius cogens*). Because of the importance of the values it protects, it has become a peremptory norm having a higher rank in hierarchy than treaty law or even ordinary customary rules. It cannot be derogated from by treaties, local or special customary law, or even general custom not endowed with the same normative force. The principle, by the same token, also overrides contrary municipal law (e.g. amnesty laws). Contrary municipal laws would be internationally unlawful and unopposable. Courts of justice in third States would not be bound by such laws and the perpetrators of torture stay criminally liable whatever the measures taken under municipal law. The *ius cogens* character of the principle leads also to universal jurisdiction for prosecuting torturers.[245] It is not possible in this article to do more than to underline the particularly sweeping and far-reaching conclusions as to the consequences of the prohibition. It may be asked to what extent, as far as terminology is concerned, it would be preferable to speak of international public order instead of *ius cogens*.[246]

(*b*) *Wilfully causing great suffering or serious injury to body or health*

[240] Ibid., paras. 470 ff.

[241] Ibid., paras. 475 ff. For the *Meija* case, see: *Inter-American Yearbook on Human Rights*, 1996–I, pp. 1120 ff. For the *Aydin* case, see ECHR, *Rep.*, 1997–VI, no. 50, pp. 1866 ff, 1886–1892.

[242] *Furundzija*, para. 140.

[243] Ibid., paras. 148–150.

[244] Ibid., paras. 151–2.

[245] Ibid., paras. 153–7. On the character as *ius cogens*, see also *Delalic*, para. 454.

[246] The reasons have been explained in R. Kolb, *Théorie du ius cogens international* Paris, 2001.

(*Article 2 ICTY Statute*). The difference of this offence with respect to torture lies in the fact that torture requires a specific purpose whereas wilfully causing etc. does not. The seriousness of the injury may be measurable by considering the incapacity to work ensuing from the offence. Thus, according to the *Delalic* case (1998), the offence is constituted by 'an act or omission that is intentional, being an act which, judged objectively, is deliberate and not accidental, which causes serious mental or physical suffering or injury'.[247]

(*c*) *Inhuman treatment* (*Article 2 ICTY Statute*). Inhuman treatment is an intentional act or omission 'which causes serious mental or physical suffering or injury or constitutes a serious attack on human dignity'.[248] This definition is relative to that of torture: 'inhuman treatment is treatment which deliberately causes serious mental and physical suffering that falls short of the severe mental and physical suffering required for the offence of torture'.[249] Both offences thus join each other, one on the top, the other beneath, leaving no gap. Whether the required threshold is reached is to be decided in the light of all the circumstances of the particular case. Guidance can be obtained through the human rights case-law which considers the level of severity of the acts in the context of, *inter alia*, the duration of the acts, their nature and effects, sex, age and state of health of the victim, etc.[250]

Inhuman treatment stems from a disdain of human dignity.[251] The term 'inhuman(e)' is best defined in relation to its opposite, 'human(e)', i.e. kind-hearted, compassionate, merciful. It can be illustrated through a non-exhaustive list of acts, e.g. non-protection against attacks, medical experiments, mutilation, exposure to public curiosity or insults, insufficient food and water rations, etc.[252] The standard to be used for measuring is objective: the humiliation or suffering must be sufficiently intense for a normal person to be hurt.[253] The severity of the acts can also be the consequence of the cumulation or repetition of acts being in themselves insufficient.[254] Finally, the *mens rea* is made up by the intention to humiliate or to injure, if the actor is conscious of the foreseeable consequences of his acts.[255] It may be thought that it is enough that the perpetrator should have been aware of these foreseeable consequences of his acts.

[247] *Delalic*, paras. 498 ff, quotation from para. 511. This sentence does not seem well constructed.
[248] Ibid., para. 543.
[249] Ibid., para. 542.
[250] Ibid., paras. 534 ff.
[251] *Aleksovski*, para. 56.
[252] *Delalic*, paras. 518 ff.
[253] *Aleksovski*, para. 56.
[254] Ibid., para. 57.
[255] Ibid., para. 56.

(*d*) *Cruel treatment* (*Article 3 ICTY Statute*). According to the *Delalic* case (1998), cruel treatment for the purposes of Article 3 ICTY Statute corresponds to the definition of inhuman treatment in the context of Article 2 ICTY Statute.[256] It has been held in *Jelisic* (1999) that beatings, cutting off of ears and cuts in the flesh of the arms constitute such cruel treatment.[257]

All these offences under the general heading of 'mistreatments' are indispensable, for it is the most common practice in modern wars to commit them. But it must be said that their open-endedness and fact-intensity ('case-by-case analysis') somewhat detracts from the necessary precision of criminal provisions (*Bestimmtheitsgrundsatz*). It is not suggested that this is avoidable; the problem must however be seen.

3. *Rape and other serious sexual assaults*

The elements of rape are the following: (i) the sexual penetration, however slight, of the vagina or anus of the victim by the penis of the perpetrator or any other object used by the perpetrator, or of the mouth of the victim by the penis; (ii) this penetration must be obtained by coercion or force, or threat of force, against the victim or a third person.[258] These elements can be gathered, in the absence of a definition of rape in international law, by looking to the various municipal legal systems. In these systems there are discrepancies only as to the legal qualification of the penetration of the mouth of the victim. But the gravity of the act accounts, in the view of the Chamber, for its being treated as rape.[259] If there is no penetration at all, the act may still qualify as serious sexual assault inflicted upon the physical and moral integrity of a person by means of coercion or intimidation in a way that is degrading and humiliating for the victim's dignity.[260] Not only women but also men can be raped.

Rape is prohibited, in times of war, by conventional and customary law entailing, in case of breach, the criminal responsibility of the perpetrator.[261] Human rights treaties ordinarily cover rape by way of their provisions on physical integrity.[262]

4. *Unlawful confinement of civilians (Article 2(g) ICTY Statute)*

In cases of international armed conflicts it is lawful to confine enemy civilians to certain areas or in camps. The conditions which must be

256 *Delalic*, para. 551.
257 *Jelisic*, paras. 41 ff.
258 *Furundzija*, para. 185.
259 Ibid., paras. 182–3.
260 Ibid., para. 186.
261 Ibid., paras. 165 ff.
262 Ibid., para. 170–1.

respected are laid down in the Geneva Convention IV of 1949, especially in Articles 5, 27 and 41–3. The question has been considered in the *Delalic* case (1998).

First, the confinement must rest on a *lawful reason*.[263] The freedom of movement of enemy civilians may be restricted or even temporarily suppressed, but only if the security of the State requires it, especially in cases of spying, sabotage, or hostile activity. The mere fact of being an enemy national cannot in itself be considered as threatening the security of the opposing party. The State must have specific reasons to feel its security threatened, e.g. by activities, special knowledge or qualifications of the individual, etc. The measures of constraint should not affect the fundamental right of persons concerned to be treated with humanity. They must moreover be necessary, no lesser means being available (proportionality *lato sensu*). The Chamber adds that States enjoy in this matter 'a great deal of discretion'.[264]

Secondly, there are *procedural safeguards* as provided for in Article 43 of the Geneva Convention IV (1949).[265] There is a right to have the necessity of the internment periodically reviewed by a court or administrative body. There is also a right to have the names of interned persons delivered to the protecting power. If those guarantees are not respected, the confinement becomes unlawful.

The Chamber concludes that States may confine enemy civilians, but must bear in mind that the measure is an exceptional one, to be taken only for reasons of security.[266] It may be wondered if these extenuating standards correspond to the generally held conceptions and practices (not abuses) on this matter. One may recall that the United Kingdom interned a great number of Argentinian nationals at the time of the Falklands/Malvinas war, this measure arousing no protest as to its legality. More fundamentally, there is some incongruity in the reasoning of the Chamber in *Delalic*. The strict standards proposed (i.e. only an exceptional measure for clear and compelling security interests) are to some extent at odds with the sweeping *dictum* on the great deal of discretion enjoyed by States. It seems in any case that the States have a somewhat greater discretion (or margin of appreciation) than it might seem on reading the judgment.

5. *Plunder (Article 3(e) ICTY Statute)*

Plunder covers all forms of unlawful appropriation of property in armed conflict, including pillage (violent appropriation) or spoliation.

263 *Delalic*, paras. 564 ff.
264 Ibid., para. 570.
265 Ibid., paras. 579 ff.
266 Ibid., para. 583.

The property may be public or private, but it must belong to the adverse party. The seizure must be linked to the armed conflict.[267] The prohibition of plunder is undoubtedly customary and gives rise, if breached, to individual criminal responsibility.[268]

Some other offences have been provisionally considered under the Rule 61 proceedings of the ICTY. Thus, for instance, in the *Martic* case (1996), the offence of indiscriminate attacks on civilians was considered. The Chamber found that such attacks constitute a grave breach of the Geneva Conventions of 1949 if committed wilfully in violation of the relevant provisions of Protocol I, and causing death or serious injury to body or health.[269] The prohibition is customary in character and applies to both international and internal armed conflict. It cannot be done away with by claiming reprisals.[270]

IX. Individual Criminal Responsibility and Forms of Participation in a Crime (Article 7(1) ICTY Statute; Article 6(1) ICTR Statute)

1. Individual criminal responsibility flows from the following five types of action: planning, instigating, ordering, committing or aiding and abetting in the commission of a crime. As has been said in the *Delalic* (1998)[271] and *Kayishema* (1999)[272] cases, each of these types of action entails disjunctively criminal responsibility; but this was, indeed, stating the obvious. In the *Rutaganda* case (1999), the meaning of these types of action was analysed. 'Planning' was not there defined. But it may be considered as the methodical preparation of an offence to be committed. 'Instigating' was defined as direct incitement of another to commit an offence; it is said that the incitement must be public, but that is quite certainly a *lapsus calami*. 'Ordering' supposes a superior/subordinate relationship and the use of the superior's authority to persuade the subordinate to commit a crime. 'Commission' of a crime is the direct act producing the result, or an omission if there is a duty to act. 'Aiding and abetting' is at the lower threshold of criminal participation to a crime and needs further analysis. It may be noted that it covers all acts of assistance in either physical form or in the form of moral support that substantially contribute to the commission of the crime.[273]

2. What are the minimum requirements for criminal participation in an offence? The question arises in the context of 'aiding and abetting'

[267] Ibid., paras. 584 ff. *Jelisic*, paras. 46 ff.
[268] *Delalic*, para. 315.
[269] *ILR*, vol. 108, pp. 44–5, para. 8.
[270] Ibid., p. 45–7, paras. 10 ff.
[271] *Delalic*, para. 321.
[272] *Kayishema*, para. 197.
[273] See *Rutaganda*, under ch. 2.1.

('aider et encourager') which constitutes the lowest form of criminal participation.

(*a*) First, the participation must have a *direct and substantial effect* on the commission of the crime.[274] The assistance need not always be physical or tangible. It may consist of moral or psychological support and encouragement of the principals in their commission of the crime.[275]

Presence at the place of the crime may be enough if it facilitates the crime, e.g. because of the authority enjoyed by the person who is present or if that person supervises the action.[276] The acts of assistance may be removed in time and space from the actual commission of the offence.[277] Thus, criminal assistance can also be given after the commission of the crime, e.g. if there was a promise to eliminate evidence.[278] Omissions may also be covered.[279] The assistance must obviously not be a condition *sine qua non* for the commission of a crime.[280] In summing up it can be said that the *actus reus* of aiding and abetting requires practical assistance, encouragement, or moral support which has a substantial effect on the perpetration of the crime.[281]

(*b*) Secondly, as to the *mens rea*, there must be an awareness of the participation in a crime, and an intention to participate in its commission. Knowledge and intent can be inferred from the circumstances.[282] It is not necessary for the accomplice to share the *mens rea* of the principal. It is enough that he has knowledge that his actions assist the perpetrator in the commission of the crime and that he acts nevertheless.[283]

The whole question may be summed up as follows: 'The accused will be found criminally culpable for any conduct where it is determined that he knowingly participated in the commission of an offence that violates international humanitarian law and his participation directly and substantially affected the commission of that offence through supporting the actual commission before, during, or after the incident'.[284]

3. The category of the '*common criminal purpose*' known in common law systems is a means of imputing the criminal results to all the participants of the group who acted to further the common criminal plan.

[274] *Tadic* (1997), paras. 678 ff, 692. *Delalic*, para. 326. *Furundzija*, paras. 217 ff. *Aleksovski*, para. 61. *Kayishema*, para. 199.

[275] *Tadic* (1997), paras. 679, 689. *Delalic*, para. 326. *Furundzija*, paras. 199 ff.

[276] *Tadic* (1997), para. 689. *Furundzija*, para. 209, *Aleksovski*, paras. 64–5. *Kayishema*, para. 200.

[277] *Delalic*, para. 327.

[278] *Aleksovski*, para. 62.

[279] *Kayishema*, para. 202 (if there is a duty to act: see e.g. Article 6(3) ICTR Statute).

[280] *Furundzija*, para. 209. *Kayishema*, para. 201.

[281] *Furundzija*, para. 235.

[282] *Tadic* (1997), paras. 675–7. *Delalic*, para. 328.

[283] *Furundzija*, paras. 236 ff.

[284] *Tadic* (1997), para. 692.

This category of collective criminality has been applied in the Nüremberg and subsequent proceedings under the heading of the 'common design' to commit crimes.[285] The conditions for its application were held at that time to be: (i) that there was a system in force to commit certain offences; (ii) that the accused was aware of that system; and (iii) that the accused participated in operating the system.[286] The whole question was taken up again in the *Tadic* (1999) Appeals judgment.[287] Two conditions must be fulfilled in order to hold criminally liable for all the acts of the group each member participating in it. First, *all participants must possess the same criminal intention*, e.g. the intent to kill on a systematic basis.[288] If this is the case, it is sufficient that the accused has participated in one aspect of the common design, e.g. the providing of material assistance. This extends especially to persons acting pursuant to a concerted plan within concentration camps. Secondly, the offences committed must at least be a *natural and foreseeable consequence of effecting that common purpose*.[289] This is important for situations where some offences committed were not those actually contemplated in the plan. Criminal responsibility for such 'ultra vires' acts may still be imputed to each member of the group if such acts were a foreseeable corollary of the common design and if the particular accused was either reckless or indifferent to the predictable consequence. At least *dolus eventualis*[290] is required. The *mens rea* is thus made up of two elements: (i) the intention to take part in a joint criminal enterprise; and (ii) the foreseeability and advertent recklessness (*dolus eventualis*) as to the commission of further crimes linked with the common purpose.

This category of the common criminal purpose has been considered customary in character by the Appeals Chamber.[291]

In summing up it may be said that the *actus reus* of the common criminal purpose consists of (i) a plurality of persons; (ii) the existence of a common design, plan or purpose to commit a crime or crimes; (iii) the participation of the accused in that system; and the *mens rea* consists (i) in an intent to perpetrate the crime(s) or at least in the knowledge that it will be perpetrated coupled to an intention to further the system, or (ii) in the foreseeability of further crimes ('ultra vires') with the accused taking willingly that risk.[292]

[285] See the *Law Reports of Trials of War Criminals*, United Nations War Crimes Commission, vol. XV (London, 1949), pp. 94 ff.

[286] Ibid., p. 95.

[287] *Tadic* (1999), paras. 190 ff.

[288] Ibid., paras. 196 ff.

[289] Ibid., paras. 204 ff.

[290] I.e. the accused willingly took the risk of further crimes being committed.

[291] *Tadic* (1999), para. 226.

[292] Ibid., paras. 227–8.

X. Command Responsibility: Responsibility of the Superior for the Acts of His Subordinates (Article 7(3) ICTY Statute; Article 6(3) ICTR Statute)

1. The criminal responsibility of the superior for the unlawful acts of his subordinates, if he failed to discharge his duty of prevention or suppression (after the fact), is well established in customary[293] and conventional international law. That type of responsibility for culpable omissions has been the object of a series of post-Second World War trials[294] and has since been codified in Articles 86–7 of Additional Protocol I (1977).[295] The duty to act—necessary for a responsibility for omission—flows from the duties inherent in the post of command.

2. Three elements must be fulfilled in order to have command responsibility.

(a) First, there must be a *superior/subordinate relationship*.[296] A superior is a person in a position of authority, whether military or civilian. Judicial case-law has recognized that non-military superiors can be held liable, be they political leaders (*Tokyo* Trial) or civil industrialists (*Flick* Trial). The control of the superior over the subordinates may be *de iure* or *de facto*. It is not the formal status which is decisive, but the actual possession of powers of control over the actions of the subordinates. It must be possible legally or factually to give orders in order to prevent the offences or to sanction their authors. For civilian authorities there is normally no direct power to take military sanctions, but the power to pass a report on the situation is sufficient. Conversely, an ineffective formal position will not lead to responsibility if the superior in fact did not have the material ability to act as requested. It is the principle of effectiveness which is controlling in this matter.

(b) Secondly, as to the *mens rea*, the superior *must have known or have had reason to know* about the commission of the offences by the subordinates.[297] The standard is two-fold. The superior may have had *actual knowledge* which may be established through direct or circumstantial evidence. But such knowledge cannot be presumed simply because the acts were widespread, numerous, or occurring over a prolonged period. Such aspects are, however, relevant indicia for knowledge. This is particularly true if the acts are committed near to the place where the superior exercises his powers. A more difficult aspect is the

[293] *Delalic*, para. 343.

[294] See in *Law Reports of Trials of War Criminals*, United Nations War Crimes Commission, vol. XV (London, 1949), pp. 65 ff.

[295] *Delalic*, paras. 330 ff.

[296] On the whole point, see *Delalic*, paras. 348 ff, 364 ff. *Aleksovski*, paras. 73 ff. *Kayishema*, paras. 208 ff, 229 ff.

[297] On this point, see *Delalic*, paras. 379 ff. *Aleksovski*, paras. 79–80. *Kayishema*, paras. 225 ff. See also the *Report of the Secretary-General*, UN.DOC. S/25704, para. 56.

second part of the standard, i.e. the '*had reason to know*'.[298] A distinction was drawn by the Chamber in the *Delalic* case (1998) between the customary law developed through the post-Second World War trials and the customary law following the adoption of Protocol I (1977). As to the traditional law the Chamber starts by saying that there is a duty on commanders to remain informed about the activities of their subordinates. Thus the superior will be responsible if he has been at fault in having failed to acquire such knowledge, especially where the superior had in his possession information which would put him on notice of the risk of offences being committed or where he was wilfully blind to the acts of his subordinates. On the other hand, Article 86(2) of Protocol I (1977) limits the responsibility of the superior to cases where he had some specific information which would have put him on notice that offences were committed or which would put him on further inquiry.[299] The Chamber concludes that this stricter standard, more favorable to the accused, must be applied. Moreover, the Chamber adds, this stricter standard must be taken to reflect customary international law at the time the offences occurred.[300] The Chamber in the *Kayishema* case (1998) tried to limit the range of that *dictum* by applying it in the first place to non-military superiors. According to this Chamber, the duties of the military commander with regard to being informed are more extensive. The old customary rules would seem to apply. For non-military superiors, on the other hand, it would be necessary to show that they consciously disregarded information which clearly indicated or put them on notice that their subordinates had committed or were about to commit crimes.[301]

The conclusion that the wording of Article 86(2) of Protocol I of 1977 corresponds to new customary law does not seem warranted. Until most recent times the only (judicial) practice available was that of the post-Second World War trials, which does not support such a holding. The adoption of a single, albeit important, conventional rule departing from a well-established principle cannot be held of its own to overturn the previous position in general international law. This does not exclude that special reasons be adduced in order to apply the law of Protocol I as the one more favorable to the accused (nor that a constant application of this law may lead to the emergence of a new customary rule).

(c) Thirdly, the duty to act of the superior is limited to *necessary and reasonable measures*.[302] This standard refers to the circumstances and cannot be further specified in the abstract. The circumstances are that of

[298] *Delalic*, paras. 387 ff. *Kayishema*, paras. 225 ff.

[299] The words of Article 86(2) Protocol I are '[if they had] information which should have enabled them to conclude . . . ' ('des informations leur permettant de conclure . . . ').

[300] *Delalic*, para. 393.

[301] *Kayishema*, paras. 227–8. The Chamber relied on the Rome Statute on an International Criminal Court of 1998.

[302] *Delalic*, paras. 394–5. *Aleksovski*, para. 81.

the time of armed conflict in which the commander found himself; due account must be taken of the harshness and limitations inherent in such situations. In particular, a commander (or superior) cannot be obliged to perform the impossible; reasonable measures are only those that the superior has the material ability to perform. This is an application of the general principle of law *ad impossibile nemo tenetur*.[303]

(d) Finally, the Chamber in the *Delalic* case (1998) rejected the requirement that the superior's failure to act must have *caused* the commission of the offence, as claimed by the defence.[304] It held that such a requirement had not been acknowledged by the previous judicial practice. For the failure to punish committed offences such an element of causation cannot in any case exist, since the failure to punish does not cause the offence but comes after the fact. The present commentator would like to stress that the whole question seems inappropriately dealt with. As a matter of logic, a failure to act (omission) is never causative of the criminal result reached. Causing something and not intervening in order to stop a chain of external causes is not the same. What the Chamber had in mind is not causality in the strict sense, but what is called, in the civil legal systems, 'improper causality'. This type of causality is not a natural fact but a legal *hypothesis*: could the criminal result very probably have been avoided if the accused had acted according to his duty? As can be seen, this is causation in a very indirect and logically profoundly different sense. The test is not that of the *conditio sine qua non* (causality proper), but that of a *conditio cum qua* (*verisimiliter*) *non*. The whole question, if at all, should have been considered in that light.

XI. Defences: The Plea of Duress

The only defence analysed so far in the case-law of the ad hoc Tribunals is that of duress. The plea of duress consists in the argument that the accused acted under an immediate threat to his life or limb when committing the acts complained of. The defence is also termed 'necessity', 'compulsion', 'coercion', or 'compulsory duress'. It has been considered in various judgments following the Second World War, as for instance in the *Krupp*, *I.G. Farben*, and *Flick* Trials.[305] At the ICTY, the question of duress was raised in the *Erdemovic* case (1997) in the context of a guilty plea. The problem to be solved was whether duress is a plea in mitigation of the sentence or a complete defence absolving criminal guilt. If it was a complete defence, the guilty plea would have been

303 See *Dig.*, 50, 17, 185, *regulae iuris* (Celsus). *Corpus iuris canonici, Liber sextus*, tit. 13, *Regulae iuris, regula* 6.

304 *Delalic*, paras. 396 ff.

305 *Law Reports of Trials of War Criminals*, United Nations War Crimes Commission, vol. XV (London, 1949), pp. 170 ff.

equivocal[306] (and thus void), since a man cannot plead guilty and not guilty at the same time. The question whether duress is a ground of mitigation or a real defence turned out to deeply split the Appeals Chamber, leaving some visible signs of friction between the judges. It also turned out to be nourished by a profound clash of legal traditions, especially between the common law and the civil law. This is regrettable.

Since it was not possible to reach a common position in the judgment, the opinions of the judges have to be analysed separately. Very broadly speaking, two positions were held. First, the traditional common law position: duress as a ground only for mitigation. Secondly, the traditional civil law tradition: duress as a ground for removal of criminal guilt if strict conditions are met (otherwise only as a ground for mitigation).

Judges McDonald and Vohrah represent the first position.[307] They start by stating that in the post-Second World War jurisprudence there is no authority for duress as a complete defence to the killing of innocent persons[308]—with only the exception of a unsubstantiated *dictum* in the *Einsatzgruppen* case.[309] As the common and civil law traditions differ on this point, a general principle can exist only to the limited extent that an accused is less blameworthy if he acts under duress (mitigation). A number of policy considerations point clearly in the same direction. The law relating to the protection of the highest value (life) is based on a moral absolute: you may not kill the innocent even in order to save your own life. One should moreover not engage in a utilitarian logic in weighing life against life, e.g. if it is pleaded that refusal to obey would not have saved the victims but would only have added the accused to the victims. As has been said the rule is a moral absolute and no exceptions should be made. In addition, more can be expected from a soldier than from a civilian. It must also be considered that the Tribunal deals with the most serious crimes; a sweeping defence of duress would be dangerous. The common law approach leaves enough flexibility, since mitigation (or even remittal of punishment) can solve hard cases. Thus, duress is not a general defence but only a ground of mitigation. Judge Li concurs in the result.[310] For him duress may be a complete defence if certain conditions are met,[311] but it may not be such in cases of heinous crimes, e.g. the killing of the innocent.

[306] A separate question was whether the guilty plea was an informed one, this being denied by four of five judges (McDonald, Vohrah, Cassese, Stephen).

[307] Joint Sep.Op. McDonald/Vohrah, paras. 32 ff.

[308] M. Erdemovic had pleaded guilty to have participated in the execution squads which had killed over 1,200 civilians after the fall of Srebenica. He pleaded that if he had refused to execute the orders, he would have been shot himself too.

[309] For that *dictum*, see *Law Reports* . . . , loc.cit., p. 174.

[310] Sep. and Diss.Op. Li, para. 5.

[311] Ibid., para. 5: (i) the act was done to avoid an immediate danger both serious and irreparable; (ii) there was no other adequate means to escape; and (iii) the remedy was not disproportionate to the evil.

Judge Cassese represents the other position, that of the civil law systems.[312] He starts by an acrimonious rejection of the policy oriented approach of his common-law colleagues. Going into policy considerations, he says, and upholding those of the common law (especially English law) is extraneous to the task of the Tribunal; these policy considerations were meta-legal and contrary to the *nullum crimen* principle. The disregard for the civil law tradition was not warranted. Moreover, if international law was really uncertain on the point at issue, recourse should be had to the law applicable in the former Yugoslavia (allowing duress as a complete defence) and not to policy considerations. The Judge then turns to the substantive point. As a special exception for murder (killing of the innocent) cannot be said to have developed in customary international law, the general rule that duress is a complete defence should have been applied. The conditions to that effect are strict: (i) there must be an immediate threat of severe and irreparable harm to life or limb motivating the acts; (ii) there must not be other adequate means of averting the evil; (iii) the crime committed was not disproportionate to the evil threatened; and (iv) the situation of duress was not voluntarily brought about by the person coerced.[313] Moreover, special duties on the part of the accused towards the victim may preclude the possibility of raising duress as a defence. The same is true if an individual voluntarily becomes a member of a unit which notoriously engages in actions contrary to international humanitarian law.[314] As can be seen, for the killing of the innocent these conditions will seldom be met, but the defence should not be cut off *a priori*. There is at least one case where the defence is clearly made out. If by refusing to obey the accused could not have saved the victims—who would have been killed by other persons—but would only have forfeited his life also, the law cannot treat him as a criminal. Judge Cassese then goes on to show that the post-Second World War jurisprudence which seems to rule out the defence is not as categorical as it was claimed and that other cases, not quoted, support the view of duress as a complete defence.[315] Returning to the policy considerations, Judge Cassese opposes those inherent in the civil law tradition to those claimed by Judges McDonald and Vohrah. Law is based on what society can reasonably expect from its members; it does not require, by criminal sanction, acts of martyrdom. Mitigation is not enough, as the behavior is then still labelled as criminal. Judge Stephen, a common lawyer, joined the civil law position.[316] He stated that the common law exception for murder in pleading duress as a complete defence—a position which he finds hardly appropriate—had been

[312] Sep. and Diss.Op. Cassese, paras. 11 ff.
[313] Ibid., para. 16.
[314] Ibid., para. 17.
[315] Ibid., paras. 19 ff, 30 ff.
[316] Sep. and Diss.Op. Stephen, paras. 24 ff.

applied to situations where the accused had a choice between his and the victim's life, not where such choice was non-existent, it being only a case of either death for one or death for both.[317] The true test seems thus to be if there was a moral choice and if this choice was proportionate. Law cannot compel the choice to die for the highest ethical principles.

As can be seen, this case raises most profound problems lying at the root of criminal law and of a philosophical nature (criminal law knows many of them).[318] It will not be surprising if the present commentator, being a civil lawyer, adheres to the position upheld by Judge Cassese. It may also be noted that the exception in the common law tradition is constantly narrowed and increasingly challenged. While respecting the profound ethical foundations upon which it rests, it seems that law (and particularly criminal law) cannot compel an individual to do what is reasonably impossible to be expected from everybody, i.e. to illuminate one's passage on earth by a heroic gesture. The law has to speak to the average man, not to the saint. In other words: criminal law requires less than morals. Thus, the legality of the killing may still be affirmed, but the author will be criminally excused (*entschuldigender Notstand*).

XII. Conclusion

Through the first eleven substantive judgments rendered, the ad hoc Tribunals on the former Yugoslavia and Rwanda have already helped in affirming and developing the law on a series of points. How much international criminal law needed to be reshaped in order to evolve towards a homogenous and constructive body of law can be wholly appreciated only after a careful reading of the post-Second World War jurisprudence. These old judgments follow each other somewhat haphazardly, based often on municipal law or an amazing intermingling of international law and municipal law. They thereby split into a kaleidoscope of different shapes and tunes. Centralization of the judicial organ administering a branch of law and thus unification of the law itself has always corresponded to a progress in social evolution. The ad hoc Tribunals have thus paved the way for a single international criminal court.

As to the achievements of the Tribunals, three short aspects may be mentioned. First, there is the tendency (whose importance it is difficult to overestimate) to merge international and non-international armed conflicts into a single unit for the purposes of the applicable criminal law. This evolution will in turn retroact on the substantive law applicable. It will strive towards a single legal régime for armed conflicts centered in

[317] Ibid., para. 25.

[318] See e.g. the reflections on problems raised by the plank of Carneades, in A. Kaufmann, *Rechtsphilosophie*, 2nd edn. (Munich, 1997), p. 228.

the protection of the individual, not on distinctions related to sovereignty and the *domaine réservé*. To what extent this constitutes progress will be appreciated in the future. Secondly, one may underline the care with which the elements of the crimes were defined. This was a useful task to be performed since the law was often extremely uncertain on that point. Thirdly, on a more technical level, it is interesting to note the importance given to the principles of effectivity and teleological interpretation on several aspects.[319] The Tribunals also tend to take into account municipal law analogies and general principles of law, this being hardly surprising if one thinks about the many *lacunae* still present in international criminal law. This course is to be welcomed.

This long journey through the case-law of the Tribunals invites other long journeys: one may thus await with interest the case-law to come.[320]

[319] e.g. on the question of nationality in the grave breaches régime; the responsibility of the superior for his subordinates; the imputation of acts of the VRS to the FRY, etc.

[320] If two criticisms may be levied, it is first the often excessive length of the judgments. It is felt that the same could be said in less words, with a simplicity which, according to Ch. De Visscher, realizes 'une véritable économie de pensée et d'action [et] tend à produire un sentiment de certitude' (*Théories et réalités en droit international public*, 4th edn. (Paris, 1970), p. 388). Second, the French or Latin words which appear in the judgments (on the website) are often misspelled or otherwise wrong.

SURRENDERING THE ACCUSED TO THE INTERNATIONAL CRIMINAL COURT

By SIMON N. M. YOUNG[1]

I. INTRODUCTION

Under the Rome Statute of the International Criminal Court,[2] the surrender of the accused is a *sine qua non* to prosecution, there being no provision for trial *in absentia*. Without its own independent police force, the International Criminal Court must rely on the cooperation of States Parties to arrest and surrender individuals. The ability of the ICC to obtain custody of accused persons is directly related to the scope of legitimate State objections to surrender. Once the Statute comes into force and the ICC is established,[3] two kinds of impediments to surrender are likely to be contentious. First, by application of the Statute's procedural mechanism for distributing prosecutions between national courts and the international forum, States Parties may object to the admissibility of a case before the ICC. Secondly, they may object on the substantive ground that surrender is prohibited by their constitution or law, e.g. on the basis that nationals may not be extradited.

Perhaps the most controversial topic during negotiations on the Statute was the ICC's jurisdiction and the mechanism for distributing national and international prosecutions.[4] Ultimately it was decided that the Court should have a broad compulsory jurisdiction over war crimes

[1] LL B (Toronto), LL M (Cantab.), Assistant Professor, Faculty of Law, University of Hong Kong, formerly Counsel, Crown Law Office–Criminal, Ministry of the Attorney General for Ontario. The author would like to thank Barry Glaspell and the Editors of the Yearbook for their many helpful comments on an earlier draft. The views expressed herein are solely those of the author.

[2] Rome Statute of the International Criminal Court, July 17, 1998, UN Doc. A/CONF.183/9*, and corrections in CN.577.1998 TREATIES–8 (Annex) and CN.357.1999 TREATIES–14 (Annex), *reprinted in* 37 ILM 999 (1998) [hereinafter Statute]. The Statute was adopted at the United Nations Diplomatic Conference of Plenipotentiaries on the Establishment of an International Criminal Court held in Rome, Italy from 15 June to 17 July, 1998. It was adopted in an unrecorded vote by 120 countries in favour, 7 against and 21 abstaining. It is reported that the United States, China, Libya, Iraq, Israel, Qatar, and Yemen voted against adoption. See Dominic McGoldrick, *The Permanent International Criminal Court: an end to the culture of impunity?*, 1999 *Crim. L. Rev.* 627, 627–8. NB: All references to article and rule numbers in this article are to the Statute and the Rules of Evidence and Procedure, *infra* n. 8, unless otherwise indicated.

[3] As of 27 May 2001, the Statute has been signed by 139 countries and ratified by 32. It comes into force following ratification by 60 States (art. 126).

[4] See generally Danesh Sarooshi, *The Statute of the International Criminal Court*, 48 *Int'l & Comp. LQ*, 387, 395 (1999); Mahnoush H. Arsanjani, *The Rome Statute of the International Criminal Court*, 93 *Am. J. Int'l L.* 22, 25 (1999); John T. Holmes, *The Principle of Complementarity*, in *The International Criminal Court: The Making of the Rome Statute Issues, Negotiations, Results*, 41, 43

and crimes against humanity, tempered by a deferential distribution mechanism that makes the Court complementary to national courts. Under this principle of complementarity, national courts have the primary responsibility for prosecuting all offences. But if States are either unwilling or unable to prosecute, the ICC may rule a case admissible and require the surrender of the accused. One of the shortcomings of the Statute is the failure to specify how the burden of proof is allocated in admissibility proceedings. Given that States are likely to be in the best position to offer evidence on this point, one might suppose that they should have the burden to demonstrate the *bona fides* of their domestic prosecution. However, many writers have tended to assume that the Prosecutor will have the burden to prove admissibility simply because of the perceived 'primacy' of national courts.[5] Without giving the Prosecutor adequate resources to inquire into the propriety of domestic prosecutions, this approach may impair the effective operation of the Court.

The substantive problem of domestic law objections to surrender cannot be dismissed simply on the basis of the orthodox position that international law trumps national law.[6] The Statute itself considers the processing of arrest and surrender requests as essentially a matter of national law. It also reflects a reluctance to interfere with existing treaty regimes, such as extradition treaties, and to affect the rights and interests of non-States Parties. But at what point will this sensitivity to a State Party's national law and international obligations give way to a finding that the Party is in breach of its obligations under the Statute? How are the legitimate interests of States Parties to be reconciled with the effective operation of the ICC? The Statute fails to address these issues in a clear manner.

This article will suggest answers to these two issues on the basis of treaty interpretation. In Part II, an interpretive framework will be established, emphasizing the object and purpose of the Statute. It will be argued that the twin principles of effective prosecution and complementarity inform the Statute's text and can help clarify interpretive problems. In Part III, the interpretive framework will be applied to the

(Roy S. Lee, (ed.), 1999) [hereinafter *Making of the Rome Statute*]; Elizabeth Wilmshurst, *Jurisdiction of the Court*, in *Making of the Rome Statute*, id. 127.

[5] See Louise Arbour and Morten Bergsmo, *Conspicuous Aspects of Jurisdictional Overreach*, in *Reflections on the International Criminal Court: Essays in Honour of Adriaan Bos* 129, 130–1 (Herman A. M. von Hebel *et al.* (eds.), 1999) [hereinafter *Reflections on the ICC*]; McGoldrick, *supra* n. 2 at 643; Holmes, ibid. at 73, 77; Marten Zwanenburg, *The Statute for an International Criminal Court and the United States: Peacekeepers under Fire?*, 10 *Eur. J. Int'l L.* 124, 131–2 (1999). But cf. Jeffrey L. Bleich, *Complementarity*, 25 *Denv. J. Int'l L. & Pol'y* 281, 287–8, 291 (1997).

[6] The orthodox position has been expressed in various sources. See generally art. 27 of the Vienna Convention on the Law of Treaties, *infra* note 7; Treatment of Polish Nationals in Danzig Case, 1932 PCIJ (ser. A/B) No. 44, 24 (4 Feb.); *Prosecutor* v. *Blaskic* (Subpoena), *infra* n. 10 at 718; *Draft Articles on State Responsibility Provisionally Adopted by the Drafting Committee of the International Law Commission*, UN Doc. A/CN.4/L.569, 12, art. 42(4) (4 Aug. 1998).

problem of burden of proof in admissibility challenges. It will be argued that there are two types of admissibility challenges which operate in tandem, giving rise in effect to a dialogue between the ICC and States over the venue of prosecution. In a preliminary ruling challenge, the Prosecutor should carry the persuasive burden of showing admissibility, while States would have a duty to produce evidence on the conditions of their own domestic prosecution. In a general challenge under article 19, States should have both the persuasive burden and evidentiary duty. In Part IV, the interpretive framework is applied to the problem of national law objections to surrender. It will be argued that the Statute permits domestic courts a very narrow sphere of authority in the processing of arrest and surrender requests. It does not permit States to evade their surrender obligations by relying on the traditional extradition-based grounds of refusal, such as nationality, the political offence doctrine, and double criminality.

II. An Interpretive Framework for the Statute

The framework of interpretation used in this article is essentially that set out in Part III of the Vienna Convention on the Law of Treaties.[7] The answers to the issues of burden allocation in admissibility challenges and national law objections to surrender do not readily emerge from the ordinary meaning of the treaty text or from the Statute's preparatory work. The Rules of Procedure and Evidence are also of limited assistance in clarifying these issues.[8] Consequently, an approach that emphasizes the object and purpose of the Statute is applied.[9] This approach is not

[7] Vienna Convention on the Law of Treaties, 23 May 1969, 1155 UNTS 331 [hereinafter VCLT]. Art. 31 of the VCLT provides that, '[a] treaty shall be interpreted in good faith in accordance with the ordinary meaning to be given to the terms of the treaty in their context and in the light of its object and purpose'. Recourse may be made to the preparatory work of the treaty in order to confirm the meaning resulting from the application of the general rule or to determine the meaning when the general rule of interpretation leaves the meaning ambiguous or obscure, or leads to a result which is manifestly absurd or unreasonable (art. 32 of VCLT).

[8] On 30 June, 2000, the Preparatory Commission for the International Criminal Court adopted its report containing the finalized draft texts of the Rules of Procedure and Evidence, UN Doc. PCNICC/2000/1 and Add.1 [hereinafter Rules]. See also *Proceedings of the Preparatory Commission at its fifth session (12–30 June 2000)*, UN Doc. PCNICC/2000/L.3/Rev.1. Pursuant to art. 51(1), the Rules enter into force upon adoption by a two-thirds majority of the members of the Assembly of States Parties, a body which is to be established upon entry into force of the Statute. Article 5(5) provides that in the event of a conflict between the Statute and the Rules, the Statute shall prevail.

[9] On the teleological approach to treaty interpretation, see generally Ian Brownlie, *Principles of Public International Law*, 637–9, 687–9 (5th edn. 1998); Gerald G. Fitzmaurice, *The Law and Procedure of the International Court of Justice: Treaty Interpretation and Certain Other Treaty Points*, 28 *Brit. YB Int'l L.* 1, 7–8, 18–20 (1951); Gerald G. Fitzmaurice, *The Law and Procedure of the International Court of Justice, 1951–4: Treaty Interpretation and Other Treaty Points*, 33 *Brit. YB Int'l L.* 203, 207–8, 210, 220–3 (1957); Edward Gordon, *The World Court and the Interpretation of Constitutive Treaties*, 59 *Am. J. Int'l L.* 794, 815–21 (1965); Hugh Thirlway, *The Law and Procedure of the International Court of Justice, 1960–1989*, 62 *Brit. YB Int'l L.* 1, 44–8 (1991). See also Case Concerning Application of the Genocide Convention (*Bosnia* v. *Yugoslavia*), 1996 ICJ 4, paras. 31–4 (11 July).

entirely teleological as it keeps within the confines of the ordinary language of the text. There is precedent for this approach from international tribunals interpreting their own constitutive instruments.[10] The Statute is clearly a law-making instrument with the characteristics of a criminal statute, a due process code, an extradition, and a mutual legal assistance treaty combined. Given the ambitious enterprise of the Statute and the considerable elements of political compromise among States with diverse criminal justice systems, interpretive problems are bound to emerge. The proposed interpretive framework can assist in addressing these problems and ensuring consistent interpretations in line with the basic tenets of the Statute.

The two central underlying purposes of the Statute are complementarity and the effective prosecution of the most serious international crimes. These principles are expressly contained in the preamble of the Statute and in the preambles of all its previous drafts since 1994.[11] To understand the specific meaning of these principles, it is necessary to consider them in light of the text and drafting history of the Statute.

1. *The Principle of Effective Prosecution*

During the drafting process, the most substantial discussion of the desirability of having an international criminal court was in 1992–3.[12] The general consensus in the International Law Commission was that such a court was desirable given the historical cases of impunity for the

[10] The International Court of Justice has on a number of occasions recognized implied powers of United Nations bodies on the basis of the purposes and functions of those bodies. See Reparation for Injuries Suffered in the Service of the United Nations, 1949 ICJ 174, 180 (11 April); Certain Expenses of the United Nations, 1962 ICJ 151 (20 July); Competence of the General Assembly for the Admission of a State to the United Nations, 1950 ICJ 4, 8–9 (3 Mar.); Namibia Case, 1971 ICJ 16, 30–2 (21 June). The Appeals Chamber of the International Criminal Tribunal for the Former Yugoslavia (ICTY) has also applied this method of interpretation in construing the ICTY Statute, although not strictly a treaty. See *Prosecutor* v. *Tadic* (Jurisdiction), 35 ILM 32, 55–8 (1995); *Prosecutor* v. *Blaskic* (Subpoena), 110 ILR 607, 694–6, 714 (1997).

[11] Paragraph 4 of the Statute's preamble provides that 'the most serious crimes of concern to the international community as a whole must not go unpunished and that their effective prosecution must be ensured by taking measures at the national level and by enhancing international cooperation'. Paragraph 10 of the preamble and art. 1 emphasize that the ICC shall be complementary to national criminal jurisdictions. These statements can be traced to similar ones in the International Law Commission's 1994 Draft Statute for an International Criminal Court, which along with commentary can be found in *Report of the International Law Commission on the work of its forty-sixth session*, 2 May–22 July 1994, UN GAOR, 49th Sess., Supp. No. 10, at 43–161, UN Doc. A/49/10 (1994) [hereinafter ILC Draft Statute].

[12] See *Report of the International Law Commission on the work of its forty-fourth session*, UN GAOR, 47th Sess., Supp. No. 10, UN Doc. A/47/10 (1992), para. 29–32; *Report of the Working Group on the Question of an International Criminal Jurisdiction*, Annex to ibid., para. 21, 25–43 [hereinafter 1992 Working Group Report]; *Topical summary of the discussion held in the Sixth Committee of the General Assembly during its forty-seventh session*, UN Doc. A/CN.4/446 (1993), para. 11–30.

most serious crimes of international concern.[13] It was felt that an international criminal court was needed to 'enhance the effective suppression and prosecution of crimes of international concern'.[14] This overriding purpose of effective prosecution was carried into and implemented in the Rome Statute.

The principle of effective prosecution requires that conditions exist to contribute to a reliable outcome at trial.[15] For example, one condition that is generally recognized as being essential is the impartiality of the judges.[16] The ICC, like many domestic systems, goes further by requiring strict impartiality and fairness from the prosecutors as well.[17] Another significant factor is a speedy trial.[18] As one court has aptly stated,

> [w]hen a trial takes place without unreasonable delay, with all witnesses available and memories fresh, it is far more certain that the guilty parties who committed the crimes will be convicted and punished and those that did not, will be acquitted and vindicated.[19]

A reliable verdict will depend on the extent to which the court receives all the evidence relevant to the issues in the case. This in turn depends on the ability of the Prosecutor and accused to gather this evidence. Under the Statute, the Prosecutor and even the accused depend on the cooperation of States Parties to provide assistance in evidence gathering.[20]

[13] See 1992 Working Group Report, *id.* at para. 39. For an historical account of the failure of prosecution through national jurisdictions, see Antonio Cassese, *On the Current Trends towards Criminal Prosecution and Punishment of Breaches of International Humanitarian Law*, 9 *Eur. J.Int'l L.* 2 (1998); M. Cherif Bassiouni, *From Versailles to Rwanda in Seventy-Five Years: The Need to Establish a Permanent International Criminal Court*, 10 *Harv. Hum. Rts. J.* 11 (1997).

[14] Paragraph 1 of preamble to ILC Draft Statute, *supra* note 11.

[15] On the truth-determining function of the Court and Prosecutor, see arts. 54(1)(a) & 69(3).

[16] See arts. 36(3)(a), 36(7), 40(2), 41(2)(a), 45–7, 70.

[17] See arts. 42(1), 42, 45–7, 70.

[18] The Statute contains a number of provisions aimed at minimizing delay. For example, upon receipt of a request for arrest and surrender, States Parties shall 'immediately' take steps to arrest the person in question (art. 59(1)). Once ordered to be surrendered or if the person consents to the surrender, he or she shall be delivered to the Court 'as soon as possible' (arts. 59(7) & 92(3)). Accused are not to be detained for an unreasonable period prior to trial due to inexcusable delay by the Prosecutor (art. 60(4)). The Trial Chamber must ensure that a trial is 'fair and expeditious' at all times (arts. 64(2) & (3)). When a unique investigative opportunity presents itself, the Court may authorize measures necessary to 'ensure the efficiency and integrity of the proceedings' (art. 56(1)(b)). If a request for assistance under Part 9 is denied, the requested State Party shall 'promptly' inform the Court of the reasons for such denial (art. 93(6)). States that accept the jurisdiction of the Court on an *ad hoc* basis shall cooperate with the Court 'without any delay or exception in accordance with Part 9' (art. 12(3)). States may only challenge the admissibility of a case once and it must be made 'at the earliest opportunity' (arts. 19(4) & (5)). Unjustified delay can be indicative of an unwillingness to prosecute, leaving it open to the Court to intervene (art. 17(2)(b)).

[19] *Regina* v. *Askov*, [1990] 2 SCR 1199 at 1221.

[20] The Statute contains provisions facilitating the optimal degree of cooperation between the ICC and States Parties. See e.g. arts. 86, 89(1), 93(1), 97, 99(4), 57(3)(d). The Prosecutor also has limited direct investigative powers, see e.g. arts. 56, 99(4), 57(3)(d).

Effective prosecution as an interpretive principle requires that the Statute be read to avoid or minimize impediments, such as partiality, delay, and lack of State cooperation, to achieving a reliable verdict at trial.

2. *The Principle of Complementarity*

While the principle of complementarity was incorporated in the ILC's 1994 Draft Statute for an International Criminal Court (ILC Draft Statute),[21] its practical significance was eclipsed by that Statute's *ad hoc* consent preconditions to acquiring jurisdiction.[22] Under the ILC's draft, once the custodial and territorial States (and possibly a third extradition-requesting State) consented, it would be unlikely that another State would try to oust the ICC's jurisdiction by launching its own prosecution. During subsequent negotiations in the Preparatory Committee and at the Rome Conference, however, complementarity came to the forefront as attention turned towards compulsory jurisdiction for the most serious crimes. Compulsory jurisdiction appeared more acceptable if, under the principle of complementarity, the Court was required to defer to *bona fide* national prosecutions.[23]

Complementarity governs the relationship between the Court and States Parties and constitutes the means by which effective prosecution is accomplished. While it is sometimes said that the principle of complementarity gives national courts primacy in jurisdiction, this description is misleading. National courts may have the primary responsibility for prosecuting international crimes; they do not have primacy in determining where the prosecution will take place. Nor does the ICC have primacy in this respect. Under the ILC Draft Statute, States would effectively have had primacy because the Court's jurisdiction in a specific case depended on the *ad hoc* acceptance of jurisdiction by the relevant States Parties. The drafters also refused to follow the approach of the International Criminal Tribunal for the Former Yugoslavia (ICTY),

[21] Paragraph 3 of the preamble to the ILC Draft Statute, *supra* n. 11, provided that the court was 'intended to be complementary to national criminal justice systems in cases where such trial procedures may not be available or may be ineffective'.

[22] Under art. 21(1) of the ILC Draft Statute, id., the acquisition of jurisdiction in a particular case required both the custodial State (State which has custody of the accused) and the territorial State (territory on which the alleged crime occurred) to be parties to the Statute and, in a separate act, to have accepted the jurisdiction of the Court for that case. The consent of a third State, such as the State of nationality of the accused, was also necessary where that State requested the extradition of the accused pursuant to an international agreement (art. 21(2)). For further background on the ILC Draft Statute see James Crawford, *The ILC Adopts a Statute for an International Criminal Court*, 89 *Am. J. Int'l L.* 404 (1995).

[23] See *Report of the Ad Hoc Committee on the Establishment of an International Criminal Court*, UN GAOR, 50th Sess., Supp. No. 22, UN Doc. A/50/22 (1995) paras. 91–101 [hereinafter Ad Hoc Committee Report].

which gives the ICC primacy.[24] Instead the drafters opted for a rule-based mechanism, which leaves the power to distribute prosecutions with a judicial organ of the ICC applying prescribed legal criteria.

The principle of complementarity is not just a procedural device for distributing prosecutions; it also reflects three substantive aims embodied in the Statute. When interpreting the Statute, these three aspects of complementarity should be kept in mind. The principle of complementarity is first and foremost a means for ensuring effective prosecution. Having national systems undertake the bulk of the prosecutions is efficient as it utilizes established resources and avoids overburdening the ICC.[25] Secondly, the principle reflects a sensitivity to various State sovereignty interests.[26] In the areas of surrender and evidence gathering, the Statute recognizes separate spheres of authority as between the Court and States and establishes a regime of cooperation to ensure the Court's effective operation. Lastly, the provisions on admissibility impose a minimum international standard of justice which States must maintain if they wish the Court to defer.[27] There are at least six elements to these standards.[28] The proceedings must be conducted in accordance with principles of due process recognized by international law. They can not be for the purpose of shielding the person from criminal responsibility. There can be no unjustified delay in the proceedings. The proceedings must be conducted independently and impartially. They must be consistent with an intent to bring the person concerned to justice. And

[24] See *Statute of the International Tribunal for the Former Yugoslavia*, SC Res. 827, U.N. SCOR, 48th Sess., Annex, 3217th mtg. at 29, UN Doc. S/RES/827 (1993), *reprinted in* 32 *ILM* 1203 (1993) [hereinafter ICTY Statute]. Article 9 of the ICTY Statute provides that the ICTY and national courts shall have concurrent jurisdiction, but the ICTY shall have primacy over national courts; it may request national courts to defer to its competence at any stage of the procedure. On the primacy of the international criminal tribunals, see generally *Prosecutor* v. *Tadic* (Jurisdiction), *supra* note 10 at 48–53; Bartram S. Brown, *Primacy or Complementarity: Reconciling the Jurisdiction of National Courts and International Criminal Tribunals*, 23 *Yale J. Int'l L.* 383 (1998).

[25] This idea has been expressed on a number of occasions by members of the drafting bodies and other commentators. See generally Ad Hoc Committee Report, *supra* n. 23 at para. 31; *Report of the Preparatory Committee on the Establishment of an International Criminal Court*, Vol. I, UN GAOR, 51st Sess., Supp. No. 22, UN Doc. A/51/22 (1996) at para. 55 [hereinafter 1996 Committee Report]; Antonio Cassese, *The Statute of the International Criminal Court: Some Preliminary Reflections*, 10 *Eur. J. Int'l L.* 144, 158 (1999); United Nations High Commissioner for Human Rights, *The High Commissioner's Position Paper on the Establishment of a Permanent International Criminal Court*, para. 62 (Geneva, 15 June 1998), which can be found at <www.unhchr.ch/html/menu2/2/icc.htm>.

[26] See, e.g., arts. 70(2), 72–3, 90(6), 93, 97–8.

[27] The drafting history reveals that an alternative approach, which required deference on demand without any review of the substantive quality of the national prosecution, was considered and rejected. See *Draft Statute for the International Criminal Court, Report of the Preparatory Committee on the Establishment of an International Criminal Court*, Addendum, Part One, UN Doc. A/CONF.183/2/Add.1 (14 April 1998), art. 15 [hereinafter Committee's Draft Statute].

[28] See arts. 17, 20(3).

finally, the justice system must have a certain capability to obtain the accused, the necessary evidence and to carry out its proceedings.

3. *Application of the Two Principles*

In applying these two principles in practice, there will be occasions when they conflict. If the principles cannot be reconciled it is suggested that the principle of complementarity should give way to that of effective prosecution, since the former principle is a means to achieving the latter. While the means (complementarity) may reflect other values, these must be subordinate to the prior value of effective prosecution. It cannot be assumed that the States Parties to the Statute would devise a mechanism to implement their collective purpose which, in its operation, undermined that same purpose.

III. Procedural Impediment: Burden of Proof in Admissibility Challenges

1. *The Problem of Allocating the Burden of Proof in Admissibility Challenges*

Allocation of the burden of proof can be of considerable practical importance to the outcome of contentious disputes. Where the evidence is evenly balanced, the burden of proof may be used by the court as a legitimate legal basis to rule against the party having the burden.[29] This aspect of the burden of proof is closely associated with the distinct concept of duty to produce evidence, although the two are often confused and in civil law jurisdictions the distinction does not exist.[30] In a particular case, it is possible that the opposing parties will each have a duty to tender evidence to the court (an evidential duty), but only one party will have the ultimate burden of proof (persuasive burden).[31] Satisfaction of an evidential duty does not necessarily satisfy the persuasive burden, as this depends on the persuasiveness of the overall evidence. Different consequences also flow from the failure to meet these two types of obligations. Failing to discharge the persuasive burden means losing one's case, failing to discharge an evidential duty may have less drastic consequences, such as an adverse inference.

[29] See Mojtaba Kazazi, *Burden of Proof and Related Issues: A Study on Evidence Before International Tribunals*, 29–30 (1996); Juliane Kokott, *The Burden of Proof in Comparative and International Human Rights Law*, 16–17 (1998).

[30] See Kazazi, ibid., at 21–38; Bernard Robertson, 'Exhaustion of Local Remedies in International Human Rights Litigation—The Burden of Proof Reconsidered', 39 *Int'l & Comp. LQ* 191 (1990); Kokott, *id.* at 9–17.

[31] Kazazi, ibid., at 35–8.

2. *The Procedural Structure Governing Admissibility*

(a) Admissibility at the Investigative Stage

Under the Statute, the Prosecutor initiates investigations *proprio motu* (art. 15) or as a result of referrals of situations by either States Parties or the Security Council acting under Chapter VII of the United Nations Charter (arts. 13–14). The Prosecutor must initiate referred investigations unless there is no reasonable basis to proceed having regard to the strength of the evidence, the admissibility of the case, and any substantial reasons to believe that an investigation would not serve the interests of justice (art. 53(1)).

Once a non-Security Council referred investigation has been initiated, the Prosecutor must notify all States Parties and those non-States Parties, which 'would normally exercise jurisdiction over the crimes concerned' (art. 18).[32] Within a month of receipt of this notice, a State may inform the Court that it is investigating or has investigated the criminal acts mentioned in the notification (art. 18(2)). 'At the request of that State, the Prosecutor shall defer to the State's investigation . . . unless the Pre-Trial Chamber, on the application of the Prosecutor, decides to authorize the investigation' (art. 18(2)). Although not expressly stated, the title of article 18, 'Preliminary rulings regarding admissibility', suggests that the Chamber is to decide this application in accordance with the admissibility criteria in article 17.[33]

It is unclear whether the requesting State may participate in the consideration of the Prosecutor's application. Article 18 neither refers to the process as a 'hearing' nor provides for the submission of information to the Court by any entities other than the Prosecutor. The Rules appear to prescribe a procedure whereby the Court will decide the Prosecutor's application on the basis of written submissions (rule 54). But rule 55(1) also provides that the Pre-Trial Chamber will have the authority to decide the procedure followed in each case and may hold a hearing if appropriate. Article 18(7) appears to contemplate a State being able to challenge a ruling of the Pre-Trial Chamber under this article. It provides that '[a] State which has challenged a ruling of the Pre-Trial Chamber under this article' has only a limited right to bring another challenge under article 19. It is unclear whether the first challenge

[32] This category of non-States Parties is limited to those that would 'normally' exercise jurisdiction, thereby obviating the need to determine if States under their domestic law would have actual jurisdiction in a particular case. The criteria obviously cannot be based on universal jurisdiction as this indiscriminate standard would be unworkable and require notification of all States. Presumably, the Prosecutor has been given the competence to define the criteria according to international law standards and the most common bases for exercising jurisdiction (e.g. territorial, nationality).

[33] This is consistent with rule 55(2), which provides that the Pre-Trial Chamber shall consider the factors in art. 17 in deciding whether to authorize an investigation.

referred to here is a challenge in the first instance during the consideration of the original application or a challenge as in the nature of an appeal. Paragraph 4 does not clarify the confusion. It simply provides that the State concerned or the Prosecutor 'may appeal' to the Appeals Chamber against a ruling of the Pre-Trial Chamber; the word 'challenge' is not repeated. Nevertheless, given the challenging State's obvious interest in the outcome of the application, the restriction on its ability to raise the issue again, and its express right of appeal, the most sensible construction is to presume that the State in question will have the opportunity to participate as a party to the original proceeding.

Even if it is decided to defer to a State's request, the Prosecutor may remain concerned with the domestic prosecution in three respects. First, the Prosecutor can review its deferral decision and re-apply for authorization after six months or at any time when there has been a significant change of circumstances in the State's unwillingness or inability genuinely to carry out the investigation (art. 18(3); rule 56). Secondly, the Prosecutor may request that the State periodically disclose the progress of its investigations and any subsequent prosecutions. States Parties must respond to such requests without undue delay (art. 18(5)). Finally, the Prosecutor may, on an exceptional basis, seek authority from the Pre-Trial Chamber to pursue necessary investigative steps for the purpose of preserving evidence (art. 18(6)).

(b) Admissibility at the Surrender Stage

At any time after the initiation of an investigation, the Prosecutor may apply to the Pre-Trial Chamber for the issuance of an arrest warrant (art. 58). The Pre-Trial Chamber must issue the warrant if satisfied on two conditions (art. 58(1)): (*a*) there are reasonable grounds to believe that the person has committed a crime within the jurisdiction of the Court; and (*b*) the person's arrest is necessary to ensure attendance at trial, to ensure non-interference with the investigation or the court proceedings, or to prevent the commission of an offence.

On the basis of the warrant, the Court may transmit a request to any State, on the territory of which the requested person may be found, and request the cooperation of that State in the arrest and surrender of that person (arts. 58(5) and 89). States Parties must, 'in accordance with the provisions of [Part 9] and the procedure under their national law', comply with the request (art. 89(1)). However, requested States are entitled to object to the admissibility of the case and there are three different situations that might arise at this stage.

1. PRELIMINARY RULING CHALLENGE

The requested State may have already received notification from the Prosecutor pursuant to the article 18 preliminary ruling mechanism. If the requested State makes a request for deferral within the one-month deadline, any subsequent issues of admissibility will be dealt with in accordance with the article 18 procedure outlined above.

II. RESTRICTED ARTICLE 19 CHALLENGE

If the requested State previously failed to secure a preliminary ruling of inadmissibility, it has only a restricted ability to bring a subsequent article 19 challenge at the surrender stage. The State may only bring this challenge on the 'grounds of additional significant facts or significant change of circumstances' (art. 18(7)). Aside from this restriction, the rest of the procedure to be followed is the same as the general article 19 challenge discussed below.

III. ARTICLE 19 CHALLENGE

Article 19 sets out the normal procedure for States, accused persons and persons named in an arrest warrant or summons to challenge the jurisdiction of the Court and admissibility of a case. This type of challenge at the surrender stage will typically concern two groups of States: those which did not receive notification under article 18 and were thus not entitled to request the Prosecutor's deferral, and those which did receive such notification but chose not to request a deferral. Unlike the preliminary ruling mechanism, article 19 challenges are still available to States and individuals even if the situation has been referred to the Court by the Security Council.

Challenges to the admissibility of a case on the grounds referred to in article 17 may be made by

(a) an accused or a person for whom a warrant of arrest or a summons to appear has been issued under article 58;
(b) a State which has jurisdiction over a case, on the ground that it is investigating or prosecuting the case or has investigated or prosecuted; or
(c) a State from which acceptance of jurisdiction is required under article 12.[34]

If a State brings a challenge, the Prosecutor shall suspend the investigation until the Court rules on admissibility under article 17. However, pending the ruling the Prosecutor may seek authority from the Court to pursue necessary investigative steps to preserve evidence in exceptional circumstances, to take a statement or testimony from a witness or complete other evidence gathering that had previously been started, and to prevent the absconding of persons named in an arrest warrant (art. 19(7) and (8)).

[34] See art. 19(2). It appears from art. 12 that category (c) States include the territorial state and the state of nationality.

The admissibility of a case may be challenged under article 19 only once by any person or State. The challenge must take place prior to or at the commencement of the trial. Victims and those who may have referred the situation to the ICC are entitled to submit observations to the Court. The Statute does not expressly provide for a hearing, but as with the article 18 mechanism, the Rules provide that the Court shall decide on the procedure to be followed and may hold a hearing (rule 58). In exceptional circumstances, the Court may grant leave for a challenge to be brought more than once or at a time later than the commencement of the trial (art. 19(4)). However, challenges at the commencement of a trial, or subsequently with the leave of the Court, can be based only on the principle of *ne bis in idem* under article 20(3).[35] In addition, States should make their challenges 'at the earliest opportunity' (art. 19(5)).

Decisions on admissibility may be appealed to the Appeals Chamber (art. 19(6)). Alternatively, if the Court has ruled a case to be inadmissible, the Prosecutor may submit a request for a review of the decision if new facts arise which negate the basis on which the case had previously been found inadmissible.

(c) Lack of Clarity in Allocation of the Burden of Proof

In the absence of express direction, one may be tempted to infer the allocation of the evidential duty and persuasive burden from the language chosen by the drafters. For example, since admissibility is not a precondition to the exercise of jurisdiction, one might infer that whoever brings the application has the burden of proof. So in the case of the preliminary ruling, the Prosecutor would have the burden, while in the normal article 19 challenge, the party that brings the challenge (State or individual) would have the persuasive burden. However this formalistic approach to the issue is problematic, and as a proposed general rule of international law it has been the subject of much criticism.[36] Such an approach ignores both the substantive law in the particular case, and the ability of the parties to obtain the evidence required.

Perhaps a more refined approach is to consider the substantive legal criteria and to ask whether it appears to divide the persuasive burden between the parties on the basis of a general proposition subject to one or more enumerated exceptions. So for example, under article 17(1)(a) the State has the burden to show that it is prosecuting the case within

[35] See art. 19(4).

[36] See Kazazi, *supra* n. 29 at 225–8; Kokott, *supra* n. 29 at 174–6; Sir Gerald Fitzmaurice, *The Law and Procedure of the International Court of Justice*, vol. II, 575–7 (1986); Case of Certain Norwegian Loans (*Fr.* v. *Nor.*), 1957 ICJ 9, 39 (6 July) (separate opinion of Judge Lauterpacht); C. F. Amerasinghe, *Local Remedies in International Law*, 278, 281–2 (1990).

jurisdiction, while the Prosecutor has the burden to show the inadequacy of that prosecution. This approach is akin to the *actori incumbit probatio* principle ('the burden of proof rests upon him who asserts the affirmative of a proposition that if not substantiated will result in a decision adverse to his contention'),[37] which some writers have characterized as a general rule of international law applied by international tribunals in inter-State disputes.[38] However the *actori* principle has also been criticized.[39] It seems arbitrary to allocate the burden on the basis of assertions of 'affirmative' propositions only. In litigation, parties will tend to assert all favourable propositions irrespective of whether they are framed in the affirmative or negative. In some instances, there may be reasons for wanting to impose a persuasive burden on a party to prove a negative proposition. For example, in criminal law, it is generally incumbent on the prosecutor not only to prove the elements of the crime but also to disprove any substantive defences raised by the accused. Since the *actori* principle does not allow for burdens to disprove propositions (i.e. prove negative propositions), it is of limited application. It also suffers from being abstract, overly formalistic, and divorced from the overall context and purposes of the Statute.

3. *Assistance from the Preparatory Work*

The preparatory work to the Statute is of limited assistance in resolving the present issue.[40] This is so for three reasons. First, the issue of burden allocation was not expressly addressed in any of the draft texts

[37] Durwand V. Sandifer, *Evidence Before International Tribunals*, 127 (*rev. ed.*, 1975).

[38] See generally Kazazi, *supra* n. 29 at 221–3; Dinah L. Shelton, *Judicial Review of State Action by International Courts*, 12 *Fordham Int'l LJ* 361, 379 (1989); H. W. A. Thirlway, *Evidence Before International Courts and Tribunals*, in *Encyclopedia of Public International Law*, vol. II, 302–4 (R. Bernhardt (ed.), 1992).

[39] Kokott, *supra* note 29 at 184–95; Kazazi, ibid., at 224–30.

[40] The preparatory work of the ICC begins with the work of the ILC in 1993–4, although there were earlier related discussions in the context of the Draft Code of Crimes Against the Peace and Security of Mankind. See *supra* n. 12. The 1994 Draft Statute was considered by an Ad Hoc Committee of the General Assembly, which prepared a report in 1995, see *supra* n. 23. Further work in drafting the Statute was continued by the Preparatory Committee (Committee), which held six formal sessions from 1996 to 1998. For a succinct summary of these sessions, see the four articles written by Christopher Keith Hall published in volumes 91 and 92 of the *Am. J. Int'l L.* at 177, 124, 331, 548 respectively (1997 and 1998). The negotiations at the Rome Conference were conducted in a number of separate working groups concerned with specific aspects of the Statute. However, given the importance of Part 2 of the Statute, dealing with jurisdiction and admissibility, negotiations on this part were held in the Committee of the Whole, in which all participating States were represented. The debates on admissibility in the Committee of the Whole can be found at *Summary Records of the 11th and 12th Meetings of the Committee of the Whole held on June 22–3, 1998*, UN Doc. A/CONF.183/C.1/SR.11 & SR.12. See also *Making of the Rome Statute*, *supra* n. 4, for a detailed account of the drafting history behind the Statute.

produced by the official bodies.[41] In the first two sessions of the Preparatory Committee in 1996, France had proposed an admissibility procedure that addressed the issue of evidential duty. In preliminary admissibility challenges, the State or person challenging would be required to provide information concerning the conduct of the investigations and the judicial procedures which might support a finding of inadmissibility.[42] However, this proposal was never discussed in the first two sessions, and it does not appear to have been mentioned again.[43] The second limitation of the preparatory work is the lack of any reported authoritative statements by States or members of the official bodies on the topic. While some non-governmental organizations recommended that States should generally carry the burden of proof, the issue does not appear to have been publicly debated amongst the delegates.[44] One reason is that much of the negotiations on the admissibility articles both in the Committee and at the Rome Conference occurred during informal sessions or other private meetings.[45] These sessions and meetings proved to be effective in identifying objections and securing agreement, but they were not officially reported. Lastly, the few public statements by States on the issue are conflicting and generally unhelpful in discerning any general opinion.[46]

[41] The 1994 ILC Draft Statute is generally recognized as the first draft Statute, although the ILC produced an earlier draft in 1993. See *supra* nn. 11 and 12. In the fourth session of the Committee, the predecessor to art. 17 was drafted in a form which came very close to the final article. See *Decisions Taken by the Preparatory Committee at its Session held in New York from 4 to 15 August 1997*, UN Doc. A/AC.249/1997/L.8/Rev.1, 1997, Annex I, art. 35. The predecessor to art. 19 was drafted in the fifth session of the Committee. See *Decisions Taken by the Preparatory Committee at its Session held in New York from 1 to 12 December 1997*, UN Doc. A/AC.249/1997/L.9/Rev.1, 1997, Annex III, art. 36 [hereinafter 5th Session Committee Report]. The preliminary ruling mechanism (art. 18) was introduced by the US in the last session of the Committee. See *Proposal Submitted by the United States of America*, UN Doc. A/AC. 249/1998/WG.3/DP.2 [hereinafter US Proposal]. All the articles drafted by the Committee were collected together in a Draft Statute, which served as the basis of negotiation at the Rome Conference. See Committee's Draft Statute, *supra* n. 27. During the drafting process at the Conference, there were two interim drafts of Part 2 prepared by the Bureau of the Committee of the Whole: see *Discussion Paper*, UN Doc. A/CONF.183/C.1/L53 (6 July 1998) and *Bureau Proposal*, UN Doc. A/CONF.183/C.1/L.59 (9 July 1998).

[42] See art. 39 proposed by France in 1996 Committee Report, vol. II, *supra* n. 25.

[43] However, evidential duties in admissibility proceedings are addressed in the Rules. See *infra* note 62.

[44] See Human Rights Watch, *Justice in the Balance: Recommendations for an Independent and Effective International Criminal Court*, 75–6, 82–3 (1998); Amnesty International, *The International Criminal Court: Making the Right Choices* art. 16 (1998).

[45] See Hall, *supra* n. 40, vol. 92 at 125 (n. 6), 332 (n. 2), 549 (n. 5); Holmes, *supra* n. 4 at 52; Roy S. Lee, *Introduction: The Rome Conference and Its Contributions to International Law*, in *Making of the Rome Statute*, *supra* n. 4 at 21–3.

[46] For example, in the Ad Hoc Committee, the view was expressed that the burden of proving an exception to the exercise of national jurisdiction should be on the ICC. See Ad Hoc Committee Report, *supra* n. 23 at paras. 42 & 49. On the other hand, in the first two sessions of the Preparatory Committee, some delegates thought that if in all cases the Prosecutor had to prove that circumstances required the Court's intervention, the Court would be reduced to 'a mere residual institution, short of necessary status and independence'. See 1996 Committee Report, *supra* n. 25 at para. 157.

Despite these problems, it is worth mentioning one aspect of the drafting process which can shed light on the rationale and background to the article 18 preliminary ruling. The article in its original form was introduced by the United States at a fairly late stage in the drafting process, in the last session of the Committee.[47] The proposal came as a surprise to many of the delegates and, because of time constraints, did not receive any consideration or debate.[48] It was simply included in bracketed form for consideration at the Rome Conference. The US representative at the Conference claimed to have proposed the article . . .

> after it had become clear in the discussions of the Preparatory Committee that there was a growing support for the concept of referrals of overall situations to the Court by the Security Council, a State Party, or the Prosecutor acting *proprio motu*. In line with the principle of complementarity, it would then seem necessary to provide for a procedure, at the outset of a referral, which would recognize the ability of national justice systems to investigate and prosecute the crimes concerned. Under the proposed article, the Prosecutor would be able to proceed immediately to conduct an independent investigation *if, in the face of a challenge by a national judicial system, the Prosecutor could persuade the judge to allow him to do so*.[49]

The article in its original form was controversial for a number of reasons. The proposal required the Prosecutor to notify the world of all its investigations; a right of appeal existed only for States and it gave States an unlimited right to challenge admissibility on a subsequent occasion. It was perceived by some States as seriously undermining the effectiveness of the ICC.

Notwithstanding these objections, the preliminary ruling mechanism in amended form was ultimately incorporated into the Statute and was seen as being 'intricately linked to the complementarity regime and the independent role of the Prosecutor'.[50] States were adamant that amendments be included to minimize any hindrance to the effective operation of the ICC.[51] However, there is no indication of any public objections by States to the U.S. representative's expressed understanding that the Prosecutor would have the burden of persuasion in preliminary ruling applications.

[47] See US Proposal, *supra* n. 41.

[48] See generally Holmes, *supra* n. 4 at 68–73; Hall, *supra* n. 40, vol. 92 at 552.

[49] See *Summary Records of 11th Meeting*, *supra* n. 40 at 6 (emphasis added). See also David J. Scheffer, *The United States and the International Criminal Court*, 93 *Am. J. Int'l L.* 12, 15 (1999).

[50] See Holmes, *supra* n. 4 at 73.

[51] Ibid. at 69–73.

4. *Analogy of the Local Remedies Rule*

The requirement of exhausting local remedies is recognized as a general rule of international law in diplomatic protection claims[52] and as an essential step in complaints procedures under multilateral human rights treaties.[53] As a rule of admissibility dealing with the 'sensible relationship between national and international courts',[54] one might be tempted to apply the law of local remedies by analogy to admissibility proceedings in the ICC. By analogy, the allocation of the burden of proof as between applicant and respondent in local remedies proceedings would be the same as between the Prosecutor and investigating State in the ICC context.

With the possible exception of the U.N. Human Rights Committee,[55] the practice of international tribunals has shown a tendency to apply what is known as a divided burdens approach to the local remedies rule. Under this approach, it is incumbent on the respondent State to raise the objection of failing to exhaust local remedies and demonstrate the existence of available domestic remedies. If this is satisfied then it falls upon the applicant to prove that the remedies in fact were exhausted, or are unavailable or ineffective in addressing the wrong alleged.[56]

Despite the apparent similarity in the two admissibility rules, there are a number a significant distinctions which caution against importing the law of local remedies into the ICC context. Arguments for imposing the

[52] See Case Concerning Elettronica Sicula S.p. A. (ELSI) (*USA* v. *Italy*), 1989 ICJ 15, 42 (July 20); Interhandel Case (*Switz.* v. *USA*), 1959 ICJ 6, 27 (21 Mar.); Ambatielos Claim (*Greece* v. *UK*), 23 ILR 306, 334–6 (Arb. Comm. 1956); Amerasinghe, *supra* n. 36; A. A. Cancado Trindade, *The Application of the Rule of Exhaustion of Local Remedies in International Law* (1983).

[53] See First Optional Protocol to the International Covenant on Civil and Political Rights, *adopted* 16 Dec., 1966, 999 UNTS 302, arts. 2, 5(2); American Convention on Human Rights, *adopted* 22 Nov. 1969, 1144 UNTS 123, arts. 46–8; Protocol No. 11 to the Convention for the Protection of Human Rights and Fundamental Freedoms, 11 May, 1994, ETS No. 155, art. 35 (in force 1 Nov., 1998); Robertson, *supra* n. 30; Jo M. Pasqualucci, *Preliminary Objections Before the Inter-American Court of Human Rights: Legitimate Issues and Illegitimate Tactics*, 40 *Va. J. Int'l L.* 1 (1999); T. Zwart, *The Admissibility of Human Rights Petitions* (1994).

[54] Brownlie, *supra* n. 9 at 509.

[55] The Human Rights Committee appears to impose the burden entirely on the respondent State to demonstrate available and effective remedies. See generally *Ramirez* v. *Uruguay* (Comm. No. 1/74), UN Doc. A/35/40, 121, 123; *C.F. et al.* v. *Canada* (Comm. No. 113/81), UN Doc. A/40/40, 217 at paras. 6.2, 10.1; *Croes* v. *Netherlands* (Comm. No. 164/84), UN Doc. A/44/40, 259 at para. 10; *A. et al* v. *S.* (Comm. No. 1/76) in Selected Decisions under the Optional Protocol, UN Doc. CCPR/C/OP/1, 18; Amerasinghe, *supra* n. 36 at 297; Zwart, *supra* n. 53 at 11–13; but see *contra* P. R. Ghandhi, *The Human Rights Committee and the Right of Individual Communication*, 273–5 (1998) and Dominic McGoldrick, *The Human Rights Committee*, 188–9 (1994).

[56] For diplomatic protection cases, see generally *supra* n. 52. For human rights case, see generally *Austria* v. *Italy*, App. No. 788/60, 1961 Y.B. Eur.Conv. on HR 116, 168 (Eur. Comm'n on HR); *Donnelly* v. *United Kingdom*, App. Nos. 5577–83/72, Eur. Comm'n HR Dec. & Rep. 4, 64 (1975); *Gussenbauer* v. *Austria*, No. 4897/71, 1972 Y.B. Eur.Conv. on HR 448, 464–6 (Eur. Comm'n on HR); *X.* v. *United Kingdom*, App. No. 5006/71, 39 Coll. Dec. Eur. Comm'n on HR 91, 93 (1972); *X.* v. *United Kingdom*, App. No. 3651/68, 31 Coll. Dec. Eur. Comm'n on HR 72, 90 (1970); Velasquez Rodriguez Case, 4 IA. Ct. H.R. (ser. C) at para. 60 (1988); Adv. Op. OC–11/90, Exceptions to the Exhaustion of Domestic Remedies, 11 IA. Ct. H.R. (ser. A) at para. 41 (1990).

persuasive burden on the applicant in both diplomatic protection and human rights cases are not readily applicable to the Prosecutor. First, the analogy fails because the focus of the inquiry in local remedies proceedings is on the applicant's conduct, whereas in the ICC context it is on the State. In local remedies proceedings, the respondent State's claim of inadmissibility focuses on what the applicant could and ought to have done to exhaust local remedies. In the ICC context, a State's inadmissibility claim focuses on its own investigation and prosecution rather than on something the Prosecutor could or ought to have done. The issue is whether the claiming State has acted or is acting in such a manner as to be entitled to carry out the prosecution, and not whether there is anything further that the Prosecutor should do before the ICC can proceed.[57] As will be seen, appreciating that the State's claim of inadmissibility relates to its own conduct is central in understanding the allocation of the persuasive burden in admissibility proceedings under both articles 18 and 19.

Secondly, consistent with this difference in the focus of the inquiry, there is a distinction in the ability of the responding party to respond to the State's claim. In local remedies proceedings, given cost and accessibility reasons, applicants will normally have made attempts to obtain redress at the domestic level and thus are keenly aware of the effectiveness of these remedies. This is to be contrasted with the Prosecutor, who lacking resources and direct access will likely have little information about the state of the domestic prosecution.

Thirdly, there are differences in the consequences to the parties as a result of an admissibility decision. If a case is inadmissible under the local remedies rule, it is generally open to the applicant to exhaust the local remedy and, if necessary, return to the international forum without prejudice.[58] By contrast, where a case is ruled inadmissible in the ICC context, there is nothing further that the Prosecutor can practically do to make the case admissible at some point in the future. The only option available to the Prosecutor is to monitor the situation, with whatever means available, and to apply for a review if there is a change in circumstances.

Lastly, it is important to highlight the differences in the procedural context in which the rules operate. In diplomatic protection and human rights cases, there is only one application process governing the local remedies issue. As already discussed, the ICC by contrast has essentially

[57] Recall that even the principle of complementarity requires that States meet minimum standards of international justice before the ICC will defer. See text accompanying *supra* n. 28.

[58] See generally *C.F. et al.* v. *Canada*, *supra* n. 55 at para. 71; *Aumeeruddy-Cziffra* v. *Mauritius* (Comm. No. 35/78), UN Doc. A/36/40, 135; *Jaona* v. *Madagascar* (Comm. No. 132/82), UN Doc. A/40/40, 184.

two admissibility procedures, roughly corresponding to the investigation and surrender stages of a proceeding. These two procedures are not the same: rather they operate in tandem, and their structure as set out in the Statute has important implications for the allocation of the burden of proof. As will be discussed more fully in the next section, these implications arise primarily from a structure that promotes a dialogue between States and the Prosecutor over claims to investigate and prosecute. The effect of this dialogue is to induce certain expectations in the respective parties, which have implications for the allocation of the burden of proof.

5. *Application of the Interpretive Framework*

The allocation of the burden of proof will tend to disadvantage the party or parties on whom the burden lies. Naturally there must be a justification for this unequal treatment of the parties. For example, in criminal law, the presumption of innocence and the abhorrence of convicting the innocent are the reasons for imposing the burden of proof on the prosecution. In the context of ICC admissibility proceedings, it is argued that the reasons for burden allocation are derived from the internal logic of the Statute's procedural structure and from its underlying purposes. Applying this framework, it is submitted that the Prosecutor should have the persuasive burden of demonstrating admissibility in article 18 preliminary rulings. However, different considerations apply to article 19 challenges and lead to the opposite position that States (or individuals where appropriate) should have the persuasive burden of showing inadmissibility in these challenges. The proposal suggested here is meant to be applied flexibly, and there may be situations, discussed below, where fairness and the purposes of the Statute require a different allocation.

It is important to emphasize the internal logic of the procedural structure. The Statute formalizes what has been earlier described as a dialogue between States and the Prosecutor concerning the appropriate forum of prosecution. This dialogue begins with the Prosecutor's duty to notify States which would ordinarily have jurisdiction (whether or not they are Parties to the Statute) of an initial investigation into a situation. The notified States have a strict one month time limit to respond to the notice by requesting a deferral. A request for deferral made within time constitutes a public claim to undertake a *bona fide* national investigation and prosecution. Without knowing anything further about the intentions of the requesting State, there are no circumstances at this point to raise any doubt about the genuineness of the State's claim. Given that article

18 proceedings will normally be conducted during the early stages of the investigation, the concerns about delay will tend to be minimal. The principle of complementarity requires that the State be given the initial opportunity to investigate the situation. The same investigations would presumably have to be carried out, with or without State cooperation, even if the Prosecutor was authorized to proceed. Effective prosecution at this early stage requires that immediate investigatory steps be taken at the local level, unless it can be demonstrated by the Prosecutor that the requesting State clearly cannot or will not comply with its undertaking. This interpretation is largely consistent with the language of article 18 and the framers' intentions.

There will be a change in circumstances in two respects upon expiry of the one month deferral deadline. For notified States that did not choose to request a deferral, the implication is that they either did not have jurisdiction to prosecute or were otherwise not interested in doing so. In other words, there is implicit acquiescence on the part of these States in allowing the ICC to proceed. The other change in circumstance relates to the expectations of the Prosecutor. For the sake of certainty and effective prosecution, the Prosecutor must be able to rely on the absence of State claims for jurisdiction. On the basis of this reliance, the Prosecutor should confidently be able to invest time and effort into the investigation without fear of losing control over the case at the mere request of a State. It follows from these two circumstances combined with considerations of fairness that it should be more difficult for States to claim jurisdiction in article 19 challenges. These circumstances ground at least an inference of doubt about the genuineness of the State's claim to prosecute, although this inference may be rebutted.

This position is also supported by the two basic principles underlying the Statute. To halt the ICC proceeding with another proceeding that requires the Prosecutor to justify its continued investigation and prosecution presents an impediment which undermines the principle of effective prosecution. Resources dedicated to the criminal investigation might have to be diverted towards an admissibility investigation, which will involve acquiring information about the conditions of the national prosecution. Given that article 19 challenges can be brought at any time before trial, and in exceptional cases even after the trial commences, the concerns about detrimental effects of delay to the reliability of the prosecution are heightened. The Statute's requirement that these challenges be brought by States at the earliest opportunity highlights this concern. Imposing the persuasive burden on States also reinforces complementarity in that it creates an incentive for States to act diligently in the spirit of effective prosecution by using the article 18 preliminary ruling mechanism. This will lead to an efficient procedure that avoids delay, clarifies expectations over the appropriate forum at the outset of the investigation, and minimizes overlapping investigations at both the national and international levels.[59]

One might object to the proposed allocation on the basis that it would be too easy for States to shield an accused by using the article 18 deferral mechanism. However, merely because the Prosecutor carries the persuasive burden under article 18, it does not follow that States have no evidentiary obligations to produce relevant evidence regarding its ability and willingness to prosecute. It is generally recognized in the practice of international tribunals that both parties will have evidentiary duties to assist the tribunal in its fact-finding role.[60] This is especially true for the party who has exclusive control over evidence that will shed the greatest light on the facts in issue.[61] To a certain extent, the Rules are consistent with this practice by imposing evidentiary duties on States to furnish the Court with information on its own prosecution in both article 18 and 19 proceedings.[62] However, the Rules are silent on the consequences of failing to discharge these duties. To reinforce their importance, detrimental consequences, short of losing the challenge, ought to follow upon their breach.[63] For example, if the State concerned refuses to provide evidence of its own investigation or an explanation of any apparent delay, then it should be permissible for the Pre-Trial Chamber to interpret this refusal as diminishing the strength of the State's rebuttal, or alternatively as strengthening the position of the Prosecutor. In addition to this evidential duty, the Pre-Trial Chamber may allow the Prosecutor some latitude in its means of proof when dealing with 'subjective facts', such as a State's intent to bring a person to justice, which would be very difficult to discern and would involve inquiries of a sensitive or even

[59] This dialogue between States and the ICC may be seen as an advantage over the present international criminal tribunals. The lack of an obligation on States to notify the ICTY or Rwanda tribunal of their own prosecutions has given rise to concerns about inefficient parallel investigations. See Frederik Harhoff,'Consonance or Rivalry? Calibrating the Efforts to Prosecute War Crimes in National and International Tribunals', 7 *Duke J. of Comp.& Int'l L.*, 571, 578–9 (1997).

[60] See arts. 64(6) & 69(3); Kazazi, *supra* n. 29 at 119–28; Kokott, *supra* n. 29 at 153–4, 188–91.

[61] See *Corfu Channel Case* (*UK* v. *Alb.*), 1949 ICJ 4, 18 (9 April) where the Court held that 'a State on whose territory or in whose waters an act contrary to international law has occurred, may be called upon to give an explanation . . . that State cannot evade such a request by limiting itself to a reply that it is ignorant . . . [t]he State may . . . be bound to supply particulars of the use made by it of the means of information and inquiry at its disposal.'

[62] In requesting a deferral under art. 18, States must provide information concerning their own investigation, taking into account art. 18(2), to the Prosecutor, who in turn must forward this information to the Court if an application for authorization is made (rules 53–4). Where a State makes a challenge under art. 19, it must apply in writing and disclose the basis for the application (rule 58). Despite these apparent impositions of mandatory evidentiary duties, rule 51 creates confusion and ambiguity by suggesting that the State has a discretion to introduce evidence on its willingness to prosecute whenever the criteria in art. 17(2) is considered by the Court.

[63] See generally Fitzmaurice, *supra* n. 36 at 576–7; Kokott, *supra* n. 29 at 154, 188–9; Robertson, *supra* n. 30 at 192.

intrusive character.[64] Finally, it should be recalled that the fear of abusing article 18 was also of concern to the drafters; consequently, many safeguards were incorporated in the procedure to prevent abuse and to permit the ICC to monitor the situation.[65]

Should the analysis be any different when it is the accused or named suspect who is bringing the article 19 challenge? In this situation, one might think that the burden should always be on the Prosecutor because of the presumption of innocence or the accused's right 'not to have imposed on him or her any reversal of the burden of proof or any onus of rebuttal'.[66] To address this argument, it is first necessary to distinguish the *ne bis in idem* ground of inadmissibility from the other three grounds mentioned in article 17(1). The latter three grounds deal either with State sovereignty interests or an internal issue concerning threshold offence seriousness. They are not concerned with human rights. A decision on these grounds does not affect the jeopardy of the accused or advance the Prosecutor's material case. Consequently, the trial rights mentioned earlier are not intended to apply in this context. If the accused claims that there exists a State willing and able to prosecute, but that State has not joined in the proceeding, then this raises some doubt over the genuineness of the claim.[67] However, if the State has joined in the proceeding then the fact of the accused's participation does not make it any different than if the State alone was bringing the challenge. In both cases, the onus should be on the parties claiming inadmissibility; this is especially so if the Prosecutor has expended efforts in the investigation. But if the accused objects to admissibility on the *ne bis in idem* ground, then the Court will be asked to decide an issue which could advance the Prosecutor's case. The decision would effectively determine a substantive defence which the accused could raise at trial.[68] Unlike the other grounds, *ne bis in idem* brings to the foreground issues of fairness and human rights.[69] Furthermore, considerations of implied acquiescence and reliance by the Prosecutor do not strictly apply in this situation since the dialogue arising from article 18 does not involve individuals. Hence, in this situation it would be incumbent on the accused to adduce evidence

[64] In the *Corfu Channel Case*, *supra* n. 61, the Court held that the 'exclusive territorial control exercised by a State within its frontiers has a bearing upon the methods of proof available to establish the knowledge of that State as to [events on its territory]. By reason of this exclusive control, the other State, the victim of a breach of international law, is often unable to furnish direct proof of facts giving rise to responsibility. Such a State should be allowed a more liberal recourse to inferences of fact and circumstantial evidence.'

[65] See text accompanying *supra* n. 51.

[66] Arts. 66 & 67(1)(i).

[67] Note that the Prosecutor's obligation to suspend an investigation only extends to challenges brought by States (art. 19(7)).

[68] Art. 20.

[69] Of the four grounds of inadmissibility in art. 17, this is the only one for which the Court may grant leave to bring a challenge post-trial or on multiple occasions.

to support a claim of *ne bis in idem*, but the burden of persuasion would lie with the Prosecutor to rebut this claim.

Another possible criticism of the proposal is to the assumption that non-States Parties which did not receive an article 18 notice acquiesced in leaving the prosecution to the ICC. It is conceded that if any State challenges admissibility within the one month deadline, under articles 18 or 19, there is no appreciable difference whether that State was notified by the Prosecutor or not. In both instances, if the State can show that it has jurisdiction over the case, the reasons for leaving the persuasive burden with the Prosecutor remain the same. However, if the non-State Party without notification brings an article 19 challenge after the one month period, there are still reasons for leaving the persuasive burden with this State (even though it is inaccurate to say that this State had acquiesced in the ICC's jurisdiction). In this situation, the considerations of effective prosecution and respect for the expended efforts of the Prosecutor in its investigation weigh in favour of imposing the burden on that State.

One final objection to the proposal might come from non-States Parties, who argue that the imposition of the persuasive burden on them is tantamount to imposing an obligation on third States and is excluded by the law of treaties. In replying to this complaint, it must first be recognized that the Statute creates a right of challenge for the non-State Party, which it might not otherwise have had. If the non-State Party wishes to exercise this right then it must agree to do so in the prescribed manner, with the attendant duties and obligations.[70]

IV. Substantive Impediment: National Law Objections to Surrender

1. *The Problem of National Law Objections to Surrender*

Assuming a prosecution is admissible in the ICC, when, if ever, may a State Party validly refuse to comply with a request to surrender an accused person in its custody? Using extradition law as an analogy, there are three kinds of objections to a surrender request. First, States might argue that their domestic procedural requirements for arrest and surrender have not been met in the particular case. For example, there may be insufficient evidence of the criminal allegation to justify surrender, or, as in the case of Senator Pinochet, the accused may be found to be unfit

[70] See VCLT, *supra* n. 7 at art. 36.

to stand trial according to domestic standards.[71] Secondly, States might appeal to substantive grounds of refusal, which in some countries are contained in their constitutions, e.g. non-extradition of nationals.[72] Lastly, States and more likely the accused may object to the Court's failure to provide the same human rights and fair trial standards as the custodial State, e.g. the State constitution may prohibit life imprisonment,[73] or provide for a right to a jury trial, both of which the Statute lacks. If a custodial State makes this argument, the obvious reply is for that State to refer the matter to its competent authorities for prosecution. But if for whatever reason the custodial State cannot or will not prosecute, then the accused may argue that he should not be prejudiced by this circumstance beyond his control. To remove him to face trial in a forum guaranteeing a lesser standard of justice than his place of residence is unfair. Surrender should only be possible if the ICC provided the same degree of rights protection as in the custodial State.

It is important to disentangle two distinct issues embedded in these objections: (*a*) what norms, other than those in the admissibility criteria, can justify precluding the trial of an accused in the ICC; and (*b*) who should decide the applicability of these norms in a specific case? For example, it may be accepted that the accused's right not to be tried twice for the same offence must be protected, but it does not necessarily follow that the custodial State should be the body to give effect to this objection. As with the earlier issue of burden allocation, the Statute *prima facie* fails to answer these two questions. With respect to the traditional grounds for refusing extradition, such as double criminality, nationality, and political offence, the Statute neither expressly prohibits nor permits them. Without express provision, one might think that they are prohibited on the basis of the well-established principle that States cannot invoke their internal law as justification for failure to perform an international obligation.[74] But the Statute contains language which could conceivably

[71] The United Kingdom claimed that the legal basis for refusing to extradite Senator Pinochet to Spain because of his unfitness arose solely from a residual sovereign discretion granted by the domestic extradition legislation. The Secretary of State presumed that the European Convention on Extradition, to which the United Kingdom is a party, did not allow for refusal on the basis of unfitness. See paragraphs 28–31 of the Home Secretary's Letter to the Spanish Ambassador, reprinted in Home Secretary Jack Straw's written answer to question asked by Paul Clark, in UK, HC *Parliamentary Debates*, col. 358W (2 March 2000), which can also be found in Home Office Press Release No. 42/2000, *Senator Augusto Pinochet Ugarte*, at <wood.ccta.gov.uk/homeoffice/hopress.nsf>.

[72] See Helen Duffy & Jonathan Huston, 'Implementation of the ICC Statute: International Obligations and Constitutional Considerations', in *The Rome Statute and Domestic Legal Orders Volume I: General Aspects and Constitutional Issues*, 29, 43–4 (Claus Kress & Flavia Lattanzi (eds.), 2000) [hereinafter *The Rome Statute and Domestic Legal Orders*], where the many countries that have this constitutional prohibition are listed.

[73] e.g. Art. 34 of the Colombian constitution prohibits life imprisonment. See 'Political Constitution of Colombia', trans. by P. B. Heller & M. W. Coward, in *Constitutions of the Countries of the World* (Gisbert H. Flanz (ed.), 1995).

[74] See sources cited at *supra* n. 6.

support a contrary position. One thing that is clear from the Statute is that it does not follow the approach of the ICTY.[75] The ICTY Statute, under the authority of Chapter VII of the UN Charter, imposes an absolute duty on States to comply with requests to surrender accused to the Tribunal.[76] Rule 58 of the ICTY Rules of Procedure and Evidence expressly provides that the State's obligation to surrender prevails over any legal impediment which may exist under the national law or extradition treaties of the State concerned.[77] The Statute, on the other hand, adopts a compromise approach which some have described as exhibiting features of both a horizontal inter-State extradition model of cooperation, and a vertical supra-national model, such as the one used by the ICTY.[78] The precise scope of legitimate national law objections to surrender will have to be determined in the context of the Statute, its drafting history and underlying purposes.

2. *Substantive Framework Governing Surrender*

(a) Basic Obligation to Surrender

States Parties have a general duty to 'cooperate fully' with the Court in its investigation and prosecution (art. 86). Specifically, they must 'comply with requests for arrest and surrender' from the Court, 'in accordance with the provisions of [Part 9] and the procedure under their national law' (art. 89). States Parties have a further duty to ensure that there are procedures under their national law for the forms of cooperation required under Part 9 (art. 88). This is the basic duty to implement the Part 9 obligations.

What does the reference to 'procedure under . . . national law' encom-

[75] A proposal to expressly prohibit legal impediments was proposed by Croatia but not accepted at the Rome Conference. *See Proposal Submitted by Croatia*, UN Doc. A/CONF.183/C.1/WGIC/L.9 (29 June 1998).

[76] See art. 29(2)(e) of the ICTY Statute, *supra* n. 24.

[77] *Rules of Procedure and Evidence, adopted* 11 Feb., 1994, 33 ILM 484 (1994). Despite these seemingly coercive powers, the practice of the ICTY and ICTR has shown many incidences where States have imposed their national laws to impede the transfer of accused. This foreshadows problems for the ICC. See generally Sheila O'Shea, 'Interaction Between International Criminal Tribunals and National Legal Systems', 28 *NYU J. Int'l. L. & Pol.* 367 (1995–6); Kenneth S. Gallant, 'Securing the Presence of Defendants before the International Tribunal for the Former Yugoslavia: Breaking with Extradition', in 'The Prosecution of International Crimes' 343–73 (R. S. Clark & M. Sann, eds., 1996); Kenneth J. Harris and Robert Kushen, 'Surrender of Fugitives to the War Crimes Tribunal for Yugoslavia and Rwanda: Squaring International Legal Obligations with the U.S. Constitution', 7 *Crim. L.F.* 561 (1996); Colin Warbrick, 'Co-operation with the International Criminal Tribunal for Yugoslavia', 45 *Int'l & Comp. LQ* 947 (1996); Hazel Fox, 'The Objections to Transfer of Criminal Jurisdiction to the UN Tribunal', 46 *Int'l & Comp. LQ* 434 (1997); Goran Sluiter, 'To Cooperate or not to Cooperate?: The Case of the Failed Transfer of Ntakirutimana to the Rwanda Tribunal', 11 *Leiden J. Int'l L.* 393 (1998).

[78] See Bert Swart and Goran Sluiter, *The International Criminal Court and International Criminal Co-operation*, in *Reflections on the ICC*, *supra* n. 5 at 97–101; *Prosecutor* v. *Blaskic* (Subpoena), *supra* n. 10 at 713–15; Cassese, *supra* n. 13 at 14–16; Cassese, *supra* n. 25 at 164–5.

pass? Are States given an unfettered discretion to define the national law which will apply to their arrest and surrender procedure? If so then will it be permissible to include all the traditional grounds for refusing extradition? Whether a national law is procedural in nature is not always easy to discern. For example, a constitutional prohibition against arbitrary arrests may be used to test the validity of the criminal process, but it is also a substantive right of the accused.

(b) State Objections to Surrender

State objections to surrender may arise from three possible sources in the Statute: the domestic arrest and surrender procedures, international obligations of the custodial State, and extradition refusal grounds applied by the custodial State.

I. DOMESTIC ARREST AND SURRENDER PROCEDURES

The Statute expressly provides that the arrest and surrender of an accused on the territory of a State Party is to be done in accordance with the domestic procedural laws of that State Party (arts. 59(1) & 89(1)). Article 59 appears to specify minimum requirements expected of domestic arrest proceedings. Upon arrest, the individual is to be brought promptly before the competent judicial authority in the custodial State which must determine three conditions: (a) the warrant applies to that person; (b) the person has been arrested in accordance with the proper process; and (c) the person's rights have been respected (art. 59(2)). The rights of persons during an investigation are specified in art. 55.

The individual also has the right to apply for judicial interim release pending surrender. While the decision to release is left to the national court, it can only be made after considering set criteria and recommendations from the Pre-Trial Chamber (art. 59(4) & (5)). One factor that the national courts cannot consider when deciding release is whether the warrant of arrest was properly issued under article 58, i.e. whether there were reasonable grounds to believe the person committed the offences and the arrest of the person appeared necessary.

The Statute contemplates the accused challenging surrender in the national courts on the basis of the principle of *ne bis in idem* (art. 89(2)). However, rather than considering the issue itself, national courts are required to defer the issue until the ICC has decided the admissibility of the case. As *ne bis in idem* is a possible ground of inadmissibility, this objection is effectively reserved for the ICC to determine prior to surrender.

II. CONFLICTING INTERNATIONAL OBLIGATIONS

Unlike the procedural limitations, the Statute clearly provides for objections where the duty to surrender conflicts with the State's other international obligations. Three specific areas are mentioned: competing extradition requests,[79] State and diplomatic immunity,[80] and status of forces agreements.[81] The Statute contemplates that issues concerning competing requests will be resolved cooperatively with the Court prior to surrender. But with the other two areas, it is unclear where and when these issues should be decided.

It is also unclear whether a State Party can make legitimate objections beyond these three areas, for example in the area of human rights. The Statute expressly recognizes that breach of a pre-existing treaty obligation is a basis for early consultation with the ICC, but this does not necessarily justify or excuse non-compliance (art. 97).

III. TRADITIONAL GROUNDS FOR REFUSING EXTRADITION

The rule of speciality is the only traditional extradition-based impediment that is expressly provided in the Statute (art. 101). The rule does not operate to prevent surrender but imposes a limit on the charges with which the ICC can proceed after surrender, subject to possible waiver by the requested State.

The other traditional extradition-based objections are neither expressly included nor excluded in the Statute. The Statute distinguishes 'surrender' from 'extradition' by providing separate definitions for each term (art. 102).[82] But for article 91, one might safely have thought that by failing to include these objections, the Statute intended their non-applicability. Oddly enough, the Statute appears to presume the possible existence of these objections in article 91, which is an article concerned with the documents the ICC must submit in support of a request for arrest and surrender. Paragraph 2 provides that the request shall contain (*a*) information to identify and locate the named person; (*b*) a copy of the warrant of arrest; and (*c*) such documents, statements or information as may be necessary to meet the requirements for the surrender process in the requested State, 'except that those requirements should not be more burdensome than those applicable to requests for extradition pursuant to treaties or arrangements between the requested State and other States and should, if possible, be less burdensome, taking into account the distinct nature of the Court'.

The practical effect of this provision is unclear. It appears to act as a

[79] Under art. 90(6) & (7), the requested State has a discretion whether to give effect to either the ICC request or a request from a non-State Party, with whom the requested State has an existing extradition agreement.

[80] See art. 98(1).

[81] See art. 98(2). The Statute does not actually use the term 'status of forces agreement'; rather, it uses the more general language of 'obligations under international agreements pursuant to which the consent of a sending State is required to surrender a person of that State to the Court'.

[82] For a discussion of this distinction, see William A. Schabas, 'Follow up to Rome: Preparing for Entry into Force of the International Criminal Court Statute', 20 *HRLJ* 157, 158 (1999); *The Rome Statute and Domestic Legal Orders*, *supra* n. 72.

constraint on the informational demands that a State can make of the ICC. However, to have this effect, it implicitly recognizes a State's authority to prescribe domestic law requirements for surrender, and expressly imposes an upper limit and caution on the exercise of this authority. This limit and caution on the State's authority is expressed only in exhortatory and not mandatory language. Are States permitted to include the traditional extradition refusal grounds as part of their domestic law requirements so long as they have deemed less burdensome requirements not 'possible' even taking into account the distinct nature of the Court? If this were so then a patchwork of different surrender regimes between the Court and States Parties might emerge. Is it possible that 'the requirements for the surrender process' refer not to all possible requirements but to a smaller subset of requirements, e.g. those that are only dependent on the receipt of information from the ICC for their verification? This approach would exclude refusal grounds such as nationality. Nevertheless, the meaning and effect of article 91(2)(c) is ambiguous; this ambiguity needs to be addressed by way of the interpretive framework. Before considering this issue from the perspective of the Statute's underlying purposes, an analysis of Part 9's drafting history can provide some guidance in understanding what was intended by article 91 (2) (c).

3. *The Drafting History*

It is helpful to view the drafting history of article 91(2)(c) in the context of the overall debate concerning whether to include extradition refusal grounds in the Statute. Like the Rome Statute, the ILC Draft Statute neither expressly prohibited nor permitted the invocation of such grounds.[83] The ILC also recognized that surrender or 'transfer' to the Court was to be distinguished from 'extradition' or other forms of surrender between two States.[84]

Two divergent views emerged in the Committee on how the surrender regime should be framed.[85] One view was that it should be broadly similar to that existing between States on the basis of extradition and legal assistance agreements. Under this approach, the framework of cooperation and the procedure by which each State meets its obligations would be largely controlled by its national law. The opposing view emphasized the unique nature of the Court's relationship to States, favouring the strict unimpeded transfer regime envisaged in the ILC

[83] This however was a natural consequence arising from the jurisdictional framework adopted in that Statute. Given that in all cases the custodial State had to accept the jurisdiction of the court, it was unlikely that the custodial State would accept jurisdiction and then try to impede the surrender of the accused.

[84] See commentary to art. 53 of the ILC Draft Statute, *supra* n. 11.

[85] See 1996 Committee Report, vol. I, *supra* n. 25, at paras. 310–25.

Draft Statute. Despite this divergence, there were two points on which there was general agreement. First, it was felt that the grounds for refusing compliance with requests from the Court should be limited to a minimum, and specifically laid down in the Statute, even though there was no agreement on what precise grounds for refusal should be included.[86] Secondly, there was general support for the view that the Statute should permit the involvement of national courts in the application of national law where those requirements were considered fundamental, especially to protect the rights of individuals, as well as to verify procedural legality.[87]

At its fifth session, the Committee drafted new provisions on surrender and cooperation[88] which were ultimately submitted for consideration at the Rome Conference.[89] Many of the provisions were bracketed, reflecting their tentative nature and the lack of consensus on them. With respect to the issue of grounds for refusing surrender two options were mentioned. The first simply stated that there would be no grounds for refusal. The second enumerated five refusal grounds, with an additional one mentioned in a footnote. These grounds provided for possible refusal if

- the State had not accepted the Court's jurisdiction in the particular case,
- the person is a national of the requested State,[90]
- the person is being investigated or prosecuted domestically,
- the information submitted does not meet the minimum evidentiary requirements of the requested State,
- compliance with the request would put the State in breach of an existing international obligation, or
- imposition of the punishment for the offence would be prohibited by the law of the requested State had it exercised jurisdiction.[91]

There was also a proposal by the Committee that the accused would be entitled to challenge surrender in the domestic courts on three bases: the lack of jurisdiction of the ICC, *ne bis in idem*, and failure to meet the evidentiary requirements of the requested State with respect to the factual allegations.[92] In the result the Statute only provides for domestic challenges on the basis of *ne bis in idem*, and even in this respect, the

[86] Ibid., at paras. 316, 324.

[87] Ibid., at para. 323.

[88] See *Report of the Working Group on International Cooperation and Judicial Assistance* in Annex IV of 5th Session Committee Report, *supra* n. 41.

[89] See Part 9 of the Committee's Draft Statute, *supra* n. 27 at 131–50.

[90] This ground was included in another set of brackets with an attached footnote, which contained the comment that this ground did not prevent the surrender to the Court so long as the person if convicted was returned to the requested State to serve the sentence. See n. 14 to art. 87 of Committee's Draft Statute, ibid., at 134.

[91] See n. 15 to art. 87 of Committee's Draft Statute, ibid. Footnote 13 to art. 87 provided that there was no agreement on the list of grounds contained in this option.

[92] See bracketed art. 97(7) of Committee's Draft Statute, ibid., at 136.

domestic court is to defer the issue until the ICC has determined admissibility.

While much of the same divergence in opinion persisted at the Rome Conference, by the end of the Conference, three significant achievements had been realized.[93] First, the qualification 'in accordance with . . . the procedure under . . . national law' was added to the duty to comply with surrender requests as a compromise for adding articles 88 (duty to implement cooperation obligations) and 97 (duty to consult with the Court).[94] It was understood that this qualification referred only to procedural laws and not the substantive laws of the State. Secondly, the term and concept of 'surrender' was favoured over that of 'extradition'. Lastly and most significantly, it was decided that there would be no enumerated grounds for refusing a surrender request.[95] The most controversial of the grounds for refusal that was removed was the one prohibiting the extradition of nationals. The majority view, even amongst many European countries which have such prohibitions in their constitutions, was that this limitation was inapplicable in the context of handing over persons to the Court. Eventually, the opposing States agreed to have their reservations about the deletion of this ground recorded in a footnote.[96] When this footnote was also deleted, nine States repeated their reservations in the Committee of the Whole.[97]

While it appears from this history that the drafters intended to remove all extradition refusal grounds from the Statute, it remains to be seen what was the intention behind article 91(2)(c). The predecessor to article 91 drafted by the Committee required the ICC in all cases to submit sufficient information to identify the person sought.[98] There were different additional submission requirements depending on whether it was a 'pre-indictment' arrest or a 'post-indictment' arrest.[99] In the former case, the request had to be supported by a copy of the arrest warrant, a statement of the reasons to believe the suspect may have committed a crime within the jurisdiction of the Court, a brief summary

[93] See generally Phakiso Mochochoko, 'International Cooperation and Judicial Assistance', in *Making of the Rome Statute*, *supra* n. 4 at 305–17.

[94] See *Report of the Working Group*, UN Doc. A/CONF.183/C.1/WGIC/L.11/Add.3 (13 July, 1998).

[95] See *Report of the Working Group*, UN Doc. A/CONF.183/C.1/WGIC/L.11/Add.4 (14 July, 1998).

[96] See Mochochoko, *supra* n. 93; ibid.; *Report of the Working Group*, UN Doc. A/CONF.183/C.1/WGIC/L.11/Add.4 /Corr.1 (July 15, 1998). The footnote reads, '[s]ome states reserved their position with respect to the deletion of this provision as this would raise problems of compatibility with constitutional provisions and domestic legislation'.

[97] See *Summary Records of the 38th Plenary Meeting of the Committee of the Whole held on July 15, 1998*, UN Doc. A/CONF.183/C.1/SR.38 at 3–4.

[98] See art. 88 of the Committee's Draft Statute, *supra* n. 27 at 139.

[99] A subsequent proposal by Canada, which appeared to be accepted by the delegates, abolished the distinction between post- and pre-indictment requests and minimized the Court's duty to supply details of the factual allegations. See *Proposal Submitted by Canada*, UN Doc. A/CONF.183/C.1/WGIC/L.1 (25 June, 1998).

of the facts of the case, a statement as to why pre-indictment arrest is urgent and necessary, and

> [such documents, statements, or other types of information regarding the commission of the offence and the person's role therein, which may be required by the laws of the requested State;] [however, in no event may the requested State's requirements be more burdensome than those applicable to requests for extradition pursuant to treaties with other States;][100]

In respect of post-indictment arrest requests, it was only necessary to submit a copy of the arrest warrant and information regarding the commission of the offence. It appears that this initial reference to burdensome State requirements was made in the context of the sufficiency of evidence requirement and was not intended to refer to all possible requirements. Further evidence supporting this narrow construction of the provision can be seen from the drafting history of the Rome Conference, which reveals that the present article 91 had already been settled before agreement was reached to eliminate all express grounds of refusal.[101] This implies that article 91 was not intended to preserve or resurrect extradition refusal grounds. If article 91(2)(c) was intended to recognize any domestic authority to refuse surrender, it was only limited to cases where the evidence supporting the commission of the offence was insufficient for surrender.[102]

4. *Application of the Interpretive Framework*

Historically, extradition treaties imposed reciprocal restraints on surrender not to protect the interests of the fugitive, but to ensure respect for the sovereign interests of States. These restraints have been described as

> largely designed to serve the interests of the requested state rather than the individual. Many states prefer not to extradite political offenders as this will impair their neutrality towards internal conflicts in foreign states. The principle of *non bis in idem* is applied to ensure respect for the judicial decisions of the requested state; the double criminality requirement secures respect for the legal system of the requested state; and the rule of speciality protects the integrity of the extradition process.[103]

[100] See art. 88(1)(b)(v) of the Committee's Draft Statute, *supra* n. 27.

[101] See *Report of the Drafting Committee to the Committee of the Whole*, UN Doc. A/CONF.183/C.1/L.68 at 3, 5 (13 July 1998). This Report shows that the decision to remove the six enumerated refusal grounds was still pending while the final text of what would become art. 91 was already adopted.

[102] In describing the drafting history, Mochochoko notes that the express refusal ground of failing to meet the minimum evidential requirements of the requested State was removed and incorporated into art. 91. See *supra* n. 93 at 312.

[103] See Committee on Extradition & Human Rights (International Law Association), *First Report*, in *Report of the 66th Conference held in Buenos Aires* 142–183 at para. 7 (1994).

However, more recently there has been greater recognition of the requested person's human rights as legitimate considerations in extradition.[104]

The Statute defines a relationship between the Court and States Parties that is fundamentally different from the bilateral relationship between States arising from extradition treaties. There are at least three significant distinctions suggesting the diminished importance of sovereignty interests in the ICC context. The most obvious is that the ICC is not a State but an entity manifesting the will of all States Parties. It could be said that when dealing with the ICC, a State Party is dealing with an international organization, of which it forms a constituent part.[105] The relationship is not intended to be reciprocal as the ICC is an instrument of the States Parties designed to serve their interests in complementary effective prosecution. Secondly, the State–ICC relationship under the Statute is much more complex and broader than the State–State relationship in extradition treaties. In the latter case, States' rights and obligations generally start and end with the request and extradition of the individual. In the ICC, States Parties have many more rights, obligations and interests beyond the realm of surrender.[106] Lastly, in contrast to extradition treaties, the Statute provides for an extensive criminal procedure that aims to guarantee a fair trial and the due process rights of the accused. Concerns about sending one's national to face an uncertain trial in some alien jurisdiction are non-existent or significantly diminished in the ICC context.[107]

The unique relationship between States Parties and the ICC supports an interpretation favouring a strict and unimpeded surrender regime in the Statute. Further support for this interpretation can also be found in the Statute's underlying purposes. The Statute represents an agreement amongst States Parties to enforce laws prohibiting the worst international crimes, in accordance with principles of effective prosecution and complementarity. Assuming a case is admissible, the principle of effective prosecution favours an expeditious and unimpeded surrender to

[104] See generally Committee on Extradition & Human Rights (International Law Association), *First Report*, ibid., *Second Report*, in *Report of the 67th Conference held in Helsinki*, 214–46 (1996), and *Third Report*, in *Report of the 68th Conference held in Taipei*, 132–63 (1998); *Soering* v. *United Kingdom*, 161 Eur. Ct. HR (ser. A) (1989); Kai I. Rebane, 'Extradition and Individual Rights: The Need for an International Criminal Court to Safeguard Individual Rights', 19 *Fordham Int'l LJ* 1636 (1996); Christine Van den Wyngaert, 'Applying the European Convention on Human Rights to Extradition: Opening Pandora's Box?', 39 *Int'l & Comp. LQ* 757 (1990); *Model Treaty on Extradition*, GA Res. 45/116, UN GAOR, 45th Sess., Annex, Agenda Item 100, at art. 3, UN Doc. A/RES/45/116 (1991).

[105] Under art. 112, every State Party is an equal member of the Assembly of States Parties, the Statute's overarching administrative body.

[106] e.g. the right to refer situations, challenge admissibility, participate in the selection of judges and the Prosecutor, challenge a decision not to prosecute a referred case, and obligations to provide judicial assistance and permit the Prosecutor to conduct on-site investigations in certain cases.

[107] See Duffy & Huston, *supra* n. 72 at 45, '[s]urrender to the Court does not entail the same degree of abandonment of one's own nationals as extradition might'.

the Court. Unless the Court is allowed to exercise jurisdiction, the accused will be free from prosecution. Effective prosecution can also be undermined by protracted domestic litigation over surrender. Delays will tend to jeopardize the truth-seeking function of the prosecution as witnesses tend to be more difficult to locate, and memories fade with time.[108]

Implicit in the principle of complementarity is the notion that States and the ICC have their respective spheres of competence. As States are responsible for executing arrest and surrender requests within their territory, it should be left to their courts to review the validity of that execution process. On the other hand, any issues relating to the conduct of the prosecution and trial should be left to be decided by the ICC after surrender. While the principle of complementarity involves some deference to state sovereignty interests, it should still be seen as a means to implement effective prosecution, not a substitute for such prosecution. Sensitivity to State interests should yield if the alternative to surrender is that the accused will go without prosecution. In other words, complementarity informs the question of whether the ICC or States should prosecute, but a prosecution there must be. Under Part 9, the Statute imposes obligations of 'ends' and leaves States to decide the 'means' to achieve them. The manner of implementation should be respected so long as the substance of the obligation is satisfied. Thus complementarity is best understood as affording a margin of appreciation to the manner in which States implement their Part 9 duties insofar as effective prosecution is not compromised, e.g. by creating undue delays or otherwise tainting the trial process.

Although the importance of sovereignty interests is diminished under the Statute, surrender remains a coercive process that uproots the accused and brings him or her before an international court, most likely located in another country. Such an interference with personal liberty must be justified at the earliest opportunity. In extradition law, this opportunity has generally been afforded to the sending State, irrespective of the safeguards in the receiving State. Human rights considerations require that there be some pre-surrender judicial determination of the validity of the arrest and the continued detention of the accused. The goal of the Court in achieving effective prosecution may conflict with these considerations. The challenge is to strike the most appropriate balance between the interests of the accused and the purposes of the ICC. For example, the interest in effective prosecution is not compelling if there is doubt that the arrested person is the person named in the arrest warrant. This kind of determination should be made at the earliest opportunity.

To complete the analysis in this part, the conclusions reached by

[108] See *Regina* v. *Askov*, *supra* n. 19 at 1220–2.

applying the interpretive framework will be summarized under four categories of possible objections.[109] Procedural objections are those derived from the processing of arrest and surrender requests in the custodial State. Substantive objections are those based on possible extradition refusal grounds in the Statute. Human rights objections are based on claims by the accused of human rights violations during both the investigative and trial process. The fourth category of objections concerns conflicting international obligations of the custodial State that impede or preclude compliance with a surrender request.

(a) Procedural Objections

As mentioned already, a State Party's duty to surrender a requested person is subject to two general qualifications: the provisions of Part 9 and national law procedures. In light of the distinct nature of the ICC, the drafting history of the Statute and the principles of complementarity and effective prosecution, national law procedures should not obstruct the surrender of accused persons to the Court. Variations from country to country in the procedural law may be respected so long as the delivery of the requested person to the court is not unreasonably delayed. As a general rule, States in implementing their Part 9 obligations should not introduce more procedural steps than are required by the Statute. States Parties are expected to act in good faith[110] and to consult promptly with the Court to resolve cooperation problems (art. 97).

The domestic procedures required by the Statute are minimal, consistent with ensuring an unimpeded and expeditious surrender to the Court. There must be procedures in place to receive and respond to arrest and surrender requests from the ICC. The Statute leaves it to States to apply their own domestic arrest law, but that law must respect the rights of a person during an investigation as set out in article 55. Upon arrest the person must be brought promptly before a judicial officer in the custodial State, who may grant the person interim release after considering the factors listed in article 59 (4) and the recommendations of the Pre-Trial Chamber. In deciding whether to grant interim release, the judicial officer is expressly prohibited from considering whether the warrant was properly issued. The arrested person is entitled to raise the issue of *ne bis in idem* in the national court; however, the issue is to be decided only by the ICC while the national court postpones the surrender proceeding.

[109] These categories do not purport to be watertight compartments. There is bound to be some overlap between them, especially since certain procedural and substantive objections, and conflicting international obligations, may have a human rights quality.

[110] On good faith in international law generally, see art. 26 of the VCLT, *supra* n. 7; *Legality of the Threat or Use of Nuclear Weapons*, 1996 ICJ 226 at paras. 98–103 (8 July); *Case Concerning the Gabčikovo–Nagymaros Project* (*Hungary* v. *Slovakia*), 1997 ICJ at paras. 141–2 (25 Sept.); Bin Cheng, *General Principles of Law as Applied by International Courts and Tribunals*, 105–60 (1987).

Before ordering the person's surrender, the judicial officer must determine that the warrant applies to the person and that the person has been arrested in accordance with the proper process.[111] It is important not to confuse the first determination with the proof of an accused's identity at trial. Determining whether the warrant applies to the arrested person is a simpler issue and should not require any examination of the criminal allegations. If the reviewing judicial officer is not satisfied that the person named in the arrest warrant is the arrested person then that person should ordinarily be released.[112] A more interesting issue arises where the judicial officer finds that the 'proper process' has not been followed during the arrest procedures. Putting aside for the moment human rights considerations, it is difficult to accept that every procedural error should lead to the refusal of a surrender request. Most procedural breaches will likely be technical ones where the individual suffers little if any prejudice in making full answer and defence to the charges. Absent such prejudice, failing to surrender due to a procedural defect undermines the principle of effective prosecution and amounts to a failure to cooperate in breach of the Statute.

(b) Substantive Objections

The text of Part 9, particularly its drafting history, and the purposes of the Statute reveal no basis for reading in the traditional extradition refusal grounds (except for the rule of speciality) or any residual discretion to refuse.[113] A wide interpretation of article 91(2)(c), which would open the door to these grounds, should not be accepted in light of its drafting history and the principle of complementary effective prosecution.

On the issue of whether States Parties may impose an evidential sufficiency requirement for surrender, the Statute is ambiguous. Two provisions expressly requiring the Court to consider evidential sufficiency were removed from an earlier draft and replaced with the more discretionary approach contained in article 91(2)(c).[114] The State's discretion to implement an evidential sufficiency requirement is limited by a duty of good faith. As expressed in article 91(2)(c), the requirement should be no more burdensome than existing requirements under

[111] Article 59(2) requires that a third determination be made, that the person's rights have been respected, but this will be discussed in the context of human rights objections.

[112] The Statute, however, does not expressly stipulate this. Instead, art. 97(b) simply lists this determination as an example of when the State Party must consult with the Court without delay in order to resolve the matter.

[113] State practice in implementing the Statute appears to be consistent with this position. See articles in *The Rome Statute and Domestic Legal Orders*, *supra* n. 72. For example, Canada's implementing legislation, Bill C–19: 'An Act respecting genocide, crimes against humanity and war crimes and to implement the Rome Statute of the International Criminal Court, and to make consequential amendments to other Acts', 2d Sess., 36th Parl., 2000 (assented to 29 June 2000, S.C. 2000, c.24), does not apply the traditional extradition refusal grounds.

[114] See arts. 87(3)(d) & 87(7)(c) of Committee's Draft Statute, *supra* n. 27.

extradition treaties for that State. Many countries, such as those parties to the European Convention on Extradition,[115] have no such sufficiency requirement and should not, in good faith, be permitted to impose one in the context of the ICC.

Finally, courts in the custodial State may be asked to address a substantive issue, having the potential to halt the prosecution, on the basis that the individual's detention should not be prolonged if the ICC would inevitably reach the same outcome at trial. An example of this is refusing to surrender on the basis of unfitness to stand trial (as in the case of Senator Pinochet).[116] Taken to its logical limit, this argument would allow States to rule on issues directly related to the accused's guilt or innocence, such as an alibi defence. The Statute clearly does not contemplate such an intrusive role for States.[117] Evidential sufficiency only concerns the question whether the prosecution has sufficient evidence to meet a threshold test (e.g. a *prima facie* case) and should not require the domestic court to weigh evidence or consider substantive defences. It is submitted that the need to respect the separate spheres of responsibility between the Court and States, the importance of maintaining uniform international trial standards, and the Statute's safeguards in favour of the individual all support the detention and surrender of the accused until the substantive issue can be decided by the ICC.

(c) Human Rights Objections

It is important to distinguish human rights complaints impugning the conduct of the arrest and surrender procedures from complaints about the conduct or fairness of the accused's trial before the ICC. While the custodial State has been given limited jurisdiction over the first category of complaints, jurisdiction over the second category of complaints should rarely if ever be exercised by the custodial State.

1. RIGHTS DURING AN INVESTIGATION

The Statute requires the domestic court to determine that the arrested person's rights have been respected before ordering surrender. Article 55 provides for a number of procedural rights during an investigation, and in particular, during questioning by the Prosecutor or by national authorities. As with the requirement to determine 'proper process', the Statute gives no indication as to the consequences of finding that the

[115] European Convention on Extradition, 13 Dec. 1957, 359 UNTS 276; ETS No. 24.

[116] See *supra* n. 71.

[117] Extradition judges in Canada have not been given such a wide scope of review. In *Argentina (Republic)* v. *Mellino*, [1987] 1 S.C.R. 536 at 553, the Supreme Court of Canada found that it 'would cripple the operation of our extradition arrangements if extradition judges were to arrogate the power to consider defences that should properly be raised at trial. How would we react to foreign courts exercising this kind of pre-emptive jurisdiction in relation to trials in this country? There are, as well, practical considerations such as the limited information available to an extradition judge and his jurisdictional inability to obtain it.'

person's rights have not been fully respected. The principle of effective prosecution implies that not every violation results in a refusal to surrender, especially since rights violation can vary greatly in severity. It must be remembered that a State's refusal to surrender, when no country is willing and able to prosecute, is equivalent to a judicial stay of proceeding, which is tantamount to an acquittal. To warrant such an outcome, the rights violation must be so egregious that it is not reasonably possible for the accused to be guaranteed a fair trial. Most rights violations do not rise to this level and can be remedied by something short of a stay of proceedings. For example, a breach of an individual's right to counsel upon arrest is generally only prejudicial if he or she consequently provides incriminating evidence. This violation might be remedied by excluding the evidence at trial without frustrating the principle of effective prosecution. Indeed, the Statute allows the Court to exclude evidence at trial if it was obtained in violation of the Statute or internationally recognized human rights (art. 69(7)).

While rights violations may be remedied by a stay of proceeding or exclusion of evidence, it is suggested that the judicial officer in a surrender proceeding should not be given the jurisdiction to order these two remedies. These remedies have significant ramifications for the trial, and accordingly its implications should be left for the ICC to decide after surrender. Without the capability of obtaining all the relevant evidence, domestic courts will often be in a difficult position to decide these issues pre-surrender.

If remedial issues for rights violation should generally be left to be decided post-surrender in the ICC, then one might ask why the custodial State should have any competence to consider such violations. It is conceivable that the custodial State may order non-trial related remedies short of releasing the individual or excluding evidence at trial, e.g. ordering damages for physical or mental harm. But more importantly, by allowing individuals to raise these issues in the domestic forum, an evidential record of the complaint may be created and used as the factual basis for an application in the ICC. The individual will likely benefit from this opportunity while memories are fresh and witnesses are more accessible. Additionally, one should not ignore the possibility of detainees filing human rights complaints against the custodial State in international fora. Where this occurs, the international human rights tribunal will require that the applicant exhaust local remedies or otherwise demonstrate that the remedies were unavailable or ineffective.[118]

A difficult issue arises when the individual raises a rights complaint which requires consideration of the merits of the allegations, such as a complaint of arbitrary detention.[119] There are a number of reasons why

[118] See discussion of local remedies rule in Part III, section 4.

[119] Art. 55(1)(d) provides for a person's right not to be subjected to arbitrary arrest or detention in respect of an investigation under the Statute.

national courts should defer determination of this issue to the ICC without exploring the factual underpinnings of the arrest warrant.[120] First, the Statute provides that in deciding an interim release application, the national court is not to consider whether the warrant of arrest was properly issued. The intent of this prohibition would be undermined if an accused could circumvent it by requiring the domestic court to go behind the warrant in a complaint about arbitrary detention. Secondly, States that do not have an evidential sufficiency requirement would nevertheless be forced to review the factual allegations in an arbitrary detention challenge. Such a result would undermine the Statute's aim to ensure the least burdensome means to surrender. Thirdly, the ICC is the more suitable forum to decide an issue of arbitrary detention. The Court would be better placed to apply definitions of international crimes to standardize the legal tests for verifying the legality of the individual's detention. Furthermore, it is only after surrender that the accused is entitled to full disclosure of the prosecution's evidence, which can be extremely helpful to the defence in preparing the complaint or in deciding whether to raise the issue. Finally, there are safeguards in the Statute which attempt to minimize the degree of impairment to the individual's liberty interest.[121]

II. FAIR TRIAL RIGHTS

In the second category of human rights objections, the accused claims that the trial process in the ICC either falls below international human rights standards or is not as favourable as in the custodial State, e.g. failing to provide for a right to a jury trial. In both cases, the national court should refrain from hearing the complaint, leaving it to be decided as a trial issue in the ICC. The ICC is the more suitable forum to decide whether the trial standards in the Statute are inconsistent with international human rights law. An attack on trial standards is essentially a

[120] The Rules appear to be consistent with this position. Rule 117 provides that challenges to the arrest warrant's validity will be referred to the Pre-Trial Chamber while the arrested person is detained in the custodial state. The Pre-Trial Chamber is to decide the challenge without delay. The basis in the Statute for the Chamber to consider this challenge is unclear. The only express pre-surrender challenges to be considered by the Pre-Trial Chamber relate to admissibility where the arrested person raises the issue of *non bis in idem* in the national courts (see art. 89(2)). It could be that the Chamber's jurisdiction is implicitly found in a duty to ensure that the detainee's procedural rights under art. 55 are respected.

[121] The arrest warrant is issued by a judicial body of the Court only if satisfied that there are reasonable grounds to believe that the person has committed a crime within the jurisdiction of the Court and the arrest appears necessary (art. 58(1)). After the person is delivered to the Court, the Pre-Trial Chamber must satisfy itself that the accused has been informed of the alleged crimes, and of his or her rights under the Statute, including the right to apply for interim release (art. 60(1)). Within a reasonable time after surrender, the Pre-Trial Chamber must hold a hearing to confirm the charges on which the Prosecutor intends to seek trial (art. 61). Before the hearing, the accused is entitled to be informed of the charges and evidence on which the Prosecutor intends to rely. To have the charges confirmed, the Pre-Trial Chamber must be satisfied that there is sufficient evidence to 'establish substantial grounds to believe that the person committed each of the crimes charged'.

claim that the accused cannot realize a fair trial in the ICC. However, in most cases, a review of such a claim will require an appreciation of the facts and issues in the case, which is something that national courts will not be in a position to obtain. Furthermore, claims of trial unfairness can often be addressed by the court in the course of the trial. The Statute clearly requires the Court to protect the human rights of accused persons.[122] In addition to protecting the specific 'minimum guarantees' listed in article 67, the Court has residual authority to 'ensure that a trial is fair and expeditious and is conducted with full respect for the rights of the accused' (art. 64(2)).

Where the custodial State refuses to hear a complaint challenging the ICC trial standards, it will be open to the accused to bring a complaint before an international human rights tribunal, to which the custodial State is party. Assuming the tribunal decides the complaint before the person is surrendered, this scenario could lead to the interesting problem of the custodial State facing inconsistent demands from the ICC (ordering the accused's surrender) and the tribunal (finding that surrender would put the State in breach of its human rights treaty obligations). It is difficult to predict what exactly the Court would do in this case; however, there appear to be at least three options. The Court could defer to the tribunal's decision by reading the Statute's analogous human rights provision(s) in a consistent manner. Conversely, it could disagree with the tribunal's decision and make a finding of non-cooperation against the custodial State, which would then become a matter for the Assembly of States Parties (arts. 87(7) and 112). Alternatively, a solution to the problem could be found through consultations pursuant to article 97.

Claims that surrender should be refused because of more favourable trial standards in the custodial State are difficult to accept if the accused would consequently go without prosecution. In such cases, the question arises as to whether the custodial State would be in breach of the Statute if, instead of surrendering, it proceeded to prosecute the accused applying its more favourable trial standards. The answer depends on whether the circumstances of this prosecution fall below the international standards of justice set out in the Statute's admissibility criteria. Where the Court decides a case to be admissible, it effectively has held that there is no State 'willing and able' to carry out the prosecution. The principle of complementarity is concerned with minimum standards of justice and not with ensuring the most advantageous trial procedures for the accused. Thus, where the Court has made a determination that a particular case is admissible, the custodial State must surrender the

[122] The fair trial rights contained in arts. 55 and 67 parallel those found in the various international human rights treaties. The application and interpretation of the applicable law by the Court must be consistent with internationally recognized human rights, and be without adverse distinction on a number of enumerated grounds (art. 21(3)).

requested person irrespective of that person's wishes. Further support for this position can be seen by contrasting the surrender provisions with those governing other forms of cooperation set out in Part 9. In the latter case, the drafters included an exception to complying with an assistance request where execution of the request 'is prohibited in the requested State on the basis of an existing fundamental legal principle of general application'. The omission of this express exception for surrender requests suggests that States Parties must comply even if it means contravening a domestic law of fundamental significance.

(d) Conflicting International Obligations

Part 9 of the Statute permits three derogations from the basic duty to surrender where the requested State is required to act inconsistently with obligations under extradition treaties, principles of immunity, and status of forces agreements. It is perhaps too early to say what other conflicting international obligations will override a State Party's surrender obligations under the Statute, e.g. Chapter VII action under the UN Charter. Rather than suggest that there might be other categories of overriding conflicting international obligations, the Statute contemplates that when conflicting obligations arise they are to be resolved cooperatively on a case-by-case basis. Article 97 provides that where compliance with a request would require the requested State to breach a 'pre-existing treaty obligation', the requested State must consult with the Court without delay to try to resolve the matter. At the end of the consultations, it will be for the ICC to decide whether the requested State Party's position is in breach of the Statute.[123]

V. Conclusion

This article has sought to apply the principle of purposive interpretation in clarifying ambiguities in the Statute's text. The principle of effective prosecution is the Court's *raison d'être*. To apply it in this context is appropriate: the criminal justice systems of States are themselves aimed at achieving reliable trial outcomes. Complementarity, on the other hand, is a new word in the international law lexicon. It is supposed to define the complex relationship between States and the ICC as set out in the Statute. To define complementarity as giving 'primacy' or 'priority' to States is to oversimplify the concept. As illustrated by the surrender issues discussed in this article, complementarity is a fluid concept that may emphasize or de-emphasize State interests depending

[123] This is to be contrasted with compliance problems with assistance requests (other than for surrender) prohibited by domestic law based on existing fundamental legal principles of general application. Art. 93(3) provides that if 'after consultations the matter cannot be resolved, the Court shall modify the request as necessary'.

on the nature of the problem. To understand how complementarity applies to a particular issue, it is necessary to identify the point where exclusive domestic jurisdiction ends and State obligation under the Statute begins. In some cases, the Statute makes it clear where this dividing point should be. For example, States must exhibit certain minimum standards of international justice before the ICC will refrain from prosecuting an otherwise admissible case. As well, obligations to cooperate with the ICC are subject to certain international obligations that a State may have. Where the dividing point is less clear, three guiding principles applied in this article are suggested. First, complementarity serves effective prosecution and must be subordinate to it. Secondly, the dialogue structure between States and the ICC sets reliance and expectation interests that affect the scope of State obligations. Thirdly, States and the ICC have separate spheres of authority based on their functional and legal expertise. In anticipation of many surrender issues and problems, these principles aim to provide durable solutions that balance the often conflicting interests of States, the ICC and accused persons.

NOTE

FALSIFICATION OF DOCUMENTARY EVIDENCE BEFORE INTERNATIONAL TRIBUNALS: AN ASPECT OF THE *BEHRING SEA* ARBITRATION, 1892–3*

By GEOFFREY MARSTON[1]

I. Introduction

While the merits phase of the case of *Maritime Delimitation and Territorial Questions between Qatar and Bahrain*[2] was pending before the International Court of Justice, Bahrain informed the Court by a letter dated 25 September 1997 of 'certain surprising and deeply concerning developments which are unprecedented in the history of the Court'. Bahrain then challenged the authenticity of 81 documents produced by Qatar as annexes to Qatar's memorial and announced that it would disregard the content of those documents in preparing its counter-memorial. In Bahrain's assessment, the challenged documents 'play an essential role in Qatar's Memorial, serving as almost the only basis for Qatar's claim to the Hawar Islands as well as, to a lesser degree, the Zubarah region'. After the respective counter-memorials had been filed on 23 December 1997, Bahrain, in a letter to the Court dated 2 February 1998, stated that Qatar had continued to rely on the challenged documents—now increased to 82—and emphasized the need for the Court to decide the question of their authenticity as a preliminary issue.

In response, the Court, by an order dated 30 March 1998, directed that Qatar should file by 30 September 1998 an interim report, to be as comprehensive and specific as possible, addressing the authenticity of each of the challenged documents and that Qatar's reply on the merits, to be filed by 30 March 1999, should contain its detailed and definitive position on the question; Bahrain's reply on the merits, also to be filed by 30 March 1999, was required to contain its observations on Qatar's interim report. On 30 September 1998, Qatar provided the Court with its interim report which ended as follows:[3]

[1] LLB, LLM, Ph.D (Lond.); Lecturer in Law, University of Cambridge; Fellow of Sidney Sussex College, Cambridge. The British archival references are to Crown Copyright documents in the Public Record Office, London (PRO), and the United States archival references are to documents in the National Archives, College Park, Maryland (NACP).

[2] The brief account below has been compiled from the information given in the Court's orders of 30 March 1998 and 17 February 1999 and from the written pleadings made publicly available on the Court's internet website (www.icj-cij.org).

[3] Order of 17 February 1999, p. 4.

. . . after receiving its various experts' reports and in the light of the conflicting views amongst the parties' experts, Qatar has decided that it will disregard all the 82 challenged documents for the purposes of the present case so as to enable the Court to address the merits of the case without further procedural complications. It does so, however, with the proviso that it does not accept Bahrain's distortion of the historical facts or its exaggerations of the effect of the challenged documents on Qatar's case.

On 27 November 1998, Bahrain supplied the Court with comments on 'the insufficiency of Qatar's explanations' while at the same time it referred to 'the effective abandonment by Qatar of all the impeached documents in the face of Bahrain's proof of forgery'. By an order dated 17 February 1999, the Court placed on record Qatar's decision 'to disregard, for the purposes of the present case, the 82 documents challenged by Bahrain'.

Qatar's decision to disregard the disputed documents, without however conceding that any of them was 'forged', as Bahrain had alleged, has apparently closed the door on an unusual aspect of procedure before international tribunals, namely the tendering by one party of documentary evidence whose authenticity is then challenged by the other party. Unusual it was, but it was not completely unprecedented. In the *Behring Sea* arbitration (sometimes referred to as the *Fur Seal* arbitration) between Great Britain and the USA in the late nineteenth century, a matter of documentary authenticity arose although it differed from that raised in the *Qatar* v. *Bahrain* case in at least one material respect, namely that it concerned the authenticity of translations of documentary evidence and not of the documentary evidence itself.

II. The Background to the Behring Sea Arbitration

By a treaty of 1867,[4] the Emperor of all the Russias ceded to the United States 'all the territory and dominion now possessed by his said Majesty on the continent of America and in the adjacent islands', the same being contained within the 'line of demarcation' set out in Articles III and IV of a Convention of 1825 between Russia and Great Britain.[5] The adjacent islands included the Pribilof Islands in the Behring Sea from which a valuable fur seal industry was carried on. The United States thereafter legislated for the regulation of sealing 'within the limits of the Alaska Territory or in the waters thereof' and, acting under this legislation, seized sealing boats flying the British flag operating both within the three-mile belt of the islands and beyond it in the deeper or 'pelagic' waters of the Behring Sea east of the line of demarcation.

This gave rise to a long-running international dispute between Great Britain (also at that period representing Canadian interests) and the United States over the limits of their respective territory and jurisdiction on the north-west coast of America. In particular, the United States asserted that it had inherited from Russia exclusive jurisdiction in the Behring Sea, and in any event that it had a property right in fur seals bred in the Pribilof Islands which was capable of protection even when the seals themselves were outside the three-mile belt.

By a treaty signed on 29 February 1892 of which ratifications were exchanged

[4] *Consolidated Treaty Series*, vol. 134, p. 331.

[5] Ibid., vol. 75, p. 95.

on 7 May 1892,[6] Great Britain and the United States agreed to create an *ad hoc* tribunal of arbitration and to refer the dispute to it. The tribunal was to consist of seven members: two named by the British Monarch and two by the President of the United States; together with one appointed by the French President on the joint request of the parties, one by the King of Italy in similar manner, and one by the King of Sweden and Norway in similar manner. The members were to be 'jurists of distinguished reputation in their respective countries' and should be, if possible, 'acquainted with the English language'. In due course, Lord Hannen, a Lord of Appeal, and Sir John Thompson, Minister of Justice and Attorney-General of the Dominion of Canada, were nominated as the British members. As the United States members, John M. Harlan, of the Supreme Court of the United States, and Senator John T. Morgan were nominated. The President of France nominated Baron de Courcel, a senator and ambassador of France, the King of Italy nominated the Marquis Venosta, an Italian senator and former Foreign Minister, while the King of Sweden and Norway nominated Gregers Gram, a Minister of State. As their respective Agents, Great Britain appointed Charles H. Tupper, Minister of Marine and Fisheries for the Dominion of Canada, and the United States appointed John W. Foster, who became Secretary of State while the arbitration was pending.

Article VI of the arbitration treaty asked the tribunal to rule initially on five points:

1. What exclusive jurisdiction in the sea now known as the Behring's Sea, and what exclusive rights in the seal fisheries therein, did Russia assert and exercise prior and up to the time of the cession of Alaska to the United States?

2. How far were these claims of jurisdiction as to the seal fisheries recognized and conceded by Great Britain?

3. Was the body of water now known as the Behring's Sea included in the phrase 'Pacific Ocean' as used in the Treaty of 1825 between Great Britain and Russia; and what rights, if any, in the Behring's Sea, were held and exclusively exercised by Russia after said Treaty?

4. Did not all the rights of Russia as to jurisdiction and as to the seal fisheries in Behring's Sea east of the water boundary, in the Treaty between the United States and Russia of the 30th March, 1867, pass unimpaired to the United States under that Treaty?

5. Has the United States any right, and, if so, what right, of protection or property in the fur-seals frequenting the islands of the United States in Behring's Sea when such seals are found outside the ordinary 3-mile limit?

Two provisions of the procedure should be mentioned at this stage. Article III read:

The printed Case of each of the two Parties, accompanied by the documents, the official correspondence, and other evidence on which each relies, shall be delivered in duplicate to each of the Arbitrators and to the Agent of the other Party as soon as may be after the appointment of the members of the Tribunal, but within a period not exceeding four months from the date of the exchange of the ratifications of this Treaty.

Article IV began:

[6] *United Kingdom Treaty Series*, 1892, No. 8.

Within three months after the delivery on both sides of the printed Case, either Party may, in like manner, deliver in duplicate to each of the said Arbitrators and to the Agent of the other Party, a Counter-case, and additional documents, correspondence, and evidence in reply to the Case, documents, correspondence and other evidence so presented by the other Party.

On 1 September 1892, the Agents delivered their respective printed cases.[7] The appendix to the case of the United States exhibited translations into English of 31 hitherto untranslated documents, written originally in the Russian language, which had been extracted from the archives of the Russian-American Company then held by the Department of State.[8] Facsimile reproductions of the original documents were included at the back of the appendix.[9] The translations had been made on behalf of the United States by one Ivan Petroff, a former employee of the Census Department who was a native Russian speaker. Petroff was already experienced in Alaskan documentation through having assisted H. H. Bancroft in preparing his history of Alaska.[10] In his memoirs, the United States Agent, John Foster, described his opinion of Petroff at the time of his hiring as 'a native Russian and an intelligent scholar, who seemed well fitted for the task'.[11]

III. The Discovery of the Falsifications

In an article published fifty years later, William Williams, who had been one of the United States' junior counsel in the arbitration, recounted his recollections of the arbitration.[12] It appeared that Williams, who knew no Russian but was familiar with the characters used in that language, decided, on a personal whim, to indicate on the facsimiles of the original documents written in Russian the significant passages which he read in the translations, using proper names as identifying indicators. He took up the story as follows:[13]

The writer attributed his failure to succeed in locating the first passage to his ineptitude and ignorance of the foreign language, but upon failing to identify the next two his suspicions were aroused and before the evening was over he became satisfied that a fraud of the first order had been practiced on the government.

Williams related that the United States' Agent, John W. Foster, who was now also Secretary of State, was thereupon recalled from the West to Washington by telegram. The United States' archives contain a fuller account of Williams'

[7] The written and oral proceedings were printed in several volumes by the United States Government Printing Office in 1895: *Proceedings of the Tribunal of Arbitration . . . for the determination of questions between the two Governments concerning the jurisdictional rights of the United States* (to be cited as *Proceedings*).

[8] *Proceedings*, vol. II, pp. 49–90.

[9] *Proceedings*, vol. XVI.

[10] In his *History of Alaska* (1886), p. xi, H. H. Bancroft acknowledged the work of his 'assistants and stenographers' in making abstracts in locations including Washington, but made no reference to particular individuals.

[11] John W. Foster, *Diplomatic Memoirs*, vol. II (1909), p. 40.

[12] William Williams, 'Reminiscences of the Bering Sea Arbitration', *American Journal of International Law*, 37 (1943), p. 562.

[13] Ibid., p. 567.

involvement about which he probably had no opportunity to refresh his memory when he wrote his article fifty years later.[14] In fact, Williams wrote the following letter, dated 19 October 1892, to Foster who was in Chicago at the time:[15]

> I regret to be obliged to announce that I have just discovered some grave inaccuracies in what we have published as translations of the Alaska Archives in Vol. I of our Appendix, and that they affect some of the important passages quoted in the text of our Case. They consist in the insertion into the English version of whole sentences which have no existence in the Russian. Following is an instance: you will remember that one paper contains a prohibition against 'killing fur seals at sea or in the passes of the Aleutian Islands'; the original, however, contains nothing which even remotely resembles this. As to several of the inaccuracies I have consulted separately both Mr Buynitzki [*sic*] and Mr Mayo, and therefore know them to exist. Mr Mayo is now making a new translation of every passage of which we have made use in the text of the Case, and in a short time I will know just how much mischief has been done. I think that eventually we will be obliged to have all translations made anew.
>
> Since this unfortunate discovery deprives some of our important quotations of all their value, you will probably wish an early opportunity to offer some explanation to the Arbitrators and to the British agent.
>
> It looks like treachery on the part of Petroff. The errors I have been able to discover are of such a character (relating as they do to jurisdiction over the Bering Sea) as to make it difficult to account for them in any other way.
>
> While I do not expect you will be able to take any action in this matter before your return to Washington, I nevertheless thought it of sufficient importance to warrant my bringing it to your attention now.

Two days later, after more re-translations had been done, Williams telegraphed Foster in Chicago as follows: 'Further examination confirms worst fears concerning matter mentioned my letter nineteenth. Believe no foundation left for our position.'[16] Foster telegraphed back on the following day to Williams: 'Have all translations in appendix revised as speedily as possible ask Bunitsky's [*sic*] entire time if Mayo needs him.'[17]

In his published memoirs, Foster took up the subsequent story as follows:[18]

> A thorough examination resulted in the discovery that in every one of the documents seeming to sustain our contention, Petroff had designedly interpolated the language in the English translations. Happily, however, he had not tampered with the Russian text of the

[14] NACP: RG 76, MLA 159 (folder: 'Petroff, Ivan'). These documents are filed in the main Department of State archive for the arbitration but how they got there deserves explanation. On 27 June 1911, Williams wrote to Foster telling him that he had found amongst his papers some which threw light on the Petroff incident, namely copies of Williams' letter to Foster dated 19 October 1892, Williams' telegram to Foster dated 21 October 1892 and Foster's telegram in reply dated 22 October 1892. Williams continued: 'I found also the original admission by Petroff of his guilt. This is a public paper and belongs on the files. I suppose the reason it was not put there at the time is that we were treating this matter as a confidential one and that later I forgot to put the paper where it belonged. A copy therefore was published in our appendix. Please feel at liberty to deal with it in any way you wish.' Foster wrote to the Secretary of State on 3 July 1911 enclosing Williams' letter of 27 June 1911, the original Petroff 'confession' and the above copies 'which I respectfully suggest should be placed on file in the Department with the other documents in said case'.

[15] Ibid. Stephen H. Buynitsky was an official of the Treasury Department, presumably familiar with the Russian language. William C. Mayo was an official of the State Department.

[16] Ibid.

[17] Ibid.

[18] Foster, op cit. above (n. 11), p. 41. In this work, written in 1909, Foster mistakenly attributed the discovery of the fraud to Mayo.

original documents which were correctly reproduced in the facsimiles, and the fraud was thus easily detected.

Foster then recalled that Petroff was called before him in the presence of witnesses when '[h]e quietly acknowledged his guilt, and did not deign to give any explanation of or excuse for his conduct'. Foster continued:[19]

I immediately asked the British Chargé to come to the [State] Department, and explained to him the imposition practiced on me, and also in a letter gave the details of it to the British agent; and as soon as possible he was furnished with specifications of the false translations and with revised translations. This act of perfidy would have given me more annoyance, if I had not shown my good faith in publishing the facsimiles, and made such timely discovery of the imposition.

The story at this point may conveniently be resumed from the diplomatic correspondence preserved in the British archives. The first news which London heard of the matter came in secret telegram No. 151 dated 31 October 1892 sent to the Foreign Office by Michael H. Herbert, the *chargé d'affaires* at the British Embassy in Washington. It read:[20]

Behring Sea Arbitration: Secret. Secretary of State told me privately to-day that he had recently discovered to his great chagrin that the translations of certain Russian documents included in appendix to the United States' Case had been incorrectly made. Fresh translations would now be made and sent to arbitrators and British Agent as soon as possible. He desired me to convey to your Lordship his deep regret at the mistake.

Within the Foreign Office, R.P. Maxwell, a member of the arbitration team, wrote a minute dated 1 November 1892 in relation to the telegram. The minute indicated that not only had the discrepancies already been spotted by the British team and a print of them made but that plans might have been made to use them to Britain's advantage in its counter-case. The minute read:[21]

This refers to the correspondence of the Russian American Co. appended to the U.S. Case. On comparison of the translations made by the U.S. with the certified copies of the originals presented by them, we found that there were numerous interpolations and mistranslations. A copy of the two translations in parallel columns is annexed on which the chief instances of interpretations or inaccurate renderings are marked in red ink. As the arguments in Part I of the U.S. Case are mainly based on these interpolated passages this admission of the U.S. almost wholly destroys their position so far as their extra-territorial claims in Behring Sea are concerned.

We had hoped that the U.S. would not have discovered the matter till it came out in our counter-case.

At the foot of the minute was written the letter 'R' in red ink, indicating that it was seen by the Secretary of State for Foreign Affairs, the Earl of Rosebery.

Accompanying the minute were twenty-four pages printed in parallel columns with the suspect translations in one column and in the other a British translation, made by G. F. Fairholme, a Foreign Office official who earlier in his career had been posted in St Petersburg. The discrepancies between the two versions were

[19] Ibid.
[20] PRO: FO 371/2181.
[21] Ibid.

underlined in red ink. The print had clearly been prepared before the news from Washington arrived.

By a letter dated 2 November 1892, Foster confirmed to Herbert his earlier oral statement and gave Herbert a letter of that date for forwarding to the British Agent, Charles Tupper, which read:[22]

I deem it my duty to bring to your attention, without delay, the fact that it has been discovered by me that a number of the documents belonging to the archives of the Territory of Alaska, now in the possession of the Department of State, and referred to in the Case of the United States before the Tribunal of Arbitration delivered to you on September 1st last, were incorrectly translated from the Russian language in which the originals appear. Lithographic reproductions of the original documents are to be found in Volume I of the Appendix to the Case of the United States, following page 591, and English translations of the same are given in Volume I, pages 49 to 90. It has within the last few days been ascertained that some of these translations are incorrect, but to what extent I have not yet been able accurately to determine. A thorough examination is now being made, and, at the earliest practicable date, I shall furnish you with revised and corrected translations, and indicate the pages in the Printed Case of the United States where the erroneous translations have been quoted or referred to. I have, however, not been content to await the result of that examination, and I hasten to inform you of the above fact, and to assure you that this announcement shall be followed by a more detailed statement with as little delay as possible.

The nature of the errors referred to seem to make it certain that the Government of the United States has been grossly imposed upon by a person employed on the work of translation. What the motive for such imposition may have been, I have no knowledge, and I forbear from any mention of my suspicions.

In a covering despatch to the Foreign Office dated 4 November 1892 enclosing Foster's letter, Herbert wrote:[23]

With reference to the last paragraph of the letter to Mr. Tupper, Mr. Foster informed me privately at our interview on the 31st ultimo that he could not understand the motives of the translator in thus imposing upon the United States' Government, unless he had contemplated the attempted sale later of the information to the British Government.

In Washington, Petroff signed a typed statement dated 11 November 1892 addressed to Foster and which was signed as witnesses by Williams and another person present, John H. Haswell. It read:[24]

Dear Sir,–

You employed me during the past summer to examine the Alaskan Records or Archives on file in the State Department, with a view to ascertaining whether they contained information which would be of use in the Bering Sea Arbitration. Upon my recommendation you ordered that certain of these records be translated. I hereby acknowledge that I misled you in important particulars as to their contents, and that in making the translations I was guilty of gross inaccuracies and interpolations, amounting to falsification.

Ivan Petroff

Translator

[22] Original in PRO: FO 115/938, f. 40: printed in *Counter-Case of the United States*, Appendix (*Proceedings*, vol. VII, p. 151).

[23] Despatch No. 314. The original has not been located in the British archives. The outgoing copy, from the Embassy's archives, is in PRO: FO 115/916, f. 30; a printed copy is in PRO: FO 881/6301, p. 246.

[24] See n. 14, above.

According to William Williams in his 1943 memoir: 'Upon being confronted with evidence of his treachery Petroff broke down, signed a full confession of his guilt and was turned over to the proper authorities for prosecution. Unfortunately the Attorney General was obliged to report that there was no statute applicable to his case.'[25]

Although one might expect the affair to have been kept secret, at least until the publication of the counter-cases, the *Washington Post* got hold of the story within a day.[26] In its edition of 13 November 1892, the newspaper carried a front-page story headlined: 'He betrayed his trust: Ivan Petroff gave false information to this government—a Bering Sea incident'. Having stated that the false translations 'formed a part of the arch upon which the United States' claim rested, although it was not the keystone by any manner of means', the report continued:

> It was at first supposed at the State Department, and this belief is still current, that Petroff had been paid by the British government to falsify the information. An official of the State Department said last night, however, that this charge had not been proven. No explanation had been given for the offense, and the most charitable conclusion of the official was that Petroff, thinking he knew the character of the information that the Department wanted, had manufactured it so as to make a strong case for this Government. The State Department officials are congratulating themselves that they have discovered the falsification. It is an embarrassing and mortifying thing for the United States to admit that it has been imposed upon, but even this is better than having the falsities pointed out by England.

The report concluded by stating that it was not possible to punish Petroff for his actions as 'there was no law upon the statute book to meet such a case as this, and Mr Petroff will simply lose his Government position, with the knowledge that never again can he re-enter official life'.

The following day, 14 November 1892, the *Washington Post* carried a short leader, entitled 'The State Department and Petroff', stating that its report of the previous day in which it had written that there was a current belief in the State Department that Petroff had been paid by the British Government was 'calculated to mislead' unless further explained in a 'correction'. It wrote:

> It was not the intention of *The Post* to convey the impression that such statement or idea was ever made or given by any official of the State Department. On the contrary, we had good reason for stating that there is no information in that Department to warrant such a belief. We intended simply to mention that there was rumour to that effect.

On 16 November 1892, the British Ambassador in Washington, Sir Julian Pauncefote, sent to the Foreign Office the cuttings of the above reports. The Earl of Rosebery noted in red ink on the back of Pauncefote's covering despatch: 'It is "not proven" that the British Govt paid Petroff'.[27] On the night of 21/22 November 1892, Pauncefote telegraphed the Foreign Office as follows:[28]

[25] Williams, loc. cit. above (n. 12), p. 567.

[26] Other newspapers carried the story (e.g. the *New York Times*, 14 November 1892), but derivative from the *Washington Post*.

[27] PRO: FO 5/2181 (unfoliated). It is more likely that Lord Rosebery was here summarizing the conclusion of the newspaper than expressing his own view or knowledge.

[28] Ibid. (telegram No. 165).

I transmit in special bag tomorrow a Note from U.S. Govt with inclosure from U.S Agent to British Agent explaining falsification of documents. Notice is given of withdrawal of twelve documents and one inclosure out of the thirty-one of which fac-similes are given at the end of Volume I of the Appendix to United States case. The remaining nineteen documents are retained in the Case and revised translations are furnished. References are given to the pages of the Case in which each document is cited.

On 22 November 1892, Pauncefote sent a despatch to the Foreign Office. It read:[29]

With reference to my Telegram No 165 of yesterday, I have the honour to enclose a copy of the note which I have received from the Secretary of State on the 20th instant transmitting a letter adressed [*sic*] by him as Agent of the United States in the Behring Sea Arbitration to the Honourable Charles Tupper, the British Agent, giving full explanations respecting the falsifications which have been discovered in the translations of certain Russian documents which appear in Volume I of the appendix to the case of the United States.

P.S. The enclosures to the Note of the 19th November are sent in Print and will be found at page 4 of the enclosed correspondence.

The documents attached consisted of prints of Foster's letters to Tupper, Petroff's 'confession' and, as 'Enclosure 2', amended translations of documents Nos. 11, 13, 14, 16, 19, 20, 21, 22, 23, 24, 25, 26, 27, 28, 29, 30 and 31.

The United States' Note to the British Ambassador, dated 19 November 1892, was signed by Foster who wrote:[30]

I transmit herewith a note and accompanying documents addressed to the Honorable Charles H. Tupper, Agent of Great Britain before the Tribunal of Arbitration at Paris relative to a correction of errors which have been discovered in the documents referred to in, and attached to, the printed Case of the United States heretofore submitted.

I beg that you will be so kind as to transmit the same to its destination at your earliest convenience.

Foster's note of 19 November 1892 to Tupper read in full as follows:[31]

Under date of the 2d instant I advised you that I had discovered that a number of documents belonging to the Archives of Alaska and referred to in the Case of the United States before the Tribunal of Arbitration were incorrectly translated from the Russian language; and I promised to give you at the earliest practicable date a detailed statement of the erroneous translations and to indicate the pages in the Case of the United States where they are quoted or referred to.

Before complying with that promise, I deem it due to my Government and to myself to state the circumstances under which these translations were introduced into the Case of the United States. When I entered upon the work of preparing the same I learned that there existed in the Archives of the State Department a large collection of documents entirely in the Russian language, which had been turned over by the Russian authorities in the Territory of Alaska at the time of the transfer of that Territory to the United States, in accordance with the treaty of cession of 1867. These documents I found to be unclassified and without indices. Desiring to ascertain whether they contained any information relevant to the work I had in hand, I made inquiry for a competent person to undertake the needed research. After considerable investigation my choice fell upon

[29] PRO: FO 5/2183 (unfoliated) (despatch 332).

[30] Original in PRO: FO 115/938, f. 101.

[31] *Counter Case of the United States*, Appendix (*Proceedings*, vol. VII, pp. 152–3).

Ivan Petroff. I learned that he was a native Russian, educated in St. Petersburg, that he had several times visited Alaska as an agent of the United States Government and had been in the employ of this Government for several years in responsible positions. He was represented to me as an accomplished linguist and the best informed person obtainable in the Russian language and history, and I was also told that he had performed a large part of the labor in the compilation of H. H. Bancroft's History of Alaska. Having entire confidence in his capacity and integrity, I entrusted to him the examination of the Alaskan Archives, with the result shown in the use made of them in the Case of the United States and Volume I of its Appendix.

Only a few weeks ago my suspicion was for the first time aroused as to the correctness of some of the passages translated by Petroff, and careful examination has revealed an astounding series of false translations. As soon as I was prepared to do so, I brought Petroff into my presence and confronted him with the proofs of his infidelity and false translations. The evidence of his dishonest conduct being over-powering, he acknowledged his guilt in the presence of witnesses and signed a full confession, of which I inclose you herewith a copy certified to by the witnesses. The only motive which he has alleged for his conduct is that he supposed by making the false translations and interpolations he would so ingratiate himself into favor and impress upon this Government the importance and value of the Alaskan Archives as to secure his employment to classify, translate, and index that voluminous collection of documents.

In making this explanation I desire to again direct attention to the fact mentioned in my note of the 2d instant that photolithographic reproductions of all the original documents, of which translations were cited or made use of, were introduced in Volume I of the Appendix to the Case of the United States, following page 593, and that the British Government and its representatives were thus furnished with the means of testing the correctness of the translations.

I now desire to give notice as Agent of the United States that I do hereby formally withdraw from the Case of the United States in their entirety the original Russian documents hereinafter designated. These documents are included in those referred to in the footnote to page 41 of the Case of the United States, of which translations are given in Volume I of the Appendix to said Case, at pages 49 to 90, and facsimiles in the same Volume following page 593.

Foster then set out the following table:

Number of document withdrawn	Where cited in U.S. Case
	Pages
1	43, 44
2	45, 46, 47
3	47, 48
4	48, 49
5	Not cited
6	44, 45
7	Not cited
8	41
9	42
10 and inclosure	53, 54, 60
12	60
15	62
Inclosure to No. 29	103, 104

Foster continued:

I inclose herewith revised translations of those of the Russian documents hereinbefore referred to which are retained in the Case of the United States, and beg to direct attention to the following pages of the Case, on which there appear falsified translations of portions of these documents:

On page 61, of document No. 14.
On pages 54, 55, of document No. 14, inclosure.
On pages 62, 66, of document No. 16.
On page 67, of document No. 17.
On page 67, of document No. 20.

I have to advise you that I will send without delay to each member of the Tribunal of Arbitration duplicate copies of my note to you of the 2d instant and of the present note, and further that a proper correction of the errors inserted in the Case of the United States will be made in the Counter Case, and the correspondence relating thereto be included in its Appendix.

Foster also enclosed a print of the witnessed copy of Petroff's 'confession'.

On 25 November 1892, Pauncefote sent despatch No. 334 to the Foreign Office as follows:[32]

With reference to my despatch No 332 of the 23rd [*sic*] instant I have the honour to enclose, at the request of Mr Foster, a communication addressed by him as Agent of the United States in the Behring Sea Arbitration to Lord Hannen one of the British Arbitrators in relation to erroneous translations of certain Russian documents referred to in the Case of the United States. Mr Foster has sent me a similar communication addressed by him to Sir John Thompson the other British Arbitrator, and I have forwarded it to His Excellency the Governor General of Canada for delivery to Sir John Thompson at Ottawa.

I have also forwarded to His Excellency six printed copies of the correspondence inclosed in the above communications, which were furnished to me by the State Department.

Foster's letter dated 23 November 1892[33] which was forwarded to Lord Hannen enclosed a copy of Foster's letters of 2 and 19 November 1892 to the British Agent 'in relation to erroneous translations of certain Russian documents referred to in the Case of the United States'. The letter to Lord Hannen went on: 'From these communications and their enclosures it will appear that certain substantial changes in Part First of the Case of the United States have been rendered necessary, which changes will be duly made in the Counter Case of the Government of the United States'.

IV. The Counter-Cases' Treatment of the Falsifications

Both parties in their respective counter-cases delivered in January 1893 referred to the falsification of the translations of the correspondence relating to the affairs of the Russian-American Company. The United States counter-case,

[32] PRO: FO 5/2183 (unfoliated).
[33] Copy in NACP: M.99/Roll 51.

having described the incident and the steps taken to remedy the falsifications, observed:[34]

Some evidence which the United States Government had relied on, to prove that for many years prior to the time of the cession of Alaska Russia had prohibited the killing of fur-seals in the waters frequented by them in Bering Sea, thus turns out to be untrue; and it now becomes necessary for the United States to restate, in part, their position in respect to some of the questions submitted to this Tribunal.

The appendix additionally printed the Foster-Tupper letters of 2 and 19 November 1892, the Petroff 'confession' and the amended translations.[35]

The appendix to the British counter-case set out in parallel columns the original and the revised translations of the Russian-American Company documents included in the appendix to the United States' case, with the material differences underlined and the interpolations both underlined and enclosed within square brackets.[36]

Not surprisingly, the British counter-case tried to make more than the United States out of the incident. In an Introduction to Part I of the British argument, it was written:[37]

Upon the first perusal of the extracts included in the United States Case, certain passages were observed which at once gave rise to the impression that the papers must have been faultily translated. The fac-similes supplied in the Appendix were consequently examined by a competent Russian scholar in the confidential employment of Her Majesty's Government, and a large number of errors and interpolations were discovered of a most important kind. Some few of these were apparently purposeless, but the great majority were of such a nature that they could only be accounted for on the supposition that some person had deliberately falsified the translations in a sense favourable to the contentions of the United States. The matter seemed of so much importance that steps were taken to obtain an independent translation by another hand, which was completed in October, and entirely confirmed the previous impression.

The United States Government independently came to the knowledge of the fact at the beginning of November, and their Agent has given the explanation of it in a communication addressed to the Arbitrators and to the British Agent on the 19th of that month. The United States Agent at the same time gave notice of the withdrawal of a certain number of the documents, and furnished revised translations of the others. Her Majesty's Government have pleasure in acknowledging that these revised translations, with the exception of one or two small errors of no moment, are perfectly accurate. But there are statements and arguments in the Case founded on the original translations, or depending mainly on them for support, which still remain to be answered, and it will therefore be necessary in the proper place to draw attention to the translations and original documents.

The successive printed drafts of the British counter-case have survived and it is interesting to compare them with the passage above. The earliest was a 'preliminary draft' bearing a stamped date of printing of 19 October 1892, that is the very day when Williams wrote to Foster of his discovery and two weeks

[34] *Counter-Case of the United States* (*Proceedings*, vol. VII, p. 14).
[35] *Counter-Case of the United States*, Appendix (*Proceedings*, vol. VII, pp. 151–74).
[36] *Counter-Case of Great Britain*, Appendix (*Proceedings*, vol. VIII, pp. 305–78).
[37] *Counter-Case of Great Britain* (*Proceedings*, vol. VIII, pp. 7–8).

before the British authorities were officially informed of the falsifications. In the context of the Russian claims to maritime jurisdiction, it read:[38]

It is much to be regretted that the advisers of the Government of the United States should have been misled in this matter by what appear to be errors of a translator or annotator of the Russian texts, which have crept into the printed translation.

The second draft, undated but evidently also printed before news of the falsifications was notified to the British team, read:[39]

It is much to be regretted that the advisers of the Government of the United States should have been misled in this and in many other instances by errors which appear to have arisen from the incompetence of the translator, or from the accidental incorporation of the comments of an annotator into the text of the translation.

The fourth draft, printed after news of the falsifications was received in London, struck a more censorious tone, though the passage below was later deleted before the final version was issued:[40]

It is much to be regretted that the advisers of the Government of the United States should have been misled in this matter by errors which it is impossible to explain away, either by alleged incompetence of the translator or from any accidental incorporation of the comments of an annotator.

V. The Legal Significance of the Falsifications

It would be possible to make an assessment of the significance to the United States argument as originally advanced in its case of each of the falsifications to be followed by an assessment of the damage caused by the withdrawal of some documents and the rectification of the translation of others. The present discussion, however, will be confined to a description of the significance of the falsifications as expressed by the parties and by contemporary commentators.

First, a flavour should be given of the sort of falsification perpetrated by Petroff. As an illustration, translations made respectively by the British official Fairholme and by Petroff of the same passage in a letter in the Russian language written on 18 July 1822 by the Russian Ministry of Finance to the Board of Administration of the Russian-American Company read as follows:[41]

Fairholme's translation

. . . to enable us to confine ourselves to exercising a control over such an extent of water only as is by common custom considered to be under the jurisdiction of any Power which has possession of the seaboard, and to introducing on the coast such a system of surveillance as may be found necessary for the protection of our territory from attack, and for the prevention of illicit trading.

[38] PRO: FO 97/544 (Preliminary Draft, p. 8).
[39] Ibid. (Second Draft, p. 10).
[40] Ibid. (Fourth Draft, p. 2).
[41] PRO: FO 5/2181 (unfoliated).

Petroff's translation

. . . we will not claim jurisdiction over coastwise waters beyond the limits accepted by any other maritime Power for the whole of our coast facing the open ocean. Over all interior waters, however, and over all waters inclosed by Russian territory, such as the Sea of Okhotsk, Bering Sea, or the Sea of Kamchatka, as well as in all gulfs, bays, and estuaries within our possessions, the right to the strictest control will always be maintained.

The general thrust of the Petroff falsifications was summarized by Foster in his memoirs published in 1909 in the following two sentences:[42]

The result of [Petroff's] labors among these archives was the production of a number of documents, the translation of which as presented by Petroff was strongly confirmatory of the alleged Russian exercise of exclusive jurisdiction in Bering Sea for the protection of seals. . . . A thorough examination resulted in the discovery that in every one of the documents seeming to sustain our contention, Petroff had designedly interpolated the language in the English translations.

Writing in 1943, Williams stated of the United States' need to revise its documentary submission in the light of the falsified translations: 'Through such amendment our position on the historical and jurisdictional questions was necessarily weakened'.[43]

Turning to the British Government's assessment of the effect of the falsifications, its counter-case concluded the Introduction to its Part I with the following paragraph:[44]

It is not possible, by a mere comparison of the correct and the erroneous translations, to form an accurate opinion of the effect of the insertion of the fictitious and interpolated passages upon the argument contained in the Case for the United States. Attention will therefore be called, in connection with each branch of the subject, to the manner in which it depends upon such interpolations and errors. When the spurious passages are expunged, and the erroneous translations corrected, it will be found that no evidence remains to support the contentions of the United States (a) that the Russian Government and the Russian-American Company claimed and exercised exclusive jurisdiction as to trading and hunting in the Behring Sea, and (b) that the Ukase of 1821 was merely declaratory of pre-existing claims which had been enforced therein for many years. The alleged pre-existing claims and their enforcement for many years, so far as they implied any extraordinary maritime jurisdiction, are merely the creations of the translator.

British counsel stressed during oral argument in Paris the significance of the falsifications in weakening the United States' argument by their withdrawal. On 12 May 1893, the Attorney-General, Sir Charles Russell QC, referred to the work of 'that very astute, but unscrupulous artist, Mr Ivan Petroff'.[45] He asserted that the Tribunal would 'see at a glance how completely and absolutely the United States have changed front upon this question since the discovery of these forgeries upon which they had based their great case of derivative title from Russia'. He went on:[46]

[42] Foster, op. cit. above (n. 11), p. 40.
[43] Williams, loc. cit. above (n. 12), p. 567.
[44] *Counter-Case of Great Britain* (*Proceedings*, vol. VIII, p. 8).
[45] *Oral Argument on behalf of Great Britain* (*Proceedings*, vol. XIII, p. 114).
[46] Ibid., p. 115.

Cut out these forgeries, and you have no reference to the fur-seals, no assertions by Russia in respect to the waters of the Behring Sea, no acts of interference asserted or suggested by Russia in that sea at all.

After Sir Charles Russell had further analysed the Petroff falsifications, the President of the Tribunal, Baron de Courcel, asked whether the United States' Secretary of State, at the relevant time Mr Blaine, had already had knowledge of the Petroff 'interpolations' when he negotiated the 1892 arbitration treaty and put forward the questions for the Tribunal to answer which became incorporated in Article VI.[47] John W. Foster, the United States Agent, replied:[48]

I will say that Mr. Blaine had no knowledge whatever of the contents of these documents. They were not known to any person in the Department, or any official of the Government of the United States, until after we began to prepare this case, when this person named by Sir Charles was called upon as an expert in the Russian language to translate them.

. . .

As to the matter of dates, they were not known until after the ratification of the Treaty, April 9, 1892.

. . .

It is not a matter of supposition. It is a fact that Mr. Blaine did not know what were the contents of the documents now under discussion.

Sir Charles Russell did not go so far as to express doubt on Foster's explanation, but he still considered that Blaine must have had 'some idea that there were in existence documents which would support the statements that there were acts of assertion by Russia which could be relied upon'. He then pointed out the fact that the United States had withdrawn the forged documents and presented new translations but had not altered the case as it was originally presented. Lord Hannen here tried to express the point which he thought Russell was making: 'Taking out the interpolated passages there does not remain the foundation for the claim of a derivative title from Russia?' Sir Charles Russell replied: 'That is it'.[49]

When the argument resumed on 16 May 1893, Sir Charles Russell observed that his mention of the falsifications had caused irritation to the other side. He continued:[50]

I wish our position in that regard to be made quite clear to the Tribunal. We do not in the least suggest, and have never suggested, that those who represent the interests of the United States were in any way blameworthy in that matter; they were simply deceived; and we accept, as I think I said before, implicitly the statement of General Foster, that when Mr. Blaine was conducting his diplomatic correspondence he was not aware of these Russian documents. But we thought it necessary, and we still think it necessary, to call attention to that fact in order to show that, according to our view, the case—the substantial case—originally presented on the part of the United States was a case of

[47] Although the President's transcribed remarks might suggest that he envisaged the possibility that Blaine knew of Petroff's falsifications at the relevant time, the context indicates that he was asking whether Blaine at the relevant time had Petroff's translations to hand.

[48] *Proceedings*, vol. XIII, pp. 117–18, *passim*.

[49] Ibid., p. 119.

[50] Ibid., p. 120.

territorial jurisdiction in Behring Sea, territorial dominion in Behring Sea; and that once these falsified documents are expunged the whole of that question depends upon the construction of the Ukase of 1821, the action following on that Ukase, and upon the construction of the Treaties of 1824 and 1825. We feel it necessary to call attention to those falsifications and to suggest—we may be right or we may be wrong, but it is the view we submit on this matter—that it is the discovery of these falsifications by which the representatives of the United States were deceived which has led to their change of front;—namely, the change, on which I have already dwelt at such length, by which the question of derivative title under Russia, the question of territorial dominion exercised by Russia, has receded into the background to make room for the different case now presented.

In its award of 15 August 1893, which upheld the British contentions, the Tribunal made no reference to the false translations.[51]

Turning to secondary sources, Professor John Bassett Moore, of Columbia University, in his classic work of analysis *History and Digest of the International Arbitrations to which the United States has been a Party*, gave some illustrations of the magnitude of Petroff's falsifications. For the sake of brevity, only one of them will be cited here:[52]

. . . on the 21st of July 1824, a special committee, consisting of Count Nesselrode and other dignitaries of the empire, made a report in response to an application of the directors of the Russian-American Company for an interpretation of the treaty concluded between Russia and the United States in that year. By the Petroff translation the report was made to say that 'the sovereignty of Russia over the shores of Siberia and America, as well as over the Aleutian Islands and the intervening sea, has long since been acknowledged by all the powers', and consequently that 'these coasts, islands and seas' could not have been referred to in the convention. By the correct translation it appears that the passage referred only to 'the coasts of Siberia and the Aleutian Islands', and did not mention either the coasts of America or 'the intervening sea.'

Moore concluded:[53]

Without giving other illustrations of the effect of the false translations it may in a word be stated that their detection and withdrawal removed practically the only evidence from destinctively [*sic*] Russian sources, apart from the ukase of 1821, of the assertion by Russia of any exceptional jurisdiction in Behring Sea.

Writing shortly after the conclusion of the arbitration, the legal *savant* Thomas Barclay noted that '[p]ar suite de procédés inconnus jusqu'alors dans les documents de chancelleries, les seuls textes importants relatifs à la question américaine avaient été l'objet d'interpolations'.[54] Referring to the translation of a Russian report of 21 July 1824 he noted that 'interpolations américaines' had been made. He went on:[55]

Ce fut ce document qui vraisemblablement suggéra l'idée que les Etats-Unis pouvaient soutenir que la Russie n'avait jamais renoncé à son droit de juridiction, qu'elle avait affirmée dans l'ukase de 1821.

Il convient de dire, à la décharge du gouvernement des Etats-Unis, que le gouverne-

[51] See, e.g., *American Journal of International Law*, 6 (1912), p. 233.

[52] Moore, Vol. I (1898), at pp. 814–15.

[53] Ibid., p. 815.

[54] 'La question des pêcheries dans la mer de Behring', *Revue de droit international et de législation comparée*, 25 (1893), p. 417, at p. 436.

[55] Ibid., p. 437.

ment de Washington remarqua l'interpolation bien avant l'arrivée de la protestation du *Foreign Office* britannique.

VI. Conclusion

As William Williams observed, 'a fraud of the first order' was practised on the United States Government by Petroff's falsifications.[56] It was a fraud which had a debilitating effect on the United States argument since, shorn of Petroff's interpolations, the Russian material did not support a claim to regard the Behring Sea as a *mare clausum*. Consequently, the United States had to fall back on its alternative argument of extra-territorial jurisdiction over seals based on 'property' in them. To this day, no authentic explanation of why Petroff behaved as he did has come to light. His written 'confession' gave no clue. Foster later wrote: 'Before [Petroff] began his labors I had explained to him the character of our contention, and it is supposed he made the interpolations in order that I might be the better pleased with his work'.[57] Thus before he started his translations Petroff knew the thrust of what the United States wanted to argue and therefore could deduce what at best it hoped to find in the Russian documents. But the falsifications were astutely made in the context of the dispute and were of the kind which would require familiarity with the techniques of international negotiations and to some extent with international law, knowledge of which would not normally be possessed by a census clerk. Possibly further research might uncover what became of Petroff. Over 60 years old at the time of the affair according to the *Washington Post*,[58] did he live out the rest of his life in ignominious poverty, or, being of what the newspaper described as an 'adventurous spirit', did he start a discreet new life of affluence funded by a secret paymaster?

[56] Williams, loc. cit. above (n. 12), p. 567.
[57] Foster, op. cit. above (n. 11), p. 41.
[58] Issue of 13 November 1892.

REVIEWS OF BOOKS

International Law, the International Court of Justice and Nuclear Weapons. Edited by LAURENCE BOISSON DE CHAZOURNES and PHILIPPE SANDS. Cambridge: Cambridge University Press, 1999. xxii + 592 pp. + annexes + index. Hardback, £60; paperback, £24.95.

The book under review is the definitive work on the two advisory opinions of the International Court of Justice of 8 July 1996 (*Legality of the Threat or Use of Nuclear Weapons*—request by the General Assembly; and the *Legality of the Use by a State of Nuclear Weapons in Armed Conflict*—request by the World Health Organisation). The myriad of issues related to and arising from the threat of use or use of nuclear weapons is mirrored by the number of essays contained in the book. The legal problems connected with nuclear weapons were linked to several issues, procedural and substantive, of a general nature, such as the Court's advisory function; the sources of international law and the link between them; the competence of international organizations; the question of *non liquet*. The essays often refer to previous jurisprudence of the World Court (or even treat it as the main subject), e.g. the *Lotus* case and its relationship with the advisory opinion in question.

The book consists of 30 essays written by specialists in different areas of international law: humanitarian law; environmental law; theory of law; the law of international organizations. Unfortunately, it is impossible to assess all the essays. The review will therefore focus on the main issues, procedural and substantive, raised. As to the procedural aspects, the essays on the law relating to international organizations provide an interesting analysis of the so-called principle of speciality (which formed the heart of the matter in the Court's answer to the WHO request), closely related to a general problem of their functions. This principle mainly concerns interpretation of the words in Article 96, paragraph 2, of the United Nations Charter 'arising within the scope of their activities'. Referring to the advisory opinion in the *Jurisdiction of the European Commission of the Danube* (1927), the Court noted that an international organization has only the powers invested in it by the Member States (G. Griffith and C. Staker, 'The Jurisdiction and Merits Phases Distinguished'; P. Klein, 'Quelques réflexions sur le principe de specialité et la "politisation" des institutions specialisées'; M. Bothe, 'The WHO Request', V. Leary, 'The WHO Case: Implications for Specialised Agencies'; E. Lauterpacht, 'Judicial Review of the Acts of International Organisations').

Especially interesting is the essay of Klein who assesses the findings of the Court in the light of the functionalist theory which is based on an assumption that political questions should not be dealt with by specialized agencies. The request of the WHO generated other interesting problems of general international law, such as interpretation of the constitutions creating international organizations. Leary, for example, criticizes the ICJ for relying on traditional means of interpretation in relation to the Constitution of the WHO and missing the opportunity of the application of other, and, in the view of this author, more suitable, means of interpretation, such as 'dynamic-revolutionary' or teleological methods (p. 117). It has to be said, however, that both approaches are controversial and not at all accepted as the basic methods of interpretation. It would have been of benefit to this interesting submission if the author had substantiated her views in greater detail. The Court assessed the functional aspect of speciality in the light of the *ultra vires* doctrine. In relation to this aspect, the Court took the position as to the WHO request that procedural propriety and the doctrine of *ultra vires* are two separate questions.

There are two interesting aspects of the WHO request which were not raised by any of the authors: one is whether, if there were an obligation owed to the WHO by Member States, under its Constitution, which would be violated by the use of nuclear weapons, the request of the WHO would be within its competence in these circumstances; and if that were the case, how the Court should approach the issue regarding whether the matters concern obligations under the WHO Convention. These problems were raised elsewhere in a stimulating article of C. F. Amerasinghe[1] and as well analysed in Judge Shahabudeen's opinion. The reasoning of the Court denying the request for an advisory opinion of the WHO is described by Bothe as 'formalistic, oversimplistic, cynical and even logically flawed' (p. 104). To illustrate the mystery surrounding the legal nature of requests for advisory opinions and their controversial character, the same decision of the ICJ received a positive assessment in the article by C. F. Amerasinghe, who wrote that '[t]he Court regarded the issue of competence of the WHO as a matter of constitutional interpretation, which cannot be faulted'.[2]

The substantive problems relating to the use or threat of use of nuclear weapons concern a great variety of aspects, such as, e.g., *jus ad bellum* and *jus ad bello* (essays of C. Greenwood and R. Mullerson, and J. Gardam); environmental law (E. Brown-Weiss and D. Momtaz); the right to life and genocide (V. Gowlland-Debbas); humanitarian law (L. Condorelli), neutrality (C. Dominicé); the problem of *jus cogens* and nuclear weapons (J. Werksamn and R. Kalastchi); the status of nuclear weapons in the light of the Court's opinion (E. David). The findings of the Court in this case were a subject of much criticism. The question, however, arises whether that criticism is fully justified. Being mindful of the fact that the Court had undertaken to deal with the problem at all (which in itself is a controversial issue), in the view of the present author, we have to agree with David that the Court's findings contain many positive aspects which have a lasting value, such as, most importantly, that there is a general rule of illegality of the use or threat of use of nuclear weapons.

Greenwood supports the view that the Court made a very important contribution to the crystallization of the relationship of *jus ad bellum* and *jus in bello*. He rightly points out several important aspects of the Court's decision, such as that the use of nuclear weapons is subject to the *jus in bello*, and the rejection of the arguments that specific *lex specialis* which have been developed over the long period of time to be used in the conduct of hostilities 'can be circumvented by reference to general provision of environmental or human rights law' (p. 265). This approach of the Court is, however, not applauded by Brown-Weiss, who states: '[m]ost regrettably in this context, it [the opinion] does not refer to the environment'. By including explicit reference to the environment, it would have taken an important step in . . . ensuring the integration of environmental considerations in implementing international law related to armed conflicts' (pp. 348–9).

In the view of the present reviewer (in agreement with Greenwood), the Court took the right approach to the problems of the applicability of the environmental law in the case of armed conflict. The Court mentioned the environmental concerns to be taken into consideration in these circumstances. Apart from the few well-established general norms (such as Principle 21 of the 1972 Stockholm Declaration), the main body of rules of environmental law is still very much in the making—it is mostly based on treaty law—with customary law playing only the secondary role. This is one of the reasons why the Court has been traditionally (and consistently) cautious in its approach to environmental

[1] C. F. Amerasinghe, 'The Advisory Opinion of the International Court of Justice in the WHO Nuclear Weapons Case: A Critique', *Leiden Journal of International Law*, 10, (1997), no. 3, pp. 525–39.

[2] Ibid., p. 534.

matters. This was evidenced by the *Gabčíkovo-Nagymaros Project (Hungary* v *Slovakia)* case of 25 September 1997. Although Brown-Weiss is right in stating that the Court in this case gave consideration to environmental matters, at the same time, the Court has proved to be a staunch supporter of the *pacta sunt servanda* rule, notwithstanding convincing pleadings of Hungary to justify the termination of the treaty in question on the basis of environmental concerns.[3]

Mention must be made of the very interesting essay concerning the relationship between the norms *jus cogens* and nuclear weapons. The authors of the essay submit an original argument that since the threat or use of nuclear weapons is governed by the principles of international humanitarian law which themselves are widely accepted as norms of *jus cogens* nature, the Court could have relied on this concept to further limit or prohibit their use (p. 184). The essay presents an in-depth study of the character of rules of *jus cogens* giving an extensive overview of relevant doctrine and of the work of the International Law Commission.

The third part of the book approaches the problem of nuclear weapons and the limited role of the Court in a wider, extra-legal context such as that of politics (D. Kennedy; M. Reisman and J.-P. Dupuy); and justice and fairness (M. Koskenniemi and T. Franck). This part of the book represents a very personal and subjective assessment, not altogether very uplifting, of the limitations of both international law and the Court. The authors of the essays, however, show a very realistic approach to the inherent problems relating to international justice and the role of the Court, illustrated by the words of Koskenniemi: '[s]o whatever the reason for the Court's silence, it was a beneficial silence inasmuch as it could only leave room for the workings of the moral impulse, the a-rational, non-foundational appeal against the killing of the innocent' (pp. 497–8). Similarly Franck, fully aware of the limitations of the Court and the (perhaps) too high expectations of States as to the Court's findings, states: '[t]he result, uncannily, was almost universally welcomed. It tended to be welcomed as Solomonic by governments with and without nuclear weapons and by the NGOs that had sparked the request' (p. 519).

In conclusion, the book under review is a most comprehensive study of the advisory opinion in question. It offers an overview of the substantive and procedural aspects of the problem of the threat or use of the nuclear weapons itself, and insight into the legal issues concerning the role of advisory opinions in general and the role of the Court. It will satisfy lawyers and non-lawyers, since the focus is not only on law but also on the issues of morality and justice.

M. FITZMAURICE

A Guide to the Human Rights Act 1998. By PAROSHA CHANDRAN. London: Butterworths, 1999. xv + 174 pp. £22.

The entry into force of the Human Rights Act 1998 on 2 October 2000 has been preceded by a fanfare of publicity in the media. The significant impact that the Act will have has been explored extensively in a vast outpouring in both the specialist and general academic literature. All the major publishers have produced guides to the Act and expositions of how the Act will affect particular branches of the law. The Judicial Studies Board has embarked on an ambitious programme to train all levels of the judiciary in the

[3] There is a plethora of articles on this subject. To mention a few: A. E. Boyle, 'The Gabčíkovo-Nagymaros Case: New Law in Old Bottles', *Yearbook of International Environmental Law*, 8 (1997), pp. 13–21; J. Klabbers, 'The Substance of Form: The Case Concerning the *Gabčíkovo-Nagymaros Project*, Environmental Law and the Law of Treaties', ibid., pp. 32–41; J. Lammers, 'The Gabčíkovo-Nagymaros Case Seen in Particular from the Perspective of the Law of International Watercourses and the Protection of the Environment', *Leiden Journal of International Law*, 8 (1998), pp. 287–321; M. Fitzmaurice, 'The Gabčíkovo-Nagymaros Case: The Law of Treaties', ibid., pp. 321–45.

effects of the Act. Legal practitioners will have to familiarize themselves with the case law of the European Convention on Human Rights. The House of Lords in several important decisions such as *Reynolds* v *Times Newspapers Ltd.* and *Ex parte Kebilene* has already begun to appreciate the significance of the Act. Seldom can an Act have received such massive attention before it has entered into force. Yet it is still clear that a large number of private and voluntary organizations fulfilling public functions are either unaware of the Act or their obligations under it.

This is the background against which Parosha Chandran's book should be evaluated. At the outset, it must be appreciated that the purpose of the book is to provide a 'simple' guide to the Act. The book is 'not intended to be a full exposition or analysis of the new law, but is instead intended as a guide to assist those who seek to make light of the significance of the Act's provisions', in the words of the author. The scheme of the guide is very straightforward. Two initial chapters provide an introduction to and explain the purpose of the Act. There follow seventeen further chapters dealing with each section of the legislation in turn. This is followed by three appendices taking in the text of the Act, the text of the European Convention (as amended by Protocol No. 11) and Protocols Nos. 1, 4, 6 and 7 and the Rules of Court of the Strasbourg Court.

There is much to commend in this guide. There has been much loose thinking about the effect of the Act. It is often stated that the European Convention will be incorporated into our law. However, as Chandran observes correctly the purpose of the Act is 'to give further effect' to rights and freedoms guaranteed under the Convention. This is illustrated vividly by an extract from *Hansard* in which the Lord Chancellor states: 'I have to make this point absolutely plain. The European Convention on Human Rights under this Bill is not made part of our law.' Thus, it is clear that the Act does not import full incorporation. The vertical or horizontal effect of the Act is discussed usefully but without any great depth of analysis. The omission of Article 13 (the right to an effective remedy before a national authority) is highlighted and the real reason therefor—'the effect on the public purse' (Jack Straw)—is revealingly exhibited by way of another extract from *Hansard*. The key requirement of section 2(1) that a court or tribunal determining a question which has arisen in connection with a Convention right *must take into account* the jurisprudence of the Strasbourg organs is analysed carefully. The interpretive obligation under section 3(1), particularly the 'so far as it is possible to do so' clause, will, of course, require a rather different approach to statutory interpretation than hitherto, as commented on by many observers. As Lord Irvine remarked in the debates: '[t]he Convention rights are the magnetic north and the needle of judicial interpretation will swing towards them'. Chandran makes the valuable point that the obligation in section 3(1) is not confined to courts or tribunals and may include any body which has the authority to read and give effect to legislation.

A large number of other important features, of which the following is only a small sample, are discussed: declarations of incompatibility; acts of public authorities (there is bound to develop considerable jurisprudence of what constitutes a public authority, and Chandran makes a number of suggestions in line with *Hansard* extracts), and raising Convention rights in legal proceedings (in which Chandran explores the relevance of the Act in proceedings between private individuals). The notion of the 'victim' inherent in section 7 is addressed and the effect of the 'victim' test on judicial review proceedings discussed. Unfortunately, there is no discussion of the Strasbourg case law on this issue, apart from the plea that legal practitioners should familiarize themselves with it!

Chandran's book relies very heavily on extracts from *Hansard* as an explanation to sections of the Act. Indeed, in her preface, she refers to 'staying in with *Hansard*'. This is both a strength and a weakness. *Hansard* is, of course, an invaluable aid to the meaning of various sections and, as such, the extracts extrapolated by Chandran illustrate her points graphically. However, it is not a substitute for analysis of pre-existing domestic or Strasbourg law for a critical assessment of the Act's impact. Chandran's treatment is largely explanatory. Accordingly, it is a 'simple' guide: the intricacies of the concept of the 'margin of appreciation' (including the propriety of its application in domestic law), the notion of the victim and the horizontal effects of the Act are not explored in any great depth or detail. However, as a straightforward guide it is successful. Whether it is better than any of the other guides will depend largely on individual taste.

P. R. GHANDHI

The Law of the Sea. By ROBIN CHURCHILL and VAUGHAN LOWE. 3rd edition. Manchester: Manchester University Press, 1999. xlix + 494 pp. £29.99.

The eleven years that have passed since the previous edition of this classic work have been an eventful time with regard to the law of the sea. The new edition of Churchill and Lowe draws these developments together and hones them into an elegant and accessible narrative and exposition that is replete with analytical insight. The structure of the work remains unaltered. After an historical introduction, a series of succinct chapters looks at the basic building blocks of the subject: baselines, internal waters, the territorial sea, straits, archipelagoes, the contiguous zone, the continental shelf, the EEZ, delimitation of maritime boundaries, the high seas, and the international seabed area. The remaining chapters deal with a number of thematic issues that cut across jurisdictional categories, these being navigation, fishing, pollution, marine scientific research, military uses, and the position of landlocked and geographically disadvantaged States. The final chapter looks at dispute settlement.

As would be expected, the text is thoroughly updated to take account of the many significant developments that have taken place in recent years. The consequences of the entry into force of the Law of the Sea Convention in 1994 naturally pervade the new text. Major changes are found in the chapters dealing with fishing and pollution control, which have been expanded considerably to take account of the plethora of new conventions addressing these questions, and the chapter on maritime delimitation, which has been extensively recast in the light of the *Denmark* v. *Norway* case of 1993 and other developments. The chapters on the international seabed area and the settlement of disputes have also been significantly developed to take account of the amendments to the former and the breathing of life into the latter (although the merits judgment in the *M/V Saiga* case came too late for inclusion). The chapters dealing with the high seas and navigation are also considerably expanded to include a more detailed coverage of IMO Conventions and activities.

There is, however, much more than mere updating (vital though that is) to this new edition. All of the text has been extensively reworked, adding greater clarity in some places and more fulsome explanations in others. In particular, the examination of maritime delimitations is a significant improvement on the previous edition. Although the authors rightly stress the difficulty of offering 'any precise account of the principles of delimitation' (p. 182), they nevertheless offer some concrete propositions reflecting the essence of recent developments. Moreover, it seems as if the authors have shifted their overall perspective somewhat. The significance of environmental concerns is stressed at many points and, at a more general level, the expanded introduction tends to portray the subject upon a broader canvas than the rather rigidly positivist picture presented previously. There is also a less bullish approach to the economic advantages to be had from deep seabed mining and, perhaps, less scepticism concerning the overall impact of the EEZ. There is in consequence a greater richness and subtlety to the whole.

Despite the widespread adherence to the 1982 Convention, the authors continue to examine carefully the extent to which various Convention provisions reflect customary international law and their conclusions, firmly rooted in careful examinations of State practice, are, on the whole, cautious. Thus they still remain hesitant to claim customary status for Article 19 concerning innocent passage (p. 87) and for the regime of transit passage (p. 113, although they recognize that rights akin to this now exist in certain straits). Given the paucity of State practice, they also conclude that the extensive jurisdictional competence granted to coastal and port States with regard to environmental regulation has not passed into custom (p. 353). On the other hand, the authors note that the provisions of Article 76, concerning the outer limit of the continental shelf, have been widely adopted in State practice and, although they still fall somewhat short of a ringing endorsement of its customary status, conclude that 'it would be difficult to argue that any . . . claim consistent with Article 76 was not compatible with customary international law' (p. 150). They also conclude that, despite some disparity in State practice, the archipelagic regime is reflected in custom (pp. 129–30).

This work will be warmly welcomed by teachers, students, practitioners, and researchers. The text is now more 'user friendly', with a greater use of subheadings, and footnotes are placed where they should be found, at the foot of the page rather than at the end of each chapter. The authors' interpretation of their self-denying ordinance restricting the overall number of footnotes seems to have been relaxed somewhat and this too is welcome. As before, each chapter is followed with extensive suggestions for further reading and these provide an excellent starting-point for those wishing to proceed further. It is difficult to believe that it would be possible to produce a better book of this length on the law of the sea. This new edition of Churchill and Lowe provides the ideal introduction—and more—into this vast and complex subject.

MALCOLM D. EVANS

The Settlement of Disputes in International Law. Institutions and Procedures. By JOHN COLLIER and VAUGHAN LOWE. Oxford: Oxford University Press, 1999. xxviii + 395 pp. £75.

International relations used to be so simple. If you had a dispute, you could huff, puff or send round a gun boat and sort the thing out. Unless, of course, you were one of those countries with a glorious history of losing nearly every conflict they have fought. Nowadays, life is simultaneously more complex and, on the whole, fairer. The use of force is excluded as a means of settling disputes and smaller States can live more easily with the big boys. Complexity has arisen, though, from the sheer volume of inter-State activity and the expanding standing of non-States in the international sphere.

Collier and Lowe accurately and most usefully reflect this state of affairs. Their book is one element in a quite rapidly expanding body of work on the subject. In the English language alone there has been the recent publication of the third edition of Merrills' *International Dispute Settlement* (reviewed below) as well as enough journal articles to keep any legal adviser far too busy to contemplate the merits of using force. With this book, the devil is in the detail, the comprehensive and authoritative treatment not just of the institutions but also the procedure of the arbitral process. Indeed, one of the most useful features is the very lucid distinction made between admissibility and jurisdiction at the beginning of Part Two. Collier and Lowe has at least two functions. It can be read as a monograph, but is sufficiently clearly laid out to function also as a primary reference work on the main institutions and techniques of dispute settlement. The very detailed footnoting augments this role by offering plenty of relevant further, and more subject-specific, reading.

The first chapter is compelling for the exposition of the authors' concept of the role of international law in the settlement of disputes. They demonstrate acute realism in stressing that recourse to law is only one option in solving many disputes, and frequently not even the most appropriate. Law, for them, serves to manage rather than suppress conflicts, but even when attempts to address a dispute avoid reliance on the legal merits, we all know that it is lurking in the background if necessary, an *eminence grise juridique*.

This chapter is therefore crucial in placing the exposition of the institutions and procedure in perspective.

What then follows is an impressive account of practice in the whole field of dispute settlement followed by another 100 pages of the most significant primary materials. There is even a chapter on dispute settlement in the law of the sea including the International Tribunal at Hamburg. This is reasonably short since, when this book was written, the Tribunal had only considered one matter, giving rise to the legitimate query: it is all very well being a judge on the Law of the Sea Tribunal, but what do they *actually do*? In the meantime, of course, they have considered the *Southern Bluefin Tuna* dispute and shown that they may well contribute effectively to the settlement of some types of dispute (although the incoherent manner in which the ruling was expressed does little for the wider appreciation of the Tribunal's contribution).

The ICJ is discussed in some detail yet, perhaps consistently with the authors' concept of international law as but one means of working out problems—and not always the best one—it is in there in at the end of the section on institutions. This is fair enough, though rather hard to take when one has been brought up on international law as providing a coherent foundation for international relations—a notion to which Collier and Lowe themselves subscribe (p. 2), with the ICJ being at the centre of that process (albeit one which has to co-exist with frequent diversions from that centre). But perhaps the authors are right: the ICJ's role in the settlement of disputes has been rather limited, whatever impact its decisions and advisory opinions have had on the development of principles and rules of international law. The book's treatment of the Court emphasizes this fact.

Part Two covers procedure: what actually happens—or does not happen, as the various grounds for challenging admissibility or objecting to jurisdiction make clear. The detailed analysis and descriptions make it plain that options for using law to solve problems these days, however plentiful, remain seriously circumscribed by the need for consent. This section of the book is very strong, its chief merit perhaps being the way the procedures of the disparate bodies, discussed discretely as institutions in the first part, are discussed so as to offer a comparative treatment of how the whole process actually works.

Finally, the footnotes: the extensive reference to websites is very helpful, particularly for those with limited access to primary materials. In this respect the book is surely in line with the trend for increasing reliance on electronic resources. Perhaps less necessary was the practice of repeating whole references even within chapters, rather than referring to the first footnote containing a particular item—hardly a major criticism of a book which excellently fulfils (in subject-matter) and exceeds (in performance) the authors' 'modest aim of introducing readers to some of the main processes for the settlement of international disputes'.

RYSZARD PIOTROWICZ

Droit de la délimitation maritime: commentaire de quelques décisions plutoniennes. By GILLES DESPEUX. Frankfurt: Peter Lang GmbH, 2000. 181 pp. DM 69.

The analysis of maritime boundary delimitation in general, and the delimitation of continental shelves, EEZs, and single maritime boundaries in particular, has tended to revolve around a relatively compact canon comprising decisions of the International Court of Justice and of a select number of *ad hoc* arbitral tribunals. The focus on the former is hardly surprising, but the reason why some of the latter attain a prominence denied to others is a more mysterious business. As its subtitle suggests, this book seeks to explore some of the decisions which have not acquired canonical status: decisions which are currently lost to the 'underworld' of delimitation and which deserve to be restored to the light. It should be said at the outset that the reason why this volume has set out to rescue so limited a range of candidates is in itself obscure, but it must be accepted that the line has to be drawn somewhere and this volume provides quite enough material to reflect upon for the time being.

The first chapter looks at the 1981 *Dubai/Sharjah* arbitration. As the author points out, if this decision has been bypassed it is because it was not until 1993 that it was officially made public and so it could hardly have played much role in the evolution of the subject. Despite this, it was known of in certain circles and its approach was substantially in line with the then current practice in that it blended together trends in conventional and customary law thinking and reflected this in the use of an equidistance line modified in the light of pertinent factors (relevant or special circumstances). The author particularly approves of the twelve-mile partial enclave given to the island of Abu Musa. The second chapter examines the *Beagle Channel* arbitration of 1977, the delimitation aspects of which were dealt with in the award in the most economical fashion. The author teases out the lessons and implications of this award with subtlety and skill, noting in particular the manner in which navigational interests justified the alteration of the equidistance line and the way in which islands and similar features were handled.

The third chapter turns to what the author describes as the 'ten commandments' of the US federal government. This complex chapter surveys ten decisions of US federal organs: five judgments of the Supreme Court in disputes concerning the course of inter-State boundaries dividing internal waters and the first three miles of territorial sea (over which the State and therefore the Supreme Court has jurisdiction) and five administrative decisions given by the Commission operating under the Coastal Energy Impact Programme to determine the seawards areas in respect of which the States were entitled to federal financial assistance to alleviate the burdens of offshore development, these areas still being under federal jurisdiction. The Supreme Court decisions are in the public domain but the administrative decisions are not published and are known from the writings of those involved in making them. This chapter presents an admirable summation of disparate and difficult material, drawing out the essential elements of the various decisions, the emphasis being on those aspects which contribute to the more general aspects of boundary delimitation. Thus those decisions which focus on historic title receive comparatively short shrift whilst the 1990 Supreme Court judgment in *Georgia and South Carolina* is considered in much greater detail and is the subject of some criticism, particularly for its apparent endorsement of the theory of coastal front projection. As regards the decisions taken for the purposes of the CEIP, the equidistance-special circumstances approach was adopted, albeit for a variety of reasons, and the various special circumstances advanced are considered, as is the manner in which the provisional equidistance line was modified to give effect to them. It is refreshing to be reminded that in two of the five decisions it was concluded that there was no reason to depart from a strict equidistance line—perhaps others will note that it is possible to exercise such restraint!

The final chapter is a rather cursory consideration of the report of the Iraq–Kuwait Boundary Commission which highlights the manner in which low-tide elevations were dealt with and how the three disparate sections of the line were connected together, this being contrasted with the manner in which a similar problem was handled in the US context.

As will by now be obvious, the decisions surveyed are, on the whole, tolerably well known (at least in outline) and so what we have is a book that delves into the apocrypha of delimitation rather than a book that reveals a lost or forgotten world. This is not just a quibble over an analogy. Given that the bulk of these decisions are not unknown to commentators, in order to fulfil its task properly the work should be indicating the place that those decisions ought to be taking in the exposition of the subject and showing how they add to our understanding of the law of maritime delimitation. As it is, the work tends to limit itself to a presentation of the decisions, explaining the background to them, highlighting and commenting upon their essential elements. Since almost all of the decisions in question have been the subject of a full presentation and authoritative analysis elsewhere (often by those intimately involved in their making), the initial impression is that the work as a whole fails in its task since the case for their collective significance remains to be made out. This, however, would be unfair. It is worth recalling that these decisions, even if not unknown, are not all well known and it is certainly very useful to have a commentary of this nature which draws them together in a convenient and accessible fashion. Moreover, the text is replete with well-conceived observations and thoughtful analysis and represents a useful contribution to the study of many of these decisions in their own right. And if the work itself fails to draw these decisions into the mainstream of study, it certainly succeeds in making the case for that task to be undertaken. To revert to the author's analogy, his descent into the underworld, like that of Orpheus before him, may not have released his Eurydice, but it has at the very least served to perpetuate the remembrance—and his goal may even yet be achieved.

MALCOLM D. EVANS

International Law and Infectious Diseases. By DAVID P. FIDLER. Oxford: Clarendon Press, 1999. xlvii + 364 pp. £60.

In this book Fidler has made a significant contribution towards producing a framework which uses the processes of international law and techniques developed by the international community to combat and prevent the spread of infectious diseases. This is an area of international law which hitherto has been very poorly represented in the literature. David Fidler is uniquely qualified to push forward the frontiers in this area as he has already written extensively on the subject. It is clear that he enjoys a remarkable grasp and has the ability to bring the framework of international law to bear. This is an area of immense practical significance in which theoretical underpinnings have not previously been exposed in a comprehensive manner. Although some of the material here has been published before as various journal articles—portions of chapters 1, 3 and 10 and an earlier version of chapter 7—this does not in any way detract from the importance of the work.

This book seeks to deal with the significant international issues arising out of our attempt to control the spread of infectious diseases and is divided into ten chapters. Chapter 1 provides a detailed analysis of why infectious diseases are now at the forefront of global public health concerns and connects this to the 'globalisation of public health'. This highlights the importance of international law principles to fight the spread of infectious diseases. In this chapter, Professor Fidler introduces us to the concept of '*microbialpolitik*', by which he means 'the international politics generated by human attempts to control infectious diseases'. He seeks throughout the book to examine the international politics that infectious diseases create. The international law examined is conditioned by this '*microbialpolitik*', which provides the political framework into which the law on infectious diseases fits. Chapter 2 provides a fascinating account of the history of international attempts to control the spread of infectious diseases from the mid-nineteenth century until the creation of the World Health Organization (WHO). Chapter 3 details and analyses the International Health Regulations (IHR) promulgated by the WHO. The history of the IHR in the setting of the WHO Constitution is examined, as are the present efforts to revise them in the light of emerging or re-emerging infectious diseases.

Chapter 4 explores the sources of international law in the context of the international mechanisms available to the global community to control infectious diseases. The study reveals an interesting and well-balanced survey of the primary sources in this regard: treaties, custom, and general principles of international law, the latter of which Fidler characterizes as 'badly suited as a source for international law on infectious disease control because their utility falls outside the public health context while their theoretical potential in this context is limited'. Subsidiary means for determination of rules of law—

judicial decisions and the writings of publicists—are also considered, in line with Article 38(1)(d) of the Statute of the ICJ. These are said not to have 'had any impact on relevant international law'. There is also a short excursus on sources of international law outside Article 38(1) in which equity and considerations of morality and humanity—which are particularly relevant in the context of the human suffering infectious diseases cause—are examined briefly, and the notion of 'soft' law related to the WHO processes on global public health is discussed. A slight criticism of this chapter is the lack of sophistication in the analysis of the sources of international law, which may well be justifiable in the context of this specific application. There also seems to be an over-dependence on two particular authorities—Brownlie and Oppenheim—with no real indication of the wealth of differing views and, accordingly, the subtle intricacies that may arise in this area.

Chapters 5, 6, 7 and 8 examine specific areas of international law in which infectious diseases cause concerns and problems—international trade, human rights, armed conflict and environmental protection. Chapter 6, which perhaps the reviewer may be permitted to single out for particular praise, is a very interesting account of how and when infectious disease control measures impinge on an individual's human rights by way of limitations imposed by public health measures, issues relating to the 'right to health' and human rights problems connected to HIV/AIDS. Professor Fidler traces the human rights implications from a historical perspective, taking into account the various human rights treaty regimes emerging in the aftermath of World War II, including international and regional instruments such as the ECHR and ACHR. The landmark decision of the ECHR in *D* v. *UK* is given prominence and the extension of the Court's Article 3 jurisprudence delineated succinctly. This decision is clearly of huge importance for the rights of individuals suffering from AIDS and facing deportation. By holding that the deportation of the applicant to St Kitts (his home State) would breach Article 3 on the ground that deporting D in his late stage of AIDS to a developing country where general public health conditions were bad and where access to AIDS treatment would not be possible and as such would constitute 'inhuman' treatment, the case is a significant step forward in human rights jurisprudence.

A number of other interferences with the rights of individuals under the jurisprudence of the Strasbourg institutions are also delineated. Whether these treaty-based restrictions on human liberty also form part of customary international law is an interesting point: the author concludes that 'customary international law mirrors the treaty rules powerfully'. In the section on the 'right to health', the question is posed as to whether D's deportation would have meant the UK Government had violated D's 'right to health'. Although the ECHR does not protect the 'right to health', the author suggests there is some reasoning in the ECHR's decision to support such a view, but wisely counsels caution because of the 'very exceptional circumstances' of the case. The chapter concludes with an extremely interesting appraisal of HIV/AIDS issues in the context of both civil and political rights and economic, social, and cultural rights and a section on '*microbialpolitik*'. The only pity is that more attention is not paid to the hugely important decision of the Human Rights Committee in this context in the *Toonen* case, which is only briefly referred to. The detailed reasoning of the Committee would have repaid a more thorough analysis.

The penultimate chapter returns to the theme of '*microbialpolitik*' with sections on '*microbialpolitik*' and international law, '*microbialpolitik*' and international relations theory and a final section on global health jurisprudence. The appendix contains a carefully drafted proposal for a World Health Organization Framework Convention on Global Infectious Disease Prevention and Control.

This monograph provides a unique account of the international law on infectious diseases. It is a long-awaited and significant addition to the literature on international law. Professor Fidler has produced an elegant text which displays his unrivalled knowledge in the field. It deserves to be read by all those seeking an understanding of this subject.

P. R. GHANDHI

Insolvency in Private International Law: National and International Approaches. By IAN F. FLETCHER. Oxford: Clarendon Press, 1999. xxlii + 465 pp., including bibliography and index. £75.

In his characteristically elegant style, Fletcher provides in this monograph a comprehensive, systematic, and critical analysis of the complex subject of cross-border insolvencies in private international law. The work, intended for practitioners dealing with problems engendered both by individual bankruptcy and by corporate insolvency, as well as for legislators, academics, and postgraduates seeking information and critical comment on the state of private international law in relation to transnational commercial transactions, will provide an invaluable source of detailed information as well as stimulating insight into the problems faced, or that may be faced, by legislators and judges alike.

Part 1 of the book examines national approaches to problems of cross-border insolvency. It is not designed to cover aspects of private international law in a multitude of States; rather, the focus of the book is on the law and practice in England and Wales with selected examples of comparable practice from other jurisdictions. It is understandable, if somewhat unfortunate, that Fletcher has chosen to draw examples only from Commonwealth jurisdictions and from the USA and has singularly avoided reference, apart from a very few instances, to civil law jurisdictions. A systematic approach is adopted, focusing on jurisdictional issues in relation to bankruptcy petitions lodged in England and Wales, but having some procedural or substantive element involving assets or interests outside this jurisdiction, and on the recognition and treatment of foreign bankruptcy proceedings within England and Wales. Fletcher then examines choice of law provisions with emphasis on the critical issues raised by the choice of anti-avoidance legislation.

A valuable and distinctive feature of the book is its contribution to developmental thinking in relation to law reform. The suggestions that are made in response to perceived problems in current legislation are always presented in an intensely practical manner with examples as to their operation in multi-jurisdictional settings. Such suggestions abound in the chapter on corporate insolvency and encompass such issues as the general principles governing the recognition of winding-up proceedings commenced outwith the jurisdiction of the English courts; the problems created by the failure to recognize automatic vesting of assets situated in this jurisdiction in a foreign liquidator; and the uncertainty surrounding the application of anti-avoidance legislation. The recommendations will surely be a stimulus to the debate on insolvency reform and provide positive and pragmatic advice in this context.

A feature of the need for a rapid response to the problems generated by cross-border insolvencies has been the willingness on the part of the judiciary of many jurisdictions to react flexibly and co-operatively when faced with potentially conflicting procedures or substantive rules. In this context, the final chapter of this part of the book examines the role of the judiciary and their record in promoting workable solutions to what would otherwise appear to be intractable problems. A detailed analysis of the scope of section 426 of the Insolvency Act 1986 is the prelude to a discussion of notable cases in which judicial assistance has been most effectively utilized, pre-eminent amongst which must be the litigation resulting from the collapse of the Bank of Credit and Commerce International SA.

The second part of the book is devoted to an exposition of the international regulation of insolvency law—an area that is greatly in need of development in the light of the growth of international commerce—but whose evolution to date has been lamentably slow. With admirable scholarship and clarity of presentation, the history of the bilateral treaties on insolvency incorporated in the Montevideo Treaties and the Nordic Bankruptcy Conventions, are discussed. Sadly, chapter 6 in which there is an analysis of the European Convention on Bankruptcy, has been overtaken by subsequent events. This was foreshadowed in the book. The Convention, whose fate was sealed by the failure of the UK to sign the Convention by the due date, has been replaced by the Regulation on International Co-operation in Insolvency Proceedings (*OJ* C221, 3 August 1999). However, apart from the obvious changes wrought by the alteration in legal instrument, the commentary on the substantive and procedural elements of the Convention, which are mirrored in the Regulation, remains valid and insightful. A chapter is devoted to the Council of Europe Convention on the International Aspects of Bankruptcy, and although the weight to be attached to particular elements is always a matter of opinion, it is perhaps surprising to see a thorough-going analysis devoted to a convention that may well be of historical significance only. The global initiative that will probably have a greater impact is the UNCITRAL Model Law on Bankruptcy and Insolvency Proceedings that is reviewed in the final substantive chapter.

Appendices containing extracts of the selected national legislation referred to in the text as well as the now defunct EU Convention, the Istanbul Convention and the UNCITRAL Model Law are a helpful feature. This work is a scholarly, well written and thoroughly documented contribution to the complex field of insolvency and private international law.

CLARE CAMPBELL

The Child and the European Convention on Human Rights. By URSULA KILKELLY. Aldershot: Ashgate, 1999. xiv + 368 pp. £50.

This monograph originated as a doctoral thesis and it retains many of the characteristics associated with that type of scholarly writing. It is thorough. It is carefully footnoted. It has an extensive bibliography. The author has considered over 750 reported and unreported cases dating from the establishment of the Strasbourg institutions over forty years ago. Each chapter concludes with a summary under the heading 'future challenges' that gives a brief overview and identifies trends. Kilkelly draws helpful parallels between the European Convention on Human Rights and the UN Convention on the Rights of the Child, and by drawing contrasts, clarifies the different expectations of the two Conventions. It is her firm belief that the potential of the European Convention to protect children will only be achieved if the detailed standards on children's rights set out in the UN Convention are used as a benchmark against which the Strasbourg decisions are measured. Readers interested in the academic study of the European Convention, and in how it has been applied in cases involving children and their families, will find this book an invaluable research tool.

The book's thirteen chapters look at the special position of children in a variety of contexts. These include the right to participate in legal proceedings, the right to identity, the right to life, the right to family life, and the right to receive health care. Chapter 10 is devoted to immigrant and refugee children and Kilkelly engages in a careful and comprehensive analysis of the compatibility of immigration measures with Articles 8 and 3. The protection of a child's right to liberty (Article 5) and to a fair trial (Article 6) are examined in chapter 3. The importance of these rights irrespective of age cannot be overstated. However, the Court's reluctance to acknowledge that children are autonomous was made explicit in *Nielsen* v. *Denmark* (1988). As Kilkelly makes plain, the Convention does not expressly recognize that children may require greater protection than adults because of their vulnerability to the powers of their parents as well as to the powers of the State. This theme is developed in the chapters on abuse and neglect, on the definition and treatment of the family, on custody and contact, on alternative care, and in the final chapter that is devoted entirely to adoption.

The right guaranteed by the rather vague and negative wording of Article 2 of the First Protocol, 'No person shall be denied the right to education', relates specifically to children. States are obliged to respect the religious and philosophical convictions of parents when providing education and teaching. This obligation originates from the desire to prevent the indoctrination of children by the State, such as occurred in Nazi Germany. However, it has the potential to undermine the child's right to receive a form of education that exposes him or her to influences other than those regarded as acceptable by the parents. Kilkelly's analysis of how the Court has handled this dilemma, and her discussion of whether this right is truly a child's right or a parent's right, is thoughtful and persuasive.

Those readers who refer to this book in order to determine how the Convention might impinge on the domestic law of their own country are likely to find the way in which it is organized difficult to handle. It is not an easy book to dip into. The analysis is very much of the type that is found in a thesis. It tends to assume that the reader is familiar with the Convention's articles and Protocols. It tends to assume a knowledge of the key facts of the relevant case law which can be difficult to discover from the text. Readers may therefore find it helpful to have a book such as *Family Law and the Human Rights Act 1998* by Swindells, Neaves, Kushner and Skilner close to hand. This volume contains a section in which the most significant cases affecting children and their families are summarized in alphabetical order.

Children in England are already starting to benefit from the growing awareness that the Human Rights Act 1998 affects everyone, regardless of age. As Kilkelly's book reveals, although relatively few applications have been made to Strasbourg on behalf of children directly, those that have succeeded, or even some that have failed such as *Costello-Roberts*, have had a major impact on domestic law. Corporal punishment is no longer permitted in British schools, and soon such punishment may also be made unlawful in the home in the light of *A* v. *United Kingdom* (1998). There is, however, a real risk that the 1998 Act may lead judges to focus closer attention on the rights and interests of parents and in doing so to lose sight of the separate rights and welfare of children. The Convention does little to encourage the treatment of children as separate persons with rights that are independent of those of their parents. How far the treatment of children as autonomous is critical to the promotion of their welfare and protection is a debate that bedevils family law and one to which Kilkelly's book makes a most useful contribution.

MARY HAYES

The Riddle of all Constitutions: International Law, Democracy, and the Critique of Ideology. By SUSAN MARKS. Oxford: Oxford University Press, 2000. 164 pp. £30.

This is a timely book by an able young scholar. The title, drawn from Marx rather than Marks, is challenging and so are the contents. The thesis propounded is attractive and persuasive to the reviewer, even if the methodology, so to speak, is more contentious.

The argument, put briefly, is as follows. An emerging norm of democratic governance in international law has become accepted. Marks is not concerned to justify it, but to examine its implications and whether 'it represents a good idea' (p. 1). The thread which runs through the work is that, important though the institutions and procedures of representative democracy clearly are, they cannot be allowed to exhaust the meaning of democracy. 'To permit that is to give up on the idea that democracy is about self-government, and not just about legitimating government by others' (p. 2). In a highly contentious excursus into ideology, to which it will be useful to return, the author analyses international legal processes 'through which asymmetrical power relations are legitimated . . . or otherwise supported' (p. 29).

She notes international law's traditional impartiality on the subject of political systems and that it has become less acceptable to take States as one finds them than formerly. Instead, they should be seen to require democratic government. Marks, while accepting the legitimacy of this development, argues that it is a limited concept of democracy which informs the international community. It is largely about elections, with few questions asked about the role of organized interest groups and civil society in influencing the terms of collective life. Particularly in relation to the new democracies, there is a danger that low-intensity democracy will ossify political and economic structures from a less than democratic past. The author is equally concerned that 'formal' politics will tend to legitimate free markets, whatever inequalities of power and influence ensue.

In short Marks is concerned about the lack of attachment to social and economic rights, to a genuine political market, to the instantiation of subsidiarity in civil society. Identity and culture are too easily overlooked. Should not international law have a positive view on these matters rather than appearing to rubber-stamp whatever emerges from electoral processes?

From this point, the author goes on to tackle the subject of globalization, or 'cosmopolitan democracy'. As the reviewer knows full well, this is perhaps the most pressing issue of our times in terms of legal and political systems. Her adoption of the term '*nebleuse*' (p. 85) to describe the network of actors and institutions which make up the global economy is instantly recognizable. What she has to say about these phenomena is both crucial and largely incontrovertible. There is a simultaneous need for efforts to deepen democracy within nation-States and extend democracy to international and transnational settings.

Marks' response to these challenges is to espouse what she calls the 'principle of democratic exclusion'. This 'is used to refer to the idea that all should have the right to a say in decision-making which affects them, and that systematic barriers to the exercise of that right should be acknowledged and removed. For this purpose, the relevant processes of decision-making and barriers to participation include not only those operating within nation-States, but also those operating among nation-States and in transnational areas' (p. 119). This is difficult to gainsay.

Some will already be familiar with these arguments, although Marks has done a service by bringing such matters clearly to the attention of a larger audience. For this she should be both widely read and congratulated. However, no review would be complete without some reservations. They are these.

It is difficult, since the book aims at a high theoretical justification for its claims, to see the epistemic foundations for outcomes which are, nevertheless, essentially well-founded. There is a certain amount of neo-Marxist mystique, and pandering to the tastes of deconstructionists and other methodological relativists. She is right that enquiry in the field of human endeavour should be motivated 'by a sense of injustice' (pp. 25, 121), but does not say why. There is plenty of theory but it is ungrounded; we are treated to a kind of theoretical ethnography. There is an excursus into the role of ideology, which, with respect, is not a second-order issue and in this context only serves to confuse issues which elsewhere she clarifies. Although she is expressly conscious of the need to relate epistemological to ethical issues, she seems sympathetic to scepticism about the possibility of 'disinterestedness'. These statements are, in fact, largely incompatible. All her concerns can be justified by an adherence to 'categorical critique'. It is ironic that its greatest contemporary exponent is nowhere mentioned. Alan Gewirth's *Community of Rights* ought rationally to be the first chapter in her biblical odyssey. When Marks gets her epistemology right she will be a fearsome and important advocate of those ideas which she rightly seeks to promote. At least one person looks forward to her future output with considerable expectation and pleasure.

DOUGLAS LEWIS

International Dispute Settlement (Third edition). By JOHN MERRILLS. Cambridge: Cambridge University Press, 1998. 342 pp. Hardback, £60; paperback, £24.95.

Professor Merrills published the original edition of *International Dispute Settlement* in 1984. A second edition followed in 1991. This new, third, edition is to be warmly welcomed. Apart from the normal updating of the previous material, major changes on the international scene have had to be accommodated, particularly with the ending of the Cold War and the parallel freeing-up of the Security Council enabling it to take a more active role in the world's trouble spots, the development of the former GATT dispute settlement panels into the more thorough-going dispute settlement procedures of the World Trade Organization, and the setting up of the new International Tribunal for the Law of the Sea.

A book of just under 350 pages (in fact, 311 if Appendices are excluded) cannot aspire to be a detailed reference work on all the dispute settlement procedures of which it treats. Although it concentrates on disputes between States, it nevertheless includes a brief discussion of international arbitration involving individuals or corporations, such as the ICSID procedures (pp. 111–15). It also excludes from its scope the unilateral coercive settlement of disputes, but has quite a lot to say about collective coercive action by the international community acting through the UN (chapter 10). Even so, the peaceful settlement of inter-State disputes is, quite properly, Merrills' subject. On this he provides a readable, stimulating, and knowledgeable overview of the place of dispute settlement processes in today's world, outlining the main features of each, and giving examples of the ways in which they have been used in recent times.

A book on the settlement of international disputes naturally places the emphasis on the available procedures of settlement. But it is the disputes themselves, in their infinite variety, which are the core of the problem. They are seldom *purely* about issues of law: there will always be an element of politics involved, and the political dimension will often predominate. A particular strength of the book is that it is firmly rooted in the behaviour of States, particularly in recent times, and takes full account of the principal political and diplomatic factors involved.

Just as international disputes are as much, if not more, a matter of politics as of law, so too are the available settlement procedures. Lawyers naturally concentrate on arbitral and judicial settlement procedures; yet as Merrills observes, 'it is clear that by comparison with domestic courts, international courts and tribunals occupy a relatively insignificant position' (p. 165). It is the other, less law-dominated and more diplomatically oriented, procedures to which recourse is more often had by States, since they are the procedures which can better take into account the political factors which gave rise to the dispute in the first place. Yet *all* the settlement procedures share one critical characteristic, in that they all depend on the consent of the States concerned. Even those to which States are bound by virtue of a treaty obligation are ultimately consensual in that their adherence to the treaty is itself an act requiring their consent. It is a sad fact, duly noted by the author, that all too often the necessary consent is not forthcoming, or is only forthcoming in too qualified a form to be helpful.

Merrills' account of the various dispute settlement procedures is complemented by assessments of their respective advantages and disadvantages. This is a most valuable feature of the book: each chapter ends with a section which, although variously titled ('limitations of . . . ', 'value of . . . ', 'significance of . . . ', etc.), in each case evaluates the particular settlement process under discussion. Those individual assessments prepare the ground for the final chapter, on 'Trends and Prospects', which combines stimulating and constructive legal and political perspectives for future improvements to the international arrangements for dispute settlement.

Before that final end-of-term report, so to speak, come eleven chapters, each of which is devoted to one particular aspect of dispute settlement (except for the ICJ, which is given two chapters, one on organization and procedure and the other on the work of the Court). These chapters cover both the various *procedures* (chapters 1–7: negotiation, mediation, inquiry, conciliation, arbitration and the ICJ) and the principal *structures* of international dispute settlement (chapters 8–11: law of the sea, trade disputes, the UN, and regional organizations).

The settlement procedures considered in the opening chapters follow the traditional list of those referred to in Article 33 of the UN Charter. It is always a problem with such a listing that it tends to impose a rigid categorization on processes which are in reality almost infinitely flexible. To some extent the categories reflect older classifications by commentators rather than the realities of State practice: States are typically more concerned with settling their disputes than with placing the procedure which suits their purposes under one or other of the traditional headings. In practice, if not perhaps in principle, the distinctions are blurred between, say, good offices, mediation, and conciliation (as noted at pp. 27, 202–4).

Good offices, incidentally, are not included in Article 33, nor does Merrills deal with them in a separate chapter, but in practice they are a very important process in international dispute settlement—given due mention, for example, in the context of trade disputes (pp. 202–4) and in connection with the role of the UN and regional organizations (e.g., pp. 224, 229 and 266). Another omission from the list in Article 33, and similarly not awarded its own chapter, is consultation. There is, as Merrills points out, a 'need to encourage consultation both as an informal practice and, where appropriate, in an institutional setting . . . [T]here are many situations where consultation, when once established, is an excellent way of promoting and protecting interests' (pp. 303–4). It plays an important role in the settlement of trade disputes (pp. 201–2) and Merrills notes that '[o]ne of the most useful functions of a regional organisation is to provide its members with a forum for consultation and negotiations in actual or potential dispute situations' (p. 266).

Whether or not Article 33 constitutes a complete list of available processes (and its formal completeness is ensured by its final inclusion of 'other peaceful means of [the parties'] own choice'), it is apparent—and Merrills' book makes it clear—that there is no shortage of available international judicial and arbitral bodies which are capable of resolving disputes, or of other more political procedures which can be equally fruitful. While existing structures can always be improved, it is not their deficiencies which at present stand in the way of effective dispute settlement but rather the unwillingness of States to have recourse to them as often as is desirable. As the author several times points out, the consensual nature of international dispute settlement, and the unwillingness of States to lose control of the management of a dispute by putting its resolution in the hands of a third party, are the real stumbling blocks.

Merrills begins his short conclusion with the observation that 'The peaceful settlement of international disputes is the most critical issue of our time' (p. 310). So it is. This latest edition of Merrills' book is an indispensable guide to the available procedures and processes, and their potential for coping with the infinite variety of disputes with which the international community is plagued.

A. D. Watts

Between Vengeance and Forgiveness: Facing History after Genocide and Mass Violence. By MARTHA MINOW. Boston: Beacon Press, 1998. xii + 214 pp. US $23. *War Crimes: Brutality, Genocide, Terror and the Struggle for Justice*. By ARYEH NEIER. New York: Times Books, 1998. xiv + 286 pp. US $25. *Making Justice Work*. By THE CENTURY FOUNDATION/TWENTIETH CENTURY FUND TASK FORCE ON APPREHENDING INDICTED WAR CRIMINALS. New York: The Century Foundation Press, 1998. viii + 354 pp. No price stated.

The bloodthirsty history of the twentieth century, witness to genocide and continuing human rights abuse, presents an on-going challenge to international human rights law. There is a burgeoning literature on human rights law and practice to which the texts under review add. The normative content of that law—largely shaped in response to the horrors of the Holocaust—is impressive but, lacking an adequate institutional framework, is not yet a fully mature legal order. All three texts concentrate upon the need for a response to mass atrocity. Each may be seen as 'committed', because each assumes that only a positive response to mass atrocity will suffice. Both Neier and the Twentieth Century Foundation devote their analysis to advocating the more effective pursuit of justice. Minow has a wider focus, analysing a whole range of societal responses to mass atrocity.

Minow's study represents the fruition of more than two years' activity with Facing History and Ourselves, which is dedicated to developing educational programmes in response to mass atrocity. The century just ended saw the novel trend of the 'invention of new and distinctive legal forms of response' (p. 1). These include trials (chapter 3); truth commissions (chapter 4); and reparations (chapter 5). The empirical focus of these core chapters is enhanced by the theoretical framework provided in the second chapter, on vengeance and forgiveness, and by the final chapter, on facing history. The author's express aim is to 'develop and deepen a vocabulary for assessing the goals and limitations of each kind of response to societal-level atrocities' (p. 4). In the face of collective violence, it is often claimed that the response is animated by the desire to obtain justice and truth. But Minow suggests there is a pair of implicit, but more basic, underlying goals—those of vengeance and forgiveness. These condition and limit the spectrum of response to collective violence and, under closer scrutiny, can be viewed as a pair of antinomies. Vengeance excludes, or at least resists, forgiveness, whilst forgiveness excludes vengeance (p. 21). However, vengeance may be seen as a component of justice—at least retributive justice, administered by a court, in accordance with the rule of law. Forgiveness, although theoretically not necessarily exclusive of punishment, often leads in practice to the negation of punishment.

In face of such an antimony Minow seeks a middle way—'what response do or could lie between vengeance and forgiveness, *if legal and cultural institutions offered other avenues for individuals and nations?*' (p. 21, original emphasis). Over the last fifty years or so, a shift has occurred, from a legal discourse of trial and punishment, to one based on psychology and healing—and the adoption of therapeutic techniques and goals guided by the tenets of restorative justice and reconciliation. Depending upon which of the underlying goals is chosen, different responses emerge, from trial and punishment, to aesthetic responses, in art and memorialization. Ultimately, it is not abstract theory which shapes societal response, but legal, political, military and economic factors. The caveat entered is: 'closure is not possible . . . and all responses to collective atrocities are characterized by incompleteness and inescapable inadequacy' (p. 5).

Chapter 3 focuses upon trials—and it is here that the precedent set by the great trials at Nuremberg and Tokyo in the aftermath of World War II come under scrutiny. Minow rehearses the well-aired criticisms often levelled against the two tribunals, viz. 'Retro-activity, policization and selectivity' (p. 31). Whatever the substance of these criticisms, it is not sufficient to outweigh the case for adopting a legal response. The positive legacy of the two tribunals lay in creating and shaping the subsequent human rights agenda. Her cautious conclusion suggests that through law it may be possible to build 'an evolving consensus about international norms' (p. 51).

Truth commissions are often seen as second-best or adjunct to prosecution. But it is not that truth commissions only substitute for prosecution when the practicalities and political realities suggest otherwise. Rather, the reason may be found in the inherent limitations of the trial process itself—the financial and emotional costs of litigation and the limited ability of a trial to produce a definitive historical record. If the purpose is to create a forum where victims receive priority, along with the aim of securing the truth, then truth commissions may be preferable to trials.

Trials aspire to justice and accountability—to retributive justice. Truth commissions shift the discourse from law and control, towards one of health and healing. The prime example of such a body is the South African Truth and Reconciliation Commission. The TRC was a complex body which, by allowing truth to be traded for amnesty, aspired to glean the truth, and build a foundation for individual and societal healing. Restorative justice displaces retributive justice. Instead of the limiting terms of truth and justice, Minow elucidates no less than twelve operative considerations. These include gaining full public acknowledgement of past events, punishing offenders, and aspiring to the maximum possible compatibility of the multiplicity of goals one with another (p. 88). Viewed through this evaluative framework, it is by no means obvious that trials should be the singular response to mass atrocity.

The therapeutic motif can also be found in the category of reparations (chapter 5). Here the distinctions between restitution, reparation and apology are analysed. Two main problems are identified: first, the poignant fact that 'no market measures exist for the value of living an ordinary life, without nightmares or survivor guilt' (p. 104). Secondly, there is the problem of 'compensating past victims without creating new ones' (p. 110). Moreover, reparation, whatever its place in the 'lexicon of potential responses' (p. 117), will fail if it be thought that it may effectuate a closure on the past.

The final chapter outlines the inherent limitations of each of the three main forms of response. Trials are seen to be about symbolism, 'rather than an affirmation of the rule of law' (p. 122). Truth commissions are perhaps best at producing the 'psychological rather than historical truth' (p. 128). Finally, reparations may be seen to elevate 'things over persons, money over dignity' (p. 131).

The remaining texts concentrate upon and prioritize the legal option. Neier analyses the prospects and potential of international human rights law through the agency of the two *ad hoc* international tribunals, ICTY and ICTR, viewed through the historical, legal and political background. The first half (chapters 1–7) deals with that historical background, outlining both the normative and institutional development of international human rights law and practice. Despite the slow progress recorded over the half century since the IMT in 1946, Neier advocates a legal response to human rights abuse. The core of the book is the analysis of the two *ad hoc* tribunals and their potential (chapters 8–14). The Epilogue outlines the prospects and potential of the proposed permanent international criminal court. This court is seen to represent the emergence of a new era in international human rights law and practice.

Neier's analysis reveals the crucial impact of politics upon the formation of the current tribunals, suggesting that both were born out of the failure of politics to find an acceptable solution to the problems in Yugoslavia and Rwanda respectively. The future of ICTY was only secured when the world had to face the reality of the massacre in Srebrenica in 1995, although resource problems, patchy co-operation and a myriad of other problems remain. To date, the tribunals have dealt with key legal issues such as the treatment of rape as a war crime, the protection of non-combatants in siege warfare, and the interface between freedom of expression and incitement to genocide, witnessed in Rwanda (chapters 10, 11, 12). Chapter 13 explores the issue of guilt—taking its theoretical cue from the classic analysis by Karl Jaspers (*The Question of German Guilt*, 1946). The impact of establishing individual and legal guilt is a prerequisite to forcing the bulk of perpetrators to 'confront their own political, moral and metaphysical guilt' (p. 228). Legal prosecution can be justified and indeed prioritized. Following a plea for greater efficiency by the ICTY (chapter 14), Neier concludes on a positive note: the record of the tribunal has exceeded expectations, 'even if governments of good conscience still have further to go to fulfil its mandate' (p. 251).

The aim of the Task Force Report is to focus attention upon the ICTY and suggest ways to render it more effective. The underlying premiss is that 'until all war criminals are arrested and brought to justice' (p. 13), there can be no lasting peace and reconciliation in the former Yugoslavia. The advantage of prosecution is seen as being in bringing individuals to account, avoiding the ascription of collective guilt, creating an accurate historical record, and thus breaking the cycle of violence and revenge. Unlike Minow, the Task Force Report clearly implies that prosecution will create the necessary closure over the past and all other responses must be adjunct to it (p. 12). Like Neier, this report relates the success of the *ad hoc* tribunal to the future prospects of a permanent international criminal court. Background papers deal, *inter alia*, with the scope of the legal obligation of States to co-operate with the tribunal (Orentlichter), and the numerous appendices cover the main source materials—UN resolutions, etc.—relevant to the recommendations advanced.

Whatever the differences of emphasis and coverage between these texts, they share the basic commitment that, in the face of mass atrocity, to do nothing is unacceptable. The law must be pitted against the seeming irrationality of mass violence. Hannah Arendt's gloomy assertion, that atrocity reveals the limits of law because no punishment can ever be condign, is forcefully challenged here.

TONY RICHARDSON

Protecting Prisoners: The Standards of the European Committee for the Prevention of Torture in Context. By ROD MORGAN and MALCOLM D. EVANS. Oxford: Oxford University Press, 1999. xix + 294 pp. £50.

Protecting Prisoners is a collection of essays on the work of the European Committee for the Prevention of Torture which arose, as the authors explain in the preface, out of a seminar on the European Convention for the Prevention of Torture held at the University of Bristol in September 1997 and attended by various experts. The experts were later asked to prepare their contributions for publication, and with the addition of two more contributions to ensure a more representative account of the Committee's work, the resulting volume serves as a useful companion to *Preventing Torture*, the earlier work by Evans and Morgan on the Committee's first ten years of operation (reviewed in last year's *Year Book*).

The contents of *Protecting Prisoners* are organized into three parts. Part One is written solely by Morgan and Evans and benefits greatly from their co-operative and cross-disciplinary experience, as well as from the fieldwork they undertook in the preparation of *Preventing Torture*. However, unlike the largely historical account contained in *Preventing Torture*, Part One of *Protecting Prisoners* provides a more recent account of the Committee's work in developing standards for the prevention of torture and other forms of ill-treatment. It also contains a comprehensive digest of the Committee's jurisprudence (up to 31 December 1998) which has been thoughtfully analysed according to the different categories of detained persons. These categories assist the reader in applying the Convention's standards to not only the different legal classes of prisoners (such as a prisoner on remand or under administrative detention), but also the different sociodemographic classes of prisoners (including women and youths). The resulting analysis is to be highly commended since it provides valuable insights into how the Convention standards and safeguards should be applied to different detainees in light of their particular vulnerabilities to ill-treatment by the State.

Part Two then considers the Committee's work within the broader framework of other international mechanisms for the prevention and prohibition of ill-treatment. It comprises contributions from both academic observers and experts working in the field and begins with a topical consideration of the relationship between the work of the Committee and that of the European Court of Human Rights, noting the fruition of a two-way jurisprudential interchange. Part Two also considers the mechanisms established by the United Nations to prevent and prohibit the torture and ill-treatment of detainees, illustrating both the connections to, and degree of divergence between, the European and UN approaches to prisoner protection. The role of the European Prison Rules is also considered, with the contributing author providing several grounds for the abandonment of the Rules in favour of an evolving digest of Committee standards and guidelines. Lastly, Part Two takes the reader outside the inter-governmental sphere to consider how non-governmental organizations, such as Amnesty International, influence, and feed off, the development of standards by bodies such as the Committee for the Prevention of Torture.

The remainder of the book is then devoted to Part Three, which consists of a series of country-specific analyses of the Committee's reports and the reactions by the governments concerned. The countries considered are Belgium, France, Hungary, the Netherlands, Turkey, and the United Kingdom, thereby giving the reader a representative sample of the different legal systems, political histories, and socio-economic realities confronting the implementation of the Convention's protections. This sample also aptly illustrates one of the central themes expressed by Morgan and Evans, namely whether the standards of the European Convention for the Prevention of Torture should operate as universally applicable minimum standards, or as aspirational standards to be applied according to the different socio-economic realities within the much-expanded Council of Europe.

In answering this question, Evans and Morgan persuasively argue for what they have termed a 'variable geometry' approach, which is an approach that essentially allows for the realization of universally applicable standards over time according to available local resources. The case studies in Part Three clearly provide the raw material to support this conclusion, although, in reading the book from cover to cover, one is struck by the absence of a concluding chapter. It is the one weakness of what is a well-written and thoughtful contribution to the scholarship concerning the protection of prisoners. However, it is a weakness which can be easily remedied by re-reading the conclusions in Part One after Part Three. Overall, *Protecting Prisoners* can be recommended as a reliable, balanced and accessible work on the rights of prisoners within Europe, which also offers something to readers with a broader interest in the implementation of universal standards.

JOANNA HARRINGTON

The Weakness in the International Protection of Minority Rights. By J. REHMAN. The Hague: Kluwer Law International, 2000. 288 pp. £58.

The title of this intense volume does not convey the full scope of Rehman's thesis and interests. The book is in essence an attempt to measure the condition of contemporary Pakistan from minority rights and human rights perspectives. The work is divided into five parts, comprising the introduction, a short section on the historical development of minority rights, two major substantive sections—established rights under international law, and emerging rights—followed by a brief concluding part five. There are also a useful bibliography, maps, and documentary appendices. Chapters on the right to existence, equality and non-discrimination, and autonomy, are followed in each case by detailed examination of the application of the norms in Pakistan. The implications of alleging 'weakness' of international protection are not always clear. The term comprises the conceptual limitations/confusions of international law in this field, weaknesses of international mechanisms, and weaknesses of implementation of international standards stemming from conceptual confusion and local reluctance to implement. Much of this approximates to the familiar grief about the failure of the international system of human rights to deliver results on the ground, to actually make a difference. Taking Rehman's evidence, the failure appears gross.

Pakistan does not emerge with much credit from the analysis, though the writer is careful to point out that minority rights in other countries are in an equal or worse condition overall. The chapters on existence are heavily critical of the recent history of Pakistan. This is coupled with a broad brush approach to other (many) possible cases of genocide (pp. 65 ff.) which require greater substantiation, and is supererogatory for Rehman's arguments, except as a lament on the human condition. The chapters on discrimination (six and seven) have a sharper focus. Sections on the application of blasphemy and analogous laws in Pakistan have conviction, evidence, and bite, and vividly picture the subversion of laws by religious bigotry and political calculation. Christians and Hindus are portrayed as faring badly; an even deeper level of oppression is reserved for the Ahmadiyyas. Chapters eight and nine on autonomy (the reviewer was never entirely clear what was meant by 'autonomy' in this context) convey the dilemma of 'recognition of a right to autonomy and the artificial nature of Pakistan' (p. 204), and consider the varied cases of Bengalis, Baluchis, Pakhtuns, Sindhis, and Muhajirs.

In advising prospective writers of books, theses and dissertation topics, the question of whether the candidate is too close to the action can be a pertinent consideration: can they stand back and be objective? On the other hand, we can only write usefully on things that interest us. In some areas, Rehman's approach approximates to a love-hate relationship with his chosen case study, but mostly the tone is properly academic, dry and substantiated. He displays considerable scholarship and great commitment to the subject. Studies of human rights performance of a particular country are always difficult; sensitivities are legion.

Rehman's moral is that international law needs to work harder to sort out the messages intended for governments, and governments should take more seriously the message of human rights. Clarification and good faith are minimal requirements for an effective regime. There are other, more disturbing implications. The book is also an essay on the limits of human rights, practically, through weak mechanisms and lack of civil space, and culturally, because of their apparent irrelevance to the forces controlling Pakistan and remoteness from the lives of people. If this portrait of a nation really 'tells it how it is', and if similar country portraits could be painted in comparable colours, we have a long way to go before human rights can truly be embraced in a common ownership transcending cultural and religious difference.

PATRICK THORNBERRY

International Environmental Law Reports. Volume I: Early Decisions. Edited by CAIRO A. R. ROBB. Cambridge: Cambridge University Press, 1999. 600 pp. Hardback, £90; paperback £40.

Early Decisions is the first volume of the *International Environmental Law Reports* to be produced by the Lauterpacht Research Centre for International Law of the University of Cambridge. Four more volumes are planned, on Trade and the Environment (volume 2), Human Rights and the Environment (volume 3), Decisions of National Courts (volume 4), and Decisions of the International Court of Justice (volume 5). The aim of the Reports, as emphasized in the Preface by the Editor (Cairo Robb) and General Editors

(Daniel Bethlehem, James Crawford, and Philippe Sands), is to reproduce in 'one easily accessible collection the key decisions from international and national tribunals' and provide 'source material that will assist in the further development' of international environmental law.

The first volume, *Early Decisions*, contains cases that have contributed to the development of principles and rules in this field of law, decided by various international and national tribunals from 1880s to the 1960s. International decisions are reproduced in the first part of the volume (with the exception of judgments given by the International Court of Justice, which will be contained in volume 5), whilst the second part reproduces decisions by national tribunals. The international decisions analysed include some very well known 'environmental' cases (for example the *Trail Smelter* case and the *Lac Lanoux* case) as well as cases whose 'environmental dimension' may be less apparent at first (such as the *Island of Palmas* case). The reader will, however, find it extremely interesting to discover that even such cases may be read in a way that emphasizes their importance for the development of international environmental law.

The national decisions included in this volume are drawn from the following jurisdictions: Austria, Germany, Italy, Switzerland, and the United States. All judgments are translated in English. The decisions analysed cover a wide range of environmental topics: rights of riparian States over international rivers, regulation of hazardous activities and substances, and air and water pollution. These judgments focus on the resolution of environmental disputes, but they also analyse broader issues of international law. Questions examined include, *inter alia*, the relationship between international law and national law, territorial sovereignty and sources of international law.

The cases are presented in an extremely accessible and clear manner: each case is introduced by digest entries, followed by a summary of the decision and by other relevant documents (compromis, notes, etc.) and the full text of the decision. Reading *Early Decisions* is a very pleasant and enjoyable experience. One can discover decisions of which one was unaware and think of well-known decisions from a different perspective. It is refreshing to read a collection of cases which is both useful and stimulating. After having read the first volume of the *International Environmental Law Reports*, one would only wish to be able to read and use the forthcoming volumes as quickly as possible.

PAOLO GALIZZI

Governmental Illegitimacy in International Law. By BRAD R. ROTH. Oxford: Clarendon Press, 1999. xxx + 439 pp., including index. £65.

The title of Professor Roth's book deserves emphasis: *Governmental Illegitimacy in International Law*. Despite much academic advocacy to the contrary, Professor Roth is not considering a qualifying standard for the legitimacy of all governments but a disqualifying one for some regimes, otherwise apparently satisfying the appropriate criteria to be regarded as a government. So, while some considerations may in some cases have a bearing on claims of illegitimacy of some governments—that they are not endorsed by a responsive democratic process, that they do not promise fulsome compliance with human rights standards, that they are not committed to good governance, that they do not adhere to the rules against the use of force and intervention—failure to satisfy any of these or all of them would not generally be a reason for denying status to an effective authority: indeed, we would find ourselves with precious few governments if the standards were applied with any degree of comprehensiveness and rigour.

As disqualifying standards, there is room for discrimination, both as to the circumstances which in fact disqualify and the consequences of 'disqualification'. If choices are to be made about which regimes should be assessed, who makes the decision to go ahead and according to which criteria? Are regimes which do not measure up to be regarded as nullities or are certain statuses, such as representation in international organizations, to be denied to them, or are the States of which they claim to be the governments to be deprived of certain of their rights, such as the protections against intervention or even the use of force? Professor Roth has things to say about many of these questions. He does not regard the answers as self-evident but, where there might be a conclusion of illegitimacy, he appreciates its destabilizing effects: there will be demands that the illegitimate regime be gone or be removed.

The traditional answer about government status is that it is properly claimed by the authorities which are in effective control of the territory of a State. Subject to their being no (probably no excessive) external involvement in the achieving of effective control, how a government came to power and how it conducted itself domestically were at the centre of a State's domestic jurisdiction. The demonstration of effective control was a pre-condition for lawful recognition of the government by other States but not a guarantee of it. Recognition being a unilateral power of the recognizing state, it did not follow as a legal entitlement from the establishment of effectiveness but from the exercise of a political decision of the recognizing government. The traditional position was the centerpiece of the Westphalian system: one government could not insist upon the satisfaction of any standard of governmental legitimacy without interfering in the internal affairs of the other State.

After a study of the classics of political theory, Roth rejects the Hobbesian equation of effectiveness and legitimacy, but neither is he content with a constitutional solution—that the administration which has gained authority through the prescribed process has a better claim to legitimacy than any other. He says that 'in an international community of peoples, recognition of a government cannot be coherently tied to respect for a given set of constitutional processes' (p. 67). If this is intended as a statement of law, then it is not quite correct—the constitutional foundation of international legal society is the sovereign equality of 'States'. It is much easier to reach the conclusion that the will of a State is legitimately expressed by the regime in effective power there than it is to say that the will of the people(s) is expressed by an entity the authority of which may owe nothing to the opinions of the population. Also, on such a basis, one can more readily reject the legitimacy of a government imposed by external forces as being contrary to the sovereign equality of States than one can support the claim to legitimacy of an authority set up as a result of a foreign intervention to set the people free (p. 68).

Roth's line is that neither in political theory nor in actual practice is the link between the effectiveness of an authority and its acceptability to the people merely a matter of chance. He does not suggest that there is a straight-line correlation between acceptability and effectiveness, rather that the less an authority is accepted by its people, the more likely it is that effectiveness will depend upon force and, therefore, be contingent on the capacity of the authority to continue to exercise the necessary force. This does not take him so far as to say that acceptance requires democratic endorsement or that only grudging acceptance (particularly when the likely alternative were taken into account) would be insufficient. Indeed, that which was once imposed may become that which is now accepted. In particular, he says, we ought to be wary of external assessments of whether a people accept their (effective) government, not just because of the paternalism and unlawfulness that might be involved, but because of the general unlikelihood that a foreign saviour (or its surrogate) will enjoy acceptance more readily. This is evidence of a more State-orientated approach than is currently fashionable in discussions in the field. Roth is conscious of the prospect that claims of illegitimacy of an effective regime will soon sound like claims that it should be replaced and then that others have a right to intervene to carry out the supersession.

For all the political theory that informs the first part of the book, Roth makes it clear he is writing as a lawyer. None the less, he denies that this excludes him from taking moral positions, not only because of the inherent uncertainty within international law, but also because, where its rules and principles can be discerned, they are not without a moral purpose. The rules of international law come from a pluralistic society, and Roth himself is concerned 'to preserve space in the world for ideological pluralism and innovation'. The problem is that claims that certain regimes are illegitimate in the sense with which Roth is concerned are invariably founded on the view that they are incompatible with international human rights standards, that is, they violate universal standards: no space for pluralism there. Roth talks of the 'aggressiveness' of the radical anti-effectiveness movement: its objectives are to be attained by replacement or overthrow, should that be necessary. By contrast, Roth's programme is conservative. Even to the extent that he shares the objectives of the radicals, he knows that they will have to be achieved within States by local governments, according to the norms and processes of international law and politics. From such a perspective, intervening by force in another State, intervening to replace a government by force, does not strike him as self-evidently the best way forward. It is easy to agree.

There follows a long chapter on recognition with the curious starting-point that there has been nothing written worth note since Lauterpacht and Chen. Such an assumption fails to take account of not only recent literature, notably Verhoven and Talmon, but also the change of practice, in which States have increasingly adopted a policy of not recognizing governments: it should not be surprising that there is less literature, given that there is less practice. Nonetheless, it is true that some distinguished writers have been unimpressed with much of the recent writing on recognition. Roth is able to answer some of the criticisms: especially, he is aware that non-recognition belongs to a different part of the international law from recognizing/not recognizing decisions: they are to do with status and relations; non-recognition is to do with sanctioning. Confusion occurs when, as a consequence of the sanctioning of an 'illegitimate' regime, it is necessary to affirm the status of an ineffective, 'legitimate' administration. Take Kuwait: the non-recognition of the Iraqi-installed government was part of the sanction process against Iraq, but the coincident confirmation of the recognition of the government of Kuwait was an exercise of the ordinary recognition process.

This chapter does go rather further than one might have anticipated, for more than half is concerned with intervention, though Roth does make useful connections between the two parts. The recognition section is rather disappointing: old-fashioned, unoriginal, incomplete, and not prepared to live with the legal idea of recognition. Recognition is a legal institution (even if the decision to recognize or not to recognize is taken on political grounds). Even though it is a wide discretion, it is not an unlimited one; whether exercised or not, there will be different legal consequences for those involved. Recognition is recognition; things which are 'like' recognition are not recognition. States know the difference: that is why some of them have said that they will no longer recognize governments and continue to insist that their relations with a particular regime are not 'recognition'.

Roth is not an unreconstructed traditionalist. He acknowledges that developments under and influenced by the Charter have affected significantly the placement of the line between the internal and external affairs of States, though he is much more cautious than some human rights enthusiasts about quite how far the displacement has been made. There might, then, be another way—a universal, minimum (?legal) standard of legitimacy, which would apply at least to changes of government. Democracy is the presently favoured candidate but, as Roth readily concedes, democracy has many shapes. He dismantles one version—'Revolutionary Democratic Dictatorship'—though he does not judge its prospects to be at an end as a result of the changes in eastern Europe and the Soviet Union. None the less, the tensions the survivor regimes face (Cuba, North Korea), and the obstacles to resurrection elsewhere, have made at least plausible the view that liberal democracy has triumphed as the universal ideology (p. 119). But Roth has his doubts about the merits of the prevalent liberal model—one embracing purely negative rights and enhancing economic advantage, so long as nominally dependent on an electoral process. Roth deals at some length with the intervention in Haiti. The limited hopes which prevailed at the time he was writing have scarcely been sustained. The situation in

Sierra Leone, which was just beginning to catch attention when Roth was finishing his book, would have been an even more interesting (but hardly less depressing) case.

In his conclusion, Roth writes, (p. 419).

> And while the international community may increasingly come to common judgments as to what is not the will of a given people, it has far less reason to affirm a particular system of government as an enforceable right.

These adverse judgments are usually reached after a government which has won a tolerably fair election is denied office or soon replaced by a group which has no such endorsement to rely on. The importance of this is that the delegitimization of the usurper does not result in a vacuum but in support for the continuingly 'legitimate', if ineffective, government. There may not often be any prospect of the government being forcibly restored (though there are some examples) but the displaced regime can be paid diplomatic tribute, can exercise the external powers of the State, can cast imprecation against its overthrower in international meetings and, just possibly, serve as a focus for activity which can one day lead the people of the State to replace the delegitimized regime. Only the last would be of much consolation to the people whom the delegitimizing policy is supposed to benefit. As far as a 'legitimate' delegitimizing standard goes, based on democratic governance, Roth has two reservations: one, that the standard lacks provenance as a rule of international law because it carries within itself a contradiction—only the liberal democratic model is permitted, but the generality of State practice does not support such a rule; the other, that this legitimacy standard, like all those invoked before, constitutes a threat to peace when it is invoked, perhaps in bad faith, but also when it is relied on by the missionary intervener against a regime, the lack of popular support for which might be highly contestable.

This has been a long review but Roth's book deserves close attention. It does not say that progress in this area cannot be made, but does indicate that it will not be easy.

COLIN WARBRICK

New Political Entities in Public and Private International Law. With Special Reference to the Palestinian Entity. Edited by A. SHAPIRA and M. TABORY. The Hague: Kluwer Law International, 1999. viii + 430 pp. £92.75.

This book is the outcome of a conference held in Tel Aviv involving scholars from the Max Planck Institutes in Heidelberg and Hamburg and Israeli officials and scholars, under the auspices of the Cegla Institute for Comparative and Private International Law. The conference, apparently held in 1996 (though the preface does not say so), focused on the status of the Palestinian Entity in public and private international law, and on certain related questions arising from the Peace Process. So too does the book, whose title and sub-title might with more accuracy have been reversed. The book is well produced. Unlike many edited collections of conference papers, it contains a comprehensive index.

The work itself is divided into three parts. Six essays in Part I focus on the 'political, legal and security framework'; four in Part II, on human rights, and four rather miscellaneously in Part III deal with 'legal assistance, economic and environmental aspects'. As might be imagined, there is considerable overlap between the parts, and especially between Parts I and II.

Part I contains a general introduction by Lapidoth, based on her earlier work on autonomous areas: she suggests that 'in case of diffusion of powers, both the central government and the regional and autonomous authorities could each be the lawful bearer of a share of sovereignty', without necessarily leading to the dismemberment of the State.

Such cases, however, do not extend to 'situations of mere administrative autonomy' (p. 15).

In a second chapter, the chief Israeli negotiator of the Declaration of Principles of 1993 (the Oslo Accord) sets out the Israeli view of its 'relatively abstract' provisions, as well as the detailed terms of the Interim Agreement of 1995. He argues that 'with regard to most of the issues involved, the Israeli interpretation of those DOP provisions was accepted' (p. 18): accordingly the position under these agreements is that of 'Palestinian autonomous areas under the supreme authority of an Israeli military government' (p. 49). Singer's account is lucid and well informed, taking the position in terms of implementation down to mid-1996. But of course much has happened since then.

Another Israeli lawyer involved in the negotiations, Daniel Reisner, shows how apparently technical issues of the transfer of civil power (issue of stamps, travel documents, electricity supply) raised fundamental political or even 'existential' problems (p. 72), owing to the conflicting aims of the two parties. Again this is a thoughtful and extremely well-informed review from its particular perspective, giving considerable insight into the negotiating process.

The first German contribution to the volume attempts to give some content to the idea of new political entities in the conflict of laws. Arguing for an autonomous concept of the State in private international law, independent of its understanding in public international law, Busse suggests that rights arising by virtue of Palestinian law or administration pursuant to the Interim Agreement should be treated as rights arising under the law of a State and recognized for the purpose of the conflict of laws (p. 120). The conclusion can hardly be doubted, since the only other candidate law, Israeli law, does not even claim to apply to such transactions. But Israeli law does claim to apply to transactions in the West Bank, and the simplistic criterion of 'effectiveness' offered by the author would hardly be a sufficient basis for resolving conflicts arising there between two putative legal systems, both of which had some effectiveness and both of which claim to apply. The criteria he proposes for dealing with actual conflicting claims between overlapping or partial legal systems are elementary, not to say jejeune, and the distinction now proposed between the 'public' and 'private' domain is simplistic. Private international law's 'autonomous' approach to the State would seem to have a considerable distance to travel—and indeed these issues effectively vanish from later chapters.

Returning to the main (as distinct from ostensible) theme of the volume, the co-editor, Tabory, briefly assesses the legal personality of what is termed 'the Palestinian autonomy'. Proceeding from the basis that 'there is no international acknowledgment of the acceptance of a state of Palestine' (p. 141), the chapter avoids analysing such questions as the controversy over the Algiers Declaration, the effect of the recognition of that Declaration by a significant number of States, or the relation between the underlying legal position of the Palestine people under the Mandate and the various arrangements which have been part of the Peace Process. Instead it is simply asserted that the PLO's claim to representative status externally 'has no basis in the constituting IA' (p. 146). The author is, no doubt, accurate in portraying the intended effect of the Interim Agreement so far as the Israeli Government is concerned—but at the level of general international law there is more to be said. The chapter thus fails to address adequately the central promise of the book's title.

A second German contribution, by Tobias Stoll, looks in some detail at the security arrangements pursuant to the various agreements, summarizing succinctly the various arrangements before going on to consider who would be legally responsible in the event of breaches of security. In effect the question is whether the Palestinian Authority is a mere delegate of the occupying power for the purposes of responsibility for security issues or more generally: the two previous essays merely assumed or asserted answers to that question, whereas Stoll analyses them with some finesse.

Part II brings together four essays under the rubric of 'human rights'. The point is, apparently, to consider the Middle East conflict 'as a confrontation over contradictory human rights claims, and not as a conflict centering on sovereignty over territory or peoples' (p. 183). But this is a false dichotomy. The international law of human rights operates in relation to the State or, more generally, the holders of public power, and it includes among its concerns the claims of peoples as well as individuals. Griegerich in the first of the essays clearly sees this, and he provides a review of issues precisely centering on sovereignty or rights over territory or people, such as one might have expected to find in Part I. While not abandoning a human rights emphasis, he deals with such issues as the characterization of the Declaration of Principles as an international treaty, the status of the Palestinians as a 'people', the conflict of 'third generation rights' (self-determination versus peace) underlying the process, and the relation between the legal personality of the PLO and the Authority.

In similar vein, Andreas Zimmermann considers the nationality of the inhabitants of the Palestinian autonomous territories. He takes the view that Palestinian nationality was abolished in 1947 by the termination of the Mandate and the creation of Israel (p. 235). Having regard in particular to Jordan's renunciation of nationality claims to the Palestinians in 1988, the result is that Palestinians who have not acquired third State nationality were stateless (p. 237). But in his view this is no longer so, since the actual and embryonic rights of Palestinians under IA are enough to justify connecting them for international law purposes to the territory of the West Bank and Gaza (p. 245).

Natan Lerner considers the question of minority rights, providing a *tour d'horizon* of developments in the field of minorities protection, but without any reference to the Peace Process. By contrast, Fania Domb from Tel Aviv University begins by asking to what extent the Peace Process itself implements the 'legitimate rights of the Palestinian people and their just requirements' (p. 263, citing Article A(1)(C) of the Camp David Agreement). The answer is a brief affirmative: the author goes on to argue that the Palestinian Authority is bound by the general customary international law of human rights as to all persons within its jurisdiction (p. 287).

Briefer notice only is required of the chapters in Part III, dealing with a miscellany of 'functional' matters. Thilo Marauhn discusses fiscal and monetary aspects of the Peace Process from the perspective of public international law; Heiner Braun surveys issues of protection of investments in the autonomous territories; Andrea Peddinghaus seeks to compare the incomparable, looking at the experience of the emergent economies of central Europe for possible guidance so far as the Palestine economy is concerned, and Nicholas Blanchard discusses the role of conflict of laws in relation to transboundary pollution of water.

It is a pity that there is no general conclusion to the volume, such as might have been provided by one or more of the Directors of the two Max Planck Institutes involved in the conference. Lacking such a conclusion, and given the rather heterogeneous subjects dealt with, the book is not more than the sum of its parts. It certainly does not fulfil the promise of its title, nor even—for that matter—of its sub-title. Its principal value lies in the insight afforded as to Israeli intentions in the Peace Process (Singer, Reisner), evolving negotiating techniques (Reisner) and questions of devolved responsibility especially in the field of human rights (Stoll, Griegerich, Zimmermann, Domb).

JAMES CRAWFORD

The Changing International Law of High Seas Fisheries. By FRANCISCO ORREGO VICUÑA. Cambridge: Cambridge University Press, 1999. 338 pp. £45.

The changing nature of the high seas fisheries regime provides the focus of this book written by a recognized authority in the field. The author most certainly succeeds in providing a thoroughly readable account of developments in this important area including the adoption of the 1995 Agreement for the Implementation of the Provisions of the UN Convention on the Law of the Sea relating to the Conservation and Management of Straddling Fish Stocks and Highly Migratory Fish Stocks (the 1995 Agreement), an agreement of crucial importance, being the first global accord to regulate straddling fish stocks and highly migratory fish stocks and to provide for the peaceful settlement of disputes that may arise in their exploitation.

The scene is set with a discussion of the evolving principles and concepts in this area of the law and, in particular, the traditional high seas freedom of fishing. It is explained that this principle has in fact for some time been recognized as not being absolute in nature, but rather subject to the principles of reasonable use and equitable allocation of resources. However, as pressures on the resources of the sea were none the less augmented by improvements in the technology utilized by fishing fleets, the author rightly notes that the extension of national jurisdiction by the adoption of exclusive economic or fisheries zones should be seen as an attempt by coastal States to ensure that stocks are managed more effectively within these 200-mile zones.

The implications of the extension of coastal State jurisdiction do not, however, provide the main focus of the book. Instead, the work goes on to highlight the importance of the 1982 Convention on the Law of the Sea in the development of broad approaches to the management of high seas fish stocks, noting that, in addition to recognizing national jurisdiction over the EEZ, this treaty also placed greater emphasis on the conservation and management of high seas fisheries in waters adjacent to and beyond the 200-mile EEZ. The author underlines that, although these new approaches lacked the detail required to regulate high seas fisheries effectively, their introduction established legal principles which proved capable of being developed at a later stage, particularly in the form of the 1995 Agreement.

In relation to the period after the signing of the Law of the Sea Convention, he goes on to note that the pressures on straddling fish stocks and highly migratory fish stocks began to be recognized as a global issue, with distant-water fishing fleets turning their attention to those stocks located in the high seas, and away from the over-exploited stocks located within areas now subject to national jurisdiction. In this context, the author highlights well the wide variety of disputes (such as the recent EC/Canada dispute in the north-west Atlantic) which have arisen between coastal States and distant-water fishing countries as to the regulation of fish stocks in the high seas, and the reasoning behind the widespread recognition that a supplementary international legal framework, building upon the general provisions of the Law of the Sea Convention, was required to regulate high seas fisheries. Discussion consequently moves on to cover the convening of the United Nations Conference on Straddling Fish Stocks and Highly Migratory Fish Stocks by resolution of the UN General Assembly in December 1992, and to provide a detailed assessment of the 1995 Agreement which, *inter alia*, establishes basic principles on the conservation and management of high seas fisheries.

The crucial influence upon the 1995 Agreement of evolving basic principles and concepts of international environmental law (such as the concept of sustainable development, the ecosystem approach, and the precautionary principle), and of the need to balance the interests of coastal States and distant-water fishing States are lucidly detailed. The added influence of international and State practice since the third UN Conference on the Law of the Sea is also addressed. The author also details the nature and extent of the duty placed on States under the 1995 Agreement to co-operate with a view to ensuring the proper conservation and sustainable use of fish stocks, and a chapter is devoted to the manner in which conservation and management measures relating to straddling and migratory stocks are to be enforced by flag, port and coastal States. The work concludes by addressing the issue of dispute settlement under the 1995 Agreement, the author rightly noting that this issue 'is the third essential pillar on which the 1995 Agreement is built, together with the principles of conservation and management, and the mechanisms on compliance.' (p. 267).

The author, who was President of the Chilean Delegation to UNCLOS III, is to be highly commended for producing a learned account of the recent significant developments in this area of the law. The point is well made that the 1995 Agreement is a compromise which accommodates the conflicting interests of coastal States and distant-water fishing nations, and only seeks to regulate particular types of fish stocks. Nevertheless the author correctly indicates that it is an agreement which has already had a significant influence on the framework of high seas fisheries generally, and will continue to do so in the future.

PETER DAVIES

International Compliance with Nonbinding Accords. Edited by EDITH BROWN WEISS. Washington, DC: The American Society of International Law, 1997. 264 pp. $25 (members); $35 (non-members).

This is a collection of papers presented at an American Society of International Law workshop held in Chantilly, Virginia, in May 1996 to study compliance with nonbinding legal accords, or 'soft law', and to explore the hypothesis that under some circumstances countries comply with nonbinding legal instruments as well as they do with binding ones. The participants set themselves a hard task: nonbinding instruments come in a variety of shapes and sizes, and are difficult to define and sometimes even to recognize (save where the instrument itself proclaims its nonbinding character, as in the case of the 1992 Statement of Forest Principles adopted by the UN Conference on Environment and Development). They give rise to an enormous diversity of methods of implementation by both international and domestic agencies. It is therefore not surprising that the conclusion of most of the papers is that more research is needed before the above hypothesis can be proved or disproved.

In her introduction to the volume, Edith Brown Weiss discusses the characteristics of nonbinding instruments, saying that they 'represent norms which may be observed even though the states and other actors are not strictly required to do so. They create an expectation that they may shape behaviour and may be used to avoid or resolve disputes', even though they cannot be enforced in courts or through other formal methods of adjudication. She gives a general introduction to the existing literature on compliance; she then summarizes the papers which comprise the rest of the volume and points to directions which further inquiries might take.

The first three of the eight papers concerns the general theoretical aspects of compliance. Peter Haas considers a range of different approaches (such as 'game theory' or 'functional institutionalism') to understanding why States choose to comply with both binding and nonbinding accords. Benedict Kingsbury seeks to relate concepts of compliance to four different theories of law: directive, constructivist, spontaneous and informal, and regulatory. Atsuko Kanehara examines developments in the concept of State sovereignty, pointing out that matters once considered to fall within domestic jurisdiction no longer do so; she looks at promotion of the common interests of States in the field of environmental law, and especially the principle of 'no harmful use of territory' articulated in Principle 21 of the 1972 Stockholm Declaration on the Human Environment—a principle which she considers 'has crystallized into a customary principle of international law'. She concludes that although the system of sovereign States may be changing, it 'still remains strong as the basic structure of international law', and that States need to be given wide discretion in taking domestic measures to attain internationally agreed goals of environmental protection.

The remaining five papers examine particular areas in which nonbinding accords play a major role. Dinah Shelton provides an illuminating analysis of the sources of soft law in the field of human rights and of methods of assessing compliance. The influence of nonbinding instruments relating to human rights cannot be doubted: readers of successive instalments of 'United Kingdom Materials on International Law' in this *Year Book* will appreciate the weight given by the UK Government to the 1975 Helsinki Final Act and 1993 Vienna Declaration in its public pronouncements on human rights. Environmental matters are dealt with by Richard Parker, who advocates a system of 'benchmark standards', by Naomi Roht-Arriaza, who considers the work of the International Organization for Standardization in establishing an environment management system for companies, and by David Wirth, who deals with the techniques adopted by the World Bank group of organizations to ensure that projects financed by the group come up to environmental 'good practice' standards. Finally, Virginia Leary discusses nonbinding accords in the field of labour, and concludes that although instruments such as ILO recommendations have an important role to play, they are less effective than binding conventions.

The point is made expressly or impliedly in many of these papers that there is a continuous process of transformation from soft law to hard law, so that today's nonbinding instrument may be (but will not necessarily be) the basis of tomorrow's treaty or rule of customary law. Compliance, as State practice and as evidence of *opinio juris*, must play an important role in this process. The contributors to this volume must be applauded for the skill with which they tackle a very amorphous area, and it is not their fault if no very firm conclusions emerge from their work.

C. A. Hopkins

DECISIONS OF BRITISH COURTS DURING 2000 INVOLVING QUESTIONS OF PUBLIC OR PRIVATE INTERNATIONAL LAW

A. Public International Law[1]

State immunity—State Immunity Act 1978, Section 16(2)—visiting armed forces—scope of State immunity under the common law—European Convention for the Protection of Human Rights and Fundamental Freedoms, Article 6—relationship between the customary international law of human rights and State immunity

Case No. 1. Holland v. *Lampen-Wolfe*, 20 July 2000, [2000] 1 WLR 1573, [2000] 3 All ER 833, <http://www.publications.parliament.uk/pa> (HL).

The appellant was a citizen of the United States and an employee of an American university who was seconded to teach courses on international relations at a United States military base in North Yorkshire. The respondent was also a citizen of the United States, and an educational services officer in the United States Department of Defence. In that capacity, he wrote a memorandum about the appellant's performance that she claimed was defamatory. The United States asserted immunity for the respondent under Section 16(2) of the State Immunity Act 1978. Section 16(2) displaces Part One of the Act in proceedings relating to 'anything done by or in relation to the armed forces of a state while present in the United Kingdom' and by doing so renders the issue of immunity one of common law.

The Lords agreed that the respondent's acts were done 'in relation to the armed forces'. As Lord Hope explained, this was determined by reference to the nature of the duties which the respondent was in the United Kingdom to perform, and those duties involved the provision of a curriculum that 'was designed to directly complement the professional military education programs of the various services'.[2]

With regard to the common law of immunity, the Lords relied on *Littrell* v. *United States of America (No. 2)* where immunity was upheld in a case involving allegedly negligent medical treatment in a United States military hospital. There Hoffmann LJ had required a close examination of the facts to determine whether the act in question was *jure imperii* or *jure gestionis*:

> The context in which the act took place was the maintenance by the United States of a unit of the United States Air Force in the United Kingdom. This looks about as imperial an activity as could be imagined. But it would be facile to regard this context as determinative of the question. Acts done within that context range from arrangement concerning the flights of the bombers—plainly jure imperii—to ordering milk for the base

[1] © Professor Michael Byers, 2001.

[2] [2000] 1 WLR 1573 at 1577, [2000] 3 All ER 833 at 836.

from a local dairy or careless driving by off-duty airmen on the roads of Suffolk. Both of the latter would seem to me to be jure gestionis, fairly within an area of private law activity. I do not think that there is a single test or 'bright line' by which cases on either side can be distinguished. Rather, there are a number of factors which may characterise the act as nearer to or further from the central military activity . . . Some acts are wholly military in character, some almost entirely private or commercial and some in between.[3]

Lord Millett considered the instant case from this perspective:

The fact that the services in question were brought in rather than provided internally is not decisive. Of greater significance are the facts that they were provided at United States military bases and involved only citizens of the United States. The courses were provided by and to United States citizens and were designed to complement military programmes and assist (*inter alia*) in the assessment of candidates for promotion. In today's conditions the education and training of military personnel so as to make them fit for promotion or service overseas or to ease their transition to civilian life on retirement from active service is a normal and necessary part of the maintenance of a nation's armed forces. In my opinion the standard of education which the United States affords its own servicemen and their families is as much a matter within its own sovereign authority as is the standard of medical care which it affords them. Neither ought to be subjected to the supervision or jurisdiction of another state.[4]

The appellant made the additional argument that under Article 6 of the European Convention for the Protection of Human Rights and Fundamental Freedoms she had a right to an effective remedy for her claim and that immunity should not therefore be granted.[5] The court disagreed, on the basis that the United Kingdom's obligation to respect the United States' right to immunity under customary international law constituted a limitation on the rights it could grant under the Convention. As Lord Millet explained:

Article 6 requires contracting states to maintain fair and public judicial processes and forbids them to deny individuals access to those processes for the determination of their civil rights. It presupposes that the contracting states have the powers of adjudication necessary to resolve the issues in dispute. But it does not confer on contracting states adjudicative powers which they do not posses. State immunity . . . is a creature of customary international law and derives from the equality of sovereign states. It is not a self-imposed restriction on the jurisdiction of its courts which the United Kingdom has chosen to adopt. It is a limitation imposed from without upon the sovereignty of the United Kingdom itself.

The immunity in question in the present case belongs to the United States. The United States has not waived its immunity. It is not a party to the Convention. The Convention derives its binding force from the consent of the contracting states. The United Kingdom cannot, by its own act of acceding to the Convention and without the consent of the United States, obtain a power of adjudication over the United States which international law denies it.[6]

[3] [1995] 1 WLR 82 at 94–5, [1994] 4 All ER 203 at 216–17, this *Year Book*, 65 (1994), pp. 491–6.

[4] [2000] 1 WLR 1573 at 1586–7, [2000] 3 All ER 833 at 836.

[5] *United Nations Treaty Series*, vol. 213, p. 221; *UK Treaty Series*, No. 71 (1953), Cmd. 8969. At the time the case was heard the Human Rights Act 1998 had not entered into force.

[6] [2000] 1 WLR 1573 at 1588, [2000] 3 All ER 833 at 847–8.

Although the Court was right to conclude that obligations to a third State under customary international law cannot be altered by a treaty to which that State is not a party, it was careful to avoid a more difficult issue that is currently before the European Court of Human Rights. Could the provisions of a human rights treaty constitute a waiver of immunity by the States that have ratified that treaty?[7] Moreover, could the customary international law of State immunity be affected by the development of human rights as well in customary international law?

Lord Cooke, in his judgment, considered the latter issue—although only in respect of the customary international law right of access to an impartial court. In *Regina* v. *Bow Street Metropolitan Stipendiary Magistrate and Others, ex parte Pinochet Ugarte (No. 1)*, similar legal developments concerning torture had led three Law Lords to deny State immunity under the common law.[8] Here, however, Lord Cooke held that the scope of properly sovereign activities could not only become more restricted as a result of changing circumstances; it could in some cases actually expand:

> At the present day, I think, a state may reasonably claim to have welfare and educational responsibilities towards the members of its armed forces. In turn the quality and efficacy of the forces may be strengthened if the state discharges those responsibilities. In their discharge the state may reasonably claim that it should not be subject to interference by other states or their courts. This is such a case. The government of the United States having reasonably claimed the immunity, I agree that it should be upheld as a modern application of the principle of *par in parem* to which Lord Wilberforce referred in *I Congreso*.[9]

Lord Cooke is right that, if changing circumstances can lead to restrictions in the scope of State immunity, this process must be able to work in the opposite direction as well. However, the consequences of this insight are likely very limited. With State functions being increasingly transferred to, or duplicated by, private actors, and with sovereign prerogatives becoming increasingly limited as a result, the overall trend is towards less rather than more immunity.

[7] Three cases on this issue are currently before the European Court of Human Rights. For the decisions on admissibility, see *Fogarty* v. *United Kingdom* (Application No. 37112/97), 1 March 2000; *Al-Adsani* v. *United Kingdom* (Application No. 35763/97), 1 March 2000; *McElhinney* v. *Ireland* (Application No. 31253/96), 9 February 2000. All available at: <http://www.echr.coe.int/>. In a recent case involving the similar issue of international organization immunity, the ECHR held that Article 6 of the European Convention did not prevail over an immunity granted by a treaty, namely the 1975 European Space Agency Convention, *United Nations Treaty Series*, vol. 1297, p. 186. See *Waite and Kennedy* v. *Germany* (Application No. 26083/94), [1999] 30 EHRR 261.

[8] [1998] 3 WLR 1456, [1998] 4 All ER 897, (1998) 37 International Legal Materials 1302, <http://www.publications.parliament.uk/pa> (HL), this *Year Book*, 70 (1999), pp. 277–83. See also, Lord Millet's judgment in *Regina* v. *Bow Street Metropolitan Stipendiary Magistrate and Others, ex parte Pinochet Ugarte (No. 3)* [1999] 2 WLR 827, [1999] 2 All ER 97, (1999) 38 International Legal Materials 581, <http://www.publications.parliament.uk/pa>, this *Year Book*, 70 (1999), pp. 283–93.

[9] [2000] 1 WLR 1573 at 1578–9, [2000] 3 All ER 833 at 838. For the decision in *I Congreso*, see [1983] 1 AC 244, [1981] 3 WLR 328, [1981] 2 All ER 1064, this *Year Book*, 52 (1981), pp. 314–19.

Act of State doctrine—'Buttes' non-justiciability—whether an English court would recognize an Iraqi resolution transferring Kuwait Airways aircraft to Iraqi Airways—effect of Iraq's admission that it had violated international law—effect of a clear expression of policy by the United Kingdom government—whether the illegal use of force between States offends English public policy so as to override the act of State doctrine

Case No. 2. Kuwait Airways Corporation v. *Iraqi Airways Company*, 10 November 2000, <http://www.courtservice.gov.uk/> (CA).

After the Iraqi invasion of Kuwait in August 1990, the Revolutionary Council of Iraq ('RCC') passed Resolutions 312 and 313 designating Kuwait as a Governate forming an integral part of Iraq. This case arose out of a claim by Kuwait Airways Corporation ('KAC') for wrongful interference with ten of its aircraft during the occupation. The aircraft, which had been at Kuwait Airport at the time of the invasion, were seized and removed to Iraq. On 17 September 1990, the RCC passed Resolution 369, which purported to dissolve KAC and transfer the assets to Iraqi Airways Company ('IAC'). IAC then treated the aircraft as its own: six were flown to Iran where they were interned by the Iranian authorities and the remaining four were partially or wholly destroyed in air raids by the coalition forces.

In interlocutory proceedings the House of Lords held that IAC, as a separate entity acting in the exercise of sovereign authority, was, under Section 14(2)(a) of the State Immunity Act 1978, entitled to immunity in respect of the taking and removal of the aircraft to Iraq. However, it also held that this immunity did not extend to any subsequent retention and use of the aircraft in consequence of the purported vesting in IAC of ownership by legislative decree. Lord Goff, speaking for the majority, said:

> Plainly, a separate entity of a state cannot ipso facto claim sovereign immunity in respect of a claim by the former owner, though it may well be able to plead, by way of defence, that its actions were not unlawful. Nor can it be said . . . that the acts done by IAC after 17 September 1990 were mere outward manifestations of a denial of title which occurred at the time of the seizure of the aircraft. As I understand the position, such acts constituted fresh acts of conversion, though the limitation period may, under the statute [a reference to the Limitation Act 1980, section 3(1)], run from an earlier date . . . .
>
> Finally, I do not think it relevant that (as was very probably the case) the Iraqi government would not have tolerated return of the aircraft by IAC to KAC. For the fact remains that IAC in treating the aircraft as its own, was doing so pursuant to the Iraqi legislation which vested the aircraft in IAC; and by doing it cannot be said to have acted in the exercise of sovereign authority.[10]

Lord Goff left open the possibility that IAC might have a defence based on its submission that the matters relied upon would involve the court in adjudicating on transactions of a foreign State in the conduct of foreign relations, or on sovereign acts done by a foreign State in respect of persons or property within its jurisdiction which were non-justiciable in the English courts.

In English law, the act of State doctrine holds that the courts will not inquire into the validity of those acts or laws of a foreign State which purport to take

[10] [1995] 1 WLR 1147 at 1163, [1995] 3 All ER 694 at 711, this *Year Book*, 66 (1995), pp. 496–501, HL.

effect within that State's territory. This doctrine prevents English courts from exercising jurisdiction in respect of such acts or laws even when the foreign State concerned is not a party to the suit.[11]

The related doctrine of non-justiciability is often referred to as '*Buttes* non-justiciability' after the leading case on the point, *Buttes Gas and Oil Co.* v. *Hammer*.[12] It holds that national courts are not competent to rule on the rights and duties of States as between themselves. Both the act of State doctrine and *Buttes* non-justiciability operate *rationae materiae* as substantive defences, as compared to immunities *rationae personae* which are preliminary objections to jurisdiction. The act of State doctrine and *Buttes* non-justiciability are questions of competence to adjudicate, rather than questions of an accorded privilege.[13] They therefore arise at a later procedural stage than issues of diplomatic or State immunity.

The act of State and non-justiciability issues raised by IAC, as well as several issues of causation and remoteness, were returned to the Divisional Court. There, in a lengthy sole judgment, Mance J concluded that acts in violation of international law or contrary to the express policy of the United Kingdom government could not benefit from either the act of State doctrine or *Buttes* non-justiciability.[14] The issues of causation and remoteness were heard separately by Aikens J.[15] Both judgments were appealed to the Court of Appeal, which heard the two cases together.

In a judgment of the court, Henry, Brooke and Rix LJJ conducted an extensive review of the case law, as well as the writings of a number of authors. In respect of the act of State doctrine they observed that there was a 'prima facie rule that a foreign sovereign is to be accorded . . . absolute authority . . . to act within his own territory'. This rule was subject to certain exceptions, one of which was that 'a penal or discriminatory act of a foreign sovereign cannot be made the basis of a claim in our courts'. However, the breadth of this public policy exception was uncertain. What was needed, according to the Court, was 'a balanced answer to the conflicting needs of private rights, sovereign immunities, and international relations'. This, the judges held, was to be found in generally accepted principles of international law:

> It ought to come as no surprise that restraints on judicial intervention that are suggested or required by considerations of what the international community of nations demands in certain situations should themselves be susceptible to exceptions which are mandated by clearly established principles of international law. If English public policy can be shown to differ from such principles, then no doubt the courts of this country will be required to follow the dictates or limits of that public policy. But there is, at any rate in the abstract, every reason to think that in most cases English public policy will be at one with, and will be illuminated by, clearly established principles of international law.

[11] See generally *Blad* v. *Bamfield*, (1674) 3 Swans. 603, 36 ER 991; *Duke of Brunswick* v. *King of Hanover*, (1848) 2 HL Ca. 1, 21–2; *Luther* v. *Sagor*, [1921] 3 KB 532; *Princess Paley Olga* v. *Weisz*, [1929] 1 KB 718.

[12] [1982] AC 888, [1981] 3 WLR 787, [1981] 3 All ER 616, this *Year Book*, 53 (1982), pp. 259–68. See also *Cook* v. *Sprigg*, [1899] AC 572.

[13] See *Kuwait Airways Corporation* v. *Iraqi Airways Co.*, [1995] 1 WLR 1147 at 1167, [1995] 3 All ER 694 at 714–15, this *Year Book*, 66 (1995), pp. 496–501, HL.

[14] [1999] CLC 31, [1999] 116 ILR 534, this *Year Book*, 69 (1998), pp. 305–14.

[15] [2000] 2 All ER 360.

In respect of non-justiciability, which applies 'whether the sovereign acts within his own territory or outside it', the Court explained that guidance

> is to be found in such considerations as whether there are 'judicial or manageable standards' by which to resolve the dispute, whether the court would be in 'a judicial no-man's land', or perhaps whether there would be embarrassment in our foreign relations, at any rate if that possibility was drawn to the court's attention by the executive.

Other situations calling for judicial restraint included '[s]ensitive issues involving diplomacy between states, or uncertain or controversial issues of international law'. And as the Court explained:

> The distinction which has been developed in the analogous area of sovereign immunity between situations where the sovereign acts by way of sovereign authority (acta iure imperii) and where he acts in the commercial sphere (acta iure gestionis) may also be of some assistance, because with the development of the restrictive theory of sovereign immunity there has come the realisation that it is not every impleading of a sovereign that requires judicial restraint or gives rise to a legitimate fear of giving offence. In essence, the principle of non-justiciability seeks to distinguish disputes involving sovereign authority which can only be resolved on a state to state level from disputes which can be resolved by judicial means.

The Court then applied these conclusions to the facts of the case, but without going so far as to adopt Mance J's conclusion that neither the act of State doctrine nor *Buttes* non-justiciability could apply when the acts in question had been deemed illegal by the UN Security Council:

> We agree that the Security Council resolutions, against the background of the Charter of the United Nations, to which both the United Kingdom and Iraq were signatories, were binding on both nations, and indeed on all member states of the United Nations, which embrace practically all the nations in the world. We agree also that this material provides clear evidence of breach by Iraq of clearly established principles of international law. Indeed, the opposite has not been asserted on behalf of IAC. The only difficulty which perhaps might be said to arise with the judge's approach in principle is that it ought in theory to be possible to decide whether KAC's claim is justiciable or not without first entering upon an adjudication of whether Iraq's conduct is or is not contrary to international law, which involves sitting in judgment on that conduct. . . . Whatever jurisdictional claim may have been the colourable pretext of Iraq's invasion and annexation of Kuwait, Iraq itself had by March 1991 foresworn its own actions, albeit under force of arms, and accepted that it was obliged to reverse its conduct.
>
> In these circumstances, there was nothing precarious or delicate, and nothing subject to diplomacy, which judicial adjudication might threaten; there could be no embarrassment to diplomatic relations, no casus belli, and nothing to vex the peace of nations in judicial investigation . . . . [T]here is no need to decide the question of international law, or to speculate about other invasions or annexations past or future, or to prejudge the applicability of the territorial act of state doctrine, in order to conclude that KAC's claim does not fall to be driven away from the courts on the ground of non-justiciability.

The Court also accorded great weight to an expressed policy of the United Kingdom Government. Pursuant to an order of the Divisional Court, the Secretary of State for Foreign and Commonwealth Affairs had been asked: 'Has Her Majesty's Government recognized at any time that the State of Iraq exercised de facto sovereign power in Kuwait as at 17 September 1990 or at any time thereafter?' The response from Sir Franklin Berman, the Legal Adviser to the Foreign and Commonwealth Office, read in part as follows:

> Her Majesty's Government in the United Kingdom have not at any time, throughout the period from the date specified in the learned Judge's Order until the expulsion of Iraqi forces from Kuwait on 26 February 1991, recognized Iraqi occupation or control over the territory of Kuwait.
>
> On 6 August 1990, four days after Iraqi invasion and occupation of Kuwait, the Security Council of the United Nations adopted Resolution No 661 (1990). This Resolution was binding on all Member States under the terms of the Charter of the United Nations and determined inter alia that Iraq had usurped the authority of the legitimate Government of Kuwait and that all States should not recognise any regime set up by the occupying Power.
>
> On 9 August 1990, the Security Council adopted Resolution No 662 (1990). This Resolution was likewise binding on all Member States . . .
>
> A subsequent decision of the Security Council of 2 March 1991 required Iraq to rescind immediately its actions purporting to annex Kuwait.
>
> The conduct of Her Majesty's Government in the United Kingdom has been strictly in conformity with the requirements of these Resolutions and all other pertinent decisions of the Security Council relating to the Iraqi invasion and occupation of Kuwait.

As the Court of Appeal explained, '[t]he Berman letter provided an opportunity for the executive branch of government to make known to the judicial branch any concern it might have felt about the non-justiciability of the issues raised by KAC's claim, and to do so against the background of the speech of Lord Wilberforce in Buttes Gas . . . '

Although there is nothing wrong with the Court's conclusion, the approach adopted by it is unlikely to be available in most cases of this kind. Simply put, those invoking the act of State doctrine or *Buttes* non-justiciability are unlikely to admit to having violated international law. Nor will the United Kingdom Government always express its views so clearly. In such circumstances, courts will still have to look to any relevant Security Council resolutions and, in the absence of such resolutions, to their own assessments of English public policy as informed by international law.

Lastly, the Court considered whether the violations of international law giving rise to this case were of such a character as to trigger a refusal to recognize a foreign government's acts or laws on the basis of English public policy:

> This case may not be concerned with individual human rights in the direct way in which they were in issue in Oppenheimer v Cattermole if only because the present claimant is a corporation. Nevertheless, the context of war and peace is one of hardly less fundamental importance to the welfare of mankind, as the preamble to the UN Charter makes abundantly clear. There the reaffirmation of fundamental faith in human rights and in the dignity and worth of the human person are sandwiched between references to the scourge of war, the need to maintain international peace and security and the need to ensure that armed force not be used save in the common interest. It is a commonplace that it is in the midst of war that human rights are often most easily trampled on. Moreover the fundamental nature of the purposes and principles of the Charter are

underlined by the provision in article 103 to the effect that its obligations are paramount.[16]

As with Mance J's judgment in the Divisional Court, the Court of Appeal's conclusion that acts in violation of international law or contrary to the expressed policy of the United Kingdom government cannot benefit from the act of State doctrine or '*Buttes* non-justiciability' is to be commended as properly situating these doctrines of limited judicial restraint within the increasingly comprehensive and detailed international legal system. At the same time, the judgment still leaves at least some questions unanswered. Is the exception for acts in violation of international law restricted to illegal uses of force and particularly serious human rights violations? If it only applies to some violations, how should the courts draw the line? Although the Court was on solid ground given the facts of this case, situations involving no expressed government policy and difficult determinations of international law will inevitably arise.

Extradition—1972 Extradition Treaty between the United States and the United Kingdom (Schedule 1 to the United States (Extradition) Order 1976), Articles III(4) & VII(4)—interpretation of extradition treaties—whether person who has served entire prison sentence but violated terms of supervised release is extraditable

Case No. 3. In Re Burke, 15 June 2000, [2000] 3 WLR 33, [2000] 3 All ER 481, <http://www.publications.parliament.uk/pa> (HL).

In 1992 the appellant pleaded guilty, in the United States, to two charges of bank robbery and was sentenced to five years in prison followed by five years of parole (i.e. supervised release). After completing the prison sentence, he left for the United Kingdom in violation of the terms of his release. He was arrested under a provisional warrant issued by the United States authorities who sought his extradition to serve the remainder of the release. The appellant sought a writ of *habeas corpus* on the basis that Articles III(4) and VII(4) of the 1972 Extradition Treaty between the United States and the United Kingdom, as set out in Schedule 1 to the United States (Extradition) Order 1976, should be read so as to restrict the extradition of persons sentenced on conviction for an extradition crime to those who remained subject to a period of imprisonment. Article III(4) reads:

> A person convicted of and sentenced for an offence shall not be extradited therefor unless he was sentenced to imprisonment or other form of detention for a period of four months or more or, subject to the provisions of article IV, to the death penalty.

Article VII(4) reads:

> If the request relates to a convicted person, it must be accompanied by a certificate or the judgment of conviction imposed in the territory of the requesting party, and by evidence that the person requested is the person to whom the conviction refers and, if the person

[16] For the decision in *Oppenheimer* v. *Cattermole*, see: [1976] AC 249, [1975] 1 All ER 538, this *Year Book*, 47 (1974–5), pp. 372–4.

was sentenced, by evidence of the sentence imposed and a statement showing to what extent the sentence has not been carried out.

When the Divisional Court ruled against the appellant, he appealed to the House of Lords.

Lord Hope, writing for the majority, regarded the treaty as 'a bargain between two contracting parties which is entitled to receive a liberal construction according to its own language, object and intent'.[17] He observed that the treaty was plainly 'designed to ensure, among other things, the return of a person who is unlawfully at large because he has escaped from custody'.[18] Since there was no express limitation to such cases, the question was 'whether a limitation to this effect is to regarded as implied'.[19] Lord Hope noted:

The only words of limitation contained in the treaty which are relevant to this issue are to be found in paragraph (4) of Article VII. These are to be found in the requirement that a request for extradition through the diplomatic channel which relates to a convicted person must be accompanied by evidence of the sentence imposed and a statement showing to what extent the sentence has not been carried out. It is implicit in the concluding phrase of this paragraph that the process of extradition is not to be resorted to in a case where the sentence has been carried out and there remains no unsatisfied element of punishment. This is consistent with the fact that extradition treaties are designed to ensure that persons who are convicted and sentenced in one country do not escape punishment by fleeing to another country before they have satisfied the sentence imposed by the court. If his sentence has been carried out, with the result that his punishment for the offence is over and done with, the person is not to be regarded as seeking to escape punishment and there is no longer any purpose to be served by his being extradited.

But it is significant that the word 'sentence' in each of the two phrases where it appears in the concluding words of this paragraph is not otherwise qualified. . . . [20]

On this basis, Lord Hope held:

[T]he word 'sentence' in the concluding phrase refers to the whole of the sentence described in the preceding phrase as 'the sentence imposed by the court'. The wording of this paragraph lends no encouragement to the idea that it is appropriate to separate out the custodial element in that sentence from the other elements.[21]

Lord Hutton, with whom Lord Hobhouse concurred, dissented. On the issue of treaty interpretation, Lord Hutton noted that in *In re Arton (No. 2)*, Lord Russell of Killowen CJ had said:

In my judgment these treaties ought to receive a liberal interpretation, which means no more than that they should receive their true construction according to their language, object, and intent.[22]

With regard to the text of the extradition treaty, Lord Hutton held:

[17] [2000] 3 WLR 33 at 38, [2000] 3 All ER 481 at 486. Lord Hope here cited *R.* v. *Governor of Ashford Remand Centre, ex parte Beese* [1973] 1 WLR 969, 973C, 974F per Lord Widgery CJ; *R.* v. *Governor of Ashford Remand Centre, ex parte Postlethwaite* [1988] 1 AC 924, 946H–947B per Lord Bridge of Harwich.

[18] [2000] 3 WLR 33 at 38, [2000] 3 All ER 481 at 486.

[19] [2000] 3 WLR 33 at 38, [2000] 3 All ER 481 at 486.

[20] [2000] 3 WLR 33 at 39, [2000] 3 All ER 481 at 487.

[21] [2000] 3 WLR 33 at 39, [2000] 3 All ER 481 at 487.

[22] [1896] 1 QB 509 at 517, quoted at [2000] 3 WLR 33 at 43, [2000] 3 All ER 481 at 490.

It is clear by reason of Article III (4) that a person convicted of an extradition offence and sentenced to pay a very large fine which he has not paid, or sentenced to make very large restitution to the victim of his crime which he has not made, cannot be extradited unless he has also been sentenced to imprisonment or other form of detention for a period of four months or more. Similarly, a person convicted of an extradition offence and sentenced only to a period of supervised release cannot be extradited . . . When Article III (4) speaks of a 'sentence' it is speaking of a sentence of imprisonment or detention. . . . [A]s a valid request cannot be made for the extradition of a convicted person unless that person has been sentenced to imprisonment or detention, I consider that when Article VII (4) requires the request to be accompanied by evidence of 'the sentence imposed' it is implicit that 'the sentence imposed' is a sentence of imprisonment or detention and therefore the requirement for 'a statement showing to what extent the sentence has not been carried out' must also relate to a sentence of imprisonment or detention.

I consider that this construction is in conformity with the intent of the relevant provisions of the treaty. It is clear that if a convicted person has been sentenced in the United States to undergo supervised release or to pay a fine (no matter how large) or to make restitution (no matter how large) he cannot be extradited unless he has been sentenced to imprisonment or detention for a period of four months or more. It is also clear that if the only sentence which has been imposed upon a convicted person has been a sentence of imprisonment or detention for a period of four months or more and he has fully served that term he cannot be extradited as a convicted person. It therefore appears to me that where a convicted person has served the full term of imprisonment for which he was sentenced and has been released from prison and is subject only to forms of correction or punishment in respect of which he could not have been extradited, it is not the intent of the treaty that he should be extradited because those other forms of correction or punishment have not been fully carried out.[23]

In this context, Lord Hutton observed that a number of other extradition statutes supported this conclusion:

Although the treaty between this country and the United States does not use the term 'unlawfully at large' in respect of a convicted person whose extradition is sought, the requirement that a convicted person should not be extradited unless he is 'unlawfully at large' is contained in a number of provisions not related to the United States contained in extradition statutes (see, for example, section 1 of the Fugitive Offenders Act 1967 and sections 1(1)(b) and 9(8)(b) of the Extradition Act 1989) and I consider that the construction of Article VII (4) contended for by the appellant is in conformity with the general intendment of an extradition statute or treaty, namely that a convicted person should be extradited when he is unlawfully at large.[24]

Of the two possible interpretations of the extradition treaty, the latter interpretation is the more compelling. Extradition treaties are not only designed to facilitate the transfer of fugitives between States; they also provide important protections to the individuals concerned.[25] There is therefore no reason to adopt a 'liberal construction' in favour of the requesting State. Instead, careful

[23] [2000] 3 WLR 33 at 41–3, [2000] 3 All ER 481 at 489–90.

[24] [2000] 3 WLR 33 at 43, [2000] 3 All ER 481 at 490.

[25] See John Dugard and Christine van den Wyngaert, 'Reconciling Extradition with Human Rights,' *American Journal of International Law* 92 (1998) pp. 187–212.

attention to the 'ordinary meaning of the terms of the treaty in their context and in the light of its object and purpose' is called for.[26]

Finally, Lord Hutton expressed concern about an affidavit received from the Assistant United States Attorney for the Northern District of Illinois, certain paragraphs of which made detailed reference to the power of the United States court to send the appellant back to prison for having violated the terms of his parole. Lord Hutton observed:

These paragraphs give rise to the inference that the United States seeks the extradition of the appellant not for the purpose of ensuring that he completes the term of supervised release to which he was originally sentenced but so that a judge may consider whether the term of supervised release should be revoked for violation of a condition of his supervised release (which violation is not an offence for which the appellant could be extradited) and the appellant sentenced to an additional term of imprisonment.[27]

It is important that extraditions not occur when they would violate the provisions of the Extradition Act 1989, for example, by concerning offences not defined as 'extradition crimes'. Lord Hutton, having identified that the extradition request may have been directed at the offence of having violated the terms of the supervised release, was properly concerned about the true intent of the United States. It is surprising that the other judges did not address this point.

Extradition—Backing of Warrants (Republic of Ireland) Act 1965, Section 2(2)—double criminality—abuse of process

Case No. 4. In Re Ellis; *In Re Gilligan*; 5 October 1999, [2000] 1 All ER 113, <http://www.publications.parliament.uk/pa> (HL).

Due to the close relationship between the Republic of Ireland and the United Kingdom, Ireland is excluded from the definition of foreign State in Section 3 of the Extradition Act 1989. There is no extradition treaty between the two countries; the process for rendition is instead modelled on the backing of warrants system long familiar to English law.

Historically, magistrates in England only had local jurisdiction and a warrant was valid only in the jurisdiction of the issuing magistrate. This meant that a new warrant had to be obtained if an accused went to another county. With time, a practice developed whereby a warrant issued by a magistrate in one county would simply be endorsed by a magistrate in another, if the accused had fled there. During the eighteenth century the process was put on a statutory footing and extended to the rendition of persons between the United Kingdom and Ireland. Rendition between the two countries was regulated, first by the Petty Sessions (Ireland) Act 1851 and then, after the achievement of Irish independence in 1949, by the Backing of Warrants (Republic of Ireland) Act 1965.

[26] See Article 31, Vienna Convention on the Law of Treaties, *United Nations Treaty Series*, vol. 1155, p. 331, *International Legal Materials*, 8 (1969), p. 679, <http://untreaty.un.org>, and discussion below, 426–31.

[27] [2000] 3 WLR 33 at 44, [2000] 3 All ER 481 at 491.

The Act of 1965 requires a magistrate in the United Kingdom to endorse a warrant issued in Ireland unless certain very limited conditions have not been met. These conditions include, most importantly, the limitations set out in Section 2(2):

> An order shall not be made . . . if it appears to the court that the offence specified in the warrant does not correspond with any offence under the law of the part of the United Kingdom in which the court acts which is an indictable offence or is punishable on summary conviction with imprisonment for six months . . .

The Secretary of State for the Home Department is not involved: the matter is dealt with between the Irish Garda Siochána and the police in the United Kingdom. The matter is heard before whatever magistrates court is in the area where the person is arrested and hearings are far less elaborate than extradition hearings before the specialized Bow Street magistrates.

The Irish government issued warrants against two individuals, Ellis and Gilligan. The warrants issued against Gilligan included a charge of common law murder, as well as seventeen other charges including possession and importation of cannabis, and illegal possession of firearms and ammunition. The warrants against Ellis included unlawful and carnal knowledge of a girl and sexual assault.

Magistrates in the United Kingdom ordered that the individuals be returned to Ireland to face proceedings against them for the crimes described in the warrants. Both men challenged the orders in separate appeals, arguing that the crimes described in the warrants did not meet the requirements of double criminality, in that they did not 'correspond' with offences under English law as required by Section 2(2) of the 1965 Act. Additionally, Gilligan argued that an abuse of process had occurred when the English police arrested him on other charges in the period immediately preceding the issuance of the Irish warrant. This, he claimed, was done with the intention of facilitating the Irish warrant.

The Divisional Court heard the appeals jointly, and dismissed them. On appeal, the House of Lords agreed that the crimes cited in the warrants reasonably corresponded with crimes found in English law and that the distinctions drawn by the defendants were not material. Lord Steyn said that the word correspond 'is not a term of art' and that determining whether statutes correspond is a relatively simple matter.[28] Lord Clyde said that 'it is sufficient that the material in the warrant specifies something similar or analogous to behaviour which constitutes an offence of the required gravity in the local jurisdiction'.[29]

As to the abuse of process argument, the Lords referred to their 1995 decision in *In re Schmidt* that there is no abuse of process jurisdiction under the Extradition Act 1989.[30] Although that decision was based in part on the protective role played by the Secretary of State's discretion under that legislation, and the Secretary of State plays no such role under the 1965 Act, the close

[28] [2000] 1 All ER 113 at 122.

[29] [2000] 1 All ER 113 at 126.

[30] [1995] 1 AC 339, [1994] 3 WLR 228, [1994] 2 All ER 65, this *Year Book*, 65 (1994), pp. 500–2.

ties between Ireland and the United Kingdom were considered sufficient to justify a streamlined procedure.

Extradition—Extradition Act 1989, Section 12—medical examination on condition of confidentiality—medical report finding the accused 'unfit to stand trial'—whether fairness required disclosure of medical report to requesting States—importance of maintaining integrity of the international criminal justice system

Case No. 5. R. v. *Secretary of State for the Home Department, ex parte Amnesty International and Others,* 31 January 2000; *R.* v. *Secretary of State for the Home Department, ex parte The Kingdom of Belgium*; *R.* v. *Secretary of State for the Home Department, ex parte Amnesty International Limited and others,* 15 February 2000, <http://www.courtservice.gov.uk/> (QBD).

Following two House of Lords decisions concerning State immunity and double criminality, Augusto Pinochet was, on 8 October 1999, committed on the remaining charges against him to await the decision of the Secretary of State as to whether he should be extradited to Spain.[31] At this stage of the process the Secretary of State has a broad scope of discretion under Section 12 of the Extradition Act 1989 which reads, *inter alia*:

(1) Where a person is committed under s. 9 above and is not discharged by order of the High Court, the Secretary of State may by warrant order him to be returned unless his return is prohibited, or prohibited for the time being, by this Act or the Secretary of State decides under this section to make no such order in his case.

(2) Without prejudice to his general discretion as to the making of an order for the return of a person to a foreign state . . .

(a) the Secretary of State shall not make an order in the case of any person if it appears to the Secretary of State in relation to the . . . offences in respect of which his return is sought that . . . (ii) by reason of the passage of time since he is alleged to have committed it . . . it would, having regard to all the circumstances, be unjust or oppressive to return him . . .

On 14 October 1999, the Secretary of State received representations from the Chilean Embassy which suggested that there had been a recent and significant deterioration in Pinochet's health. The Home Department invited Pinochet to submit to a medical examination so as to provide the information necessary for the decision on whether to allow the extradition. Pinochet agreed, on the condition of strict confidentiality.

Upon receiving the medical report, the Secretary of State indicated that Pinochet had been found unfit to stand trial. The Secretary of State indicated that he was 'minded' not to allow the extradition. However, he refused to release

[31] For the House of Lords decisions, see *Regina* v. *Bow Street Metropolitan Stipendiary Magistrate and Others, ex parte Pinochet Ugarte (No. 1)*, 25 November 1998, [1998] 3 WLR 1456, [1998] 4 All ER 897, (1998) 37 International Legal Materials 1302, <http://www.publications.parliament.uk/pa>; *Regina* v. *Bow Street Metropolitan Stipendiary Magistrate and Others, ex parte Pinochet Ugarte (No. 3)*, 24 March 1999, [1999] 2 WLR 827, [1999] 2 All ER 97, (1999) 38 International Legal Materials 581, <http://www.publications.parliament.uk/pa>; reviewed together in this *Year Book*, 70 (1999), pp. 277–95.

the medical report itself, which prompted the Kingdom of Belgium and six human rights organisations to seek judicial review—with the ultimate aim of reviewing the report and being allowed their own medical examination.

The Divisional Court ruled on the issue twice. First, Maurice Kay J held that, although in some situations the public interest can outweigh an obligation of confidentiality, in this situation it did not. He found that the Secretary of State had acted within his discretion when he refused to release the medical results, that the examination procedure and methods were impartial, and that it was inappropriate for the appellants to call for an independent medical examination. Additionally, Maurice Kay J examined the question of standing and found that neither the human rights organizations nor Belgium had enough of an interest at stake for them to be entitled to see the medical report.

The appellants renewed their application, conceding that the human rights organizations did not need to see the report but that all four of the States seeking extradition of Pinochet (i.e. Spain, Belgium, France and Switzerland) should have the opportunity to review it under conditions of strict confidentiality. This time, Simon Brown LJ, Dyson and Latham JJ ruled in their favour, with Simon Brown LJ indicating:

> [T]here is but a single question for our determination: does fairness require disclosure of this report to the requesting states? This is not a question which we can shirk on the footing that the procedure to be followed by the Secretary of State is substantially a matter for him. It is not.

He held that maintaining the integrity of international criminal law was a goal of sufficient importance to require disclosure:

> The decision which the Secretary of State is 'minded to' take is, it need hardly be emphasised, one of very great moment. Its consequence would be that Senator Pinochet, accused though he is of the most terrible crimes, would be effectively untriable anywhere in the world. He would not be extradited to Spain. No more would he be extradited to any of the other three requesting states . . . If ever there were a case in which the integrity of the international criminal justice system needed to be demonstrated, a case calling for the highest standards of fairness and transparency, this is it. It is simply not satisfactory that this all-important medical report should be seen only by four office-holders within a single state.

The other two judges came to similar conclusions in their judgments, with Dyson J making specific reference to the 'enormity of the alleged crimes' and the 'monumental importance of the decision that the Secretary of State is poised to make'.

Refugee—1951 Convention relating to the Status of Refugees, Article 1A(2)—persecution by non-State agents—whether absence of State protection a constituent element of persecution—degree of State protection required

Case No. 6. Horvath v. *Secretary of State for the Home Department,* 6 July 2000, [2000] 3 All ER 577, [2000] 3 WLR 379, <http://www.publications.parliament.uk/pa> (HL).

The appellant, a Roma (or gypsy) from Slovakia, left his country of citizenship and entered the United Kingdom. He and his accompanying wife and child applied for asylum, claiming that they feared persecution by violent gangs of skinheads, against whose acts the Slovak authorities failed to provide protection for Roma. The Secretary of State refused his application for asylum and the Special Adjudicator dismissed the appeal. The Immigration Appeal Tribunal and the Court of Appeal did likewise, finding that, although the appellant had a well founded fear of violence from skinheads, this did not amount to persecution because he had failed to prove that the Slovak authorities would not protect him.[32]

On appeal, the House of Lords looked to the 1951 Geneva Convention relating to the Status of Refugees, Article 1A(2) of which provides that the term 'refugee' shall apply to any person who

> owing to a well-founded fear of being persecuted for reasons of race, religion, nationality, membership of a particular social group or political opinion, is outside the country of his nationality and is unable or, owing to such fear, is unwilling to avail himself of the protection of that country . . . .[33]

Lord Hope, with whom Lords Browne-Wilkinson and Hobhouse concurred, relied upon the 'principle of surrogacy' identified by James Hathaway as the underlying purpose of the Refugee Convention: i.e. to provide protection only where there is a failure of protection by the home State.[34] As Lord Hope explained:

> If the principle of surrogacy is applied, the criterion must be whether the alleged lack of protection is such as to indicate that the home state is unable or unwilling to discharge its duty to establish and operate a system for the protection against persecution of its own nationals.[35]

Lord Hope also relied upon the analysis provided by Lord Lloyd in the 1998 case of *R.* v. *Secretary of State for the Home Department, ex parte Adan* to the effect that two tests, of 'fear' and 'protection', must be satisfied:

> If category (1) [i.e. nationals who are outside their country owing to a well-founded fear of persecution for a Convention reason, and are unable to avail themselves of the protection of their country] were confined to refugees who are subject to state persecution, then I can well see that such persons would, ex hypothesi, be unable to avail themselves of state protection. On that view the words would indeed serve no purpose. But category (1) is not so confined. It also includes the important class of those who are sometimes called 'third party refugees' i.e. those who are subject to persecution by factions within the state. If the state in question can make protection available to such persons, there is no reason why they should qualify for refugee status. They would have satisfied the fear test, but not the protection test. Why should another country offer asylum to such persons when they can avail themselves of the protection of their own

[32] The Court of Appeal judgment is reported at (2000) INLR 15.

[33] *United Nations Treaty Series*, vol. 189, p. 137, Cmd. 9171, as modified by the 1967 Protocol relating to the Status of Refugees, Cmd. 3906. The question of the application of the Geneva Convention in national law arose for determination on account of Section 8(1) of the Asylum and Immigration Appeals Act 1993, which provides that: 'A person who is refused leave to enter the United Kingdom under the . . . [Immigration Act 1971] may appeal against the refusal to a special adjudicator on the ground that his removal in consequence of the refusal would be contrary to the United Kingdom's obligations under the [Geneva] Convention.'

[34] *The Law of Refugee Status* (Toronto: Butterworths, 1991), pp. 124–34.

[35] [2000] 3 All ER 577 at 581, [2000] 3 WLR 379 at 383.

country? But if, for whatever reason the state in question is unable to afford protection against factions within the state, then the qualifications for refugee status are complete. Both tests would be satisfied.[36]

Lord Hope concluded that 'in the context of an allegation of persecution by non-state agents, the word "persecution" implies a failure by the state to make protection available against the ill-treatment or violence which the person suffers at the hands of his persecutors'.[37]

In terms of the level of protection required, Lord Hope again looked to the principle of surrogacy:

The surrogacy principle rests upon the assumption that, just as the substitute cannot achieve complete protection against isolated and random attacks, so also complete protection against such attacks is not to be expected of the home state. The standard to be applied is therefore not that which would eliminate all risk and would thus amount to a guarantee of protection in the home state. Rather it is a practical standard, which takes proper account of the duty which the state owes to all its own nationals.[38]

The Immigration Appeal Tribunal had found that the institutions of government in Slovakia are 'effective and operating', that the 'violent attacks on Roma are isolated and random attacks by thugs' and that, although the police 'do not conduct proper investigation in all cases', there was evidence that they 'have intervened to provide protection when they have been asked to do so and that stiff sentences are imposed at times for crimes that are racially motivated'.[39] Lord Hope consequently refused the appeal.

Lord Clyde, who concurred in the result, questioned the merits of distinguishing between the fear and protection tests:

[I]n deciding whether a fear of persecution is well-founded it seems to me that account must be taken of the availability of the forces of the state to counter the fear. And if that is correct it is no longer possible to confine the consideration of protection to the so-called 'protection test.' For a fear to be well-founded it seems to me that all the circumstances relating to the fear have to be taken into account. In assessing the existence of a real risk of the violation of rights occurring anything which may bear on the likelihood of the incidence of the violation will be relevant. It is the applicant's fear which is in issue, and so matters particularly relating to him will be important. . . . [40]

Lord Lloyd also concurred in the result, but dissented on the issue of whether the availability of State protection should be factored into the determination of persecution:

It is the severity and persistence of the means adopted, whether by the state itself, or factions within the state, which turns discrimination into persecution; not the absence of state protection. It is surely simpler, and therefore better from every point of view, not least that of an appellate court considering an appeal on a question of law, that the fact-finding tribunal should first assess the ill-treatment, and answer the question whether it amounts to persecution for a Convention reason, and then, as a separate question,

[36] [1998] 2 All ER 453 at 458–9, [1999] 1 AC 293 at 305–6, [1998] 2 WLR 702 at 708, (1998) 37 International Legal Materials 1090 at 1095, <http://www.publications.parliament.uk/pa>, this *Year Book*, 69 (1998), pp. 321–5.

[37] [2000] 3 All ER 577 at 583, [2000] 3 WLR 379 at 385.

[38] [2000] 3 All ER 577 at 586, [2000] 3 WLR 379 at 388.

[39] [2000] 3 All ER 577 at 582, [2000] 3 WLR 379 at 384.

[40] [2000] 3 All ER 577 at 598–9, [2000] 3 WLR 379 at 401–2.

evaluate the protection available to the applicant. I can see no advantage in running these two questions together.[41]

A peculiar aspect of this case is that the Law Lords dismissed the Canadian cases on point as unhelpful, due to minor differences between Article 1A(2) of the Refugee Convention and the legislation implementing that provision into Canadian law. For example, Lord Hope said, with regard to the 1993 Supreme Court decision in *Canada (Attorney General)* v. *Ward*:

I would be cautious about drawing conclusions from that case about the approach to be taken to the definition in article 1A(2) in view of the fact that this definition has been reproduced in a different form in section 2(1) of the Canadian Immigration Act 1976 by breaking it down into sub-paragraphs.[42]

Yet Section 2(1) closely mirrors Article 1A(2), with the separation into sub-paragraphs having no obvious effect on the definition. Section 2(1) reads:

'Convention refugee' means any person who
(*a*) by reason of a well-founded fear of persecution for reasons of race, religion, nationality, membership in a particular social group or political opinion,
(i) is outside the country of the person's nationality and is unable or, by reason of that fear, is unwilling to avail himself of the protection of that country, or
(ii) not having a country of nationality, is outside the country of the person's former habitual residence and is unable or, by reason of that fear, is unwilling to return to that country, ...

Had the Law Lords fully considered the Canadian cases, they would have found a somewhat different approach being applied there. Instead of a two part analysis, the second element, State protection, is considered essential to determining whether the first element, fear, is 'well-founded'. La Forest J, in *Canada (Attorney General)* v. *Ward*, wrote for the Supreme Court:

It is clear that the lynch-pin of the analysis is the state's inability to protect: it is a crucial element in determining whether the claimant's fear is well-founded, and thereby the objective reasonableness of his or her unwillingness to seek the protection of his or her state of nationality.[43]

However, La Forest J also held that the absence of State protection must be proved:

[C]lear and convincing confirmation of a state's inability to protect must be provided. For example, a claimant might advance testimony of similarly situated individuals let down by the state protection arrangement or the claimant's testimony of past personal incidents in which state protection did not materialize. Absent some evidence, the claim should fail, as nations should be presumed capable of protecting their citizens. Security of nationals is, after all, the essence of sovereignty. Absent a situation of complete breakdown of state apparatus . . . it should be assumed that the state is capable of protecting a claimant. . . . Refugee claims were never meant to allow a claimant to seek out better protection than that from which he or she benefits already.[44]

[41] [2000] 3 All ER 577 at 589, [2000] 3 WLR 379 at 391.
[42] [2000] 3 All ER 577 at 585, [2000] 3 WLR 379 at 387. The Immigration Act 1976 may be found in Revised Statutes of Canada 1985, c. I–2. *Canada (Attorney General)* v. *Ward* is reported at [1993] 2 SCR 689.
[43] [1993] 2 SCR 645–6.
[44] [1993] 2 SCR 650–2.

Separating the definition of refugee into separate elements for the purpose of analysis serves little purpose. If what matters is the well-founded character of the individual refugee claimant's fear of persecution, the existence or absence of State protection cannot be accorded a secondary role. Although the conclusion in this case would likely have been the same either way, the approach taken by the Supreme Court in *Canada (Attorney General)* v. *Ward* is preferable to that taken by the House of Lords.

Refugee—persecution by non-State agents—deportation to third country not recognizing persecution by non-State agents where State not complicit—whether third country 'safe'—Asylum and Immigration Act 1996, Section 2(2)(c)—1951 Convention relating to the Status of Refugees, Articles 1A(2) and 33

Case No. 7. R. v. *Secretary of State for the Home Department, ex parte Adan; R.* v. *Secretary of State for the Home Department, ex parte Aitseguer*, 19 December 2000, <http://www.publications.parliament.uk/pa> (HL).

The United Kingdom and 137 other States have undertaken, by way of Article 33 of the 1951 Geneva Convention relating to the Status of Refugees, not to 'expel or return ("*refouler*") a refugee in any manner whatsoever to the frontiers of territories where his life or freedom would be threatened on account of his race, religion, nationality, membership of a particular social group or political opinion'.[45] However, Section 2(2) of the Asylum and Immigration Act 1996 enables the Secretary of State to remove expeditiously from the United Kingdom claimants for asylum who have arrived from a 'safe third country', if he certifies that the following conditions have been fulfilled:

(a) That the person is not a national or citizen of the country or territory to which he is to be sent;
(b) That his life and liberty would not be threatened in that country or territory by reason of his race, religion, nationality, membership of a particular social group, or political opinion; and
(c) That the government of that country or territory would not send him to another country or territory otherwise than in accordance with the Convention [i.e. the 1951 Refugee Convention].

The two respondents had travelled to the United Kingdom by way of Germany or France respectively. In each instance the Secretary of State had certified that they were returnable as both those States were 'safe third countries'. Moreover, the United Kingdom, Germany and France had all ratified the 1990 Dublin Convention which provides that the first Member State

[45] *United Nations Treaty Series*, vol. 189, p. 137, Cmd. 9171, as modified by the 1967 Protocol relating to the Status of Refugees, Cmd. 3906. The question of the application of the Geneva Convention in national law arose for determination on account of Section 8(1) of the Asylum and Immigration Appeals Act 1993, which provides that: 'A person who is refused leave to enter the United Kingdom under the . . . [Immigration Act 1971] may appeal against the refusal to a special adjudicator on the ground that his removal in consequence of the refusal would be contrary to the United Kingdom's obligations under the [Geneva] Convention.'

that an asylum seeker enters is the one responsible for hearing his claim.[46] Section 2 of the Asylum and Immigration Act 1996 was designed to implement the Dublin Convention into English law.

The two respondents feared persecution from non-State agents in their country of origin, but there was no evidence of State complicity in the persecution feared. Adan (a different Adan from the appellant in a 1998 House of Lords judgment[47]) was a member of a minority clan in Somali and feared persecution from an armed group in a situation where all forms of legitimate government had broken down. Aitseguer was a citizen of Algeria who feared persecution at the hands of an Islamic fundamentalist group there.

The position taken in Germany and France on persecution by non-State agents differed markedly from that taken in the United Kingdom and elsewhere. Germany and France subscribed to what has been called the 'accountability' theory whereby the classes of cases in which claimants can obtain refugee status are limited to situations where the persecution alleged can be attributed to the State. Most parties to the Refugee Convention apply the 'protection' theory whereby persecution by non-State agents, combined with an absence of State protection, can give rise to refugee status. For example, in the 1998 case of *R.* v. *Secretary of State for the Home Department, ex parte Adan*, Lord Lloyd identified four categories of refugees under Article 1A(2), the first of which was 'nationals who are outside their country owing to a well-founded fear of persecution for a Convention reason, and are unable to avail themselves of the protection of their country'. Of this category, he said:

> If category (1) were confined to refugees who are subject to state persecution, then I can well see that such person would, ex hypothesi, be unable to avail themselves of state protection. On that view the words would indeed serve no purpose. But category (1) is not so confined. It also includes the important class of those who are sometimes called 'third party refugees', ie those who are subject to persecution by factions within the state. If the state in question can make protection available to such persons, there is no reason why they should qualify for refugee status. They would have satisfied the fear test, but not the protection test. Why should another country offer asylum to such persons when they can avail themselves of the protection of their own country? But if, for whatever reason, the state in question is unable to afford protection against factions within the state, then the qualifications for refugee status are complete. Both tests would be satisfied.[48]

In the case under review here, the Court of Appeal held that the scope of Article 1A(2) extends to those who fear persecution by non-State agents in circumstances where the State is neither complicit in the persecution nor willing or able to afford protection. As Lord Woolf explained:

[46] Convention determining the State responsible for examining applications for asylum lodged in one of the Member States of the European Communities, *International Legal Materials*, 30 (1991), p. 425. See Agnès Hurwitz, 'The 1990 Dublin Convention: A Comprehensive Assessment,' *International Journal of Refugee Law*, 11 (1999), p. 646.

[47] *R.* v. *Secretary of State for the Home Department, ex parte Adan* [1998] 2 All ER 453, [1999] 1 AC 293, [1998] 2 WLR 702, (1998) 37 International Legal Materials 1090, <http://www.publications.parliament.uk/pa>, this *Year Book*, 69 (1998), pp. 321–5.

[48] [1998] 2 All ER 453 at 457–9, [1998] 2 WLR 702 at 706–8, [1999] 1 AC 293 at 304–6, this *Year Book*, 69 (1998), pp. 321–5.

We entertain no doubt but that such persons, whose case is established on the facts, are entitled to the convention's protection. This seems to us to follow naturally from the words of article 1A(2): '. . . *is unable to or, owing to such fear, is unwilling to avail himself of the protection of that country*'; and this involves no technical or over-legalistic reading of the provision.[49]

The Court of Appeal concluded that in these circumstances the Secretary of State was not entitled to certify that Germany and France were 'safe third countries'.

The House of Lords unanimously upheld the decision of the Court of Appeal. Lord Steyn noted that it is a long standing principle of English law that 'if it would be unlawful to return the asylum seeker directly to his country of origin where he is subject to persecution in the relevant sense, it would equally be unlawful to return him to a third country which it is known will return him to his country of origin'.[50]

Turning to the 1996 Act, Lord Steyn considered Section 2(2)(c) to be 'drafted in plain words':

It requires certification by the Secretary of State that the third country would not send the asylum seeker to his country of origin 'otherwise than in accordance with the Convention'. The section does not express the condition in terms that refer to 'the Convention as legitimately interpreted by the (third) country concerned'.

Lord Steyn continued:

It follows that the enquiry must be into the meaning of the Refugee Convention approached as an international instrument created by the agreement of contracting states as opposed to regulatory regimes established by national institutions. It is necessary to determine the autonomous meaning of the relevant treaty provision. . . . The rules governing the interpretation of treaties are articles 31 (General rule of interpretation) and article 32 (Supplementary means of interpretation) of the Vienna Convention on the Law of Treaties which codify already existing public international law.[51]

It followed that there can, in principle, 'be only one true interpretation of a treaty'. Lord Steyn, noting that '[t]he subject of the Refugee Convention is fundamental rights', considered that

if Parliament had intended to introduce in 1996 the relativist and imprecise notion of 'the Convention as legitimately interpreted by the third country concerned,' which tends to undermine the protections guaranteed by the Refugee Convention, it would have made such legislative intent clear by express words.

The Secretary of State had accepted that, if Article 1A(2) had to be given one autonomous interpretation, the House of Lords' 1998 decision in *Adan* v.

[49] [1999] 2 WLR 1274 at 1296, [1999] 4 All ER 774 at 795, this *Year Book*, 70 (1999), pp. 301–4 (emphasis in original).

[50] Lord Steyn cited with approval *R.* v. *Secretary of State for the Home Department, ex parte Bugdaycay* [1987] AC 514 at 532D-E.

[51] Lord Steyn cited with approval *Fothergill* v. *Monarch Airlines Ltd.* [1981] A.C. 251, [1980] 2 All ER 696, [1980] 3 WLR 209, this *Year Book*, 51 (1980), pp. 316–25. The Vienna Convention may be found at *United Nations Treaty Series*, vol. 1155, p. 331, *International Legal Materials*, 8 (1969), p. 679, <http://untreaty.un.org>.

Secretary of State for the Home Department represented that interpretation.[52] Lord Steyn consequently dismissed the appeal.

Lord Hutton came to a similar conclusion, and likewise placed a great deal of weight on the human rights character of the Refugee Convention:

On the Secretary of State's case, section 2 of the 1996 Act constitutes a diminution in a human right given to an asylum-seeker by an international convention incorporated into the law of the United Kingdom by a United Kingdom statute. Under the law of the United Kingdom, as decided by this House in *Adan* v. *The Secretary of State for the Home Department*, an asylum-seeker is entitled to the protection of Article 33 notwithstanding that the state in whose territory he fears persecution is not complicit in that persecution. This is an important human right and, because the courts of Germany and France will rule that Article 33 does not give this right, the effect of section 2, if the construction contended for by the Secretary of State were held to be correct, would be to take away that right from Ms. Adan and Mr. Aitseguer.

Lord Hutton noted that Parliament could always enact legislation to remove a right given by the Refugee Convention and incorporated into English law. Here, however, he affirmed the following statement by Lord Hoffmann in the 1999 case of *R.* v. *Home Secretary, ex parte Simms*:

Parliamentary sovereignty means that Parliament can, if it chooses, legislate contrary to fundamental principles of human rights. The Human Rights Act 1998 will not detract from this power. The constraints upon its exercise by Parliament are ultimately political, not legal. But the principle of legality means that Parliament must squarely confront what it is doing and accept the political cost. Fundamental rights cannot be overridden by general or ambiguous words. This is because there is too great a risk that the full implications of their unqualified meaning may have passed unnoticed in the democratic process. In the absence of express language or necessary implication to the contrary, the courts therefore presume that even the most general words were intended to be subject to the basic rights of the individual.[53]

Lord Hutton considered that the wording of Section 2(2)(c) was ambiguous in this respect, and therefore incapable of removing the important human right in issue.

Lord Slynn concurred, holding that:

The question is not whether the Secretary of State thinks that the alternative view is reasonable or permissible or legitimate or arguable but whether the Secretary of State is satisfied that the application of the other state's interpretation of the Convention would mean that the individual will still not be sent back otherwise than in accordance with the Convention.

Lord Hobhouse also concurred, and pointed out that this decision rendered unauthoritative two recent Court of Appeal cases. In *R.* v. *Secretary of State for the Home Department, ex parte Kerrouche*[54] and *R.* v. *Secretary of State for the Home Department, ex parte Iyadurai*,[55] Lord Woolf, writing for that Court, had

[52] [1998] 2 All ER 453, [1998] 2 WLR 702, [1999] 1 AC 293, this *Year Book*, 69 (1998), pp. 321–5. See quotation above, at 423.

[53] [1999] 3 WLR 328 at 341F.

[54] [1997] Imm. AR 610, [1998] INLR 88, this *Year Book*, 69 (1998) 326–7.

[55] [1998] Imm. AR 470, [1998] INLR 472, [1998] Times LR 382, this *Year Book*, 69 (1998) 325–30.

accorded a wide margin of discretion to third States in their interpretation of the Refugee Convention.

The Law Lords, in this case, have refused to move away from the principle they first established in *In re Musisi*, that judges are required to subject decisions of this kind to the 'most anxious scrutiny'.[56] By defining and applying limits on the 'safe third country' concept, the Court of Appeal has reaffirmed that the Refugee Convention's provisions are binding on the United Kingdom as international law.[57]

That said, Parliament has, as Lord Hutton indicated it could, recently changed English law so as to avoid the very issue brought forward in this appeal, namely the removal of asylum seekers to third States under the Dublin Convention. Section 169(3) of Schedule 16 to the Immigration and Asylum Act 1999 repeals Sections 2 and 3 of the 1996 Act. By Section 11 of the 1999 Act, a member State of the European Union with which there are standing arrangements such as the Dublin Convention for determining which State is responsible for considering asylum applications, is to be regarded as a place from which a person will not be sent to another State otherwise than in accordance with the Refugee Convention. On the basis of the judgments analysed here, these provisions violate the United Kingdom's international obligations. Unfortunately, neither other States nor the British public are likely to express much concern, given prevailing attitudes towards applicants for refugee status.

Stateless person—refugee—1951 Convention relating to the Status of Refugees, Article 1A(2)—is a stateless person unable to return to the country of his former habitual residence by reason of his statelessness alone a 'refugee'

Case No. 8. Revenko v. *Secretary of State for the Home Department*, 31 July 2000, [2000] 3 WLR 1519 (CA).

Moldova became an independent State in 1991, upon the dissolution of the Soviet Union. It quickly adopted new immigration rules. The appellant, who had been born in Moldova, was denied citizenship there under the new rules. He left the country and, being unable to return, claimed asylum in the United Kingdom. He based his claim on the theory that statelessness—in and of itself—entitles stateless persons to asylum under the 1951 Geneva Convention relating to the Status of Refugees.[58]

A special adjudicator denied the appellant's claim on the basis that he did not have a present well-founded fear of persecution were he to be returned to

[56] [1987] AC 514 at 531, [1987] 1 All ER 940 at 952, this *Year Book*, 58 (1987), pp. 433–8.

[57] For another example of judicial willingness to limit political discretion in defining 'safe third countries', see: *Mohammed A.S. Al-Mass'ari* v. *Secretary of State for the Home Department*, this *Year Book*, 68 (1997), pp. 562–7.

[58] *United Nations Treaty Series*, vol. 189, p. 137, Cmd. 9171, as modified by the 1967 Protocol relating to the Status of Refugees, Cmd. 3906. The question of the application of the Geneva Convention in national law arose for determination on account of Section 8(1) of the Asylum and Immigration Appeals Act 1993, which provides that: 'A person who is refused leave to enter the United Kingdom under the . . . [Immigration Act 1971] may appeal against the refusal to a special adjudicator on the ground that his removal in consequence of the refusal would be contrary to the United Kingdom's obligations under the [Geneva] Convention.'

Moldova. Article 1A(2) reads (with the bracketed words having been deleted as a result of Article 1(2) of the 1967 Protocol):

For the purposes of the present Convention, the term 'refugee' shall apply to any person who . . . (2) [As a result of events occurring before 1 January 1951 and] owing to well-founded fear of being persecuted for reasons of race, religion, nationality, membership of a particular political group or political opinion, is outside the country of his nationality and is unable or, owing to such fear, is unwilling to avail himself of the protection of that country; or who, not having a nationality and being outside the country of his former habitual residence [as a result of such events], is unable or, owing to such fear, is unwilling to return to it.

The appellant's argument focussed upon the fact that the words 'owing to well founded fear of being persecuted for reasons of race, religion, nationality, membership of a particular political group or political opinion' do not appear in the clause pertaining to stateless persons that follows the semi-colon. The Immigration Appeal Tribunal, however, also denied his claim.

The Court of Appeal did likewise, with Pill LJ, who wrote the principal judgment, applying Articles 31 and 32 of the 1969 Vienna Convention on the Law of Treaties as a widely accepted codification of the customary international law of treaty interpretation.[59] Article 31 reads, *inter alia*:

1. A treaty shall be interpreted in good faith in accordance with the ordinary meaning to be given to the terms of the treaty in their context and in the light of its object and purpose.

However, Pill LJ also considered that judicial precedent required him to take a broad approach to interpretation that focussed on the purposes the drafters had sought to achieve. As Lord Lloyd had explained in the 1998 case of *R.* v. *Secretary of State for the Home Department, ex parte Adan*:

[W]e are here concerned with the meaning of an international Convention. Inevitably the final text will have been the product of a long period of negotiation and compromise. One cannot expect to find the same precision of language as one does in an Act of Parliament drafted by parliamentary counsel . . . It follows that one is more likely to arrive at the true construction of article 1A(2) by seeking a meaning which makes sense in the light of the Convention as a whole, and the purposes which the framers of the Convention were seeking to achieve, rather than by concentrating exclusively on the language. A broad approach is what is needed, rather than a narrow linguistic approach. But having said that, the starting point must be the language itself.[60]

But instead of starting with the language of Article 1A(2), Pill LJ began his analysis by considering the fact that the conference that adopted the Refugee Convention had also engaged in negotiations on a protocol concerning statelessness. The conclusion of those particular negotiations was postponed, with the Final Act of the Conference stating:

[59] *United Nations Treaty Series*, vol. 1155, p. 331, International Legal Materials, 8 (1969), p. 679, <http://untreaty.un.org>.

[60] [1999] 1 AC 293 at 305, [1998] 2 All ER 453 at 457, [1998] 2 WLR 702 at 706, this *Year Book*, 69 (1998), pp. 321–5. Pill LJ also referred to a similar statement by Lord Clyde in *R.* v. *Secretary of State for the Home Department, ex parte Horvath*, [2000] 3 All ER 577 at 593–4, [2000] 3 WLR 379 at 395, <http://www.publications.parliament.uk/pa>, reviewed above at 418–22.

With respect to the draft Protocol relating to the Status of Stateless Persons, the Conference adopted the following resolution:

'THE CONFERENCE,

'HAVING CONSIDERED the draft Protocol relating to the Status of Stateless Persons,

'CONSIDERING that the subject still requires more detailed study,

'DECIDES not to take a decision on the subject at the present conference and refers the draft Protocol back to the appropriate organs of the United Nations for further study.[61]

A Convention relating to the Status of Stateless Persons was eventually adopted in 1954.[62] That Convention entitles stateless persons to certain privileges, but not the same privileges that are accorded to 'refugees' under the 1951 Refugee Convention. In particular, there is no obligation of non-refoulement in the 1954 Convention.[63]

Pill LJ also considered a 'Joint Position' adopted by the Member States of the European Union in 1996, which reads, *inter alia*:

The determining factor for granting refugee status in accordance with the Geneva Convention is the existence of a well-founded fear of persecution on grounds of race, religion, nationality, political opinions or membership of a particular social group . . .[64]

He attached considerable importance to the United Nations High Commissioner for Refugees' *Handbook on Procedures and Criteria for determining Refugee Status*, which states, *inter alia*:

It will be noted that not all stateless persons are refugees. They must be outside the country of their former habitual residence for the reasons indicated in the definition. Where these reasons do not exist the stateless person is not a refugee.[65]

Pill LJ did not accord any weight to the *travaux préparatoires* to the Refugee Convention, observing that Lord Lloyd had expressed reservations about their value in the 1998 *ex parte Adan*,[66] and that Lord Steyn had found them unhelpful in *ex parte Shah*.[67] He also noted that the appellant had not identified anything in the *travaux* which supported the view that the intention of Article 1A(2) was to provide protection for stateless persons generally.

Pill LJ did, however, accord significance to the views of academic writers on

[61] Article III, Final Act of the United Nations Conference of Plenipotentiaries on the Status of Refugees and Stateless Persons, held at Geneva, from 2 July 1951 to 25 July 1951. *United Nations Treaty Series*, vol. 189, p. 138 at 144, Cmd. 9171.

[62] *United Nations Treaty Series*, vol. 360, p. 130, Cmd. 1098.

[63] Article 33(1) of the Refugee Convention reads: 'No Contracting State shall expel or return ("*refouler*") a refugee in any manner whatsoever to the frontiers of territories where his life or freedom would be threatened on account of his race, religion, nationality, membership of a particular social group or political opinion.'

[64] Joint Position of the Member States of the European Union on the Harmonized Application of the Definition of the Term 'Refugee' (*Official Journal*, 1996, L63, 4 March 1996), paragraph 3.

[65] (1988) paragraph 102.

[66] *R.* v. *Secretary of State for the Home Department, ex parte Adan* [1999] 1 AC 293, [1998] 2 All ER 453, [1998] 2 WLR 702, this *Year Book*, 69 (1998), pp. 321–5, HL.

[67] *Islam* v. *Secretary of State for the Home Department; Regina* v. *Immigration Appeal Tribunal and another, ex parte Shah*, [1999] 2 AC 629, [1999] 2 WLR 1015, [1999] 2 All ER 545, <http://www.publications.parliament.uk/pa>, this *Year Book*, 69 (1998), pp. 295–301.

this issue, noting that only one, Atle Grahl-Madsen, had expressed a view in favour of the appellant's position.[68] The following passage written by James Hathaway was, in Pill LJ's opinion, more reflective of the majority view:

[I]t was agreed to restrict the scope of the Convention to those persons who required protection from a state to which they were formally returnable, and to leave the problems of the stateless population to be dealt with by a later and less comprehensive conventional regime. It is thus clear that statelessness per se does not give rise to a claim to refugee status.[69]

In addition, Pill LJ relied heavily on judicial precedent, including the following statement by Lord Lloyd in the 1998 *ex parte Adan*:

It was also common ground that article 1A(2) covers four categories of refugee: (1) nationals who are outside their country owing to a well-founded fear of persecution for a Convention reason, and are unable to avail themselves of the protection of their country; (2) nationals who are outside their country owing to a well-founded fear of persecution for a Convention reason, and, owing to such fear, are unwilling to avail themselves of the protection of their country; (3) non-nationals who are outside the country of their former habitual residence owing to a well-founded fear of persecution for a Convention reason and are unable to return to their country, and (4) non-nationals who are outside the country of their former habitual residence owing to a well-founded fear of persecution for a Convention reason, and, owing to such fear, are unwilling to return to their country.[70]

But what seems to have been particularly decisive was a judgment by Katz J of the Federal Court of Australia, who dealt with the very same issue in the 2000 case of *Savvin* v. *Minister for Immigration and Multicultural Affairs*.[71] Katz J engaged in a lengthy grammatical analysis of the meaning of the semi-colon that precedes the clause pertaining to stateless persons in Article 1A(2) and separates that clause from the words 'owing to well founded fear of being persecuted for reasons of race, religion, nationality, membership of a particular political group or political opinion':

The use of semicolons is discussed by Quirk and others in their authoritative work, A Comprehensive Grammar of the English Language (1985) . . . The authors point out . . . that, typically, the semicolon is used as a replacement for the word 'and,' in order to show that 'two independent clauses are regarded as being sufficiently related to belong to one sentence.' They further point out, however . . . , that the use of a semicolon may sometimes be followed by the use of the word 'and,' 'but' or 'or.' As to the use of the semicolon in the latter circumstances, they say (emphasis added): 'Such a use (*in effect, replacing a comma*) is chiefly found in rather formal writing and in sentences whose complexity already involves the use of one or more commas and whose major divisions call for a hierarchically superior punctuation mark if the reader is not to be momentarily puzzled or misled . . .

When one reads the words which relate to stateless persons in the later part of article 1A(2) as being part of one complete clause, rather than as comprising in themselves an

[68] Atle Grahl-Madsen, *The Status of Refugees in International Law* (Leyden: A. W. Sijthoff, 1966), vol. 1, para. 66.

[69] *The Law of Refugee Status* (Toronto: Butterworths, 1991), pp. 60–1.

[70] *R.* v. *Secretary of State for the Home Department, ex parte Adan* [1999] 1 AC 293 at 304, [1998] 2 All ER 453 at 457, [1998] 2 WLR 702 at 706, this *Year Book*, 69 (1998), pp. 321–5.

[71] [2000] 171 ALR 483.

independent clause, then I consider that the appropriate way to approach their construction is as follows: it is apparent that those words describe a person whose circumstances are to be contrasted with those of the person described in the earlier part of the clause. So much is apparent from the first six of those words, 'or who, not having a nationality.' However, not only do the words in the later part of article 1A(2) describe a person of contrasting circumstances to the person described in the earlier part of the clause. They also suggest naturally a particular point in the description of the first person's circumstances at which the reader is to begin to mark that contrast of circumstances. That point in the description of the first person's circumstances is at the words, 'is outside the country of his nationality' and not earlier. That that is the particular point in the description of the first person's circumstances at which the reader is to begin to mark the contrast of circumstances is demonstrated by the use in the later part of article 1A(2) of the words, 'or who, not having a nationality and being outside the country of his former habitual residence, is . . . ' The form of words which I have just quoted, beginning the contrast of circumstances between the two classes of person part way through the description of the first person's circumstances, avoids the necessity, in what is already a very long clause, to repeat, so far as a stateless person is concerned, the phrase, 'Owing to a well-founded fear of being persecuted for reasons of race, religion, nationality, membership of a particular social group or political opinion,' which opens the clause. That opening phrase is instead taken to be impliedly applicable to a stateless person simply by reason of the form of words used in relation to such a person in the later part of the clause.[72]

In light of this analysis, Pill LJ concluded:

The paragraph in article 1A(2) should be read as a whole and does, in my judgment, set out a single test for refugee status. When the words in the first part of the paragraph 'is unable or, owing to such fear, is unwilling' were repeated in the second part of the paragraph, it was intended that the entire paragraph should be governed by the need to establish a well-founded fear of persecution on a Convention ground. The existence of a well-founded fear was intended to be a pre-requirement of refugee status. It is significant that both categories, nationals and stateless persons, were dealt with in the same paragraph and indeed in the same sentence. I cannot conclude that, by the order of words in the last part of the paragraph, the need for the fear was intended to be excluded in the case of what could be a large category of persons.[73]

Both Clarke LJ and Bennett J concurred.

There are two general points that can be made about this judgment. First, the judges assumed, on the basis of the existence of the 1954 Convention relating to the Status of Stateless Persons, that the object and purpose of the 1951 Refugee Convention was solely to protect those who have a well-founded fear of persecution. In fact, the two instruments are directed at different situations. The 1954 Convention speaks to the relationship between the stateless person and a State in which he or she is lawfully found; it does not speak to the stateless person's relationship to any other State, nor does it deal with the situation of a stateless person who is illegally present in the State in which he is found. For these reasons it does not contain a provision on non-refoulement equivalent to Article 33 of the Refugee Convention. In contrast, the Refugee Convention is designed to protect those who are outside their State of habitual residence and unable or unwilling to return there—and unable to benefit from its protection—

[72] [2000] 171 ALR 483 at 500–1.
[73] [2000] 3 WLR 1519 at 1536.

regardless of whether they are lawfully within the State in which they are found. A need for protection may arise in several situations: when the State of origin is itself persecuting an individual, when that State is failing to protect the individual against persecution by others, or when that State is refusing to accept any responsibility for the individual on the basis that he or she is not one of its nationals. Unlike a person who is outside his or her State of nationality, who may or may not require protection, a stateless person who is denied entry to his or her State of habitual residence and who has no right to live elsewhere is *prima facie* in need of protection. The criteria of 'well-founded fear' as a reason for being or remaining outside one's State of habitual resistence is rendered redundant by a proven inability to return.

Secondly, it is striking that the judges, while stating that they would do so, did not in fact follow the requirements of the Vienna Convention on the Law of Treaties concerning interpretation. All three focussed on the object and purpose of the Refugee Convention when, in fact, Article 31(1) of the Vienna Convention indicates that the object and purpose are ancillary to the ordinary meaning of the terms.[74] In addition, and notwithstanding their expressed reluctance to engage in a detailed analysis of the *travaux*, all three judges accorded considerable weight to the postponement of the protocol on stateless persons at the 1951 Conference. Pill LJ, in fact, considered the historical context first, leaving any consideration of the ordinary meaning of the terms to the very end of his judgment.

Armed forces—criminal injuries—war operations or military activity by warring factions—compensation to military personnel for criminal injuries sustained abroad—Criminal Injuries Compensation (Overseas) Scheme 1979

Case No. 9. Regina v. *Ministry of Defence, ex parte Walker*, 6 April 2000, [2000] 1 WLR 807, [2000] 2 All ER 917, <http://www.publications.parliament.uk/pa> (HL).

The appellant was a British soldier stationed in Bosnia in 1995 as part of a United Nations peacekeeping force. He was injured when a Serbian tank fired a shell into a UN accommodation block. He sought compensation under the Criminal Injuries Compensation (Overseas) Scheme 1979, a discretionary ex-gratia programme which provides compensation to members of the armed forces injured abroad as a result of crimes of violence.

In 1980 the Ministry of Defence had articulated an exception to the scheme whereby compensation would not be paid where a 'state of war exists or a warlike situation is declared to exist'. In 1994, the Minister of Defence announced that operations in Bosnia fell into that category. The Ministry consequently refused to provide compensation to the appellant when he applied

[74] On this point, see this *Year Book*, 68 (1997), pp. 307–11 (reviewing *Sidhu* v. *British Airways plc; Abnett (known as Sykes)* v. *British Airways plc*, [1997] AC 430, [1997] 2 WLR 26, [1997] 1 All ER 193, HL and *Semco Salvage and Marine Pte. Ltd.* v. *Lancer Navigation Co. Ltd. (The Nagasaki Spirit)*, [1997] AC 455, [1997] 2 WLR 298, [1997] 1 All ER 502, [1997] Times LR 57, HL).

for it in 1996. An application for judicial review was rejected by the Divisional Court and subsequently by the Court of Appeal.

On appeal to the House of Lords, the appellant relied on the 1994 Convention on the Safety of United Nations and Associated Personnel.[75] Article 9 of the Convention requires each State party to make criminal, under its national law, intentional attacks on UN personnel and attacks on official UN premises that are likely to endanger UN personnel.

The Convention was implemented into United Kingdom law by the United Nations Personnel Act 1997. Section 1 of the Act makes it an offence to assault, causing injury, a UN worker outside the United Kingdom. According to Section 2, it is an offence to attack premises used by a UN worker, when a UN worker is on the premises, if that attack would constitute a breach of the Criminal Damage Act 1971.

The appellant argued that the Court should assume that Parliament intended to fulfil the United Kingdom's international obligations and therefore construe the exception elaborated by the Ministry of Defence as complying with those obligations.[76]

Lord Slynn, with whom Lords Nicholls, Hoffmann and Saville concurred, accepted that the attack may have been criminal under the Convention but nonetheless found that it constituted military activity for the purposes of the exception:

> [T]he Convention of 1994 . . . still leaves open the question of what compensation is paid under national schemes. . . . What happened was criminal under international law, but it is still 'military activity' for the purposes of the exclusion to the scheme.[77]

Lord Hobhouse dissented, holding that the attack, even if it appeared military, was wholly criminal and compensation was therefore required. He said:

> Sergeant Walker was injured as a result of . . . a deliberate attack by a Serbian tank upon a UN accommodation block. It was not part of any attack on the Muslim forces. Sergeant Walker was not engaged on any combatant activity nor in assisting one side or the other. By accepted norms, the attack on the civilian non-combatant UN peacekeepers was criminal. Further it had been declared to be such by the United Nations Convention on the Safety of United Nations and Associated Personnel, of 9 December 1994 . . . He was injured as the result of a criminal act of violence. He was not injured by an 'enemy'. He was not injured as a result of a 'war' operation or some military activity by a 'warring' party.[78]

[75] (1995) 34 International Legal Materials 482, Cmd. 3363.

[76] This argument is consistent with the approach set out by Lord Diplock in *Garland* v. *British Rail*, [1983] 1 AC 751 at 771A, [1982] 2 All ER 402 at 415, [1982] 2 WLR 918 at 934–5, this *Year Book*, 53 (1982), pp. 291–3. See also: *R.* v. *Secretary of State for the Home Department, ex parte Brind*, [1991] 1 All ER 720 at 722–3 and 733–4, [1991] 2 WLR 588 at 591–2 and 603–4 (*per* Lord Bridge and Lord Ackner), this *Year Book*, 62 (1991), pp. 437–40; *Mortensen* v. *Peters*, (1906) 8 F(JC) 93 at 103–4 (*per* Lord Kyllachy).

[77] [2000] 2 All ER 917 at 923, [2000] 1 WLR 806 at 812.

[78] [2000] 2 All ER 917 at 929, [2000] 1 WLR 806 at 818–19.

Overseas protectorate—removal of indigenous persons from territory—royal prerogative—peace, order and good government

Case No. 10. R. v. *Secretary of State for the Foreign and Commonwealth Office, ex parte Bancoult*, 3 November 2000, *The Times*, 10 November 2000, <http://www.courtservice.gov.uk/> (QBD).

In 1965 the United Kingdom formed the British Indian Ocean Territory (BIOT) by way of the British Indian Ocean Territory Order 1965, which was an Order in Council made under the powers of the royal prerogative. The BIOT is made up of those islands in the Indian Ocean that form the Chagos Archipelago. The territory had previously been governed under the British Colony of Mauritius, although the island of Mauritius is more than a thousand miles away.

At the request of the British Government and pursuant to his powers under the Order of 1965, the Commissioner of the BIOT issued the Immigration Ordinance of 1971. This ordinance compulsorily removed the entire civilian population of the BIOT to Mauritius. Most of the residents of the islands belonged to the indigenous Ilois people. The number of Ilois was not agreed upon, although the Divisional Court cited a 1971 report that numbered them at 829. The appellant was an Ilois who argued that the expulsions were illegal.

In his judgment, Laws LJ explained that the United Kingdom formed the BIOT in order to secure the island of Diego Garcia for a United States military base at a time when Mauritius was about to achieve independence. Documentation presented to the court revealed that the United Kingdom was aware that developing the base would require the expulsion of the Ilois and might therefore conflict with obligations under the United Nations Charter.

Laws LJ, however, focussed on whether the expulsions were compatible with British law. He held that the Order of 1965 was made under the royal prerogative and that the Commissioner thus had a broad discretion, including the right to make laws for the colony, to ensure the 'peace, order, and good government' of the territory. But he also held that the Order in question went too far:

> [T]he 'peace, order, and good government' of any territory means nothing, surely, save by reference to the territory's population. They are to be governed: not removed. In the course of argument Gibbs J gave what with respect seems to me to be an illuminating example of the rare and exceptional kind of case in which an order removing a people from their lawful homeland might indeed make for the territory's peace, order and good government: it would arise where because of some natural or man-made catastrophe the land had become toxic and uninhabitable. Short of an extraordinary instance of that kind, I cannot see how the wholesale removal of a people from the land where they belong can be said to conduce to the territory's peace, order and good government. The people may be taxed; they should be housed; laws will criminalise some of the things they do; maybe they will be tried with no juries, and subject to severe, even brutal penalties; the laws made for their marriages, their property, and much besides may be far different from what obtains in England. All this is vouchsafed by the authorities. But that is not all the learning gives. These people are subjects of the Crown, in right of their British nationality as belongers in the Chagos Archipelago. As Chitty said in 1820, the Queen has an interest in all her subjects, who rightly look to the Crown—today, to the rule of law which is given in the Queen's name—for the security of their homeland within the Queen's dominions. But in this case they have been excluded from it. It has been done

for high political reasons: good reasons, certainly, dictated by pressing considerations of military security. But they are not reasons which may reasonably be said to touch the peace, order and good government of BIOT, and in my judgment this is so whether the test is to be found in our domestic public law, exemplified by the Wednesbury doctrine or in a more, or less, intrusive approach. In short, there is no principled basis upon which section 4 of the Ordinance can be justified as having been empowered by section 11 of the BIOT Order. And it has no other conceivable source of lawful authority.[79]

Gibbs J concurred:

Each of the words 'peace', 'order' and 'good government' in relation to a territory necessarily carries with it the implication that citizens of the territory are there to take the benefits. Their detention, removal and exclusion from the territory are inconsistent with any or all of those words. To hold that the expression used in the Order could justify the provisions of the Ordinance would thus in my judgment be an affront to any reasonable approach to the construction of language.[80]

The Court consequently quashed the part (Section 4) of the Immigration Ordinance of 1971 that had compulsorily removed the residents of the Chagos Archipelago, thus paving the way for their return.

This decision, while focussing on the incompatibility of the expulsions with British law, constitutes an important footnote to the history of British imperialism. It is widely accepted that the duties owed by States under international law to the residents of their overseas territories have increased substantially over the course of the last century, with self-determination being but one of the concomitant rights. This judgment helps bring British law up to date with these developments—a matter of no small relevance for the Ilois, and the residents of the few other British overseas territories that remain.

[79] Paragraph 57.

[80] Paragraphs 69–71.

B. Private International Law*

1 *Forum conveniens and the impecunious claimant:* Lubbe *v.* Cape plc[1]

Last year we noted the decision of the Court of Appeal[2] in this piece of international asbestos litigation, in which two major issues had to be resolved. On the first, the court had held that where a foreign court was put forward as the natural forum, it could still be regarded as an available court even though as a matter of foreign law, it was open to the claimant to sue there by reason of the voluntary submission of the claimant only and not as a matter of jurisdictional right. On the second, it had held that the fact that the claimants would lose the reasonable certainty of external funding[3] for the prosecution of their claim, and be faced instead with a far lower and much less certain level of financial support, was not enough of a reason to consider a stay to be unjust. Accordingly the Court of Appeal had stayed the action in favour of the courts of South Africa. The House of Lords agreed with the court's assessment on the first point, but disagreed on the second, regarding it as a denial of justice that these impecunious claimants should be left to pursue their claims in South Africa. It therefore lifted the stay. The result was a claim in which over 3,000 claimants—those injured, or representatives of those killed—in the asbestos industry may proceed to prove their claims in England, even though all the claimants bar one were South African nationals, the mines and processing plants in and around which this disaster befell them were located in South Africa, and the English corporate defendant was no more than a holding company, which had in 1979 disposed of its shares in the South African companies which carried out the operations, and which had no assets in South Africa. From this brief summary it may be seen that the argument about financial support had a great deal of work to do to overcome the case for a stay; and that it did so demonstrates the weight which it must be seen to have. We will examine this, as the second point, below.

On the first point, however, there was a reassuring and authoritative return to orthodoxy. It had been assumed from the time of the decision in *Spiliada Maritime Corporation* v. *Cansulex Ltd*[4] that the availability of a natural forum in another country was a requirement which was satisfied by showing that the claimant could commence proceedings there, and that it was nothing to the point that the precise legal basis for his entitlement to do so was the submission of the defendant to that court's jurisdiction. A malign decision of the Court of Appeal[5] had cast doubt on this, appearing to hold that a court was not available, in the material sense, unless the claimant had an absolute and unqualified right to hale the defendant into court. The death of this notion was proclaimed last year,[6] but wild asses can now be seen dancing on its grave. It is a welcome development, for it was always contrary to principle that the operation of the English doctrine

[1] [2000] 1 WLR 1545, HL: Lords Bingham of Cornhill, Steyn, Hoffmann, Hope of Craighead, and Hobhouse of Woodborough.

[2] [2000] 1 Lloyd's Rep 139, CA; noted in this *Year Book*, 70 (1999), p. 319.

[3] In the form of legal aid or a conditional fee arrangement.

[4] [1987] AC 460, HL.

[5] *Mohammed* v. *Bank of Kuwait and the Middle East KSC* [1996] 1 WLR 1483, CA.

[6] In this *Year Book*, 70 (1999), p. 319.

of *forum conveniens* should be hostage to the unpredictable civil procedural rules of foreign courts, which will have been designed with no eye to the *Spiliada* doctrine. It was a reasonable view that if the defendant held up his hand and undertook to submit to the jurisdiction of the foreign court, that rendered the court an available one: the laws of Scotland and the United States were to this effect,[7] and English law is now in line with them. It is true that this may leave the claimant feeling that the defendant, by volunteering an undertaking to submit, has rather shot his fox; but this is too bad. English law stopped loading the jurisdictional dice in favour of the claimant some time ago, and if the natural forum is shown to the judge to be available,[8] it is irrational to expect him to act as if it were not. True, if the undertaking is offered only at the hearing of the application for a stay, the claimant may fairly ask what else he was supposed to have done if not to start against the defendant in England. But the right response is that a victory secured only by a late change of position by a defendant may properly lead to a costs order in favour of the losing claimant. The common sense of commercial judges ought to be a sufficient basis for the prevention of such limited injustice as may arise from a late but effective undertaking.[9]

So South Africa was an available forum, and, obviously, one whose judgments would in principle be enforceable in England by reason of the defendant's submission. But the claimants wanted to sue in England where, it may be surmised, the defendant's assets were, the damages awarded to a successful claimant would be higher, and financial support would underwrite both the preparation of the scientific evidence and the costs of litigation. In South Africa the level of financial support would be much lower, if it existed at all.[10] Lord Bingham of Cornhill was clear that in those circumstances it would be unjust to send the claimants to a forum, admittedly natural, in which their impecuniosity would mean that their claim would fail for want of a proper hearing. Though similar reasoning had also led to the refusal of a stay in *Connelly* v. *RTZ Corp plc*,[11] in circumstances described as exceptional, it has become clear that facts such as these are perhaps not so rare after all; and that wherever a stay will lead to a claim being stifled on grounds of impecuniosity, it will not be ordered.[12] Lord Bingham made no bones about it:[13]

> For reasons already given, I have concluded that a stay would lead to a denial of justice to the plaintiffs. Since as the *Spiliada* case makes clear, a stay will not be granted where it is established by cogent evidence that the plaintiff will not obtain justice in the foreign forum, I cannot conceive that the court would grant a stay in any case where adequate funding and legal representation of the plaintiff were clearly judged to be necessary to the doing of justice and these were clearly shown to be unavailable in the foreign forum although available here.

[7] Convincingly demonstrated by Lord Hope of Craighead at pp. 1562–6.

[8] At the time of the hearing of the application: pp. 1565–6.

[9] For a good illustration of this, see *Amoco (UK) Exploration Co* v. *British American Offshore Ltd* (Langley J, 12 December 2000).

[10] The evidence as summarized by Lord Bingham seemed somewhat unclear. But it sufficed to discharge the burden of proof which, on this point, lies on the claimant seeking to overcome the case for a stay.

[11] [1998] AC 854, HL.

[12] An analogy may lie with the circumstances in which an order for security for costs will and will not be made under CPR r. 25.12.

[13] At p. 1561.

That being so, it was unnecessary to proceed to ask whether Article 6 of the European Convention for the Protection of Human Rights and Fundamental Freedoms had any bearing on the decision: it did not, because the common law had got there first.

After the decision in *Connelly*, the Lord Chancellor's Office had embarked on a campaign to have the effect of that decision reversed by legislation,[14] fearing that English solicitors would be empowered to write themselves cheques drawn on the legal aid fund, as impecunious claimants arrived in England with no assets apart from a cause of action. It is unlikely that the decision in *Lubbe* will be regarded in the same way as that in *Connelly*. For one thing, the legislative reversal of a decision specifically recorded as being in line with the Human Rights Convention would be—or should be—legally and politically difficult. For another, the effective removal of legal aid has meant that the account is now closed and most cheques will bounce; the external support which will increasingly underwrite such personal injury claims lies in the field of conditional professional fees.

Even so, two substantial doubts remain. First, though Lord Bingham was careful to eschew any intention to make disparaging comparisons between the provision made by the legal systems in England and South Africa, it was undeniable that this was the very thing which he needed to do to reach the conclusion that it would be unjust to stay the English proceedings. Even if it were said that it does not disparage the South African system of civil justice to say that a claimant will be fatally disadvantaged by the understandable lack of external financial support for his claim, the conclusion nevertheless is that there will be a denial of justice if the claimant is required to sue there. In his conclusion, therefore, the comparison is made clearly and precisely: these claimants cannot obtain justice in the courts of South Africa; and that is a judicial holding which should give very considerable pause. For there is no unassailable line which can be drawn to circumscribe it. Moreover, Lord Bingham considered that the absence of a developed procedure for class actions in South Africa contributed to the conclusion that there would be a denial of justice in South Africa, albeit because the uncertainty wrought by this would risk discouraging any prospect of funding by conditional fees. But if this is an admissible point, it opens the door to the argument, so assiduously rejected in case after case, that comparisons between systems of civil procedure are to be made. After all, Lord Bingham referred to 'the expert evidence which would be essential if these claims were to be justly decided', and that the inability of the claimants to fund it in South Africa would lead to a denial of justice. It appears to follow that the minimum requirements for a just determination may include expert evidence, and a tribunal which can make a proper evaluation of it. So what if the foreign court would limit or exclude expert evidence and proceed on some less sophisticated basis of evaluation? Or if the tribunal of decision were to be a civil jury, manifestly incapable of understanding the complex science which underpins the claim? One supposes that there will be little judicial encouragement for any attempt to roll back *Spiliada* in this way. But it is harder to be confident that its defence will be easy. Perhaps the truth is, however, that the proposition that one can operate the *Spiliada* principles without making this

[14] Referred to in this *Year Book*, 70 (1999) p. 319, 321.

form of comparison is naive, for in the English analysis comparison will, at some level, precede and motivate the decision.[15] At least *Lubbe* is open about it. Whether it is a correct reading of Lord Bingham's speech to say that it limits the inroad it makes to arguments which can be said to concern the financing of litigation is unclear; but if this is not the answer, there will be some hard cases before long.[16]

The second doubt concerns the application of *Lubbe* to cases where the jurisdiction of the court is founded on service out of the jurisdiction with the permission of the court, obtained under CPR r. 6.20. Suppose that a claimant has obtained an order for service, and the defendant applies under CPR 11 for a declaration that the court has no jurisdiction and for orders to give effect to that decision. Suppose the claimant, though unable to show that England is the natural forum, can show that he lacks the means to prosecute the claim in the place where the defendant is resident: will this make England 'the proper place in which to bring the claim'? It might appear to be so, for if England is the only place in which justice can be done, it will be difficult to deny that England is the proper place if it is in practice the *only* place where the claim can be brought. But this would serve to widen, with more dramatic effect, the jurisdiction of the English courts to any case in which a local conditional fee arrangement will offer a claimant an advantage which he lacks overseas, and will risk turning England into a courthouse for the world. Given the appalling disadvantages this offers to all except local lawyers,[17] it is to be supposed that it will not happen.[18] But how not? It might be argued that the availability of funding cannot by itself suffice[19] to make England *the* proper place to bring the claim unless it is shown that there is no other court, from China to Peru, in which such possibilities exist. This will

[15] This is one reason why the High Court of Australia, considering that this comparison is inappropriate for an Australian court, has focused its attention on the local question whether the Australian court is inappropriate.

[16] It cannot really be said that where the funding of a claim is concerned, there is advantage to the claimant without concomitant disadvantage to the defendant, so that the court is not taking sides in paying attention to it. It is evident that the prospect of defending a claim brought by a contingency-fee funded claimant, say in the shameless fora of Texas and Louisiana, is more terrifyingly expensive for a defendant who will not have a corresponding opportunity to have his costs underwritten by lawyers on his side.

[17] If there is any doubt about it, see *Smith Kline & French Laboratories Ltd* v. *Bloch* [1983] 1 WLR 730, CA.

[18] It was argued that a court should be entitled to take account of factors of public interest—such as that if actions lacking a strong connection to England are allowed to proceed in England local claims will be delayed in getting a hearing—in deciding whether to stay proceedings. Such concerns were voiced most clearly by Spiegelman CJ in *James Hardie Industries Pty Ltd* v. *Grigor* (1998) 45 NSWLR 20, 43, NSW CA, but he felt unable, in the light of *Oceanic Sun Line Special Shipping Co Inc* v. *Fay* (1988) 165 CLR 197, to give effect to them. Lords Bingham and Hope agreed that such factors were inadmissible in England also, notwithstanding their relevance in the law of the United States: *Piper Aircraft Co* v. *Reyno* (1981) 454 US 235. As long as the law does not permit a stay in cases where the parties are agreed that the proceedings should be brought in England, this is probably inevitable: to make such an evaluation only where the parties disagree about trial in England may not be wholly rational; and it may be that there are no manageable standards by which this factor could be properly regulated. But if this is so, any further widening of the doors to cases which are not otherwise most closely connected to England will be at the expense of local litigants waiting in the queue.

[19] But consider the fact that it was single-handedly able to prevent a stay of proceedings in the instant case.

be difficult. But even if there are other places outside England and the place of the defendant's residence where such financial support may be found, how could it be said that the court should set aside the order permitting service, still leaving the claimant without a court in which he can be sure to get a hearing? Or, to put it another way, can a court be permitted or required to make an order which will deny justice to a claimant when the defendant is properly, albeit without having submitted to the jurisdiction,[20] before the court? It is as well to confess that this trouble can be seen coming, but that no convincing antidote is immediately to hand to deal with it. Yet it will widen the exorbitant jurisdiction of the English courts if all that is required of a claimant is a good arguable case that the claim falls within one of the paragraphs of rule 6.20, and the prospect of a local conditional fee agreement.

Two final points may be noted. First, in the light of the decision on the impact of funding, it was not necessary for the court to give a definitive view of the manner in which the claimant had elected to plead a case against the English parent company, rather than against the separately incorporated South African operating companies. It was easy to infer that this manipulative pleading had been adopted in order to skew the analysis of where the natural forum lay in favour of England. All that Lord Bingham said of this was that the trial judge had been entitled to conclude that it did, or that it did not, serve to make England the natural forum, and that it was probably not open to an appellate tribunal to interfere as the Court of Appeal had.[21] This suggests that there was not a point of law at the root of it. The conclusion appears to be that a judge may choose to look at the reality of the case, perhaps including the possibility of amendment, in coming to a practical decision about where the case does have its natural forum. It does not support the argument that the court is rigidly tied to the formulation of the claim as put forward by the claimant, but neither does it say that a judge may wholly disregard the careful structure of the claim. In this respect the analysis in *Berezovsky* v. *Michaels*[22] may have more to say on the issue. Secondly, the decision to lift the stay meant that there was no decision to stay a claim brought against a defendant domiciled in England in favour of the courts of a non-Contracting state to the Brussels Convention,[23] and there was therefore no need to consider the correctness of the decision in *Re Harrods (Buenos Aires) Ltd*[24] that this was permissible. But Lord Bingham stated that had he come to the conclusion that the common law required a stay of proceedings, he would have referred to the Court of Justice of the European Communities a question whether Article 2 of the Convention permitted this to be done, as he considered the answer to the question, as a matter of European law, to be unclear. No plainer indication can be given that it is time for the issue raised in *Re Harrods* to be referred for an authoritative ruling.

[20] CPR r. 11.1(5).

[21] In the first of its two reported decisions in the case: [1999] ILPr 471, CA.

[22] [2000] 1 WLR 1004, HL; noted below.

[23] Civil Jurisdiction and Judgments Act 1982 Sch 1. The Brussels Convention is replaced by an EC Regulation which will come into effect on March 1st 2002.

[24] [1992] Ch 72, CA.

2 *Jurisdiction over international defamation:* Berezovsky *v.* Michaels[25]

Last year we noted that the Court of Appeal[26] had upheld an order permitting service out of the jurisdiction on a defendant American magazine publisher and its editor, at the behest of a Russian businessman who complained that those few copies of the magazine which circulated in England had defamed him. The House of Lords dismissed the further appeal of the publisher and editor, with the result that the claimant should be free to proceed to prove his case in the English courts. The striking result is that a Russian oligarch may sue his alleged American defamers in the English courts, though no complaint was made against the publication of the same material in the same number of the magazine in Russia or the United States. Great must have been the rejoicing at the defamation Bar; and when this corner of the legal world sees something to rejoice in, one may fairly ask whether the broader public interest has been well served by whatever it was which gave rise to it.

There can be no serious doubt that *if* it was properly open to Berezovsky to limit the scope of his pleading and the court's attention to a defamatory statement circulated only in England, there was no real reason to object to his bringing an action in the English courts, and to institute it by service out if need be. That he was entitled to plead as he chose had already been established in the *Shevill* litigation.[27] So the real issue for the court was whether it was required on a jurisdictional application to focus on only the 2000 copies sold in England, and to put out of its mind the fact that close on a million were sold and read elsewhere, overwhelmingly in America. If, as seems to follow from the decision, the answer is that it was, it lends strong support to the view that a claimant is entitled to plead selectively and by doing so expect to win the jurisdictional battle. If this is so, it is worth asking whether this feature is peculiar to defamation, or extends to claimants generally.

The discussion of this issue in relation to *Lubbe* v. *Cape plc*[28] came to the conclusion that the trial judge appeared to have a broad and general margin of appreciation, which allowed him to regard the fact that the case was pleaded against only one potential defendant as making or not making England the natural forum for the claim.[29] But in *Berezovsky* the trial judge had made a similar broad assessment of the claim, and had found that the Russian and American elements—which were inescapably raised for evaluation, as the justification of the statements, or the question whether they were fair comment, was bound to involve a close inspection of matters which went to the heart of the Russian government and state—outweighed the English ones. It was in effect upon this point that Lords Hoffmann and Hope of Craighead dissented, but their being in the minority makes it clear that the task for the judge is much more circumscribed by the pleading than the minority, or perhaps *Lubbe*, would

[25] [2000] 1 WLR 1004, HL: Lords Steyn, Nolan, and Hobhouse of Woodborough; Lords Hoffmann and Hope of Craighead dissenting.

[26] *Sub nom Berezovsky* v. *Forbes Inc* [1999] ILPr 358, CA; noted in this *Year Book*, 70 (1999) p. 323.

[27] *Shevill* v. *Presse Alliance SA* [1996] AC 959; [1995] ECR I–415.

[28] Discussed above, as Case 1 in this survey.

[29] *Supra*, text to notes 21 and 22.

accept or suggest. It had been suggested[30] that such an approach would serve as an open invitation to forum shoppers; and it is hard to dissent from the view that what was foreseen has come to pass.

Most rational people will accept that this dispute has nothing whatever to do with England, and the attempt by the claimant to establish that he had a significant English reputation was peculiarly incredible. The basis of the difficulty in erecting this sentiment into a legal principle was, however, that domestic English libel law regards each publication as a separate tort. Each such tort will, presumably, have its own characteristics and will also point, if this is then elevated to the plane of private international law, to its own natural forum and governing law. So Berezovsky was libelled 2000 times in England, and where other than England is such a claim to be regarded as naturally belonging? To get round this argument it is presumably necessary to contend that the publication should be regarded, for jurisdictional purposes,[31] as if it were one tort, and that this notional omnibus tort serves to define and locate jurisdictional contacts. Lord Steyn saw this as a technique which had nothing to commend it, but he may have been too unkind, at least if one is grasping for an analysis which would allow a court to do as Popplewell J. did, and say that this case does not have enough to do with England to make England the proper place in which to bring it.[32] An alternative analysis, but to the same effect, would be to say that Berezovsky has only one reputation, and that the proper place to bring an action with international points of contact is where that single reputation is located, and therefore, necessarily, damaged. After all, and as Lord Hoffmann was sharply aware, the claimant was seeking the decision of an English court to vindicate his reputation: it was all Lombard Street to a China orange that an English verdict in his favour would be used as evidence or proof that his reputation, not just his *English* reputation, had been wrongly impugned, by the same lies and to the same extent.

As against this view of the matter, it is not clear that it is proper to look at a tort which damages reputation as (in any sense) a single tort. For it may be wrong to consider that Berezovsky has *a* reputation, as opposed to there being as many reputations of him as there are readers who have a view of Berezovsky: in other words, the reputations are held by them, not owned by him. If that is so, the lowering of Berezovsky in the eyes of these individuals is a series of separate acts which strike at and damage the separate measures of esteem accorded by these individuals. Or, to use an analogy, if a large number of English debtors default on sums owed by them to Berezovsky, this would not be seen as a single diminution of his patrimonial estate (located at the place where he resides),[33] but as a number of acts, each separately actionable, done by separate individuals, each separately suable. If this is translated to the context of defamation, it would mean that each withdrawal of esteem is separately actionable. If there are as

[30] Reed and Kennedy, [1996] LMCLQ 108.

[31] It need not follow that it be so regarded for choice of law purposes, still less for the purposes of English domestic law.

[32] This being the test now imposed by CPR r. 6.21(2A), in statutory substitution for the common law requirement that England be shown, clearly or distinctly, to be the natural forum for the trial of the action.

[33] Cf. the interpretation which might be taken in Italian law: *Marinari* v. *Lloyd's Bank plc* (Case C–364/94) [1995] ECR I–2719.

many causes of action as there are debtors, there may also be thought to be as many causes of action as there are those who withdraw their esteem.

But again, there is a material difference between defamation and this analogy: in defamation, the cause of action does not lie against the several individuals who choose to withdraw their esteem, but against the one individual who caused this to happen. Any analogy with the case of several contracts is therefore illusory. Neither is there an analogy with a product manufacturer whose dangerous article is sold in many jurisdictions to several claimant-victims, for there there will be as many torts as there are victims. It is right that each instance of personal injury be seen as a separate, and separately actionable, tort, with the result that the manufacturer faces being made to answer for his fault, or lack of it, in many different jurisdictions. By contrast, in defamation, there is one tortfeasor and one victim, no matter how many times and to how many people the statement is published; it is the act of a single individual which establishes his liability. In that light, it is not so strange that this should be seen as constituting a single tort, for the purposes of the conflict of laws if not also for domestic law. From this perspective, there was something attractive in the proposition that the claim stemming from publication in a magazine with a predominantly American audience was not one whose natural forum was England, even if the complaint were restricted to publication to readers in England. It is respectfully submitted that the dissentients were absolutely right in their conclusion that the judge had asked himself the right question and had given it the right answer: the claim form alleged a tort which had nothing of any credible substance to do with England. Permission to serve the claim form out of the jurisdiction should not have been given and should have been set aside.

Given that the majority decided otherwise, however, the question must be to identify the ratio of the decision. It is almost certainly limited to defamation, for with no other tort does a single defendant have the potential to inflict thousands of separate torts on the hapless claimant, nor in any other tort is the party who elects, unjustifiably, to cause loss not the tortfeasor. More broadly, it may be that the case stands for the proposition that a judge is limited, in his assessment of where the natural forum lies, by the factual ambit of the claim as asserted by the claimant, and is not permitted to look to extrinsic material in order to draw the conclusion that, seen in a broader context, the natural forum is not where it appears to be. As suggested above, the fact that the Court of Appeal was held by the majority to have been entitled to reverse Popplewell J. on this point would appear to be at odds with the approach of the first instance judge in *Lubbe*, which was thought to be unimpeachable and which closely resembled the approach of Popplewell J.

The majority also approved the reasoning of Hirst LJ below, when he applied *Cordoba Shipping Co Ltd* v. *National State Bank, Elizabeth, New Jersey ('The Albaforth')*,[34] a decision on negligent misrepresentation which pre-dated *Spiliada*, to the effect that the place where a tort is committed may be presumed to be the natural forum for the litigation of liability arising from it. Though it could be, and was, argued that a decision of this vintage should be no more than a stepping stone to *Spiliada* and which was now *functus*, it was far from clear that there was anything wrong with it. Though not all torts depend on the evidence

[34] [1984] 2 Lloyd's Rep 91, CA.

of those who were present to bear witness to their commission, and though not all torts are governed by the *lex loci delicti commissi*, most are; and a presumption that the *locus delicti* is the natural forum for a tort claim is hard to criticize.[35] Even the dissentients did not appear to dispute this, reserving their criticism for the conclusion of the majority that, despite the very terms of his judgment, Popplewell J. had failed to give effect to this point.

In the final analysis, the practical significance will be that as long as a publication has an appreciable circulation in England, which will also mean, one imagines, a body of English internet readers,[36] the English courts will be open to the claimant, whether or not the defendant is present in England. Perhaps this is right, for it should in principle be no answer to an allegation that a tort was committed in England to argue that no tort was committed in the United States. But the incentive to forum shop at the defamation Bar is now clear and obvious and, some will think, obviously wrong.

3 *Ordering the sale of a bankrupt's land in Portugal:* Ashurst *v.* Pollard[37]

The Brussels Convention excludes bankruptcy from its scope;[38] but where it does apply, proceedings which have as their object rights *in rem* in land in another contracting state are within the exclusive jurisdiction of the courts of that state.[39] It is therefore something of a surprise to find that the Court of Appeal concluded that the Brussels Convention allowed it to order, as against legal owners of the land, that they do what was needed to allow a trustee in bankruptcy to sell land in Portugal: after all, as a matter of Portuguese law, the land was vested in the defendants. But this was the order sought and made in *Ashurst* v. *Pollard*.[40]

Pollard had been made bankrupt in England in 1993, at which time he owned, jointly with his wife, an estate in Portugal, and of which he was registered as joint proprietor. As a matter of English law, the bankruptcy caused all his assets to vest in his trustee, but this obviously had no effect on the Portuguese land register. The trustee wished to sell the land. In order to do so he needed to enforce an incident of his ownership *qua* trustee in bankruptcy against another legal owner: either the legal ownership which the Insolvency Act gave him, or the perfection[41] of his title against Pollard who now held his legal title as trustee

[35] At this broad level of generality it is not necessary to examine separately the torts whose governing law is identified by the Private International Law (Miscellaneous Provisions) Act 1995, or by the common law rule in *Boys* v. *Chaplin* [1971] AC 356.

[36] Lord Steyn did not find the need to deal with the impact, if any, which might have flowed from the fact that copies of the article had been read on the internet. But he would presumably have considered that any person who accessed this virtual material from a computer terminal with a physical location in England read it in England and, in doing so, assisted the conclusion that there was a further separate tort committed by the defendant.

[37] [2001] 2 WLR 722, CA: Kennedy, Potter and Jonathan Parker LJJ, affirming [2000] 2 All ER 772, Jacob J.

[38] Article 1, second paragraph, point (2).

[39] Article 16.1.

[40] The case is reported as a jurisdictional challenge, but it appears that the court considered jurisdiction and merits in a single proceeding, and that there was to be no resumed hearing once jurisdiction had been established.

[41] Cf. paragraph 16 of the judgment, citing with approval Jacob J.'s use of this expression.

for the trustee in bankruptcy. The Court of Appeal, affirming Jacob J., held that the claim was within the Brussels Convention and was not subject to exclusive Portuguese jurisdiction, and made the orders for the sale of the land.

As to the question whether such a claim by a trustee in bankruptcy meant that Article 1, second paragraph, point (2) removed it from the domain of the Convention, the Court stated that the governing test was whether bankruptcy was the principal subject matter of the proceedings, and held that it was not, for it arose after the declaration of bankruptcy, and not as part of the decision to make a bankruptcy order. Though this had also been the approach of Rattee J. in *Re Hayward*,[42] there must still be some doubt whether it was the right question to ask. As bankruptcy lies outside the Convention, it ought to follow that nothing in the Convention cuts across or interferes with the bankruptcy law of the English court. If as a matter of English bankruptcy law a court would have jurisdiction to make the order which it was asked to make, there is much to be said for the view that the Convention cannot contradict it by, for example, removing the court's jurisdiction to make the order. Though this argument has become rather bogged down in the analogous[43] context of arbitration, where it was never completely clear whether an issue of arbitration immunised the entire underlying claim from the Convention,[44] the fundamental decision of the Court of Justice in *Hoffmann* v. *Krieg*[45] clearly means that a court is not obliged by the Convention, whether directly or indirectly, to contradict its own law on bankruptcy, any more than in *Hoffmann* it was obliged to contradict its own law on status. Had that reasoning been applied here, there would have been no scope for the Convention to be applied. But for some reason, this argument, which is squarely founded on the Court's own jurisprudence, has been shaded by the proposition that the *exclusions* particularised in the second paragraph to Article 1 are to be read as if they were *exceptions* to a general rule of the Convention, and therefore given a narrow or restrictive meaning, so that they will only be engaged if they are the principal subject matter of the proceedings. One wearies of saying it, but even if this is what Jenard may have proposed,[46] this is not what the Convention says; it is not what the Court said in *Hoffmann*; and it is baffling to see the English judges electing to be *plus royalistes que la cour*. But the tide is probably too strong for reason to turn it back now. Even so, the principal issue in the case was whether the trustee in bankruptcy in this case should be granted an order for sale of the land. If this proceeding did not have bankruptcy as its principal subject matter, it is hard to know what it did have. The court will be required to apply principles of insolvency law to determine whether to make the order for sale, and one would have thought that this placed bankruptcy at the heart of the claim. All the court said by way of answer was that it was not so, and the fact that the claimant was a trustee did not make it so. But even if this last point is correct, what, apart from the substantive and procedural law of

[42] [1997] Ch 45, noted this *Year Book*, 67 (1996), p. 557.

[43] Similarly outside the Convention: point (4) of the second paragraph of Article 1.

[44] See the discussion in Dicey and Morris *The Conflict of Laws* (13th edn. 2000), paragraphs 11–023 to 11–029, and 12–128 to 12–131.

[45] Case 145/86 [1988] ECR 645.

[46] 1979 OJ C59/1 at 10.

bankruptcy, will the court have applied in deciding whether the order should be made? It is all very strange.

But on the footing that the proceedings were within the scope of the Convention, an order that Portuguese land be sold, and that steps be taken to have the Portuguese land register amended prior to the sale, might be thought to be orders whose making was within the exclusive jurisdiction of the Portuguese court. But the Court of Appeal disagreed, relying on the principle established in *Webb* v. *Webb*,[47] namely that claims to enforce rights *in personam*, albeit that they relate to land, are not actions which have rights *in rem* as their object: the *jus actionis* is not the vindication of a pre-existing legal right, indefeasible as against all the world, but is brought on some other basis to acquire such a right. Insofar as founded on a right *in personam*, it is not founded on a right *in rem*, good against the entire world. It was appalling reasoning in *Webb*,[48] but it represents the law, and proves that if hard cases make bad law, bad lawyers can make worse. True, if this dichotomy held, an action by a trustee against a joint legal owner, who is held to hold as bare trustee for the trustee in bankruptcy, may appear to fall on the personal rights side of the line. But the effect of English bankruptcy law was that the trustee had already become legal owner of all property of which the bankrupt had been legal owner; and that being so, he was asserting an incident (albeit one which he had only because he was trustee) of his pre-existing legal title.[49] That should have served to place the case on the other side of the line: a legal owner, albeit a rather special one, was seeking to enforce an incident of his legal ownership, albeit against another who also has legal ownership. That is a matter which has a right *in rem* as its object, and Article 16.1 should have led to the conclusion that, if the Convention applied to the action at all, the Portuguese courts had exclusive jurisdiction over it. It is true that if this reasoning were followed, the Portuguese courts would have been dealing with a case which might not involve intricate principles of Portuguese land law. But on the footing that the sale in Portugal would need to be for a proper price, it might well be more appropriate for a Portuguese court to conduct the necessary factual investigation and supervision. The Court of Appeal did not think so. It distinguished *Re Hayward* extremely briefly: although Rattee J. had there held that Article 16.1 did apply, Jonathan Parker LJ said:[50]

> By contrast, the proceedings in the instant case do not raise any issue as to title to land. The trustee in the instant case is not seeking to establish or protect, let alone perfect, his title to Mr Pollard's interest in the Portuguese land.

This is very difficult to understand, for perfecting his title is exactly what the trustee appeared to be doing. As a matter of Portuguese law, title to the land was vested in Pollard; as a matter of English law it was vested in the trustee and, as

[47] Case C–294/92 [1994] ECR I–1717.

[48] See the note in *Year Book of European Law*, 14 (1994) 563.

[49] After all, this is presumably why the bankruptcy exclusion was not relevant in the first place.

[50] At paragraph 60 of the judgment.

Jacob J had put it, he needed to perfect that title by having steps taken by Pollard under order of the court. If this curt sentence is meant to demonstrate the distinction between *Pollard* and *Re Hayward*, it will not be met with universal regard.

As to Article 16.3, it seems almost impossible to deny that the action had as its object the entry on the Portuguese register of title. If so Article 16.3 would have reconfirmed exclusive Portuguese jurisdiction over it. And *Re Hayward* had also conceded the application of Article 16.3 in such a case. But all the Court of Appeal said was that *Re Hayward* was distinguishable on the basis recited above, and Article 16.3 was not sensibly mentioned. If the court considered that the subject-matter of the action in *Pollard* was the relationship between the parties, to which the state of the Portuguese land register was an incidental and remote consequence, it is no more convincing than the reasoning which purported to sidestep Article 16.1. The action was brought in order to obtain an order that the Portuguese register of title should be amended: that was, in effect, all it sought, so that the trustee could then proceed to sell. For the Court of Appeal to conclude that the rectification of the register was not the principal subject matter of the action is simply incomprehensible. It does not merit further examination.

4 *Being 'sued' in the context of the Brussels Convention:* Canada Trust Co *v.* Stolzenberg (No 2);[51] National Justice Compania Naviera S.A. *v.* Prudential Assurance Co. Ltd. (No. 2) (*The Ikarian Reefer*)[52]

The House of Lords affirmed the decision of a majority of the Court of Appeal[53] that the date for determining whether the defendant Stolzenberg was domiciled in the United Kingdom, for the purpose of deciding whether he could serve as the hook on which to hang a claim against co-defendants domiciled in other contracting states, was that of the issue of process, and not the later date of service. The case was examined in some detail in the context of the decision of the Court of Appeal, and it is not necessary to repeat what was said there. It suffices to say that, in a claim advanced against a very large number of defendants, only one was even arguably domiciled in England; those co-defendants domiciled[54] in other contracting states objected to their being

[51] [2000] 3 WLR 1376, HL: Lords Steyn, Hoffmann, Cooke of Thorndon, Hope of Craighead, and Hobhouse of Woodborough.

[52] [2000] 1 WLR 603, CA: Simon Brown, Waller and Tuckey LJJ.

[53] [1998] 1 WLR 547, CA, noted this *Year Book*, 68 (1997), p. 343.

[54] There was also an appeal by co-defendants who were not domiciled in any contracting state, and whose liability to be sued in England depended on RSC Order 11 rule 1(1)(c), now re-enacted in significantly amended form as CPR r. 6.20(4). It was held (at 1386) that as one defendant had submitted to the jurisdiction of the English courts, the others were capable of being seen as necessary or proper parties to the claim against that defendant. This is not easy to accept, for the simple fact of a late submission by one defendant cannot establish that he had been duly served when the application for permission to serve out was made. But as CPR r. 6.20(4) removes the requirement of prior due service on a defendant, it is not proposed to examine the issue further.

joined under Article 6.1 of the Convention[55] on several grounds, of which two[56] may be mentioned: first, that the date on which the anchor defendant should be required to have a domiciliary connection to England[57] should be the date on which he was served with the claim form and the court accordingly became seised of a claim against him; and secondly, that the standard of proof on disputed issues of jurisdiction should be higher than that of a good arguable case.[58]

Article 6.1 of the Convention allows that a defendant domiciled in a contracting state may be sued 'where he is one of a number of defendants, in the courts for the place where any one of them is domiciled'. The appellants contended that this required that Stolzenberg be domiciled in England when he was served,[59] for it was only then that it could be said that he was being sued and that the intended co-defendants became jurisdictionally liable to be brought in. The argument was supported at two levels: that it was simply inaccurate to say that Stolzenberg was being sued until he had been served with process, and the appellants could not be co-defendants with someone who was not being sued. But the court disagreed, giving two broad reasons for this conclusion: that it was correct to say that the engine of litigation had been turned as soon as a claim form was issued; and that if it were later, it might encourage a devious defendant to cast off his English domicile and so frustrate the intending claimant. The first of these is right enough, if matters are measured from the standpoint of English procedural law: the process of litigation has undeniably begun, time periods start[60] to run and stop running,[61] and it is difficult to say that a defendant is not being sued. The second, however, was manifestly weak as a justification: the thought of a defendant being willing and able to flee, casting off an English[62] domicile in the gap between issue and service, depends upon so many improbable factors that it was unhelpful, even as a makeweight, quite apart from the fact that it is bizarre to regard a change of domicile as a matter for adverse comment. Moreover, it calls to mind the defendant who, in ignorance of the fact that a claim form has been issued, winds up his affairs and leaves England for good, only to find, several months later, that he is liable to come back to England to defend himself, by reason of article 2.[63] Nor is it enough to say that he should

[55] In fact the Lugano Convention, as the appellants were domiciled in Switzerland. The material provisions are identical, save that it is not possible to make a reference to the Court of Justice for a preliminary ruling in a case governed by the Lugano Convention.

[56] It was also contended that, quite apart from the date of domicile, Article 6 required that service be made on the anchor defendant before a co-defendant may be served. The submission was rejected, and needs no examination.

[57] Technically, to the United Kingdom as a matter of the Convention, and to England as a matter of internal United Kingdom law.

[58] This is the standard fixed for cases governed by common law and other statutory rules: *Seaconsar Far East Ltd* v. *Bank Markazi Jomhouri Islami Iran* [1994] 1 AC 438, HL.

[59] Which he was not, if he ever had been: Lord Hoffmann at 1388.

[60] For service of the claim form.

[61] Limitation, for example, will not happen.

[62] Lord Hope of Craighead delivered a speech almost completely devoted to Scots law which appeared to show that there were no such difficulties in Scotland.

[63] Lord Steyn saw the point at 1385, but was unmoved by it. The extraordinary result is that the law has been fashioned to deal with a person who repudiates his English domicile *mala fide*, whatever that may mean, and at deliberate cost to the many who do so in good faith. Hard cases make bad law.

be aware of this and therefore runs the risk with his eyes deemed to be open. The same reasoning would hold that a consumer, sued by a supplier in the courts for the place where he used to be domiciled, ought to be cheerfully aware that he remained liable to be so sued.[64] It is implausible and it is wrong.

The appellants' best argument, according to the court, was that consistency of approach with Article 21 required that a defendant not be regarded as sued until he was served. In *Dresser (UK) Ltd* v. *Falcongate Freight Management Ltd*[65] the Court of Appeal had held that, as a matter of English law and for the purpose of Article 21 of the Convention, an English court was seised of an action, which was therefore only then definitively pending,[66] only when process had been served; and that there was sense in aligning the definition of when a defendant was sued with the time at which the action became pending. The court disagreed, though not for very convincing reasons. Lord Steyn saw Article 21 as a 'tie-break' rule,[67] different in focus and purpose from the rule about where a defendant may be sued. It is undeniable that this is a possible view to take, and that there need be no elegance or harmony in the interpretation of the Convention. Lord Hoffmann,[68] by contrast, embarked upon a remarkable linguistic analysis of the German language original of the decision in *Zelger* v. *Salinitri*,[69] in order to demonstrate that the Court of Appeal in *Dresser* may have taken too simplistic a view of what *Zelger* had decided, and of J. L. Austin's concept[70] of 'trouser words' to explain that the concept of an action being *definitively* pending may have been more complex than it seemed at first sight. But after all that, he reached the same conclusion as Lord Steyn by abandoning linguistics in favour of recourse to a balancing of advantage and disadvantage which, in the end, put paid to the argument for the appellants. But as the question was evidently difficult, one may legitimately wonder what positive interest is served by the separation of the two concepts of a defendant being sued and a court being seised of an action. Maybe the court was aware, at the back of its mind, that even if the appellants were right, Article 6.1 was still a rule capable of doing bad things. After all, there was nothing to prevent a claimant issuing a claim form naming Stolzenberg as defendant, but having no real intention of pursuing him to judgment, or even discontinuing the claim against him, once jurisdiction had been established over the co-defendants. It is admittedly hard to see what a court could do to prevent this, unless there is a residual or national law power to prevent abusive exercise of legal rights. True, the proposition that Article 6.1 should be available only if the anchor defendant is the 'main' defendant would encourage argument and complexity. Perhaps the truth is that the rule is one

[64] Lord Steyn instanced, at 1382, the case of actions brought by a consumer in his new court, without mentioning the other side of the coin, which is that all actions brought against the consumer will be brought in the courts for the place where he was domiciled when the supplier issued the writ and not, if he has since moved, where he now is. The example, attributed to Lord Cooke of Thorndon, is singularly unconvincing.

[65] [1992] 1 QB 502, CA.

[66] This being the meaning of 'seised' put forward by the Court of Justice in *Zelger* v. *Salinitri* (Case 129/83) [1984] ECR 2397.

[67] At 1383.

[68] With whose speech the other members of the House did not express their concurrence.

[69] (Case 129/83) [1984] ECR 2397.

[70] *Sense and Sensibilia* (1962), at p. 70, cited by Lord Hoffmann at 1392.

open to criticism, but is one which is hard to show to be wrong. As with the decision in the case.

But on the requisite standard of proof, the court was so unwilling to examine whether the standard of a good arguable case should be departed from that it did not call on counsel for the respondent.[71] This is extraordinary. The result is that an English court will irrevocably accept jurisdiction and hear a case even though it believes, on balance, that the Convention provides that it does not have jurisdiction and that the courts of another contracting state do. How can this possibly be correct? There appear to be two sensible alternatives. One is to accept that the standard should be a balance of probabilities; the second is to allow a court to make a provisional assessment that it may have jurisdiction, but to postpone a final decision until the evidence has been heard and then, if the supposed jurisdictional basis was unfounded after all, to dismiss the claim on jurisdictional grounds. The first alternative was criticised[72] on the ground that it risked provoking a substantive hearing at the jurisdictional stage, but this is unconvincing. It is clear that, wherever the standard of proof is set, the parties may and will deploy evidence to show that it has or has not been met: the issue of where the line is drawn has no necessary or obvious relationship to the manner in which the parties will argue that it has or has not been met. The second, not uncommon in other jurisdictions, is precluded by the traditional approach of English civil procedure, now enshrined in CPR Part 11, which is to give a final and unreviewable ruling on jurisdiction before the defendant serves his defence. But taking all this together, an English court sets a low standard for the taking of a jurisdictional decision which is thereafter irreversible, even if it is wrong. This does not look sensible; and in the context of the Convention it is unacceptable. It is true that as a matter of common law, jurisdiction may be established if the court considers that there is a good arguable case that the jurisdictional requirements of the law have been met. That is fair enough: the rules of the common law explain when jurisdiction exists, and that is all they do. They take no account of whether other countries would have jurisdiction as well: this lies almost completely outside the scope and concern of the common law on jurisdiction; but in the rare case in which the common law actually contains a rule which *denies* the existence of jurisdiction, the standard to be met is a balance of probabilities.[73] But the Convention is wholly different from the autocephalous common law régime. It confers and it deprives of jurisdiction, doing both equally. It denatures the Convention for an English court to accept that it has jurisdiction if only[74] 30 per cent certain that jurisdiction exists, but to conclude that it has no jurisdiction only if 70 per cent certain that jurisdiction has been taken away by some other Article. From this point of view the pretended consistency with the common law on jurisdiction is a dangerous illusion, and to say, as Lord Steyn did,[75] that jurisdictional issues under the Convention are very important is to miss the point that it is not issues under, but the structure of, the

[71] At 1387.

[72] At 1387.

[73] *Re Polly Peck International (in administration) (No 2)* [1998] 3 All ER 812, CA, noted this *Year Book*, 69 (1998), p. 356.

[74] The figures are taken for illustration, in an impressionistic attempt to quantify the meaning of a good arguable case.

[75] At 1387.

Convention which is the most important. The argument may, most unfortunately, now be regarded as settled by the House of Lords, and therefore as binding on all lower courts. It is much to be regretted, for the right answer would have caused little trouble and would have been much more faithful to the obligations placed on the United Kingdom as a contracting state.

The question of whether a defendant was being sued also arose in *The Ikarian Reefer*. Proceedings in the English courts had resulted in the defendant insurer succeeding against the claimant Panamanian shipowner,[76] and obtaining an order for costs in its favour. Failing to recover the full sum assessed, the insurer sought an order under the Supreme Court Act 1981 s 51 against one Comninos, the principal behind the shipowner, and moving spirit in the conduct of the litigation. Section 51 allows a court to make an order for the payment of costs against a non-party, but Comninos was domiciled in Greece and contested the jurisdiction of the court over him, claiming that he was liable to be sued in Greece but not in England. The Court of Appeal rejected the submission on the basis that he was not being sued at all, so that Article 2 was irrelevant, or (if that was wrong and he was being sued) on the basis that Article 6 gave the English court jurisdiction over him. It is submitted that the court got the right answer, but for two wrong reasons.

Explaining why Comninos lost, Waller LJ was inclined to prefer the reasoning that he was not being sued, and that the issue of a summons in relation to costs did not involve suing the respondent. This was because it did not involve pursuing a substantive cause of action, or the making of orders ancillary to proceedings pending before the court.[77] It is not clear whether this was intended as a guide to the meaning of 'sued' only within the context of the Brussels Convention, but his proposition[78] that proceedings against an alleged contemnor do not involve suing suggest that it was seen as a general explanation of what it means to be sued. With great respect to the judge, it is suggested that this line of reasoning has the potential to lead to unwelcome difficulty. If the key to an understanding of what is meant by being sued is the pursuit of a substantive cause of action, would a defendant be sued (*a*) in proceedings for a declaration of non-liability, or (*b*) as respondent to an anti-suit injunction in cases where the only basis for obtaining it is his allegedly oppressive or vexatious behaviour, or (*c*) in proceedings for the enforcement of a judgment? In the case of (*a*), there is some authority[79] for the view that there is no substantive cause of action if all that is sought is a declaration that there is no liability owed, and in (*b*) that such an injunction is not based on a legal or equitable right at all.[80] By contrast, in (*c*) it appears to be supposed by Article 16.5 that proceedings to enforce a judgment—which means proceedings concerning measures of execution[81]—do involve the respondent, and presumably others, such as garnishees, in being sued and, that being so, Article 16.5 takes away any jurisdictional objection they

[76] Who was found to have ordered the grounding and arson of its own ship.

[77] At 137.

[78] At 137.

[79] *The Maciej Rataj* [1991] 2 Lloyd's Rep 458 (affirmed [1992] 2 Lloyd's Rep 552, CA, but now to be read in the light of *The Tatry* (Case 406/92) [1994] ECR I–5439).

[80] *South Carolina Insurance Co* v. *Assurantie Maatschappij 'De Zeven Provicien' NV* [1987] AC 24; *Amoco (UK) Exploration Co* v. *British American Offshore Ltd* [1999] 2 Lloyd's Rep 772.

[81] Jenard: 1979 OJ C59/1 at 36.

may have. It might have been possible to argue that what was really going on in *The Ikarian Reefer* was the enforcement of a judgment (which expression includes an order for costs[82] which had been made against the shipowner), and that this enforcement lies within the exclusive jurisdiction of the courts in which the enforcement is sought. In this case enforcement was sought in England, whose procedural law had a rather useful measure, namely the making of further orders against a non-party. Article 16.5 appears to provide that this is a matter within the exclusive jurisdiction of the English court *qua* enforcing court; and that there was therefore no need to answer the difficult question whether such post-judgment measures are to be seen as involving someone being sued. It is to be hoped that any intricacy which might seek to take advantage of the suggestion that it requires a substantive cause of action before someone can be said to be sued will not be allowed to take root in the law. Without the proposition having been tested to destruction, it is suggested that proceedings which are brought for the purposes of obtaining a judicial order against him do involve suing the defendant or respondent, and that no elaboration of this broad and general proposition is necessary.

For much the same reason as that just given, it is doubtful whether it was right to point to Article 6.2 in order to hold that Comninos was a third party against whom a warranty, guarantee, or other third party claim was being advanced. Waller LJ considered that seeking an order for costs against a non-party was a third party proceeding, but this may not be quite right. A third party proceeding in the context of Article 6.2 more naturally refers to a passing-on claim by a losing party, who argues that if he goes down to the claimant, someone else owes him and should be ordered to perform a duty of contribution or indemnification. But here the claim against Comninos was by the successful party, albeit that his success should be underwritten, and in this sense guaranteed, by another. Here as well the slightly uneasy manner in which the law was held to work suggests that the court was not quite asked to focus on what should have been seen as the real issue, which was one of the enforcement of judgments, as distinct from the establishing of original liability, which it did not concern.

5 *Matters relating to an avoided contract and the Brussels Convention*: Agnew *v.* Länsförsäkringsbolagens AB[83]

Yet another twist in the debate whether Article 5.1 of the Brussels and Lugano Conventions may be relied on by a claimant who seeks a declaration that he was not contractually bound to another was provided by this case on the avoidance of a contract of reinsurance. Agnew, domiciled in England, carried on its reinsurance business there. The defendant, LAB, was a Swedish entity which reinsured certain risks with Agnew. When Agnew discovered what it took to be material non-disclosure by LAB, it brought proceedings in London for a declaration that it was entitled to avoid the contracts of reinsurance, relying on

[82] Article 25.

[83] [2001] 1 AC 223, HL: Lord Nicholls of Birkenhead, Lord Woolf MR and Lord Cooke of Thorndon; Lord Hope of Craighead and Lord Millett dissenting.

Article 5.1 of the Lugano Convention[84] as the basis for special jurisdiction over LAB. Affirming the decision of the Court of Appeal,[85] the House of Lords held that the matter was one relating to a contract; and a bare majority held that the pre-contractual obligation to make a fair presentation of the risk was the obligation in question which fell to be performed in London. The English courts therefore had special jurisdiction over the defendant.

For the claim to have fallen within Article 5.1 it was necessary to hold that the matter was one relating to a contract, and to locate the obligation in question as being performed or performable in England: the conditions may be taken as distinct and cumulative.[86] It may have seemed too obvious for words that an action to avoid a contract on the ground that its making was flawed by the telling of half-truths and lies was a matter relating to a contract, but the House of Lords had only recently held that an action for the recovery of money paid pursuant to a supposed contract later discovered to be wholly void was not a matter relating to a contract. In *Kleinwort Benson Ltd* v. *Glasgow City Council*[87] a bare majority had either held that this was not a matter relating to a contract because there was no contract for it to relate to, or that because the obligation sought to be enforced did not arise *ex contractu*, there was no relevant obligation in question. The effect of *Agnew* must be that while *Kleinwort Benson* may still be applicable in cases of supposed contracts wholly void, or maybe only those whose voidness is common ground,[88] it is of no application to voidable ones which are, obviously, actual contracts. It was probably hoping for too much that *Kleinwort Benson* should be overruled, but it is still calamitous where it does apply: the claimant who sues for breach, but claims alternatively for the return of money if it be held that there never was a contract, will be able to advance the first argument on the basis of Article 5.1, but may be debarred from advancing the second; and if that is generally bad, for a consumer[89] it is considerably worse. An action brought to rescind or avoid a contract must be a matter relating to a contract: if it does not relate to the contract which lies at the heart of the action, what on earth does it relate to? On this point at least, all members of the court were in agreement that the claimant won.

So the critical question was to identify the obligation in question. There was no doubt what the obligation in question was as a matter of fact: the duty cast on the proposer to make a fair presentation of the risk to be insured. But did this count as 'the obligation in question' for the purpose of Article 5.1? A majority considered that it did, declining the invitation to adopt a construction which restricted the term to an obligation created by the contract, or an obligation created by the contract which the contract obliged the other to perform. Lord

[84] At the date of the proceedings the Convention of Accession by which Sweden became a contracting state to the Brussels Convention was not in force (it came into force in the United Kingdom on 1 January 2001).

[85] [1997] 4 All ER 937, CA, noted this *Year Book*, 68 (1997), p. 331.

[86] Certainly for the dissentients they were separate and cumulative. It is less clear that the majority would need to take this view, but in the light of the decision in the case, nothing turns on it.

[87] [1999] 1 AC 153, HL, noted this *Year Book*, 68 (1997), p. 331.

[88] By the time the claim was pleaded it was common ground that the supposed contract was and had always been a nullity.

[89] Relying on the jurisdictional privileges granted by Section 4 of Title II in proceedings relating to a contract made by a consumer.

Woolf MR eloquently explained[90] why the view of common sense, that the obligation in question was that to make a fair presentation, and that the obligation to make a fair presentation was the obligation in question, was not affected by the authorities: any attempt to distinguish between duties of good faith which arise before the contract from those which continue after its creation[91] would be unmeritorious and unduly doctrinaire; and any attempt to distinguish between duties created by the contract from those imposed by the general law, or equity, on parties by reason of their having entered into a contract[92] would be just as pointless. So sensible was the speech that it is difficult to say much about it; and that it led to special jurisdiction being found in the place where the obligation to make a fair presentation called for performance was a predictable bonus. The dissentients, Lord Hope of Craighead and Lord Millett, though accepting that the matter was one relating to a contract,[93] imposed a further theoretical limitation on what counted as an obligation. For Lord Hope it had to be 'an obligation which one party has undertaken to perform to the other under the contract'.[94] According to Lord Millett, 'it must be limited to an obligation non-performance of which gives rise to contractual liability, and does not extend to what, when properly analysed, is merely a condition precedent to the formation of a fully binding contract.'[95] The reason for the disagreement is hard to ascertain, for the practicalities favour Lord Woolf MR. It cannot be said to be driven by any of the judgments of the Court of Justice on the interpretation of Article 5.1, for as a matter of fact none had had to deal with a void or a voidable contract. Given that all the precedent cases had dealt with contracts which were undeniably valid, or which the adjudicating court was to treat as valid,[96] it would be no surprise to find 'the obligation in question' and 'the contractual obligation in question' used interchangeably, for in that context, interchangeable is what they are. What these cases cannot do is throw reliable light on the way to reason a case in which the validity of the contract is denied by the claimant.

In the end, and all theorising aside, there are two potential justifications for the dissentient view: that it is imperative that Article 5.1 be given a narrow construction, or that it may be difficult to locate the place where one of these pre-contractual obligations required to be performed. As to the first objection, the narrowing of Article 5.1 is not necessarily a social good, and certainly not a dominating concern. It was devised to allow claims to be litigated where performance of the relevant obligation was due. At one level this will serve the purpose of having a dispute litigated where it has its factual heart.[97] Some decisions have indeed insisted on a restrictive reading, but the correct position

[90] At 505–10.

[91] At 506–7.

[92] At 506.

[93] At 516 and 527 respectively.

[94] At 519.

[95] At 531.

[96] The nearest the Court of Justice had come to the present case was in *Effer SpA* v. *Kantner* (Case 38/81) [1982] ECR 825, where the defendant had alleged that the contract was ineffective and that as a result, Article 5.1 was inapplicable. The Court held that his bare assertion was not conclusive, and that the national court had to examine its jurisdiction for itself.

[97] Cf. *Custom Made Commercial Ltd* v. *Stawa Metallbau GmbH* (Case C–288/92) [1994] ECR I–2913.

is that the construction should be no wider than is justified to secure the aims of the Article. It is very hard to see that the approach of Lord Woolf MR violates that prescription. As to the second, it may sometimes be difficult to see where a pre-contractual obligation was required to be performed. But it will not usually cause problems. It was plain and obvious to the majority that the proposer's obligation to tell the truth, the whole truth, and nothing but the truth to the reinsurer was to be performed where the reinsurance was to be placed, in London.[98] In fact, the difficulties of location lie not with pre-contractual obligations, but rather more with negative obligations, such as a contractual promise not to compete with the other party. A negative obligation, plainly contractual in nature, may appear to present problems of location, but it has not been suggested that a claim founded on one of these is carried outside the scope of Article 5.1.[99] It is submitted that this is the reason why an obligation not to use duress or undue influence may have appeared problematic to Lord Millett: not on account of its pre-contractual nature, but because it is essentially negative: an obligation not to exercise duress of C's goods, or to coerce by other illegitimate means, wherever these might be brought to bear. But if the particular allegation is that D coerced C by doing an act in a particular place, that place ought to be the place for performance of the obligation in question. True, in *Kleinwort Benson*[100] there was more scope for debate about the obligation and its place, but it was not impossible to see this as the duty to repay money transferred on the mistaken belief that there was a contractual justification for the original payment: that was, as a matter of fact, the obligation sued on, and to concede it was the obligation but deny that it was contractual would be very unattractive.[101]

It follows that *Kleinwort Benson* has probably been, as we say, 'confined to its own special facts', and that actions which are brought to enforce, rescind, dissolve, annul, or otherwise affect,[102] or obtain damages or other relief in respect of the breach of a contract, will be within Article 5.1: no further limitation to a narrower class of obligations than that relied on to found the claim will serve to exclude the case from that provision. Claims based on misrepresentation, equitable mistake, duress, undue influence, and frustration will therefore be liable to attract special jurisdiction under Article 5.1. Had the minority prevailed it is unlikely that any of these would have given rise to special jurisdiction. The position in relation to common mistake, failure of offer and acceptance, lack of consideration, and illegality will be likely to be within the

[98] As was accepted by the parties: Lord Woolf MR at 505.

[99] Cf. *Boss Group Ltd* v. *Boss France SA* [1997] 1 WLR 351, CA, with which none of their Lordships expressed disagreement.

[100] It is ironic that in the Court of Appeal in that case, Millett LJ, as he then was, had been happy to accept that the claim for repayment in consequence of the voidness of a contract was within article 5.1: see [1996] QB 678, CA, reversed [1999] 1 AC 153.

[101] Lord Millett denied that such an obligation could be the one to which Article 5.1 referred because it did not sound in damages; he therefore referred to it as a 'so-called obligation' at 529–31, and sought by this means to distance the 'so-called obligation' to make a fair presentation from the French and German law obligations to negotiate in good faith which, though extra-contractual, were said by his Lordship to sound in damages and hence, it is to be inferred, to be within Article 5.1. There appears to be no precedent, save some unexplained theory, which imposes this as a limitation on the plain meaning of the words.

[102] The words are those of the former RSC Order 11 rule 1(1)(d).

Article, at least where this issue is raised as a defence to an attempt to enforce the contract; but where it is common ground that there never was a contract, *Kleinwort Benson* will still hold sway.

It is necessary to mention two further points. First, the court dealt briefly with the proposition that the case fell within Section 3 to Title II, as it was concerned with reinsurance. This all members of the court denied, and the correctness of their decision was later confirmed by the Court of Justice.[103] Second, there remained the argument that the claim fell within Article 5.3. It was inevitable that this was rejected, for as all members of the court agreed that the matter was one relating to a contract, it followed that it could not relate to tort, delict or quasi-delict. The case therefore adds nothing to the debate whether the Court of Justice meant what it said in *Kalfelis* v. *Bankhaus Schröder Münchmeyer Hengst & Co*[104] when it explained that Article 5.3 covered all actions which sought to establish the liability of a defendant and which were not matters relating to a contract within the meaning of Article 5.1.

6 *Negative declarations in the conflict of laws*: Messier-Dowty Ltd *v.* Sabena SA[105]

The traditional view of the common law is that a court may certainly grant a declaration that a claimant owes no liability to a defendant, but that it will be slow to do so for two reasons: there may be more than a trace of forum shopping involved when a 'natural defendant' brings a claim for a declaration in a court which he has chosen, so preventing his opponent, the 'natural claimant' exercising the traditional privilege of deciding where to launch proceedings; and there may be oppression or vexation on the part of a claimant who insists on bringing a claim to court long before his opponent has decided on, or has threatened, litigation as a means of dispute resolution. The first of these was reflected in the court's generally exercising its discretion against the assertion of jurisdiction by service out,[106] or in support of a stay of proceedings; the second in the inherent power of the court to strike out claims for declarations which it was unprepared to grant.[107]

Two facts of modern commercial life had brought pressure to bear on this tradition of uncooperative hostility to declaratory proceedings. First, the Brussels Convention had been interpreted as meaning that proceedings for a negative declaration could not be specially attacked or disparaged for alleged jurisdictional impropriety: an action brought in a court with jurisdiction under the Convention was an action brought in a court with proper and appropriate jurisdiction, which was not to be qualified or read down.[108] Secondly, the practice of the Commercial Court appeared to regard proceedings for negative declaratory relief as part of the common currency of litigation, and not as a

[103] *Groupe Josi Reinsurance Co* v. *Compagnie d'Assurances Universal General Insurance Co* (Case C–412/98) [2001] 1 QB 68, ECJ.
[104] [1988] ECR 5565.
[105] [2000] 1 WLR 2040, CA: Lord Woolf MR, Lady Justice Hale, Lord Mustill.
[106] Hitherto by reference to RSC Order 11 rule 4(2); now by reference to CPR 6.21(2A).
[107] RSC Order 15 rule 16 (preserved in Schedule 1 to the Civil Procedure Rules).
[108] *The Tatry* (Case C–406/92) [1994] ECR I–5439.

matter for remark or blame.[109] The landmark decision of the Court of Appeal in *Messier-Dowty Ltd* v. *Sabena SA* makes it clear that the previous hostility is now to be treated as a thing of the past, and that courts should not be reluctant to make declarations in any case in which the making of such an order would be useful.

When an aircraft owned and operated by Sabena (a Belgian company) and manufactured by Airbus GIE (a French entity) in which BAA (an English company) had an interest, crashed at Brussels Airport, the finger of blame pointed at the landing gear which had been manufactured by Dowty (an English company). A complex web of contracts surrounded the manufacture and fitting of the landing gear, and the sale of the plane to Sabena. But Dowty contended that its landing gear had failed because of inadequate information supplied to it by Airbus and/or BAA, and rather than wait around to be sued in respect of the damage caused to the plane and consequential losses, estimated at $50 million, it brought proceedings for a declaration that it owed no liability to Sabena, Airbus, and BAA. Sabena contested the jurisdiction of the court, pointing to Article 2 of the Brussels Convention; and argued that the claim was in any event an abuse of process, pointing to the alleged fact that Dowty had no cause of action against it. The court accepted that if the case fell within the jurisdictional provisions of the Convention there was no jurisdictional objection open to Sabena; and that there was no other basis for objection save the general and neutral exercise of the court's discretion. But it held that on the facts, the Convention did not render Sabena liable to the jurisdiction of the English courts, and on that ground the claim against it was dismissed.

In its application of the Brussels Convention the court was called upon to apply basic and well-understood principles of law. Jurisdiction over Sabena had to be founded on Article 6.1, and that in turn required the link between the claims against Sabena and against the defendant being sued in the court of its domicile, BAA, to be so close that it was expedient to hear them together to avoid the risk of irreconcilable judgments.[110] But the court had already concluded that it was not expedient as a matter of English practice to allow the claim against Sabena to proceed at all, for reasons which will be examined below, and, that being so, it was not expedient to try the case at all, let alone with that against BAA to avoid the risk of irreconcilable judgments resulting from separate trials. The sense of this is plain enough, though the suspicion remains that it involves using the term 'expedient' to serve two distinct purposes, one defined by reference to the consistency of two judgments and the other to reflect the propriety of the claim as a matter of English procedural law when viewed alone. It is to be questioned whether this aspect of the judgment is quite right, for it may have been better simply to say, as Lord Woolf MR did,[111] that as the claim against Sabena stood to be dismissed as a matter of English law, the threshold condition for the satisfaction of Article 6.1 could not be met at all, for Sabena was not a defendant. After all, it has been established by the Court of Justice[112] that a national court may apply the standards set by its own procedural

[109] See, for example, *Gulf Bank KSC* v. *Mitsubishi Heavy Industries Ltd* [1994] 1 Lloyd's Rep 323.

[110] *Kalfelis* v. *Bankhaus Schröder Münchmeyer Hengst & Co* (Case 189/87) [1988] ECR 5565.

[111] Page 435.

[112] *Kongress Agentur Hagen GmbH* v. *Zeehaghe BV* (Case C–365/88) [1990] ECR I–1845.

law in deciding whether the conditions of Article 6 have been met, just as long as these do not contradict the practical effect of the Convention;[113] and if as a matter of English procedural law there was no basis for allowing the claim for a declaration to proceed, there was no claim against Sabena by which Sabena was being sued, and therefore Article 6.1 had no application.

Of more immediate interest was the reasoning which led the court to strike out the claim against Sabena. The court repudiated[114] the tradition of hostility particularly as articulated by Kerr LJ in *The Volvox Hollandia*[115] and *First National Bank of Boston* v. *Union Bank of Switzerland*,[116] certainly in the particular context of a case where jurisdiction was defined by the Convention, but also generally.[117] In this the judgment is to be warmly applauded. If the Convention gives jurisdiction there is no jurisdictional objection to be taken; and it also follows that there is no reason to seek to distort the Convention so that its rules are rendered inapplicable to a claim for negative declaratory relief, either by reading them so that they cannot apply to actions for declaratory relief,[118] or by criticizing the claimant for seeking to win a jurisdictional race.[119] The practical impossibility—never mind the theoretical inadequacy—of defining an action as one for negative declaratory relief[120] ought to be proof enough of the wisdom of the new jurisprudence on this point. But as said before, there was a separate strand of argument, not anchored in the Convention, and which bespoke a general hostility to the idea that a natural claimant could be forced into the role of actual defendant. This the court repudiated. Lord Woolf MR preferred to ask whether it would be useful to make the declaration,[121] as other cases[122] had admittedly done, but—and this is the point where the case takes the law in a new direction—taking as his point of departure the proposition that a declaratory judgment is an entirely useful form of resolution to a dispute. This encapsulates the novelty of the decision. He could see no reason whatever for hostility to proceedings for a declaration; observed that they were particularly useful in cases which came up through the Family Division; and recognised that the law should be able to respond to commercial needs.[123] It was for the court to exercise its discretion to ensure that proceedings were not inappropriate, or were not a misuse of the court's procedures,[124] but it was not to do so against a

[113] Such as by declining to allow the claim on jurisdictional grounds.

[114] Page 434; paragraph 36 of the judgment.

[115] [1988] 2 Lloyd's Rep 361, 391, CA.

[116] [1990] 1 Lloyd's Rep 32, CA.

[117] See in particular at p. 434, paras 36, 41, and 42 of the judgment.

[118] See for an earlier confirmation of this view, *Boss Group Ltd* v. *Boss France SA* [1997] 1 WLR 351, CA.

[119] At p. 435, paragraph 44 of the judgment.

[120] If the claim is brought for a declaration that the goods were delivered, or that the price was paid, or that the contract was lawfully rescinded, or was vitiated by a common mistake, or procured by duress, or that it was lawful to set off a debt owed, or that the claimant was a bona fide purchaser for value, and so on, all of these may appear to be negative declaratory in form. But they raise disputed issues of substance. And a declaration that a contract was discharged by performance, though not negative, is nevertheless declaratory in form; and it is hard to see that any rational ground of distinction can be found in this area.

[121] Page 432.

[122] In particular *Camilla Cotton Oil Co* v. *Granadex SA* [1976] 2 Lloyd's Rep 10, HL.

[123] Page 432.

[124] Page 435, paragraph 43 of the judgment.

backdrop of hostility. The result is therefore that the test of utility is retained but reoriented. A judge who applies the test of utility but who does so with the words of Kerr LJ at the back of his mind will not have applied the law established by *Messier Dowty*.

If one sees claims as being the peculiar property of those who are injured, it is probably wrong to allow the party said to have done the wrong to seize the role of *dominus litis* for himself. The common law does tend to see the world in this way: a right of action is property, and for this to be reduced to the status of a right to counterclaim by the further action of the alleged wrongdoer is to adversely affect it. But there is no wrongdoing until a court has established it, only alleged wrongdoing; and it may be as wrong to falsely accuse of injuring as to injure. Once that is understood, proprietorship in a claim has to be seen as joint tenancy of a dispute; and the question who moves to bring it before a judge a largely neutral one. In that light there is every reason to deal with the issues as the Court of Appeal did, and to regard the form of the action, whether in the context of the Convention or otherwise, as largely irrelevant. Of course a court should strike out vexatious claims, brought by parties who had no real reason to fear being sued by an opponent; but it always had those powers, now afforced by the case management duties of the Civil Procedure Rules,[125] and these are not uniquely directed at proceedings for a declaration of non-liability.

One point at which the context—Convention, non-Convention—may appear to be important is where a claimant appears to have launched proceedings at an inappropriately early stage in the drama. The argument may be put this way: if the case is one where the English courts' jurisdiction is a matter for the common law, a court may be entitled to conclude that the proceedings were brought so early that they should be struck out as being vexatious without regard to the Convention; but where the jurisdictional basis for the claim lies in the rules of the Convention, no criticism can be made of a claimant who starts early, so as to avoid forfeiting jurisdiction as a result of Article 21 and its first-seised rule to prevent parallel claims. Lord Woolf MR acknowledged that there was good sense in the claimant not dawdling but in being the first to seise his chosen court.[126] It is important to give this aspect of the judgment its full scope, however. For Article 21 must be applied by an English court, even in relation to proceedings in another contracting state founded on the traditional jurisdictional rules of that state, and even though the English court has been asked to take jurisdiction by reason of Article 4 of the Convention.[127] Because Article 21 applies without regard to the jurisdictional basis on which either court has acted, there is, in truth, no separate category of case to which Article 21 is inapplicable or irrelevant;[128] and that being so, the criticism that a claimant was too quick off the mark should in every case be read subject to the 'good sense' to which Lord Woolf MR referred.

[125] To which Lord Woolf MR made specific reference at p. 435, paragraph 43 of the judgment.

[126] Page 433, paragraphs 30–2 of the judgment.

[127] *Overseas Union Insurance Ltd* v. *New Hampshire Insurance Co* (Case C–351/89) [1991] ECR I–3317.

[128] Unless, of course, the case is one in which there is no credible reason to suppose that the opponent was intending to sue in a contracting state: it may be difficult to make that confident judgment in advance.

The reason why Sabena prevailed was, therefore, not on account of any hostility to the nature or timing of, or of the motive behind, the proceedings brought by Dowty. But Lord Woolf MR identified two principal reasons why the declaratory proceedings should not be allowed to proceed. First, it was not possible to justify the action on the basis that it would allow all the parties to be bound into a single and consistent proceeding: Sabena had a claim against Airbus, from whom it purchased the plane; and the contract of sale had a jurisdiction agreement for the French courts which could not be overridden by Article 6.1.[129] That being so, Sabena was compelled, in effect, to sue Airbus in France and defend against Dowty in England. There was therefore no possibility of a single and all-embracing proceeding, as often happens when jurisdiction agreements bind some but not all those involved, and this weakened the claimed utility of the proceedings which Dowty had brought,[130] to say nothing of the injustice done to Sabena by this division of litigation. Secondly, it was far from clear that Sabena intended to claim against Dowty, for its principal target was its seller, Airbus; and the complaint about the landing gear and its specification was really between Dowty, Airbus, and BAA. All that being so, it was too early to justify bringing a claim against a party who had not made any serious threat to sue and who, as a matter of commercial common sense, could well be understood to have no such intention. This was therefore a classic and proper case for the exercise of the court's discretion to say that it was inexpedient to allow the claim against Sabena to be advanced, at least at this premature stage.

The decision is a far-reaching one, and one which both recognizes the arguments which have been made inadmissible by the Convention, and re-states English law on granting relief in negative declaratory form. Whether it will lead to an explosion of such actions is much to be doubted, for the dismissal of the actual claim in the case shows that the court's discretion still stands sentinel against the misuse of the court's procedures to advance such claims. But the days of contrived hostility to such proceedings are now, thankfully, at an end.

7 *The scope and effect of an exclusive jurisdiction clause*: Donohue *v.* Armco Inc[131]

The law on the scope, effect, and enforcement of exclusive jurisdiction clauses continues to generate excitement. Two years ago we noted[132] that an English court may decline to grant specific enforcement[133] of an exclusive jurisdiction clause which nominated the English courts in circumstances where to do so would have a damaging effect on the general desirability of having a multi-partite dispute tried in an all-encompassing single proceeding. The law may be

[129] *Hough* v. *P & O Containers (Bloem + Voss Holding AG, third parties)* [1999] QB 834, noted this *Year Book*, 69 (1998), p. 342.

[130] In this respect the common law, as exemplified in *Bouygues Offshore SA* v. *Caspian Shipping Co* [1998] 2 Lloyd's Rep 461, CA, noted this *Year Book*, 69 (1998), p. 342, is more flexible.

[131] [2000] 1 Lloyd's Rep 579, CA: Stuart-Smith and Sedley LJJ; Brooke LJ dissenting in part.

[132] In relation to *Bouygues Offshore SA* v. *Caspian Shipping Co* [1998] 2 Lloyd's Rep 461, CA, noted this *Year Book*, 69 (1998) p. 342.

[133] It remains untested whether an action for damages for breach would be available at common law.

characterised as holding the clause to be strictly binding as far as the parties to it are concerned, but not necessarily binding on the judge, whose public obligations include, but also extend further than, the enforcing of private contracts; and it was also there noted that this made the common law more flexible than the corresponding provision of the Brussels Convention. But the opposite tendency, of the energetic enforcement of jurisdiction agreements, is demonstrated by the vigorous judgment of the Court of Appeal in *Donohue* v. *Armco Inc.*

A number of companies formed the Armco group, a rich and powerful American conglomerate. In 1990 Armco decided to sell some insurance companies in its direct or indirect ownership to the then management of the said companies: a management buy-out. One of the purchasers[134] was Donohue. It was later alleged by Armco that it had been the victim of a fraudulent scheme, stitched together by Donohue and others and which involved, among other things, causing Armco to inject huge sums of money into the companies being sold, and tricking Armco into agreeing to English jurisdiction clauses in the sale and purchase agreements.[135] Armco made further allegations of fraudulent behaviour by and coordinated by Donohue and his associates; and as a result brought proceedings in the US District Court, alleging fraud, and claiming punitive and treble damages under the Racketeer Influenced and Corrupt Organisations Act ('RICO'). Donohue and his associates denied the conspiracy, and argued that the US proceedings were either vexatious or oppressive or brought in violation of the exclusive jurisdiction clauses in the sale and purchase agreements. Donohue applied to the English courts for an anti-suit injunction; and his various associates (some party to the sale and purchase agreement, others not) applied to be joined to the claim for this relief. A majority of the Court of Appeal, reversing Aikens J, granted much of the relief sought; Brooke LJ would have made a more limited form of order.[136]

The facts of the case are complex, but the case featured a number of important points. First, the exclusive jurisdiction clauses were contained in the contracts of sale and purchase and could not, on the face of it, have any effect on strangers to those agreements.[137] Secondly, the claims in the US courts were brought by and against parties who were not privy to the sale and purchase agreements. Thirdly, the claims in the US proceedings were capable of being said to fall outside the material scope of the exclusive jurisdiction clauses. Fourthly, the validity of the clauses, insofar as they bound Armco, had been challenged by

[134] In fact the purchase was effected by means of a corporate vehicle, Wingfield, which was incorporated under the law of Jersey. In the end this wrinkle was of little practical relevance.

[135] This bizarre allegation was maintained before Aikens J at first instance, but abandoned on appeal.

[136] Though he disagreed with the majority about the scope *ratione materiae* of the jurisdiction clauses in question, Brooke LJ also considered that Donohue had delayed for far too long in seeking the relief, and that as a result of general equitable principle, which may also be seen as an aspect of what comity requires, and *The Angelic Grace* [1995] 1 Lloyd's Rep 87, CA, such delay was fatal to the claim for injunctive relief. The point is an important one, but its essentially impressionistic character means that it is not examined further here.

[137] However, with contracts made after the coming into force of the Contracts (Rights of Third Parties) Act 1999, the benefit of a contract may in certain circumstances be taken by a non-party for whose benefit the contract was intended. This may make it easier for a non-party to claim the benefit of a jurisdiction agreement.

Armco, in America and at first instance. And fifthly, a judge in the District Court had heard and rejected a motion to have the US proceedings dismissed on jurisdictional grounds derived from the jurisdiction agreements themselves.

In a forthright judgment, Stuart-Smith LJ staked out an orthodox point of departure: that where foreign proceedings are brought in unwaived breach of a jurisdiction clause which nominates the English courts, an anti-suit injunction will be ordered unless strong reason or strong cause is shown why this relief should not be granted.[138] He detected the possibility, hitherto unnoticed by commentators, that this determined approach had been watered down by Millett LJ in *The Angelic Grace*,[139] who had referred to the need to show 'good reason' why the order not be made. But Stuart-Smith LJ was having none of it: the injunction would be granted unless there was strong cause not to do so. Given this starting point, the factors identified in the previous paragraph can be assessed to see whether they constituted, separately or all together, a strong reason not to make the order. Before doing so, it is useful to have confirmation from the Court of Appeal that the practice of the Commercial Court[140] is to be taken as correct. It means that a single and undifferentiated test of enforceability applies to jurisdiction clauses at common law, whether for the English courts (where effective enforcement will usually be by injunction to restrain foreign proceedings) or for foreign courts (where effective enforcement will usually be by the stay or dismissal of English proceedings). In this regard the law on jurisdiction clauses departs from the rest of the law on jurisdiction, which is constructed on the basis that a stay of English proceedings is very different from (and easier to obtain than) an injunction to restrain foreign proceedings.[141] But a commercially minded court may well be expected to see the summary and effective enforcement of all jurisdiction agreements as serving an important social goal.

So was there strong cause not to do so? Well, as to the scope *ratione personae* of the clauses, privity of contract meant that they could not be binding on non-parties to the agreements which contained them, and could not be taken advantage of by non-parties either.[142] This, after all, was the principal reason why the clauses nominating England had not been enforced in *Bouygues Offshore SA* v. *Caspian Shipping Co*:[143] as they could not affect the litigational freedom of the various non-parties, there was strong reason not to enforce them as between the two actual parties. But Stuart-Smith LJ applied a gloss to this. In *Bouygues*, the non-parties had been independent of those who were bound by the clause; but in *Donohue* he suspected that the entities suing in the District Court who were not party to the sale and purchase agreement had been put up to it by Armco (which was bound by it). Such actions by 'friends and relations' of Armco stood on a rather different footing. He said:[144]

Furthermore I do not think that a party to an exclusive jurisdiction agreement should be able to defeat its effect by causing subsidiaries or affiliates to bring other actions on

138 At pp. 588–9, paragraphs 33–5 of the judgment.
139 [1995] 1 Lloyd's Rep 87, CA.
140 The cases are numerous and are not listed here.
141 Cf. *Soc Nat Ind Aérospatiale* v. *Lee Kui Jak* [1987] AC 871, PC.
142 NB the future effect of the Contracts (Rights of Third Parties) Act 1999 s. 1.
143 [1998] 2 Lloyd's Rep 461, CA.
144 At p. 590, paragraph 43 of the judgment.

different subject matter against the other party to the exclusive jurisdiction agreement. This is what Mr Leaver calls the 'friends and relations' point. Moreover, if the subject matter of the New York proceedings formed the subject of a fraud trial in England, I have little doubt that the judge would sever the collection agreement from the management buy-out aspect of the case. They are in any event, it seems to me, separate conspiracies. But that merely emphasizes that the subject matter is different. Accordingly the existence of the collection agreement claims, and the fact that they may be litigated in New York is not good reason, let alone strong cause, for refusing the anti-suit injunction in respect of those matters to which it does apply.

The threads of this paragraph perhaps need to be disentangled. First, the fact that friends and relations have been put up to institute a spoiling action is irrelevant, unless it is treated as somehow prejudicial, to the party who is breaking the agreement himself: the *Bouygues* principle is inapplicable if the non-parties are not independent of the contractually bound parties. But this does not mean that the jurisdiction clause is held to bind those who were not privy to it, so that they may also be restrained; and Stuart-Smith LJ did not suggest otherwise. If they are to be restrained, it will have to be on the basis that their behaviour is oppressive or vexatious and that England is the natural forum for their claims.[145] Stuart-Smith LJ did not actually say this, but in principle it must be correct. It will be undeniable that such claims fall, for reasons of privity at least, outside the jurisdiction agreement: but this does not by itself insulate them from the allegation that they are vexatious or oppressive; and if the court has[146] personal jurisdiction over those who are acting oppressively, there is no particular reason not to restrain them by injunction.

As to the scope of the clauses *ratione materiae*, it was arguable in principle that even as between the parties bound by them, some or all of the complaints in the American action fell outside their definitional scope. It is clear that on this question of construction, reasonable minds may differ. Aikens J, at first instance, had held that the claims of a conspiracy to defraud did not 'arise out of or in connection with' the sale and purchase agreement, but out of the conspiracy to defraud.[147] Stuart-Smith LJ referred to the line of authority[148] which attributes the widest practical scope to such words, and assisted by this general canon of construction, held that the judge's interpretation was wrong. In this he was probably correct: if the question is asked whether the parties, all presumed to be sensible men of business, intended to leave a gap in or around the edges of such a clause, so as to allow carefully crafted complaints to steer a devious path around the provision for dispute resolution, only one answer ought to be countenanced. There are some deeply inept clauses out there, which no amount of sensible judicial interpretation will ever to be able to mend. But the wording used in *Donohue* seemed pretty clear, and it was perhaps a surprise that a

[145] *Airbus Industrie GIE* v. *Patel* [1999] 1 AC 119, HL.

[146] If it has to establish this by service out under CPR r. 6.20, there may be difficulty in finding a substantive cause of action at all, and (separately) difficulty in fitting the claim within one of the paragraphs of rule 6.20: cf. *Amoco (UK) Exploration Co* v. *British American Offshore Ltd* [1999] 2 Lloyd's Rep 772; and see Brooke LJ at p. 599, paragraphs 89–92 of the judgment.

[147] Brooke LJ appeared to be close to Aikens J in his interpretation of the clause.

[148] Most notably *Ashville Investments Ltd* v. *Elmer Contractors Ltd* [1989] QB 488, CA; *Harbour Assurance Co (UK) Ltd* v. *Kansa General International Insurance Co Ltd* [1993] 2 QB 701, CA. And see also *National Westminster Bank plc* v. *Utrecht-America Finance Co* (27 November 2000).

respected commercial judge[149] was taken in by the submission which appears to have persuaded him. Moreover, the clauses were held to encompass the RICO claims, which were really only fraud actions by any other name. Sedley LJ appeared to consider that this was enough to dispose of the argument; Stuart-Smith LJ preferred to reason that if and insofar as facts and matters fell within the jurisdiction clause, that same material was precluded from introduction into or use in a RICO claim; one imagines that a similar principle may come to be applied to other American statutory causes of action which cover ground which is in England the province of the common law of tort.[150] True, this principle of broad construction of jurisdiction clauses is technically limited to cases in which the law governing the agreement is English law. But the reasoning used to generate the result is not governing law-specific; and it is to be supposed that an English judge will proceed by similarly practical reasoning when confronted by a clause in a contract governed by a foreign law.

As to the alleged invalidity of the clauses, this point was pursued before Aikens J, but was abandoned before the Court of Appeal. But had it been maintained, it would presumably have been held that before a final injunction could be based on an exclusive jurisdiction clause, the court would need to conclude, to the ordinary civil standard of a balance of probability, that the clause was valid and binding on the party against whom the injunction was sought: a good arguable case upon the issue of validity, such as is needed when jurisdiction is contested, will not suffice.

A larger problem was that the judge in the District Court had heard and rejected a motion by Donohue to dismiss the US action on jurisdictional grounds derived from the jurisdiction clauses.[151] Stuart-Smith LJ was not deflected from what he reasoned to be the correct answer by this: it is accurate to say that the American judgment was not regarded as binding, nor even influential. This is in one, but only in one, respect puzzling. The starting point is that an English court will not recognise a foreign judgment given in breach of a jurisdiction agreement, and the view of the foreign court that there has been no breach of the agreement is irrelevant.[152] It follows that where a foreign court entertains an action in breach of a jurisdiction agreement, there is some statutory encouragement for an English court to prevent the coming about of a judgment which will be denied recognition, even if the foreign court will take a different view.[153] And traditionally the judgment of a foreign court on a jurisdictional motion will not be recognized, for the issue is not determined by it as final and conclusive, or as *res judicata*. Though there are cases which hold that an interlocutory decision of this sort could still be recognised as giving rise to an

[149] And a respected Lord Justice of Appeal.

[150] In competition law, for example. For the proposition that a direct action by a victim against the tortfeasor's insurer is within the scope of a jurisdiction agreement in the contract, see *Youell* v. *Kara Mara Shipping Co Ltd* [2000] 2 Lloyd's Rep 102.

[151] That he had done so after the decision of Aikens J, which judgment was reversed, allowed it to be said that he had proceeded on a basis which now allowed for reconsideration.

[152] Civil Jurisdiction and Judgments Act 1982 s. 32.

[153] Though when a similar argument was advanced in support of an application for an injunction to restrain an American action for treble damages, which would be denied recognition in England under the Protection of Trading Interests Act 1980 s. 5, the argument failed and it was said that the Act furnished no basis for an injunction: *British Airways Board* v. *Laker Airways Ltd* [1985] AC 58, HL, approving (on this point) the view of Parker J at first instance.

estoppel,[154] it was clear that this was not appropriate in *Donohue*, for the District Court judge was reported[155] as having said that 'a party seeking to avoid enforcement of [a forum selection clause is] entitled to have the facts viewed in the light most favourable to it and no disputed fact should be resolved against that party until it has an opportunity to be heard'. This appears to indicate that the District Court did not make its ruling on the balance of probabilities, but as one which was slanted by virtue of its interlocutory character: this could not possibly satisfy the English criteria for regarding the judgment as *res judicata*. But the uncomfortable fact for Donohue remained that he had applied to the District Court for an interpretation of and a ruling on the jurisdiction clause, had obtained a ruling which went against him, and he now sought to disavow that ruling before the English courts. In *Desert Sun Loan Corp* v. *Hill*[156] a majority of the Court of Appeal, including Stuart-Smith LJ, had been prepared in principle to recognise such a ruling, obtained in very similar circumstances from an American court, as being *res judicata* against the party who made the application. This was a very controversial, and probably wrong, conclusion to attach to a judgment from a court in which the loser had appeared as defendant, only to argue that the court had no jurisdiction.[157] At least in *Donohue* there was no repetition of the nonsense that this American ruling was entitled to recognition as *res judicata*. It followed that it presented no formal obstacle to the court's coming to its own conclusion about the scope and effect of the clause. To the argument that it presented an indirect obstacle, and that comity required the English court to defer to the expressed conclusion of the American judge, Stuart-Smith LJ, correctly it is submitted, neatly sidestepped the point: he reformulated the issue as being whether the party in breach should be allowed to create a situation in which there would be parallel litigation and the risk of conflicting judgments. This, he concluded, should not be permitted, and if as a consequence of responding to that problem the court diverged from the view of the District Court, that was not a fatal objection. It is submitted that there is nothing to complain about here.[158] First, if the foreign judgment is not entitled to recognition, as it was not, it would be unexpected, and unprincipled, for backdoor recognition to occur via the shadowy requirements of comity. Secondly, although the Canadian[159] approach to anti-suit injunctions requires prior application to the foreign court, and allows the making of the order only if the jurisdictional rules of the foreign court do not contain a limitation resembling the Canadian doctrine of *forum non conveniens*, that structure is not part of the English law on anti-suit injunctions, where the requirement to respect comity is met in a completely different way.[160] So the expressed conclusions of the

[154] Cf. *The Sennar (No 2)* [1985] 1 WLR 490, HL; *Desert Sun Loan Corp* v. *Hill* [1996] 2 All ER 847, CA.

[155] By Stuart-Smith LJ at p. 592, paragraph 50 of the judgment.

[156] [1996] 2 All ER 847, CA.

[157] Roch LJ saw the point, which is vouched for by the Civil Jurisdiction and Judgments Act 1982 s. 33; see also *A/S D/S Svendborg* v. *Wansa* [1997] 2 Lloyd's Rep 559, CA.

[158] It also echoes the conclusion of Thomas J in *Akai Pty Ltd* v. *People's Insurance Co Ltd* [1998] 1 Lloyd's Rep 90.

[159] *Amchem Products Inc* v. *British Columbia (Workers' Compensation Board)* [1993] 1 SCR 897.

[160] For details of this, see Briggs in Rose (ed.), *Lex Mercatoria: Essays on International Commercial Law in Honour of Francis Reynolds*, p. 219.

American judge would not be something which would be recognised or required prior to an application for an anti-suit injunction, and no more needed to be said about it.[161]

Finally, but here mystifyingly, an injunction was also sought by associates of Donohue, who wished to take advantage of the effect of the jurisdiction agreement to which Donohue was bound, but some of whom were not privy to it. By a process of reasoning which can only baffle and confuse, the majority agreed that they could apply to be joined to the action under CPR r. 19.1(2), and that it was not necessary for them to show that they had a substantive cause of action which furnished a legal basis for them to be added into Donohue's claim. But the only claim brought by Donohue was for an anti-suit injunction; these associates had no discernible basis for obtaining such an injunction (certainly they had none on the basis of the jurisdiction clauses to which they were not party); and it surely cannot be correct that they could be added in as claimants who had no substantive cause of action against the defendants and whose claim should presumably have been promptly struck out under CPR r. 3.4 or r. 24.3. It is one thing to want an injunction, but unless there is a cause of action to justify the claim for it, there is no basis for applying for it. Brooke LJ saw this clearly,[162] and his incomprehension at the submission, and at the conclusion of the majority, is easy to share.

The result of this complex collection of analyses is that the privity limitation on the effect of jurisdiction agreements has been loosened to an uncertain extent; and it is clear that more loosening may yet be expected if the courts continue along the path of devising means to make these agreements more and more completely effective. Injunctions to enforce such clauses will be granted almost as a matter of routine against those bound by them, and collusive attempts to get friends to engage in spoiling tactics will be ineffective, at least so far as the bound parties are concerned. If it also means that the erratic majority judgments in *Desert Sun Loan Corp* v. *Hill* have been weakened, that can only be for the good and the rigour of the law.

8 *Title to movable property*: Glencore International AG *v.* Metro Trading Inc;[163] Raiffeisen Zentralbank Oesterreich AG *v.* Five Star General Trading LLC[164]

Two decisions at first instance highlighted the distinction between the rules for the acquisition and loss of title to tangible and intangible movable property, in that the passing of property in tangible movables is still governed by rules of the common law, whereas title to intangible property, if that expression now has any coherent meaning, is largely governed by the Rome Convention.

[161] And in *The Ivan Zagubanski* (16 November, 2000) Aikens J granted an anti-suit injunction in aid of an arbitration agreement, notwithstanding the fact that a French court had already concluded that it was not binding.

[162] At p. 599, paragraphs 89–92 of the judgment.

[163] [2001] 1 Lloyd's Rep. 283, Moore-Bick J.

[164] [2000] 1 All ER (Comm) 897, Longmore J.

Glencore International AG v. *Metro Trading Inc*[165] was one small part of the web of litigation which followed the financial collapse of an oil storage operation in and off the coast of Fujairah, and which was owned by Metro Trading International Inc. Over thirty separate actions were brought, which is to say nothing of the interlocutory applications which each managed to spawn. Metro's business lay in the purchase, blending, and sale of fuel oil, acquiring its supplies from several sources, selling to all and sundry and providing temporary storage facilities for quantities of oil. All this mixing of property was bound to prove embarrassing when it came to light that a gigantic hole had appeared in Metro's reserves. Claims of ownership far exceeded the amounts of oil actually held by Metro, and questions of competing titles therefore arose for decision. As the deliveries of oil to Metro had taken place in Fujairah, but certain of the contracts by which it had been delivered or sold were governed by other laws, the judge had to make a choice of law. In essence, Moore-Bick J applied the traditional rule of the common law, that transfer of title is governed by the *lex situs* of the property at the time of transfer, and extended it to acquisition of title otherwise than by derivative transfers: by the original means of *accessio*, *commixtio*, *confusio*, *specificatio*, and so forth; he held that the law governing the contracts which were associated with these transfers and other acquisitions did not govern the title unless the *lex situs* so provided. The judgment is a ringing and reassuring statement of orthodoxy, coupled with a sensible extension into the field of original acquisition as proposed by Dicey and Morris.[166]

The argument had been put forward that where a particular transfer of oil was made pursuant to a contract governed by a specific law, the passing of property was, as a matter of English choice of law rules, and never mind what the *lex situs* would have said about it, governed by the *lex contractus* rather than by the *lex situs*. The submission was that as between the contracting parties, the *lex contractus* should apply, albeit that where third parties were involved, the *lex situs* would apply instead. The practical complexity of this was obvious, and it is hard to see how it could have been accepted: indeed, in a case where the transactions were as factually messy as they were here, such a division of governing laws would have produced a complicated and unpredictable answer of advantage to nobody. As a matter of authority it was not open to the judge: *Cammell* v. *Sewell*,[167] *Castrique* v. *Imrie*,[168] *Re Anziani*,[169] *Bank voor Handel en Scheepvart NV* v. *Slatford*,[170] *Hardwick Game Farm* v. *Suffolk Agricultural Poultry Producers' Association Ltd*,[171] *Winkworth* v. *Christie Manson &*

[165] Much of the judgment was occupied with a detailed analysis of the law of Fujairah. The judge referred to the basic rule of English law that foreign law is a matter of fact, but added the sensible rider that, as with all questions of fact, the court is not inhibited from using its own intelligence. He also reaffirmed that foreign legal texts need to be interpreted by expert witnesses, and that the expert's role extends to interpretation as well as to application in the light of the law of the country. This aspect of the case, though illustrating the real complexity with which a judge may have to deal, is not examined further here.

[166] *The Conflict of Laws* (13th edn., 2000).

[167] (1860) 5 H & N 728.

[168] (1870) LR 4 HL 414.

[169] [1930] 1 Ch 407.

[170] [1953] 1 QB 248.

[171] [1966] 1 WLR 287, CA.

Woods,[172] and *Macmillan Inc* v. *Bishopsgate Investment Trust plc (No 3)*[173] had all applied the *lex situs* to the acquisition and loss of title, as had *Inglis* v. *Robertson*.[174] Though *Winkworth* had proposed certain exceptions,[175] none of these came anywhere near the facts of the present case: the arguments in favour of the legal certainty which flowed from the application of the *lex situs* were far too strong to be overthrown by the allegation that in a particular case, these two parties should have their property rights determined by the law of the contract which they made. Had the facts of the case been less complex, and *dramatis personae* fewer in number, there might have been a better prospect of success for this misguided argument. But on these facts there was none. The judge also explained why the policies underpinning the rule—the control exercised by the *situs*, the public and private interest in the security of transactions—were compelling, and maintained the traditional rule.

But the case concerned the acquisition of title not only by transfer but also by original means. No English case had specifically dealt with this, but the current edition of Dicey and Morris[176] had proposed that the *situs* rule should also apply where it was contended that a new title had been acquired by *accessio*, etc. The judge simply approved the Dicey text on this point, and it is submitted that he was right to do so, for there is, in truth, no alternative to this solution: the two policies mentioned above apply with equal force in this context. It is worth observing that the effect of retention of title clauses will therefore be dealt with on the same basis: if it is alleged that the use or incorporation of a thing into another, or the making of a new thing, has had the effect of conferring a new title on the maker, or of vesting it in the owner of the former rude materials,[177] the answer is found by looking at the *lex situs* of the thing when the process took place.[178] If the *lex situs* chooses to allow the contract to affect the passing of property, that is its prerogative; but it is incompetent for the *lex contractus*, of its own force, to prevail over the *lex situs*.

So the law of Fujairah was to be applied. Whether this meant the domestic law of Fujairah, or the law of that state including its rules of the conflict of laws, was left undecided. The judge observed that Millett J[179] had made the extraordinary[180] assertion that the doctrine of renvoi had been 'largely discredited'. Only if one considers that the noise of ignorance can discredit the wisdom of principle can this be so. The judge found as a fact that the law of Fujairah would, in this case, not refer to any other law before coming to a conclusion. He therefore

[172] [1980] 1 Ch 496.

[173] [1996] 1 WLR 387, CA.

[174] [1898] AC 616, HL.

[175] Regarded rather doubtfully by the judge, at least where they were not simply statements of other well-established rules of the conflict of laws.

[176] *The Conflict of Laws* (13th edn, 2000), paragraph 24–010.

[177] Cf. *Institutes*, 2.1.25.

[178] Any suggestion in *Zahnrad Fabrik Passau GmbH* v. *Terex Ltd* 1986 SLT 84, Outer House, that the effect should be governed by the *lex contractus* as such (rather than as part of the *lex situs*), or at first instance in *Armour* v. *Thyssen Edelstahlwerke AG* 1986 SLT 452, (reversed [1991] 2 AC 339, HL), that it should be the *lex situs* at the time of the asserting of the claim, was rejected by the judge. It is submitted that he was entirely correct in so doing.

[179] At first instance in *Macmillan Inc* v. *Bishopsgate Investment Trust plc (No 3)* [1995] 1 WLR 978.

[180] This writer's characterization, not that of the judge.

contented himself with the observation that the leading textbooks[181] still support its application, that the policy of applying the law which prevails at the place where effective control is exercised may also do so, and left it at that. It is a matter of mild regret that he did not take the opportunity to denounce the assertion of Millett J, but if that would be unbecoming for a puisne judge in examining an utterance of one now a Lord of Appeal in Ordinary, a commentator need not pull his punches. Millett J was wrong. After all, if the effect of the passing of property under the law of Fujairah was held by that law to be governed by the law of the contract to transfer, no serious argument could be got up to deny the application of that law which the Fujairah judge would himself have applied: Moore-Bick J said as much. If this is not renvoi it is hard to think what else to call it. The matter should be considered as closed, at least for as long as the question is governed by the rules of the common law.

The common law has been superseded in relation to intangible movable property, and this to such an extent that it must be open to question whether this expression still has any meaning. The point is starkly illustrated by *Raiffeisen Zentralbank Oesterreich AG* v. *Five Star General Trading LLC*. An Austrian bank, RZB, lent money to Five Star to finance the purchase of a ship, the Mount Athos I. As part of the bargain, Five Star mortgaged the ship to the bank, and executed a notice of assignment of the insurance on the ship to the bank: the insurance was agreed to be governed by English law, and the insurers were French. In due course the ship collided with another and was a total loss. Cargo owners attached the insurance moneys in France, but the bank brought proceedings in England for a declaration that as assignee of the insurance it was entitled to recover on this to the extent of its interest, even though the notice of assignment had not been served on the insurers in accordance with French law. Longmore J had to decide whether the bank's claim was governed by English law, as the law governing the insurance, or French law, as the *situs* of the chose in action which had been assigned. Longmore J held that the issue was one of the assignment of a contract, which fell within the Rome Convention,[182] and was one of whether the assignment could be invoked against the debtor, which was governed by Article 12.2 of the Convention. As a result English law applied to the issue, and under that law the assignee bank had a good claim to the money.

A preliminary puzzle is as to why the Rome Convention applied at all. The claim concerned a policy of marine insurance, and Article 1.3 states that 'the rules of this Convention do not apply to contracts of insurance which cover risks situated in the territories of the Member States of the European Economic Community. In order to determine whether a risk is situated in these territories the court shall apply its internal law'. The internal law of the United Kingdom is set out in the Insurance Companies Act 1982 s 96A(3).[183] If the ship was to be regarded as a vehicle, the risk was situated where the vehicle was registered:[184] despite being named the Mount Athos I, it is not stated in the judgment that the ship was registered in Greece. If not a vehicle, the risk was situated in the

[181] Dicey and Morris at para 27–007; Cheshire and North, *Private International Law* (13th edn 1999), pp. 948–50.

[182] Contracts (Applicable Law) Act 1990, Sch 1.

[183] As to which, see Dicey and Morris, paragraph 33–141.

[184] s. 96A(3)(b).

member state in which the establishment of the policy-holder to which the policy relates is situated.[185] If the risk was not situated in a member state the Convention would apply. But the judgment gives no clues, and it is therefore impossible to verify that the choice of law régime in the Rome Convention required to be applied. Had the Convention been inapplicable, the decision might have been different: the point is considered below.

But if the Convention did apply, Article 12 appeared to provide a complete answer to the question. Article 12 deals with voluntary assignment; and Article 12.2 provides that: 'the law governing the right to which the assignment relates shall determine its assignability, the relationship between the assignee and the debtor, the conditions under which the assignment can be invoked against the debtor and any question whether the debtor's obligations have been discharged.'

As a matter of first impression, that covered the case exactly: the question was whether or in what circumstances the assignee bank could invoke the assignment against the debtor insurance companies, and in particular whether it required the service of a notice of assignment in formal fashion, as required by French law; and Longmore J did indeed conclude that this was the correct approach. But the argument against it was that though the Rome Convention might apply to contractual issues, it had no application to proprietary questions;[186] the particular question whether the bank was now entitled to enforce the insurance in its favour was a proprietary question; and proprietary questions were, as a matter of common law, governed by the *lex situs*.[187]

In order to convince, this argument would have had to succeed at two levels. It would in practice first have to be correct as a matter of common law; and then it would have to be shown to be unaffected by the Rome Convention. As to the first, the common law was obscure and undeveloped. Though Dicey and Morris had traditionally discussed the question under the rubric of intangible movable property, and though choses in action are to some extent regarded as property in English domestic law, the distinction between owning a debt and being owed a debt—the latter being a contractual issue—may well have been no more than semantic. True, the effect of contractual debts and other obligations is in some circumstances affected by the law on security and insolvency, and there may be aspects of that law which make more sense if a debt is treated as property; but none of this entails the conclusion that they must be seen as property for the purpose of the conflict of laws. Perhaps in reflection of this, Dicey and Morris laid down the law—the cases being too incoherent to dictate any rational answer—in terms of the intrinsic and internal validity of the assignment as being a matter for its proper law, and the assignability of the debt itself being a matter for its governing law. This reflected in general terms the essentially contractual nature of the territory. This analysis was opposed by certain writers[188] who approached the question more from the standpoint of a commercial practitioner, and who took the view that the rights were proprietary, and that the *lex situs* was an appropriate and rational choice of law rule for a property issue. But it was never accepted judicially, nor did it command general scholarly agreement.

[185] s. 96A(3)(d).
[186] Giuliano and Lagarde: 1980 OJ C282/1 at 10.
[187] This would be French law, as the place where the debtor insurer was resident.
[188] Principally Goode, *Commercial Law* (2nd edn 1995), p. 1126.

However that may be, the Rome Convention supplants the common law wherever it claims to apply. Given that the factual infrastructure of the decision was the effect of the voluntary assignment of a contract of insurance, there was no way round the application of Article 12. Pressed with the argument[189] that the domain of the Convention is restricted to contractual matters, and does not extend to proprietary ones, Longmore J quoted with general approval the leading textbooks,[190] which both doubted the proposition that, when dealing with the assignment of contracts, or intangibles in general, there is any proprietary issue, distinct in any way from the contractual issue, at all: as the judge put it, 'if it is relevant to consider title to such choses in action at all (as it could be in cases e.g. of insolvency or competing priorities) it is difficult, if not impossible, to divorce the concept of title from the underlying contract which has created the chose in action in the first place'. Dicey and Morris submit that the question of who is entitled to enforce the debtor's obligation is simply and only contractual, certainly for the purposes of the Rome Convention, but also, in all probability, as a matter of common law as well. It may be that the decision marks the beginning of the end for the proposition that, as far as the conflict of laws is concerned, the assignment of contracts is to be seen as anything other than a contractual issue. And it follows from the general analysis of Longmore J that if he had found that Article 1.3 of the Convention directed him away from Rome and back to the common law, he would have applied the law governing the insurance contract to determine whether the insurers were now obliged to the bank.

The decision is to be welcomed for its return to basic common sense. Its consequence is that a supposed rule about the assignment of intangible property will be confined to cases which do not involve the assignment of contractual rights. Even then, it is to be doubted whether there is much use for a single rule to govern such peripheral and residual cases. The assignment of intellectual property rights will usually be governed by the *lex creationis*. The assignment of shares is governed by the *lex incorporationis*, and not by Article 12;[191] though the true reason for this may be that shares are not, in fact or in law, assigned.[192] And in the case of what Dicey and Morris describe as 'more complex assignments',[193] such as the transactions which take place within the structure of indirect holdings of shares and other financial instruments, it is unlikely that a simple rule can produce answers which correspond to the commercial reality which the law ought to support. So if the analysis in *RZB* v. *Five Star* stands the test of time, as it is submitted that it should, the proposition that there is a generic category of intangible movable property, of which contractual rights form the major part, will have been overturned. A good day's work will have been done.

[189] Supported by Giuliano and Lagarde: 1980 OJ C282/1 at 10.

[190] Dicey and Morris, pp. 978–9; Cheshire and North, pp. 957–8.

[191] Cf. *Macmillan Inc* v. *Bishopsgate Investment Trust plc (No 3)* [1996] 1 WLR 387, CA.

[192] It is not possible to assign burdens of contracts, and shares are an inextricable mix of benefits and burdens. The truth is that the shares are surrendered and cancelled, and shares are registered by the company in the name of the 'assignee'; but they are in no sense the same shares. For this insight I am indebted to Maisie Ooi, successful doctoral candidate in the University of Oxford.

[193] Paragraph 24–063.

9 *Choice of law in equitable wrongs and restitutionary claims*: Kuwait Oil Tanker SAK *v*. Al Bader;[194] Grupo Torras SA *v*. Al Sabah[195]

Two very long judgments from the Court of Appeal dealt with the choice of law issues in equitable and/or restitutionary claims at the end of extremely long analyses of complex facts and the law of tort. This presumably reflects the fact that the typical pleading will allege fraud and conspiracy in myriad ways, and may only add a claim seeking the imposition of a constructive trust at the end. In neither case, unfortunately, can it really be said that the judgment advances our understanding of the law.

Part of the reason for this lies in the confusion between the several categories of cause of action in this area. Dicey and Morris provide a choice of law rule for restitutionary claims,[196] and this has been generally approved in recent cases. But it is less certain that the category of 'restitutionary claims' is complete and coherent within the conflict of laws. Dicey and Morris also raise[197] the choice of law difficulties in equitable suits which are founded on the dishonest assistance of a breach of trust, or on the knowing receipt of trust property. There is authority for the view that all equitable claims are governed by the *lex fori*, with any foreign law being looked to only for the limited purpose of deciding whether the conduct of the defendant should be counted as unconscionable.[198] Another strand holds that equitable wrongs are close to torts[199] for choice of law purposes, and are not restitutionary: this because they are based on and generated by wrongdoing and not on and by receipt. Stir into the mixture the fact that the discussion in the judgments may come after scores of pages of complex fact and findings of liability for fraud, and it is small surprise that the analysis may be less than completely clear.

In *Kuwait Oil Tanker SAK* v. *Al Bader*, a massive claim was pleaded primarily as a tort of unlawful conspiracy, but it was also alleged that the actions of the defendant were independently actionable as breaches of the duty of good faith and honesty, and that these had led to his unjust enrichment. The analysis offered by the court for the breach of fiduciary duty was that four questions had to be asked: (1) what was the proper law of the relationship between the defendant and the person for whose benefit the powers and duties were imposed? (2) what are the duties imposed by that law? (3) do these duties, ascertained by reference to that proper law, have the general appearance of being fiduciary when held up against English standards? and (4) is it unconscionable for the defendant to retain the assets? As to point (1) the court appeared to approve and apply the law of Kuwait, but by reference to Rule 200(2)(c), as the place where the enrichment occurred. But if this is what was done it is hard to understand, for the law which governs the relationship is not necessarily the same as that of

[194] *The Times*, [2000] 2 All ER (Comm.) 271, CA: Nourse, Potter, and Clarke LJJ.

[195] [2001] CLC 221, CA: Robert Walker, Tuckey and Stuart Smith LJJ; affirming [1999] CLC 1469, Mance J, noted in this *Year Book*, 70 (1999), p. 344.

[196] Rule 200 in the 13th edn.

[197] Paragraph 34–032.

[198] Most authoritatively by the Full Court of the Federal Court of Australia: *Paramasivam* v. *Flynn* (1997–8) 160 ALR 203.

[199] In all cases decided to date, the relevant choice of law rules will have been those of the common law, the material facts pre-dating the coming into force of the Private International Law (Miscellaneous Provisions) Act 1995, the impact of which in this area is untested.

the place where the enrichment occurred.[200] It is, indeed, difficult to reconcile this with the Dicey and Morris rule at all, for according to this there is only a single law to be applied, not a combination of English and proper laws; it appears to meld the approach taken to choice of law for equitable claims with the choice of law rule for restitutionary ones. It is nevertheless possible to approve of the decision at the practical level of setting out a series of questions which ought to produce a rational answer when breach of fiduciary duty is said to have led to an unjust enrichment: the proper law decides whether there was a duty and whether it was breached; English law decides whether it should be seen as a fiduciary duty; and if so, English law may impose a constructive trust to reverse the enrichment. It is just that this combination of questions is not quite what one might have expected.

But it is a model of rational clarity when contrasted with *Grupo Torras SA* v. *Al Sabah*. The equitable tail to the pleading was that the defendant had dishonestly assisted another's breach of trust, and the court denied that the choice of law rules for restitutionary claims, nor those for tort claims, were applicable. Insofar as the foundation of the claim was fault rather than receipt, this may be well understood. But rather than explain the basis on which a choice of law rule was to be constructed, the court applied Spanish law, seeming to do so on the basis that this was the law of the place where the defendant had done the acts which were alleged to found his liability. It having been ascertained that his conduct gave rise to liability under Spanish law, his liability under English law was taken as established. It is impossible to say exactly what path led the court to this conclusion. It may have been that English law was applied subject to its being shown that there was in Spanish law the basis for an adverse finding in relation to the defendant. It may have been the common law tort choice of law rule.[201] It may have been *sui generis*. Indeed, the only point on which the court did appear to be clear was that it was not applying the choice of law rule for restitutionary claims.

It is possible to read the two cases as authority for the need to draw a line which separates claims which are essentially based on receipt of property whose retention is unjust (for which Dicey's Rule 200 may be appropriate) from those which are based on wrongdoing for which compensation is due (for which a choice of law rule more akin to that for torts will be applied). Indeed, in the latter case, it may even be that the statutory choice of law rule for torts will be held to be wide and rational enough to be applied. And as a single claim may make both allegations, a court may need to be astute to prevent double recovery. But it cannot yet be said that the textbooks, or the cases, have seen a clear and straightforward basis for the analysis of claims which have their roots in equity.

Adrian Briggs

[200] Cf. *Arab Monetary Fund* v. *Hashim* [1996] 1 Lloyd's Rep 589, CA.

[201] It being unclear whether the 1995 Act would apply were the material facts more recent than 1995.

DECISIONS OF THE EUROPEAN COURT OF HUMAN RIGHTS DURING 2000*

In view of the number of decisions now handed down by the European Court of Human Rights, the practice of providing a note of each case has ceased to be practical. Thus, this survey will no longer cover all cases decided during the period under review; instead it will highlight only a proportion of the cases on grounds of their significance in reflecting or developing the current law. The cases will be grouped by reference to article number. Since Protocol 11 came into effect the Court has been responsible for admissibility decisions. Unless these are of special interest, they will not be included in the review.

'Disappearance' in custody—ineffective investigation—right to life—Article 2 impact on relatives—inhuman and degrading treatment—Article 3—failure to cooperate—Article 28(1)(a)

Case No. 1. Timurtas case.[1] In this case against Turkey, the Court concluded, by six votes to one, that there had been a violation of Articles 2 and 3 as regards both the disappearance of the applicant's son and the failure of the authorities to investigate. The Court held unanimously that there had been a violation of Article 5.

The applicant's son, A.T., was taken into custody on 14 August 1993 and has since disappeared. The applicant filed a complaint with the Turkish authorities, but this was not investigated. The applicant then brought a complaint under the Convention, claiming violations of Articles 2 and 5 regarding A.T.'s rights and Article 3 regarding the anguish suffered by the applicant. The applicant argued that he had had no effective remedy for these violations contrary to Article 13 and, further, that the Turkish Government had not complied with its obligations under Articles 18 and 34. The Government disputed the applicant's version of events.

The Court noted that the Commission had carried out a hearing of witnesses but there had been no eye-witness account of A.T. being taken into custody. Thus, the documentary evidence was crucial. Although there was a possibility that the documentary evidence supporting the applicant's version of events had been tampered with, the Court also noted that the Contracting States were under an obligation to cooperate and to furnish all necessary facilities to access relevant information, especially as in some instances the Contracting State would be the only body to have access to that information. A failure on a Government's part to submit such information as was in its hands without sufficient explanation, as here, might well give rise to the conclusion that the applicant's allegations were well founded. The Court therefore agreed with the

[1] ECHR, judgment of 13 June 2000.

Commission's assessment of the facts and its conclusions that Turkey had failed to comply with the former Article 28(1)(a).

In assessing the claim under Article 2, the Court had first to determine whether, in a case of disappearance, a violation could arise solely from the authorities' failure to provide a plausible explanation of a detainee's fate.[2] In principle, the answer would be 'yes', although the finding in each case would depend on the facts. The length of time since the detainee had last been heard of would be a factor; the longer the period of time without news, the more likely it would be that the detainee was dead. Given the expiry of six-and-a-half years in this case, there was a presumption that A.T. had died. In the absence of an explanation, the Government was responsible for that death, resulting in a violation of Article 2. Such an approach is, of course, crucial for the effectiveness of the protection of the right in question. An approach which denied such a possibility would allow a State to escape censure by the expedient of hiding or destroying victims' bodies. Clearly, an unacknowledged detention also constitutes a severe violation of Article 5.

As with previous cases in this area,[3] the Court included within the scope of Article 2 an obligation on the authorities to investigate claims of this nature effectively. The Court had no difficulty in finding that there had been a violation of this aspect of Article 2 and, indeed, of Article 13.

Following its approach in similar cases,[4] the Court also confirmed that there had been a violation of Article 3 as regards the applicant's suffering consequent on his son's disappearance. Not only was there a close family relationship but the attitudes of the authorities in failing to investigate the matter carefully and in lying to the applicant about A.T.'s fate showed a callous disregard for the applicant's concerns which exacerbated the distress caused by A.T.'s disappearance. It is interesting to contrast this case with *Çakici*[5] in which the Court emphasized that Article 2 is not to be seen as entailing a general rule that the disappearance of a close relative alone constituted inhuman and degrading treatment. It suggested that factors such as the attitude of the authorities would be crucial. Such factors were, the Court noted, present here. It is, however, debatable whether on the facts the difference in treatment between this case and *Çakici* was very different or whether this constituted a response to criticism of the ruling in *Çakici* to the effect that insufficient weight was given to the suffering of the brother of the victim.[6]

[2] In taking into custody the Government has assumed a certain responsibility for the individual; the situation of a detainee is different from that, for example, of an individual killed on the street. The presumption of the Contracting State's responsibility is that much stronger in the case of the detainee: contrast, for example, the position in *Tanrikulu* v. *Turkey*, ECHR, judgment of 8 July 1999 and this *Year Book*, 70 (1999), p. 350.

[3] *Çakici* v. *Turkey*, ECHR, judgment of 8 July 1999 and this *Year Book*, 70 (1999), p. 349, *Kaya* v. *Turkey*, ECHR, judgment of 19 February 1998, *Reports and Decisions*, 1998–I and this *Year Book*, 69 (1998), p. 378 and *Yasa* v. *Turkey*, ECHR, judgment of 2 September 1998, *Reports and Decisions*, 1998–VI.

[4] *Kurt* v. *Turkey*, ECHR, judgment of 25 May 1998, *Reports and Decisions*, 1998–III, and this *Year Book*, 69 (1998), p. 361.

[5] *Çakici* v. *Turkey*, above, n. 3.

[6] See *Çakici*, ibid, dissenting judgment.

Shooting by unidentified persons—right to life—positive obligations—effective investigation—Article 2—risk of ill-treatment—positive obligations—Article 3

Case No. 2. Mahmut Kaya case.[7] In this case against Turkey, the Court held that there had been a violation of Article 2 both as regards the right to life (six votes to one) and the requirement for an effective investigation (unanimously). The Court also found, by six votes to one, that there had been a violation of Articles 3 and 13. It did not consider the arguments arising under Article 14. The Court made an order in respect of non-pecuniary damage together with an award for costs.

The applicant's brother, H, was a doctor. In February 1993 he, together with a lawyer friend, went out to attend to a wounded member of the PKK. Neither returned, their bodies being found some days later. They had been bound and shot. Both had indicated previously that they believed that they were under surveillance and that their lives were in danger. Autopsies were carried out, revealing some bruising and indicating prolonged exposure of H's feet to water or snow. The applicant's father lodged various petitions with the prosecuting authorities claiming that the police had abducted H and that the murders had been committed by contra-guerrillas operating with official approval; one particular individual had been seen receiving assistance from the gendarmes. Unsuccessful efforts were made to arrest the suspects and the file was transferred a number of times because of jurisdictional questions. A delegation from the European Commission of Human Rights took evidence from witnesses.

The Court accepted the Commission's assessment of the facts. In considering the arguments under Article 2, the Court noted that it had not been proved beyond reasonable doubt that any State agent had been involved in the killing. The question was whether the authorities had failed in a positive duty to protect H from a risk to his life. Given that at the relevant time there were rumours that contra-guerrillas were targeting those suspected of assisting the PKK, H, as a doctor suspected of providing such assistance, was at particular risk and that risk could be regarded as real and immediate. The authorities were aware of that risk and knew or should have known that the contra-guerrillas were acting with the knowledge or acquiescence of certain members of the security forces. Although there was a system of measures in place which should have protected H, in reality these had been undermined by factors such as the series of failures on the part of the authorities to investigate allegations of wrongdoing by the security forces; the transfer of jurisdiction to administrative councils; and the attribution of many actions to the PKK. These factors resulted in a lack of accountability in the security forces, which was incompatible with the rule of law in a democratic society. The authorities in permitting these defects to go uncorrected had failed to take reasonable steps to prevent a real and immediate threat to life thus violating Article 2. Similar concerns arose in relation to Article 3. The authorities must have been aware that H was at risk of ill-treatment as well as extra-judicial execution from those who were not being held accountable for their actions. In the Court's view, the Government was therefore also responsible for treatment which the medical evidence revealed to be, at the least,

[7] ECHR, judgment of 28 March 2000.

inhuman or degrading, whether this had been the intention or not. Although the case concerns H's death, it should be noted that the steps required under Articles 2 and 3 do not seem to relate to that specific incident but seem more a criticism of the approach of the authorities to the situation in general.

The authorities failed to investigate the matter with any degree of effectiveness, responding to the complaints in a limited and superficial way. Thus, there was a second violation of Article 2 in respect of the obligation to undertake adequate investigations.[8] The failure to investigate resulted also in a violation of Article 13: the applicant's claim was an arguable one, even though the responsibility of state agents for the killing had not been proven, and therefore there was an obligation to investigate as a precursor to the provision of an effective remedy.

Mahmut Kaya (and equally *Timurtas* (Case No. 1)) may not advance the law under the Convention very far. Sadly, they are, however, representative of a string of cases brought against Turkey over the last few years, emphasizing the problems arising in that country. *Mahmut Kaya* serves as an example of Contracting States' positive obligations to ensure that individuals' lives are not at risk. In this case, the danger arose from the activities of contra-guerrillas, operating with the support of some element of government forces, where the Court held the element of risk was clear.[9] Contrast the finding in *Mahmut Kaya* with the admissibility decision in *Case No. 3. Bromley*,[10] in which the applicant's daughter was killed by a psychopath, K.W., who had escaped after being allowed out on home leave. The applicant claimed that the authorities had failed in their positive obligations under Article 2 by negligently releasing K.W. early, but the Court rejected this. Relying on the fact that the prisoner had returned from previous home leaves without incident and there was no medical diagnosis that he posed a risk to life, the Court held that there was no evidence that the authorities knew or ought to have known that K.W. posed a threat to life.[11] Further, it was not apparent that the authorities had failed to take any reasonable step available to them which would have secured K.W.'s capture before he committed any further crimes. In this decision, we can see the Court reaffirming its approach in *Osman*[12] and the concerns about imputing to the authorities greater knowledge than they actually possess and imposing on the authorities disproportionate burdens. Although not raised by the Court, and by contrast to the position in, for example, *Mahmut Kaya* (Case No. 2), it is also questionable

[8] As regards the level of investigation required, it is not necessary that the investigation be perfect: see *Grams* v. *Germany*, ECHR, decision of 5 October 1999 in which a complaint concerning the loss of evidence during an inquest was declared inadmissible.

[9] A number of cases involving the UK relating to allegations of unlawful killings by the security forces or with their connivance were declared admissible during the year: *Jordan*, *McKerr*, *Kelly* and *Shanaghan* v. *UK* (Applications 24746/94, 28883/95, 30054/96 and 37715/97), ECHR, decision of 4 April 2000.

[10] *Bromley* v. *UK*, ECHR, decision 23 November 1999.

[11] On the issue of whether there was sufficient risk see e.g. *Osman* v. *UK*, ECHR, judgment of 28 October 1998 and this *Year Book*, 70 (1999), p. 351, *Andronicou and Constantinou* v. *Cyprus*, ECHR, judgment of 9 October 1997 and this *Year Book*, 69 (1998), p. 375 and *Chahal* v. *UK*, ECHR, judgment of 15 November 1996, *Reports of Judgments and Decisions*, 1996–V and this *Year Book*, 68 (1997), p. 380.

[12] *Osman* v. *UK*, above, n. 11.

whether the daughter in this case was at greater risk than any other member of the general public.[13]

It is clear that the circumstances in which positive obligations can arise are not limited to criminal cases,[14] and this is true also of the procedural obligation regarding the need to investigate effectively. The scope of this obligation has been clarified to some extent during the period under review, as several cases arose in respect of Contracting States' obligations as regards the provision of medical care. It seems that, in principle, the positive obligations under Article 2 include a requirement to have in place rules that ensure medical professionalism so as to protect patients' lives. Further, States should also ensure there is a system in place whereby allegations of medical malpractice can be effectively investigated. Clearly, though, this obligation cannot result in a finding of liability every time a medical accident occurs.[15]

Alleged ill treatment in prison—inhuman and degrading treatment—effectiveness of investigation—Article 3—detention on remand—delay in release—Article 5—censorship of correspondence—Article 8—restrictions on freedom of movement—Protocol 4, Article 2—temporary suspension of voting rights—Protocol 1, Article 3—compensation for 'unjust detention'—status as victim—Article 34

Case No. 4. Labita case.[16] In this case against Italy, the Court, in a decision of the Grand Chamber, found that there had been no violation of Article 3 in respect of the conditions of detention (nine votes to eight as regards one period of detention and unanimously concerning the other) but, unanimously, that there had been a violation regarding the effectiveness of the investigation. The Court further found unanimously that there had been a violation of both Articles 5(1) and 5(3) and of Article 8, Article 2 of Protocol No. 4 and Article 3 of Protocol No. 1. It also concluded that it was not necessary to examine the claims under Article 6(3). It made an award for non-pecuniary damage together with an award for costs.

The applicant was arrested on suspicion of belonging to the mafia on the basis of uncorroborated statements of a former member of the Mafia ('*pentito*'), whose information itself was second-hand. The applicant was detained on remand for more than two-and-a-half years. When he was acquitted, he was not released until the following morning as the officers needed to process his release were not available when he returned to the prison. The applicant claimed that he was subjected to ill-treatment during his detention and that such ill-treatment was systematic. Amongst other claims, he alleged that he was regularly slapped, his testicles were squeezed, and he was often subjected to body searches when showering. He had to wait very lengthy periods to see a doctor and remained handcuffed during medical examinations. Further, the warders warned prisoners that they would be subjected to reprisals were they to tell their lawyers or

[13] See further *Mrs W* v. *UK*, (1983) *Decisions and Reports*, vol. 32, p. 190 and contrast with the facts in *Osman*, ibid.

[14] *LCB* v. *UK*, ECHR, judgment of 9 June 1998, and this *Year Book*, 69 (1998), p. 374.

[15] See *Erikson* v. *Italy*, ECHR, decision of 26 October 1999 and *Powell* v. *UK*, ECHR, decision 4 May 2000, both declared inadmissible.

[16] ECHR, judgment of 6 April 2000.

other prisoners about the treatment they were receiving. Although the applicant and other prisoners complained and a judge's report criticized the conditions at the prison, the matter was never successfully prosecuted as the perpetrators were not identified.

The applicant was, furthermore, kept under a special security regime and his correspondence was censored. Even after the applicant's acquittal, certain measures (including curfew, prohibition on going to bars, or associating with persons with a criminal record) were applied for three years. The applicant was also deprived of his voting rights. In January 1998 the applicant was awarded 64 million lire as compensation for his 'unjust' detention.

The applicant alleged that the conditions in which he was held constituted a violation of Article 3. The Court began by reaffirming that the principle that Article 3 enshrines is one of the most fundamental values in democratic societies and no derogation from it is possible, notwithstanding the offence with which the applicant had been charged.[17] Nonetheless, ill-treatment must attain a minimum level of severity if it is to fall within the scope of Article 3, the assessment of this point being dependent on the facts in each case. In respect of a person deprived of his liberty, physical force, which has not been made strictly necessary by his own conduct, diminishes human dignity and is therefore, in principle, contrary to Article 3.[18] In the case of punishment, however, the suffering or humiliation involved must in any event go beyond that inevitable element of suffering or humiliation connected with legitimate punishment. Additionally, the applicant must prove beyond a reasonable doubt that the ill-treatment took place, taking into account circumstantial evidence and unrebutted presumptions of fact.[19] In this case, although the Court stated that it would examine whether the alleged treatment was sufficiently serious, in the event the question turned into one of proof. In the Court's assessment, the applicant did not adduce conclusive proof of the ill-treatment, despite the judge's report concerning general conditions in the prison in which the applicant was held. In particular, the applicant did not complain about the ill-treatment until a hearing a year after the most recent of the incidents, a delay for which he did not give any explanation. Moreover, the applicant did not suggest that he was ever refused permission to see a doctor.

The Court then went on to consider the level of investigation into the applicant's allegations. Given the general circumstances operating with the prison at the time, and the media attention on this matter, it would seem that there had been reasonable cause for suspecting that the applicant had been subject to improper treatment. The Court reiterated that Article 1 in conjunction with Article 3 requires that there be in such circumstances an effective investigation and, referring to its existing case law on Article 2,[20] stressed that

[17] See *Selmouni* v. *France*, ECHR, judgment of 28 July 1999, *Reports of Judgments and Decisions* 1999–V, and this *Year Book*, 70 (1999), p. 355, n. 32 and *Assenov and Others* v. *Bulgaria*, ECHR, judgment of 28 October 1998, *Reports of Judgments and Decisions* 1998–VIII, p. 3288 and this *Year Book*, 70 (1999), p. 356. See also *T and V* v. *United Kingdom* (Case No. 5).

[18] *Tekin* v. *Turkey*, ECHR, judgment of 9 June 1998, *Reports of Judgments and Decisions* 1998–IV, pp. 1517–18, and this *Year Book*, 69 (1998), p. 379 and *Assenov and Others* v. *Bulgaria*, above n. 17, p. 3288.

[19] *Ireland* v. *United Kinngdom*, ECHR, judgment of 18 January 1978, Series A, No. 25, p. 65.

[20] For example, *McCann and Others* v. *United Kingdom*, ECHR, judgment of 27 September 1995, Series A No. 324, p. 49. See also *Timurtas* (Case No. 1) and *Mahmut Kaya* (Case No. 2).

such an investigation in the interests of ensuring the effectiveness of the Convention rights in practice should be capable of leading to the identification and punishment of those responsible. In this case, although some investigation was undertaken, it did not seem to have been adequate. Little action was taken and it was taken late. In particular, although the applicant claimed he would recognize the warders if he saw them in person, no meeting took place and, shortly after the applicant made this claim, the file was closed on the grounds that the perpetrators had not been identified. Moreover it was clear from the media that the applicant's claim was not an isolated one.

The Court went on to consider the applicant's claims under Article 5, first, that he had not been brought promptly before a judge as required by Article 5(3) and Article 5(1) on the basis that he had not been freed immediately after his acquittal. The Government claimed that the Italian courts had awarded him compensation for his 'unjust' detention and the applicant could therefore no longer claim to be a victim. The Court referred to its previous case law, stating that:

> a decision or measure favourable to the applicant is not in principle sufficient to deprive him of his status as a 'victim' unless the national authorities have acknowledged, either expressly or in substance, and then afforded redress for, the breach of the Convention.[21]

Although Italian law provided for payment of compensation, this was not necessarily based on the fact that the detention did not satisfy the conditions of Article 5, but rather on the fact that the applicant was ultimately acquitted and that the detention had been unjust. Further, the national court made no mention of the fact that detention had been for an excessive period. The applicant could therefore still be considered as a victim for the purposes of Article 5(3).

Turning to the merits of the applicant's claim under Article 5(3), the Court noted that the period to take into consideration was almost two years and seven months. The Court reiterated its previous case law in this area: that although a reasonable suspicion of an offence having been committed might initially justify detention, the longer the detention the greater the need for the national authorities to show special factors applied in the case. Further, the national authorities must also demonstrate that they acted with special diligence.[22] The Court here considered whether there remained reasonable grounds for suspicion or whether other grounds for detention arose. Considering the first issue, the Court noted the importance of statements of '*pentitos*' in the fight against the Mafia, but noted that these statements also create problems, not least the fact that they may be manipulated or made for personal reasons. Thus such statements must be corroborated. Here, not only were the statements uncorroborated, but contradictory evidence existed. Compelling reasons would therefore be required to justify further detention, which on the facts the Court did not find to be shown.

[21] *Amuur* v. *France,* ECHR, judgment of 25 June 1996, *Reports of Judgments and Decisions* 1996–III, p. 846 reaffirmed during the period under review in the decision of the Grand Chamber in *Dalban* v. *Romania,* ECHR, judgment of 28 September 1999, *Reports of Judgments and Decisions* 1999–VI in respect of Article 10, and in *Rotaru* (Case No. 17) in respect of Article 8.

[22] *Contrada* v. *Italy,* ECHR, judgment of 24 August 1998, *Reports of Judgments and Decisions* 1998–V, p. 2185, and *I.A.* v. *France,* ECHR, judgment of 23 September 1998, *Reports of Judgments and Decisions* 1998–VII, p. 2978.

As regards the applicant's detention after he was acquitted, the Court noted that the exceptions contained in Article 5(1) are to be construed narrowly so as to minimize the risk of anyone being arbitrarily deprived of their liberty.[23] Although administrative formalities may permit some delay in release when they constitute a first step in the process of releasing the applicant, in this case the delay was also caused by the absence of the appropriate officer. The delay, therefore, did not fall within Article 5(1)(c).

The Italian Government, in the light of the Court's previous judgments finding a violation of Article 8 in *Calogero Diana* v. *Italy*[24] and *Domenichini* v. *Italy*[25] concerning the same legislation on which the interception of the applicant's correspondence was based, did not contest the point in this case.

The Court noted that the applicant was for three years subjected to very severe restrictions on his freedom of movement, which undoubtedly amounted to an interference with his rights guaranteed by Article 2 of Protocol No. 4.[26] Given that the restrictions were based on Italian law and aimed at maintaining public order and for the prevention of crime, the question then was whether they were necessary in a democratic society within the meaning of Protocol 4, Article 2(3). The Court stated that preventative measures could be legitimate, even in respect of a person who had been acquitted, 'as concrete evidence gathered at trial, though insufficient to secure a conviction, may nonetheless justify reasonable fears that the person concerned may in the future commit criminal offences.'[27] In this case, however, there seemed to be insufficient evidence to show that the applicant was a threat. In particular, the fact that the applicant's wife was the sister of a now deceased mafia boss, in the absence of other evidence, was insufficient.

The final issue related the applicant's right to vote, the Government arguing that the restrictions were necessary to exclude Mafia influence over elected bodies. The Court noted that the rights granted by Article 3 of Protocol No. 1 are not absolute and that the Contracting States have a significant margin of appreciation in organizing their electoral systems.[28] Ultimately, however, it is for the Court to determine whether the rights guaranteed are protected and not deprived of their effectiveness.[29] In this case, although the Court had no doubt that taking action against the Mafia is a legitimate aim, it noted that these measures were only imposed after the applicant had been acquitted and there was therefore no concrete evidence on which a 'suspicion' that the applicant belonged to the Mafia could be based.

[23] e.g. *Manzoni* v. *Italy*, ECHR, judgment of 1 July 1997, *Reports of Judgments and Decisions* 1997–IV, p. 1191, and *Quinn* v. *France*, ECHR, judgment of 22 March 1995, Series A No. 311, p. 17.

[24] *Calogero Diana* v. *Italy*, ECHR, judgment of 15 November 1996, *Reports of Judgments and Decisions* 1996–V, p. 1775–6 and this *Year Book* 68 (1997), p. 424.

[25] *Domenichini* v. *Italy*, ECHR, judgment of 15 November 1996, *Reports of Judgments and Decisions* 1996–V, p. 1799–80 and this *Year Book* 68 (1997), p. 425.

[26] See e.g. *Guzzardi* v. *Italy*, ECHR, judgment of 6 November 1980, Series A No. 39, p. 33 and *Raimondo* v. *Italy*, ECHR, judgment of 22 February 1994, Series A No. 281–A, p. 19.

[27] *Labita* (Case No. 4) at para 195.

[28] *Mathieu-Mohin and Clerfayt* v. *Belgium*, ECHR, judgment of 2 March 1987, Series A No. 113, p. 23.

[29] *Gitonas and Others* v. *Greece*, ECHR, judgment of 1 July 1997, *Reports* 1997–IV, p. 1233 and this *Year Book*, 68 (1997), p. 410, and *Matthews v. United Kingdom*, ECHR, judgment of 18 February 1999, *Reports* 1999–I and this *Year Book*, 70 (1999), p. 381.

Although this case developed the jurisprudence on freedom of movement, an area in which there is not yet much case law, it raises real questions regarding the approach of the Court to Article 3, as the closeness of the Grand Chamber's decision indicates.[30] Despite the Court's emphasis on the centrality and non-derogability of Article 3, in this case the Court turns the issue into one of proof alone rather than the level of ill-treatment. This is especially problematic if the difficulties that a prisoner may face in challenging his or her captor (including access to information and the threat of reprisals) are not taken into account. The level of proof required often causes problems for applicants to show an actual violation of Article 3. In another case decided the same month, although the victim could produce medical evidence, the Court noted that it was not possible to ascertain whether the injuries were caused by the police or whether the torture was as severe as the applicant claimed.[31] The Court has held, as it did in this case, that the burden of proof is 'beyond all reasonable doubt', but it is surely not appropriate to see this as the same standard of proof as that used in criminal cases.[32] There the high burden of proof operates to protect individuals; here it would work to undermine their rights.

Furthermore, despite the Court's previous statements about the presumptions to be applied as to the ill-treatment of detainees during the period of their detention, which were reiterated here,[33] the Court seemingly did not adopt that approach. Although one could argue that the delay in the applicant claiming ill-treatment distinguished this from previous cases, such as *Tomasi*[34] where the applicant showed his injuries to an investigating judge more or less immediately, the approach here is still surprising given the widespread concern about the conditions in the prison during the relevant period. This is especially so when one considers the level of proof accepted in other cases under Article 3.[35]

The dissenting judges castigated the approach of the majority as 'inadequate, possibly illogical and even unworkable'. Their concern was that, because of the absence of adequate investigation, the applicant was precluded from obtaining evidence and from having the opportunity to identify the guards responsible for the attacks. The dissenting judges also pointed out that an approach which accepts that a violation of Article 3 must be proved beyond reasonable doubt would encourage Contracting States not to investigate these matters properly, as to do otherwise could provide applicants with the evidence they need to bring a successful claim. Of course, an inadequate investigation itself can now constitute a violation of Article 3. The question of the adequacy of the investigation thus becomes even more significant, as it constitutes a mechanism for finding a

[30] Judges Pastor Ridruejo, Bonello, Makarcyk, Tulens, Strážnická, Butkevych, Casadevall, and Zupancic dissented on this point from the majority.

[31] *Veznedaroglu* v. *Turkey*, ECHR, judgment of 11 April 2000.

[32] *Ribitsch* v. *Austria*, ECHR, judgment of 4 December 1995, Series A No. 336, opinion of the Commission, p. 37, cited by the dissenting judges in *Labita* (Case No. 4).

[33] See e.g. *Tomasi* v. *France*, ECHR, judgment of 27 August 1992 Series A No. 241.

[34] Ibid.

[35] See e.g. *Kurt* v. *Turkey*, above, n. 4. In his partly dissenting opinion Judge Matscher commented that the Commission's reporting on the facts in that case were 'superficial and insufficient' and the analysis of the facts 'clearly unsatisfactory'. *Çaciki* v. *Turkey*, above, n. 3 relied on a witness's description of the condition of the victim together with hearsay evidence. See also *Mentes* v. *Turkey*, ECHR, judgment of 28 November 1997, Reports, 97–VIII and this *Year Book*, 69 (1998), p. 364.

violation of this article where the applicant's claim is arguable but not capable of satisfying a relatively high burden of proof. The difficulty with this argument is, however, that in such a case the violation is procedural and, as the dissenting judges commented, a procedural violation is 'obviously less serious than a violation for ill-treatment'.

The dissenting judges also expressed concerns about the severity of treatment shown to have occurred which they felt was sufficiently severe to find a violation of the substantive aspect of Article 3. This was an issue the majority of the Court did not focus on—despite the fact that the Italian Government itself contested none of the applicant's factual allegations and described the conduct of the prison warders as 'appalling'. Indeed, it was these factors that were crucial in the Commission's conclusion that there had been a violation. The question of the level of ill-treatment required to show a violation of Article 3 was raised in a number of cases during the period under review, notably in *T* and *V* v. *UK* (Case No. 5) and *Smith and Grady* (Case No. 18).

Trial of children in adult court—length of sentence—inhuman and degrading treatment—Article 3—detention of child 'at Her Majesty's pleasure'—absence of review of detention—Article 5—effective participation of child in trial—Article 6

Case No. 5. T. and V. case.[36] In this case involving the United Kingdom, the Grand Chamber of the Court found, by twelve votes to three, that there had been no violation of Article 3 in relation to the trial and, by ten votes to seven, in relation to the sentence. The Court further held, by sixteen votes to one, that there had been no violation of Article 6(1) in relation to the trial but, unanimously, that there had been a violation of that article in relation to the sentence. The Court was unanimous in finding that there had been no violation of Article 5(1) but that there had been a violation of Article 5(4). The Court made an award of costs to both applicants.

The applicants were convicted in 1993 of the abduction and murder of a two-year-old boy. At the time of the offence T and V were 10 and at the time of their trial, 11. The case attracted a very high level of media coverage. Following their conviction, T and V were sentenced to be detained indefinitely 'at Her Majesty's pleasure'. In practice, this means that the convicted prisoners must serve a 'tariff' period, set down by the Home Secretary, and thereafter the prisoners must be released unless a parole board hold that they represent a danger to the public. The Home Secretary set a tariff of fifteen years, a decision which was quashed by the House of Lords on 12 June 1997. No new tariff was set.

The applicants argued that in view of their age at the time, trial in public in an adult court, as well as the punitive nature of the sentence, were violations of Article 3. The Court began by repeating the general rules regarding the application of Article 3: that it prohibits in absolute terms torture or inhuman or degrading treatment or punishment, irrespective of the victim's conduct.[37] Thus the nature of the crime committed by the applicants is immaterial in this

[36] ECHR, judgment of 16 December 1999.

[37] *Chahal* v. *UK*, ECHR, judgment of 15 November 1996, *Reports of Judgments and Decisions* 1996–V, p. 1855 and this *Year Book*, 68 (1997), p. 380. See also *Labita* (Case No. 4).

context. A minimum level of severity is required to trigger Article 3, the assessment of which depends on all the facts of the case, including (especially where degrading treatment is concerned) whether the intention of the treatment was to degrade the victim.[38]

In this context the Court considered whether the imposition of criminal liability at the age of 10 would violate Article 3. In assessing this point, the Court had regard to the standards applicable in other Contracting States. Although many chose to impose criminal responsibility at a later age, equally other States chose the same or a younger age and, further, international conventions on the subject provided no definitive guidance. Thus, given that the United Kingdom had not fixed the imposition of criminal liability at a disproportionately low age, the attribution of such liability in itself could not constitute a violation of Article 3. Regarding the trial itself, the Court noted that the tendency was to seek to try to safeguard the privacy of juvenile offenders. Although this might constitute a factor to be taken into account, it was not enough to show sufficiently severe treatment, especially given that there had been no intention on the part of the UK Government to humiliate the applicants. To the contrary, the authorities had taken special measures to try to mitigate the impact of the trial process on them. Although there was evidence that proceedings such as those applied to the applicants could be expected to have a harmful effect on an 11-year-old child, this was more a consequence of the need to deal with the murder case in question, and any exacerbation of the applicants' feelings of guilt or distress was not beyond that necessitated by that need.

The applicants' claims as regards the sentence 'at Her Majesty's pleasure' contravening Article 3 were also dismissed. The sentence was not one of life imprisonment without the possibility of release, instead requiring the serving of a specified period after which continued detention was subject to review by the parole board. Furthermore, States have a positive obligation, notably under Article 2, to take measures for the protection of the public from violent crime.[39] In itself, the imprisonment of a child for the purposes of deterrence or punishment in such circumstances would not contravene Article 3. Although in principle a long period of punitive detention might constitute inhuman and degrading treatment, as might indeed a continued failure to fix the tariff leaving a prisoner in uncertainty as to the length of the prison sentence, this was not yet the case here.[40]

Article 6 guarantees a fair trial and this includes the right of the accused to participate in his trial.[41] Although this principle has been established in respect of adults, this was the first time the Court had to consider how this principle

[38] *Raninen* v. *Finland*, ECHR, judgment of 16 December 1997, *Reports of Judgments and Decisions* 1997–VIII, pp. 2821–22 and this *Year Book*, 69 (1998), p. 365, n. 13.

[39] *A.* v. *UK*, ECHR, judgment of 23 September 1998, *Reports* 1998–VI, p. 2699, and this *Year Book*, 70 (1999), p. 355 and *Osman* v. *UK*, above, n. 11.

[40] The power of the Home Secretary to set a whole life tariff as regards adults was challenged before the English courts in the cases of Anthony Anderson and John Taylor following the entry into force of the Human Rights Act in England and Wales: *R.* v. *Secretary of State for the Home Department, Ex parte Anderson and Taylor*, judgment of 22 February 2001, *Times*, 27 February 2001 in which the High Court held that the Home Secretary's powers were unaffected by the Human Rights Act and Article 6(1) of the Convention as the setting of the tariff was not a sentencing exercise.

[41] *Stanford* v. *UK*, ECHR, judgment of 23 February 1994, Series A No. 282–A, pp. 10–11.

might apply to criminal trials involving children. The Court noted that the trial, and particularly the media and public interest in it, affected the ability of the applicants to participate in the trial, which, together with the formality of the trial, seemed to have intimidated the applicants to the point where they were unable to follow the trial, instruct counsel or take decisions in their own best interests. The fact that counsel was within 'whispering distance' of the applicants could not ameliorate the fault in proceedings, as it was unlikely that the applicants would have had the temerity to consult their legal advisors during the trial. In this regard, the Court distinguished this case from *Stanford*,[42] where although the defendant could not hear all the evidence, counsel could and, importantly, could also take his client's instructions. On this basis the Court held that there had been a violation of Article 6(1). The Court did not consider Article 6(1) in conjunction with Article 14. Another issue raised in connection with Article 6(1) was that the determination of the sentence was not carried out by an 'independent and impartial' tribunal[43] but by the Home Secretary. The Court found a clear violation of Article 6 as the Home Secretary was not independent of the executive. On independence, see also *McGonnell* (Case No. 13).

The applicants raised a number of arguments under Article 5 in relation to the sentence. The Court rejected the argument that the sentence was unlawful or arbitrary for the purposes of Article 5(1). As regards Article 5(4), since the Home Secretary set the tariff, there was no judicial supervision in the determination of the applicants' sentences at the time that they were set. The subsequent review by the House of Lords could not change this. Since no new tariff had been set, the children were denied access to review of their detention, as this right was triggered by the expiry of the tariff. In the current circumstances it would be impossible to tell when this would be. There was therefore a violation of Article 5(4).

The issues under Article 5 seem to be pretty clear. Those under Articles 3 and 6 call for further comment. It appears that, in principle, the attribution of criminal responsibility to a young child (rather than the trial of such a child) could itself constitute inhuman and degrading treatment within the scope of Article 3, though the Court did not explain why. Many of the issues discussed in relation to this point related to the trial rather than the impact of the attribution of criminal responsibility as such. These are, however, separate issues. We are left with the possibility that the imposition of too low an age of criminal responsibility could constitute a violation of Article 3, but with no clear idea as to the basis on which this might occur.

The mechanisms of the trial—and the circumstances in which it was conducted—raise further points, quite apart from the adverse psychological impact on the applicants. The Court drew on a number of factors to determine that the applicants had not been able to participate effectively in their trial: the impact of the media and public interest and the length and complexity of proceedings. Although the court trying the matter could have excluded the public and the media from the court room,[44] it is questionable whether, whatever the measures

[42] Ibid.

[43] *Eckle* v. *Germany*, ECHR, judgment of 15 July 1982, Series A No. 51, pp. 34–5.

[44] The Practice Direction that was issued in response to this case suggested that public and media access should be so limited, with media access being given via video link.

the courts took to lessen the formality of proceedings, children—especially those in circumstances similar to T and V here—would ever fully understand the trial or be capable of properly instructing their lawyers whether this be during or prior to trial. It would also seem that the inability to concentrate and the intimidation felt by T and V during the trial itself might on its own be sufficient to constitute a violation of a right to a fair trial, even if the children were better able to instruct their lawyers away from the public eye. If this is the case, questions about viability of trying children of this age arise. In any event, the case illustrates clearly the difficulties in involving children in the trial process—whether this be as defendant or as witness. Further, if the impact on the defendant and the defendant's ability to cope are central to the notion of a fair trial rather than objective considerations about trial procedure, arguably some adults would equally not be able to participate in their defence, especially during trial, and would therefore also not have had a fair trial.

One issue which the court did not directly address is the problem of 'trial by media', although the Court quite clearly recognized the potential impact of the intense media interest, as the trial judge had done. Although the media is often seen as the guarantor of a defendant's rights, the reverse seems to have been the case here.[45] During the period under review the issue of a biased jury was raised, but not in connection with media interest (*Sander*, Case No. 12). The issue of a fair trial was raised in numerous other cases this year, including *Rowe and Davis* (Case No. 8), *Fitt* (Case No. 9). *Condron* (Case No. 10) and *Averill* (Case No. 11), all of which concern criminal proceedings.

Another aspect of Article 3 is the limit it imposes on the deportation or expulsion of individuals. In this respect several cases deserve note. These are based on the surprising decision of the Court in *D.* v. *UK*,[46] in which the Court held that the deportation of D, who was suffering from AIDS, back to St Kitts would constitute a violation of Article 3, as the effect of the withdrawal of the medical treatment and lack of family support would be to leave him living in conditions of adversity such as to constitute inhuman treatment. In passing, the Court also referred to the fact that the UK had assumed responsibility for D, giving him treatment from 1994 onwards, and noted that D had become accustomed to the idea that he would die in the UK in a caring environment and had become reliant on the palliative treatment offered to him.[47] Clearly, this extended the potential scope of Article 3, taking it beyond the intentionally inflicted actions of government, or even beyond those of other bodies. Presumably seeking to quiet Contracting States' concerns as to the extent of this ruling, the Court in *D* stated that it was not creating a right for aliens to remain in a State so as to claim the benefit of medical, social or other assistance. The question then was, where would the line be drawn? Two admissibility decisions this year offered some light on the scope of *D*.

[45] Press interest in T and V continues. The Court of Appeal recently granted an injunction against the publication of the boys' whereabouts. *Jon Venables and Robert Thompson* v. *News Group Newspapers Limited, Associated Newspapers Limited and MGM Limited*, judgment of 9 January 2001 (CA).

[46] *D.* v. *UK*, ECHR, judgment of 2 May 1997 and this *Year Book*, 68 (1997), p. 407.

[47] *D.* v. *UK*, ibid, at para 52.

Right to medical treatment—AIDS—return to country of origin—inhuman treatment—Article 3

Case No. 6. S. C. C case.[48] In this case against Sweden, the Court declared the application under Article 3 and Article 6(1) inadmissible. The case concerned a Zambian national who had lived in Sweden from 1990 to 1994 as the wife of a Zambian diplomat. After his death she applied for a residence permit but was rejected. She challenged the decision relying on the fact that she had contracted HIV and should be granted a permit on humanitarian grounds. The doctor refused treatment unless she had a residence permit, although eventually, as her condition deteriorated, treatment was started. By this time, however, all her appeals had been rejected. Her claim under Article 3 was also rejected. When the matter came before it, the Court focused on the use of Article 3 when the risk arises from factors which cannot directly or indirectly engage the responsibility of public authorities. Responsibility would only be engaged in limited circumstances. It then took into account the following factors: HIV diagnosis was itself not enough; AIDS treatment was available in Zambia; the applicant's family, including her children, lived there; and the applicant's treatment had only recently started. Clearly, a number of factors distinguish this case from *D*[49] but it is not clear which are determinative.

Right to medical treatment—AIDS—return to country of origin—inhuman treatment—Article 3

Case No. 7. Tatete case.[50] In this case against Switzerland, the Court declared the application admissible, but subsequently struck the case off the lists following a friendly settlement. In this case, the admissibility of which was decided prior to *S.C.C.*, it seemed as if some further light might be shed on the issues raised above. The applicant, who was born in the Congo, was illegally resident in Switzerland. On 8 October 1997, one month before she was to leave the country, she discovered she had contracted AIDS and was suffering from pneumonia; her permit was extended by a month and a half and then again when she was re-admitted to hospital. In January 1998, she requested that the Swiss authorities reconsider their decision requiring her to leave as she required tri-therapy to improve her chances of survival; any abrupt end to treatment would have dramatic adverse consequences on her condition. The Swiss authorities refused on the basis that treatment for her condition was available in the Congo and that there was as yet no cure for her condition anywhere. The authorities considered that returning to her family would have beneficial effects on the applicant and offered to provide her with the necessary medicine and therapeutic advice. The applicant relied on *D*[51] to claim that there had been a violation of Article 3 and the Court declared the case admissible.

The crucial difference between this case and *S.C.C.* (Case No. 6), unless there are differences in the state of medical care and the family situation which are not

[48] *S.C.C.* v. *Sweden*, ECHR, decision 15 February 2000.
[49] *D.* v. *UK*, above, n. 47.
[50] *Tatete* v. *Switzerland*, ECHR, decision of 18 November 1999.
[51] *D.* v. *UK*, above, n. 47.

apparent on the face of the decisions, seems to be the length of time the two applicants received treatment. In *S.C.C.*, the Swedish authorities refused treatment initially and only started treatment shortly before the due date for deportation because of the applicant's deterioration in health. By contrast, the Swiss provided a greater degree of medical care for a longer period, albeit not as long as in the case of *D.*[52] Although one might also seek to distinguish the cases on the basis that *S.C.C.* was simply not as ill as *Tatete*, the message seems to be that if Contracting States do not want to find themselves violating Article 3 for seeking to deport sick non-nationals for whom they have cared (or alternatively be left with the responsibility of caring for an alien), then they should refrain from treating ill aliens in the first instance. Given the purpose of Article 3, this cannot be right. *Tatete* has been struck off the list of cases, which does leave some worrying unanswered questions. It may be that some of them will be answered in *Taskin*, a case which was communicated during the period under review and which concerned another deportation challenged on the grounds of ill-health, albeit not AIDS.[53]

Non-disclosure of evidence—decision by prosecution—impact on defence—equality of arms—right to a fair trial—Article 6(1)

Case No. 8. Rowe and Davis case.[54] In this case concerning the UK, the Court sitting as a Grand Chamber held unanimously that there had been a violation of Article 6(1). The Court made an award for costs but the remainder of the claim for just satisfaction was dismissed.

The applicants were found guilty of a number of serious criminal offences, against which they appealed on various grounds. At the first hearing before the Court of Appeal the prosecution handed a document to the court which was not shown to the defence. Despite changes in the English law regarding disclosure, the Court of Appeal consistently refused to order disclosure. The matter was subsequently referred to the Criminal Cases Review Commission which revealed, *inter alia*, that one of the witnesses relied on by the prosecution was a long-standing police informer who had received £10,300, police protection and immunity from prosecution in relation to his participation in the offences in question. The nature of the evidence he gave was not revealed on the basis of public interest immunity.

The applicants alleged that the failure to disclose this evidence undermined their right to a fair trial as protected by Article 6. The Court, referring to earlier case law, noted that the specific guarantees in Article 6(3) were aspects of the right to a fair trial enshrined in Article 6(1).[55] The issue the Court had to resolve was whether the proceedings were fair in their entirety. In this context, the Court stated that the fundamental element of a fair trial was equality of arms

[52] Ibid.

[53] *Taskin* v. *Germany*. ECHR, decision of 6 April 2000.

[54] ECHR, judgment of 16 February 2000.

[55] *Edwards* v. *UK*, ECHR, judgment of 16 December 1992, Series A No. 247–B, at para 33.

between prosecution and defence in an adversarial system.[56] This required that both prosecution and defence must be given the opportunity to have knowledge of and comment on observations filed and evidence adduced by the other party.[57] The prosecution particularly must disclose all evidence, whether favourable or not.[58] The role of the Court was not to assess whether the withholding of the evidence itself is necessary, instead it was to review the procedure overall to ensure equality of arms. Here, the fact that it was the prosecution which assessed the importance of concealed evidence to the defence and weighed it against the public interest in keeping the information secret entailed a breach of Article 6(1).

The appeal procedure did not rectify the unfairness caused by the lack of scrutiny of the trial judge of the evidence for a number of linked reasons. The Court of Appeal was dependent for their understanding of the importance and relevance of the disputed evidence on the account given by the prosecution and from transcripts of the first instance hearing. The fact that the evidence was not disclosed at first instance denied the defence the opportunity to review its strategy in the light of new evidence. The Court of Appeal's appraisal of the case was *ex post facto* and was made in the light of a guilty verdict. It is thus possible to distinguish this case from the previous *Edwards* case:[59] in *Edwards* the defence received most of the non-disclosed evidence prior to the appeal hearing, thus enabling it to put before the Court arguments as to the impact of the new material. In this case, the material was only disclosed after the Court of Appeal had ruled on the case.

Non-disclosure of evidence—decision by court—impact on defence—equality of arms—right to a fair trial—Article 6(1)

Case No. 9. Fitt case.[60] In this case involving the UK, the Court found that there had been no violation of Article 6(1).

The applicant was charged and found guilty of certain criminal offences. Prior to the trial the defence was notified that the prosecution applied *ex parte* to the trial judge for an order that the prosecution should not be required to disclose certain material to the defence. The defence were told that the material related to sources of information. The judge refused to order disclosure. A second *ex parte* application was made by the prosecution, which was followed immediately by an *inter partes* hearing, regarding the question of whether a witness statement taken from a co-accused after his guilty plea should be disclosed to the defence. Again the judge refused to order disclosure of the statement, but the defence

[56] Note that in *Krmčar v. Czech Republic,* ECHR, judgment of 3 March 2000, in the context of civil proceedings, the Court commented that adversarial proceedings require that the defence should have access to and the opportunity to familiarize itself with and comment on all evidence before the court, even where this evidence, as it had been gathered by the court, had not been available to the prosecution.

[57] *Brandstetter* v. *Austria*, ECHR, judgment of 28 August 1991, Series A No. 211 at paras 66–7.

[58] *Edwards* v. *UK*, above, n. 55 at para 36.

[59] *Edwards* v. *UK*, above, n. 55.

[60] ECHR, judgment of 16 February 2000. See also *Jasper* v. *UK*, ECHR, judgment of 16 February 2000.

were served with a summary of the statement, omitting any reference to sources of information. On appeal, the defence challenged the conviction on the basis, *inter alia*, that they should have had the full text of the co-accused's statement. The appeal was unsuccessful.

The applicant brought a claim under Article 6(1), alleging his right to a fair trial had been undermined, using similar arguments to those put forward in *Rowe and Davis* (Case No. 8). The Court applied the same tests as it had in *Rowe and Davis*, this time coming to a different conclusion: that there had been no violation of Article 6. A central factor was that the decision not to disclose had been made by the trial judge (by contrast to the prosecution making that decision in *Rowe and Davis*) and that the defence had been kept informed and had had the opportunity to make submissions and participate in the decision-making process as far as possible in the light of the public interest.

The judgment was not, however, unanimous. The question how much information the defence needs to be able to participate on equal terms is a difficult one. The dissent pointed out that the defence were not fully informed of the judge's reasoning for withholding the evidence; by definition they were excluded from *ex parte* proceedings. The subsequent *inter partes* hearing did not remedy this defect, as the defence, again, did not know exactly what arguments they would need to put forward and the points they were arguing against. On this basis, the inability of the defence to put forward full arguments undermined the ability of the judge to monitor effectively the need for disclosure and therefore vitiated the procedural safeguards provided by the involvement of the judiciary. Furthermore, the Court's approach did not comply with the decision in *van Mechelen*[61] which required that the least restrictive approach to the defendant's rights be taken: according to the dissenting judge:

> if it can be shown that there is a viable alternative way of proceeding which is less restrictive of an applicant's right to a fair trial and to proceedings adversarial in character, it should be taken. In my opinion, where the applicant can establish on a *prima facie* basis that such an alternative way exists, the onus shifts to the respondent to show why it cannot use or adapt such a way.[62]

In this case, Fitt argued for the 'special counsel' procedure. The UK Government argued that the introduction of such a system would raise insoluble practical difficulties. This position the dissenting judges seemed to view with scepticism, an understandable position given that a special counsel procedure was being introduced in the UK in a number of policy areas. It should be noted that the problem of the withholding of evidence is not limited to the UK: a number of cases in this area were brought on similar points;[63] and that, indeed, the problems of identifying secret evidence may be just as great if not greater in the continental inquisitorial system.[64]

[61] *Van Mechelen* v. *Netherlands*, ECHR, judgment of 23 April 1997, *Reports* 1997-III and this *Year Book*, 68 (1997), p. 405.

[62] *Fitt*, above, n. 60. Dissent of Judge Hedigan.

[63] See e.g. *Voisine* v. *France*, ECHR, 8 February 2000, *Krmčar* v. *Czech Republic*, above, n. 56, *Kuopila* v. *Finland*, ECHR, judgment of 27 April 2000.

[64] See comments of Dissenting Judge Zupančič.

Self-incrimination—drawing of adverse inferences by a jury—right to a fair trial–Article 6(1)

Case No. 10. Condron case.[65] In this case against the UK, the Court concluded unanimously that there had been a violation of Article 6(1) but that the applicants' claims under Articles 6(2) and 6(3) amounted to a restatement of the argument in respect of a right to a fair trial. The Court made an order for costs.

The applicants were drug addicts. Together with a third party, Curtis, they were charged with the supply of proscribed drugs. The applicants had been videotaped passing packages to Curtis and, when their flat was searched, sixteen 'wraps' of heroin of between 0.07 and 0.09 grams were found, together with a further 1.19 grams of heroin. After their arrest, their solicitor noticed that the applicants were in the early stages of withdrawal and he expressed concern that they were consequently not fit to be questioned. The police medical examiner examined the applicants and confirmed that they were fit to be questioned. The applicants were cautioned and were advised that if they felt unwell they should say so and the questioning would be stopped. The applicants consistently responded 'no comment' to police questions. At trial, the applicants claimed that they had bought the heroin in bulk the evening before for their own use; that the package shown on the video tape was a packet of cigarettes and that they had refused to answer questions originally on the advice of their solicitor who thought they were in no condition to answer questions. The judge in summing up commented to the jury:

> The law is . . . that you may draw such inferences as appear proper from a defendant's failure to mention the points I have referred to in their respective interviews. . . . You do not have to hold it against him or her. It is for you to decide whether it is proper to do so. Failure to mention the points in interview cannot on its own prove guilt but depending on the circumstances you may hold it against him or her when deciding whether he or she is guilty. You should decide whether in the circumstances which existed at the time of the interview the matters were ones which the defendant concerned could reasonably be expected then to mention.

The applicants appealed against their convictions on the basis of the inclusion of their interviews with the police as evidence and on the basis of the trial judge's summing up. They were unsuccessful.

The applicants claimed that their right to a fair trial had been violated. The Court noted that the starting point in this area of law was the case of *John Murray*,[66] where the Court confirmed that the right to silence is not absolute. Whether drawing adverse inferences from an accused person's silence infringes Article 6 should be determined in the light of all the circumstances. Given the centrality of the right to silence to the notion of a fair trial, caution must be exercised before an accused's silence can be used against him and, in particular, silence cannot be the sole or main reason for conviction. Nonetheless the Court noted that, 'the right cannot and should not prevent that the accused's silence, in situations which clearly call for an explanation from him, be taken into

[65] ECHR, judgment of 2 May 2000.

[66] *John Murray* v. *UK*, ECHR, judgment of 8 February 1996, *Reports of Judgments and Decisions* 1996–I.

account when assessing the persuasiveness of the evidence adduced by the prosecution.'[67]

This case can be distinguished from *Murray*.[68] The applicants, unlike Murray, gave evidence at their trial and put forward an explanation as to why they had been silent. Further, this case was heard before a jury. Although these were all considered relevant facts, none were determinative of the question on their own. Other factors were that the applicants were under no legal compulsion to speak, they were cautioned clearly and they were allowed access to legal advice and their solicitor was present during interview. This in itself raises a difficult question, as it was on the advice of the solicitor that the applicants exercised their right to remain silent. In what circumstances will it not be appropriate for a defendant to rely on his solicitor's advice, especially given solicitors' duties of good faith to the court? Here, the solicitor expressed concern about his clients' well-being, albeit a view at variance with that of the medical examiner. Does a difference of opinion (and a cautious approach on the part of the legal adviser) necessarily mean that the solicitor was wrong, or even acting in bad faith? The issue deserves much careful attention as limiting the right of an accused to rely on the advice of legal advisers could undermine their rights to that advice in the first place, especially given the emphasis given by the Court in its jurisprudence to the need for access to legal advice.[69]

The Court noted that the judge in his summing up to the jury followed the existing guidance but questioned whether this achieved the appropriate balance set down in *Murray*.[70] In particular, the judge left the jury free still to draw an adverse inference, even if the jury was satisfied as to the reasonableness of the defendants' arguments as to why they stayed silent. The Court took the view that the jury should have been directed that it could only draw an adverse inference if satisfied that the only sensible reason for the defendants' silence during police interview was their having no answer or none that would stand up to cross examination. The appeal process could not cure this defect, as the Court of Appeal had no way of reviewing the jury's decision-making. Further, the Court of Appeal was concerned with a different question from whether the applicants had a fair trial; it was concerned with the safety of the applicants' conviction, and in this case there was additional evidence suggesting a finding of guilty. There had been on this basis a violation of the right to a fair trial. These issues were raised again, in different circumstances, in *Averill* (Case No. 11).

Right to silence—inferences drawn from silence—right to a fair trial

Case No. 11. Averill case.[71] In this case involving the UK, the Court held by six votes to one that there had been no violation of Article 6(1) or 6(2) but, unanimously, that there had been a violation of Article 6(1) in conjunction with Article 6(3)(c).

[67] *Condron*, above, n. 65 at para 56.
[68] *John Murray* v. *UK*, above, n. 66.
[69] *Averill* (Case No. 11).
[70] *John Murray* v. *UK*, above, n. 66.
[71] ECHR, judgment of 6 June 2000.

The applicant was arrested under the Prevention of Terrorism (Temporary Provisions) Act 1989. The applicant was repeatedly interviewed by the police, but he remained silent. At each interview he was cautioned in accordance with the relevant legislation as to the possible consequences of his remaining silent. The applicant was not permitted to have a solicitor in the interviews with him although, after an initial twenty-four hour period, he was allowed daily access to legal advice. During the twentieth interview he was again cautioned and then asked to account for his presence at a given location at a specified time. He was also asked to account for the presence of certain fibres found on him and again cautioned as to the inferences that might be drawn if he failed to do so. Subsequently he was charged and found guilty of a number of criminal offences, including murder. Although the finding was based on circumstantial evidence of a forensic nature, the judge drew 'a very strong adverse inference' from the applicant's failure to explain away the forensic evidence until the trial itself. The applicant's appeal was unsuccessful.

This case again concerns the scope of the limitations on the right to silence[72] and takes the judgment in *John Murray* as its starting point. As in *Condron* (Case No. 10), a finding of guilty should not be based wholly or mainly on a suspect's silence. As with *Condron*, *Averill* can be distinguished from *Murray* on the basis that the applicant in this case did testify, although he did not have an as immediately obvious explanation for not explaining the forensic evidence away when asked about it as the applicants in *Condron* did. Averill claimed that he had not understood the importance of the forensic evidence as he was not given sufficient information. The Court did not focus on this point but highlighted the fact that Averill had clearly been cautioned.[73] Against this should be balanced the fact that Averill did not have access to legal advice for twenty-four hours, although he subsequently was able to consult a solicitor. The Court then noted that the trial judge was not obliged to draw adverse inferences from the silence of an accused. Here, the judge gave detailed reasons for doing so which were scrupulously reviewed on appeal. Averill was not convicted purely on his silence but on strong forensic evidence.

The Court did, however, criticize the delay in giving Averill access to legal advice. Although this delay was shorter than in *John Murray*,[74] it was still incompatible with the right to a fair trial.[75] Access to a lawyer at an early point may be critical as early decisions may have long term strategic consequences for the defence.

These two cases illustrate the narrow boundary between the need to protect the rights of an accused and the need to guard against activities such as ambush defences. One could seek to distinguish between *Condron* and *Averill*, which came to different decisions, on the basis that the former concerned a jury trial; the latter did not. That, however, is not the main point in issue—there is nothing inherent in a jury trial that is contrary to the right to a fair trial, although there

[72] In his dissent, Judge Loucaides reiterated his view that the right to silence should be absolute.

[73] Although this on its own is not decisive: see *John Murray* v. *UK*, above, n. 66 at p. 50.

[74] *John Murray* v. *UK*, above, n. 66.

[75] See also e.g. *Magee* v. *UK*, judgment of 6 June 2000 which concerned a refusal to allow a prisoner to see his lawyer for forty-eight hours. The Court found a violation of Article 6(1) in this case, too.

may be difficulties with the way juries operate and how jury decisions are reviewed (see also Case No. 12 *Sander*). In *Condron* the issue was whether the jury should hold the applicants' silence against them even if the jury found their reasons for remaining silent plausible, a possibility the judge's directions left open. In *Averill*, the judge followed in his reasoning the formal requirements of the right to a fair trial and so we know that he did not rely on Averill's silence alone. *Condron* concerned a jury trial, and because the jury's reasoning is not revealed, it is impossible to review their decisions on appeal. Whether, had the judge directed the jury more specifically, it would have come to a different verdict is, of course, also unknown.

Allegedly racist jurors—judge's direction—right to a fair trial—Article 6(1)

Case No. 12. Sander case.[76] In this case involving the UK the Court held, by four votes to three, that there had been a violation of Article 6(1).

During the trial of the applicant, an Asian, one of the jurors alleged that two of the other jurors had made openly racist remarks and jokes. After discussing the matter with counsel in chambers, the judge raised the matter with the jury, asking them to indicate whether they thought that they would be able to reach a verdict without racial bias. The jury the next day confirmed this, and in doing so refuted the original allegations. The letter making these points was signed by all the jurors. A separate letter was received from one of the jurors, explaining he had made the jokes, apologizing for any offence caused but claiming that he was not racially biased. The judge decided not to discharge the jury. The applicant was subsequently convicted and his appeal was unsuccessful.

The Court in assessing the case started by noting that the requirement for impartiality had two elements, a subjective and an objective element: this is so whether a criminal or civil matter is in issue (see e.g. *McGonnell* (Case No. 13)). The first related to the actual impartiality (or lack thereof) of the tribunal, the second to whether in the circumstances there were sufficient guarantees to exclude any objectively justified or legitimate doubts as to the impartiality of the court. Although the perspective of the accused is important in this context, it is not decisive.[77]

In the absence of evidence to the contrary, the subjective impartiality of the jury must be assumed[78] and, although one member of the jury had made racist jokes, this was in the opinion of the Court (with one dissent) insufficient to show bias on the part of the jury. Assuming that making racist jokes equates with being racist, this raises the question as to what level of proof is required. Only two out of twelve of the jurors were involved in the incident: is this enough to taint the entire jury?

As regards the objective impartiality requirement, the letter from all the jurors was, in the Court's opinion, insufficient to discredit all the original allegations. The Court made three linked points to support this view: that jokes take on a very different hue when made in the context of a trial; that, given his identity

[76] ECHR, judgment of 9 May 2000.

[77] *Gregory* v. *UK*, ECHR, judgment of 25 February 1997, *Reports of Judgments and Decisions* 1997–I and this *Year Book*, 68 (1997), p. 433.

[78] *Piersack* v. *Belgium*, ECHR, judgment of 1 October 1982, Series A No. 53, pp. 14–15.

was known, the juror who originally complained might have felt his position was compromised; and it is unlikely that the average person would admit to being racist. In this regard it was, according to the Court, possible to distinguish the present case from that of *Gregory*,[79] in which an allegation of a racially biased jury had been found not to violate Article 6(1). In that case, however, it was not clear which juror had complained about the racism, nor who the offender was. Furthermore, in this case, counsel for the defence had continued to insist on the need to discharge the jury. However strong the judge's admonition, it would be unlikely to counter racist views overnight.

Although intuitively it seems that the Court came to the 'right' conclusion in this case, its reasoning, as noted by Judges Sir Nicolas Bratza, Costa, and Fuhrmann, is not persuasive, especially as regards its attempts to discredit the letter written by the jury and in its attempts to distinguish *Gregory*.[80] Perhaps a more straightforward approach might be to reconsider whether the Court in *Gregory* itself took a sufficiently robust approach to the question of racism. As the Court noted here, racism is not an evil which can be easily uprooted by judicial admonition.

Separation of powers—impartial tribunal—planning appeal—right to a fair trial—Article 6(1)

Case No. 13. McGonnell case.[81] In this case involving the UK the Court, having dismissed the Government's preliminary objections, held unanimously that there had been a violation of Article 6(1).

The applicant bought the Calais Vinery and made numerous applications to permit residential use of the land. These were unsuccessful as the local development plan adopted by the States of Deliberation, the island's legislature, prohibited residential development. The applicant then moved into a converted packing shed and subsequently was found guilty of changing the use of the shed without permission and was fined. The applicant complained that at the determination of his planning appeal by the Royal Court of Guernsey, the close connection between the judicial and executive and legislative functions of the Bailiff deprived the Bailiff of the independence and impartiality required by Article 6(1). The Bailiff, as well as presiding over the Royal Court and the Court of Appeal, is head of the island's administration and president of the States of Deliberation. The Guernsey courts had previously ruled on the separation of powers, the Court of Appeal holding that there is no structural conflict between the Bailiff's judicial duties and his role in the States of Deliberation.

The Government was held to be precluded from relying on non-exhaustion of domestic remedies as it had not raised the issue before the Commission. The Government further contended that the applicant had waived his rights because he failed to raise an objection to the tribunal when it was open to him to do so. In this context, seeing as the applicant had not expressly waived his rights, the question was whether there had been a tacit waiver within the sense of the ruling

[79] *Gregory* v. *UK*, ECHR, above, n. 77.
[80] *Gregory* v. *UK*, ECHR, above, n. 77.
[81] ECHR, judgment of 8 February 2000.

in *Håkansson and Sturesson*.[82] The question is essentially one of what was reasonable in the circumstances. Given the clear statement of the Guernsey Court of Appeal in previous case law which ran contrary to the applicant's arguments and the fact that the point was not raised by the Government until a late stage of the proceedings, the Court found that the applicant's failure to challenge the Bailiff in Guernsey could not be said to have been unreasonable, and therefore did not amount to a tacit waiver of his right to an independent and impartial tribunal.

As regards compliance with Article 6(1) and the right to an impartial tribunal, the Court referred to its decision in *Findlay*,[83] noting that, as in that case, the issues of independence and impartiality were closely linked. Independence goes to the make up and appointment of the tribunal, whereas impartiality relates to freedom from bias, both as a matter of fact and also as regards appearances.[84] The Court noted that there was no argument that the Bailiff was personally biased. The issue related to the question whether the Bailiff had the required appearance of independence, in other words the required level of objective impartiality. Clearly, the Bailiff has non-judicial as well as judicial responsibilities. The Government argued that in the case of the former, the Bailiff merely occupied positions rather than exercising functions. This the Court rejected: even a purely ceremonial constitutional role must be classified as a 'function'.

In reviewing whether on the facts of the case, the various responsibilities of the Bailiff were consistent with Article 6(1), the Court referred to its previous case law, likening the situation to those in cases such as *Procola*[85] and *De Haan*.[86] The Court concluded that the mere fact that the Deputy Bailiff presided over the States of Deliberation when the planning policy was adopted in 1990 was capable of casting doubt on his impartiality when he subsequently determined, as the sole judge of the law in the case, the applicant's planning appeal.

There are clear parallels between this case and *Procola*[87] which concerned the Judicial Committee of the Luxembourg Conseil d'État. In that case, four out of five members who sat on an administrative law matter had given a pre-legislative opinion on the matter. Although the Court has repeatedly held that it does not require strict adherence to the separation of powers doctrine, equally clearly the Court will take a stringent approach when reviewing such cases. This point can be illustrated by the Court's emphasis on perceived, as well as actual, impartiality and the fact, made clear in this case, that the Court will not accept that individuals can have a purely formal role. In *Procola*,[88] the judges in both circumstances were acting in their capacity as lawyer, affecting the substance of the law. In *McGonnell*, the Bailiff was, in effect, presiding officer of the debates

[82] *Håkansson and Sturesson* v. *Sweden*, ECHR, judgment of 21 February 1990, Series A No. 171, p. 20.

[83] *Findlay* v. *United Kingdom*, ECHR, judgment of 25 February 1997, *Reports* 1997–I, p. 198 and this *Year Book*, 68 (1997), p. 433.

[84] On the question of subjective and objective impartiality during the period under review, see Case No. 12 *Sander*. On the issue of independence see *Khan* (Case No. 15) and *T and V* (Case No. 5).

[85] *Procola* v. *Luxembourg*, ECHR, judgment of 28 September 1995, Series A No. 326, p. 16.

[86] *De Haan* v. *The Netherlands*, ECHR, judgment of 26 August 1997, *Reports* 1997–IV, pp. 1392, 1393.

[87] *Procola* v. *Luxembourg*, above, n. 85.

[88] *Procola* v. *Luxembourg*, ibid.

rather than formulating the policy—although it should be noted that he did have the right to vote. Further, the fact that Guernsey is a small community and could therefore not be expected to have the elaborate structures (or indeed the persons to man them) found in larger communities was not a relevant factor.[89]

Notwithstanding questions of size, the approach in this judgment might affect a number of Contracting States' constitutional arrangements, for example the House of Lords in the United Kingdom and the Conseil d'État in France. There are possible limitations to the scope of this ruling. In *McGonnell* the key was the fact that the Bailiff personally had both been involved in the planning discussions and adjudicated on the planning appeal based on that policy. Furthermore, the Bailiff was sole adjudicator in the appeal. Similar points can be made in relation to *Procola*: again the majority of those with responsibility for determining the administrative action had been involved in the pre-legislative opinion. One might argue that provided the judges do not act (or perhaps do not constitute the majority) in cases involving legislation when they have been involved in the legislative process, there will be no conflict. Problems arise with this view, however: what if the minority 'partial' judge is determinative for the outcome where a panel of judges is split fairly evenly?[90] Further, is such an approach not the equivalent of saying that, for example, the Law Lords may not become involved in the enactment of legislation, or otherwise risk limiting their jurisdiction to legislation enacted before they became Law Lords? Perhaps one solution to this problem might be that adopted by Sir Nicholas Bratza in his concurring opinion to the Commission's report, to the effect that 'different considerations would . . . apply . . . in cases involving a dispute between private parties'. Presumably, in such an instance the authorities would not in effect be defending their own policy choices, minimizing the likelihood that the judges would be perceived as having their own axe to grind.[91] Even such an approach does not, however, resolve all the difficulties.

Public servant—fixed term contract—civil rights—applicability of Article 6

Case No. 14. Pellegrin case.[92] In this case involving France the Court held, by thirteen votes to four, that there had been no violation of Article 6, as that article was not applicable to the case.

The applicant was recruited as a technical adviser to the Minister for the Economy, Planning and Trade of Equatorial Guinea. Subsequently he contested a decision by the French Minister for Cooperation and Development that he was not to work as a technical adviser overseas on the basis that he had failed a medical examination and had been declared unfit to work overseas. Legal proceedings instituted by the applicant on 16 May 1990 were still pending. The

[89] See Dissenting Opinion of Commissioner Alkema.

[90] Similar problems have already been noted with respect to jury deliberations (*Sander* Case No. 12): save as regards juries, it is not possible to tell which voters voted guilty and which not guilty.

[91] This would seem also to be consistent with *Procola*, which also concerned an administrative law action.

[92] ECHR, judgment of 8 December 1999.

applicant brought an application under the Convention arguing that there had been a breach of his right to a hearing within a reasonable time.

The scope of Article 6, which applies to civil rights, has long been the subject of contention as regards public servants. Normally a contract of employment would constitute a civil right for the purposes of Article 6; a number of governments, notably the French government, have argued that public servants, however, by the nature of their employment, fall outside Article 6. The Court reviewed its case law in this area and, in the hope of ending the disputes between public servants and the employing state, decided to adopt a new 'functional' test, based on the nature of the employee's duties and responsibilities. Only those disputes raised by public servants whose duties typified the specific activities of the public service in so far as the latter was acting as the depositary of public authority responsible for protecting the general interests of the State or other public authorities would be excluded from the scope of Article 6(1). Disputes between administrative authorities and employees who occupy posts involving participation in the exercise of powers conferred by public law will not fall within the scope of Article 6. Clearly the armed forces and the police would thus be excluded. The Court expressly stated, however, that all disputes regarding pensions should come within Article 6(1), as on retirement employees break the special bond between them and the authorities.[93] Applying this test to the case in hand, the Court noted that the applicant's post, involving as it did the drawing up of a budget for state investment together with a three year plan and programme of public investment, fell within the field of the State's public finances, a field in which the State exercised sovereign power. Article 6 was, therefore, not applicable.

In adopting a functional test, the Court's approach parallels that of the European Court of Justice in determining the scope of public authority for the purposes of Article 39(3) EC.[94] On the face of it, there seems to be a significant difference between the two, however. The European Court of Justice looks at each job individually to see if it is connected with the exercise of sovereign power, the Court here seems to be taking whole sectors—for example, the armed forces and the police—together. Although one might suggest that the difference in approach relates to the different reason for which public servants are being excluded from the protection of the Convention and the EC Treaty respectively,[95] the comparison does raise the question whether it would be appropriate to exclude, for example, army cleaners from Article 6(1), which would seem to be the result of applying a sector-based functional test. It would seem from subsequent cases that this was not intended to be the case. In *Frydlender*,[96] the Grand Chamber in reviewing the activities of the applicant, who had been

[93] See e.g. *Lambourdiere* v. *France*, ECHR, judgment of 2 August 2000.

[94] See e.g. Case C–4/91 *Bleis* v. *Ministere de L'Education Nationale* [1991] ECR I–5627 and the Commission Notice, OJ [1998] C–72/2.

[95] The provisions in the EC Treaty relate to prohibitions on grounds of nationality as regards access to employment.

[96] *Frydlender* v. *France*, ECHR, judgment of 27 June 2000, *Castanheira Barros* v. *Portugal*, ECHR, judgment of 26 October 2000, in which the applicant was a civil servant, initially at the Coimbra Institute of Criminology and subsequently at the National Institute of Criminology. His dispute of his employment terms fell within Article 6(1). *Satonnet* v. *France*, ECHR, judgment of 2 August 2000 concerned a public servant employed under an individual contract to work for a publicly managed body. Article 6(1) was found to apply.

posted to the New York economic development office as head of an autonomous section to handle the promotion of French wines, beers and spirits, considered that he was not carrying out any task which could be said to entail, either directly or indirectly, duties designed to safeguard the general interests of the State. Clearly, seniority is also in itself not a decisive factor. Further, the Court in reaching this decision commented that the *Pellegrin* decision had been adopted with a view to restricting cases in which public servants could be denied the 'practical and effective protection afforded to them, as to any other person, by the Convention, and in particular by Article 6'.

Evidence obtained using a listening device—third party—conviction based on evidence—right to private life—Article 8—right to a fair trial—Article 6(1)

Case No. 15. Khan case.[97] In this case against the UK, the Court held unanimously that there had been a violation of Article 8 and of Article 13 but, by six votes to one, that there had been no violation of Article 6(1). A request for a revision of the judgment was rejected on 4 October 2000.

Khan was charged with certain offences relating to the import of proscribed drugs. His conviction was dependent on evidence gained by using a listening device installed on B's property. The bug had been installed under the authorization of the Chief Constable of South Yorkshire, but related to suspicions the police had of B; the police had neither expected nor foreseen that Khan would visit B. At trial, the judge ruled the evidence was admissible, although there had been civil trespass in attaching the device. Following this ruling, Khan pleaded guilty but subsequently appealed on the basis that the evidence ought to have been inadmissible. The matter eventually came before the House of Lords which ruled that there was no right to privacy in the UK and, further, the common law permitted the admissibility of improperly obtained evidence. Although Article 8 was relevant to the question of admissibility, in the House of Lords' view it was not determinative.

The principal issue in this case was whether the interference that had clearly occurred complied with Article 8(2); that is, was it 'in accordance with the law' and 'necessary in a democratic society'? The requirement that an interference be in accordance with the law, according to the Court's long-standing jurisprudence, includes a qualitative element.[98] This means that the domestic law must provide protection against arbitrary interference with individuals' rights under Article 8, and be sufficiently clear in its terms to give an adequate indication of the circumstances in which the authorities are entitled to resort to covert operations.[99] In this instance, there was no statutory system, the matter being dealt with by Home Office Guidelines. These Guidelines were neither legally

[97] ECHR, judgment of 12 May 2000.

[98] See e.g. *Halford* v. *UK*, ECHR, judgment of 25 June 1997, *Reports* 1997–III at para 49 and this *Year Book*, 68 (1997), p. 408. See, similarly, *Amann* (Case No. 16) and *Rotaru* (Case No. 17) and also cases on Article 10(2), for example, *Hashman and Harrup* (Case No. 22).

[99] *Malone* v. *UK*, ECHR, judgment of 2 August 1984, Series A No. 82 and this *Year Book*, 55 (1984), p. 387.

binding nor directly publicly accessible. This together with the fact that the House of Lords held that there was nothing unlawful about a breach of privacy meant that there was no national law concerning the use of covert listening devices and therefore these actions could not be in accordance with the law.[100]

Looking at the issue of Article 13, the Court noted that there was no real remedy for the violation of Article 8, as the criminal courts could only review the fairness of proceedings. The Government argued that remedies could be obtained by the Police Complaints Authority (PCA) but, as the Commission noted in *Govell*,[101] it is only in limited circumstances that matters must be referred. In the majority of cases it is the Chief Constable who would decide whether matters should be referred. Furthermore, given that the PCA's members were appointed by the Chief Constable and the PCA itself was obliged by statute to have regard to the Secretary of State's advice as to preferring and withdrawing disciplinary or criminal charges, it would seem that the PCA lacked independence.[102]

It should be noted that Part III of the Police Act 1997 is now in force, thus satisfying the principal concern regarding a lack of law in this area. Nonetheless, *Khan* will remain important in this area as significant gaps in statutory protection remain. The question of surveillance will become increasingly important as different technological means for communication, as well as those for intercepting and monitoring, increase. The linked issue of data storage is dealt with below in *Amann* (Case No. 16) and *Rotaru* (Case No. 17).

The Court then went on to consider the domestic court's failure to exclude the evidence. It reiterated that, whilst Article 6 guarantees a right to a fair hearing, it does not deal with questions of admissibility, as such.[103] The question the Court will review is whether the proceedings as a whole were fair. Here the Court noted that, by contrast to the position in some of the previous cases decided on this point,[104] the fixing of the listening device was not contrary to domestic law and there was nothing unlawful about the breach of privacy. Further, Khan's statements were made voluntarily; there was no question of entrapment.[105] Khan also had the opportunity to challenge both the authenticity and use of recording before the courts, which opportunity he used. The Court therefore concluded that there was no violation of the right to a fair trial; the unlawfulness of the bugging went to Article 8(2) and not to Article 6(1). The sole dissenting judge[106] did point out that it would be somewhat strange to argue that it is necessary to break the law in order to uphold it. Should a conception of fairness, which includes respect for the rule of law, permit a conviction solely on evidence obtained illegally? Further, allowing the admissibility of such evidence

[100] See also *Govell* v. *UK*, Application No. 27237/95, *Commission Rep.*, 14 January 1998.

[101] Ibid.

[102] For the Court's approach to independence see *McGonnell* (Case No. 13).

[103] See e.g. *Teixara de Castro* v. *Portugal*, ECHR, judgment of 9 June 1998 and this *Year Book*, 69 (1998), p. 406.

[104] *Schenk* v. *Switzerland*, ECHR, *Reports* 1988–II.

[105] Contrast *Teixara de Castro* v. *Portugal*, above, n. 103.

[106] Judge Loucaides.

provided no deterrent to the police from repeating their conduct, thus undermining the effectiveness of the Convention rights.

Interception of phone call—creation and storage of information card—right to private life—Article 8

Case No. 16. Amann case.[107] In this case against Switzerland, the Court held unanimously that there had been a violation of Article 8 regarding both the interception of the phone call and the creation and storing of the information card. It similarly held that there had been no violation of Article 13. The Court made an award for non-pecuniary damages and legal costs.

The applicant imported depilatory appliances into Switzerland for sale. In 1981 he received a call from a woman at the former Soviet embassy who wanted to order a 'Perma Tweez'. The call was intercepted by the Federal Public Prosecutor's Office (FPP), which requested an investigation into the applicant and the goods he sold. As a result, the FPP drew up a 'card' on the applicant based on the investigation and on the national security card index. In 1990 the applicant learned of the card's existence and asked to see his card, some items on which turned out to have been censored. The applicant brought a claim for compensation and then an administrative law action. All were unsuccessful.

The Court commenced by referring to *Halford*,[108] reconfirming that phone calls, whether on private or business premises, fall within the scope of 'private life'. It was not disputed that the interference in the form of the interception took place; the question is, as often in such cases, justification. As noted in *Khan* (Case No. 15) the first element of Article 8(2) is that the interference be 'in accordance with the law', which requires a certain quality of law.[109] By contrast to the earlier case of *Kopp*,[110] however, which also concerned Switzerland and concerned a similar point, in which the Court ruled that there was sufficient legal base to satisfy the qualitative requirement, the judicial authorities in this case did not examine in the same detail whether the surveillance was lawful. It would therefore be possible to distinguish *Kopp*. The Court, however, considered that it was unnecessary to do so as the 'foreseeability'[111] element inherent in the notion of law was not satisfied. The Court re-emphasised, as it had done in *Kopp*, that with increasingly sophisticated tapping techniques the need for sufficiently precise law became ever more important. Here national law contained no indication as to the persons concerned by the measures, the circumstances in which the measures may be used, the means to be employed or the procedures to be observed.

As regards the card index, the storage of data fell within Article 8[112] and, as noted regarding the phone tap, the Court found no reason to interpret private

[107] ECHR, judgment of 20 February 2000.

[108] *Halford* v. *UK*, above, n. 98.

[109] See *Kopp* v. *Switzerland*, ECHR, judgment of 25 March 1999, *Reports* 1998–II which concerned a similar case and in which the Court found that the interference was in accordance with the law.

[110] *Kopp* v. *Switzerland*, ibid.

[111] *Malone* v. *UK*, above, n. 99.

[112] *Leander* v. *Sweden*, ECHR, judgment of 26 March 1987, Series A No. 116, p. 22.

life restrictively so as to exclude business life. It suggested that such an approach was in line with the terms of the Council of Europe Convention of 28 January 1981 for the protection of individuals with regard to automatic processing of personal data,[113] personal data being defined in Article 2 of that convention as 'any information relating to an identified or identifiable individual'. The fact that it is the creation of the record that falls within the scope of Article 8(1), means the subsequent use to which it is put is irrelevant; it is therefore not necessary to prove that the data was sensitive in any way.[114] The question then arose as to whether the intrusion was justified. Given that the same national rules were in issue as regards the interception of the phone call, the Court held that the requirement of foreseeability had not been satisfied. Similar concerns arose regarding the storing of the data.

Considering Article 13, the Court restated the general principles of the law in this area, as it did in *Smith and Grady* (Case No. 18). In this case, the applicant was able to consult his card as soon as he asked to do so and, when he complained, the courts before which he brought his action were competent to examine the questions and did so. The mere fact that all of the applicant's claims were dismissed is not in itself sufficient to determine whether or not the administrative-law action was 'effective'.

Storage of personal data in security files—private life—Article 8

Case No. 17. Rotaru case.[115] In this case against Romania, the Grand Chamber of the Court held unanimously that there had been a violation of Article 6(1) and Article 13 and, by sixteen votes to one, that there had been a violation of Article 8.

During legal proceedings brought by the applicant, one of the defendants, the Ministry of the Interior, submitted a letter containing details of the applicant's political activities between 1946 and 1948. The letter also alleged that the applicant had been a member of the Christian Students' Association, an extreme right wing movement. The applicant claimed that some of the information, notably his membership of the Christian Students' Association, was false and defamatory. He brought an action against the Romanian Intelligence Service (RIS), which had originally provided the information, but the Romanian courts held that they had no power to order amendment or destruction of the information. Subsequently RIS discovered some of its statements were inaccurate. As a result the Bucharest Court of Appeal quashed the previous judgments, declared the information about the applicant's membership of the Christian Students' Association to be null and void, but it did not rule on the question of damages. The applicant alleged a violation of his right to private life. He also claimed the lack of an effective remedy.

The Court noted that insofar as the Bucharest Court of Appeal's judgment afforded the applicant some redress, it was only partial and therefore, following

113 On which the EC Data Protection Directive is based.

114 See Government's arguments outlined by the Court at para 68 of the judgment.

115 ECHR, judgment of 4 May 2000.

the Court's previous rulings on similar points, the applicant could still be considered to be a victim under Article 34.[116]

The Government in this case denied that Article 8 was applicable, arguing that (by contrast to, for example, *Amann* (Case No. 16)) the information in the RIS's letter of 19 December 1990 related not to the applicant's private life but to his public life. The Court rejected this argument, re-emphasizing that 'the storing of information relating to an individual's private life in a secret register and the release of such information comes within the scope of Article 8(1)'.[117] As with *Amann*, the Court explained that Article 8 applies also to business life and considered the impact of the Data Protection Convention. It also then added, 'public information can fall within the scope of private life where it is systematically collected and stored in files held by the authorities'.[118] In the Court's view, the material collected, collated, and stored by RIS fell within the scope of Article 8, especially given the length of time for which it was stored and given that some of it was inaccurate and likely to be defamatory. Given this approach, there had clearly been an interference with the rights protected by Article 8(1). The Court then turned to the question of Article 8(2).

The Court accepted that intelligence services could legitimately exist in a democratic society, but qualified this by stating that powers of secret surveillance of citizens are tolerable under the Convention only in so far as strictly necessary for safeguarding the democratic institutions.[119] Taking the same line as it has in numerous other judgments, including *Amann* (Case No. 16) and *Khan* (Case No. 15), the Court confirmed that the interference was based on the law, law which was accessible but which did not satisfy the requirements of foreseeability.

This series of cases together emphasizes the limitation on governmental freedom to collect and to store information on citizens. Although the Court clearly accepts that the imperatives of national security and law enforcement may involve such activities, they must be subject to clear, accessible guidelines. This is important as the Convention on Data Processing, and more specifically the EC Data Protection Directive (95/46/EC), exclude the activities of law enforcement bodies from their scope.[120] In this context it should be noted that the Contracting States are negotiating a convention on 'cybercrime', a document which has already been heavily criticized for not respecting individuals' rights. The UK authorities have, for example, suggested that under the convention it should be permissible to require that all emails be stored for seven years, against the possibility of their becoming relevant for law enforcement or security purposes. Such a proposal seems unlikely to be compatible with Article 8, as currently interpreted. Of course, it will not only be these authorities that are caught by such requirements; other governmental bodies may also, in principle, be caught—for example, medical authorities.

[116] See e.g. *Amuur* v. *France*, ECHR, above, n. 21. See also this year, *inter alia*, *Labita* (Case No. 4).

[117] ECHR, judgment, at para 43.

[118] Ibid.

[119] *Klass and Others* v. *Germany*, ECHR, judgment of 6 September 1978, Series A No. 28, p. 21.

[120] See Council Resolution of 17 January 1995 on the Lawful Interception of Telecommunications which identifies the requirements of law enforcement agencies [1996] OJ C 329/1.

It should also be noted that the subject matter of the information collected does not matter; it can relate to issues that clearly fall within an individual's private life (*Amann*), to information relating to criminal activities (*Khan*) and even in relation to the storage of information about an individual's public aspect, such as their political views (*Rotaru*). Importantly, the information does not need to be confidential. If the definition in the Data Protection Convention is adopted, as it seems it is, virtually any information relating to individuals may be caught by this, provided it is organized into a file of some description.

One question that the Court did not address, however, is whether the individual needs to be identifiable from the data, or whether anonymized data will not fall within the scope of Article 8. Anonymized data can occur in a variety of forms: from a file in which a name has been blanked out through to statistical reports. The former would clearly seem to fall within Article 8's ambit. The position regarding the latter is less clear: statistical data is excluded from the concept of 'personal data' for the purposes of the EC Directive. This of course need not be determinative for the Court's purposes. One of the Contracting State's constitutional courts has already taken a fairly robust line regarding the protection of statistical information derived from personal data, arguing that if you can use a computer to produce statistical reports, you can use similar programming to reverse that process. Should the Court accept this argument, or include anonymized data within Article 8 for any other reason, possibilities which are currently *not* excluded, the impact on many areas of governmental activity would be significant.

Military service—intrusive questioning—dismissal—private life—Article 8

Case No. 18. Smith and Grady case.[121] In this case involving the UK, the Court unanimously found that there had been a violation of Article 8 but that the facts did not give rise to any separate issues in respect of Article 14 in conjunction with Article 8. The Court further held unanimously that there had been no violation of Article 3 whether alone or in conjunction with Article 14 and that it was not necessary to consider Article 10, whether alone or in conjunction with Article 14. The Court subsequently ruled on the matter of just satisfaction,[122] holding by six votes to one that the UK Government should make an award to both applicants in respect of pecuniary loss (£19,000), non-pecuniary loss (£59,000 and £40,000 respectively) and costs.

Smith and Grady were members of the UK armed forces and are homosexual. The Ministry of Defence operated a policy that excluded homosexuals from the armed forces. Each of the applicants were the subject of an investigation which resulted in their admitting their homosexuality. They were discharged on the sole ground of their sexual orientation. Their judicial review applications (following a ruling from the European Court of Justice on a related issue)[123]

[121] ECHR, judgment of 27 September 1999. See also *Lustig-Prean and Beckett* v. *UK*, ECHR, judgment of 27 September 1999.

[122] ECHR, judgment of 25 July 2000.

[123] Case C–249/96 *Grant* v. *South West Trains Ltd* [1998] 1 CMLR 993; [1998] All ER (EC) 193. The reference to the European Court of Justice on this point in *R.* v. *Secretary of State for Defence, ex parte Perkins*, was also withdrawn. Contrast the approach of the European Court of Justice in Case C–13/94 *P.* v. *S. and Cornwall County Council* [1996] ECR I–2143, [1996] All ER (EC) 397.

were dismissed, despite some reservations by the national courts as to the compatibility of their dismissal with the Convention.[124]

The Court, reviewing the evidence, considered the investigations and, in particular, the interviews of the applicants to have been exceptionally intrusive. Further, the administrative discharges had a profound effect on the applicants' careers and prospects. The Court also noted the absolute and general character of the policy. Taking these factors into account, the Court found that there had been especially grave interferences with the private life of the applicants.[125]

There was no doubt that the restriction was in accordance with the law, both domestic and that of the European Community. The Government's main argument to justify this rule was that the presence of homosexuals in the armed forces would have a substantial and negative effect on morale and, consequently, on fighting power. The Court held that it had no reason to doubt that the policy was designed with a view to ensuring the operational effectiveness of the armed forces or that investigations were, in principle, intended to establish whether the person concerned was a homosexual and to this extent were, therefore, pursuing the legitimate aims of 'the interests of national security' and 'the prevention of disorder' within Article 8(2). The question then was whether the measures were necessary in a democratic society. In coming to a negative conclusion, the Court began by underlining that a democratic society respects pluralism, tolerance and broadmindedness.[126] Although the Contracting States retain a significant margin of appreciation in respect of national security issues, they should not frustrate the exercise by individual members of the armed forces of their right to respect for their private lives, a right which applies to service personnel as it does to others within the jurisdiction of the State. When Contracting States seek to claim a risk to operational effectiveness, they must refer to specific examples. The Report on which the Government relied in support of its contention, in the view of the Court showed only negative attitudes of heterosexuals towards homosexuals and in so far as they constituted a predisposed bias on the part of the heterosexuals, the Court considered that, on their own, these views were not enough to justify this policy. The Court further noted that the policy was not based on any moral standpoint and nor were the physical capability, courage, dependability or skills of the personnel in question. The Court suggested that any difficulties arising out of a change of policy could be dealt with by the imposition of a strict code of conduct. Finally, the Court noted the changing views in the domestic laws of the Contracting States supported the admission of homosexuals into the armed forces.

The Court considered the investigations, which continued after the applicants had admitted their homosexuality, as a separate issue. The Government's argument, that this was to prevent individuals from using homosexuality as an excuse to leave the armed forces, was rejected as the applicants wished to remain in the armed forces. Further, the applicants had very little choice but to cooperate with the interview process, as they wanted the investigations to be kept as discreet as possible, thus there was no arguable claim that the applicants

[124] *R.* v. *Ministry of Defence, ex parte Smith* [1996] QB 517.

[125] *Dudgeon* v. *UK*, ECHR, judgment of 22 October 1981, Series A No. 45, pp. 18–19, *Vogt* v. *Germany*, ECHR, judgment of 26 September 1995, Series A No. 323, p. 23.

[126] *Vereinigung Demokratischer Soldaten Österreichs and Gubi* v. *Austria*, ECHR, judgment of 19 December 1994, Series A No. 302 and *Dudgeon* v. *UK*, ibid.

had consented to the process, thereby waiving their rights. On this basis, the continued investigation was unjustified.

The Court accepted that, in principle, treatment grounded on a bias of the heterosexual majority against a homosexual minority could constitute a violation of Article 3. It also noted that the interviews were particularly humiliating and distressing for the applicants. Nonetheless, in the Court's opinion, this did not reach the level of severity required to fall within Article 3. In passing, it should be noted that this case, as do *T and V* (Case No. 5) and *Labita* (Case No. 4), illustrates the subjective element in the assessment of severity for the purposes of Article 3. The Court also rejected the arguments based on Article 10: freedom of expression was subsidiary to the applicants' right to respect for their private lives.[127]

Finally, the applicants complained of a violation of Article 13, in that they had no effective remedy before a national authority in respect of the violations of which they were victims. The Government referred to the earlier ruling in *Vilvarajah*,[128] arguing that proceedings by way of judicial review afforded an effective remedy to the applicants. The Court reviewed the scope of Article 13, stating that it required the provision of a domestic remedy allowing the competent national authority both to deal with the substance of the relevant Convention complaint and to grant appropriate relief, whilst allowing the Contracting States a margin of appreciation as to the form by which this end might be secured. Article 13 did not require the certainty of a favourable outcome for the applicant.[129] In this case, where there had been a violation of the rights protected by Article 8, the only test open to the English courts was whether the policy was irrational, that is that it was beyond the range of responses open to a reasonable decision-maker. Although human rights considerations would be taken into account, they were not determinative, and the threshold for irrationality was high. Although the Court of Appeal clearly had doubts about the policy, the judges in that court did not consider it to be irrational. The Court concluded that the irrationality test was so strict that it effectively excluded any consideration by the English courts of whether the interference with the applicants' rights answered a pressing social need or was proportionate to the national security and public order aims pursued. These are principles respect for which lies at the heart of the Court's analysis of Article 8. There was thus a violation of Article 13.

The ruling in this case as regards Article 8, given the gradual change in attitudes towards homosexuals reflected in the Court's Article 8 jurisprudence,[130] should come as no great surprise, especially given the sweeping nature of the prohibition and the intrusive investigation techniques. Several points are, however, worth noting. The first relates to the margin of appreciation: the Court

[127] It took a similar approach in respect of religion and freedom of expression: *Kokkinakis* v. *Greece*, ECHR, judgment of 25 May 1993, Series A No. 260–A, p. 23, and *Larissis and Others* v. *Greece*, ECHR, judgment of 24 February 1998, *Reports* 1998–I, p. 383 and this *Year Book*, 69, (1998), p. 400. See also this year, *Serif* (Case No. 19).

[128] *Vilvarajah and Others* v. *The United Kingdom*, ECHR, judgment of 30 October 1991, Series A No. 215.

[129] *Vilvarajah and Others* v. *The United Kingdom*, ibid.

[130] See also *Salguiro da Silva Monta* v. *Portugal*, ECHR, judgment of 21 December 1999. At the time of writing a copy of the judgment of this case was not available in English.

found a violation here despite the fact that the measure fell within the area of national security, an area in which Contracting States have a comparatively wide margin of appreciation. (See also *Rotaru*, Case No. 17.) The second relates to the role of the European Court of Justice; these cases show yet another area of law in which human rights protection within the scope of Community law has proved lacking,[131] although the position may be improved following the introduction of the EU Charter of Fundamental Rights. Further, this ruling has clarified that the notion, held by some judges to the effect that proportionality is the same as the *Wednesbury* unreasonableness test (irrationality), is not correct. It should be noted that in this case the Court distinguished between the previous caselaw, which had concerned individual decisions regarding expulsion from the UK, in which there was individual and exhaustive review in accordance with the Court's principles, with the situation, such as the present case, where a general policy is under review. Judicial review may thus in some cases still satisfy Article 13. Given the number of similar cases which might be brought following the substantive ruling, the policy will no doubt cost the UK Government dear.

State interference in religious affairs—conviction for usurping functions of a minister—freedom of religion—Article 9

Case No. 19. Serif case.[132] In this case against Greece the Court held unanimously that there had been a breach of Article 9. It further held that it was not necessary to examine the issues under Article 10. The Court made an award in respect of pecuniary and non-pecuniary damage.

The state appointed T to a vacant post of mufti of Rodopi. Five years later two Muslim members of Parliament requested the State, in accordance with relevant domestic legislation, to organize elections to fill the posts of mufti of Rodopi and mufti of Xanthi. Receiving no response to their request, they decided to organize their own elections. Prior to the elections, however, the President of the Republic changed the law regarding the procedure for the appointment of muftis, who were thereafter to be appointed by presidential decree. The President used a procedure to change the law which is available 'when extremely urgent and unforeseeable need arises'; such legislation must be approved by Parliament within forty days. The applicant was elected mufti in the elections organized by the Muslims. He challenged the validity of T's appointment. Meanwhile, the Parliament enacted a law retroactively validating the legislative act adopted by the President. The applicant was subsequently convicted for usurping the functions of a minister of a 'known religion' by issuing a message about the religious significance of a feast, delivering a speech at a religious gathering, issuing another message on the occasion of a religious holiday and wearing the uniform of the office of mufti without having the right to do so. He brought a claim under the Convention claiming that his freedom of religion as guaranteed by Article 9 had been infringed.

The Court commenced by noting that, although religious freedom is

[131] See *Grant* and *P.* v. *S*, above, n. 123. See also e.g. Case C–150/90 *Society for the Protection of Unborn Children Ltd* v. *Grogan* [1991] ECR 4685.

[132] ECHR, judgment of 14 December 1999.

primarily a matter of individual conscience, it also includes freedom, in community with others and in public, to manifest one's religion in worship and teaching.[133] Looking at the facts underlying the applicant's conviction, the Court held that there had been a violation of the applicant's rights of expressing his religion in public. As the claim concerned the manifestation of belief it was, in principle, subject to limitation under Article 9(2). The question was whether such interference was justified in an area where the Court has typically allowed Contracting States a rather wide margin of appreciation. As with other articles (such as Articles 8 and 10), interference can be justified under Article 9(2) only if it is prescribed by law, necessary in a democratic society, and aims to achieve certain goals. As regards the first point, both sides put forward arguments regarding the obligations of Greece under the Treaty of Peace of Athens, entered into shortly after the First World War for the protection of Muslims within Greece. The Court declined to rule on this issue, as it held that the interference did not comply with Article 9 on other grounds.[134] The Court did, however, accept that the interference was seeking to protect public order, given that the applicant was not the only person claiming to be the religious leader of the local Moslem community and that the matter was the subject of dispute.

As to whether the restriction was necessary, the Court re-emphasized the importance of pluralism, but noted that some restrictions on freedom of religion could be justified in order to reconcile the interests of the various religious groups.[135] Referring to the *Wingrove* case,[136] and borrowing the tests used in Article 10 cases, the Court noted that any such restrictions must correspond to a 'pressing social need' and must be 'proportionate to the legitimate aim pursued', thus continuing the common themes between these articles. Given the functions that the applicant had actually carried out, the Court held that punishing a person for the mere fact that he acted as the religious leader of a group that willingly followed him could not be considered compatible with the demands of religious pluralism in a democratic society. The Government expressed concerns regarding the religious tension in the area between the Muslims and Christians, but the Court held that such tensions were the result of pluralism, and that there was no evidence that the split in the Moslem community had exacerbated matters. The Government put forward further arguments relating to the need to protect the legal functions carried out by the mufti and that the applicant's actions undermined the system put in place by the State for the organization of the religious life of the Moslem community in the region. As regards the former point, the Court noted that the applicant had not, in fact, carried out any of the functions which carried legal responsibilities. As to the second point, the Court commented that in its view, in democratic societies it is not necessary that the State take measures to ensure that religious communities remain or are brought under a unified leadership.

This position will obviously have implications for any system where the government of a Contracting State seeks to regulate and control the organization

[133] *Kokkinakis* v. *Greece*, ECHR, judgment of 25 May 1993, Series A No. 260–A, p. 17.

[134] *Manoussakis and Others* v. *Greece*, ECHR, judgment of 26 September 1996, *Reports of Judgments and Decisions* 1996–IV, p. 1362.

[135] *Kokkinakis* v. *Greece*, above, n. 133 at paras 31 and 33.

[136] *Wingrove* v. *The United Kingdom*, ECHR, judgment of 25 November 1996, *Reports of Judgments and Decisions* 1996–V, p. 1956, para 53 and this *Year Book*, 68 (1997), p. 391.

of religions, a point which is supported by the ruling by the Grand Chamber in *Hasan and Chaush*.[137] This case concerned the election of the Chief Mufti, there being two rival candidates between whom the Bulgarian state did not maintain impartiality. The Court here interpreted Article 9, by reference to Article 11, to hold that the freedom of religion encompasses the notion that a religious community should be allowed to function free from arbitrary or biased State interference. The State's refusal to recognize one of the rival candidates and to try to impose a unified religious community constituted an interference with the applicants' freedom of religion. The extent of these rulings is, as yet, not clear as the Court merely refers to 'unjustified' interference: the issue is discussed further in *Cha'are Shalom ve Tsedek* (Case No. 20).

As a general point, the Court has tended to avoid ruling on Article 9, often characterizing cases brought under it as involving Articles 10, 11, or even Article 5[138] and Protocol 1, Article 1.[139] In the cases during the period under review, however, we can see that the reverse is also possible: Articles 10 and 11 were subsumed into the issues arising under Article 9. This series of cases has allowed the Court to elucidate some aspects of what has been a relatively underdeveloped area of law. Given the number of cases concerning Article 9 working their way through the Convention system,[140] it seems this trend may continue.

Ritual slaughter—freedom of religion—Article 9

Case No. 20. Cha'are Shalom ve Tsedek case.[141] In this case involving France, the Court held by twelve votes to five that there had been no violation of Article 9, taken alone, and by ten votes to seven that there had been no violation of Article 9 taken together with Article 14.

In 1987 the applicant association requested that it be given the official approval it needed in order to be able to perform ritual slaughter in accordance with the strict religious prescriptions of its members, for whom meat is not kosher unless it is '*glatt*'. National law permitted ritual slaughter only when it was carried out by slaughterers authorized by an approved religious body. The application was refused by the *Conseil d'État* on the basis that the applicant could not be considered a 'religious body' within the meaning of the decree. The Paris Central Consistory ('the ACIP'), the association which represented the vast majority of Jews in France and which was authorized to carry out the slaughter of animals did not, in the applicant's opinion, carry out a sufficiently thorough examination of the meat they certified as kosher. The applicant claimed that the refusal of its application infringed its freedom to manifest its

[137] *Hasan and Chaush* v. *Bulgaria*, ECHR, judgment of 26 October 2000.

[138] See *Riera Blume*, ECHR, judgment of 14 October 1999 concerning the detention and 'deprogramming' of individuals thought to belong to a sect. Given the finding of a violation of Article 5, the Court did not rule on the Article 9 point.

[139] *Chassagnou* v. *France*, ECHR, judgment of 29 April 1999 and this *Year Book*, 70 (1999), p. 378.

[140] See e.g. *Dahlab* v. *Switzerland*, Application No. 42393/98, *United Christian Broadcasters Ltd* v. *United Kingdom*, Application No. 44802/98, *Mitrpolia Basarabiei Si Exharhatul Plaiurilor* v. *Moldovia*, Application No. 45701/99, *I.S.* v. *Bulgaria*, Application No. 32438/96.

[141] ECHR, judgment of 27 June 2000.

religion through observance; furthermore, the fact that ACIP had approval constituted discrimination.

The Court noted that an ecclesiastical body could bring an action on behalf of its members.[142] It was not contested that the dietary requirements of the association's members constituted part of the practice of Judaism; thus ritual slaughter in principle could fall within the scope of protection of Article 9. There were two linked elements to be considered, the rules relating to the slaughtering of animals, and the refusal of the authorities to grant the applicant association authorization to carry out ritual slaughter. As regards the first point, the Court did not consider that the system itself, which aimed to eliminate unregulated slaughter of animals in the interests of hygiene and public health, constituted an interference with religious freedom. Indeed, it expressly permitted ritual slaughter. As regards the refusal to grant the applicant permission to slaughter animals, the Court noted that the applicant would slaughter animals the same way as ACIP, the distinction being the thoroughness of the subsequent examination of the quality of the meat. Further, it transpired that '*glatt*' meat was available on the market, imported from Belgium. The Court concluded that there would be a violation of Article 9 only if it were impossible to obtain '*glatt*' meat: freedom of religion in these circumstances does not extend to the right to take part in person in the performance of ritual slaughter and the subsequent certification process.

In any event, even were there to have been an interference with the applicant's freedom of religion, this could be justified according to Article 9(2). The measure complained of was prescribed by law and pursued a legitimate aim, namely the protection of public health and public order. Further, given the margin of appreciation granted to Contracting States, the measure could not be considered excessive or disproportionate.

The Court then considered Article 9 in conjunction with Article 14. Although Article 14 was dependent on a right protected by the Convention being in issue to come into play itself, there was no presumption that there had to be a violation of that right. Although the matter clearly fell within the scope of Article 9, the Court noted the difference of treatment which resulted from the measure was limited in scope and in so far as there was a difference of treatment, it pursued a legitimate aim. Consequently there was 'a reasonable relationship of proportionality between the means employed and the aim sought to be realised'.[143]

It should be noted that the Court in this case expressly stated that Article 9 did not include the right to slaughter the animals personally (although over a vigorous dissent). Presumably this is based on the fact that the ritual slaughter of animals is a mechanism for achieving compliance with religious codes rather than being an essential part of the practice of the religion itself. Thus, the fact that meat of the relevant quality was available was sufficient to respect the right to religious observance. The Court did not address the point, made by the dissent, that in limiting the scope of Article 9 in this way it was contradicting its approach in *Serif* (Case No. 19), holding that States should not impose unity on religious groups. One might argue that there is a qualitative difference

[142] *Canea Catholic Church* v. *Greece*, ECHR, judgment of 16 December 1997, *Reports of Judgments and Decisions*, 1997–VIII, p. 2856, para 31.

[143] See, for example, *Marckx* v. *Belgium*, ECHR, judgment of 13 June 1979, Series A No. 31, p. 16.

between rules relating to leadership and the rules in issue here, given their instrumental nature. Nonetheless, this ruling puts the applicant in the position of having to trust other groups with the task of ensuring the quality of the meat, a task which was necessary to ensure that its members were abiding by their religious convictions. Any other approach—at least where there were no reasonable grounds for distrust—could, however, lead to an unworkable situation, as many different groups sought to have their different concerns recognized. As the dissent noted, the fact that the State would seek to avoid dealing with an excessive number of negotiating partners so as not to dissipate its efforts and in order to reach concrete results more easily, is not illegitimate in itself, or disproportionate.[144]

Exclusion from profession—Jehovah's Witness—conviction for failing to enlist—freedom of religion—Article 9—discrimination—Article 14

Case No. 21. Thlimmenos case.[145] In this case against Greece, the Court unanimously found that there had been a violation of Article 14 in conjunction with Article 9 and that it was not necessary to consider Article 9 alone. It further found that there had been a violation of Article 6(1) due to the excessive length of proceedings.

A court martial convicted the applicant for insubordination in refusing to wear a uniform. He served half of a four-year prison sentence. A few years later the applicant entered a competitive examination for a position as an accountant. He came second out of sixty candidates. Although there were twelve positions available, the Board did not appoint him on the ground that he had been convicted of a felony. His appeals were unsuccessful.

Article 14 is dependent on the other rights granted by the Convention; an applicant cannot claim discrimination in its own right. The question then was, did the situation fall within any of the rights granted by the Convention? The applicant was not claiming that he had a right to a profession under the Convention but that the discrimination related to his right to freedom of religion. The applicant suggested that the authorities in Greece should have distinguished between his conviction, which arose out of religious grounds, and convictions which did not arise out of religious conviction. In effect, his disqualification from accountancy arose out of the applicant's exercise of his right to freedom of religion. The Court thus accepted that the facts in issue fell within the ambit of a Convention right.

The Court confirmed that the right not to be discriminated against is triggered not just when like situations are not treated alike but when dissimilar situations are treated the same. Although one could agree that there should be some restrictions as to who could practise as an accountant, the offence in question here, as it included no element of dishonesty or moral turpitude, was not such as would undermine the accountancy profession. In this case then, the applicant's exclusion from the accountancy profession was not justified. Fur-

[144] *Swedish Engine Drivers' Union* v. *Sweden*, ECHR, judgment of 6 February 1976, Series A No. 20, at p. 17.

[145] ECHR, judgment of 6 April 2000.

thermore, given that the applicant had already served a prison sentence, further sanction for the same offence would be disproportionate. The State could legislate more precisely so as to exclude cases such as this from the legislation prohibiting those convicted of a felony from practising accountancy.

In this case we see the Court applying its usual approach to discrimination, that of considering whether the policy has a legitimate aim and whether it is proportional. The difference here is, of course, rather than arguing that the two groups, 'normal' convicts and those convicted of a religious crime, were in an analogous situation the Court argued that the reverse was true. This decision would seem to be necessary if the right against discrimination is to be effective; to have held otherwise would in effect have allowed indirect discrimination on the basis of the applicant's religious freedom to continue indefinitely. Note, however, that this will not be true of all professional limitations, if there is a link between the nature of the religious belief and the goal pursued.[146] The Court has also ruled, in an admissibility decision, that where an individual was kept in custody for longer than the normal national rules permitted, this was not discrimination on the basis of the individual's membership of the Communist Party but related to the nature of the offences with which he was charged: terrorism.[147] Whether this rule was applied in an unequal manner so as to discriminate in practice against certain political views was not discussed.[148] *De facto* discrimination was, however, raised in a number of cases concerning the security forces in Northern Ireland, declared admissible this year.[149]

Hunt saboteurs—bound over to keep the peace—freedom of expression—quality of law—Article 10

Case No. 22. Hashman and Harrup case.[150] In this case against the UK, the Court held by sixteen votes to one that there had been a violation of Article 10 and unanimously that it was not necessary to discuss Article 11. The Court unanimously made an order for costs.

The applicants were hunt saboteurs. They were bound over to keep the peace and be of good behaviour. The concept of breach of the peace is a common law concept, which has been developed by case law. Behaviour '*contra bonos mores*' similarly has its basis in the common law. The applicants argued that there had been a violation of their freedom of expression and that had not been 'prescribed by law' as required by Article 10(2).

[146] See *Riondel* v. *Switzerland*, ECHR, decision of 14 October 1999; withdrawal of licence to run a private agency due to connections with a sect was declared inadmissible. Private security agencies have more power and authority than ordinary citizens and the sect was potentially destabilizing for public order.

[147] *Sanli & Erol* v. *Turkey* (Application 36760/97), ECHR, decision of 17 October 2000.

[148] See also *Mutlu and Yildiz* v. *Turkey* (Application 30495/96), ECHR, decision of 17 October 2000 and *Kalin, Gezer and Tebay* v. *Turkey* (Applications 24849, 24850 and 24941/94), ECHR, decision of 18 January 2000.

[149] See *Shanaghan and Kelly* v. *UK*, *supra* n. 9.

[150] ECHR, judgment of 25 November 1999.

The Court began its assessment by referring to the earlier case of *Steel*,[151] which had also concerned the activities of hunt saboteurs. Again it held that disrupting a hunt could constitute freedom of expression for the purposes of Article 10.[152] The binding over constituted an interference with that expression; the issue was whether the restriction was prescribed by law. The Court has repeatedly held that this element of Article 10(2) involves a qualitative element, as indeed we find in cases involving Articles 8, 9, and 11. The qualitative element relates to the precision of the domestic law—is its operation foreseeable in a given set of circumstances? Although the binding over order in *Steel* was considered 'lawful', the Court noted crucial differences between that case and this. In *Steel* the breach of the peace had occurred, here the binding over order was against potential future breaches of the peace and the Court has noted that particular care would be required when dealing with cases of prior restraint. The considerations identified in *Steel* regarding the imprecise nature of the requirement 'to be of good behaviour' were relevant. However, the phrase '*contra bonos mores*' is more imprecise than a requirement that somebody refrain from behaviour 'likely to cause annoyance', which is conduct defined by reference to its likely effects. Behaviour '*contra bonos mores*' may not have any such effects, and the assessment of such behaviour is much more subjective, being judged by what is wrong rather than right in the opinion of the majority of fellow citizens. For that reason, the national rules in this case were held not to have satisfied the qualitative requirement of being in accordance with 'law'.

This area is especially problematic because public order offences by their nature are hard to define in advance, so that rules that deal with this area need to some extent to be flexible to prevent evasion. Nonetheless, individuals need to know what rules would apply to them and when. Unlike *Steel*, *Hashman and Harrup* fell on the wrong side of the line as to the acceptable degree of flexibility in domestic law.

Broadcasting licence—cable networks—freedom of expression—Article 10

Case No. 23. Tele 1 Privatfernsehgesellschaft mbH case.[153] In this case against Austria, the Court held unanimously that there had been a violation of Article 10 in respect of the period prior to 1 August 1996 but no violation in respect of the period thereafter. The Court made an award of costs but dismissed the rest of the claim for just satisfaction.

The applicant applied for a broadcasting licence for the Vienna area. The Telecommunications Office dismissed the request on the basis that only ORF, the Austrian national broadcasting corporation, had been authorized under federal law. Tele 1's appeals were dismissed. It claimed that there had been a

[151] *Steel* v. *The United Kingdom*, ECHR, judgment of 23 September 1998 and this *Year Book*, 70 (1999), p. 375.

[152] One of the Commissioners dissented from this viewpoint, stating that the hunt saboteurs were not exercising a right, but infringing on the rights of others. There is, however, a qualitative difference between a fundamental right such as freedom of expression and the right to hunt, as the Court has noted in previous case law: see *Chassagnou* v. *France*, above, n. 139.

[153] ECHR, judgment of 21 September 2000.

violation of Article 10, relying on a number of the Court's previous decisions in this area.[154]

Before the Court it was accepted that the refusal of a broadcasting licence was an interference with the applicant's freedom of expression; the question was whether the interference was justified. Note that Article 10(1) specifically refers to the right of Contracting States to require the licensing of broadcasting, television or cinema, to satisfy not only concerns about spectrum scarcity but also other public policy concerns regarding quality and balance of programming. As the Court made clear in *Lentia*,[155] however, this proviso must be understood in the light of Article 10(2). In principle the monopoly system in Austria could contribute to such policy objectives, as the Court had previously held.[156] The question therefore was whether the requirements of Article 10(2) were additionally satisfied. The first element of Article 10(2) was satisfied, as it was clear that the refusal was based on Austrian legislation that the Austrian federal constitutional court had consistently interpreted to mean that broadcasting must be specifically authorized by federal legislation. It was not contested that the aim of the legislation was legitimate. It remained to determine whether the restrictions were proportionate.

The Court dealt with the case in three periods. During the first period, until 1 August 1996, the position in Austria was the same as in the *Lentia* decision in which the Court had found a violation of Article 10, ORF having a monopoly over all forms of broadcasting. The Court accordingly found a violation in this case in respect of that period.

During the second period, private broadcasters were allowed to broadcast via cable networks, whilst terrestrial analogue capacity was reserved to ORF, a division which the Government claimed was justified on the basis of spectrum. The Court has held that given technological changes, a monopoly over all forms of broadcasting can no longer be justified on spectrum scarcity grounds. Such a monopoly is not in issue here; the question is whether the reservation of terrestrial capacity to ORF was acceptable. In this context the applicant argued that cable is not comparable to terrestrial broadcasting in terms of viewer accessibility. Implicitly this is an argument that it is not enough to be able to broadcast; people must be able to access the broadcasts. The Court implicitly accepted that this was a relevant point, reflecting its stance in earlier judgments that the corollary of freedom of expression is the right to receive information.[157] It seems, however, that there is a limit to this argument; the Court noted that almost all households receiving television in Vienna have the possibility to be connected to the cable network, although in practice only 50 per cent did so. The applicant emphasized this latter point, highlighting the costs associated with connection to the network. Nonetheless, the Court held that because the private operators had a viable alternative to broadcast via the cable networks, the restriction of the terrestrial capacity to ORF was not disproportionate to the aims pursued.

[154] *Informationsverein Lentia* v. *Austria*, ECHR, judgment of 24 November 1993, Series A No. 276 and this *Year Book*, 65 (1994), p. 517. See also *Radio ABC* v. *Austria*, ECHR, judgment of 20 October 1997, *Reports of Judgments and Decisions* 1997–VI and this *Year Book*, 69 (1998), p. 391.

[155] Ibid.

[156] Ibid.

[157] *Autronic AG* v. *Switzerland*, ECHR, Series A No. 178.

The third period related to the new legislation permitting cable and satellite broadcasting. Given the applicant had not notified any cable activities nor applied to broadcast by satellite, the Court held it unnecessary to rule on the third period, as it is not its task to rule *in abstracto* whether legislation is compatible with the Convention.[158]

There has been a tendency among private broadcasters to use both European Community law[159] and Convention rights to try to gain access to broadcasting networks and to dismantle the advantages of the former state broadcasting monopolies. The Court has accepted that spectrum scarcity arguments alone will no longer justify absolute monopolies, but it is equally clear that private broadcasters cannot use Article 10 to demand specific types of access. The precise consequences of the ruling in this case as regards the viability of cable networks are not clear. In particular, to what extent is the ability of the audience to access the network relevant; would the Court have ruled similarly where there was no cable network, or where a cable operator had been granted the right to lay a cable network, but where that operator had not done so yet?

Campaign of harassment against newspaper—positive obligations—freedom of expression—Article 10

Case No. 24. Özgür Gündem case.[160] In this case against Turkey the Court held unanimously that there had been a violation of Article 10 but that there was no violation of Article 14. The Court made an award in respect of pecuniary and non-pecuniary loss together with an award for damages.

The application was brought by the editor-in-chief, assistant editor-in-chief and the owners of a newspaper, 'Özgür Gündem'. The newspaper ceased publication in 1994, as a result of a systematic campaign against it which had involved the killing, harassment and intimidation of journalists and distributors as well as acts of arson, detention of journalists and the use of unjustified legal proceedings such as the seizure of assets. Numerous petitions to the authorities remained unanswered. The Government denied State involvement in any of these actions, denied that some of them took place and further argued that investigations and, in some cases, criminal proceedings were pending. A report commissioned by the Prime Minister, the *Susurluk* report, however, described acquiescence by State authorities in unlawful activities, some of which targeted Özgür Gündem.

In this case, the Government challenged the applicants' and the Commission's assessment of facts. It denied that any weight could be given to the *Susurluk* report. The Court noted that although the report could not be relied upon to prove any particular incident, it had to be regarded as a serious attempt to provide information on problems associated with the fight against terrorism. To that extent it supported the applicants' claims that they and the newspaper were at risk from unlawful violence. The Court concluded that from 1992 onwards there were numerous acts of violence towards the newspaper and those

[158] See *Radio ABC* v. *Austria*, above, n. 154.

[159] See e.g. Case C–260/89 *Ellinkiki Radiophonia Tileorassi AE (ERT)* v. *Dimotiki Etairia Pliroforissis (DEP) and Sotirius Kouvelas* [1991] ECR I–2925.

[160] ECHR, judgment 16 March 2000.

associated with it and that these acts were, at the least, tolerated by the authorities.

The Court went on to refer to its jurisprudence in respect of many articles, such as Articles 8[161] and 11[162] and, more recently, Articles 2[163] and 3,[164] to the effect that there may be positive obligations inherent in an effective respect for the rights concerned. In the case of Article 10, given the key role freedom of expression plays in the proper functioning of democracy, effective protection of this right may not be limited to the State's abstention from interference but may also require positive measures, even as regards the sphere between individuals, as it has previously been found to do in the context of Article 8.[165]

In this case the authorities must have been aware that the newspaper and those associated with it were under attack. Very little was done in response, especially given the seriousness of the attacks. In particular, the investigations of indiviual prosecutors into specific incidents could not constitute an adequate response to a concerted campaign against the newspaper, which was tolerated, if not supported, by the authorities. Even were the newspaper supporting the PKK, as the Government alleged, this did not justify the failure on the authorities' part to take any action.[166] Given the general situation in Turkey and that Government's attempts to disassociate itself from certain events, this extension of Article 10 is not surprising.

The Court then considered a particular incident in which the police raided the newspaper. The Court found this incident, which disrupted the newspaper for two days, to be an interference with the right to freedom of expression which, although 'prescribed by law' for a legitimate aim, was disproportionate. The Court criticized, in particular, the seizure of the newspaper's archives, documentation and library, for which no justification was provided, and the blanket detention of all employees, including the cook and cleaner. The Court then reviewed in detail the prosecutions brought on various occasions by the authorities in respect of articles and cartoons published in the paper. Although the interference in the shape of these prosecutions might be based on law for the purposes of a legitimate aim, given the importance of the press, the Court found many of these prosecutions to be disproportionate and unjustified.

LORNA WOODS

[161] *Gaskin* v. *The United Kingdom*, ECHR, judgment of 7 July 1989, Series A No. 160, at paras. 42–9.

[162] *Plattform 'Ärzte für das Leben'* v. *Austria*, ECHR, judgment of 21 June 1988, Series A No. 139, at para. 32.

[163] *McCann and Others* v. *The United Kingdom*, above, n. 20 at para. 161 as regards the obligation to take steps to undertake an effective investigation and *Osman* v. *The United Kingdom*, ECHR, above, n. 11, pp. 3159–61, at paras. 115–17 regarding the right to life.

[164] *Assenov and Others* v. *Bulgaria*, ECHR, above, n. 18.

[165] *X and Y* v. *The Netherlands*, ECHR, judgment of 26 March 1985, Series A No. 91, at para. 23 and this *Year Book*, 56 (1985), p. 344.

[166] Contrast with the admissibility decision in *Hogefeld* v. *Germany* (Application 3502/97), ECHR, decision of 20 January 2000.

UNITED KINGDOM MATERIALS ON INTERNATIONAL LAW 2000*

Edited by GEOFFREY MARSTON[1]

[*Editorial Notes*:

1. From its start in 1978 and up to and including 1996, the materials in UKMIL were classified on the basis of the *Model Plan for the Classification of Documents concerning State Practice in the Field of Public International Law* adopted by the Committee of Ministers of the Council of Europe in its Resolution (68) 17 of 28 June 1968. The Committee of Ministers considered that developments in public international law since 1968 made it necessary to amend the Model Plan. Accordingly, by Recommendation (97)11 of 12 June 1997, it adopted an Amended Model Plan as a contribution by the Council of Europe towards implementing General Assembly Resolution 2099(XX) on technical assistance to promote the teaching, study, dissemination and wider understanding of international law and towards the United Nations Decade of International Law from 1990 to 1999. The present issue of UKMIL is based on the 1997 Amended Model Plan.
2. The structure of Parts Thirteen and Seventeen has been considerably revised.
3. Attention is drawn to the editorial note in UKMIL 1983, p. 361. Delay in the appearance of the bound volumes of the *Parliamentary Debates* has not made it possible to make any corrections which might be necessary to the column references in volumes 358 and 359 of the House of Commons Debates and in volume 620 of the House of Lords Debates.]

[1] LL M, Ph.D. (Lond.): Lecturer in Law, University of Cambridge; Fellow of Sidney Sussex College. The assistance of Ms S. C. Hulton of the Legal Advisers, Foreign and Commonwealth Office, the Treaty and News Departments, Foreign and Commonwealth Office, and the staff of the Official Publications Department, University Library, Cambridge, is gratefully acknowledged.

Index

Appendices

Abbreviations

HC Debs.	*Hansard*, House of Commons Debates (6th series)
HL Debs.	*Hansard*, House of Lords Debates (5th series)
Cmnd.	Command Paper (5th series)
Cm	Command Paper (6th series)
UKMIL	*United Kingdom Materials on International Law*
TS	*United Kingdom Treaty Series*
EC	European Community
EU	European Union
FCO	Foreign and Commonwealth Office
WA	Written Answers
W	Written Answers (HC from vol. 339)
WH	Westminster Hall, debates held in

Part Two: II. *Sources and codification of international law—acquisition, preservation and loss of rights*

2/1

In reply to a question, the Minister of State, FCO, wrote:

We have established a good working relationship with the new Argentine Government. The Prime Minister has met President De la Rua twice. My right hon. Friend the Secretary of State has met Rodriguez Giavarini. I attended the Argentine Presidential inauguration and the Secretary of State for Defence has met the Argentine President and Defence Minister.

On these and other occasions both sides have reaffirmed their commitment to the Joint Statement of July 1999 and to continue our dialogue on issues of common interest.

This does not affect our sovereignty of the Falkland Islands or our commitment to the Islanders' right to determine their own future.

(HC Debs., vol. 345, col. 724W: 8 March 2000)

2/2

On 4 July 2000, the UK and the French Republic signed an Agreement concerning fishing in the Bay of Granville. An Exchange of Notes of the same date contained the following provision:

. . . the conclusion of the Agreement is without prejudice to the position of either Government on the legal regime applicable to fishing activities in the Sark Box or on historic fishing activities in the Sark Box.

(Cm 5025, p. 37)

Part Three: I. B. *The law of treaties—definition, conclusion and entry into force—conclusion, including signature, ratification and accession*

3/1

In June 2000, the FCO issued a further edition of a booklet entitled *Treaties and MOUs: Guidance on Practice and Procedures* from which the following passages are taken:

SIGNATURE OF TREATIES

Unless the treaty provides that it enters into force on signature, by signing a treaty a State shows that it is in agreement with the text, but it is not bound by it until the treaty has been ratified and has entered into force. The State is not obliged to ratify it. The United Kingdom, however, does not sign a treaty unless it has a reasonably firm intention of ratifying.

In international law a Head of State, Head of Government or Foreign Minister may sign a treaty in his or her own right. Anyone else needs to produce 'Full Powers' from one of those three. In UK practice, the Queen does not sign treaties, but the Prime Minister sometimes does. Full Powers are normally signed by the Foreign and Commonwealth Secretary except for certain EU treaties which are drawn up between Heads of State and therefore require a Queen's Full Power. FCO Ministers and certain UK Representatives hold general Full Powers giving them authority to sign any treaty (subject to the approval of the Foreign and Commonwealth Secretary in each case). Anyone else signing a treaty on behalf of the UK requires a special Full Power enabling them to sign the specific treaty.

The Full Powers document is drawn up by FCO Treaty Section and (unless it is for signature by the Queen) submitted by the lead FCO department to the Foreign and Commonwealth Secretary for signature. Other Government Departments should therefore approach the appropriate FCO department in the first instance at Director level requesting Full Powers. They should give the name, title, position and any decorations of the person to be named in the Full Power and also attach a copy of the treaty.

Full Powers are not required for a treaty in the form of an Exchange of Notes. But a non-FCO Minister or official should not sign without the specific authorisation of the Foreign and Commonwealth Secretary or an FCO Minister.

RATIFICATION OF TREATIES

Treaties are frequently subject to ratification, acceptance, approval, or the mutual notification of the completion of procedures. In addition, multilateral treaties may be acceded to, which does not involve signature. The date of entry into force is determined by the provisions of each treaty. It is important to note that from the date a treaty enters into force for the United Kingdom, it places international obligations on the UK vis-à-vis the other party or parties. It is essential therefore that the UK is in a position to fulfil its obligations as from that date, and does not become legally bound until it has the necessary domestic powers to give effect to the provisions of the treaty; otherwise it will be in breach of its international obligations. Pleading insufficiency of domestic law is not, in international law, an acceptable excuse for failure to implement the provisions of a treaty.

Ratification: follows signature and signifies the consent of a State to be bound by the treaty.

Signature: is the act whereby a State expresses its agreement in principle with a treaty, but not its consent to be bound by it, unless the treaty provides that it will come into force on signature. A State which has signed a treaty which is subject to ratification is not obliged to ratify. However, UK policy is not to sign without a reasonably firm intention to ratify.

(Text provided by the FCO)

3/2

The Legal Adviser, FCO, Mr M. C. Wood, gave evidence to the HC Procedure Committee considering the Parliamentary scrutiny of treaties. Speaking on 13 July 2000, Mr Wood stated:

Just to be clear about the scope of the Ponsonby Rule, it does not of course apply to treaties that are not subject to this two-stage process of signature followed by ratification or other equivalent procedure. There are treaties that enter into force directly upon signature or upon exchange of notes. These are very often the ones of least importance. Certainly in our case they are the ones that do not require any Parliamentary legislation. There can occasionally be more important ones, the urgent ones, but I just wanted to clarify that there are a proportion of treaties, perhaps a third, that come into force on signature and are not subject to the Ponsonby Rule. But then it is very important to recall the point that the Minister made at the outset. Under our system any treaty that has to take effect as part of United Kingdom law requires legislation. The legislation has to be in place before we commit the Government in to this. So the absolutely standard practice of the Government is to never move to undertake a legal obligation under a treaty that requires implementation in our law without first ensuring that the necessary legislation is in place. That is a very important safeguard in the system.

(*Parliamentary Papers*, 1999–2000, *HC, Paper 210*, pp. 21–3)

Part Three: I. C. *The law of treaties—definition, conclusion and entry into force—reservations, declarations and objections*

(See also **9/6**, **17/8**)

3/3

On 17 May 1999, the depositary of the Protocol Additional to the Geneva Convention of 12 August 1949 and relating to the Protection of Victims of International Armed Conflicts (Protocol I) received the following declaration from the UK Government:

The Government of Great Britain and Northern Ireland declares that it recognises *ipso facto* and without special agreement, in relation to any other High Contracting Party accepting the same obligation, the competence of the International Fact-Finding Commission to inquire into allegations by such other Party, as authorised by Article 90 of Protocol I Additional to the Geneva Conventions of 1949.

(TS No. 88 (1999): Cm 4677, p. 51)

3/4

On its accession on 9 September 1998 to the Vienna Convention on the Law of Treaties, 1969, the Republic of Cuba made the following reservation:

The Government of the Republic of Cuba enters an explicit reservation to the procedure established under article 66 of the Convention, since it believes that any dispute should be settled by any means adopted by agreement between the parties to the dispute; the Republic of Cuba therefore cannot accept solutions which provide means for one of the parties, without the consent of the other, to submit the dispute to procedures for judicial settlement, arbitration and conciliation.

On 19 November 1999, the UK Government sent the following Communication to the depositary:

The Government of the United Kingdom of Great Britain and Northern Ireland objects to the reservation aforementioned. The Government of the United Kingdom wishes in this context to recall their declaration of 5 June 1987 (in respect of the accession of the Union of the Soviet Socialist Republics) which in accordance with its terms applies to the reservation above, and will apply similarly to any like reservation which any other State may formulate. Accordingly, the United Kingdom does not consider that the treaty relations between it and the Republic of Cuba include Part V of the Convention.

(TS No. 88 (1999); Cm 4677, p. 43: see also UKMIL 1987 pp. 578–9)

3/5

In reply to the question whether Her Majesty's Government planned to lift any of the reservations which it had made to UN treaties, the Minister of State, FCO, wrote:

We are committed to the international rule of law and to the United Kingdom's obligations under international law. We keep those commitments and the terms in which they are entered into under review. We have no specific plans at the present time to lift any reservations to United Nations treaties.

(HC Debs., vol. 354, col. 425W: 24 July 2000)

3/6

Speaking on 26 October 2000 in the UN General Assembly in a debate on the subjects of oceans and the law of the sea, the representative of France, on behalf of the EU, stated in respect of the Convention on the Law of the Sea:

. . . we note with concern that some States have acceded to the Convention and not to the Agreement relating to the implementation of Part XI. We call upon those States to accede to the Agreement as soon as possible. Moreover, a number of States have made statements that affect the legal scope of provisions of the Convention. Article 309 of the Convention states that no reservations or exceptions may be made to the Convention. The European Union thus stresses that such statements are without legal force. Similarly, the espousal or introduction in the national law of States parties or in international agreements of provisions that run counter to the Convention is unacceptable to us.

(A/55/PV. 42, p. 9 (translation))

Part Three: II. A. *The law of treaties—observance, application and interpretation—observance*

3/7

In reply to the question whether it is the policy of Her Majesty's Government to assist British companies to enforce judgments made against other Governments by the International Centre for the Settlement of Investment Disputes, the Minister of State, FCO, wrote:

We cannot comment on cases which are the subject of legal proceedings at the International Centre for the Settlement of Investment Disputes (ICSID). Her Majesty's Government expects any State with whom we have a Investment Promotion and Protection Agreement, to take seriously its treaty obligations and, where such a State is involved in a dispute covered by that treaty, to co-operate fully with any international arbitration procedures and rulings.

(HC Debs., vol. 352, col. 227W: 21 June 2000)

3/8

In the course of a radio interview on 25 August 2000, the Secretary of State for Foreign and Commonwealth Affairs, Mr Robin Cook, was asked about matters concerning the British Indian Ocean Territory. He replied:

There is a treaty with the United States which was signed in the nineteen sixties which did give them use of the islands for fifty years for defence purposes and we take our treaty obligations very seriously. And we can not unilaterally walk away from that treaty obligation nor do I intend to do so.

(Text provided by the FCO)

Part Three: II. B. *The law of treaties—observance, application and interpretation—application*

(See **6/2**)

Part Three: IV. *The law of treaties—breach and its consequences*

3/9

The following question was asked:

Whether any treaty provisions have been broken by any of the other member states of the European Union which sought to impose sanctions against Austria; if so, which treaty provisions were broken; and by whom?

In reply, the Parliamentary Under Secretary of State, FCO, wrote in material part:

The European Court of Justice has from time to time found that member states have breached the EC Treaties. Details are contained in the European Commission's 16th Annual Report on monitoring the application of Community law 1998. A copy of the report, which was submitted to Parliament on 20 September 1999, is available in the Library of the House.

(HL Debs., vol. 610, *WA 207*): 15 March 2000)

3/10

In reply to the question whether Austria has broken any law which would justify sanctions by the other 14 members of the EU, including the UK, the same Minister wrote:

We are not aware that Austria has breached any European Community law or any of its international commitments. However, the measures introduced by the 14 member states of the EU were intended to send a signal of concern over the inclusion of a far-Right party in the new Austrian Government. Along with our EU partners we are committed to act against xenophobia and discrimination and have the obligation to express concern where we see the danger of this arising.

(HL Debs., vol. 611, *WA 35*: 23 March 2000)

3/11

In reply to the question what are the basic principles attached to EU membership, breach of which encourages EU sanctions, the Minister of State, FCO, wrote:

The principles on which the EU is founded are listed in Article 6(1) of the Treaty on European Union (TEU). These are liberty, democracy, respect for human rights and fundamental freedoms, and the rule of law. A serious and persistent breach of these principles can lead to measures under Article 7 TEU.

(HC Debs., vol. 355, col. 147W: 23 October 2000)

Part Three: V. C. *The law of treaties—invalidity, termination and suspension of treaties—termination and suspension of operation, denunciation and withdrawal*

3/12

On 4 July 2000, the UK and the French Republic signed an Agreement concerning fishing in the Bay of Granville. Article 9 of this Agreement reads:

Earlier Agreements

Upon the entry into force of this Agreement, the following treaties or other agreements, to the extent that they are still in force, shall automatically terminate:

— the Convention, done at Paris on 2 August 1839, for defining and regulating the limits of the Exclusive Right of the Oyster and other Fishery on the Coasts of Great Britain and France;
— the Declaration, adopted at London on 23 June 1843, approving the Fishery Regulations of 24 May 1843 for the guidance of the Fishermen of Great Britain and of France in the Seas lying between the Coasts of the two Countries;
— the Declaration, done at London on 20 December 1928, regarding the Limits of French Fisheries in Granville Bay;
— the Agreement, done at London on 30 January 1951, regarding Rights of Fishery in areas of the Ecrehos and Minquiers;
— the Exchange of Notes, done at London on 10 April 1964, concerning the Status of Previous Fisheries Agreements in relation to the Fisheries Convention opened for signature in London from 9 March to 10 April 1964; and
— the Exchange of Notes, done at Paris on 24 February 1965, concerning the question of the habitual rights of French fishing vessels within British fishery limits.

(Cm 5025, p. 11)

Part Three: VIII. *The law of treaties—consensual arrangements other than treaties*

3/13

The following passages appear in a booklet published by the FCO in June 2000 entitled *Treaties and MOUs: Guidance on Practice and Procedures:*

WHAT IS AN MOU?

An MOU records international 'commitments', but in a form and with wording which expresses an intention that it is not to be legally binding. An MOU is used where it is considered preferable to avoid the formalities of a treaty—for example, where there are detailed provisions which change frequently or the matters dealt with are essentially of a technical or administrative character; in matters of defence or technology where there is a need for such documents to be classified; or where a treaty requires subsidiary documents to fill out the details. Like a treaty, an MOU can have a variety of names and can also be either in the form of an Exchange of Notes or a single document. However, the formalities which surround treaty-making do not apply to it and it is not usually published. The term 'MOU' is short for Memorandum of Understanding, which is the most common name for non-legally binding instruments. (NB: Confusingly some treaties also have that name.)

. . .

Memorandum of Understanding (MOU) or Arrangement: a form frequently used to record informal arrangements between States on matters which are inappropriate for inclusion in treaties or where the form is more convenient than a treaty (e.g. for confidentiality). They may be drawn up as a single document using non-treaty terms, signed on behalf of two or more Governments, or consist of an exchange of notes or letters recording an understanding reached between two Governments.

(Text provided by the FCO)

Part Four: II. A. *Relationship between international law and internal law—application and implementation of international law in internal law—treaties*

4/1

In reply to the question why Her Majesty's Government has decided not to subscribe to the 1970 UNESCO and 1995 Unidroit Convention on the illicit traffic of cultural materials, the Government Minister in the House of Lords wrote:

As Her Majesty's Government announced in another place on 7 February 2000, after a lengthy inter-departmental consultation, we concluded that the UK should not become a signatory to the Unidroit Convention due to the conflicts with our current law. We noted that, in order to implement the convention, changes to our limitation periods and to our personal property law would be required, resulting in a special regime for cultural objects and arguably a less generous position for the original, rightful owners of objects which were later stolen. However, Her Majesty's Government have undertaken to consider the possible options for an alternative legislative approach which would share some of the objectives of the Unidroit Convention.

Following representations made by the noble Lord, I also said that I was willing to look again at the difficulties of implementing the UNESCO convention and that we would be looking at a range of options which might form the basis of an alternative approach to the convention.

(HL Debs., vol. 612, *WA 216*: 8 May 2000)

4/2

In reply to a question, the Secretary of State for the Home Department wrote:

The Human Rights Act 1998 gives further effect in United Kingdom law to rights and freedoms in the European Convention on Human Rights. Successive Governments have sought to comply with the provisions of the Convention since 1951. Therefore we should not expect major changes to have to be made once the Human Rights Act is fully in force. Following its enactment, Departments have reviewed their legislation, and procedures in the light of the Human Rights Act. Where changes have been judged appropriate, these have been made or are in hand.

(HC Debs., vol. 354, col. 180W: 19 July 2000)

4/3

In moving the approval by the House of Lords of the European Communities (Definition of Treaties) (Agreement between the European Community and its Member States and the Swiss Confederation on the Free Movement of Persons) Order 2000, the Parliamentary Under-Secretary of State, Home Office, Lord Bassam, observed:

. . . this order enables the United Kingdom to press ahead with ratification of an agreement with Switzerland on the free movement of people. The agreement is one of seven bilateral agreements between the EU member states and Switzerland which are the culmination of several years of careful negotiation.

It is the latter agreement which concerns us today. This agreement is the only one of the seven agreements which requires individual ratification by each member state. The ratification process is necessary because the agreement combines Community and national competence.

The free movement of persons agreement was laid before Parliament as a treaty earlier this month. The draft Order in Council is the next significant step in the process. The order provides for the implementation of the agreement by specifying it as a Community treaty under the European Communities Act 1972.

The United Kingdom hopes to show its commitment to those agreements by early ratification. All seven agreements will come into force simultaneously once ratification of the free movement of persons agreement has been completed in all member states. So far as we know, only Austria and Switzerland are ahead of the United Kingdom in completing their ratification procedures.

The agreements will lead to an approximation between Switzerland and the member states of the EU which will be of benefit to us all. The individual agreements are concerned with air transport, land transport, trade in agricultural products, elimination of technical barriers to trade, public procurement, research in science and technology, and free movement of people.

(HL Debs., vol. 619, cols. 1088–9: 24 November 2000)

Part Five: I. A. 3. *Subjects of international law—States—status and powers—territorial integrity*

5/1

In reply to the question put to Her Majesty's Government 'whether they regard Maskhadov's government as the only legitimate authority of Chechnya', the Parliamentary Under-Secretary of State, FCO, wrote:

We recognise Chechnya as an integral part of the Russian Federation. The UK position is shared by our international partners. President Maskhadov was elected in 1997 in a process recognised as democratic by the Organisation for Security and Co-operation in Europe (OSCE).

(HL Debs., vol. 611, *WA 135*: 5 April 2000; see also ibid., vol. 612, *WA 25*: 11 April 2000)

5/2

In reply to a question, the Parliamentary Under-Secretary of State, FCO, wrote in part:

As all Ministers he met made clear, the UK fully supports Belize's sovereignty and territorial integrity. We welcome the talks currently taking place between Belize and Guatemala under the auspices of the Organisation of American States. We also welcome the meeting that took place on 7 July between the Guatemalan and Belizian military, and hope that this signals the full resumption of peaceful military to military contacts, and a positive dialogue to resolve this dispute.

(HL Debs., vol. 615, *WA 94*: 19 July 2000)

5/3

In reply to a question, the Minister of State, FCO, wrote:

We welcome the withdrawal of Israeli troops from Lebanon, in compliance with UNSCRs 425 and 426, as demanded by UNSCR 520. We look forward to the Lebanese Government taking measures to assert its authority throughout its territory. We support UNSCR 520's call for the sovereignty, territorial integrity, unity and political independence of Lebanon to be respected. We also support the Resolution's reaffirmation of support for the rights of the civilian population of Lebanon.

(HC Debs., vol. 354, col. 187W: 19 July 2000)

5/4

In reply to a question on the subject of the territorial dispute between Belize and Guatemala, the Minister of State, FCO, wrote in part:

The United Kingdom continues to support Belize's sovereignty and territorial integrity and will continue to provide legal assistance in Belize's efforts to demarcate its land and maritime boundaries.

(HC Debs., vol. 356, col. 182W: 7 November 2000)

Part Five: I. A. 4. *Subjects of international law—States—status and powers—non-intervention in domestic jurisdiction*

5/5

In reply to a question on the subject of Mr James Mawdsley, a British national detained in Burma (Myanmar), the Minister of State, FCO, wrote:

We continue to do all we properly can to ensure that James's rights are respected but we cannot intervene in the Burmese judicial process just as we would not allow them to intervene in ours.

We remain appalled by the lack of democracy and human rights in Burma: we are at the forefront of international action to press the Burmese regime to improve the situation.

(HC Debs., vol. 346, col. 135W: 14 March 2000)

Part Five: I. B. 4. *Subjects of international law—States—recognition—non-recognition and its effects*

5/6

In the course of a debate on the subject of Taiwan, the Minister of State, FCO, Mr John Battle, said in part:

It is fair to say that the question of Taiwan's relationship with WHO, or with any other international organisation or element in the international community, cannot be considered without taking into account the complex issue of Taiwan's international status and the effect that that has on Taiwan's ability to play a fully recognised international role. The whole international community, not only the UK, are involved in that issue.

The House will be aware of the UK Government's formal policy on the status of Taiwan, which was laid down in 1972 when the UK upgraded relations with the People's Republic of China to ambassadorial level. In a joint communique agreed with the Chinese Government and announced on 13 March 1972, the UK Government of the day stated that the UK recognised the Government of the People's Republic of China as the sole legal Government of China, and acknowledged the position of the People's Republic of China that Taiwan is a province of China. That remains our policy and forms the foundation of our dealings with Taiwan.

It follows that the UK has no formal political or diplomatic relations with Taiwan. That is not an unusual or unique position; it is shared by most other countries in the world, including our European partners and other close partners such as the United States. Although the precise formulation may differ slightly from one country to another, all have adopted a similar view and operate under similar constraints in their political dealings with Taiwan and its authorities. Only a handful of countries currently afford full diplomatic recognition to Taiwan as the 'Republic of China'. That position is unlikely to change significantly in the near future.

Taiwan's lack of widespread international recognition has obvious consequences for Taiwan's aspirations to membership of international organisations, especially those, such as WHO, whose membership is limited to states. As neither the UK nor the United Nations, where the People's Republic of China has had a seat since 1971, recognises Taiwan as a state, it follows that we cannot support Taiwan's membership of international organisations that only states may join.

(HC Debs., vol. 343, cols. 247–8WH: 2 February 2000)

5/7

In reply to an oral question, the Minister of State, FCO, Mr John Battle, stated:

East Timor was invaded by Indonesia in 1975. The United Nations never recognised Indonesia's annexation of East Timor. In the UN-organised ballot of 30 August 1999, the East Timorese voted by an overwhelming majority to reject the autonomy proposal put forward by the Indonesian Government and in so doing indicated their clear desire for independence. The subsequent violence led to the intervention of a peacekeeping force. Indonesia relinquished all claim to East Timor on 20 October. UNTAET—the United Nations Transitional Administration in East Timor—is now established and is carrying out its mandate to prepare East Timor for independence.

(HC Debs., vol. 344, col. 764: 15 February 2000)

5/8

In reply to an oral question, the Parliamentary Under-Secretary of State, FCO, Baroness Scotland of Asthal, stated in material part:

Like most countries, we do not recognise Taiwan as an independent state. We acknowledge the position of the Chinese Government that Taiwan is a province of the People's Republic of China and recognise the Chinese Government as the sole legal government of China. Taiwan and the UK nevertheless enjoy an excellent relationship, particularly in the commercial and cultural spheres. We wish to build on that to our mutual benefit. We believe that the issue of Taiwan should be solved peacefully through dialogue by the Chinese people on the two sides of the Taiwan Strait. We are firmly opposed to the use of military means, and we make that view clear to the Chinese on every appropriate occasion.

(HL Debs., vol. 612, col. 75: 11 April 2000)

5/9

In the course of a press interview on the subject of Cyprus, held on 3 October 2000, the Minister of State, FCO, Mr Peter Hain, stated:

We have never recognised the so-called Republic of Northern Cyprus and we have no intention of doing so.

(Text provided by the FCO)

5/10

In reply to a question, the Government spokeswoman in the House of Lords wrote:

We do not recognise Taiwan as a state and therefore do not maintain diplomatic relations. In accordance with this position, neither the staff of the Taipei Representative Office in London nor their counterparts in the British Trade and Cultural Office in Taipei have diplomatic status. The tax and legal status of the staff of the Taipei Representative Office in London have been reviewed on a number of occasions. However, because of the constraints imposed by the special position of the Taipei Representative Office, it has not so far proved possible under UK law to find a way to accord staff working in the office tax and employment concessions comparable to those enjoyed by the UK staff of the British Trade and Cultural Office in Taipei.

(HL Debs., vol. 617, *WA 100*: 18 October 2000)

Part Five: I. D. 5. (b). (vii). *Subjects of international law—States—formation, identity, continuity, extinction and succession of States—effects of State succession—responsibility*

5/11

In reply to an oral question on the subject of the Belize-Guatemala border dispute, the Minister of State, FCO, Mr John Battle, stated in relevant part:

I want to emphasise that the United Kingdom has no legal responsibilities in relation to Guatemala's border dispute with Belize, which goes back to 1859. However, we are ready to give diplomatic assistance to both sides to bring about a peaceful solution. That is our role, and we will continue to work towards it.

(HC Debs., vol. 348, col. 174: 11 April 2000)

Part Five: II. A. 1. (b). *Subjects of international law—international organizations—general—status and powers—privileges and immunities of the organization*

5/12

In moving the consideration by the Third Standing Committee on Delegated Legislation of the draft Organisation for Joint Armament

Co-operation (Immunities and Privileges) Order 2000, the Minister of State, FCO, Mr John Battle, stated:

That the Committee has considered the draft Organisation for Joint Armament Co-operation (Immunities and Privileges) Order 2000.

The order was laid before the House on 7 March. It will enable the Government to ratify the convention on the establishment of the Organisation for Joint Armament Co-operation, which the Government provisionally accepted on 9 September 1998. The draft order is made under the International Organisations Act 1968 and will give effect in United Kingdom law to the privileges and immunities granted by the convention. The privileges and immunities granted are necessary for the organisation, its staff and experts, as well as the representatives of member states, to carry out their functions. In accordance with section 1(6)(a) of the International Organisations Act 1968, the privileges and immunities conferred by the draft order are no greater in extent than those required by the convention or those authorised by the Act. The headquarters of the organisation are in Bonn, Germany. The organisation currently employs 30 staff, including five British nationals.

The Organisation for Joint Armament Co-operation is known by its French acronym, OCCAR. It was launched under the previous Conservative Government as a defence procurement collaboration between the United Kingdom, Germany, France, and Italy in November 1996. In joining this work, the United Kingdom aimed to participate in setting up a body which, in the words of the then Minister for Defence Procurement:

> Added value not bureaucracy; one which will lead to more efficient and effective collaborative ventures than those seen to date, producing equipment which can compete with the best in the world.

The aim of the organisation is to bring the best together and the purpose of its formal status is to allow it to place and manage contracts in its own name and to employ its own staff. That should lead to synergy in the range of skills and techniques based on best international practice.

All four member states signed the OCCAR convention at the Farnborough air show on 9 September 1998. The text was published and presented to Parliament, Command Paper 4367, in June 1999, under cover of an explanatory memorandum, approved by the then Minister for Defence Procurement. Subsequently, the House of Commons Defence Committee has examined the development of OCCAR and the implications of the convention. The Committee's report was published on 6 December 1999 and recommended that, subject to certain provisos that will be met, the convention should be ratified. The report concluded that the House should give its approval to the present order to allow for United Kingdom ratification.

The convention is open to other European states, and the Netherlands and Belgium have already indicated their interest in becoming partners in due course. It sets out, among other things, the founding principles, and the general organisation and objectives of OCCAR. The key aim is to strengthen the competitiveness of European defence technology and its industrial base, pulling together where possible.

An important commitment in article 6 is that each member state is obliged to give preference to equipment in whose development it has participated within OCCAR when meeting the requirements of its armed forces. The basic principle of OCCAR is to improve the effectiveness of project management in collaborative projects. The order ensures that its staff can move backwards and forwards in Britain under privileges and immunity regulations. All four member states have signed the convention and agreed that OCCAR shall have a legal personality and that its staff and experts, as well as representatives of member states, shall enjoy the privileges and immunities set out in annex I to the convention, article 40. The privileges and immunities are similar to those accorded to all the other international organisations, and are necessary for us to conform with our international obligations. There are 33 other organisations that have the same privileges and immunities. The proposal would bring OCCAR into line with them.

I strongly commend the draft order to the Committee. It is not about defence procurement strategy, but about the team of people in the organisation having access to privileges and immunities. I hope that this modest, non-controversial proposal will have the full support of all members of the Committee.

(HC Debs., Third Standing Committee on Delegated Legislation, 23 March 2000, cols. 3–4)

5/13

The Organisation for Joint Armament Cooperation (Immunities and Privileges) Order 2000 (Statutory Instrument No. 1105 of 2000) was made on 19 April 2000. An Explanatory Note attached to the Order read:

This Order confers privileges and immunities on the Organisation for Joint Armament Cooperation, on representatives of its Members, its members of staff and experts. These privileges and immunities are conferred in accordance with the Convention between the Government of the United Kingdom of Great Britain and Northern Ireland, the Government of the French Republic, the Government of the Federal Republic of Germany and the Government of the Italian Republic on the Establishment of the Organisation for Joint Armament Cooperation (Organisation Conjointe de Cooperation en Matière d'Armament) OCCAR (Cm. 4367). The Order will enable Her Majesty's Government to give effect to that Convention and will come into force on the date on which that Convention enters into force.

5/14

In moving the approval by the House of Lords of the European Court of Human Rights (Immunities and Privileges) Order 2000 and the International Seabed Authority (Immunities and Privileges) Order 2000, the Government spokesman, Lord Bach, remarked:

The first draft order is required to enable the Government to ratify two Council of Europe international agreements relating to the practical functioning of the new permanent European Court of Human Rights which came into being in Strasbourg on 1st November 1999. The draft order is made under the

International Organisations Act 1968 and will give effect in UK law to the privileges and immunities granted by the agreements. The privileges and immunities granted are necessary for the efficient functioning of the court. The draft order will confer only those privileges and immunities which we are internationally obliged to confer under the two agreements. The United Kingdom signed the agreements on 27th October 1999.

The two agreements concerned are: first, the European agreement relating to persons participating in proceedings of the European Court of Human Rights; and, secondly, the sixth protocol to the General Agreement on Privileges and Immunities of the Council of Europe. The text of each agreement was published and presented to Parliament in June under cover of explanatory memoranda.

Each agreement replaces a previous agreement to similar effect, which relates to the previous part-time commission and court. The changes made are designed simply to reflect the new situation where there is one single judicial body whose members are permanently resident in Strasbourg. The United Kingdom was party to the predecessor agreements and participated in the negotiations and voted for the adoption of the texts with a view to becoming party to the new agreements.

The European Agreement 1996, like its predecessor, is designed to give persons taking part in proceedings before the court—whether as parties, their lawyers or advisers, or as witnesses, experts or interveners—immunities and facilities to enable them fully to participate in the proceedings. The main immunities and facilities are: first, immunity from legal process in respect of statements made and documents submitted to the court; secondly, a right to correspond freely with the court, including for persons in detention; and, thirdly, free and unimpeded movement and travel for the purpose of attending and returning from proceedings before the court.

Previously the second, fourth and fifth protocols to the General Agreement on Privileges and Immunities guaranteed the necessary privileges and immunities to the members of the commission and the old court. The purpose of the sixth protocol is to do the same for the members of the new court. Because, however, they are permanent appointees and reside permanently in Strasbourg, it was considered appropriate to increase their privileges and immunities, to bring them in line, essentially, with those enjoyed by diplomatic envoys. In addition, under the protocol, documents and papers of the court, judges and registry that relate to the business of the court are inviolable.

The second draft order, the International Seabed Authority (Immunities and Privileges) Order 2000, will enable the Government to ratify the protocol on the privileges and immunities of the International Seabed Authority, which was published and presented to Parliament in February under cover of an explanatory memorandum.

The authority is an institution created by the United Nations Convention on the Law of the Sea, known as UNCLOS, to organise and control activities on the deep seabed beyond the jurisdiction of any state, protecting its resources as the common heritage of mankind. The UK is a member of the authority by virtue of its accession to UNCLOS in August 1997.

UNCLOS provides that the authority, to enable it to exercise its functions, shall enjoy in the territory of each state party certain privileges and immunities. The International Seabed Authority (Immunities and Privileges) Order 1996

(SI 1996/270), gives effect to those privileges and immunities in UK law. The states parties to UNCLOS, however, have recognised that certain additional privileges and immunities are necessary for the effective exercise of the functions of the authority. The protocol provides for those additional privileges and immunities. It is based substantially on Articles I, II, IV, V, VI and VII of the conventions on the privileges and immunities of the United Nations and of the specialised agencies. The proposed order will give effect in UK law to the protocol and the relevant provisions of UNCLOS in one instrument and will, therefore, revoke the 1996 order.

The order is also made under the International Organisations Act 1968 and in accordance with Section 1(6) (a) of that Act, the privileges and immunities conferred are no greater in extent than those required by UNCLOS and the protocol or those authorised by the Act. I very much hope that your Lordships will in due course approve these orders, which are modest and non-controversial.

(HL Debs., vol. 614, cols. 1270–2: 30 June 2000)

5/15

The European Court of Human Rights (Immunities and Privileges) Order 2000 (Statutory Instrument No. 1817 of 2000) was made on 12 July 2000. An Explanatory Note attached to the Order read:

This Order confers privileges and immunities on the European Court of Human Rights, its judges, Registrar and Deputy Registrar, and on persons participating in proceedings before the Court or the Committee of Ministers of the Council of Europe. It will enable Her Majesty's Government to give effect—

(i) to the Sixth Protocol to the General Agreement on Privileges and Immunities of the Council of Europe (Cm. 4727.);

(ii) to the European Agreement relating to Persons Participating in Proceedings of the European Court of Human Rights (Cm. 4728.).

5/16

In moving the approval in the House of Lords of the draft EUTELSAT (Immunities and Privileges) (Amendment) Order 2000, the Parliamentary Under-Secretary of State, FCO, Baroness Scotland of Asthal, stated:

The noble Baroness said: My Lords, the European Telecommunications Satellite Organisation—EUTELSAT—is based in Paris. It was established in 1977 and ranks as one of the world's leading satellite operators, with reach across Europe, Africa, large parts of Asia and connectivity with America. EUTELSAT provides TV and radio broadcasts and pioneered the delivery of Internet services. It also provides capacity for corporate networks, satellite news gathering, telephony and mobile voice, data and positioning services. Forty-eight countries are shareholders in EUTELSAT, the largest being Italy, with 20.3 per cent, followed by France, with 20 per cent, and the UK, with 19 per cent.

The draft order will enable the Government to notify their acceptance of the amendments to the convention and the operating agreement relating to the

European Telecommunications Satellite Organisation—EUTELSAT. These amendments were presented to Parliament, in Cm. 4572, in February 2000, under negative procedure, by the Secretary of State for Trade and Industry. The present draft order is made under the International Organisations Act 1968 and will give effect in UK law to those additional privileges and immunities, which we are obliged to confer under the convention and operating agreement, as amended.

As an intergovernmental organisation, EUTELSAT already enjoys the usual privileges and immunities, including tax free status, under the EUTELSAT (Immunities and Privileges) Order 1988. Agreement was reached in 1999 for EUTELSAT to be split into a privatised French company and a residual, three to four person, intergovernmental organisation to oversee its obligation to provide public service telephony. The former will be called EUTELSAT SA (*Société Anonyme*), to distinguish it from the latter which will retain the title EUTELSAT.

The draft order will exempt the residual intergovernmental organisation, after EUTELSAT is put on a commercial footing, from all customs duties on goods and publications of the organisation imported by the organisation into the UK in the course of its official activities. It does not apply to or affect employees of EUTELSAT or any other individual connected with EUTELSAT. The newly formed commercial company, EUTELSAT SA, will not enjoy any privileges and immunities.

In accordance with Section 1(6)(a) of the International Organisations Act 1968, the privileges and immunities conferred by the draft order are no greater in extent than those required by the convention and operating agreement, as amended, or those authorised by the Act.

(HL Debs., vol. 620, col. 907: 21 December 2000)

Part Five: II. A. 3. *Subjects of international law—international organizations—general—legal effect of the acts of international organizations*

5/17

In the course of the case of *Tharcisse Muyunyi* v. *Bow Street Magistrates' Court and the Governor of Her Majesty's Prison, Belmarsh*, the following witness statement was made by Mr M. C. Wood, Legal Adviser, FCO, on 21 September 2000:

1. I am currently the Legal Adviser at the Foreign and Commonwealth Office ('FCO') and have worked as one of the legal advisers in the FCO since 1970. From 1991 to 1994, I was Counsellor (Legal Adviser) at the United Kingdom Mission to the United Nations in New York, where I worked extensively on Security Council matters, including the drafting and negotiation of resolutions of the Security Council. I am the author of articles on a number of international legal issues, including on the practice and procedures of the Security Council and the interpretation of Security Council resolutions.

2. I am authorised by the Secretary of State for Foreign and Commonwealth Affairs to make this Witness Statement in response to the submissions of the Applicant with regard to the *vires* of the United Nations (International

Tribunal) (Rwanda) Order 1996, SI 1996/1296 ('the 1996 Order in Council'). To the extent that the matters set out herein are within my own knowledge, they are true. To the extent that they are not within my own knowledge, they are true to the best of my information and belief.

3. I have read a copy of the Affirmation of Mr John Michael Fisher, dated 19 February 2000. At paragraph 4 of that Affirmation, Mr Fisher states that Security Council resolution 955 (1994), a copy of which is now produced and shown to me marked 'MCW 1', makes no reference to Article 41 of the United Nations Charter.

4. The powers of the Security Council to take decisions binding upon States are set out in Chapter VII of the United Nations Charter. A copy of the United Nations Charter is now produced and shown to me marked 'MCW 2'. Article 39 gives the Security Council the responsibility for determining the existence of a threat to the peace, breach of the peace or act of aggression. On making such a determination, the Council then has the powers, under Articles 41 and 42, to decide what measures shall be taken to maintain or restore international peace and security. Under Article 41, the Council has the power to decide upon measures 'not involving the use of armed force'.

5. A decision of the Security Council taken in the exercise of its Chapter VII powers is binding upon the United Kingdom and all Member States of the United Nations by virtue of Article 25 of the Charter. The power to give effect in the law of the United Kingdom to decisions of the Security Council requiring the imposition of measures not involving the use of armed force is contained in the United Nations Act 1946.

6. For over thirty years it has been the practice of the Security Council, in exercising its powers under Chapter VII of the Charter, not to refer, in the resolutions which it adopts, to specific articles of the Charter, but rather to make a general reference to the fact that it is 'acting under Chapter VII'. Where, however, the Council takes a decision to impose measures not involving the use of armed forcc, it is clearly understood by all concerned that it is acting under Article 41 of the Charter. This is the only provision within Chapter VII of the Charter under which the Security Council can impose such measures.

7. There is now produced and shown to me marked 'MCW 3' a schedule of the principal resolutions of the Security Council imposing measures under Article 41 of the Charter. From that schedule, it will be seen that, with the exception of three resolutions (resolution 232 (1966), resolution 277 (1970) and resolution 409 (1977), concerned with Southern Rhodesia), the invariable practice of the Council has been to refer to Chapter VII as a whole, rather than to Article 41 in particular.

8. There is now produced and shown to me, by way of example, marked 'MCW 4', Security Council resolution 661 (1990), by which the Council decided that States should impose measures against Iraq following Iraq's invasion of Kuwait. While this resolution makes no express reference to Article 41, it was clearly based upon that provision.

9. The measures on which the Security Council has decided, in the exercise of its powers under Article 41 of the Charter, are not confined to the imposition of economic sanctions, but have included political sanctions and measures such as calling upon States to surrender suspects for trial in other States, calling upon the United Kingdom and the Netherlands to agree upon conditions for a

Scottish court to sit in the Netherlands for the purpose of trying the two men accused of causing the Lockerbie bombing and calling upon States to co-operate with the International Criminal Tribunal for the Former Yugoslavia. None of these resolutions expressly refers to Article 41 of the Charter, but, in each case, the measures were, in fact, imposed pursuant to Article 41.

10. Where the implementation in the United Kingdom of one of these Security Council decisions under Article 41 requires legislation, the normal practice has been to make an Order in Council under the United Nations Act 1946. This was done, for example, in the case of the International Criminal Tribunal for the Former Yugoslavia.

11. By Security Council resolution 955 (1994), the Security Council established the International Criminal Tribunal for Rwanda and called upon States to co-operate with it. Like the other resolutions listed in 'MCW 3', resolution 955 refers to Chapter VII as a whole, rather than to a specific article within Chapter VII. The establishment of a criminal tribunal to try persons accused of international crimes such as genocide and requiring States to give effect to its orders is, however, clearly a measure not involving the use of armed force and, as such, falls within Article 41 of the Charter. It was accordingly given effect in the United Kingdom by means of the 1996 Order in Council.

I believe that the facts stated in this Witness Statement are true.

(Text provided by the FCO)

Part Five: II. A. 4. *Subjects of international law—international organizations—personnel and experts of international organizations, including privileges and immunities*

(See also **5/12–16**)

5/18

In reply to a question, the Parliamentary Under-Secretary of State, FCO, wrote:

The immunity from legal proceedings enjoyed by European Commissioners extends only to acts performed by them in their official capacity, including words spoken or written. Commissioners are entitled to such immunity in the territory of each member state and continue to enjoy this immunity after they have ceased to hold office.

(HL Debs., vol. 610, *WA 63*: 29 February 2000)

Part Five: II. B. 3. *Subjects of international law—international organizations—particular types of organizations—organizations constituting integrated (e.g. economic) communities*

5/19

In reply to a question asking about the treaty base for the development of the EU defence policy, the Minister of State, FCO, wrote in part:

Article 2 and Title V of the Treaty on European Union provide the legal base for the EU's CFSP activity, including military crisis management. The Government are satisfied that the Treaty provides a sufficient legal base for the European defence initiative as defined in successive decisions of the European Council.

(HC Debs., vol. 356, col. 767W: 16 November 2000)

Part Five: III. B. *Subjects of international law—entities and groups other than States and international organizations—overseas territories and dependencies*

(See also **2/1**, **5/24**, **6/2–3**, **9/3–7**)

5/20

On 9 February 2000, the UK Government filed an *Amicus Curiae* Brief in support of the appellee, III Finance Ltd., a corporation organized under the Companies Law of the Cayman Islands, in the case of *III Finance Ltd.* v. *Aegis Consumer Finance, Inc., et al.* in the US Court of Appeals for the Second Circuit, on appeal from the US District Court for the Southern District of New York. The Brief included the following passages:

C. *The Constitutional Relationship Between the United Kingdom and the Cayman Islands*

The panel in *Matimak* said the 'fact that the Hong Kong Companies Ordinance may be ultimately traceable to the British Crown is too attenuated a connection.' *Matimak*, 118 F. 3d at 76. The implication is that the constitutional relationship as a whole between the United Kingdom and its Overseas Territories is in some sense 'too attenuated' for Overseas Territories corporations to be 'subjects' of the United Kingdom.

In fact, the constitutional relationship between the metropolitan United Kingdom and the Overseas Territories is close and wide-ranging and extends far beyond responsibility for external affairs and defense. In the Cayman Islands, the special responsibilities of the Governor also include internal security, the police, and the public service. These are *core* areas of government.

The Cayman Islands have been under the sovereignty of the United Kingdom since 1670. Their Constitution is set out in Schedule 2 to the Cayman Islands (Constitution) Order 1972, which is an Order in Council made by the Queen in Council under powers contained in the West Indies Act 1962. Section 1 of the Cayman Islands' Constitution provides that there shall be a Governor of the Cayman Islands who shall be appointed by Her Majesty. Section 17 provides that there shall be a Legislature Assembly for the Cayman Islands.

Any bill passed by the Legislative Assembly becomes law only when assented to by the Governor or Her Majesty. Furthermore, any law assented to by the Governor may be disallowed by Her Majesty through a Secretary of State. This is not a ceremonial procedure. Every law passed in every Overseas Territory is referred to the Foreign and Commonwealth Office to be scrutinized and considered for disallowance. Laws are regularly referred back to Overseas Territories for clarification or amendment.

In addition to legislation passed by the Legislative Assembly, the United Kingdom legislates frequently for the Overseas Territories by Order in Council in many areas: *e.g.*, civil aviation, merchant shipping, United Nations sanctions, and extradition arrangements. In 1991, the United Kingdom abolished the death penalty for murder in the Caribbean Overseas Territories against the wishes of the territory governments. Ultimate legislative authority over the Overseas Territories is vested in the United Kingdom Parliament.

There is, therefore, no sense in which the relationship between the United Kingdom and a corporation organized under the laws of the Cayman Islands is 'too attenuated.'

(Text provided by the FCO)

5/21

On 9 February 2000, the UK Government filed an *Amicus Curiae* Brief in support of the appellant, ART 57 Properties, Inc., in the case of *ART 57 Properties, Inc.* v. *57 BB Property L.L.C., et al.* in the US Court of Appeals for the Fifth Circuit, on appeal from the US District Court for the Northern District of Texas, Dallas Division. The Brief included the following passages:

STATEMENT OF THE CASE

The complete background of this proceeding has been reviewed by Appellant in its principal brief. The case involves a suit for breach of contract brought by Appellant ART 57 Properties, Inc., a Nevada corporation, against a Delaware limited liability corporation and five Appellees which are corporations organized as international business companies under the laws of the British Virgin Islands.

C. *The Constitutional Relationship Between the United Kingdom and the British Virgin Islands*

The court in *Matimak* said that the 'fact that the Hong Kong Companies Ordinance may be ultimately traceable to the British Crown is too attenuated a connection.' *Matimak*, 118 F. 3d at 76. The implication is that the constitutional relationship as a whole between the United Kingdom and its Overseas Territories is in some sense 'too attenuated' for Overseas Territories corporations to be 'subjects' of the United Kingdom.

In fact, the constitutional relationship between the metropolitan United Kingdom and the Overseas Territories is close and wide-ranging and extends far beyond responsibility for external affairs and defense. In the British Virgin Islands, the special responsibilities of the Governor also include internal security (including the Police Force), the public service, and the administration of the courts. These are *core* areas of government.

The British Virgin Islands have been under the sovereignty of the United Kingdom since 1672. Their Constitution is set out in The Virgin Islands (Constitution) Order 1976 (as amended) which is an Order in Council made by the Queen in Council under powers contained in the West Indies Act 1962. Section 3 of the British Virgin Islands' Constitution provides that there shall be a Governor of the Virgin Islands who shall be appointed by Her Majesty. Section 13(1) provides that '[t]he executive authority of the Virgin Islands shall be vested in Her Majesty' and Section 25 provides that '[t]here shall be a Legislature of the Virgin Islands which shall consist of Her Majesty and a Legislative Council.'

Any bill passed by the Legislative Council becomes law only when assented to by the Governor or Her Majesty. Furthermore, any law assented to by the Governor may be disallowed by Her Majesty through a Secretary of State. This is not a ceremonial procedure. Every law passed in every Overseas Territory is referred to the Foreign and Commonwealth Office to be scrutinized and considered for disallowance. Laws are regularly referred back to Overseas Territories for clarification or amendment.

In addition to legislation passed by the Legislative Council, the United Kingdom legislates frequently for the Overseas Territories by Order in Council in many areas: *e.g.*, civil aviation, merchant shipping, United Nations sanctions, and extradition arrangements. In 1991, the United Kingdom abolished the death penalty for murder in the Caribbean Overseas Territories against the wishes of the territory governments. Ultimate legislative authority over the Overseas Territories is vested in the United Kingdom Parliament.

There is, therefore, no sense in which the relationship between the United Kingdom and a corporation organized under the laws of the British Virgin Islands is 'too attenuated.' This point is confirmed by the Statement of the Attorney General of the British Virgin Islands which is attached to this *amicus* brief as Exhibit 3.

5/22

In reply to a question, the Government Minister in the House of Lords wrote:

The Channel Islands (and the Isle of Man) are self-governing Crown Dependencies. My noble friend Lord Bassam of Brighton used the term 'dependent or associated territories' in the reply he gave to the noble Lord on 17 April (*Official Report, WA 79–80*), because this is the generic term used for the non-metropolitan territories of member states of the European Union by the European Union Code of Conduct Group on Business Taxation.

(HL Debs., vol. 612, *WA 179*: 3 May 2000)

In reply to a further question, the same Minister wrote:

The Crown is ultimately responsible for the good government of the Crown Dependencies. This means that, in the circumstances of a grave breakdown or failure in the administration of justice or civil order, the residual prerogative power of the Crown could be used to intervene in the internal affairs of the

Channel Islands and the Isle of Man. It is unhelpful to the relationship between Her Majesty's Government and the Islands to speculate about the hypothetical and highly unlikely circumstances in which such intervention might take place.

(Ibid., *WA 180*)

5/23

In reply to questions, the Parliamentary Under-Secretary of State, FCO, wrote:

Consensual homosexual acts between adults in private remains a criminal offence in Anguilla, the British Virgin Islands, the Cayman Islands, Monserrat and the Turks and Caicos Islands. No measures to de-criminalise these acts have been taken or are being contemplated in those Territories. However, an Order in Council to do so was made by Her Majesty at the Privy Council meeting on the 13 December 2000 and will come into force on 1 January 2001.

(HL Debs., vol. 620, *WA 84*: 21 December 2000)

[*Editorial Note*: In a Command Paper entitled *Partnership for Progress and Prosperity: Britain and the Overseas Territories*, presented to Parliament in March 1999 (Cm 4264), by the Secretary of State for Foreign and Commonwealth Affairs, the following passage had appeared:

Some of the Overseas Territories need to make progress in reforming and modernising human rights provisions—notably judicial corporal punishment, capital punishment and laws affecting homosexual conduct. We would prefer to see Overseas Territory governments enact the necessary reforms themselves.]

Part Five: III. F. *Subjects of international law—Entities and groups other than States and international organizations—self-determination units and the concept of self-determination*

(See also **9/6–7**)

5/24

In the course of a debate on the subject of Gibraltar, the Minister of State, FCO, Mr Keith Vaz, stated:

As the formal response to the report makes clear, the Government are strongly committed to our relationship with Gibraltar and its people. We view that relationship as a partnership, with all that that implies in terms of responsibilities and obligations. There can be no dilution of the British Government's commitment to Gibraltar as set out in the preamble to the 1969 constitution.

My hon. Friend the Member for Tooting (Mr Cox) spoke with his customary passion. He used the example of his visit to Argentina and his conversations there about the Falkland Islands to argue that our commitment to Gibraltar is less strong than our commitments elsewhere. Let me reassure him and the House that Her Majesty's Government will never—and I mean never—enter into arrangements under which the people of Gibraltar would pass under the sovereignty of another state against their freely and democratically expressed wishes. I want to make that absolutely clear.

I hope that my hon. Friend will accept that, and that I shall not need to repeat it. That was and remains our view.

(HC Debs., vol. 351, cols. 144–5WH: 8 June 2000)

5/25

In reply to a question, the Minister of State, Ministry of Defence, wrote in part:

The rule of the British Forces in the Falkland Islands is to demonstrate the United Kingdom's continued commitment to the islands and uphold the right of the islanders to self-determination.

(HC Debs., vol. 355, col. 275W: 30 October 2000)

5/26

In reply to a question, the Minister of State, FCO, wrote:

We recognise the right of the people of Western Sahara to self-determination over their own future and will continue to support international efforts to achieve a just and durable solution in the territory.

(HC Debs., vol. 356, col. 281W: 8 November 2000)

Part Six: I. *The individual (including the corporation) in international law—nationality*

6/1

The British Embassy, Washington DC, presented the following Note (No. 13/2000) dated 2 February 2000 to the US Department of State:

Her Britannic Majesty's Embassy presents its compliments to the U.S. Department of State and would like to bring to the attention of the Department of State its concern about a number of judicial decisions which have denied corporations of United Kingdom Overseas Territories access to United States Federal Courts. The principal decision in question is the Judgement of the Court of Appeals for the Second Circuit in the case of *Matimak Trading Co.* v. *Khalily*, 118 F. 3d 76 (2d Cir. 1997).

The United Kingdom wishes to make clear its position that corporations incorporated under the laws of any of its Overseas Territories are subjects of the United Kingdom. The United Kingdom is therefore of the view that such corporations ought to be amenable to the alienage jurisdiction of United States Federal Courts under section 1332(a)(2) of title 28 of the United States Code, whether as plaintiffs or defendants. Court decisions which fail to recognise such jurisdiction may have a serious detrimental effect on the trading relationship between the United States and the United Kingdom Overseas Territories. The United Kingdom also views with great concern the potential application of the

Matimak rationale to individual Overseas Territories residents, as well as to commercial enterprises.

The United Kingdom notes that all corporations validly incorporated under the laws of the United States and its territories are entitled to sue and be sued in the courts of the United Kingdom and its Overseas Territories. As a matter of international comity and reciprocity, the United Kingdom considers that United States Federal Courts should be open to corporations established in United Kingdom Overseas Territories.

The United Kingdom appreciates the very helpful efforts of the United States Government in submitting briefs *amicus curiae* to United States courts on these matters which support the United Kingdom's position and hopes that those efforts as well as the efforts of the United Kingdom to the same end will be successful.

Her Britannic Majesty's Embassy avails itself of this opportunity to renew to the U.S. Department of State the assurances of its highest consideration.

(Text provided by the FCO)

6/2

The UK Government filed an *Amicus Curiae* Brief, dated 9 February 2000 in support of the appellee, III Finance Ltd., in the case of *III Finance Ltd.* v. *Aegis Consumer Finance, Inc., et al.* in the US Court of Appeals for the Second Circuit, on appeal from the US District Court for the Southern District of New York. The Brief included the following passages:

STATEMENT OF THE CASE

The complete background of this proceeding has been reviewed by the parties in their principal briefs. The case involves a suit for breach of contract brought by III Finance Ltd., a corporation organized under the Companies Law of the Cayman Islands, against a Delaware limited liability corporation.

SUMMARY OF ARGUMENT

The United Kingdom Government regards corporations organized under the laws of the Cayman Islands as United Kingdom nationals and, therefore, as 'citizens or subjects' of the United Kingdom for purposes [of] alienage jurisdiction. The United Kingdom Government's officially declared position as to the status of such corporations, which accords with the position of the United States Government, should be dispositive. Defendants below rely heavily on *Matimak Trading Co.* v. *Khalily*, 118 F.3d 76 (2d Cir. 1997), *cert, denied*, 522 U.S. 1091, 118 S.Ct. 883 (1998), which the Governments of the United Kingdom and the United States agree was wrongly decided. *Matimak* was based on incorrect interpretations of United Kingdom company and nationality law, and a misapprehension of the constitutional relationship between the United Kingdom and its Overseas Territories. These misinterpretations led to the erroneous conclusion that there was no foreign sovereign concerned about the panel's decision. The United Kingdom's position derives support from its Consular

Convention with the United States, the trading interests of the two countries concerned, and considerations of international comity.

ARGUMENT

I. Introduction

This case raises important questions concerning whether the United States federal courts will have the authority to exercise alienage jurisdiction over numerous corporations organized under the laws of the United Kingdom Overseas Territories, which are territories under the sovereignty of the United Kingdom. The United Kingdom Government urges this Court to rule that § 1332(a)(2) extends to corporations organized in the Cayman Islands and other United Kingdom Overseas Territories.

II. Position of the United Kingdom Government

The position of the United Kingdom Government is that entities incorporated in any territory for which the United Kingdom is internationally responsible are regarded by the United Kingdom Government as United Kingdom nationals and, therefore, are 'citizens or subjects' of the United Kingdom for purposes of alienage jurisdiction. The Cayman Islands is such a territory. Although the United Kingdom Government believes that it makes no difference whether an entity established under the laws of an Overseas Territory is a 'citizen' or a 'subject,' the term 'subject' will be used in this *amicus* brief to conform to what the United Kingdom Government understands is United States usage. The United States Supreme Court has held that the term 'citizen' is analogous to the term 'subjcct.' *United States* v. *Wong Kim Ark*, 169 U.S. 649, 663–64, 18 S. Ct. 456, 462–63 (1898).

For domestic constitutional purposes the 'United Kingdom,' or as it is sometimes called the '*metropolitan* United Kingdom,' consists of Great Britain and Northern Ireland. 'Great Britain' is the collective term for England and Wales, and Scotland. However, as a State and subject of international law, the 'United Kingdom' also includes the United Kingdom Overseas Territories and the Crown Dependencies.[4] For example, when the United Kingdom becomes party to a treaty, that treaty will apply, unless a contrary intention is specified, to all parts of the United Kingdom's territory, including the Overseas Territories and Crown Dependencies.

The United Kingdom consists of a number of law districts for the purpose of the conflict of laws. The metropolitan United Kingdom consists of three separate law districts: England and Wales, Scotland, and Northern Ireland. The Overseas Territories and Crown Dependencies are each separate law districts. As such, they are entitled to enact their own laws in accordance with their constitutions. These separate law districts have separate laws, but they all belong to the one State: the United Kingdom. It follows that, in international law, the United Kingdom Overseas Territories are not independent States, but are parts of the United Kingdom, and are subject to United Kingdom sovereignty.

Conclusive evidence of the United Kingdom's position *vis-à-vis* the Overseas Territories is contained in the United Kingdom's Rules Applying to International Claims which are contained in the United Kingdom Government's Diplomatic Service Procedure Manual, Vol. 7, Annex 1 (Mar. 1996) (a copy of which is attached to this brief as Exhibit 2). Rule 1(b) provides a definition of the term 'United Kingdom national' which encompasses '[c]ompanies incorporated under the law of the United Kingdom or of any territory for which the United Kingdom is internationally responsible.' In practice, this means that if, for example, a corporation incorporated in any of the United Kingdom's Overseas Territories is expropriated by a foreign State or denied justice in the courts of a foreign State, the United Kingdom Government has the right to take up the claim of that corporation in much the same way as it would have the right to exercise consular protection over an individual from an Overseas Territory.

The United States Supreme Court has held unequivocally that, '[I]t [cannot] be doubted that it is the inherent right of every independent nation to determine for itself, and according to its own constitution and laws, what classes of persons shall be entitled to its citizenship.' *United States* v. *Wong Kim Ark*, 169 U.S. 649, 668, 18 S. Ct. 456, 464 (1898). See also *Murrarka* v. *Bachrack Bros. Inc.*, 215 F.2d 547, 551–53 (2d Cir. 1954) ('It is the undoubted right of each country to determine who are its nationals, and it seems to be general international usage that such a determination will usually be accepted by other nations.').

The 'generally accepted test for determining whether a person is a foreign citizen for purposes of 28 U.S.C. § 1332(a)(2) is whether the country in which citizenship is claimed would so recognize him.' *Autocephalous Greek-Orthodox Church of Cyprus* v. *Goldberg and Feldman Fine Arts, Inc.*, 917 F.2d 278, 285 (7th Cir. 1990); *Sadat* v. *Mertes*, 615 F.2d 1176, 1183 (7th Cir. 1980).

International law also recognizes that the United Kingdom as a sovereign nation has the inherent right to determine who should and should not be considered its citizens or subjects. The United Kingdom Government considers corporations created in the United Kingdom Overseas Territories, including the Cayman Islands, to be 'subjects' of the United Kingdom for purposes of alienage jurisdiction.

. . .

D. *Entanglement with a Foreign Sovereign*

The *Matimak* panel was wrong to conclude that Hong Kong corporations, and by implication all corporations incorporated in United Kingdom Overseas Territories, are 'stateless' and that there was, therefore, no danger of entanglement with a foreign sovereign. On the contrary, corporations incorporated in Overseas Territories such as the Cayman Islands are not 'stateless.' The United Kingdom takes responsibility for them as 'subjects.' That is why the United Kingdom, as demonstrated by its Diplomatic Note to the United States Government and by its participation in these proceedings, is thoroughly "entangled" in this issue.

---

[4] The United Kingdom Overseas Territories comprise the following territories: Anguilla, Bermuda, The British Antarctic Territory, The British Indian Ocean Territory, The British Virgin Islands,

The Cayman Islands, The Sovereign Base Areas in Cyprus, The Falkland Islands, Gibraltar, Montserrat, Pitcairn, St. Helena and dependencies, South Georgia and The South Sandwich Islands, and The Turks and Caicos Islands. The Channel Islands and The Isle of Man are also territories over which the United Kingdom has sovereignty. They are termed 'Crown dependencies' and have a broadly similar constitutional relationship with the United Kingdom.

(Text provided by the FCO)

The UK Government filed an *Amicus Curiae* Brief, dated 9 February 2000, in support of the appellant, ART 57 Properties, Inc., in the case of *ART 57 Properties, Inc.* v. *57 BB Property, L.L.C., et al.* in the US Court of Appeals for the Fifth Circuit, on appeal from the US District Court for the Northern District of Texas, Dallas Division. The Brief followed the lines of the UK *Amicus Curiae* Brief in the III Finance Ltd. case in **6/2** above with the following other passages:

Under Rule 29(a) of the Federal Rules of Appellate Procedure, the Government of the United Kingdom of Great Britain and Northern Ireland (the 'United Kingdom Government') has obtained the consent of the parties and submits this brief as *amicus curiae* in support of Appellant ART 57 Properties, Inc.[1]

STATEMENT OF INTEREST

The United Kingdom Government has a substantial interest in expressing to the Court its views with respect to this proceeding. Appellees are corporations organized under the laws of the British Virgin Islands. At all times pertinent to the jurisdictional issue raised by this appeal, the British Virgin Islands were a United Kingdom Overseas Territory.[2] The question presented on appeal—whether a corporation formed under British Virgin Islands' law is a 'citizen or subject' of a 'foreign state' for purposes of 28 U.S.C. § 1332(a)(2)—turns in large part on the view taken by the United Kingdom Government of the relationship between the United Kingdom and British Virgin Islands corporations.

The question before the Court is an important one for the United Kingdom Government. There are hundreds of thousands of corporations organized under the laws of United Kingdom Overseas Territories which would be exempt from the jurisdiction of United States federal courts or would be denied access to those courts under the interpretation of alienage jurisdiction advocated by Appellees. The United States and the United Kingdom are major trading partners of one another and have a close working relationship on both commercial and foreign policy matters. In order to express its concern over this issue, the United Kingdom Government has submitted a Diplomatic Note to the United States Government concerning this matter. That Note is attached to this *amicus* brief as Exhibit 1 [**6/1** above]. The United Kingdom Government submits that it would not be in the interest of its trading relationship with the United States for the corporations of the United Kingdom Overseas Territories to be excluded from United States federal courts. It, therefore, appreciates the Court's consideration of this *amicus* brief in support of Appellant.

[1] The United Kingdom Government submits this brief in support of Appellant on the limited issue of whether a corporation formed under the law of the British Virgin Islands as a United Kingdom Overseas Territory is a 'citizen or subject' of the United Kingdom for purposes of alienage jurisdiction under 28 U.S.C. § 1332(a)(2). The United Kingdom Government takes no position on any other issue on appeal in these proceedings.

[2] In February 1998, the United Kingdom Government announced that all 'Dependent Territories' would in the future be known as 'Overseas Territories.' There is no practical difference between the term 'Overseas Territory' used here in reference to the British Virgin Islands and the term 'Dependent Territory.' Nor is there any practical difference between these terms and the terms 'dependency,' 'colony,' or 'crown colony.'

(Text provided by the FCO)

6/4

In reply to the question why the UK is not a signatory to the Optional Protocol of the Vienna Convention on Diplomatic Relations Concerning Acquisition of Nationality, the Parliamentary Under-Secretary of State, FCO, wrote:

FCO research indicates that the UK originally chose not to become a party to the Optional Protocol on the Acquisition of Nationality for two main reasons:

(i) It was felt that nationality provisions were out of place in a convention dealing with privileges and immunities; and
(ii) It was considered preferable to rely on the general rules of customary international law in this area.

(HL Debs., vol. 612, *WA 202*: 8 May 2000)

Part Six: VII. A. *The individual (including the corporation) in international law—immigration and emigration, extradition, expulsion, asylum—immigration and emigration*

6/5

The Parliamentary Under-Secretary of State, FCO, wrote in reply to a question:

The UN Interim Administration Mission (UNMIK) intends to introduce travel documents for residents of Kosovo as soon as practicable. These do not have implications for the status of Kosovo but reflect the practical necessity of providing people resident in Kosovo with acceptable documentation in advance of the UN Mission completing a comprehensive registration exercise. Many Kosovo Albanians had passports and other documents destroyed by the Serbs.

(HL Debs., vol. 610, *WA 139–40*: 8 March 2000)

Part Six: VII. B. *The individual (including the corporation) in international law—immigration and emigration, extradition, expulsion, asylum—extradition*

6/6

The Secretary of State for the Home Department, Mr Jack Straw, made a statement on the circumstances of his decisions in respect of Senator Pinochet. It read in part as follows:

The current position is as follows: Senator Pinochet was arrested in London on 16 October 1998, pursuant to a warrant issued by the fifth central magistrates court in Madrid, and he has been held since that date on bail.

On 14 April 1999, following the second judgment of the Appellate Committee of the House of Lords the previous month, I issued a second authority to proceed in respect of offences of torture and conspiracy to torture alleged to have been committed by Senator Pinochet after December 1988. On 16 May last year, Senator Pinochet's solicitors applied for permission for a judicial review of my decision. The state of Senator Pinochet's health was not among the grounds advanced by his legal representatives.

At the hearing on 27 May 1999, the application for permission for judicial review against me was dismissed. The extradition hearing took place between 27 and 30 September at the Bow Street magistrates court. On 8 October, the Bow Street magistrates committed Senator Pinochet on all charges to await my decision on surrender.

Reports about Senator Pinochet's medical condition were taken into account by me in taking both decisions on the authorities to proceed, but at those stages I had no reason to doubt his fitness to stand trial. Since the authority-to-proceed stages, Senator Pinochet has not made direct representations to me about his medical condition. However, on 14 October last year, representations were submitted by the Chilean embassy, attaching recent medical reports on Senator Pinochet. They suggested that there had been a recent and significant deterioration in his medical condition.

I have a clear legal duty to operate the Extradition Act 1989 in full. In the light of the information from the Chilean embassy, that duty included involving myself in and informing myself fully of the true facts about Senator Pinochet's health. I therefore asked him to undergo a thorough and extensive medical examination, to be undertaken by an independent team of clinicians. Senator Pinochet gave his consent. He was entitled to the usual patient confidentiality, and he has chosen to exercise that right. He did however agree to the disclosure of the report to me and to the United Kingdom prosecuting authorities.

On the advice of the Government's chief medical officer, I appointed a team of clinicians of outstanding national and international reputation.

. . .

My officials received the team's report late on 6 January. I considered it with advice over last weekend.

The unequivocal and unanimous conclusion of the three medical practitioners and the consultant neuropsychologist was that, following a recent deterioration in the state of Senator Pinochet's health, which seems to have occurred principally during September and October 1999, he is at present unfit to stand trial, and that no change to that position can be expected. I have therefore told Senator Pinochet's legal representatives that, subject to any representations that I may receive, I am minded to take the view that no purpose would be served by continuing the present extradition proceedings.

I have written formally to the Crown Prosecution Service as representative of the Kingdom of Spain, to the Government of Chile, as well as to France, Belgium and Switzerland, each of these three countries having outstanding extradition requests before us. Letters have also gone to a number of human rights organisations, inviting them to submit any further representations that they consider that I should take into account, and to do so within the next seven days.

(HC Debs., vol. 342, cols. 277–8: 12 January 2000)

6/7

In reply to a question, the Secretary of State for the Home Department, Mr Jack Straw, made the following written statement:

I have today decided that I will not order the extradition of Senator Pinochet to Spain. I made this decision under section 12 of the Extradition Act 1989. I have referred the case to the Director of Public Prosecutions for consideration of a domestic prosecution, in accordance with Article 7 of the United Nations Convention Against Torture and Other Cruel, Inhuman or Degrading Treatment or Punishment. I have also decided not to issue Authorities to Proceed in respect of the extradition requests from Switzerland, Belgium and France. Full reasons for my decisions are contained in the letters to the parties concerned from one of my officials as set out:

Letter to the Spanish Ambassador:

2. I am writing to inform you that the Secretary of State has this morning decided pursuant to section 12 of the Extradition Act 1989, to make no order for the return of Senator Pinochet to Spain. This letter sets out the Secretary of State's reasons. He reserves the right to expand on them should it become necessary to do so.

The Secretary of State's approach to his decision

3. On 14 April 1999, the Secretary of State issued an Authority to Proceed under section 7 of the Act on certain of the charges made in Spain's extradition request. On 8 October 1999, Senator Pinochet was committed by the Bow Street Magistrate on all charges covered by the Authority, to await the decision of the Secretary of State as to whether he should be extradited to Spain. A habeas corpus application was made on Senator Pinochet's behalf on 22 October 1999, which has not yet been heard.

4. The Secretary of State is precluded by the Act from making an order for Senator Pinochet's extradition while his habeas corpus application is still pending. In the ordinary course, the Secretary of State would not make a

decision to refuse such an order until all proceedings arising out of the habeas corpus application had been completed. However, he has a discretion to do so in appropriate cases and a duty to consider whether this is such a case. In approaching that discretion, he has proceeded on the basis that he should not at this stage decide against making an extradition order unless it is already clear that there is some decisive factor which would lead him to refuse such an order at the end of the day. The only factor militating against the extradition of Senator Pinochet which is potentially decisive at this stage is the state of his health, and in particular his mental fitness to stand trial.

Representations

5. On 11 January 2000, the Secretary of State informed those acting for Senator Pinochet and the Kingdom of Spain that he had commissioned a medical report on Senator Pinochet, which had been delivered to the Home Office on 6 February 2000. He informed them that the report indicated that Senator Pinochet was unfit to stand trial, and that no significant improvement to that position could be expected. Subject to representations to be received at the Home Office by 5 pm on Tuesday 18 January 1999, he said that he was minded to conclude that no purpose would be served by continuing the current extradition proceeding arising from the Spanish request. Similar letters were sent to representatives of Amnesty International, Human Rights Watch, and other human rights organisations, which invited them to make such representations if they wished. A statement to the same effect was made to the press on 11 January 2000, and in the House of Commons on the following day.

6. The Secretary of State has received representations from most of those who were expressly invited to make them, as well as from a large number of other parties. He has taken careful account of them. He has also taken account of the points in recent judicial review proceedings in the High Court. In addition, he has reminded himself of the representations which were made to him on the two occasions, in December 1998 and April 1999, when he considered whether an Authority to Proceed should issue under section 7 of the Act in respect of Spain's extradition request.

7. On 15 February 2000, the High Court decided that the Secretary of State was bound to disclose copies of the medical report in confidence to the authorities of Spain, Belgium, France and Switzerland, all of whom have made requests for the extradition of Senator Pinochet. Copies of the report, together with certain ancillary material, were supplied to the Crown Prosecution Service on behalf of Spain and to the embassies of Belgium, France and Switzerland later on the same day. They were invited to make any representation on the report by 5 pm on Tuesday 22 February 2000. Representations were received in response to this invitation from all four requesting states. In the case of Spain, Belgium and France these included opinions from medical practitioners about the material sent to them on Tuesday 15 February 2000. In addition, some other representations on the medical report have been received. The Secretary of State has carefully considered these representations and the opinions annexed to them, with the benefit of expert advice.

Senator Pinochet's health

8. At the time when the Secretary of State was considering his first and second Authorities to Proceed, he received representations and a certain amount of information about Senator Pinochet's state of health from his solicitors. The tenor of this material was that Senator Pinochet was in some respects frail, as was to be expected in a man of his age. It did not, however, suggest that he was either physically or mentally unfit to stand trial. The Secretary of State did not regard this information as justifying the refusal of either of the Authorities to Proceed which he then issued.

9. The first sign that a serious problem about Senator Pinochet's health might be developing came on 6 October 1999, when, two days before judgment was given in the committal proceedings, the Bow Street Magistrate excused him from attending the judgment in person. This decision was based on evidence given to the court by the general practitioner attending Senator Pinochet.

10. On 14 October 1999, shortly after the decision of the Magistrate to commit Senator Pinochet, the Secretary of State received through diplomatic channels representations from the Chilean Embassy, supported by medical reports, which suggested that there had been a recent and significant deterioration in Senator Pinochet's health. The Secretary of State did not regard this material as conclusive. It did, however, suggest the possibility that Senator Pinochet might be unfit to stand trial. He therefore decided to invite Senator Pinochet to submit to a medical examination by a team of clinicians appointed by him. The object was to obtain an independent, comprehensive and authoritative report on the relevant clinical facts. Senator Pinochet consented to undergo an examination, and the Secretary of State then selected, with the assistance of the Chief Medical Officer's advice, a team of clinicians to carry it out, having the required range of specialisations and no inappropriate personal interest in the case.

. . .

11. The clinicians were instructed to undertake the examinations and procedures which they judged desirable in order to provide the Home Secretary with a fully comprehensive report on the state of Senator Pinochet's health. In particular, they were asked to advise the Secretary of State whether, in their view, there were any aspects of Senator Pinochet's state of health which, separately or together, suggested that he was not then fit, or was likely to become unfit, to stand trial in Spain. They were told that the Secretary of State was particularly interested in Senator Pinochet's ability to follow a line of questioning, to recall events, some of which took place as long ago as the 1970s, and to give coherent evidence. To the extent that any of the contents of their report were influenced by observation of Senator Pinochet's conduct and manner, they were asked to advise the Secretary of State on the extent to which that conduct and manner were capable of being consciously influenced by the Senator himself.

12. It should be pointed out that the clinicians were not expected, in reaching their conclusions, to take responsibility for the legal test of fitness for trial, nor does the Secretary of State consider them to have done so. Their function was to ascertain the clinical facts. The test of fitness for trial which has been applied, both in framing their instructions and in assessing their report, is the responsi-

bility of the Secretary of State, who in turn has drawn extensively upon the opinions of his legal advisers.

13. The medical examination was conducted in Spanish at the Northwick Park Hospital in London over a period of some six hours on 5 January 2000, and the report was delivered to the Home Office on the following day. Certain information supplementing the report was supplied afterwards. This comprised (i) a short account of the procedures followed at the examination, which was supplied by Professor Grimley Evans on 7 January 2000; (ii) a copy of the neuropsychological report of Dr. Wyke, which had been summarised in the principal report but not annexed to it; and (iii) an explanation of neuropsychological testing by way of introduction to Dr. Wyke's report. This material was supplied to the four requesting states with the principal report on 15 February 2000. In addition, the Secretary of State has referred to Professor Grimley Evans and his colleagues the representations received on their report, and medical opinions annexed to those representations, and he has received their comments.

14. As the Secretary of State disclosed in his announcements on 11 and 12 January 2000, the conclusions of the medical report indicated that Senator Pinochet was unfit to stand trial and that no significant improvement to that position could be expected. The Secretary of State has considered the matter afresh in the light of all the material referred to in the preceding paragraph, and in the light of representations which he has received on the subject. Having done so, he is satisfied that the conclusions of the original report were correct and that it is right to regard Senator Pinochet as unfit to stand trial.

15. The critical facts are as follows:

(1) Senator Pinochet was born on 25 November 1915. He is 84 years old. The Secretary of State does not regard Senator Pinochet's age as being in itself a sufficient basis for his present decision. But he has taken account of it in assessing the significance of other aspects of his state of health.

(2) The clinicians instructed by the Secretary of State concluded that Senator Pinochet would not at present be mentally capable of meaningful participation in a trial. In reaching that conclusion, they were obliged to make assumptions about what kind of participation in a criminal trial would in law be regarded as 'meaningful' in determining the fitness of an accused. Those assumptions are apparent from the conclusion of their report and are considered in sub-paragraphs (3) and (4) below. So far as the Secretary of State has attached weight to them, he is satisfied that they are appropriate.

(3) The clinicians expressed their opinion about Senator Pinochet's capacity for meaningful participation in a trial on the basis of (i) Senator Pinochet's memory deficit for both recent and remote events: (ii) his limited ability to comprehend complex sentences and questions owing to memory impairment and a consequent inability to process verbal information appropriately; (iii) his impaired ability to express himself audibly, succinctly and relevantly; and (iv) easy fatiguability. The Secretary of State considers that all of these factors are potentially relevant to Senator Pinochet's mental capacity to participate in a trial. In this context, he attaches particular importance to Senator Pinochet's memory deficit for recent events, which would affect his ability to relate and understand items of information given to him at a trial, and to his limited ability

to comprehend complex sentences and questions and to process verbal information. The Secretary of State has not attached weight to the impairment of Senator Pinochet's capacity to remember remote events, save in so far its recent deterioration is symptomatic of brain damage having a wider significance: see sub-paragraph (6) below.

(4) With these impediments Senator Pinochet would be unable to follow the process of a trial sufficiently to instruct Counsel. He would have difficulty in understanding the content and implications of questions put to him and would have inadequate insight into this difficulty. He would have difficulty in making himself understood in replying to questions.

(5) In assessing the significance of the above matters, the Secretary of State has considered the nature of the issues which would be likely to arise in a criminal trial on the serious charges for which Senator Pinochet has been committed. He has also assumed that at any trial reasonable steps would be taken to mitigate Senator Pinochet's disabilities, for example, by attending to his physical comfort and medical needs, by adjusting the timetable of hearings, and by endeavouring to simplify the proceedings so far as their nature permitted. He has reminded himself that the burden of proof at any trial would be on the prosecution. The Secretary of State does not consider that these matters are capable of mitigating to a significant degree the difficulties to which Senator Pinochet's disabilities would give rise.

(6) The disabilities identified in the medical report are due to widespread brain damage, the major episodes of which seem to have occurred during September and October 1999 when Senator Pinochet suffered a number of strokes. They are not due to the ordinary processes of ageing.

(7) The examination took place on a single day, but the clinicians had access to reports prepared by reputable British general practitioners and specialists attending Senator Pinochet who had examined him on a number of occasions in September and October 1999. These enabled them to cross-refer their observations on 5 January 2000 to earlier observations and to evaluate a characteristic pattern of illness as it had evolved over a period of several months.

(8) The clinicians considered that further deterioration in both his physical and his mental condition was likely to occur, but were unable to express an opinion on the effect (if any) which a trial would have on the rate of deterioration. Their view was that although some day-to-day fluctuation in functional abilities was characteristic of brain damage due to cerebrovascular disease, further sustained functional improvement of a significant degree was unlikely.

16. The Secretary of State has always attached great importance to being able to satisfy himself that the results of the medical examination were not influenced by feigning of any kind. His instructions to the clinicians drew attention to the point and he is satisfied that they have been conscious of it throughout. They have advised him that there was no evidence that Senator Pinochet was trying to fake disability. The impediments were coherent in nature and consistent in manifestation, and the neuropsychological testing showed none of the features of deliberate exaggeration. In particular, those neuropsychological tests which were indicative of original intelligence and educational level showed superior performance. The Secretary of State is advised that there is no practical possibility that the results of the neuropsychological tests were influenced by

coaching. He is also advised that while it is possible to simulate with drugs the symptoms of a global impairment of cognitive functions, (i) this is a problem with which geriatricians are particularly familiar, and (ii) Senator Pinochet's cognitive impairment was focal rather than global, a pattern not seen in drug-induced impairment. It is important to point out that the outward manner of Senator Pinochet is not necessarily a reliable guide to his mental condition. It is characteristic of persons with a high level of original intelligence that they are able to mask superficially a significant impairment of cognitive functions.

17. The report of the clinicians who examined Senator Pinochet has been criticised by a number of medical practitioners whose opinions have been transmitted by the examining magistrates responsible for criminal investigations of Senator Pinochet in Spain, Belgium and France, and by certain other parties. In considering these criticisms, the Secretary of State has borne in mind that those who have made them have not examined Senator Pinochet, as the authors of the report of 6 January 2000 did, nor have they had the advantage which the clinicians enjoyed of studying records of Senator Pinochet's recent medical history. The Secretary of State is advised that most of the criticisms made of the report are irrelevant to its conclusions, and certainly to the conclusions that are critical to Senator Pinochet's fitness for trial (see paragraph 15). He is advised that those criticisms which are relevant are medically unjustified. The Secretary of State is satisfied that the advice he has received on these points has been based on a careful and objective analysis of the criticisms. He accepts that advice.

18. The medical report on Senator Pinochet of 6 January 2000 is an entirely independent report by highly qualified specialist practitioners on the relevant clinical facts. In commissioning it, the Secretary of State did not set out to prove any particular point and had no expectation of any particular outcome. He is satisfied that the clinicians who prepared it undertook their task in the same spirit.

19. Letters of request from the examining magistrates in Belgium and France have been transmitted to the United Kingdom, each of which seeks a further medical examination. In addition, Judge Garzon, the examining magistrate in Spain, has called in his representations for a further examination of Senator Pinochet. Senator Pinochet has consistently declined to comply with the invitations addressed to him by requesting states for a further medical examination. The Secretary of State, having taken advice on the point, does not consider that a further examination would yield further material of significance. He does not therefore regard it as either necessary or appropriate to commission one in order to determine whether Senator Pinochet is fit to stand trial.

Unfitness to stand trial

20. The conclusions to which the Secretary of State has come mean that in a criminal trial in England, Senator Pinochet would be found unfit to stand trial, and there would not therefore be any trial of the charges against him on their merits. If this were a peculiarity of English criminal law, the Secretary of State would not attach as much weight to it as he does. However, in the view of the Secretary of State, the principle that an accused person should be mentally capable of following the proceedings, instructing his lawyers and giving

coherent evidence is fundamental to the idea of a fair trial. He is advised that the attempted trial of an accused in the condition diagnosed in Senator Pinochet, on the charges which have been made against him in this case, could not be a fair trial in any country, and would violate Article 6 of the European Convention on Human Rights in those countries which are party to it.

21. After receiving the initial representations of Spain, the Secretary of State asked for further information from those representing Spain about the principles governing these matters in the Spanish system of criminal justice. This information has satisfied him that while the procedure differs in significant respects from that which would be followed in England, the underlying principle is substantially the same. The test of fitness to stand trial in Spain depends mainly on whether the accused is capable of understanding and following the charges against him, answering questions put to him, understanding the oral and documentary evidence for the defence and the prosecution, defending himself and instructing his lawyers. This is consistent with the representations as to Spanish law made on behalf of Senator Pinochet and on behalf of human rights organisations represented by Bindman & Partners. If Senator Pinochet were to be extradited to Spain, his fitness for trial would be assessed there by an objective process of clinical examination and testing. There is no reason to believe that that process would lead to conclusions any different in substance from those of the medical report commissioned by the Secretary of State in England. The Secretary of State is conscious that in Spain as in England, a 'trial' may include the process of assessing the Defendant's fitness for trial. However, on the material before him, it is reasonable to assume that if Senator Pinochet were to be extradited to Spain, a trial there on the merits of the charges against him would be found impossible.

22. In considering whether to decide against extradition on account of Senator Pinochet's unfitness to stand trial, the Secretary of State has given careful thought to the alternative possibility of leaving that question to be determined in accordance with Spanish judicial procedures in Spain, in the event that there was no other objection to extraditing him there. He has been advised and has concluded that on the basis of English law he is bound to form a view of his own on Senator Pinochet's fitness to stand trial, and that he cannot refrain from reaching a concluded view on this point on the basis that the question can be determined in Spain. In the light of his conclusion that no improvement in Senator Pinochet's condition can be expected, he considers that no purpose would be served by the continuance of the current extradition proceedings in England. These would involve the continued detention of Senator Pinochet here for a period which, allowing for the habeas corpus proceedings and any appeal arising out of them, might be substantial. Any order for the extradition of Senator Pinochet which might then be made would involve the compulsory removal to another country of a man of 84 years of age who must at this stage be presumed innocent, for the purpose of a trial which could not result in any verdict on the charges against him, for reasons that are already apparent to the Secretary of State as the extradition authority in the United Kingdom. The Secretary of State considers that that course would serve no purpose of any substantial value to the interests of justice and that it would be oppressive to Senator Pinochet.

23. The Secretary of State would not necessarily have taken the same view if

there had been any realistic prospect that Senator Pinochet's condition would improve, either spontaneously or as a result of treatment. He is aware that in Spanish law the effect of a finding that an accused is unfit to stand trial is to suspend a prosecution for as long as that state of affairs subsists, but it is not tantamount to an acquittal.

Section 12 of the Extradition Act 1989

24. Section 12(2)(a) of the Act provides that the Secretary of State may not order the extradition of the accused in relation to any alleged offence if it appears to him that: (i) by reason of its trivial nature; or (ii) by reason of the passage of time since he is alleged to have committed it . . . ; or (iii) because the accusation against him is not made in good faith in the interests of justice, it would, having regard to all the circumstances, be unjust or oppressive to return him.

25. The Secretary of State considers that this provision has no application to the present question. Although it would in his view be oppressive to order Senator Pinochet's extradition given his unfitness to stand trial this state of affairs has not arisen by reason of the passage of time since he is alleged to have committed the offences. But for the lapse of time since the alleged offence, a decision under section 12 might possibly have fallen to be made before Senator Pinochet became unfit, but the cause of his unfitness is the supervening brain damage which appears to have occurred in September and October 1999. That damage was not itself either caused or aggravated by the lapse of time since the alleged offences. Neither of the other two factors identified in the sub-section is relevant.

26. It follows that Senator Pinochet's unfitness for trial is not an absolute bar to his extradition. It is a matter to be addressed as part of the general discretion of the Secretary of State under section 12(1).

The European Convention on Extradition

27. The United Kingdom and Spain are parties to the Convention.

28. The Convention requires extradition in all cases to which it applies, subject only to specific and limited exceptions, and to any reservations made by particular contracting states on their accession. In cases falling outside these exceptions and reservations, there is no general discretion. There is no express exception applicable to this case, nor is there any relevant reservation of the United Kingdom or Spain. The Secretary of State is advised that it is open to argument whether the Convention is subject to an implicit exception for cases where the primary purpose of any extradition, namely the trial of the charges alleged against the accused, could not be served. In the circumstances of this case, the Secretary of State considers it unnecessary to form a concluded view about that. He has assumed, in reaching his decision, that the Convention does not allow for the refusal of extradition on the ground that the accused is and will remain unfit to stand trial in the requesting state.

29. The Convention is not incorporated into English domestic law save to the limited extent provided for by the European Convention on Extradition Order

1990, SI 1990/1507. This provides simply for the Extradition Act 1989 to apply as between the United Kingdom and other parties to the Convention, and for it to do so on the basis contemplated in section 9(8)(a) of the Act that a prima facie case need not be shown on the committal hearing. Section 12 of the Act therefore applies, as a matter of English law, to extradition proceedings arising out of requests from states party to the Convention. The discretion conferred by it on the Secretary of State must be exercised in such cases.

30. Although the Convention is not part of English domestic law, the Secretary of State attaches great importance to the international obligations of the United Kingdom, and in the exercise of his discretions under the Extradition Act he regards those obligations as both relevant and entitled to considerable weight. In most cases to which the Convention applies they will be decisive. However, the Secretary of State recognises that given the breadth of his discretion under section 12 of the Act there may be some occasions on which the requirements of the Convention are outweighed by other compelling considerations peculiar to particular cases. The Secretary of State considers that they are outweighed by such considerations in this case, having regard in particular to the nature of Senator Pinochet's condition in a man of his age, to its probable permanence, and to its impact on the possibility of a trial of the charges against him.

31. The experience of the Home Office has been that in practice parties to the Convention operate its provisions in a more flexible fashion than its absolute language suggests, and in accordance with basic principles of justice which are common to all of them. It is consistent with this approach that Belgium should have been recorded in the judgment of the High Court on their recent application for judicial review as having

> clearly stated that they would support the Secretary of State's decision if only they could be satisfied that Senator Pinochet is indeed shown by the report to be permanently unfit to stand trial:

and that Spain should have informed the Secretary of State that they will respect any decision made by the Secretary of State in the exercise of his discretionary powers. In making his decision, the Secretary of State has not attached weight to the matters summarised in this paragraph, but he considers it right that they should be recorded.

Other countervailing considerations

32. The main consideration which has been urged upon the Secretary of State in favour of allowing the current extradition proceedings to take their course is the importance of ensuring *so far as possible* that the allegations made against Senator Pinochet should be tried. The Secretary of State agrees that this is important. The scope of the charges against Senator Pinochet was substantially reduced as a result of the decision of the House of Lords in R *v.* Bow Street Metropolitan Stipendiary Magistrate ex p. Pinochet (No. 3) [1999] 2 WLR 827, but the remaining charges are extremely serious. The Secretary of State attaches great importance to the principle that universal jurisdiction against persons charged with international crimes should be made effective, and he is aware that the practical consequence of refusing to extradite Senator Pinochet to Spain on

account of his unfitness to stand trial is that he will probably not be tried anywhere. The Secretary of State is also mindful of the sense of injury which will be felt by those who suffered from breaches of human rights in Chile in the past, as well as their relatives. All of these are matters of legitimate concern, and he has had them very much in mind when considering the evidence about Senator Pinochet's state of health. They are among the reasons why he has required the evidence of Senator Pinochet's condition to satisfy a high standard of expertise, thoroughness, objectivity and cogency before he was prepared to act on it. Ultimately, however, the reservation 'so far as possible' cannot be brushed aside. A trial of the charges against Senator Pinochet, however desirable, is no longer possible.

33. The Secretary of State has considered other factors, including a wide variety of matters raised in representations received at the Home Office. This letter has dealt in terms only with those matters which have had a significant bearing on the Secretary of State's decision. It is, however, right to mention the following further points:

(1) The Secretary of State understands that if Senator Pinochet were convicted in Spain of the offences charged against him, victims of those offences might be entitled to recover civil damages in proceedings ancillary to the criminal trial. The Secretary of State doubts whether this point could be relevant to a decision whether to extradite a person on a criminal charge, but he has reached no concluded view on its legal relevance, because he does not in any event feel able to attach significant weight to it. It is right to add that the point assumes the possibility of a verdict on the charges.

(2) The Secretary of State has not had regard to the possibility, if indeed it is a real one, that Senator Pinochet might be tried in Chile.

(3) The Secretary of State considers that in some circumstances it may be appropriate for him to have regard to political, economic or diplomatic interests of the United Kingdom in exercising his discretions under the Extradition Act. He has not had regard to such factors in making his present decision.

Referring the decision to the Court

34. The Secretary of State has been urged by a number of those who have made representations to him to leave to the Courts the question whether Senator Pinochet should be discharged on account of unfitness to stand trial. He has considered this possibility but does not propose to adopt it.

35. The High Court has power to discharge accused persons who are being unlawfully detained, and such further powers as are specifically conferred on it by the Extradition Act 1989. It has no inherent supervisory power over extradition. Under section 11(3) of the Act, the High Court on the hearing of a habeas corpus application has a duty similar to that of the Secretary of State under section 12(2)(a) to discharge an accused if by reason of the lapse of time since the offences are alleged to have been committed it would in all the circumstances be unjust or oppressive to order his extradition. If the Secretary of State had regarded these provisions as applicable he would have been bound to refuse to extradite Senator Pinochet. However, the facts making it oppressive to extradite Senator Pinochet do not arise from the lapse of time since the alleged

offences. Therefore neither section 11(3) nor section 12(2)(a) applies. The Secretary of State is the only authority on whom a general discretion is conferred whether to order extradition. He has had regard in exercising it to the principle expressed by the courts on a number of occasions that the proper exercise of that discretion by the Secretary of State is the principal safeguard for the accused against oppression.

36. The Secretary of State would not, even if the Court had concurrent jurisdiction in the circumstances of this case, have thought it right to refrain from performing a duty or exercising a discretion conferred on him by statute, which he was in a position to exercise on material which he had commissioned for that purpose, simply because at some future stage another authority might take the decision instead.

Domestic prosecution

37. Article 7 of the Convention against Torture and other Cruel Inhuman or Degrading Treatment or Punishment requires the Secretary of State, if he does not order the extradition of a person accused of torture, to submit the case to the United Kingdom prosecuting authorities for the purposes of a domestic prosecution. The Secretary of State has supplied papers in advance to the Solicitor General and the Director of Public Prosecutions for that purpose and has this morning referred the case to them under Article 7. Their functions in the matter are entirely independent of his.

Letters rogatory

38. The only additional matter is the application of Judge Garzon by letters rogatory of 15 January 2000 for Senator Pinochet to be required to appear in court to respond to a request for a statement. The Home Secretary has decided not to give effect to this request on the grounds that Senator Pinochet is not a compellable witness as a matter of English law.

Letter to the Belgian Ambassador:

39. The Secretary of State has today made a final decision not to issue an Authority to Proceed under section 7 of the Extradition Act 1989 in respect of the two requests of Belgium for Senator Pinochet's extradition, transmitted on 15 December 1998 and 11 November 1999. In making this decision, the Secretary of State has treated the 'Elaborative Memorandum' transmitted on 3 February 2000 as supplementing those requests and has had regard to the full range of offences alleged against Senator Pinochet in all three documents.

40. Under 7(4) of the Extradition Act 1989, the Secretary of State is required to refuse an Authority to Proceed if an order for the extradition of Senator Pinochet could not lawfully be made or would not in fact be made in accordance with the provisions of the Act. Under those provisions, extradition is available only in respect of extradition crimes. The Secretary of State has directed himself on this point in accordance with the decision of the House of Lords in R *v.* Bow

Street Metropolitan Stipendiary Magistrate ex p. Pinochet (No. 3) [1999] 2 WLR 827. An offence committed outside the United Kingdom is not an extradition crime unless it was punishable in the United Kingdom at the date when it is alleged to have been committed. Torture outside the United Kingdom and conspiracy to torture outside the United Kingdom first became punishable in the United Kingdom on 29 September 1988 when section 134 of the Criminal Justice Act 1988 came into force.

41. None of the matters set out in the two extradition requests of Belgium and the Elaborative Memorandum disclose offences of torture or conspiracy to torture committed after 29 September 1988. In the Elaborative Memorandum, attention is drawn to three cases in which persons disappeared in circumstances which have never been disclosed to their families. It is alleged that their disappearance constituted torture of themselves and their families, which in the absence of news of them continued, or must be treated as continuing, to the present day. It is an essential requirement of the offence of torture in English law that the accused should, by some act or omission, have intentionally inflicted severe physical or mental pain or suffering on another person or been party to the infliction of such pain or suffering. The Secretary of State does not regard the two extradition requests or the Elaborative Memorandum as alleging (i) any act or omission inflicting severe pain or suffering and occurring on or after 29 September 1988, or (ii) that any intention to inflict pain or suffering was continuing until 29 September 1988 or any later date, or (iii) an intention existing at any time to inflict pain or suffering on any one other than those who disappeared. Furthermore, the Secretary of State does not regard any such allegations as being implicit in the facts alleged.

42. There are no offences other than torture or conspiracy to torture disclosed in the two extradition requests or the Elaborative Memorandum which have at any time been punishable in the United Kingdom if committed outside the United Kingdom. The requirement that offences alleged in an extradition request should be punishable under the law of the requested state is of course reflected in the European Convention on Extradition.

43. If the Secretary State had regarded the two extradition requests and the Elaborative Memorandum as disclosing extradition crimes, he would nevertheless have refused to issue an Authority to Proceed in this case because he is satisfied that Senator Pinochet is unfit to stand trial and that there is no likelihood of significant improvement. He has today decided on that ground that he will not order the extradition of Senator Pinochet to Spain. It appears to him that even had the Belgian extradition requests and the Elaborative Memorandum disclosed extradition crimes Senator Pinochet's unfitness to stand trial would have precluded his extradition to Belgium for the same reasons as it precluded his extradition to Spain. The enclosed copy of my letter this morning to the Spanish Ambassador sets those reasons out.

44. In these circumstances, the question whether Senator Pinochet could claim state immunity in respect of the offences alleged against him does not arise.

45. I refer to the three letters of request issued by the examining magistrate Mr. Vandermeersch and transmitted on 19 and 24 January and 22 February 2000. The first of these seeks a further medical examination of Senator Pinochet. It has been executed in accordance with English law by inviting Senator Pinochet to submit voluntarily to the examination sought. He has declined to comply. In the

light of the judgment of the High Court on 15 February 2000, the second letter of request has been executed so far as it seeks disclosure of the medical report. The Secretary of State does not propose to give effect to the second letter of request to any greater extent, having regard to the terms of that judgment and to his decision to refuse an Authority to Proceed in respect of Belgium's extradition requests. If Senator Pinochet were at some future stage to enter Belgium or to be extradited there from a third country, the Secretary of State will consider what further assistance might be appropriate. The third letter of request invites the Secretary of State or other competent authority to carry out an assessment of the frontal functions and of the autobiographical recall capacities of Senator Pinochet with the latter's consent. This letter has been executed so far as it can be by inviting Senator Pinochet's consent. He has declined. There is accordingly nothing more by way of execution to be done.
46. As indicated, I am enclosing a copy of the letter which I have sent this morning to the Spanish Ambassador.

Letter to Swiss Ambassador:

47. The Secretary of State has today made a final decision not to issue an Authority to Proceed under section 7 of the Extradition Act 1989 in respect of the request of Switzerland for Senator Pinochet's extradition, received on 11 November 1998 and renewed on 7 October 1999.
48. Under section 7(4) of the Extradition Act 1989, the Secretary of State is required to refuse an Authority to Proceed if an order for the extradition of Senator Pinochet could not lawfully be made or would not in fact be made in accordance with the provisions of the Act. Under those provisions, extradition is available only in respect of extradition crimes. The Secretary of State has directed himself on this point in accordance with the decision of the House of Lords in R *v.* Bow Street Metropolitan Stipendiary Magistrate ex p. Pinochet (No. 3) [1999] 2 WLR 827. An offence committed outside the United Kingdom is not an extradition crime unless it was punishable in the United Kingdom at the date when it is alleged to have been committed. Torture outside the United Kingdom and conspiracy to torture outside the United Kingdom first became punishable in the United Kingdom on 29 September 1988 when section 134 of the Criminal Justice Act 1988 came into force.
49. The requirement that offences alleged in an extradition request should be punishable under the law of the requested state is of course reflected in the European Convention on Extradition. None of the offences alleged in the extradition requests of Switzerland are alleged to have been committed after that date.
50. If the Secretary of State had regarded the extradition request of Switzerland as disclosing extradition crimes, he would nevertheless have refused to issue an Authority to Proceed in this case because he is satisfied that Senator Pinochet is unfit to stand trial and that there is no likelihood of significant improvement. He has today decided on that ground that he will not order the extradition of Senator Pinochet to Spain. It appears to him that even had the request of Switzerland disclosed extradition crimes Senator Pinochet's unfitness to stand trial would have precluded his extradition to Switzerland for the same reasons as

it precluded his extradition to Spain. The enclosed copy of my letter this morning to the Spanish Ambassador sets those reasons out.
51. In these circumstances, the question whether Senator Pinochet could claim state immunity in respect of the offences alleged against him does not arise.
52. As indicated, I am enclosing a copy of the letter which I have sent this morning to the Spanish Ambassador.

Letter to French Ambassador:

53. The Secretary of State has today made a final decision not to issue an Authority to Proceed under section 7 of the Extradition Act 1989 in respect of the requests of France for Senator Pinochet's extradition, transmitted on 13 November 1998 and 4 February 1999.
54. Under section 7(4) of the Extradition Act 1989, the Secretary of State is required to refuse an Authority to Proceed if an order for the extradition of Senator Pinochet could not lawfully be made or would not in fact be made in accordance with the provisions of the Act. Under those provisions, extradition is available only in respect of extradition crimes. The Secretary of State has directed himself on this point in accordance with the decision of the House of Lords in R *v*. Bow Street Metropolitan Stipendiary Magistrate ex p. Pinochet (No. 3) [1999] 2 WLR 827. An offence committed outside the United Kingdom is not an extradition crime unless it was punishable in the United Kingdom at the date when it is alleged to have been committed. Torture outside the United Kingdom and conspiracy to torture outside the United Kingdom first became punishable in the United Kingdom on 29 September 1988 when section 134 of the Criminal Justice Act 1988 came into force.
55. The requirement that offences alleged in an extradition request should be punishable under the law of the requested state is of course reflected in the European Convention on Extradition. None of the offences alleged in the extradition requests of France are alleged to have been committed after that date.
56. If the Secretary of State had regarded the extradition requests of France as disclosing extradition crimes, he would nevertheless have refused to issue an Authority to Proceed in this case because he is satisfied that Senator Pinochet is unfit to stand trial and that there is no likelihood of significant improvement. He has today decided on that ground that he will not order the extradition of Senator Pinochet to Spain. It appears to him that, even had the requests of France disclosed extradition crimes, Senator Pinochet's unfitness to stand trial would have precluded his extradition to France for the same reasons as it precluded his extradition to Spain. The enclosed copy of my letter this morning to the Spanish Ambassador sets those reasons out.
57. In these circumstances, the question whether Senator Pinochet could claim state immunity in respect of the offences alleged against him does not arise.
58. A letter of request of 22 February from Judge Le Loire sought a further medical examination of Senator Pinochet. That request was forwarded to Senator Pinochet's legal representatives on 29 February. They confirm that he does not propose to comply.

59. As indicated, I am enclosing a copy of the letter which I have sent this morning to the Spanish Ambassador.

(HC Debs., vol. 345: cols. 357–71W: 2 March 2000)

6/8

Speaking later in the Chamber of the House of Commons, the Secretary of State remarked:

With permission, Madam Speaker, I should like to make a statement about the case of Senator Pinochet, former Head of State of Chile.

This morning, I informed the House by written answer that I had discharged Senator Pinochet from the Spanish extradition request, on the grounds that he was unfit to stand trial and that no significant improvement in his condition could be expected. I also reported my decision not to issue an authority to proceed in the competing extradition requests from Belgium, France and Switzerland, because none of those disclosed an extradition crime. A detailed explanation of my reasons is included in my answer.

The House will also now be aware, from the written answer given earlier today by my hon. and learned Friend the Solicitor-General, that the Director of Public Prosecutions has decided, on the material available to him, that there is no realistic prospect of a conviction in this jurisdiction, and that in any event, in the light of the medical condition of Senator Pinochet, no court here would allow a trial to take place. My hon. and learned Friend will be making a statement to the House immediately after mine.

Senator Pinochet departed from his bail address at Wentworth, Surrey, this morning. He was driven under police escort to RAF Waddington in Lincolnshire. A plane provided by the Chilean Government and carrying Senator Pinochet took off at about 1.10 this afternoon. The senator has now left the jurisdiction of the United Kingdom.

Let me now give the House a full account of what has happened in this case, as I said I would once the proceedings were concluded. I begin by making some general observations. My role under the Extradition Act 1989 is a quasi-judicial one. Although not generally incorporated into our domestic law, both the European extradition convention and the United Nations torture convention place important obligations on the United Kingdom, but I have to discharge those obligations within the powers and responsibilities placed upon me by United Kingdom law.

All the decisions which I have taken have been mine alone, and have not been decisions of Her Majesty's Government. Throughout, I have been keenly aware of the gravity of the crimes allegedly committed by Senator Pinochet and of the desire for justice by those who suffered at the hands of the former Chilean regime.

This has been an unprecedented case. Both I and the courts have had to navigate in uncharted territory. Two judicial committees of the House of Lords took different views about what offences constituted extradition crimes. More recently, Mr. Justice Maurice Kay ruled that my refusal of Belgium's request for disclosure of the medical report which I had commissioned was correct. Shortly afterwards, a full divisional court, while acknowledging strong arguments on both sides, came to the opposite view.

The following is the chronology of the significant events. Senator Pinochet landed at Heathrow airport on 22 September 1998, for a private visit to the United Kingdom. On 16 October, the Metropolitan police received an extradition request from a Madrid court for the provisional arrest of Senator Pinochet for serious offences, including the murder of Spanish citizens. The police were advised by officials of the Foreign and Commonwealth Office that Senator Pinochet did not enjoy diplomatic immunity from arrest. Bow Street magistrates court then issued a provisional arrest warrant, and Senator Pinochet was arrested that evening.

Senator Pinochet's solicitors made representations to me on 21 October 1998, asking me to cancel the provisional arrest warrant. I declined to do so, on the basis that the issues raised at that stage were a matter for the court. Senator Pinochet's solicitors challenged my decision. A divisional court, headed by the Lord Chief Justice, rejected that challenge and awarded me my costs. The court nevertheless quashed the warrant on the grounds that Senator Pinochet did have sovereign immunity as a former head of state and that the warrant did not disclose an extradition crime.

The Crown Prosecution Service, acting on behalf of Spain, then entered an appeal to the House of Lords. In a unique feature of the case, the issue was considered twice by the House of Lords, first in November 1998 and then, after the first judgment was vacated, in March 1999. The key majority finding of the second court was that torture was an international crime over which the parties to the torture convention had universal jurisdiction, and that a former Head of State did not have immunity from such crimes. That ruling was a landmark judgment in human rights law, whose impact has been felt far beyond our shores. It will be a permanent legacy of the Pinochet case.

The second House of Lords judgment restricted the scope and number of the alleged crimes in respect of which Senator Pinochet could be extradited for torture and conspiracy to torture committed in Chile after the UK'S ratification of the torture convention in December 1988. The charges were, of course, still extremely serious.

I issued a second authority to proceed on 14 April 1999, giving my reasons. A second judicial challenge to my decision was made by Senator Pinochet's representatives, but was again rejected by the divisional court. On 8 October 1999, Senator Pinochet was committed by the Bow Street Magistrate to await my decision on whether to extradite him to Spain. Senator Pinochet's solicitors applied for habeas corpus, and a hearing date was set for 20 March this year.

On 14 October 1999, I received representations from the Chilean embassy, supported by medical reports which suggested that there had been a recent and significant deterioration in Senator Pinochet's health. I commissioned a medical examination of Senator Pinochet by a team of independent practitioners of outstanding national and international reputation in their fields. The team consisted of Professor Sir John Grimley Evans, Professor Andrew Lees and Dr. Michael Denham. On the team's advice, Dr. Maria Wyke, a consultant neuropsychologist, was also brought in.

I want to put on record my gratitude to Sir John Grimley Evans and his team for their assistance. They have performed a very significant public service. They have not been able to speak freely in explaining and, where necessary, defending their findings, despite widespread public scrutiny.

The clinicians were instructed to undertake an examination and to provide me with a fully comprehensive report on the state of Senator Pinochet's health. In particular, they were asked to advise whether any aspects of Senator Pinochet's health suggested that he was not then fit, or was likely to become fit, to stand trial in Spain. They were told that I was particularly interested in Senator Pinochet's ability to follow a line of questioning, to recall events—some of which took place as long ago as the 1970s—and to give coherent evidence. They were also asked to advise me on whether Senator Pinochet could be feigning any of his symptoms.

As I disclosed in my statement on 12 January, the conclusions of the medical report, applying the tests that I had outlined, indicated that Senator Pinochet was unfit to stand trial and that no significant improvements in that position could be expected. The Government's chief medical officer, Professor Liam Donaldson, confirmed the quality and thoroughness of the report. I am placing a copy in the Library of the House.

I informed the interested parties on 11 January that, in the light of the medical evidence and subject to any representations received by 18 January, I was minded to conclude that no purpose would be served by continuing the Spanish extradition request.

On 25 January, a judicial review application was made by Belgium and Amnesty International for disclosure of the medical report. In inviting Senator Pinochet to undertake the medical examination, officials had, on my behalf, given an undertaking of confidentiality. I indicated to the divisional court that although I would have preferred to disclose the medical report to the requesting states, I considered myself bound by the undertakings that I had given, subject to any overriding public interest.

Mr. Justice Maurice Kay held that the report should not be disclosed, but a full divisional court, in a judgment of 15 February, said that while the issue had been a very difficult one, the need for transparency to the requesting states in this exceptional case outweighed any duty of confidentiality. It said, however, that I should disclose the report to Spain, Belgium, France and Switzerland only in terms of strict confidence. I complied with the judgment. I regret to say that the content of that report was almost immediately leaked to the press.

Requesting states were invited to make any representation on the medical report by Tuesday 22 February. The representations included opinions from medical practitioners questioning the conclusions of the report. I asked Professor Sir John Grimley Evans and his team to review those medical opinions, and received their advice on 27 February. The team's advice was also reviewed on 28 February by the Government's chief medical officer, Professor Liam Donaldson. He commented:

> I was very impressed with the care with which Sir John (and his team) has responded to each of the points of criticism of their report. This is not a crude rebuttal—it is a sound and logical reply supported by clinical evidence. I believe it is a further reflection of the skill, integrity and independence with which this task has been carried out by the clinicians.

I considered the matter afresh in the light of all the material. Having done so, I was satisfied that the conclusion of the original report was correct. I intend to place the medical representations and the team's response in the Library once I have secured the agreement of the requesting states.

The principle that an accused person should be mentally capable of following the proceedings, instructing lawyers and giving coherent evidence is fundamental to the idea of a fair trial. The trial of an accused in the condition diagnosed in Senator Pinochet, on the charges that have been made against him in this case, could not be fair in any country, and would violate article 6 of the European convention on human rights in those countries that are party to it.

A number of the representations that I received argued that even if there were questions about Senator Pinochet's fitness for trial, those should be determined in Spain and not here. I looked at that matter with great care. However, I was advised, and I concluded, that on the basis of English law I was bound to form a view of my own on Senator Pinochet's fitness to stand trial and that I could not refrain from reaching such a view on the basis that the question could be determined in Spain.

In any event, I established, with the assistance of the Spanish authorities, that Spain's principles for determining the fitness of an accused to stand trial are similar to ours. I therefore concluded that given the advice that no improvement in Senator Pinochet's condition could be expected, no judicial purpose would be served by the continuation of extradition proceedings for the objective of a trial in Spain which could not result in any verdict on the charges against him.

Of the 70,000 letters and e-mails from the public which I have received from all over the world, and many letters from Members of Parliament and organisations, almost all have urged me to allow the extradition proceedings to take their course, so that the allegations made against Senator Pinochet could be tried. I attach great importance to the principle that universal jurisdiction against persons charged with international crimes should be effective.

I am all too well aware that the practical consequence of refusing to extradite Senator Pinochet to Spain is that he will probably not be tried anywhere. I am very conscious of the sense of injury that is bound to be felt by those who suffered from breaches of human rights in Chile in the past, as well as their relatives.

All of these are matters of great concern, and I had them very much in mind when considering the evidence about Senator Pinochet's state of health. They have been among the reasons why I required the evidence of Senator Pinochet's medical condition to satisfy a high standard of expertise, thoroughness, objectivity and cogency before I was prepared to act on it. Ultimately, however, I was driven to the conclusion that a trial of the charges against Senator Pinochet, however desirable, was simply no longer possible.

The case has taken 17 months, much of that in court proceedings. While the House of Lords hearings on state immunity were indeed an exceptional feature, that period is not an unusual one in a complex, contested extradition matter. The Extradition Act 1989 is now more than a decade old and I believe that the time has come to review it. Work on that was in fact already under way before the Pinochet case began, and I intend to publish a consultation paper in due course on the options for streamlining our extradition procedures.

As I have already made clear, this case is unprecedented. Throughout the process, I have sought to exercise my responsibilities in a fair and rational way in accordance with the law. The case has understandably aroused great debate and feeling. Its impact has been felt worldwide. It has established, beyond question, the principle that those who commit human rights abuses in one country cannot assume that they are safe elsewhere. That will be the lasting legacy of this case.

(Ibid., cols. 571–5: see also Part Thirteen: III.D., below)

In the course of the same debate, the Secretary of State remarked:

. . . in my study of British extradition law over 17 months, I have never spotted even in a footnote that one of the considerations that I have to take into account is 'the ancient rule of hospitality'. That was not one of our considerations.

(Ibid., col. 585)

6/9

In reply to the question what criteria are applied to requests for extradition of British nationals to India in cases where the request concerns an Indian-born national, the Minister of State, Home Office, wrote:

The Extradition Act 1989 contains certain general restrictions on a person's return. But the United Kingdom does not operate a barrier to the extradition of its own nationals.

(HC Debs., vol. 357, col. 350W: 24 November 2000)

Part Six: VIII. *The individual (including the corporation) in international law—human rights and fundamental freedoms*

(See also **4/2**, **5/5**)

6/10

On 11 January 2000, the EU Presidency issued a statement about the decision by Ukraine's Constitutional Court on 30 December 1999 concerning the death penalty. The statement read in part:

The Union finds that this decision shows Ukraine's willingness to join a positive trend towards the universal abolition of the death penalty, which is the ultimate goal of the European Union as set forth in the EU declaration and the EU guidelines adopted at the General Affairs Council in Luxembourg in June 1998.

This far-reaching decision is well in line with the aims of the common strategy on Ukraine as regards the promotion of human rights, as well as the letter and the spirit of the European Convention for the Protection of Human Rights and all other relevant international legal instruments which call for the abolition of this inhumane practice.

(*Bulletin of the European Union*, 1/2–2000, p. 91)

6/11

In reply to a question, the Minister of State, FCO, wrote:

The European Court of Justice has for many years taken account of the case law of the European Court of Human Rights, although not formally bound by it. Instances where the two courts have differed in their interpretation of the European Convention on Human Rights have been very rare. The Government are working to ensure that the risk of conflict does not increase as a result of the current discussions about a European Union Charter of Fundamental Rights.

(HC Debs., vol. 348, col. 112W: 11 April 2000)

6/12

In reply to a question, the Parliamentary Under-Secretary of State, Home Office, wrote in relevant part:

The Government have no present plans to grant new rights of petition under any United Nations human rights treaty. This reflects the outcome of a thorough review of our obligations under international human rights treaties in March 1999. We will review the position again when the Human Rights Act 1998 has been implemented and is properly bedded down.

(HL Debs., vol. 612, *WA 49*: 12 April 2000)

6/13

In reply to an oral question, the Solicitor-General, Mr Ross Cranston, stated in material part:

The United Kingdom ratified the European convention for the protection of human rights and fundamental freedoms in 1951, and is bound in international law to respect and observe convention rights.

Section 19 of the Human Rights Act 1998 provides for a statement of compatibility from Ministers introducing legislation into Parliament. That is already in force. It requires that when legislation is introduced in either House for a Second Reading, the Minister responsible for the legislation must make a written statement that he or she considers the Bill to be compatible with convention rights, or is unable to make the statement but wishes Parliament to proceed with the Bill anyway. It is primarily for the Minister who is responsible for a Bill to ensure that the provisions are compatible. On reaching a view on these matters, the Minister would act on the advice of his or her officials and legal advisers, and sometimes the Law Officers become involved.

(HC Debs., vol. 348, cols. 495–6: 13 April 2000)

6/14

On 5 May 2000, the EU Presidency issued a statement on the bombings of civilian targets by the Sudanese air force. It read in part:

The European Union welcomes the recent announcement by the Sudanese President that he had ordered the cessation of aerial bombing of targets in south Sudan. The European Union calls on the Government of Sudan to fulfil that commitment in full and to abstain from any such actions in the future. The European Union will continue to watch closely on the fate of civilian populations in this area.

While reiterating its commitment to the renewed political dialogue, the European Union has called the attention of the authorities of Sudan to the fact that the respect of international humanitarian law is an essential sign of their willingness to create an atmosphere conducive to the successful continuation of that dialogue and their commitment to peace.

The European Union also calls upon the SPLM/A to comply with its responsibility to fully respect the rules and principles of international humanitarian law and to abstain from using civilian premises for military purposes.

(*Bulletin of the European Union*, 5–2000, p. 69)

6/15

In the course of her reply to an oral question on the subject of human rights in Tibet, the Parliamentary Under-Secretary of State, FCO, Baroness Scotland of Asthal, stated:

My Lords, the human rights situation in Tibet remains a matter of serious international concern. We, in common with the United States and our EU partners, use every available opportunity to press the Chinese Government to respect international human rights standards in Tibet. We also continue to press the Chinese Government to enter into a genuine dialogue with the Dalai Lama with the aim of finding a long-term political solution.

(HL Debs., vol. 612, col. 1720: 11 May 2000)

6/16

In the course of a press conference held in Moscow on 17 May 2000, the Secretary of State for Foreign and Commonwealth Affairs, Mr Robin Cook, referred to the talks which he had just held with the Russian foreign minister. He went on:

Our talks covered a number of areas in which we were concerned. I raised, of course, our concerns over Chechnya, I welcomed the assurance by the Russian foreign minister that the investigation of violations of human rights in Chechnya will be thorough and that if and where a prosecution is appropriate, prosecution will proceed where there have been violations of human rights law in Chechnya. It is very important that Russia demonstrates to the world that it takes those international obligations seriously if it is to convince us those actions in Chechnya were justified and were within the international law.

(Text provided by the FCO)

6/17

The EU Presidency issued a statement on 23 May 2000 on the human rights and humanitarian situation in Colombia. The statement read in part:

The European Union strongly condemns the persistent grave violations and human rights abuses as well as acts of terrorism and breaches of international humanitarian law committed by all armed groups and emphasises the need to bring those responsible for human rights violations to justice.

While supporting the current peace process in Colombia, the European Union urges all armed groups to end all acts of violence, to respect human rights, to comply with international humanitarian law and to engage in serious and constructive peace talks with the government, with a view to achieving a sustainable peace in Colombia.

The central and east European countries associated with the European Union, the associated countries Cyprus, Malta and Turkey, and the EFTA countries Iceland and Liechtenstein, members of the European Economic Area align themselves with this declaration.

(*Bulletin of the European Union*, 7/8–2000, p. 65)

6/18

In reply to a question, the Parliamentary Under-Secretary of State, Home Office, wrote:

The Human Rights (Jersey) Law 2000, which incorporates the European Convention on Human Rights into Jersey law, received the Royal Assent on 17 May. In Guernsey, a motion proposing the introduction of similar legislation was approved by the States of Deliberation on 5 April and this legislation is expected to be introduced shortly. The Isle of Man's Human Rights Bill received its Second Reading in the House of Keys on 9 May. The Guernsey and Isle of Man legislation is expected to receive the Royal Assent before the end of this year.

(HL Debs., vol. 613, *WA 90*: 24 May 2000)

6/19

Speaking in a television interview on 19 June 2000, the Secretary of State for Foreign and Commonwealth Affairs, Mr Robin Cook, was asked about the Charter of Fundamental Rights in Europe. He replied:

We are not at all nervous about Fundamental Human Rights, indeed Britain is the cradle of liberty and freedom and therefore we approached this discussion with great confidence. We did after all draft the European Convention on Human Rights and we are very happy to engage in discussion about a declaration of European values, European Human Rights. We are clear that this should be not a legal text, we already have a legal text in the European Convention, we do not want to see any rival to that that might undermine it, but we will certainly engage in the discussion and engage in the discussion with confidence.

(Text provided by the FCO)

6/20

In reply to the question why the European Convention on Human Rights is not extended to the UK Sovereign Base Areas in Cyprus, the Minister of State, Ministry of Defence, wrote:

The Sovereign Base Areas are retained solely for military purposes, and it has therefore been considered inappropriate to include them in the notifications of the extension of the European Convention on Human Rights.

(HC Debs., vol. 352, col. 38W: 19 June 2000)

6/21

In reply to a question, the Minister of State, FCO, wrote:

This year is the 50th Anniversary of the European Convention on Human Rights. The Convention has now been ratified by all 41 member states of the Council of Europe. It has become the Europe-wide standard for fundamental rights and freedoms providing, as its founders hoped, cohesive values and a bulwark against tyranny. In the UK, the Human Rights Act 1998, which comes into force on 2 October 2000, will enshrine in UK law the guarantees provided by the Convention.

Since the Convention's entry into force, a series of additional protocols have been adopted. Where these elaborate the rights set out in the Convention or add new rights, they are optional. Like other EU and Council of Europe states, the UK keeps under review its position with regard to those protocols it has not already ratified.

(HC Debs., vol. 353, col. 6W: 3 July 2000)

6/22

On 14 July 2000, the EU Presidency issued a statement on the situation in Afghanistan. The statement read in part:

The European Union is seriously concerned that the military operations are impeding the provision of humanitarian assistance to the Afghan population. The deliberate denial of access to humanitarian aid constitutes a breach of international humanitarian law. The European Union calls upon all factions involved in the conflict to guarantee safe and unhindered access to the civilian population.

(*Bulletin of the European Union*, 7/8–2000, p. 75)

6/23

On 26 July 2000, the EU Presidency issued a statement about the trial of Miroslaw Filipovic. The statement read in part:

The European Union condemns in the strongest terms Mr. Filipovic's imprisonment, his trial, the conditions in which it was held, behind closed doors by an expeditious procedure, and the verdict, which marks a further escalation in the repression of the independent press in Serbia and in the flagrant violations of press freedom by the Belgrade regime.

It would point out that freedom of expression, the right and the duty to impart information freely and the right to a fair and public hearing by an independent and impartial tribunal are basic human rights laid down in a great many international texts, of which the foremost is the Universal Declaration of Human Rights.

(*Bulletin of the European Union*, 7/8–2000, p. 81)

6/24

On 18 August 2000, the EU Presidency issued a statement about the bombing of civilian targets in Sudan. The statement read in part:

The European Union is deeply concerned at the recent bombings, carried out by Sudanese aircraft, which hit civilian installations, in particular the bombings close to a large UN base at Mapel on 7 and 8 August.

The European Union welcomes the new Sudanese security guarantees that have allowed flights for Operation Lifeline Sudan (OLS) to resume. It hopes that the Government of Sudan will scrupulously honour its undertakings to the UN. It appeals to the warring parties to comply with the principles of international humanitarian law, particularly those relating to the safety of UN personnel, as laid down in the convention of 9 December 1994, and to free access for NGOs to civilian populations in distress.

(*Bulletin of the European Union*, 7/8–2000, p. 82)

6/25

In reply to the question why Her Majesty's Government have no present plans to sign and ratify Protocol No. 12 to the European Convention on Human Rights, the Parliamentary Under-Secretary of State, Home Office, wrote:

The Government are in principle in favour of extending Article 14 of the European Convention on Human Rights to provide a free-standing right against discrimination. But we consider that the text of Protocol 12 is too general and open-ended. In particular, it does not make clear whether 'rights set forth by law' include international as well as national law; it does not make provision for positive measures; and it does not follow the case law of the European Court of Human Rights in allowing objective and reasonably justified distinctions.

(HL Debs., vol. 617, *WA 37*: 11 October 2000)

6/26

In the course of an EU Presidency statement on the subject of Colombia, made on 25 October 2000, it was stated:

The European Union is particularly aware of the serious deterioration in the human rights situation and in that of international humanitarian law. It reiterates its 'Declaration on the human rights and humanitarian situation in Colombia' of 23 May 2000 and its condemnation of violations of human rights and of international humanitarian law, whoever commits them. It intends to consider ways of participating in the financing of the United Nations Office and practical ways of assisting those who protect human rights, which are at this time under threat. In this spirit, it will continue to support the peace communities.

(*Bulletin of the European Union*, 10–2000, p. 73)

6/27

In reply to the question 'what steps Her Majesty's Government have taken to consolidate the United Kingdom's national criteria against which they assess licence applications to export arms and dual-use equipment with those of the European Union Code of Conduct on Arms Exports', the Parliamentary Under-Secretary of State, FCO, wrote in part:

CRITERION TWO

The respect of human rights and fundamental freedoms in the country of final destination

Having assessed the recipient country's attitude towards relevant principles established by international human rights instruments, the Government will:

(a) not issue an export licence if there is a clear risk that the proposed export might be used for internal repression:
(b) exercise special caution and vigilance in issuing licences, on a case-by-case basis and taking account of the nature of the equipment, to countries where serious violations of human rights have been established by the competent bodies of the UN, the Council of Europe or by the EU.

For these purposes, equipment which might be used for internal repression will include, *inter alia*, equipment where there is evidence of the use of this or similar equipment for internal repression by the proposed end-user, or where there is reason to believe that the equipment will be diverted from its stated end-use or end-user and used for internal repression.

The nature of the equipment will be considered carefully, particularly if it is intended for internal security purposes. Internal repression includes, *inter alia*, torture and other cruel, inhuman and degrading treatment or punishment; summary, arbitrary or extra-judicial executions; disappearances; arbitrary detentions; and other major suppression or violations of human rights and fundamental freedoms as set out in relevant international human rights instruments, including the Universal Declaration on Human Rights and the International Covenant on Civil and Political Rights.

The Government consider that in some cases the use of force by a government within its own borders, for example to preserve law and order against terrorists or other criminals, is legitimate and does not constitute internal repression, as long as force is used in accordance with the international human rights standards described above.

(HL Debs., vol. 618, *WA 84*: 31 October 2000)

6/28

In reply to a question about the European Court of Human Rights, the Minister of State, FCO, wrote:

There are no instances where member states' governments have refused to accept the judgment of the Court, although there have been significant delays in the implementation of judgments. Such delays may result from the need to amend domestic law or be attributed to difficulties in a wider political context. However, the Government expect all member states to fully comply with the Court's judgments, and we regularly make our position clear to those concerned. The Government plays their part in the Committee of Ministers of the Council of Europe in carrying out the task of supervising the implementation of judgments and taking the necessary measures to ensure that they are implemented, and supports the principle that all cases should remain open until the committee is fully satisfied that they have been properly addressed.

(HC Debs., vol. 357, col. 274W: 23 November 2000)

6/29

The following question was asked of Her Majesty's Government:

With respect to the Charter of Fundamental Rights of the European Union, what are their reasons for not approving incorporation of the Charter in the Treaties of the European Union; and what they consider to be the main differences in practice between a Declaratory Charter and a Treaty Charter?

In reply, the Parliamentary Under-Secretary of State, FCO, wrote:

The Government believe that incorporation of the charter in the EU treaties is neither necessary nor desirable. It is not necessary because most of the substantive charter articles are based on existing law in the EU treaties or the European Convention on Human Rights. It is not desirable because a text incorporated into the treaties requires legal precision. The charter uses a breadth of language well suited for a political declaration enhancing the visibility of rights, freedoms and principles recognised within the EU.

The differences between a declaratory charter and one incorporated in the treaties would depend on the terms of the incorporation; at present the European Court of Justice is not obliged to have regard to the charter.

(HL Debs., vol. 619, *WA 142*: 29 November 2000)

Part Seven: I. A. *The State and its organs—the composition of the State—Heads of State*

(See also **6/6–9**, **13/11–12**)

[*Editorial Note*: The following item should be regarded as part of UKMIL 1999]

7/1

In the course of the proceedings in the case of *Re Pinochet (No. 3)*, in the Appellate Committee of the House of Lords, the following letter, dated 21 January 1999, was sent to the Crown Prosecution Service by the Head of Protocol Department, FCO:

RE: AUGUSTO PINOCHET UGARTE

1. I am directed by the Secretary of State to respond to the letter of 20 January 1999 signed by Counsel for the Appellants (the Government of Spain) and Counsel for the Respondent (Augusto Pinochet Ugarte) in the case of *R* v. *the Government of Spain and Others ex parte Augusto Pinochet Ugarte*, asking the following questions:

1) Did Her Majesty's Government recognise the Respondent, Augusto Pinochet Ugarte, as Head of State of the Republic of Chile?
2) If so, from what time was he so recognised?

2. At the time, Her Majesty's Government still adhered to the policy (abandoned in 1980, see Hansard HC Vol. 983 col. 277) of according recognition to new Governments which came to power unconstitutionally, provided that they met certain conditions, in particular that the new regime had effective control over most of the State's territory, and that it was, in fact, firmly established. Recognition was not understood to be a judgement on the constitutional or other legitimacy of the governing authorities in question. Its effect was to signal Her Majesty's Government's willingness to deal with the authorities in question as the government of the State concerned. There was no practice of according separate or express recognition to Heads of State.

3. It follows from the general material set out above that there was no express act of recognition of a Head of State following the coup in Chile in 1973. Nor is there any evidence that any enquiry was made by Her Majesty's Government into the constitutional functions assumed by General Pinochet in 1973 or thereafter, or the date from which any particular functions had been exercised by him. The Court may, however, find it of assistance to know the following.

4. The coup which brought to power the military junta took place on 11 September 1973. The new Government was recognised by Her Majesty's Government on 22 September the same year, through the medium of a Diplomatic Note from the British Embassy responding to a Note from the Ministry of Foreign Affairs the day after the coup. The Ministry's Note (enclosed, together with the Embassy's 'free translation') informed the Embassy that with effect from 11 September the Government of the Republic had been taken over by a military junta formed by four named persons, one of whom was General Pinochet. The Embassy were instructed to reply acknowledging receipt of the Ministry's Note and referring to the information regarding the institution of a new government.

5. The first Chilean Ambassador to the Court of St James's after the coup was appointed in October 1973. On 10 October 1973 the Foreign and Commonwealth Office asked the British Ambassador at Santiago to notify the Chilean Foreign Ministry that The Queen had granted agrément for the new Chilean Ambassador. The new Ambassador's Credentials, headed 'Augusto Pinochet Ugarte, Presidente de la Junta de Gobierno de Chile', were dated 26 October 1973. On 5 November 1973, the Foreign and Commonwealth Office wrote to the Ambassador acknowledging his Credentials and informing him that his name had been entered in the Diplomatic List. Some weeks later, General Pinochet, again styling himself as 'Presidente de la Junta de Gobierno de Chile', sent a message to The Queen on the occasion of New Year 1974. Her Majesty

responded in January 1974 by a telegram addressed to 'the President of the Governing Council of Chile'. Later, on 17 September 1974, Her Majesty sent a message to General Pinochet on the occasion of Chile's National Day, again addressing him as 'President of the Governing Council of Chile'. On 26 September 1974, General Pinochet acknowledged this message, this time under the style 'Jefe Supremo de la Nacion'.

6. I am directed to request you to ensure that copies of this letter and its enclosure are passed immediately to the Appellate Committee, the representatives of Senator Pinochet and the Intervenors, and the *amicus*.

(Text provided by the FCO)

Part Seven: I. E. *The State and its organs—the composition of the State—diplomatic missions and their members*

7/2

Speaking on 18 October 2000 in the Sixth Committee of the UN General Assembly considering the Report of the International Law Commission, the representative of France, on behalf of the EU and associated States, stated:

The rising number of breaches of the provisions of international law relating both to the security of diplomatic and consular staff and the inviolability of their properties has led the Sixth Commission to study this problem since 1980. Owing to numerous incidents, it became urgently necessary to reassert the principles of international law relating to diplomatic and consular relations and investigate new modalities of application capable of putting a stop to these violations. Unfortunately, this task remains relevant today, as illustrated by the Report by the Secretary-General, which gives evidence of some recent cases of breaches of international law relating to diplomatic and consular protection.

The European Union reasserts, as in previous examinations of this matter, the crucial importance of effective protection of diplomatic and consular staff in the conduct of international relations. The privileges and immunities enjoyed by diplomatic and consular staff and premises form an essential guarantee against various obstacles and pressures. They are mutually beneficial to all States in that their purpose is to facilitate contacts.

The rules of international law concerning diplomatic protection, long before being codified, have their roots far back in history. Since antiquity, intermediaries among nations have had to be protected in the interests of building peace among states. Everyone is aware of the eminent contribution made by diplomatic relations to the establishment of relations of trust among nations and concord among peoples. Any acceptance of lessened protection under the system of diplomatic and consular immunities would amount to endangering those objectives.

The obligation of guaranteeing the physical safety of staff obviously remains the most important one. The European Union is prepared to participate in all efforts aimed at guaranteeing and strengthening the right of diplomatic and consular staff to protection and security.

For this reason we consider it highly useful to reassert by a United Nations Resolution, as in 1998 by Resolution 53/97, that States must strictly observe and implement the provisions of international law relating to diplomatic and consular relations. More especially, host States are responsible for ensuring the protection of diplomatic and consular staffs and missions against groups or organizations whose intention it might be to threaten their security. This message, regularly reaffirmed by the international community, is a reminder of the absolute obligations incumbent on every State to guarantee diplomatic and consular relations free of all pressure on persons and property alike.

(Translated text provided by the FCO; see also A/C.6/55/SR. 10, p. 2)

Part Seven: IV. A. *The State and its organs—privileges and immunities—State immunity (including head of State immunity)*

7/3

The FCO delivered the following Note, dated 25 January 2000, to the Embassy of the Ukraine in London:

Eastern Department of the Foreign and Commonwealth Office presents its compliments to the Embassy of Ukraine and has the honour to refer to the Embassy's Note No. 151/BK3/1919/21–99 of 29 December 1999 regarding the dispute between Ukraine and Clin Finance Ltd. The Foreign and Commonwealth Office have notified the solicitors for the company that the British Government are not involved in the dispute and are unable to intervene on behalf of their client. Legal proceedings in the United Kingdom against a foreign state are governed by the State Immunity Act 1978. This grants immunity to a foreign state from the jurisdiction of our courts, but creates various exceptions which reflect the terms of the European Convention on State Immunity. The application of the provisions of the Act in any particular case is a matter to be determined by the courts of the United Kingdom, not by the British Government. The Foreign and Commonwealth Office are therefore unable to take any action in this matter. Legal advice on your position should be sought from your solicitors.

(Text provided by the FCO)

Part Seven: IV. B. *The State and its organs—privileges and immunities—diplomatic privileges and immunities*

7/4

The Times of 15 January 2000, p. 13, reported that armed Russian 'tax police' raided the Anglo-American School in St. Petersburg. According to the report: 'British and American envoys protested at the five-hour search, claiming that the school has diplomatic immunity.'

7/5

At a press conference held on 9 March 2000, the Minister of State, FCO, Mr Peter Hain, was asked about the incident at Harare Airport where diplomatic baggage destined for the British High Commission in Harare was detained and opened by the Zimbabwean authorities. The following exchange took place:

MR HAIN:

Could I say that I have just summoned the Zimbabwean High Commissioner to tell him in the strongest possible terms that we protest as a British government at this illegal act. It is a grave and serious breach of the international Vienna Convention. Zimbabwe should be in no doubt that this is unacceptable behaviour. Accordingly, we have decided to recall our High Commissioner from Harare for consultations. I shall also be summoning the High Commissioner, as I did today, to protest at this unprecedented action. This is a matter of the most serious concern to all countries. Every country across the world now is at risk of having its international bags, diplomatic bags, seized illegally by the Zimbabwean government which is behaving increasingly like a rogue state.

This is not an act of a civilised country and it is with great sadness that I have watched the tragedy of Zimbabwe unfold, potentially one of Africa's strongest economies and the uniting political forces. Zimbabwe has instead descended into economic chaos and increasing social instability and political isolation. The level of paranoia with which it views the international community could not be more ably demonstrated than by its need to open a diplomatic bag, without our consent, illegally, against international law and all norms of civilised conduct between countries. The bag in fact contained protective screening equipment for communications, as well as tools for its installation. This is routine equipment in all our diplomatic missions right across the world. Despite this, we will continue our efforts of dialogue with Zimbabwe in an attempt to help the country out of economic turmoil and to find political stability. As Zimbabwe's oldest friend we owe that to its people. We want Zimbabwe to succeed, but it cannot do so while it shuns the rule of law.

Q.:

What reasons have Zimbabwe given for opening the diplomatic baggage?

MR HAIN:

Absolutely no reasons have been given at all. The baggage was opened under duress. Our Deputy High Commissioner refused permission for it to be opened, in the presence of armed guards. This is the act of a rogue state, not the act of a civilised nation. It is in defiance of international law, the Vienna Convention, and Zimbabwe is acting illegally and every other country around the world will now be extremely concerned that their own diplomatic bags will be similarly seized.

Q.:

Can you just clarify what protective screening equipment is?

MR HAIN:

Protective screening equipment which was coming into Harare for our High Commission there is of exactly the same kind for our posts throughout the world to ensure that our own communications, telegrams and so on, are perfectly secure and safe. Every other country in the world does that, so do we.

(Text provided by the FCO)

7/6

In reply to a question, the Minister of State, FCO, wrote:

From a community of over 17,500 persons entitled to immunity, 36 serious offences, allegedly committed by such persons, were drawn to the attention of the Foreign and Commonwealth Office in 1999. 'Serious offences' are defined in accordance with the 1985 White Paper on Diplomatic Immunities and Privileges; i.e. as offences that would in certain circumstances carry a penalty of 12 months or more imprisonment.

(HC Debs., vol. 352, col. 580W: 29 June 2000)

Part Eight: I. D. *Jurisdiction of the State—bases of jurisdiction—universality*

8/1

In the course of a debate on the subject of Senator Pinochet's departure from the UK to Chile, the Secretary of State for the Home Department, Mr Jack Straw, was asked the following question:

Does he agree that although many people will find it difficult to understand why it was not possible to see justice done in this case, we should not lose sight of the fact that this country facilitated the process whereby important principles of international law were established—first, that there should be universal jurisdiction for human rights abuses, and secondly, that heads of state cannot automatically rely upon immunity? Does my right hon. Friend agree that important principles have been established none the less?

In reply, the Secretary of State observed:

Yes, I entirely agree with my hon. Friend that the principle of universal jurisdiction in respect of very serious crimes such as torture is now established as, too, is the principle that former heads of state are not immune from a process for such alleged crimes.

(HC Debs., vol. 345, col. 585: 2 March 2000)

Part Eight: III. A. *Jurisdiction of the State—extra-territorial exercises of jurisdiction—general*

8/2

On 29 May 2000, the UK and French Governments signed an Additional Protocol to the Sangatte Protocol on the establishment of bureaux responsible for controls on persons travelling by train between the UK and France (Cm 5015). An Explanatory Memorandum was presented to Parliament in December 2000 by the FCO. It read in material part:

The Additional Protocol supplements the Sangatte Protocol, of 25 November 1991, between the United Kingdom and France*. The Sangatte Protocol provided, in particular, for the establishment of control bureaux by each State on the territory of the other State ('juxtaposed controls'). The Additional Protocol permits the establishment of juxtaposed immigration controls at certain railway stations in France and the UK. The Governments of the United Kingdom and France signed the Additional Protocol on 29 May 2000.

The Sangatte Protocol permitted the establishment of frontier controls: by France, at Cheriton in Kent; and by the United Kingdom, at Coquelles in France. It also regulated the exercise of frontier controls on through trains between the UK and France.

The Additional Protocol extends the jurisdiction of United Kingdom immigration controls, and relevant French police controls, to railway stations at Paris Gare du Nord, Lille-Europe, Calais-Fréthun, Ashford, Waterloo and St Pancras. The extension is for the purpose of checking documentation and determining whether a person fulfils other conditions for entry to French or UK territory.

---

* Protocol Concerning Frontier Controls and Policing, Co-operation in Criminal Justice, Public Safety and Mutual Assistance Relating to the Channel Fixed Link (Cm 1802).

(Text provided by the FCO)

Part Eight: III. C. *Jurisdiction of the State—extra-territorial exercises of jurisdiction—military and other personnel abroad*

8/3

In reply to the question whether the provisions of s.9 of the Offences Against the Person Act 1861 operate fairly in relation to British soldiers under NATO command, the Minister of State, Ministry of Defence, wrote:

Yes. British troops remain subject to English law under whomsoever they serve and wherever they serve in the world.

(HL Debs., vol. 616, *WA 71*: 27 July 2000)

Part Nine: I. B. *State territory—territory—good-neighbourliness*

9/1

In a news release dated 8 December 2000 by the Department of the Environment, Transport and the Regions, it was stated:

An important step in protecting the global environment from harm during the movement and disposal of hazardous wastes was taken yesterday.

The UK has become one of the first countries to sign the Basel Convention Protocol on Liability and Compensation for Damage Resulting from Transboundary Movements of Hazardous Wastes and their Disposal. Once fully ratified the protocol will mean that any exporter of hazardous waste must be insured to cover any damage that may be caused on the journey to the recycler or disposer of that waste.

It establishes a comprehensive regime not only for liability but also for adequate and prompt compensation for damage resulting from transboundary movement of hazardous waste and will take effect when it has been ratified by 20 countries.

The UK is a strong supporter of the Basel Convention and the Government remains firmly committed to the objectives of environmentally sound management of hazardous waste.

. . .

The Basel Convention on the Control of Transboundary Movements of Hazardous Wastes and their Disposal is concerned with the environmentally sound management of hazardous waste. The UK ratified the Convention on 7 February 1994, the same date as the European Community and most other Community Member States. At present there are 143 Parties to the Convention. The Convention provides a system of prior informed consent to exports of hazardous wastes. Where exports do occur the onus is on the exporting state to ensure that the wastes are managed in an environmentally sound manner.

Article 12 of the Basel Convention provides for Parties to the Convention to co-operate with a view to adopting a protocol covering liability and compensation for damage resulting from the transboundary movements and disposal of hazardous wastes. This Protocol (the Basel Convention Protocol on Liability and Compensation) was adopted in Basel, Switzerland on 10 December 1999 at the 5th Conference of the Parties to the Basel Convention.

The Protocol establishes a system of strict liability for damage caused by transboundary movements of wastes, whereby the person initiating the transboundary movement will be strictly liable for any damage caused until the waste is delivered to the person recycling or disposing of that waste, when they become liable until completion of that operation. In order to ensure that the persons strictly liable can meet their financial obligations under the Protocol they will be required to carry insurance up to the limit of their strict liability. The Protocol will enter into force, for those who have ratified it, 90 days after the 20th ratification is received.

The Protocol will only enter into force in the UK following ratification. The UK will only be in a position to ratify the Protocol when we have a liability regime in place which enables the UK to meet the requirements of the Protocol. This will require new UK legislation.

Part Nine: II. A. *State territory—boundaries and frontiers—delimitation*

9/2

On 4 July 2000, the UK and the French Republic signed an Agreement concerning the establishment of a maritime boundary between France and Jersey (Cm 5024, with map annexed for information purposes only).

Part Nine: II. B. *State territory—boundaries and frontiers—demarcation*

(See **5/4**)

Part Nine: III. B. *State territory—territorial sovereignty—acquisition and preservation*

(See also **2/1**, **5/20–1**)

9/3

In the course of answering an oral question on the subject of the garrisoning of the Falkland Islands, the Minister for the Armed Forces, Mr John Spellar, stated:

> We very much welcome the restoration and development of democracy in Argentina. Indeed, my right hon. Friend the Secretary of State recently visited Argentina, and had very constructive discussions with Ministers there. He also visited the Falkland Islands and, again, had very useful discussions there, reinforcing our policy that the Falkland Islands are British and that sovereignty over the islands is not for negotiation. Accordingly, it is right that we should maintain a military presence as long as Argentina claims sovereignty over the islands.

(HC Debs., vol. 348, col. 686: 17 April 2000)

9/4

In reply to a question, the Parliamentary Under-Secretary of State, FCO, Baroness Scotland of Asthal, stated:

> . . . there have been no talks between Her Majesty's Government and the Government of the Republic of Cyprus with regard to the withdrawal of British sovereign base areas in Cyprus, nor do we have any intention to hold such talks. The sovereign base areas are British sovereign territory, as recognised by the 1960 Treaty of Establishment of the Republic of Cyprus between the United Kingdom, Greece, Turkey and the Republic of Cyprus.

(HL Debs., vol. 613, col. 176: 16 May 2000)

9/5

In reply to a question about the future of the British Indian Ocean Territory, the Minister of State, FCO, wrote in part:

We shall maintain our sovereignty over the BIOT for as long as our treaty obligations require it. Thereafter, we stand by the undertaking we have made that we would cede sovereignty of the territory to Mauritius.

(HC Debs., vol. 354, col. 145W: 18 July 2000)

9/6

The Permanent Representative of Argentina sent the following 'interpretative declaration', dated 8 September 2000, to the President of the UN General Assembly:

With regard to paragraph 4 of the Millennium Declaration, the Argentine delegation wishes to reiterate, in keeping with General Assembly resolutions 1514 (XV) and 2625 (XXV), its full support for the right to self-determination of peoples which remain under colonial domination and foreign occupation.

At the same time, it wishes to recall that the General Assembly has in numerous resolutions recognized the existence of a sovereignty dispute between the Argentine Republic and the United Kingdom concerning the Malvinas, South Georgia and South Sandwich islands and the surrounding maritime spaces, defining it as a special colonial situation which must be resolved through negotiations between the two Governments, by reconciling respect for the territorial integrity of Argentina with the interests of the population of the islands.

The UK Permanent Representative replied on 8 November 2000 as follows:

The British Government is pleased at the continued strengthening of our bilateral relations with Argentina, including this year through meetings between Prime Minister Blair and President De la Rua and between our Foreign Ministers.

The Joint Statement signed between our two countries in July 1999 demonstrates clearly that the United Kingdom and Argentina can manage our differences on sovereignty while making practical arrangements on matters of common interest in the South Atlantic.

However, we wish to recall that there is nothing in the agreement that compromises the position of the United Kingdom in relation to its sovereignty over the Falkland Islands: we have no doubt about Britain's sovereignty over the Falkland Islands and the other British overseas territories in the South Atlantic.

We have a duty to respect and defend the right to self-determination of the people of the Falkland Islands. The elected representatives of the Islanders once again expressed their views clearly when they visited the United Nations for this year's debate in the Committee of 24 on 11 July. They asked the Committee to recognize that they, like any other democratic people, were entitled to exercise the right to self-determination. They reiterated that the people of the Falkland Islands wanted to remain British and did not want to be part of Argentina.

The British Government remains committed to the Joint Statement and despite our differences with Argentina on the subject of sovereignty we are confident that we will build on this agreement and that our relations will continue to flourish in the spirit of reconciliation, cooperation and mutual interest.

(UN Document A/55/550)

9/7

Also on 8 November 2000, the UK Permanent Representative sent the following letter to the President of the UN General Assembly:

I have the honour to refer to the annex to the letter dated 8 September 2000 from the Permanent Representative of Argentina to the United Nations addressed to the President of the General Assembly and circulated by him (A/55/371).

The British Government fully supports the right to self-determination outlined in paragraph 4 of the Millennium Declaration. The wishes of the people of the Falkland Islands on their relationship with the United Kingdom are clear. Their views have been expressed before the Committee of 24. The people of the Falkland Islands do not want to be part of Argentina.

We have no doubt about Britain's sovereignty over the Falkland Islands and our other Overseas Territories in the South Atlantic. The British Government is confident that our relations with Argentina will continue to flourish in a spirit of reconciliation, cooperation and mutual interest that will enable us to manage our differences on sovereignty while making practical arrangements on matters of common interest in the South Atlantic.

I should be most grateful if you would have this letter distributed as a document of the General Assembly under agenda item 60(b).

(UN Document A/55/549)

9/8

In reply to a question, the Parliamentary Under-Secretary of State, FCO, wrote:

UNSCR 1244 makes it clear that Kosovo is currently part of the Federal Republic of Yugoslavia (FRY), but leaves its final status open. It will be up to the representatives of the residents of Kosovo, and the authorities in Belgrade, to agree on final status in due course, with the support of the international community.

(HL Debs., vol. 619, *WA 144*: 29 November 2000)

Part Eleven: II. *Seas and vessels—territorial sea, including overflight*

11/1

On 18 September 2000, the Crown Estate Office re-issued a press statement which contained the following item:

The Crown Estate owns around 55% of the foreshore (between mean high and mean low water) and approximately half of the beds of estuarial areas and tidal rivers in the United Kingdom. It also owns the seabed out to the 12-mile territorial limit, including the rights to explore and exploit the natural resources of the UK Continental Shelf, excluding oil, gas and coal.

The Crown Estate does not own the water column, oil, gas and coal, or govern public rights such as navigation and fishery over tidal waters.

(Text provided by the Crown Estate Office)

11/2

On 18 September 2000, the Crown Estate Office issued a press statement which read in part as follows:

On 7th July, the Crown Estate granted a lease of the seabed at Blyth, Northumberland for the UK's first offshore windfarm. The lease, to *Blyth Offshore Wind Ltd*, allows the erection of two Vestas V66 wind turbines each of 2.0MW rated capacity approximately 1 Km from the East Pier at Blyth on which the existing Blyth coastal windfarm is located. The project has been a number of years in planning and has involved extensive consultation and environmental assessment involving statutory and other bodies. The project is expected to be completed by the end of this summer.

(Text provided by the FCO)

11/3

In reply to a question on the subject of an exclusion zone around and above Diego Garcia, the Minister of State, FCO, wrote in part:

There are no exclusion zones. Diego Garcia has a three mile territorial sea, within which activities are restricted in accordance with the UN Convention on the Law of the Sea, and an area of controlled airspace that extends five miles out and 2,500ft upwards from the runway there.

(HC Debs., vol. 356, col. 685W: 15 November 2000)

11/4

The following notice was issued by the UK Hydrographic Office on January 2001:

12/01

NATIONAL CLAIMS TO MARITIME JURISDICTION.

Former Notice 12/00 is cancelled

The following list shows the breadth of sea (measured from the appropriate baselines) claimed respectively as territorial sea (TS), contiguous zone (CZ), exclusive economic zone (EEZ) and fishery zone (FZ), where no EEZ is claimed, as being under the state's jurisdiction. The information is compiled from various, sometimes unofficial sources, the absence of a limit from this list indicates that the information is not held.

The claims are published for information only. Her Majesty's Government does not recognise claims to territorial seas exceeding twelve nautical miles, to contiguous zones exceeding twenty four nautical miles or to exclusive economic zones and fisheries zones exceeding two hundred nautical miles.

Country	*TS*	*CZ*	*EEZ*	*FZ*
Albania[1]	12**	—	—	12
Algeria[1]*	12**	—	—	52[22]
Angola*	12	24	200	—
Antigua and Barbuda[2]*	12**	24	200	—
Argentina[1]*	12	24	200	—
Australia[1]*	12[11]	24	200	—
Australian Antarctica	12	—	—	12
Bahamas[2]*	12	—	200	—
Bahrain*	12	24	—	—
Bangladesh[4]	12**	18	200	—
Barbados*	12**	—	200	—
Belgium*	12	—	—	200
Belize[1]*	12[16]	—	200	—
Benin*	200	—	—	200
Brazil*[1]	12**	24	200	—
Brunei*	12	—	200	—
Bulgaria*	12**	24	200	—
Burma[1]*	12**	24	200	—
Cambodia[1]	12**	24	200	—
Cameroon*	50	—	—	—
Canada[1]	12	24	200	—
Cape Verde Islands[2]*	12	24	200	—
Chile[1]*	12	24	200	—
China				
PRC[1]*	12**	24	200	—
ROC (Taiwan)[1]	12	24	—	200
Colombia[1]	12	—	200	—
Comoros[2]*	12	—	200	—
Congo				
Brazzaville*	200	—	—	200
Kinshasa* (Zaire)	12	—	200	—
Cook Islands*	12	—	200	—
Costa Rica*	12	—	200	—
Croatia[1]*	12	—	200	—
Cuba[1]*	12	24	200	—
Cyprus*	12	—	—	12

Country	*TS*	*CZ*	*EEZ*	*FZ*
Denmark[1]	12**	—	200	—
Greenland[1]	3	—	—	200
Færoe Islands[1]	3	—	—	200
Djibouti[1]*	12	24	200	—
Dominica*	12	24	200	—
Dominican Republic[1]	6	24	200	—
Ecuador[1]	200	—	—	200
Egypt[1]*	12**	24	200	—
El Salvador	200	—	—	200
Equatorial Guinea*	12**	—	200	—
Eritrea[1]	12[12]	—	—	—
Estonia	12**[20]	—	200	—
Federated States of Micronesia*	12	—	200	—
Fiji[2]*	12	24	200	—
Finland[1]*	12**[13, 20]	14	—	12[21]
France[1]*	12	24	200[14]	12[14]
French Antarctica	12	—	—	—
Gabon[1,] *	12	24	200	—
Gambia*	12	18	200	—
Georgia*	12	—	200	—
Germany[1, 9]*	12	—	200	—
Ghana*	12	24	200	—
Greece*	6	—	—	6
Grenada*	12**	—	200	—
Guatemala*	12	—	200	—
Guinea*	12	24	200	—
Guinea Bissau[1]*	12	—	200	—
Guyana*	12**	—	200	—
Haiti*	12	24	200	—
Honduras[1]*	12	24	200	—
Iceland[1]*	12	—	200	—
India*	12**	24	200	—
Indonesia[2]*	12	24	200	—
Iran[1]	12**	24	200	—
Iraq*	12	—	—	—
Irish Republic[1]*	12	—	—	200
Israel	12[17]	—	—	—
Italy[1]*	12	—	—	12
Ivory Coast*	12	—	200	—

Country	*TS*	*CZ*	*EEZ*	*FZ*
Jamaica[2]*	12	24	200	—
Japan[1]*	12[23]	24	200	—
Jordan*	3	—	—	3
Kenya[1]*	12	—	200	—
Kiribati[2]	12	—	200	—
Korea (North)	12**	—	200	—
Korea (South)[1]*	12[6]**	24	200	—
Kuwait*	12	—	—	—
Latvia	12	—	200	—
Lebanon*	12	—	—	—
Liberia	200	—	—	200
Libya[5]	12**	—	—	20
Lithuania	12	—	200	—
Madagascar[1]	12	24	200	—
Malaysia[1]*	12	—	200	—
Maldives[2]*	12**	24	200	—
Malta[1]*	12**	24	—	25
Marshall Islands[2]*	12	24	200	—
Mauritania[1]*	12	24	200	—
Mauritius[1]*	12**	—	200	—
Mexico[1]*	12	24	200	—
Monaco[3]*	12	—	—	12
Morocco[1]	12	24	200	—
Mozambique[1]*	12	—	200	—
Namibia*	12	—	200	—
Nauru*	12	24	200	—
Netherlands[1]*	12	—	200	—
Netherlands Antilles	12	—	—	to median lines
Aruba	12	—	—	to median lines
New Zealand*	12	—	200	—
Ross Dependency	12	—	—	—
Nicaragua	200**	—	—	200
Nigeria*	12**	—	200	—
Norway[1]*	4	10	200	—
Svalbard	4	—	—	200
Oman[1]*	12	24	200	—
Pakistan[1]*	12**	24	200	—
Palau (Belau)*	3	—	—	200
Panama*	12	24	200	—
Papua New Guinea[2]*	12[15]	—	—	200
Peru	200	—	—	200

Country	*TS*	*CZ*	*EEZ*	*FZ*
Philippines[2, 3]*	12	—	200	—
Poland*	12**	—	200	—
Portugal[1]*	12	24	200	—
Qatar	12	24	—	to median lines
Romania[1]*	12**	24	200	—
Russia[1]*	12	—	200	—
St. Kitts-Nevis*	12	24	200	—
St. Lucia*	12	24	200	—
St. Vincent and the Grenadines[2]*	12**	24	200	—
Sao Tome and Principe[2]*	12	—	200	—
Saudi Arabia[1]*	12	18	—	—
Senegal[1]*	12	24	200	—
Seychelles*	12	24	200	—
Sierra Leone*	200	—	—	200
Singapore*	3	—	—	324
Slovenia*	12	—	—	—
Solomon Islands[2]*	12	—	200	—
Somalia*	200**	—	—	200
South Africa[1]*	12	24	200	—
Spain[1]*	12	24	200[14]	to median lines[14]
Sri Lanka*	12**	24	200	—
Sudan*	12**	18	—	—
Surinam*	12	—	200	—
Sweden[1]*	12	—	200	—
Syria	35**	41	—	—
Tanzania*	12	—	200	—
Thailand[1]	12	—	200	—
Togo*	30	—	200	—
Tonga[3]*	12[3]	—	200[3]	—
Trinidad and Tobago[2]*	12	24	200	—
Tunisia[1]*	12	24	—	12[8]
Turkey[1]	12[7]**	—	200[18]	12[7]
Tuvalu[2]	12	24	200	—
UAE[1]	12**	24	200	—
UK[1]*	12	—	—	200
Anguilla*	3	—	—	200
Bailiwick of Guernsey*	3	—	—	12
Bailiwick of Jersey*	12	—	—	3
Bermuda*	12	—	200	—
British Antarctic Territory*	3	—	—	3
British Indian Ocean Territory*	3	—	—	200

Country	*TS*	*CZ*	*EEZ*	*FZ*
British Virgin Islands*	3	—	—	200
Cayman Islands*	12	—	—	200
Cyprus (Sovereign Base Areas)	3	—	—	3
Falkland Islands[1]*	12	—	—	200[10]
Gibraltar*	3	—	—	3
Isle of Man*	12	—	—	12
Montserrat*	3	—	—	200
Pitcairn*	3	—	200	—
St. Helena and Dependencies*	12	—	—	200
South Georgia[1]*	12	—	200	—
South Sandwich Islands*	12	—	200	—
Turks and Caicos Islands[1]*	12	—	—	200
Ukraine[1]*	12	—	200	—
Uruguay*	12	24	200	—
USA	12	24	200	—
Vanuatu[2]*	12	24	200	—
Venezuela[1]	12	15	200	—
Vietnam[1]*	12**	24	200	—
Western Samoa*	12	—	200	—
Yemen*	12**	24	200	—
Yugoslavia[1, 19]*	12	—	—	12

Limits of dependent territories have not been listed unless they differ from those of the metropolitan state.

1 employs straight baseline systems along all or a part of the coast.
2 claims archipelago status.
3 claims waters within limits defined by geographic co-ordinates not related to distance from the coastline.
4 claims straight baseline system between points along the 18 metre isobath.
5 claims all water south of 32° 30'N. in the Gulf of Sirte as internal waters.
6 claims 3 M in Korea Strait.
7 claims 6 M in Aegean Sea.
8 fishery limit extends to 50 metre isobath off the Gulf of Gabes.
9 special claim extends limit to include the deep water anchorage west of Helgoland.
10 150 M in west with a rhumb line between 52° 30'.00S, 63°19'.25W and 54° 08'.68S, 60° 00'.00W.
11 certain islands in the Torres Strait retain 3 M territorial sea limit.
12 jurisdiction claimed to the limit of the pearl and sedentary fishery grounds.
13 Bogskar has a 3 M territorial sea limit.
14 does not claim an EEZ in the Mediterranean, France only claims a 12 M fishery limit and Spain a fishery limit to median lines.

[15] reduced to 3 M in the Torres Strait area.
[16] reduced to 3 M in the Gulf of Honduras.
[17] reduced to 3 M off Gaza.
[18] only claims an EEZ in the Black Sea.
[19] Republic of Serbia and Montenegro.
[20] TS limit reduced in parts of the Gulf of Finland to preserve a 6M wide high seas corridor.
[21] to maritime boundaries in areas exceeding 12 M.
[22] reduced to 32 nm west of the longitude of Ras Térés.
[23] TS limits reduced in the following international straits to retain a high seas corridor: La Perouse (Soya), Tsugaru, Osumi, Eastern and Western Channels, and Tsushima.
[24] and beyond TS limits to treaty limits.

* indicates a state which has ratified or acceded to the UN Convention on the Law of the Sea (UNCLOS), which came into force on 16 November 1994.

** indicates a state which requires prior permission or notification for entry of foreign warships into the territorial sea. The United Kingdom government does not recognise this requirement.

(Published in *Annual Summary of Admiralty Notices to Mariners in Force on 1 January 2001*, pp. I–81–5).

Part Eleven: III. *Seas and vessels—straits, including overflight*

11/5

In reply to the question whether he will assess the benefits of reconvening the conference which led to the Treaty of Montreux in order to reconsider its provisions, the Minister of State, FCO, wrote:

The UK keeps all Treaties to which it is a signatory under review. We do not believe there is a need for changes to the Montreux Convention at present. No other party to the Convention has asked for the conference to be reconvened.

(HC Debs., vol. 350, col. 300W: 19 May 2000)

Part Eleven: V. *Seas and vessels—contiguous zone*

(See **11/4**)

Part Eleven: VI. *Seas and vessels—exclusive economic zone*

(See **11/4**)

Part Eleven: VII. *Seas and vessels—exclusive or preferential fisheries zones*

(See **11/4**)

11/6

On 4 July 2000, the Governments of the UK and France signed an Agreement concerning fishing in the Bay of Granville. In a press release issued by the FCO it was stated in part:

The Agreement replaces the 1839 Granville Bay Agreement. It should ensure the effective conservation and management of the fishery in the Bay of Granville area. It formally defines zones and fishing rights within the Bay for Jersey and French fishermen. In addition, there is a separate Agreement delimiting the median line between France and Jersey.

(Text provided by FCO)

Part Eleven: IX. A. *Seas and vessels—high seas—freedom of the high seas, including overflight*

11/7

A press report described a plan to refloat for salvage two British warships, *Repulse* and *Prince of Wales*, sunk by enemy action about 50 miles from the east coast of Malaysia in 1941. A spokesman for the Ministry of Defence was reported to have remarked:

As things stand, it is illegal for war graves to be disturbed in UK waters, or by British subjects in international waters.

Within the past week we have reinforced and related existing standing instructions to the British High Commission in Singapore and Kuala Lumpur to make representations to host governments, relaying our concerns over the activities of divers and salvage operators which have been recently taking place in thc vicinity of both vessels.

It is true, however, that as both British vessels lie in international waters, we must rely on the co-operation of both governments.

The [Ministry of Defence] is sympathetic to the campaign's call for additional recognition for the graves under the Protection of Military Remains Act, but acknowledges that there would be little chance of preventing determined scavengers unless the Act was adopted internationally.

(*The Sunday Telegraph*, 27 August 2000, p. 14)

11/8

In reply to a question, the Minister of State, Ministry of Agriculture, Fisheries and Food, wrote in part:

The Rockall fisheries zone (RFZ) was relinquished in 1997 when the UK acceded to the UN Convention on the Law of the Sea (UNCLOS). Article 121(3) of UNCLOS prevents 'rocks which cannot sustain human habitation or economic life of their own' being used to generate exclusive economic zones. Maintenance of the RFZ would not therefore have been compatible with UNCLOS and so would have been open to legal challenge.

(HL Debs., vol. 616, *WA 210*: 3 October 2000)

Part Eleven: XIV. *Seas and vessels—protection of the marine environment*

11/9

In the course of a debate on the subject of marine pollution, the Parliamentary Under-Secretary of State, Environment, Transport and the Regions, Mr Chris Mullin, stated:

It may be helpful if I remind hon. Members of some of the background to OSPAR's consideration of radioactive discharges. As my hon. Friend explained, the Oslo and Paris commission was set up to protect the marine environment of the north-east Atlantic; it came into force in 1998. The UK is a contracting party and supports the commission's aim of reducing discharges of radioactivity.

(HC Debs., vol. 352, col. 95WH: 21 June 2000)

Part Eleven: XIX. C. 4. *Seas and vessels—vessels—jurisdiction over vessels—exercises of jurisdiction other than by flag, coastal and port State*

[*Editorial Note*: The following item should be regarded as part of UKMIL 1995]

11/10

On 10 March 1995, the EC and its Member States sent a Note Verbale to the Government of Canada which included the following passages:

The arrest of a vessel in international waters by a State other than the State of which the vessel is flying the flag and under whose jurisdiction it falls, is an illegal act under both the NAFO Convention and customary international law, and cannot be justified by any means. With this action Canada is not only flagrantly violating international law, but is failing to observe normal behaviour of responsible States.

This act is particularly unacceptable since it undermines all the efforts of the international community, notably in the framework of the FAO and the United Nations Conference on Straddling Fish Stocks and Highly Migratory Fish Stocks, to achieve effective conservation through enhanced cooperation in the management of fisheries resources.

This serious breach of international law goes far beyond the question of fisheries conservation. The arrest is a lawless act against the sovereignty of a Member State of the European Community. Furthermore, the behaviour of the Canadian vessels has clearly endangered the lives of the crew and the safety of the Spanish vessel concerned.

The European Community and its Member States demand that Canada immediately release the vessel, repair any damages caused, cease and desist from its harassment of vessels flying the flag of Community Member States and immediately repeal the legislation under which it claims to take such unilateral action.

(These passages were reproduced in the Judgment of the International Court of

Justice in the *Fisheries Jurisdiction Case (Spain* v. *Canada)*, 4 December 1998, paragraph 20)

Part Twelve: III. A. *Air space, outer space and Antarctica—Antarctica—limits and status*

12/1

In March 2000, the FCO published a booklet entitled *Britain and Antarctica*, from which the following passages are taken:

BRITISH ANTARCTIC TERRITORY

The British Antarctic Territory (BAT) is the oldest territorial claim to a part of the continent, although most of it is now counter-claimed by either Chile or Argentina. There is no indigenous population, but the BAS has three research stations there and the Royal Navy maintains an ice patrol vessel, HMS Endurance, in the area during the austral summer. The Territory has its own legal system and legal and postal administrations. Revenue from income tax and the sale of postage stamps means that it is financially self sufficient.

ANTARCTIC TREATY SYSTEM

By the 1950s, five-sixths of the continent was claimed by seven States (. . .). None of the claims was recognised by non-Claimant States, however, and the Antarctic Treaty was negotiated to put in place a mechanism to defuse the escalating disputes over sovereignty. It followed the unprecedented scientific cooperation in Antarctica demonstrated by 12 countries during the International Geophysical Year, 1957/58.

Britain was the first to sign the Antarctic Treaty, which entered into force in 1961. Covering the area south of 60 degrees latitude south, its objectives are:

- to keep Antarctica demilitarised, to establish it as a nuclear-free zone, and to ensure that it is used for peaceful purposes only;
- to promote international scientific cooperation in Antarctica; and
- to set aside disputes over territorial sovereignty.

The Treaty provides for confidence-building procedures, including exchanges of information about Antarctic activities and on-site inspections. It also provides means of consulting on matters of common interest.

The Treaty remains in force indefinitely; it has the possibility for review after 30 years (ie after June 1991), but no Party has indicated a desire for such a review. It is open for accession to all Member States of the United Nations (UN), and to others by agreement of the Treaty States. Thirty-two countries have now joined the original 12 (see Annex), and between them these now represent 80 per cent of the world's population and include both Claimants and non-Claimants, and developed and developing countries.

Consultative (voting) status is open to all countries which have demonstrated their commitment to Antarctica by conducting significant research there. Twenty-seven, including Britain, have Consultative status; they meet at annual (previously biennial) Antarctic Treaty Consultative Meetings (ACTMs), to which non-Consultative Parties and international organisations with appropriate expertise are also invited. This includes participation of environmental non-governmental organisations. Twenty-three such Meetings, held since 1961, have adopted more than 200 regulatory measures—known until 1995 as Recommendations (because they were largely non-mandatory), but now called Measures, Decisions or Resolutions to differentiate between mandatory, administrative or non-mandatory decisions respectively. More than half of those adopted have dealt with conservation and environmental protection, while others have covered subjects such as telecommunications, postal services, air safety and meteorological cooperation. Special Consultative Meetings address issues which cannot be adequately examined at the regular gatherings.

Five separate international agreements have been negotiated which, together with the original Treaty and the suite of Measures, Decisions and Resolutions, provide the framework governing all activities in Antarctica. Collectively known as the Antarctic Treaty System, the five agreements are:

- Agreed Measures for the Conservation of Antarctic Fauna and Flora (adopted June 1964);
- Convention for the Conservation of Antarctic Seals (adopted December 1972 and entered into force March 1978);
- Convention on the Conservation of Antarctic Marine Living Resources (CCAMLR) (adopted May 1980 and entered into force April 1982);
- Convention on the Regulation of Antarctic Mineral Resource Activities (CRAMRA) (adopted June 1988, but superseded by the Environmental Protocol (see below) and unlikely to enter into force); and
- Protocol on Environmental Protection to the Antarctic Treaty (adopted October 1991 and entered into force January 1998).

(Text provided by the FCO)

Part Thirteen: II. A. 1. (a). *International responsibility—responsibility other than criminal—responsible entities—States—the elements of responsibility*

13/1

Speaking on 23 October 2000 in the Sixth Committee of the UN General Assembly discussing the Report of the International Law Commission, the Legal Adviser, FCO, Mr M. C. Wood, stated with regard to the draft articles on State responsibility:

As to the *content*, the text of draft article 41 appears to combine what we understand to be different categories of obligations: namely, obligations owed *erga omnes* and obligations arising from peremptory norms of international law. It seems to create a new category of supernorm. The criteria for inclusion are both 'general and not very precise', as the Chairman of the Drafting Committee conceded in his statement. If the intention is to codify the Court's *dictum* in the *Barcelona Traction* case, this could have been done more simply. We do, of course, accept the basic concept that there are certain obligations which States owe to all States, or if you like, to the international community of States as a whole. I stress the international community of *States* as a whole. The expression currently used in the draft articles—'the international community as a whole'—is potentially misleading. Wherever this expression occurs in the text (eg article 26) it could be replaced by 'the international community of States as a whole' (c.f. article 53 of the Vienna Convention on the Law of Treaties) or, even better, by 'all States'.

I turn now to the *consequences* that it is suggested should flow from serious breaches of obligations owed to all States, however defined. It is generally accepted that all States have standing to bring a claim in respect of a breach of an obligation owed to all States. That proposition is reflected in article 49.1 (b) of the draft articles and, rightly, in our view, is not there limited to serious breaches of such obligations. We have doubts, however, about the three consequences specifically ascribed by the Commission to the category of 'serious breaches', which are set out in draft articles 42 and 54.2.

The first proposed consequence is the possibility of an award of damages reflecting the 'gravity of the breach'. To the extent that this is a reference to punitive damages, we would question whether such damages have a place in international law. If they do, surely they are potentially applicable to certain breaches of *any* international obligation.

The second proposed consequence concerns the obligations arising for third States. We are troubled by two aspects of the Commission's enumeration in article 42.2. It is inspired, no doubt, by the Advisory Opinion in the *Namibia* case. But that case concerned the legal consequences for States of an occupation of territory which had been declared by the Security Council to be illegal. We do wonder whether it is possible to speak of a single rule for all purposes. One way round this difficulty might be to provide a less prescriptive formulation, as in draft article 42.1. Our second concern with this enumeration of consequences for other States is that their inclusion in a separate chapter devoted to 'serious breaches' would seem to imply that they cannot apply to any other breaches of obligations, whatever the circumstances.

The most difficult issue, as we see it, concerns the proposal made in draft article 54.2. This would permit any State, in the case of this category of breach, to take countermeasures 'in the interest of the beneficiaries of the obligation breached'. Even if we accept the proposition, on the basis of the *Barcelona Traction dictum*, that there is a legal interest of States at large in respect of violations of certain obligations, it does not necessarily follow that all States can vindicate those interests in the same way as directly injured States.

The present proposals are potentially highly destabilising of treaty relations. Is it really the case that any (and every) State should be able to contravene any of its treaties, including—for example—those of a technical nature such as postal service agreements and the like, in response to any serious breach by another State of any *erga omnes* obligations? What happens if the State most directly affected does not want countermeasures to be taken? How would the principle of proportionality operate in such a situation?

(Text provided by the FCO; see also A/C.6/55/SR. 14, p. 7)

Part Thirteen: II. A. 1. (c). *International responsibility—responsibility other than criminal—responsible entities—States—diplomatic and consular protection*

13/2

In reply to a question, the Minister of State, FCO, wrote:

Her Majesty's Government have entered into 93 Investment Promotion and Protection Agreements. Of these, 84 are in force and nine are awaiting entry into force. There are 22 OECD member states with which an Investment Promotion and Protection Agreement is not required. Protection of investments is generally considered to be satisfactory under the domestic legislation of OECD member states.

The countries which have signed an Investment Promotion and Protection Agreement with the UK and which are in force are (date of entry into force in parenthesis):

Albania (30 August 1995)
Antigua and Barbuda (12 June 1987)
Argentina (19 February 1993)
Armenia (11 July 1996)
Azerbaijan (11 December 1996)
Bahrain (30 October 1991)
Bangladesh (19 June 1980)
Barbados (7 April 1993)
Belarus (28 December 1994)
Belize (30 April 1982)
Benin (23 November 1987)
Bolivia (16 February 1990)
Bulgaria (24 June 1997)
Burundi (13 September 1990)
Cameroon (7 June 1985)
Chile (21 April 1997)
China (15 May 1986)
Congo (9 November 1990)
Cote d'Ivoire (9 October 1997)
Croatia (16 April 1998)
Cuba (11 May 1995)
Czech and Slovak Republics (24 October 1991, amended 26 October 1992)
Dominica (23 January 1987)
Ecuador (24 August 1995)
Egypt (24 February 1976)
Estonia (16 December 1994)
Georgia (15 February 1995)
Ghana (25 October 1991)
Grenada (25 February 1998)
Guyana (11 April 1990)
Haiti (27 March 1995)
Honduras (8 March 1995)
Hong Kong (12 April 1999)

Hungary (28 August 1987)
India (6 January 1995)
Indonesia (24 March 1977)
Jamaica (14 May 1987)
Jordan (24 April 1980)
Kazakhstan (23 November 1995)
Kenya (13 September 1999)
Korea (4 March 1976)
Kyrgyzstan (18 May 1998)
Laos (1 May 1995)
Latvia (15 February 1995)
Lesotho (18 February 1981)
Lithuania (21 September 1993)
Malaysia (21 October 1988)
Malta (4 October 1986)
Mauritius (13 October 1986)
Moldova (30 June 1998)
Mongolia (4 October 1991)
Nepal (2 March 1993)
Nigeria (11 December 1990)
Oman (21 May 1996)
Pakistan (30 November 1994)
Panama (7 November 1985)
Papua New Guinea (22 December 1981)
Paraguay (23 April 1992, amended 13 June 1997)
Peru (21 April 1994)
Philippines (21 February 1981)
Poland (14 April 1988)
Romania (10 January 1996)
Senegal (9 February 1984)
Singapore (22 June 1975)
Slovenia (12 May 1999)
South Africa (27 May 1998)
Soviet Union (3 July 1991, now applies to Russian Federation)
Sri Lanka (18 December 1980)
St. Lucia (18 January 1983)
Swaziland (5 May 1995)
Tanzania (2 August 1996)
Thailand (11 August 1979)
Tonga (22 October 1997)
Trinidad and Tobago (8 October 1993)
Tunisia (4 January 1990)
Turkey (22 October 1996)
Turkmenistan (9 February 1995)
Uganda (24 April 1998)
Ukraine (10 February 1993)
UAE (15 December 1993)
Uruguay (1 August 1997)
Uzbekistan (24 November 1993)

Venezuela (1 August 1996)
Yemen (11 November 1983).

The nine countries which have signed Investment Promotion and Protection Agreements with the UK, which have yet to enter into force are:

Brazil
Colombia
Costa Rica
El Salvador
Lebanon
Morocco
Nicaragua
Sierra Leone
Zimbabwe.

The 22 OECD member states with whom an Investment Promotion and Protection Agreement is not required are:

Australia
Austria
Belgium
Canada
Denmark
Finland
France
Germany
Greece
Iceland
Ireland
Italy
Japan
Luxembourg
Netherlands
New Zealand
Norway
Portugal
Spain
Sweden
Switzerland
USA.

(HC Debs., vol. 346, cols. 600–2W: 22 March 2000)

13/3

Following the arrest in Montenegro of four policemen, including two British citizens, who were seconded to the Organization for Security and Co-operation in Europe as part of the UN Mission in Kosovo, a spokesman of the FCO stated on 3 August 2000:

It is . . . unacceptable that the Yugoslav authorities have still not informed the British Interests Section in the Brazilian Embassy in Belgrade of these arrests, or provided any information. This is in clear breach of international obligations. This afternoon the head of the Yugoslav Interests Section of the Cyprus High Commission in London was summoned to the Foreign and Commonwealth Office to [receive a] protest at this behaviour.

(Text provided by the FCO)

13/4

The Minister of State, FCO, Mr Keith Vaz, stated at a press conference held on 8 August 2000:

We will take whatever action we deem to be necessary. The action we are taking at the moment is the right action. We are making a plea on the basis of bilateral conventions and indeed the Vienna Convention which talks about people having access to consular help without delay.

What we want them to do is what we said that we wanted them to do on 3 August, which is to provide the same consular access and legal advice and assistance that any other person would expect to have under the Vienna Convention and under bilateral arrangements.

(Text provided by the FCO)

13/5

In a radio interview held on 10 August 2000 on the same subject, Mr Vaz stated:

It's quite clear in the Vienna Convention and in all the bilateral conventions that have been signed that when a citizen of another country is held there must be immediate consular access and that is what we have got to see.

(Text provided by the FCO)

13/6

On 22 August 2000, the Liberian Chargé d'Affaires, Mr Dowana, was called to the FCO where the Minister of State, Mr Peter Hain, expressed concern to him about the treatment by the Liberian authorities of four UK television journalists charged with espionage. Mr Hain stated:

Despite the assurances that their lawyer would be present, the four journalists were charged yesterday afternoon shortly after their lawyer had been sent away. I told the Liberian Chargé that this was totally unacceptable. Access to their lawyer has only been obtained today following an application to a court in Monrovia to enforce what is a basic element of Liberian law.

Despite their obligations under the Vienna Convention, the Liberian authorities have also denied consular access to the journalists. I told Mr Dowana that we expected our Embassy official from Abidjan to be given immediate access.

(Text provided by the FCO)

13/7

A press statement issued by the FCO on 25 October 2000 read as follows:

The Cuban Chargé d'Affaires, Mr Oscar de los Reyes, was summoned to Foreign and Commonwealth Office on 25 October to enable us to raise HMG's serious concerns at the denial of consular access to the seven British nationals detained in Cuba.

After the meeting, Foreign Minister Peter Hain said:

> 'I am pleased that the Chargé said that access to the detainees would be granted imminently. But I received no satisfactory explanation as to why the British Embassy in Havana had been unable to offer consular assistance to the seven British nationals detained by the Cuban authorities since 9 October in breach of the Vienna Convention governing diplomatic relations. This is most unsatisfactory. I also asked either that charges be brought against the detainees straightaway or that they be released. I hope that the Cuban authorities will resolve this matter speedily. Relations between Britain and Cuba are good and this incident is unusual and unfortunate. I hope that it can be quickly resolved.'

(Text provided by the FCO)

Part Thirteen: III. A. *International responsibility—criminal responsibility—definition of an international crime*

13/8

In the course of a debate on the subject of the situation in Burma, a speaker asked if the Minister would state that the actions of the regime in Burma amounted to genocide 'according to the legal definition.' In reply, the Minister of State, FCO, Mr Keith Vaz, stated:

> I understand why the hon. Gentleman raises the matter. The descriptions that he has given us are appalling, but he must know that the term 'genocide' has a precise meaning in international law. To be frank, under international law and all the rights and responsibilities that bind one under that law, genocide is difficult to prove. I understand the point that the hon. Gentleman makes and I can assure him that we will keep looking at this point, but genocide is a legal term and has a particular definition. I know that he does not use the word loosely. Defining the actions of the Burmese regime as genocide is important to him and to what he hopes that the Government and the international community can do. I assure him that we have noted what he has said and will continue to monitor the situation closely.

(HC Debs., vol. 347, col. 220WH: 5 April 2000)

13/9

Speaking in June 2000 in the Preparatory Commission for the International Criminal Court while it was considering the definition of the crime of aggression, the UK delegate, Ms Elizabeth Wilmshurst, stated:

> The first proposal I would like to consider is that in WGCA/DP1 (it is also to be found in the compilation but in a less accessible form). It provides in essence

that aggression constitutes the use of armed force against the sovereignty, territorial integrity or political independence of a State in violation of the Charter of the United Nations. The definition relies upon the undoubted fact that the Charter outlaws the use of force except in certain circumstances and draws the conclusion that all uses of force contrary to the Charter will involve individual criminal responsibility for aggression in respect of persons participating in those unlawful uses of force. That is a neat conclusion and it would simplify our task if it were the right one, but my delegation does not believe that it is.

If we adopted this proposal or anything along similar lines we would be bringing within the Court's jurisdiction individual participation in any unlawful use of force by a State. But there is nothing in international law to say that participation in any such use of force by an individual amounts to the crime of aggression. An act of aggression which is not part of an aggressive war (whether declared or undeclared) may give rise to State responsibility. But my delegation remains to be convinced that it constitutes a crime for an individual under international law. Certainly we have not found convincing international authority for that proposition. And it does not accord with the concept of what the Court should be doing. Should we really be giving the ICC jurisdiction in relation to participation in border skirmishes, for example? For these reasons my delegation has difficulty with the proposal in WGCA/DP1 and proposals of that nature.

(Text provided by the FCO)

13/10

In reply to a question on whether Her Majesty's Government recognised the Armenian massacre of 1915 as genocide within the meaning of the Genocide Convention, the Parliamentary Under-Secretary of State, FCO, wrote:

The Government's position on this topic is well known and was discussed in the House of Lords on 14 April 1999. The British Government condemned the massacre of 1915–16 at the time and viewed the sufferings of the Armenian people then as a terrible tragedy. The current Government in no way dissents from that view. But in the absence of unequivocal evidence to show that the Ottoman administration took a specific decision to eliminate the Armenians, British Governments have not recognised the events of 1915–16 as genocide.

(HL Debs., vol. 615, *WA 49*: 13 July 2000)

Part Thirteen: III. B. 2. *International responsibility—criminal responsibility—responsible entities—entities other than States (e.g. individuals and corporations)*

13/11

In reply to a request for a statement concerning the Crown Prosecution Service as prosecuting authority in the case of Senator Pinochet, the Solicitor-General, Mr Ross Cranston, wrote:

The Crown Prosecution Service as prosecuting authority for England and Wales has advised the Metropolitan Police Service that the material provided by the Kingdom of Spain for the purposes of the extradition proceedings would not be admissible in a criminal prosecution in England and Wales and could not be put into admissible form without a full police investigation. On the material presently available to the CPS, therefore, there is no realistic prospect in this jurisdiction of convicting Senator Pinochet of any criminal offence.

The Crown Prosecution Service has also advised the Metropolitan Police Service that, in view of the independent medical report on Senator Pinochet commissioned by the Home Secretary and taking into account representations made to the Home Secretary concerning the reports, no court in England and Wales would allow a trial of Senator Pinochet to take place, whatever the evidence.

The CPS advised the police further that the allegations contained in the Swiss, both French and both Belgian requests did not disclose offences which could be tried here since the conduct alleged in each of the requests occurred before the relevant legislation came into force.

I was consulted about this matter by the DPP and agree with these conclusions.

(HC Debs., vol. 345, cols. 336–7W: 2 March 2000)

13/12

Speaking later in the Chamber of the House of Commons, Mr Cranston stated:

With permission, Mr Deputy Speaker, I should like to make a statement about the role of the Crown Prosecution Service in respect of Senator Pinochet.

Earlier today, the CPS, as prosecuting authority for England and Wales, advised the Metropolitan police service that the material provided by the Kingdom of Spain for the purposes of extradition proceedings would not be admissible in a criminal prosecution in England and Wales and could not be put into admissible form without a full police investigation. On the material available to the CPS, therefore, there is no realistic prospect in this jurisdiction of convicting Senator Pinochet of any criminal offence.

The CPS also advised the Metropolitan police service that, in view of the independent medical report on Senator Pinochet, commissioned by the Home Secretary, and in view of representations made to the Home Secretary concerning the report, no court in England and Wales would allow a trial of Senator Pinochet to take place, whatever the evidence. Following that advice, the MPS decided that no purpose would be served in seeking to effect an arrest of Senator Pinochet.

Those decisions were necessary because of article 7 of the United Nations convention against torture and other cruel, inhuman or degrading treatment or punishment. The convention provides that if a state does not extradite, it must consider whether to prosecute the person itself. Accordingly, following the Home Secretary's decision not to extradite Senator Pinochet to Spain, the Spanish extradition papers were submitted formally to the CPS as the independent prosecuting authority for England and Wales. The CPS in turn formally referred the papers to the MPS, which is responsible for investigating offences and deciding whether to arrest or charge people.

In fact, the papers had previously been supplied to the CPS and the police and had been carefully studied by them, so both the CPS and the police were in a position to announce their decisions today. However, before I say more about that, I should set out the involvement of the CPS in the case. The CPS had a role as agent for the Kingdom of Spain, which arose after Senator Pinochet's arrest on 16 October 1998, pursuant to a warrant issued by the fifth central magistrates court in Madrid. On 18 October 1998, the CPS commenced acting as agent on behalf of the Kingdom of Spain in the extradition proceedings, and it has continued to act for the Kingdom of Spain throughout the extradition process.

In its role as agent for the Kingdom of Spain, the CPS acted in accordance with the instructions of the requesting state, which is in accordance with long-standing reciprocal arrangements between this jurisdiction and other countries. In doing so, it has been quite independent of the Government. In performing its role as agent for the Kingdom of Spain, the CPS has given confidential legal advice on the extradition proceedings and received instructions.

Let me turn to the separate and distinct function of the CPS in this matter, which is the main focus of this statement. That function is its role as the independent prosecuting authority for England and Wales, and its involvement in that regard arose in two ways. First, in October 1998 two firms of solicitors, acting for a number of individuals, applied to the then Attorney-General, my right hon. and learned Friend the Member for Aberavon (Sir J. Morris), for consent to prosecute Senator Pinochet in this jurisdiction for offences of torture, contrary to section 134 of the Criminal Justice Act 1988, and for offences of hostage taking, contrary to the Taking of Hostages Act 1982.

The papers in one of these applications were also copied by the solicitors to the MPS, which in turn sought the advice of the CPS as prosecuting authority. In those circumstances, my right hon. and learned Friend deemed it appropriate to liaise with the CPS before reaching a final conclusion on the applications for Law Officer consent to prosecute. The Attorney-General also received advice from senior Treasury counsel. Subsequently, he advised the solicitors that decisions on whether or not to grant Law Officer consent to prosecute are made by applying the tests set out in the code for Crown prosecutors, and that the legislation criminalising torture and hostage taking is not retrospective—a point later confirmed by a decision of the Appellate Committee of the House of Lords. He also advised that the material submitted in support of the applications contained insufficient admissible evidence against Senator Pinochet to justify the granting of Law Officer consent to prosecute for either offence. Consent to prosecute was, accordingly, refused.

I should add that a third firm of solicitors, acting for a number of Chileans, applied last week for my consent to prosecute Senator Pinochet for offences of torture. That application has been carefully considered and the advice of counsel was obtained. Again, the code of Crown prosecutors was applied to the decision-making process. The first requirement of the code is that there should be sufficient admissible evidence for a realistic prospect of conviction before a prosecution may follow. The application contained no evidence of a kind admissible in this jurisdiction, and I accordingly declined to grant my consent.

The second function of the CPS as prosecuting authority has been to consider the case for prosecution of Senator Pinochet in this jurisdiction under article 7 of the UN convention against torture and other cruel, inhuman or degrading treatment or punishment. The CPS and police recognised that article 7 might come into operation in respect of the Spanish extradition papers. To prepare for that contingency, the CPS obtained copies of all the relevant Spanish extradition papers in March and April 1999 in its capacity as the prosecuting authority for England and Wales. The MPS, as investigating authority, was also supplied with a copy of those papers. All that was done with the agreement of the Kingdom of Spain and the Home Office.

The Spanish extradition papers were allocated to lawyers in the CPS separate from those acting for the Kingdom of Spain. The provisional conclusion of the CPS was that the material provided by the Kingdom of Spain for the purposes of the extradition proceedings would not be admissible in a criminal prosecution in England and Wales, and that the material could not be made admissible without a full police investigation. The CPS advised the police along those lines. Whether or not the MPS institutes a full investigation in this or any other case is a matter for it to decide.

It may help the House to understand the provisional CPS conclusion if I explain that in European extradition proceedings it is not necessary to bring evidence before a court to show that a person has committed the offences of which he or she is accused. All that is necessary is that the court here must be satisfied that the allegations amount to an extradition crime and that the formal request complies with the requirements of the Extradition Act 1989 and the European convention on extradition of 1959. That explains why the CPS reached its provisional conclusion that, in the absence of a full investigation by the police, there was no admissible evidence for the purpose of a prosecution here.

In addition to those evidential considerations, the CPS—again in its role as independent prosecuting authority—received, in January, and with the consent of Senator Pinochet, a copy of the medical report prepared by the independent experts commissioned by the Home Secretary. The CPS has also seen representations made to the Home Secretary concerning that report.

The report and subsequent advice make it clear that Senator Pinochet's ill health is such that he would not be able to defend himself properly in any criminal prosecution brought in this country. The provisional CPS conclusion in the light of the material was that no court in England and Wales would allow a trial of Senator Pinochet to take place because of his ill health, whatever the evidence. Again, the CPS advised the police of that.

In reaching its provisional conclusions, the CPS consulted me and I agreed with them, after taking the best independent legal advice available. My right hon., noble and learned Friend the Attorney-General has not involved himself as a Law Officer in this case. He and I agreed that his previous patronage of Redress, from which he resigned on taking ministerial office in May 1997, meant that it would be more appropriate if I handled the case. The solicitors acting for Senator Pinochet were advised of that in September last year.

Following today's formal submission of the Spanish extradition papers to the CPS under article 7, the CPS has confirmed its provisional conclusions. First, the material in the possession of the CPS would not be admissible in any criminal prosecution in England and Wales, and could not provide a realistic prospect of conviction. Secondly, an investigation for which the police are responsible would be required to gather evidence admissible in this jurisdiction. Thirdly, whatever the evidence that might be available, no court in England and Wales would allow a trial of Senator Pinochet to take place in view of his ill health. I agree with those conclusions.

Accordingly, the CPS did not apply for my consent, in respect of the Spanish extradition material, to prosecute Senator Pinochet for torture. The Metropolitan police service and Senator Pinochet's lawyers were advised of the CPS's conclusions. The MPS, which has taken its own legal advice, decided not to arrest Senator Pinochet earlier today.

The House will also be aware that on 11 and 13 November and on 15 December 1998 my right hon. Friend the Home Secretary received requests for the extradition of Senator Pinochet from Switzerland, France and Belgium. Further requests were received from France on 4 February last year and from the Kingdom of Belgium on 12 October last year.

On 9 December 1998, my right hon. Friend decided not to issue an authority to proceed with regard to the requests from France and Switzerland. On 27 January 1999, he decided not to issue an authority to proceed with regard to the request from Belgium. On 22 February 1999 and 19 November 1999 respectively, he decided not to issue an authority to proceed in respect of the second French and second Belgian requests.

Following my right hon. Friend's decisions, the extradition papers were submitted to the CPS as the prosecuting authority under article 7. The CPS, in turn, referred the papers to the MPS to enable the investigating authorities to consider them. The CPS also advised the police that the allegations contained in the Swiss, both French and both Belgian requests did not disclose offences that could be tried here, as the conduct alleged in each of the requests occurred before the relevant legislation came into force. Accordingly, the CPS did not apply for Law Officer consent to prosecute Senator Pinochet for torture in respect of the Swiss, French and Belgian extradition material.

In performing its role under article 7 of the convention in respect of the Swiss, French and Belgian material, the CPS also took into account the medical report commissioned by my right hon. Friend and the representations made to the him about Senator Pinochet's medical condition. As I said, the CPS concluded that no court in England and Wales would permit a trial of Senator Pinochet to take place in those circumstances, whatever the evidence.

The CPS consulted me about those matters and I agree with its conclusions.

(HC Debs., vol. 345, cols. 589–92: 2 March 2000; see also Part Six: VII. B., above)

13/13

The following question was asked of Her Majesty's Government:

Whether they are giving consideration, under Article 2 of the 1948 Convention on the Prevention and Punishment of the Crime of Genocide, to the institution of genocide charges against the Burmese military leadership?

In reply, the Government Minister in the House of Lords wrote:

We are deeply concerned about human rights violations in Burma and are at the forefront of international action to press the military regime to improve the situation. But no international criminal tribunal exists at present which has competence to hear genocide charges against the Burmese military leadership. It is because of the need to end impunity for war crimes, crimes against humanity and genocide wherever they occur that the UK strongly supports the establishment of a permanent International Criminal Court.

(HL Debs., vol. 610, *WA 179*: 13 March 2000)

13/14

The following oral question was asked:

In so far as the United Nations has miserably failed to enforce its own resolutions and not stopped sanction busting by Saddam Hussein, enabling him to raise the money to fund his illegal regime, could we not consider a change in policy away from the enforcement of sanctions, which some of us have supported through thick and thin for nearly 10 years, towards a policy of indicting Saddam Hussein in the international court for war crimes, murder, genocide and crimes against humanity? Should not that be the new approach?

In reply, the Secretary of State for Foreign and Commonwealth Affairs, Mr Robin Cook, stated:

No international court would be competent to pursue those charges. We could pursue them only through a United Nations Security Council resolution to establish a special tribunal on Iraq. As I have said before, I see no realistic prospect of our obtaining agreement to such a resolution. Because of that, Britain was in the lead in supporting the formation of an International Criminal Court, which would have prosecutors who could decide for themselves who should be brought before the court, and which would end the arrangement by which special UN clearance was needed for anybody to be indicted. Once we have such a court, the way will be clear to proceed against dictators such as Saddam in the way my hon. Friend wishes.

(HC Debs., vol. 348, col. 176: 11 April 2000)

13/15

Speaking on 18 October 2000 in the Sixth Committee of the UN General Assembly discussing the Report of the International Law Commission, the representative of France, on behalf of the EU and associated States, examined the topic of the International Criminal Court. He stated in part:

The Court will have competence over war crimes committed in international and non international armed conflicts, in which women, children and the elderly are too often the principal victims. It also gives the Court competence over crimes of genocide and crimes against humanity. The Statute will therefore also apply when a government massacres its own citizens in cold blood. It contains, among others, major provisions for punishing violence of a sexual or sexist nature and contributes to the fight against the use of children as soldiers.

The Rome Statute entrusts in the first place States with the responsibility for applying international humanitarian law and human rights and for sanctioning their violations. In many states a culture of responsibility is growing. This may be seen from the greater recourse to domestic jurisdictions in these states and the strengthening of effective legal cooperation among them. This culture of responsibility should help the Court to better perform its role, i.e. prevent the most serious crimes which affect the international community, act in complement to national systems in punishing them, and intervene efficiently where States fail to take action.

The Rome Statute respects the balance among the different legal traditions. It fully guarantees the rights of accused persons to a fair trial. The European Union notes with satisfaction its insistence on the protection and rights of victims, especially their right to compensation and their participation in the proceedings of concern to them.

(Translated text provided by the FCO: see also A/C. 6/55/SR. 9, p. 3)

13/16

The FCO provided Explanatory Notes for the International Criminal Court Bill when it was introduced in the House of Lords on 14 December 2000. These contained the following passage:

BACKGROUND

3. The International Criminal Court ('ICC') will be a permanent Court, situated in The Hague, to try individuals for genocide, crimes against humanity and war crimes. The ICC will be 'complementary' to national courts; this means that relevant States will retain jurisdiction unless they are unable or unwilling genuinely to investigate and prosecute a crime. The ICC will have 18 judges and its own Prosecutor. The ICC will be able to investigate crimes committed by nationals, or on the territory, of States Parties, or of non-State Parties who have given consent. It will also have jurisdiction over crimes, wherever committed, which are referred to the ICC by the United Nations Security Council. The ICC will work with the assistance of States; States Parties are obliged to co-operate with the ICC, including by gathering evidence and arresting suspects.

4. Following several years of negotiation, the inter-governmental treaty which forms the Rome Statute of the International Criminal Court ('ICC Statute') was adopted on 17 July 1998. (The ICC Statute has been published as Cm 4555.) Once the Statute has been ratified by 60 States, the ICC will itself be created. The Foreign Secretary announced in the House of Commons on 20 July 1998 that the Government intended to introduce legislation to enable the UK to ratify

the Statute and wished to be among the Court's founding members. The UK signed the Statute on 30 November 1998 and this Bill is intended, together with corresponding legislation in the Scottish Parliament, to enable the UK to comply with all its obligations under the Statute and accordingly to ratify.

(Text provided by the FCO)

Part Fourteen: II. A. *Peaceful settlement of disputes—means of settlement—negotiations*

14/1

In reply to the question whether Her Majesty's Government support the UN resolutions pertaining to Kashmir, the Parliamentary Under-Secretary of State, FCO, wrote:

We believe that India and Pakistan should build on both the UN resolutions and the 1972 Simla Agreement in their search for a solution to Kashmir. We continue to encourage both countries to return to bilateral dialogue to find a just and lasting solution acceptable to the people of Kashmir.

(HL Debs., vol. 612, *WA 147*: 2 May 2000)

14/2

In reply to an oral question, the Parliamentary Under-Secretary of State, FCO, Baroness Scotland of Asthal, stated in part:

We condemn the return to hostilities between Ethiopia and Eritrea. Fighting can only bring further suffering to the people of both countries. We urge both sides to cease fighting and to re-enter into negotiations with the Organisation for African Unity to achieve a lasting peaceful settlement.

(HL Debs., vol. 613, col. 769: 24 May 2000)

Part Fourteen: II. F. 2. *Peaceful settlement of disputes—means of settlement—arbitration—arbitral tribunals and commissions other than the Permanent Court of Justice*

14/3

On 12 April 1999, there came into force an Agreement between the Governments of the UK and the Hong Kong Special Administrative Region of the People's Republic of China for the promotion and protection of investments. Articles 8 and 9 of the Agreement read:

Article 8

Settlement of Investment Disputes

A dispute between an investor of one Contracting Party and the other Contracting Party concerning an investment of the former in the area of the latter which has not been settled amicably, shall, after a period of three months from written notification of the claim, be submitted to such procedures for settlement as may be agreed between the parties to the dispute. If no such procedures have been agreed within that three month period, the parties to the dispute shall be bound to submit it to arbitration under the Arbitration Rules of the United Nations Commission on International Trade Law as then in force. The parties may agree in writing to modify these Rules.

ARTICLE 9

Disputes between the Contracting Parties

(1) If any dispute arises between the Contracting Party relating to the interpretation or application of this Agreement, the Contracting Parties shall in the first place try to settle it by negotiation.
(2) If the Contracting Parties fail to reach a settlement of the dispute by negotiation, it may be referred by them to such person or body as they may agree on or, at the request of either Contracting Party, shall be submitted for decision to a tribunal of three arbitrators which shall be constituted in the following manner:

(a) within thirty days after receipt of a request for arbitration, each Contracting Party shall appoint one arbitrator. A national of a State which can be regarded as neutral in relation to the dispute, who shall act as President of the tribunal, shall be appointed as the third arbitrator by agreement between the two arbitrators, within sixty days of the appointment of the second;
(b) if within the time limits specified above any appointment has not been made, either Contracting Party may request the President of the International Court of Justice, in a personal and individual capacity, to make the necessary appointment within thirty days. If the President considers that he is a national of a State which cannot be regarded as neutral in relation to the dispute, the most senior Vice-President who is not disqualified on that ground shall make the appointment.

(3) Except as hereinafter provided in this Article or as otherwise agreed by the Contracting Parties, the tribunal shall determine the limits of its jurisdiction and establish its own procedure. At the direction of the tribunal, or at the request of either of the Contracting Parties, a conference to determine the precise issues to be arbitrated and the specific procedures to be followed shall be held no later than thirty days after the tribunal is fully constituted.
(4) Except as otherwise agreed by the Contracting Parties or prescribed by the tribunal, each Contracting Party shall submit a memorandum within forty-five days after the tribunal is fully constituted. Replies shall be due sixty days later. The tribunal shall hold a hearing at the request of either Contracting Party, or at its discretion, within thirty days after replies are due.
(5) The tribunal shall give a written decision within thirty days after completion of the hearing or, if no hearing is held, after the date both replies are submitted. The decision shall be taken by a majority vote.

(6) The Contracting Parties may submit requests for clarification of the decision within fifteen days after it is received and such clarification shall be issued within fifteen days of such request.
(7) The decision of the tribunal shall be binding on the Contracting Parties.
(8) Each Contracting Party shall bear the costs of the arbitrator appointed by it. The other costs of the tribunal shall be shared equally by the Contracting Parties including any expenses incurred by the President or Vice-President of the International Court of Justice in implementing the procedures in paragraph 2(b) of this Article.

(Cm 4598, pp. 6–7; TS No. 9 (2000))

14/4

On 4 July 2000, the UK and the French Republic signed an Agreement concerning fishing in the Bay of Granville. Article 8 of the Agreement reads:

Settlement of Disputes

(1) Any Party may give notice to the other Party that a difference between them has arisen over a matter involving the interpretation or application of this Agreement. Except where the difference involves the failure of the Joint Management Committee to adopt a decision, the matter shall be referred by either Party to that Committee; the latter shall give its decision on the matter within six months of the date on which notice was given by the one Party to the other.
(2) Where the matter is not resolved to the satisfaction of both Parties by way of such reference to the Joint Management Committee, or where the difference involves the failure of that Committee to adopt a decision, either Party may, except for matters governed by the emergency procedure or the emergency arbitration procedure referred to in paragraph (3) of Article 4, give notice to the other Party that it wishes to refer the matter to arbitration as provided for in Article 3 of Annex D to this Agreement.

(Cm 5025, p. 11)

Part Fourteen: II. G. 1. *Peaceful settlement of disputes—means of settlement—judicial settlement—International Court of Justice*

14/5

In reply to oral questions about the intentions of Her Majesty's Government towards the proceedings brought in the International Court of Justice by the Federal Republic of Yugoslavia, the Parliamentary Under-Secretary of State, FCO, Baroness Scotland of Asthal, stated:

. . . the Government are confident of the strength of their case should the Yugoslav application ever reach the Merits stage. We regard this case as a shameless and opportunistic abuse of the Court, whose jurisdiction was accepted by Belgrade only three days before launching its application. The UK has substantial legal arguments for resisting the Federal Republic of Yugoslavia's application at the preliminary stage.

. . . the Federal Republic of Yugoslavia's case is a propaganda measure. It accepted the Court's jurisdiction only three days before it launched its application and seeks to deflect the blame by suggesting that NATO has responsibility for what happened in Kosovo. Milosevic is clearly responsible and has been indicted. We are confident that we have a strong legal case and will fight the Yugoslav case on its merits if we have to. We have a strong and substantial argument on jurisdiction and admissibility. If we have to send a clear message it must be that people like Milosevic cannot seek to take adventitious advantage of the procedure, which is precisely what he seeks to do in this case. We cannot let him get away with it.

(HL Debs., vol. 609, col. 232: 2 February 2000)

Part Fourteen: III. *Peaceful settlement of disputes—compensation aranegements*

14/6

On 12 April 1999, there came into force an Agreement between the Governments of the UK and the Government of the Hong Kong Special Administrative Region of the People's Republic of China. Articles 4 and 5 of the Agreement read as follows:

ARTICLE 4

Compensation for Losses

(1) Investors of one Contracting Party whose investments in the area of the other Contracting Party suffer losses owing to war or other armed conflict, revolution, a state of national emergency, revolt, insurrection or riot in the area of the latter Contracting Party shall be accorded by the latter Contracting Party treatment, as regards restitution, indemnification, compensation or other settlement, no less favourable than that which the latter Contracting Party accorded to its own investors or to investors of any other State. Resulting payments shall be freely convertible.

(2) Without prejudice to paragraph (1) of this Article, investors of one Contracting Party who in any of the situations referred to in that paragraph suffer losses in the area of the other Contracting Party resulting from:

(a) requisitioning of their property by its forces or authorities; or
(b) destruction of their property by its forces or authorities, which was not caused in combat action or was not required by the necessity of the situation;

shall be accorded restitution or reasonable compensation. Resulting payments shall be freely convertible.

ARTICLE 5

Expropriation

(1) Investors of either Contracting Party shall not be deprived of their investments nor be subjected to measures having effect equivalent to such deprivation in the area of the other Contracting Party except lawfully, for a public purpose related to the internal needs of that Party on a non-discriminatory basis and against compensation. Such compensation shall amount to the real value of the investment immediately before the deprivation or before the impending deprivation became public knowledge, whichever is the earlier, shall include interest at a normal commercial rate until the date of payment, shall be made without undue delay, be effectively realizable and be freely convertible. The investor affected shall have a right, under the law of the Contracting Party making the deprivation, to prompt review, by a judicial or other independent authority of that Party, of the investor's case and of the valuation of the investment in accordance with the principles set out in this paragraph.
(2) Where a Contracting Party expropriates the assets of a company which is incorporated or constituted under the law in force in any part of its own area, and in which investors of the other Contracting Party own shares, it shall ensure that the provisions of paragraph (1) of this Article are applied to the extent necessary to guarantee compensation referred to in paragraph (1) in respect of their investment to such investors of the other Contracting Party who are owners of those shares.

(Cm 4598, pp. 4–5; TS No. 9 (2000))

Part Fifteen: I. A. *Coercive measures short of the use of force—unilateral measures—retorsion*

15/1

In reply to a question, the Secretary of State for Foreign and Commonwealth Affairs wrote:

The Government's policy on export licence applications for Zimbabwe was set out in my statement to the House of Commons on 3 May 2000, *Official Report*, columns 149–62.

As I informed the House, the Government decided last week, in the light of the deteriorating situation in Zimbabwe, to refuse from 3 May all applications for new licences for Zimbabwe for goods and technology listed in part III, schedule 1, of the Export of Goods (Control) Order 1994, as amended (commonly known as the Military List).

This included all new licence applications for spare parts in connection with previous contracts. We also began a review of all extant export licences for Zimbabwe.

In line with my right hon. Friend the Prime Minister's statement of 9 February 2000, *Official Report*, columns 184–85W, the Government will not grant export licences for dual-use equipment where there is a clear risk that the equipment would be used in the Democratic Republic of the Congo. Other applications for Standard Individual Export Licences to export dual-use equipment to Zimbabwe will be considered on a case-by-case basis against the national criteria and those in the EU Code of Conduct.

We have now completed the review of extant licences foreshadowed in my statement of 3 May. The Government place considerable importance on UK companies being able to honour their contractual obligations. They do not, therefore, revoke existing licences except in exceptional circumstances. Zimbabwe has now regrettably placed itself in that category. We have, therefore, decided to revoke all extant Standard Individual Export Licences for goods and technology on the Military List (with the possible exception of one extant licence for de-mining equipment already in Zimbabwe) and to remove Zimbabwe as a permitted destination from all Open Individual Export Licences for goods and technology on the Military List.

In addition, Zimbabwe is a permitted destination on four Open General Export Licences (OGELs) and two Open General Transhipment Licences (OGTLs) which allow the export of goods and technology on the Military List. Zimbabwe will now be removed from the coverage of these licences. Amended copies of these licences will be placed in the Library of the House.

We will remove Zimbabwe as a permitted destination from the coverage of extant Open Individual Export Licences for dual-use equipment. Exporters affected by this measure may, however, submit applications for Standard Individual Export Licences for this equipment. Such applications will be considered on a case-by-case basis against the criteria as described above.

We will also be prohibiting transhipment of goods on the Military List to Zimbabwe via the United Kingdom without a licence, by means of an amendment to schedule 3 of the EG(C)O.

The effect of this is that we now have a national arms embargo on Zimbabwe. We will be requesting the Crown Dependencies and Overseas Territories to take the necessary measures to implement the same embargo.

The Government will continue to monitor events in Zimbabwe closely.

(HC Debs., vol. 349, cols. 493–4W: 12 May 2000)

15/2

In reply to a question asking about sanctions against Austria, the Minister of State, FCO, wrote:

Measures were implemented by the 14 member states to limit the bilateral relationship as an expression of our concern at the inclusion of a far right party in the Austrian Government. Chancellor Schuessel has now accepted the EU 14's proposal that a group of 'three wise persons', appointed by the President of the European Court of Human Rights, should report on the Austrian Government's commitment to common European values and on the evolution of the Freedom Party. We fully support this initiative, and will, together with our other EU partners, consider the report and its implications when it is submitted.

(HC Debs., vol. 353, cols. 648–9W: 13 July 2000)

15/3

In reply to a question, the Minister of State, FCO, wrote:

Following the release of the hostages on 13 July and the armed overthrow of Fiji's democratically elected government we recalled our High Commissioner in Fiji for consultations. We also summoned the Fijian High Commissioner in London to make clear our disappointment that the new Fijian administration included individuals associated with Speight and that the 1997 Constitution had been abrogated and to insist that Speight and his gang be brought to justice. We and EU partners made similar representations locally.

On 21 July we announced a number of targeted measures against Fiji,

urging EU partners to open consultations under article 366a of the Lome Convention to establish a timetable for return to democracy; all new EU aid to Fiji is currently on hold;
pressing our EU partners to impose restrictions on travel by Speight and his associates;
cancelling all FCO-funded assistance to Fiji's government;
cancelling of naval visits and joint military exercises. All defence cooperation with Fiji will remain under review.
no licenses for any arms or security equipment for export to Fiji where there is a clear risk that it will be used for internal repression.

We are consulting Commonwealth and EU partners on the next steps and on ways to promote an early return to constitutional and democratic government in Fiji. The Commonwealth Ministerial Action Group, of which the UK is a member, meets in New York on 14 September to review its decision on 16 June to suspend Fiji from its councils, and to monitor Fiji's progress in drawing up a roadmap back to democracy.

(HC Debs., vol. 354, cols. 1082–3W: 28 July 2000)

Part Fifteen: I. B. *Coercive measures short of the use of force—unilateral measures—counter-measures*

15/4

Speaking on 23 October 2000 in the Sixth Committee of the UN General Assembly discussing the Report of the International Law Commission, the Legal Adviser, FCO, Mr M. C. Wood, observed:

Mr. Chairman, I turn now to the question of *countermeasures*. We welcome the inclusion of an article (draft article 23) recognising the taking of lawful countermeasures as a circumstance precluding wrongfulness. Countermeasures play an important role in inducing compliance with international law. Their validity has been recognised by international tribunals, including the International Court of Justice. We have serious concerns, however, with some of the provisions regulating resort to countermeasures proposed in Chapter II of Part Two *bis*, insofar as these depart from existing law.

I take first draft article 51, entitled 'Obligations not subject to countermeasures'. There are indeed certain obligations the performance of which cannot be suspended by way of countermeasures. But care needs to be taken in the way this proposition is reflected in the draft articles. The chapeau is perhaps misleading in asserting that countermeasures shall not involve 'any derogation' from the enumerated obligations. Some of the relevant provisions, such as those for the protection of human rights, themselves allow derogation in certain circumstances. And, in some instances, States have entered reservations preserving the right to take countermeasures. We think it preferable to say that countermeasures may not involve the breach of those obligations of a State listed in the article.

We would invite the Commission to look at the list itself rigorously. The objective of these provisions on countermeasures must be to facilitate the resolution of disputes rather than to serve to complicate them. We must therefore aim to avoid vagueness and duplication.

I turn now to the conditions relating to resort to countermeasures set out in draft article 53, paragraphs 2 to 5. Here we find the approach taken in the draft articles frankly misconceived; they do not form an acceptable basis for the law in the field and are, I fear, rather removed from the realities of international life.

The alleged duty to offer to negotiate before taking countermeasures, and to suspend countermeasures while negotiations are being pursued, does not reflect the position under general international law. It will be recalled that the Arbitral Tribunal in the *Air Services Agreement* case between France and the United States stated that it 'does not believe that it is possible, in the present state of international relations, to lay down a rule prohibiting the use of countermeasures during negotiations'. The position has not changed since then. Nor, in our view, would such a rule be either practical or desirable *de lege ferenda*. It would force the victim State to have recourse to one particular method of dispute settlement, and might even be inconsistent with Article 33 of the Charter. It might encourage States to break their obligations in order to force another State to the negotiating table. And what scope to negotiate is there where, say, genocide is being committed? Paragraph 3, allowing for provisional and urgent countermeasures, does not solve the matter.

The alleged duty not to take or to suspend countermeasures if the dispute has merely been submitted to arbitration or judicial settlement (article 53.5(b)) is equally ill-founded. It, too, finds no support in general international law. It could discourage recourse to third-party dispute settlement. And it fails to take account of the possibility that jurisdiction may be disputed.

Mr. Chairman, we would urge the Commission to revise these provisions on the exercise of countermeasures to reflect accurately existing law on the subject.

(Text provided by the FCO; see also A/C. 6/55/SR. 14, pp. 7–8)

Part Fifteen: II. A. *Coercive measures short of the use of force—collective measures—United Nations*

(See also **5/17**)

15/5

In reply to a question, the Minister of State, FCO, wrote:

The UN Security Council resolutions provide the framework for the Government's policy on Iraq and sanctions. Our position has always been that sanctions can be lifted only when Iraq complies with its obligations under those resolutions, including disarmament. The latest resolution, SCR 1284, which the UK was key in driving through the Security Council, sets out a clear path towards the lifting of sanctions, by allowing for their suspension while the disarmament programme is underway. I urge Saddam Hussein to accept it.

(HC Debs., vol. 346, col. 47W: 13 March 2000)

15/6

In reply to a question, the Minister of State, FCO, wrote:

A number of sanctions measures are in place against the Federal Republic of Yugoslavia (FRY). United Nations Security Council resolution 1160 (1998) imposed an arms embargo on the FRY. The EU has imposed a number of measures on the FRY, including an arms embargo, a ban on the sale or supply of equipment which might be used for internal repression or terrorism, a ban on the sale and supply of petroleum and petroleum products, financial sanctions, a ban on flights and a targeted visa ban. These measures have included humanitarian exemptions where appropriate. Montenegro and Kosovo have been exempted from the flight ban and oil embargo, and from some aspects of financial sanctions. The flight ban on the remainder of the FRY has been suspended until the end of August.

Sanctions have put pressure on and isolated the Milosevic regime and its associates, and have limited Milosevic's ability to build up weaponry for use for external aggression or internal repression. Humanitarian exemptions and the targeting of sanctions measures on the regime have been designed to minimise the effect of sanctions on the general public of the FRY.

(HC Debs., vol. 348, col. 114W: 11 April 2000)

15/7

In reply to a question, the Minister of State, FCO, wrote:

UN Security Council resolution 1160 (1998) imposed an embargo on the supply of arms and related material to the Federal Republic of Yugoslavia and a ban on arming and training for terrorist activities there. There are no other UN sanctions measures in force in relation to Serbia.

Under the current terms of the 'Oil-for-Food' programme, established by Security Council resolution 986, Iraq can sell unlimited quantities of oil to buy a wide range of humanitarian goods, including the kind of equipment mentioned in the question. Iraq is expected to raise $10 billion this year from oil sales. Each contract is checked to ensure that the goods will be used for their stated purpose.

(HC Debs., vol. 349, col. 258W: 8 May 2000)

15/8

In reply to a question, the Parliamentary Under-Secretary of State, FCO, wrote:

UN Security Council Resolution 1160 (1998) imposed an embargo on the supply of arms and related material to the Federal Republic of Yugoslavia and a ban on arming and training for terrorist activities there. SCRs 1203 and 1244 allow supplies to the verification missions and the international civil and security presences respectively. UN member states are responsible for implementing and enforcing these sanctions. Resolution 1160 established a UN committee which is tasked with, inter alia, seeking information from all member states regarding action taken by them to implement the sanctions and to consider information brought to its attention by any state concerning violations of the prohibitions and to recommend appropriate measures thereto.

The European Union has a series of measures in place against the FRY. These impose mandatory obligations on EU member states and include appropriate exemptions on humanitarian grounds and for Kosovo and Montenegro. EU member states are responsible for enforcing these measures. The General Affairs Council of the European Union regularly reviews EU policy towards the Federal Republic of Yugoslavia. At the General Affairs Council of 14 February EU Foreign Ministers agreed to tighten financial sanctions and at the same time suspend the EU flight ban for six months.

(HL Debs., vol. 612, *WA 225–6*: 11 May 2000)

15/9

In reply to a question, the Minister of State, FCO, wrote:

In its resolution 1298 (2000) adopted on 17 May, the United Nations Security Council demanded that Ethiopia and Eritrea cease all military action, withdraw military forces, and reconvene proximity talks under the auspices of the Organisation of African Unity. The Security Council imposed, in relation to those two States, a mandatory arms embargo and a ban on the provision of related technical assistance or training.

The embargo is established for twelve months. At the end of this period the Security Council will decide whether the Governments of Ethiopia and Eritrea have complied with its demands and, accordingly, whether to extend the embargo for a further period. The embargo will be terminated immediately if the Secretary-General reports that a peaceful definitive settlement has been concluded.

The United Kingdom co-sponsored this resolution, which was adopted in response to the further outbreak of hostilities between Eritrea and Ethiopia. The Security Council has noted with concern the serious humanitarian implications of the fighting for the civilian population.

The European Union imposed an arms embargo against Ethiopia and Eritrea on 15 March 1999 in response to a United Kingdom proposal, following the adoption on 10 February 1999 of UN Security Council resolution 1227, which urged all States to end all sales of arms and munitions to both countries.

(HC Debs., vol. 350, col. 225W: 18 May 2000)

15/10

In the course of a debate on the subject of sanctions against Serbia and Iraq, the Minister of State, FCO, Mr Peter Hain, stated:

When we last debated the situation in Iraq on 24 March, I commended to the House the provisions of United Nations Security Council resolution 1284. After months of intensive effort, Britain secured adoption of that ground-breaking new resolution in December last year. It establishes a new platform for the UN's dealings with Iraq. It deals comprehensively with a range of issues, notably the humanitarian situation, disarmament, and Kuwaiti issues, including stolen property and missing civilians. It represents the collective will of the Security Council and has the force of international law.

(HC Debs., vol. 350, cols. 837–8: 22 May 2000)

15/11

In the course of a debate on the subject of the Ethiopia/Eritrea conflict, the Parliamentary Under-Secretary of State, FCO, Baroness Scotland of Asthal, stated:

We urge all UN member states to implement fully and to enforce effectively the mandatory arms embargo and the ban on related technical assistance and training imposed by the Security Council in Resolution 1298. We will continue to provide humanitarian aid to the region.

(HL Debs., vol. 613, col. 769: 24 May 2000)

15/12

In reply to a question relating to the members of the Revolutionery United Front in Sierra Leone, the Minister of State, FCO, wrote:

UN sanctions are already designed to target the Revolutionary United Front. UN Security Council resolution 1171 (1998) imposes a travel ban on leading members of the former military junta and of the Revolutionary United Front. It also imposes an embargo on the supply of arms and related material to Sierra Leone other than to the Government of Sierra Leone (with certain exemptions). We have not discussed the option of freezing the bank accounts of leading members of the Revolutionary United Front and their families with the US Administration or with European counterparts. However, the UK will ensure that the Security Council keeps the impact and effectiveness of sanctions under review and will make proposals for modification of the sanctions regime as we consider appropriate.

(HC Debs., vol. 350, col. 413W: 23 May 2000)

15/13

In reply to a question, the Parliamentary Under-Secretary of State, FCO, Baroness Scotland of Asthal, wrote:

The UK currently implements mandatory UN sanctions in relation to Iraq, Angola (UNITA), Liberia, Rwanda, Sierra Leone, Somalia, Sudan, Afghanistan (the Taliban), Ethiopia, Eritrea and the Federal Republic of Yugoslavia. UN sanctions against Libya have been suspended.

In addition, we implement EU sanctions in relation to Afghanistan, Bosnia, Burma, China, Croatia, the DRC, the Federal Republic of Yugoslavia, Libya and Sudan.

The UK also implements the OSCE arms embargo on Azerbaijan and Armenia, and national arms embargoes on Iran and Zimbabwe.

The sanctions are imposed on various grounds, for example as a response to a conflict which constitutes a threat to international peace and security.

We have some concerns about the human rights situation in most of these countries.

(HL Debs., vol. 615, *WA 52*: 13 July 2000)

15/14

In reply to the question whether the UN has introduced an embargo on the import of rough diamonds from Sierra Leone, the Parliamentary Under-Secretary of State, FCO, wrote:

The United Nations Security Council adopted Resolution 1306(2000) on 5 July which prohibits the direct or indirect import of all rough diamonds from Sierra Leone to the territory of member states. The resolution also decides that rough diamonds controlled by the Government of Sierra Leone through a certificate of origin regime shall be exempt from the measures when the UN Sanctions Committee on Sierra Leone has reported to the council that an effective regime is fully in operation.

Britain played a leading role in promoting Resolution 1306 in the UN Security Council. Diamonds are at the heart of the tragedy in Sierra Leone and this resolution sends a powerful signal about the need to end the trade in conflict diamonds from Sierra Leone.

The embargo on Sierra Leone rough diamonds is established for an initial period of 18 months. At the end of this period the Security Council will review the situation in Sierra Leone, including the extent of the Government's authority over the diamond-producing areas, in order to decide whether to extend the restrictions for a further period and, if necessary, to modify them or adopt further measures.

The embargo is implemented in the UK by means of an amendment to the Open General Import Licence. It is implemented in a similar manner in the Isle of Man. Orders in Council under the United Nations Act 1946 have been made to implement the restrictions in the other Crown Dependencies and in the Overseas Territories.

(HL Debs., vol. 616, *WA 18*: 24 July 2000)

15/15

In reply to a question, the Minister of State, FCO, wrote:

The UK implements the provisions of United Nations Security Council resolution 1160 (1998), which imposed an arms embargo on the Federal Republic of Yugoslavia and a prohibition on arming and training for terrorist activities there.

The UK also implements the following measures, imposed by the European Union in relation to the Federal Republic of Yugoslavia, which are designed to target the Milosevic regime.

an arms embargo and an embargo on the supply of equipment which might be used for internal repression or terrorism
a selective visa ban
a ban on the provision of Government-financed export credit and other forms of export finance
a selective freeze of funds and investment ban
an oil embargo (with specified exemptions including in relation to Kosovo, Montenegro and the EU's Energy for Democracy programme).

The EU flight ban in relation to the Federal Republic of Yugoslavia has been suspended until 31 March 2001.

(HC Debs., vol. 354, col. 641W: 26 July 2000)

15/16

In reply to a further question, the same Minister of State wrote:

As of today's date, the United Kingdom implements mandatory UN sanctions, imposed by the UN Security Council acting under Chapter VII of the Charter of the United Nations, in relation to Afghanistan, Angola, Eritrea, Ethiopia, Iraq, Liberia, Rwanda, Sierra Leone, Somalia, Sudan and the Federal Republic of Yugoslavia. UN sanctions in relation to Libya have been suspended.

The United Kingdom implements, in addition, sanctions imposed by the European Union in relation to Afghanistan, Bosnia and Herzegovina, Burma, China, the Democratic Republic of Congo, Croatia, Libya, Sudan and the Federal Republic of Yugoslavia.

In accordance with a decision of the OSCE, the United Kingdom implements arms embargoes on Armenia and Azerbaijan. There are also national arms embargoes on Iran and Zimbabwe.

A list of sanctions regimes and arms embargoes implemented by the UK is in the Library of the House. Annexed to this is a summary of additional UK restrictions on the export of strategic goods. These documents are also available on the FCO website and are updated each time there are changes to sanctions regimes implemented by the UK, or to UK restrictions on the export of strategic goods.

(Ibid.)

15/17

In reply to a question, the Parliamentary Under-Secretary of State, FCO, wrote:

The UK implements the provisions of United Nations Security Council Resolution 1160 (1998), which imposed an arms embargo on the Federal Republic of Yugoslavia and a prohibition on arming and training for terrorist activities there.

The UK also implements the following measures, imposed by the European Union in relation to the Federal Republic of Yugoslavia, which are designed to target the Milosevic regime.

an arms embargo and an embargo on the supply of equipment which might be used for internal repression or terrorism
a selective visa ban
a ban on the provision of government-financed export credit and other forms of export finance
a selective freeze of funds and investment ban
an oil embargo (with specified exemptions including in relation to Kosovo, Montenegro and the EU's Energy for Democracy programme).

The EU flight ban in relation to the Federal Republic of Yugoslavia has been suspended until 31 March 2001.

(HL Debs., vol. 616, *WA 176*: 27 September 2000)

15/18

In reply to a question, the Parliamentary Under-Secretary of State, FCO, wrote in part:

We also have reason to believe that Victor Bout continues to supply arms to Angola in breach of the UN arms embargo. We call on all states to fulfil their international obligations to implement and enforce mandatory sanctions imposed by the Security Council of the United Nations; there can be no excuse for any state to provide support for Bout in his continued flouting of UN sanctions.

(Ibid., *WA 172–3*)

15/19

In reply to a question, the Minister of State, FCO, wrote in part:

There have been changes to the following sanctions regimes:

. . .

Ethiopia and Eritrea

UN Security Council resolution 1298 (2000), which was adopted on 17 May, imposed an arms embargo and a ban on the provision of related technical assistance and training in relation to Ethiopia and Eritrea. Since then, two further Security Council resolutions have been adopted which set out exemptions for demining and peacekeeping purposes.

UNSCR 1312 (2000) was adopted on 1 August and exempts the UN Mine Action Service (UNMAS) from the prohibitions imposed by UNSCR 1298. UNSCR 1320 (2000) was adopted on 15 September and allows equipment and other material, including technical assistance and training to be provided for demining within Ethiopia and Eritrea under the auspices of UNMAS. It also allows the sale and supply of arms and related material for the sole use of the United Nations in Ethiopia and Eritrea.

Sierra Leone

UNSCR 1306 (2000), which was adopted on 5 July, imposed a ban on the import of all rough diamonds from Sierra Leone.

The resolution provided for an exemption from the ban for diamonds controlled by the Government of Sierra Leone through a Certificate of Origin regime when the UN Sanctions Committee on Sierra Leone had reported to the Security Council that an effective regime was fully in operation.

The Committee Chairman reported to the President of the Security Council on 6 October that the Committee had no objection to the procedures to be implemented by the Government of Sierra Leone. Therefore, diamonds controlled through the Government's Certificate of Origin regime are now exempt from the prohibition on the import of all rough diamonds from Sierra Leone imposed by UNSCR 1306.

(HC Debs., vol. 355, cols. 107–8W: 24 October 2000)

15/20

In reply to the question 'what steps Her Majesty's Government have taken to consolidate the United Kingdom's national criteria against which they assess licence applications to export arms and dual-use equipment with those of the European Union Code of Conduct on Arms Exports', the Parliamentary Under-Secretary of State, FCO, wrote in part:

CRITERION ONE

Respect for the UK's international commitments, in particular sanctions decreed by the UN Security Council and those decreed by the European Community, agreements on non-proliferation and other subjects, as well as other international obligations

The Government will not issue an export licence if approval would be inconsistent with, *inter alia*:

(a) the UK's international obligations and its commitments to enforce UN, OSCE and EU arms embargoes, as well as national embargoes observed by the UK and other commitments regarding the application of strategic export controls;
(b) the UK's international obligations under the Nuclear Non-Proliferation Treaty, the Biological and Toxin Weapons Convention and the Chemical Weapons Convention;
(c) the UK's commitments in the frameworks of the Australia Group, the Missile Technology Control Regime, the Nuclear Suppliers Group and the Wassenaar Arrangment;
(d) the Guidelines for Conventional Arms Transfers agreed by the Permanent

Five members of the UN Security Council, the OSCE Principles Governing Conventional Arms Transfers and the EU Code of Conduct on Arms Exports;
(e) the UK's obligations under the Ottawa Convention and the 1998 Land Mines Act;
(f) the UN Convention on Certain Conventional Weapons.

(HL Debs., vol. 618, *WA 83–4*: 31 October 2000)

15/21

The Iraq (United Nations Sanctions) Order 2000 (Statutory Instrument No. 3241 of 2000) came into force on 14 December 2000. An Explanatory Note attached to the Order read:

This Order makes provision to give effect to a decision of the Security Council of the United Nations in Resolution 661 of 6th August 1990. It prohibits the making of funds available to the government of the Republic of Iraq or persons resident in Iraq, and the remission or removal of funds to Iraq from the United Kingdom (article 3). Provision is also made for the Treasury (or a person acting on their behalf—see article 12) to require certain suspected Iraqi funds to be frozen (article 4). Article 6 makes it an offence to facilitate the commission of an offence under article 3 or 4(8).

Provision is made with respect to the granting of licences (articles 5 and 7) and for the obtaining of information for the purposes of enforcement (articles 8 to 10). Article 11 provides for penalties and proceedings for offences under the Order.

(See also in the same respect Statutory Instrument No. 3242 (Overseas Territories), No. 3244 (Channel Islands) and No. 3245 (Isle of Man).)

Part Fifteen: II. B. *Coercive measures short of the use of force—collective measures—outside the United Nations*

(See also **15/8, 13–17**)

15/22

In reply to a question, the Parliamentary Under-Secretary of State, FCO, wrote:

The member states of the European Community agreed, in a European Declaration on 7 April 1993, to impose an embargo on the sale of arms to Zaire, now the Democratic Republic of Congo (DRC).

Implementation and enforcement of the EU arms embargo is a matter for individual member states.

The EU Code of Conduct on Arms Exports requires EU member states to circulate through diplomatic channels details of licences refused. This includes licences for exports which fall within the scope of the DRC arms embargo.

The UK implements this embargo by prohibiting the export to the Democratic Republic of Congo of all goods and technology on the UK Military List which forms Part III of the Export of Goods (Control) Order. HM Customs and Excise is responsible for investigating all suspected breaches of the embargo.

(HL Debs., vol. 610, *WA 85*: 2 March 2000)

15/23

In reply to the question what changes have been made to measures in place against the Federal Republic of Yugoslavia, the Parliamentary Under-Secretary of State, FCO, wrote:

The European Union's EcoFin Council on 28 February adopted a Common Position and Council Decision implementing changes to the EU sanctions regime on the Federal Republic of Yugoslavia which had been agreed at the General Affairs Council on 14 February. Council Decision 2000/177/CFSP introduced, with immediate effect, a revised and expanded list of FRY citizens (representing an increase to a total of 794 names) against whom the EU visa ban applies, and Common Position 2000/176/CFSP suspended the EU flight ban on the FRY for a period of six months. The suspension of the flight ban will come into effect when the necessary amendments have been made to the relevant Council regulations. In parallel, we are working with our partners to tighten up the implementation of financial sanctions targeted against the regime.

Further to the Written Answer given by my honourable Friend the Member for Manchester Central—the then Minister of State for Foreign and Commonwealth Affairs—on 13 July 1999 (*Official Report*, cols. 141–142), the Government have decided to introduce a case by case approach to consideration of export licence applications for dual use goods to the Federal Republic of Yugoslavia, including Kosovo and Montenegro. There are humanitarian developmental and commercial reasons for doing so and it brings us into line with the practice of our major partners. Reconstruction in Kosovo is crucial to the province's development and the UK contribution to Kosovo could potentially be hindered without a change in practice. Applications will be considered consistent with the national export licensing criteria announced in July 1997 and those in the EU Code of Conduct on Arms Exports. We will not approve any dual use goods licence applications which could benefit the armed forces, internal security forces or similar entities of the authorities in Belgrade.

(HL Debs., vol 610, *WA 209–10*: 15 March 2000)

15/24

In reply to a question, the Minister of State, FCO, wrote:

The UK remains committed to the OSCE arms embargo against both Azerbaijan and Armenia, which the UK interprets as covering all goods and technology controlled under entries in Part III of schedule 1 to the Export of Goods (Control) Order 1994 (commonly known as the military list).

We have recently approved the export of 60 protective vests for demining operations to Azerbaijan. These will be used by the United Nations Development Programme during humanitarian land mine clearance operations. While the grant of this licence constitutes an exception to the UK's interpretation of the scope of the embargo, it is in no way inconsistent with the purpose of the embargo and our continuing commitment to uphold it. It also reflects the determination of the Government to eliminate the scourge of land mines.

(HC Debs., vol. 347, col. 631W: 7 April 2000)

15/25

In reply to a question, the Parliamentary Under-Secretary of State, FCO, wrote:

The UK remains committed to the OSCE arms embargo against both Azerbaijan and Armenia, which the UK interprets as covering all goods and technology controlled under entries in Part III of Schedule 1 to the Export of Goods (Control) Order 1994 (commonly known as the military list).

We have recently approved the export of 60 protective vests for demining operations to Azerbaijan. These will be used by the United Nations Development Programme during humanitarian landmine clearance operations. While the grant of this licence constitutes an exception to the UK's interpretation of the scope of the embargo, it is in no way inconsistent with the purpose of the embargo and our continuing commitment to uphold it. It also reflects the determination of the Government to eliminate the scourge of landmines.

(HL Debs., vol. 612, *WA 1–2*: 10 April 2000)

15/26

In reply to a question on the subject of the implementation of EU financial sanctions against the Federal Republic of Yugoslavia, the Minister of State, FCO, wrote:

EC Regulation 723/2000 amending EC Regulation 1294/1999 concerning a freeze on funds and a ban on investment in relation to the Federal Republic of Yugoslavia (FRY) was adopted by the Council of the EU on 6 April. The Regulation, which enhances the implementation of the existing financial sanctions against the FRY, came into force on 8 April. Among other changes, it clarifies the scope of the freeze of funds by tightening the definition of 'the Government of the FRY' and 'the Government of the Republic of Serbia'.

(HC Debs., vol. 348, col. 281W: 13 April 2000)

15/27

In the course of answering an oral question about the promotion of democratic rights in Burma, the Secretary of State for Foreign and Commonwealth Affairs, Mr Robin Cook, stated in part:

We are deeply concerned at the brutality of the military in Burma, the systematic use of forced labour and the displacement of ethnic minorities. Within the European Union, Britain recently proposed measures that have toughened Europe's common position against the regime in Burma. Within the International Labour Organisation, we have vigorously supported the decision to invoke article 33—for the first time in the organisation's 80–year history—against Burma.

(HC Debs., vol. 350, col. 137: 16 May 2000)

15/28

In the course of a debate on the subject of sanctions against Serbia and Iraq, the Minister of State, FCO, Mr Peter Hain, stated:

We continue to believe that a policy of isolating the Governments of Serbia and the Federal Republic of Yugoslavia—FRY—and making use of a range of targeted sanctions must be the key element in our strategy. In addition to the UN arms embargo, which has been in force since 1998, Britain implements the following EU sanctions: a visa ban on Milosevic and his cronies that covers about 800 named individuals; a ban on new investment which does not affect existing EU investments; a freeze on the assets of the FRY and Serbian Governments that extends to individuals and companies deemed to be associated with the regime, and a prohibition on making funds available to the targets of the asset freeze; a ban on the sale or supply of petroleum and petroleum products: and a ban on the sale or supply of equipment that might be used for international repression or terrorism. There are also UK national export controls on dual-use goods and on televisual equipment that is destined for the state media. The EU flight ban is currently suspended.

The sanctions regime bears no resemblance to the comprehensive international sanctions regime that was imposed on the FRY from 1992 until shortly after the signing of the Dayton agreement in 1995. I should make it clear that it does not include a comprehensive trade embargo.

The implementation of the financial sanctions regime is being revised to make clearer which Yugoslav companies are deemed to be owned or controlled by the FRY and Serbian Governments. There will be a 'white list' of those companies in Serbia that are not deemed to be under such control or ownership. We will do our utmost to ensure that no companies are persecuted because of their presence on the new EU white list. However, it should be remembered that many companies in Serbia which do not align themselves with the ruling parties already suffer discrimination and harassment.

(HC Debs., vol. 350, cols. 840–1: 22 May 2000)

15/29

In reply to a question relating to Burma, the Minister of State, FCO, wrote:

On 26 April the Council of the European Union adopted a Common Position (2000/346/CFSP) which enhanced EU sanctions against Burma by strengthening the existing visa ban, imposing a freeze on the funds of those individuals subject to the visa ban and imposing a ban on the supply of equipment which might be used for internal repression or terrorism.

Following from this Common Position, the Council adopted Regulation 1081/2000 on 22 May. The Regulation prohibits the sale, supply, export or shipment of goods listed in an Annexe to the Regulation, directly or indirectly, whether or not originating in the Community, to any person or body in Burma or to any person or body for the purpose of any business carried on in, or operated from, the territory of Burma.

The Regulation also provides that all funds belonging to individual listed in an annexe to the Regulation shall be frozen and that no funds shall be made available, directly or indirectly, to or for the benefit of those persons.

The Regulation applies within the territory of the Community including its air space and on board any aircraft or any vessel under the jurisdiction of a member state and, to any person elsewhere who is a national of a member state and any body which is incorporated or constituted under the law of a member state.

The Regulation entered into force on 24 May and is directly applicable in the UK. Legislation to provide for enforcement, including penalties, will shortly be in effect.

(Ibid., col. 580W: 25 May 2000; see also HL Debs., vol. 613, *WA 116*: 5 June 2000)

15/30

The Burma (Freezing of Funds) Regulation 2000 (Statutory Instrument No. 1472 of 2000) which came into force on 7 June 2000, provides that breaches of certain provisions of Council Regulation (EC) No. 1081/2000 of 22 May 2000 are to be criminal offences.

15/31

In reply to a question, the Minister of State, FCO, wrote:

United Nations Security Council resolution 1171 (1998) imposed an embargo on the sale and supply of arms and related material to Sierra Leone other than to the Government of Sierra Leone through named entry points. There are exemptions in that resolution and in resolution 1299 (2000) for supply to the United Nations and the Military Observer Group of the Economic Community of West African States (ECOMOG) as well as UN member states co-operating with UNAMSIL and the Government of Sierra Leone.

The UK fully supports and rigorously implements the embargo. We are discussing with Security Council colleagues ways to ensure that is implemented more effectively by all states.

(HC Debs., vol. 352, cols. 154–5W: 20 June 2000)

15/32

In reply to a question, the Parliamentary Under-Secretary of State, FCO, wrote:

The United Nations Security Council adopted Resolution 1306 (2000) on 5 July which prohibits the direct or indirect import of all rough diamonds from Sierra Leone to the territory of member states. The resolution also decides that rough diamonds controlled by the Government of Sierra Leone through a certificate of origin regime shall be exempt from the measures when the UN Sanctions Committee on Sierra Leone has reported to the council that an effective regime is fully in operation.

Britain played a leading role in promoting Resolution 1306 in the UN Security Council. Diamonds are at the heart of the tragedy in Sierra Leone and this resolution sends a powerful signal about the need to end the trade in conflict diamonds from Sierra Leone.

The embargo on Sierra Leone rough diamonds is established for an initial period of 18 months. At the end of this period the Security Council will review the situation in Sierra Leone, including the extent of the Government's authority over the diamond-producing areas, in order to decide whether to extend the restrictions for a further period and, if necessary, to modify them or adopt further measures.

The embargo is implemented in the UK by means of an amendment to the Open General Import Licence. It is implemented in a similar manner in the Isle of Man. Orders in Council under the United Nations Act 1946 have been made to implement the restrictions in the other Crown Dependencies and in the Overseas Territories.

(HL Debs., vol. 616, *WA 18*: 24 July 2000)

15/33

In reply to the question what recent changes have been made to EU sanctions against the Federal Republic of Yugoslavia and to retain specific targeted measures, the Minister of State, FCO, wrote:

Following the election of Vojislav Kostunica as President of the Federal Republic of Yugoslavia (FRY), European Union Foreign Ministers agreed at the General Affairs Council on 9 October to revise EU sanctions against the FRY and to retain specific targeted measures.

The EU oil embargo and flight ban were lifted with effect from 9 October.

On 10 November the Council of the EU adopted a Common Position to restrict financial sanctions and the visa ban to Milosevic and persons associated with him.

The provisions on financial sanctions were implemented by an EC Regulation adopted on 10 November. This Regulation repeals EC Regulations 1294/99 and 607/2000 as well as Article 2 of EC Regulation 926/98. The Regulation will come into force this week with its publication of the *Official Journal of the European Communities*.

The new Regulation provides that all funds held in the EU belonging to individuals listed in the annex to the Regulation shall be frozen and that no funds shall be made available, directly or indirectly, to or for the benefit of any person listed in the annex.

Under the new Regulation all EU financial sanctions in relation to FRY companies will be lifted. All EU restrictions on the provision of export credit support finance and on investment in the FRY will also be lifted.

UK legislation providing penalties for breaches of the financial sanctions will be amended to take account of the new Regulation.

The individuals subject to financial sanctions are identical to those subject to the EU visa ban, which is the subject of a Council Decision of 10 November.

The EU arms embargo and embargo on the supply to the FRY of equipment which might be used for internal repression or terrorism are unaffected. The

UN arms embargo against the FRY and prohibition on the arming and training for terrorist activities there remain in force.

(HC Debs., vol. 356, cols. 505–6W: 15 November 2000)

15/34

In reply to a question, the Parliamentary Under-Secretary of State, FCO, wrote:

European Foreign Ministers agreed at the General Affairs Council on 20 November that the EU arms embargo against Croatia should be lifted with immediate effect.

This is in recognition of Croatia's continuing progress towards implementing her Dayton responsibilities. These include the removal of discriminatory legislation against Croatian Serbs and assistance in war affected areas, the adoption of legislation encouraging refugee return, the establishment of a transparent relationship with the HVO (Bosnian Croat army) in Bosnia and civilian oversight of the Defence Ministry. Croatia joined Partnership for Peace in May 2000 and will soon begin negotiations with the EU on a Stabilization and Association Agreement.

On 20 November the Council of the EU adopted a new Common Position amending 96/184/CFSP so that Croatia is no longer subject to the EU arms embargo against states of the former Yugoslavia. Applications for licences to export defence equipment to Croatia will be considered on a case by case basis against the consolidated EU code of conduct and national arms export licensing criteria.

(HL Debs., vol. 619, *WA 67*: 21 November 2000)

15/35

In reply to a question, the Parliamentary Under-Secretary of State, FCO, wrote:

Following the election of Vojislav Kostunica as President of the Federal Republic of Yugoslavia (FRY), European Union Foreign Ministers agreed at the General Affairs Council on 9 October to revise EU sanctions against the FRY and to retain specific targeted measures.

The EU oil embargo and flight ban were lifted with effect from 9 October.

On 10 November the Council of the EU adopted a Common Position to restrict financial sanctions and the visa ban to Milosevic and persons associated with him.

The provisions on financial sanctions were implemented by an EC Regulation adopted on 10 November. This Regulation repeals EC Regulations 1294/99 and 607/2000 as well as Article 2 of EC Regulation 926/98. The Regulation will come into force this week with its publication in the Official Journal of the European Communities.

The new Regulation provides that all funds held in the EU belonging to individuals listed in the annex to the Regulation shall be frozen and that no funds shall be made available, directly or indirectly, to or for the benefit of any person listed in the annex.

Under the new Regulation, all EU financial sanctions in relation to FRY companies will be lifted. All EU restrictions on the provision of export credit support finance and on investment in the FRY will also be lifted.

UK legislation providing penalties for breaches of the financial sanctions will be made to take account of the new Regulation.

The individuals subject to financial sanctions are identical to those subject to the EU visa ban, which is the subject of a Council Decision of 10 November.

The EU arms embargo and embargo on the supply to the FRY of equipment which might be used for internal repression or terrorism are unaffected. The UN arms embargo against the FRY and prohibition on the arming and training for terrorist activities there remain in force.

(HL Debs., vol. 619, *WA 116*: 27 November 2000)

Part Sixteen: IV. *Use of force—use of force other than self-defence and under the UN Charter*

[*Editorial Note*: the following item should be regarded as part of UKMIL 1999]

16/1

The transcript of a press conference given on 25 March 1999 by Mr George Robertson, Secretary of State for Defence, read in part as follows:

Over the past year the international community, with Britain at the forefront, has made intensive efforts to see a peaceful resolution to the crisis in Kosovo. President Milosevic has either rebuffed the approaches or made deals that he has reneged on. The result, as we have all seen, has been a developing humanitarian catastrophe in which Yugoslav and Serb security forces are destroying whole villages and making tens of thousands homeless. Only yesterday, before we had to embark on the air strikes, the Ministry of the Interior Special Police were reported to be razing villages in central Kosovo and the areas around Poclujevo, Srbica and Komorane.

The diplomatic track came to an end on Tuesday this week when Ambassador Holbrooke had a final unsuccessful meeting with Milosevic. Throughout this period NATO has been supporting these initiatives because it was only the credible threat of force which led to the agreements last October which Milosevic ultimately failed to observe.

Seven weeks ago, on 30 January, the North Atlantic Council reaffirmed its readiness to take action and passed to NATO Secretary General Javier Solana the power to order air strikes against targets in Yugoslav territory in order to underpin international efforts to bring about a resolution. On Tuesday of this week, following the failure of two rounds of talks in France and after a final round of consultations and with great reluctance, he directed SACEUR to begin operations.

The military objective of these operations is absolutely clear cut, it is to avert an impending humanitarian catastrophe by disrupting the violent attacks currently being carried out by the Yugoslav security forces against the Kosovar

Albanians and to limit their ability to conduct such repression in the future. This action is supported by all 18 NATO states, 13 of which had planes and support assets committed to the operation.

Last night the Air Forces of Belgium, Canada, Denmark, France, Germany, Italy, the Netherlands, Norway, Portugal, Spain, Turkey and the United Kingdom and the United States were all involved in the allied military action. We are in no doubt that NATO is acting within international law and our legal justification rests upon the accepted principle that force may be used in extreme circumstances to avert a humanitarian catastrophe. NATO's action has received support inside the UN Security Council from the United States, France, Argentina, Slovenia, Malaysia, Gambia, Bahrain, the Netherlands and Gabon. Outside of Russia and China, only Namibia disagreed with the military action in the Security Council, and in the wider United Nations we know of only opposition from India and understandably Belarus and the Former Republic of Yugoslavia itself.

We believe that military action is clearly justified in the circumstances of Kosovo given the undisputed humanitarian emergency and the rejection by Milosevic of all diplomatic efforts. Yesterday the time came for NATO to act in a clear and determined way and if yesterday Milosevic still doubted the Alliance's resolve, he has now in the damage to his military machine the evidence of our determination to take action to avert a human tragedy in Kosovo. But Milosevic should, even at this late stage, think again and should stop the violence in Kosovo, withdraw his troops and sign the peace accord. And let me make it clear that NATO has the will, the determination and the stomach to see this through and to stop the flow of blood and human misery in Kosovo. So let Mr. Milosevic understand this, we will be watching how he behaves and British and allied aircraft will resume their attacks later today unless he stops the violence against the Kosovo population.

The decision to use force was not taken lightly. We are well aware of the considerable risks involved and we salute the bravery of our Servicemen and women who are undertaking these operations on our behalf. But we will not stand idly by and watch a tragedy continue to unfold in our own continent, a tragedy which could all too easily lead to a wider conflict.

(FCO Website <www.fco.gov.UK/news/newstext.asp? 2167>)

16/2

In the course of a speech given at the London School of Economics on 13 January 2000, the Secretary of State for Foreign and Commonwealth Affairs, Mr Robin Cook, referred to the conclusion of the Convention relating to the International Criminal Court. He continued:

What they were doing was something enormously historic in the relationship between states, they were accepting the creation of an international judicial system with supremacy over state court systems, based on the fundamental principle that gross offences to humanitarian law are not the sole business of the state in which they occur, but they are the business of all humanity.

If we are to take that forward we need to do so in the context in which we recognise that it is no longer sufficient for states to claim they have the sovereign right to decide what is going to be legal and what is going to be illegal. The international community can both determine that and enforce that. I think the most important diplomatic debate we will have over the first decade of this new century is to take forward when is it right, and how do we decide when it is right, for the international community to intervene against the consent of any one individual state. The first responsibility for ending conflict, for observing humanitarian law, must rest with the state and of all forms of intervention, military intervention must be the last resort. But we now have an obligation to recognise that the international community does have a right to intervene where the sovereign state is permitting or practising genocide or gross humanitarian violations. And that is only possible because we have now, since 1989, arrived at an international community which is no longer divided into blocks, but it composes of individual states willing together globally to come to an agreement on global governance, not in the sense of a global government but in the global rule of law.

(FCO reference 007/FS/2000, p. 4)

16/3

In the course of a radio interview on 28 January 2000, the following exchange took place between the interviewer and Mr Cook:

INTERVIEWER:

You talk also about when intervention should be necessary, should be used and how it should be used. On what basis and where should countries intervene in the affairs of another country?

FOREIGN SECRETARY:

I set out the points that we have submitted to Kofi Annan, the Secretary General of the United Nations. Essentially what those principles state is that the first responsibility for containing conflict rests with the state in which it happens. Armed intervention by the international regime must always be a last resort, but that where there is sustained humanitarian suffering, we should have the right to decide to intervene, provided we have the capacity to do so and provided such action would be proportionate to the problem we are resolving.

INTERVIEWER:

So why aren't we going into Chechnya? There are a quarter of a million refugees in Ingushetia, they are not being very well looked after by all accounts, why are we not doing something there?

FOREIGN SECRETARY:

Well we are doing something, we have actually provided assistance for the humanitarian aid to those refugees and I have spoken repeatedly and regularly to the Russian Foreign Minister to bring home to him our deep concern. Only last Monday at the European Union meeting of Foreign Ministers we agreed to suspend the European Union's economic assistance to Russia to bring home our deep message of concern on Chechnya.

INTERVIEWER:

But we are not intervening as such, not as we did for example in Kosovo.

FOREIGN SECRETARY:

Are you asking me to bomb Russia? Do you really think that a single listener out there would believe that that would help the problem and not make the problem worse?

INTERVIEWER:

I want to know how you are going to make the decisions in the future about where one does get bombed and where one doesn't?

FOREIGN SECRETARY:

The decision would have to be taken on a collective basis and that I made clear in the speech. But I also did say that we would have to have the ability to resolve the problem before we embark on armed force. We must approach this very clearly and very firmly with our feet on the ground, and nobody listening to this programme would imagine for one minute that it would be a sane or sensible policy to proceed to armed intervention in Russia.

(FCO reference O14/FS/2000, pp. 4–5)

16/4

On 28 January 2000, the Secretary of State made a speech at Chatham House on the subject of foreign policy and national interest. In the course of the speech, Mr Cook stated:

INTERVENTION

The biggest unresolved question in upholding universal values is when is it right for the international community to intervene and who decides that it is right? The United Nations Charter declares that "armed force shall not be used, save in the common interest". But what is the common interest, and who shall define it? We need to establish new rules of the road.

The UK has submitted to the UN Secretary-General in response to those questions a set of ideas to help the international community decide when it is right to act.

- first, any intervention is by definition a failure of prevention. Force should always be the last resort;
- second, the immediate responsibility for halting violence rests with the state in which it occurs;

- but, third, when faced with an overwhelming humanitarian catastrophe and a government that has demonstrated itself unwilling or unable to halt or prevent it, the international community should act;
- and finally, any use of force in this context should be collective, proportionate, likely to achieve its objective, and carried out in accordance with international law.

Britain will be seeking the broadest possible agreement on these principles to take forward the debate on intervention at the UN Millennium Summit in the autumn.

(Text provided by the FCO)

16/5

In reply to the question to Her Majesty's Government 'which United Kingdom proposals for international action in response to humanitarian crises which [they are] discussing with international partners', the Secretary of State for Foreign and Commonwealth Affairs wrote:

My right honourable friend the Prime Minister made clear in his speech at the Mansion House on 22 November that the international community needs an agreed framework on when and how it is appropriate to intervene in the face of massive violations of human rights and international humanitarian law. The United Nations Charter declares that armed force should not be used, save in the common interest. We need to build consensus on what that common interest is and how we define it.

We believe that the development of a set of pragmatic understandings on action in response to humanitarian crises would help the Security Council—acting on behalf of the Members of the United Nations—to reach consensus when such crises occur, thus ensuring effective and timely action by the international community. In this context, we have put to the UN Secretary-General and to key international partners a set of ideas, of which the key elements are:

first, any intervention is by definition a failure of prevention. Force should always be the last resort;
second, the immediate responsibility for halting violence rests with the state in which it occurs;
but, third, when faced with an immediate and overwhelming humanitarian catastrophe and a government that has demonstrated itself unwilling or unable to prevent it, the international community should take action;
and finally, any use of force in this context must be collective, proportionate, likely to achieve its objective, and carried out in accordance with international law.

The detail of these preliminary ideas is still under discussion with partners. Once we have had time to take account of their views and develop our proposals further, we will place a copy in the Library of the House.

(HC Debs., vol. 343, cols. 459–60W: 31 January 2000)

16/6

In a press statement released on 19 May 2000, the Minister of State, FCO, Mr Peter Hain, remarked in part:

British forces are in Sierra Leone at the request of the Government of Sierra Leone and with the blessing of the United Nations. They are evacuating British nationals. They are complying fully with domestic and international law.

It is the [Revolutionary United Front] who are consistently operating outside domestic and international law and who have committed gross human rights abuses. Harangues from such people on spurious legal points will be seen for what they are worth.

(Text provided by the FCO)

16/7

In a press statement issued on 7 June 2000 which commented on the HC Foreign Affairs Committee Report on Kosovo, the Secretary of State for Foreign and Commonwealth Affairs, Mr Robin Cook, stated in part:

The report deals at some length with the legal basis for the NATO action, while acknowledging that disputes about international law are not ones that the Committee can resolve. The Government is confident that its action was consistent with international law and I welcome the Committee's conclusion that 'NATO allies did all they could to make the military intervention in Kosovo as compliant with the tenets of international law as possible'.

(Text provided by the FCO)

16/8

In the course of a debate on an oral question about humanitarian intervention by the United Nations, the Parliamentary Under-Secretary of State, Baroness Scotland of Asthal, stated:

Her Majesty's Government firmly believe that we have a shared responsibility to act when confronted with massive violations of international humanitarian law and crimes against humanity. Indeed, we have made that absolutely clear. We note the developments in the areas that the noble Lord has just highlighted, which, of course, are matters of great concern. For that reason, we feel it essential to build the broadest possible consensus on the conditions and circumstances that make international action appropriate and, thereby, strengthen the ability of the Security Council to respond effectively and promptly. As I said earlier, we are discussing these issues to try to achieve that consensus. However, we must bear in mind the fact that any intervention must be focused so that it does more good than harm. We must be very balanced in the way we proceed in this area.

(HL Debs., vol. 615, cols. 1005–6: 19 July 2000)

16/9

On 19 July 2000, the Secretary of State for Foreign and Commonwealth Affairs, Mr Robin Cook, delivered a speech to the American Bar Association meeting in London. Mr Cook made reference to the US Secretary of State, Mrs Madeleine Albright, and continued:

HUMANITARIAN INTERVENTION

I would have welcomed hearing Madeleine address our topic for today—the conceptual and legal basis for intervention. How can the international community avert crimes against humanity while at the same time respecting the rule of international law and the sovereignty of nation states? The question of when it is right to use or threaten force is perhaps the most difficult issue with which political leaders have to grapple.

No-one can claim any longer that massive violations of humanitarian law or crimes against humanity fall solely within a state's domestic jurisdiction. The UN Charter itself was written after the Holocaust. It begins 'We the Peoples', not 'We the States'. It explicitly recognises the importance of protecting and promoting the rights of individuals.

And there is now a well-established body of international law on genocide, crimes against humanity and war crimes. The Tribunals for War Crimes in Rwanda and Yugoslavia operate in this context. So will the new International Criminal Court. They illustrate the growing international determination not to allow state sovereignty to act as a shield for war criminals.

But it is not enough to react after the event. It is far better to prevent genocide than to punish the perpetrators after the grisly evidence and mass graves are discovered. It is not good enough to have UN Blue Helmets standing aside while acts of unspeakable cruelty are carried out. We cannot accept another Srebrenica.

Exceptional circumstances demand an exceptional response. Just such circumstances arose in Kosovo. Regrettably, the threat of veto by two of the Permanent Members made Security Council action impossible despite majority support for our cause. But, under these exceptional circumstances, we were still justified, in every respect, in intervening as we did through NATO.

CHALLENGE FOR THE NEW CENTURY

Kofi Annan has said that the core challenge to the United Nations in the new century is 'to forge unity behind the principle that massive and systematic violations of human rights—wherever they may take place—should not be allowed to stand'. He has challenged us all to 'think anew'.

My answer to Kofi's challenge, and my contribution to this debate, is that we should set down guidelines for intervention in response to massive violations of humanitarian law and crimes against humanity. In doing so, I want to reinforce the Security Council's ability to do what is right and to fulfil its duties. If we cannot do this, and the Security Council cannot respond to the most serious aspects of modern conflict, it risks becoming irrelevant. This is in no-one's interest. The Security Council must continue to act in the interests of the members of the UN. It must do so on the basis of a common understanding that, when given circumstances arise, military action is justified and necessary.

The stronger the likelihood that the international community will act, the more we deter future perpetrators of crimes against humanity.

BRITAIN'S FRAMEWORK TO GUIDE INTERVENTION

The international community is more likely to act if there are clear principles to guide us when to act. Britain has submitted to the UN Secretary General a framework to guide intervention by the international community. Today, I want to share with you six of the principles on which we can build such a framework.

First, any intervention, by definition, is an admission of failure of prevention. We need a strengthened culture of conflict prevention. Last week I was in Japan for the G8 Foreign Ministers' Meeting where we agreed that a 'comprehensive approach' integrating all the policies at our disposal is the right one for conflict prevention. We need to stop the trade in small arms, and the illicit trade in diamonds which often fuels conflict—and I am proud that Britain played a leading part earlier this month in passing a Security Council resolution aimed at doing just that. We need to use development policies to eliminate the causes of conflict—poverty above all. And we need to end the use of children as soldiers.

Second, we should maintain the principle that armed force should only be used as a last resort. Intervention may take many forms, including mediation, as in Cyprus, sanctions, as in Angola, observer missions, as in Georgia, and international condemnation, as in more countries than I care to mention.

Third, the immediate responsibility for halting violence rests with the state in which it occurs. Sometimes a state would like to act but cannot. Then the international community should be ready to help if asked, as we were in Sierra Leone. But other states refuse to halt the violence, or are themselves the cause of the violence—as with Milosevic's Serbia.

Fourth, when faced with an overwhelming humanitarian catastrophe, which a government has shown it is unwilling or unable to prevent or is actively promoting, the international community should intervene. Intervention in internal affairs is a sensitive issue. So there must be convincing evidence of extreme humanitarian distress on a large scale, requiring urgent relief. It must be objectively clear that there is no practicable alternative to the use of force to save lives. But we should act on the principle that a UN member state should not be able to plead its sovereign rights to shield conduct which is inconsistent with its obligations as a member of the UN. We need to strike the correct balance between the sovereign rights of states and the humanitarian right of the international community to intervene where necessary, as it was in Kosovo.

Fifth, any use of force should be proportionate to achieving the humanitarian purpose and carried out in accordance with international law. We should be sure that the scale of potential or actual human suffering justifies the dangers of military action. And it must be likely to achieve its objectives.

Sixth, any use of force should be collective. No individual country can reserve to itself the right to act on behalf of the international community. Our intervention in Kosovo was a collective decision, backed by the 19 members of

NATO and unanimously by the 42 European nations which attended the Washington NATO Summit in April 1999. Our own preference would be that, wherever possible, the authority of the Security Council should be secured.

The first and best way of dealing collectively with conflict remains the United Nations. When conflict prevention fails, the UN usually takes the blame. But failures of the UN are no more and no less than failures of the UN's members—all of us. We need to do better if we are not to undermine the credibility of collective international efforts.

The Security Council itself needs to be more representative of the membership of the United Nations. It cannot do its job properly in the 21st century if its membership still reflects the geopolitical realities of the 1940s. Britain has been advocating the enlargement and modernisation of the Council for some time, and I welcome the United States' willingness to look at formulae which involve a Security Council of more than 21 members. A more effective and representative Security Council must be a key part of any strategy for modernising the UN.

CONCLUSION

As the world grows smaller, national interests and global interests are converging. The international community is moving towards the principle that when crimes are committed against humanity, it is in the interests of the whole of humanity to deal with them. During the dark days of appeasement that preceded the Second World War, one Prime Minister famously described Czechoslovakia as a far-away country of which we know little. In the modern world, there is no such a place as a far-away country of which we know little.

Yet the international law under which we still operate dates from the aftermath of the Second World War. It was drawn up to deal with the threat to international order of the time—aggressive invasion by a foreign power of another country. In response, it gave central importance to the sovereignty of governments and non-interference across borders. These are vital concepts of international law and they have helped make aggressive invasion a rarity in modern times.

But they do not help us address the more common threat to peace and stability in today's world. Millions have died in conflict over the past decade, overwhelmingly civilians rather than combatants. They have been the casualties not of international war but of internal strife. We need new rules of the road to guide us on when to intervene to halt casualties within a nation which we would not tolerate between nations.

When is it right for the international community to intervene and who decides that it is right? The United Nations Charter declares that 'armed force shall not be used, save in the common interest'. But what is the common interest, and who shall define it?

These are not questions which politicians can attempt to answer by themselves. We need a global debate on these crucial questions on how to develop international law to meet the needs of the modern world. And we need help to find answers that establish a new international consensus.

Where better to turn for that help than to such a distinguished gathering of the American Bar. It is traditional for the speaker to end by answering questions from his audience. This time I am going to get my retaliation in first by putting those questions to my audience. And if you can help us get nearer to the answers, then I will regard my lunch break as time well spent.

(Text provided by the FCO)

16/10

In August 2000, the Secretary of State for Foreign and Commonwealth Affairs presented to Parliament his response to the Fourth Report from the HC Foreign Affairs Committee, Session 1999–2000, which concerned Kosovo. The conclusions of the Committee are printed in bold type below, followed by the response of the Secretary of State.

Was military intervention legal?

(18) Our conclusion is that *Operation Allied Force* was contrary to the specific terms of what might have been termed the basic law of the international community—the UN Charter, although this might have been avoided if the allies had attempted to use the Uniting for Peace procedures. (Paragraph 128)

(19) We conclude that, at the very least, the doctrine of humanitarian intervention has a tenuous basis in current international customary law, and that this renders NATO action legally questionable. (Paragraph 132)

(20) We conclude that, faced with the threat of veto in the Security Council by Russia and China, the NATO allies did all that they could to make the international intervention on Kosovo as compliant with the tenets of international law as possible. (Paragraph 134)

The Government has made clear that use of force is justified as an exceptional measure when it is the only means to avert an immediate and overwhelming catastrophe and is in support of objectives set by the UN Security Council, even if the express authorisation of the Council has not been possible. Such cases would in the nature of things be exceptional and depend on an objective assessment of the factual circumstances at the time and on the terms of relevant decisions of the Security Council bearing on the situation in question.

The 'Uniting for Peace' resolution has been used to convene emergency General Assembly (GA) sessions when decisions in the Security Council were blocked by a veto. Under the UN Charter, the GA can only make recommendations for action. Such recommendations cannot of themselves constitute a legal basis for the use of force.

(21) We recommend that the Government examine whether any new legal instruments necessary to allow NATO to take action in future in the same manner as it did in Kosovo (Paragraph 135)

The Government does not believe that it is necessary to develop a new instrument of the kind suggested. The Government's aim is to build the political will within the Security Council and beyond—to use to full effect those instruments that already exist. This involves playing a part in the international debate on when and how to respond to situations of severe humanitarian crisis.

(22) We conclude that NATO's military action, if of dubious legality in the current state of international law, was justified on moral grounds. (Paragraph 138)

The Government welcomes the Committee's conclusion that the NATO intervention was morally justified. The Government is also satisfied that it was legally justified.

(Cm 4825, pp. 7–8)

16/11

The Government's Observations, dated 12 October 2000, made in response to the HC Defence Committee's Thirteenth Report of Session 1999–2000, which dealt with Iraqi No-Fly Zones, contained the following passage:

Legal basis for the no-fly zones (Para 31)

2. The Government welcomes the Committee's endorsement of the continuing need for the no fly zones and in particular their recognition that the zones are justified on moral and humanitarian grounds. We welcome in particular the Committee's recognition that military action is only ever undertaken in response to direct threats from Iraqi forces against coalition aircrew carrying out their humanitarian patrols. The Government remains satisfied that the no fly zones are legally justified as a measure to prevent a humanitarian crisis.

(*Parliamentary Papers*, 1999–2000, HC 930, Special Report)

Part Seventeen: I. D. *The law of armed conflict—international armed conflict—belligerent occupation*

17/1

In reply to an oral question, the Secretary of State for Foreign and Commonwealth Affairs, Mr Robin Cook, stated in part:

It has been the long-standing view of Governments of both complexions that the settlements in the occupied territories are illegal under international law and are a block to the peace process.

(HC Debs., vol. 344, col. 754: 15 February 2000)

17/2

Speaking on 28 March 2000 in the UN Commission on Human Rights, the representative of Portugal, on behalf of the EU, stated:

The European Union maintained its position on the Fourth Geneva Convention relative to the Protection of Civilian Persons in Time of War and observed that that Convention was fully applicable to the occupied territories, including East Jerusalem, and had force of law within that conflict.

(E/CN.4/2000/SR. 13, p. 9)

Part Seventeen: I. E. *The law of armed conflict—international armed conflict—termination, treaties of peace*

17/3

In reply to a question, the Parliamentary Under-Secretary of State, FCO, wrote in part:

The Cessation of Hostilities Agreement signed on 18 June by both Ethiopia and Eritrea provides for the return of civilian administration and the return of populations to those areas affected by the conflict. With our international partners, we will continue to press both sides to implement the agreement swiftly.

(HL Debs., vol. 614, *WA 158–9*: 6 July 2000)

Part Seventeen: III. C. *The law of armed conflict—aspects of the law of armed conflict—mercenaries*

17/4

In reply to a question, the Minister of State, FCO, wrote:

Her Majesty's Government have no plans to sign the 1989 International Convention on Mercenaries. We do not consider that it would be enforceable in the UK courts. Although the Convention was adopted more than ten years ago, it has not yet attracted sufficient ratifications to enter into force.

(HC Debs., vol. 351, cols. 703–4W: 15 June 2000)

Part Seventeen: III. D. *The law of armed conflict—aspects of the law of armed conflict—conventional weapons*

17/5

In reply to a question, the Secretary of State for Defence wrote:

In accordance with our obligations under the Ottawa Convention and the Landmines Act 1998, the Government's policy is not to use any weapon incorporating anti-personnel mines as defined in the Ottawa Convention. This obligation extends to airfield runway denial weapons and anti-tank land mines, and the UK does not retain stocks of any such weapons which contravene the Ottawa Convention.

(HC Debs., vol. 348, col. 294W: 14 April 2000)

Part Seventeen: III. E. *The law of armed conflict—aspects of the law of armed conflict—nuclear, bacteriological and chemical weapons*

17/6

In the course of answering an oral question, the Government spokeswoman in the House of Lords, Baroness Ramsay of Cartvale, stated:

. . . the Government have made crystal clear the fact that our goal is the global elimination of nuclear weapons. In principle, we have no problem with the idea of a nuclear weapons convention as the ultimate legal underpinning of a nuclear weapons-free world. However, we cannot wish away present political realities and pretend that in present circumstances negotiations on such a convention can be expected to make headway. By all means, let us be ambitious in this area but, as recognised by the NPT Review Conference, let us also focus on goals which are achievable.

(HL Debs., vol. 614, cols. 619–20: 26 June 2000)

17/7

In reply to a question, the Parliamentary Under-Secretary of State, Department of Defence, wrote:

The Chemical Weapons Convention (CWC) permits the retention of toxic chemicals and their precursors, where they are intended for purposes not prohibited under the Convention. Such permitted purposes include research, medical, pharmaceutical and protective purposes. Toxic chemicals and precursors are classified according to three Schedules, primarily on the basis of their usability as chemical weapons, the risk they pose to the Convention, and their commercial utility.

The UK, as a State Party to the CWC, is permitted to hold up to an aggregate of 1 tonne of Schedule 1 chemicals. The Chemical and Biological Defence Sector of the Defence Evaluation and Research Agency at Porton Down is licensed by the CWC National Authority to hold Schedule 1 chemicals for permitted purposes and is required to make an annual declaration of holdings and usage.

The declaration is not made public for reasons of national security and so I am withholding information about specific quantities under Exemption 1 of the Code Of Practice on Access to Government Information. However, total holdings are substantially less than the permitted maximum of 1 tonne.

(HC Debs., vol. 354, col. 550W: 25 July 2000)

17/8

In December 2000, the FCO presented to Parliament an Explanatory Memorandum in respect of the African Nuclear-Weapon-Free-Zone Treaty (the Treaty of Pelindaba). The Memorandum contained the following passages:

The Treaty of Pelindaba creates a nuclear-weapon-free-zone consisting of the territory of all of the African States. The primary obligations for States Parties to the Treaty are not to manufacture or acquire nuclear weapons or other nuclear explosive devices, not to test such weapons or devices, and to prohibit the stationing of such weapons or devices in their territory. However, each State Party remains free to allow foreign ships and aircraft (carrying nuclear weapons or devices) to visit its ports and airfields, to transit its airspace, and to navigate in its territorial sea or archipelagic waters.

Protocols I and II to the Treaty are open for signature and ratification by the five nuclear-weapon States. Protocol I requires States Parties not to use or threaten to use nuclear weapons against any State Party to the Pelindaba Treaty. Each Protocol I Party also undertakes not to contribute to any violation of the Treaty or of Protocol I. Protocol II prohibits Parties from testing nuclear weapons or devices within the zone, and from contributing to any violation of the Treaty or of Protocol II. The UK signed Protocols I and II on 11 April 1996. It now intends to ratify them.

. . .

(iii) Reservations and Declarations

The UK intends to make the following Declaration upon ratification of Protocols I and II:

a) Generally

(i) the Government of the United Kingdom believe that universal adherence to and compliance with international agreements seeking to prevent the proliferation of weapons of mass destruction are vital to the maintenance of world security;
(ii) the Government of the United Kingdom have no doubt as to their sovereignty over the British Indian Ocean Territory and do not accept the inclusion of that Territory within the African nuclear-weapon-free-zone without their consent. The Government of the United Kingdom do not accept any legal obligations in respect of that Territory by their adherence to Protocols I and II;
(iii) the Government of the United Kingdom understand that nothing in the Treaty affects rights under international law with regard to transit of the African nuclear-weapon-free-zone or visits to ports and airfields within that zonc by ships and aircraft;
(iv) the Government of the United Kingdom understand the term 'inland waters' as used in the Treaty to exclude waters used in connection with maritime navigation;

b) Re: Protocols I and II, first preambular paragraph

the Government of the United Kingdom understand the obligations referred to in the context of the provisions of Article VI of the Treaty on the Non-Proliferation of Nuclear Weapons of 1 July 1968;

c) Re: Protocol I, Article 1

the Government of the United Kingdom will not be bound by their undertaking under Article 1 of Protocol I,
(i) in the case of an invasion or any other attack on the United Kingdom, its dependent territories, its armed forces or other troops, its allies or a State towards which it has a security commitment, carried out or sustained by a Party to the Treaty in association or alliance with a nuclear-weapon State, or

(ii) if any Party to the Treaty is in material breach of its own non-proliferation obligations under the Treaty;

d) Re: Protocols I and II, Article 2

the Government of the United Kingdom accept this obligation on the understanding that it means that each party undertakes not to contribute to any act of a party to the Treaty which constitutes a violation of the Treaty, or to any act of another party to a Protocol which constitutes a violation of that Protocol;

e) Re: Protocols I and II, Article 6

the Government of the United Kingdom reserve the right to withdraw from these Protocols under the conditions specified on giving notice of withdrawal to the Depositary three months in advance.

Most of these Declarations were made by the UK at the time of signature of Protocols I and II to the Pelindaba Treaty in 1996. Only declarations (a)(iii) and (a)(iv) are new.

Declaration (a)(iii) sets out the UK understanding that nothing in the Treaty affects rights under international law with regard to the transit of the zone or visits to ports and airfields within the zone. Declaration (a)(iv) sets out the UK understanding that nothing in the Treaty prohibits transit through waters used in connection with maritime navigation.

(Text provided by the FCO)

Part Seventeen: III. F. *The law of armed conflict—aspects of the law of armed conflict—protection of the individual (international humanitarian law)*

(See also **16/5, 8–9**)

17/9

In the course of a debate on the subject of British prisoners of war of Japan during the Second World War, the Parliamentary Under-Secretary of State for Defence, Dr Lewis Moonie, stated:

The treatment of prisoners of war was governed at the time by the 1929 Geneva convention. Japan had not ratified it, but said that it would, in general, recognise its provisions. However, as we know, it did not do so.

As a safeguard to the prisoners of war, the Japanese should have permitted inspection visits by the protecting power and the Red Cross. In many areas that was refused and even where, with considerable obstructions, visits were permitted, little could be achieved. That avenue, which in Europe produced improvements in the conditions and treatment of prisoners of war in a number of cases, achieved little for those held in the far east.

The British Government were, however, able to make the point strongly that the ill-treatment of the POWs was unacceptable. That was done by means of war crimes trials and, through the Tokyo trials, a number of those held responsible for the ill-treatment of POWs were brought to justice for their crimes.

Uniquely among British POWs, the far east POWs received some compensation after the war for their ill-treatment. They received it from their captors under the terms of the 1951 peace treaty with Japan. They also received the money that the British Government received under the treaty and that they decided to distribute to the POWs and to British civilian internees. The question has been raised many times of the possibility of reopening the peace treaty to seek a higher level of compensation. That is of course a matter for my right hon. Friend the Foreign Secretary, but I will say that the Government, having examined the position most carefully, accept the legal advice that the peace treaty is closed and cannot now be reopened.

There have also been calls for an inquiry to be set up into the perceived failure of the then Conservative Government to invoke article 26 of the treaty and seek more compensation on the grounds that other countries had signed more favourable agreements. However, the records, which have been publicly available for many years, show that that decision was not taken solely because of the weak position of the Japanese economy at that time and the wish, which was in Britain's interest, to see it recover. It was also very much influenced by the fact that it was extremely difficult to ascertain what, if any, additional benefits this country would in practice be entitled to and what their worth might be. It is by no means clear, had the treaty been re-opened, that the British Government would have received any additional funds with which to provide compensation. Furthermore, there is no basis on which to reopen the issue of compensation for the far east POWs, because Japan signed no subsequent agreements conferring greater benefits upon the POWs of other countries than those awarded under the treaty.

The Government are very much aware of the depth of feeling that the ill-treatment of the far east POWs continues to evoke and we continue to raise the issue with the Japanese Government and to seek ways to build reconciliation as a means of helping to overcome the past.

At the end of the war, the pressure and support for compensation for the far east POWs was strong. The then Government suggested that the funds likely to be realised under the treaty should be shared on the basis of giving most to those who had suffered most. However, the representatives of the far east POWs wanted a simple per capita distribution, accepting that that might mean only small individual payments.

Those speaking on behalf of the POWs made it clear in the House that in establishing the principle of compensation from the captor, they made no claim of any sort on the British taxpayer. Brigadier Smythe, a leading champion for the cause of the POWs in the House said that on no account would they accept money from the British taxpayer. He went on:

> The important thing about this claim is its moral principle. The Far Eastern prisoners of war do not mind so much about the money side as they do that the principle should be established that no nation shall treat the nationals of another when they have them in captivity as the Japanese treated our men.—[*Official Report*, 10 May 1951; Vol. 487, c. 2226.]

It is clear from the views now being expressed on behalf of the far east POWs and their widows that that belief has now changed. They are seeking what is termed an 'ex-gratia gratuity,' from the British Government, and thus the British taxpayer. In essence, such a gratuity would be compensation.

It is a policy of long standing that British Governments do not make compensation payments to those who have been prisoners of war on account of their imprisonment. There are many risks implicit for those engaged in conflict and the risk of being captured is sadly one of them. It is unrealistic to suppose that Governments could effectively insure individuals against that risk. Terrible through the conditions suffered by the far east POWs were, it is unrealistic to think that it would be possible to ring-fence just that one group of POWs.

(HC Debs., vol. 345, cols. 1290–1: 9 March 2000)

17/10

In reply to a question, the Government Minister in the House of Lords wrote:

The UK does not have diplomatic relations with the Federal Republic of Yugoslavia (FRY) so is unable to make effective representations to the FRY authorities on behalf of the Albanian prisoners (believed to be some 1,540) held in Serbia. The International Committee for the Red Cross (ICRC), as an impartial body, has access to the Kosovar prisoners. Through its contacts with the authorities, the ICRC is making strenuous efforts to ensure that those facing prosecution benefit from the legal safeguards laid down in international law. We strongly support their important role in this matter. The UN representative in Kosovo, Bernard Kouchner, has frequently made public calls for the release of the Albanian prisoners in Serbia.

(HL Debs., vol. 610, *WA 178*: 13 March 2000)

17/11

By a letter dated 1 September 2000 addressed to the UN Secretary-General, the Secretary of State for Foreign and Commonwealth Affairs wrote:

I have the honour to refer to the United Kingdom of Great Britain and Northern Ireland's signature of the Optional Protocol to the Convention on the Rights of the Child on the involvement of children in armed conflict and to make the following declaration on behalf of the United Kingdom.

The United Kingdom of Great Britain and Northern Ireland will take all feasible measures to ensure that members of its armed forces who have not attained the age of 18 years do not take a direct part in hostilities.

The United Kingdom understands that Article 1 of the Optional Protocol would not exclude the deployment of members of its armed forces under the age of 18 to take a direct part in hostilities where

a) there is a genuine military need to deploy their unit or ship to an area in which hostilities are taking place; and
b) by reason of the nature and urgency of the situation

i) it is not practicable to withdraw such persons before deployment; or
ii) to do so would undermine the operational effectiveness of their ship or unit, and thereby put at risk the successful completion of the military mission and/or the safety of other personnel.

(Text provided by the FCO; see also UN Document C.N. 902.2000. TREATIES–76)

Part Seventeen: III. I. *The law of armed conflict—aspects of the law of armed conflict—war crimes*

(See also **16/9**)

17/12

In reply to the question what is Her Majesty's Government's definition of a war crime, the Parliamentary Under-Secretary of State, Home Office, wrote:

There is no single legal definition of a war crime.

In the domestic law of England and Wales, the Regulations for the Trial of War Criminals attached to the still extant Royal Warrant of 14 June 1945 define a war crime as 'a violation of the laws and usages of war committed during any war in which His Majesty has been or may be engaged at any time since the 2nd September 1939'. War crimes include grave breaches of the Geneva Conventions and their First Additional Protocol, which are punishable as criminal offences in the United Kingdom under the Geneva Conventions Act 1957. The War Crimes Act 1991 provides for the prosecution of offences of murder, manslaughter or culpable homicide in Germany or under German occupation during the Second World War, where the offences 'constituted a violation of the laws and customs of war' (Section 1).

The position under international law is complex, but the International Criminal Court, the statute for which was agreed at a United Nations conference in July 1998, will have jurisdiction to try war crimes. Such crimes are now defined for the purposes of the Court's jurisdiction in article 8 of the statute. The Government will during the current session of Parliament publish for public consultation a draft Bill implementing the United Kingdom's obligations under the statute.

(HL Debs., vol. 610, *WA 197–8*: 14 March 2000)

17/13

In reply to a question on the subject of the prosecution for war crimes of a Latvian citizen, the Minister of State, FCO, wrote in part:

We take our international obligation to bring to account those responsible for war crimes very seriously and have been in the forefront of international efforts to achieve restitution for victims of Nazi persecution. While the UK has no jurisdiction in the case, we have been assisting the Latvian authorities with their inquiries into Konrad Kalejs.

(HC Debs., vol. 346, col. 289W: 16 March 2000)

APPENDICES

I. Multilateral Agreements Signed by the United Kingdom in 2000[1]

Title	*Place and Date*	*UK Signature*	*Text*[2]
European Charter for Regional or Minority Languages	Strasbourg, 5.11.1992	2.3.2000	Misc. No. 16 (2000) (Cm 4750)
Agreement concerning the establishing of Global Technical Regulations for Wheeled Vehicles, Equipment and Parts which can be fitted and/or be Used on Wheeled Vehicles	Geneva, 25.6.1998	10.1.2000	TS No. 127 (2000) (Cm 4925)
International Convention for the Suppression of the Financing of Terrorism	New York, 10.1.2000	10.1.2000	
Basel Protocol on Liability and Compensation for Damage Resulting from Transboundary Movements of Hazardous Wastes and Their Disposal	Berne, 6.3.2000	8.12.2000	
European Convention on the Promotion of Transnational Long Term Voluntary Service for Young People	Strasbourg, 11.5.2000	19.9.2000	
Cartagena Protocol on Biosafety to the Convention on Biological Diversity	Nairobi, 15.5.2000	24.5.2000	
Optional Protocol to the Convention on the Rights of the Child on the Sale of Children, Child Prostitution and Child Pornography	New York, 25.5.2000	7.9.2000	

[1] Information supplied by the Foreign and Commonwealth Office. The table includes some agreements signed by the United Kingdom before 2000, where information was not previously available. The information is correct as at January 2001, although in some cases information available since that time has been included.

[2] Publication is in the Miscellaneous Series (Misc.) and Treaty Series (TS) of UK Command Papers. Cm = Command Paper number.

Title	*Place and Date*	*UK Signature*	*Text*
Optional protocol to the Convention on the Rights of the Child on the Involvement of Children in Armed Conflict	New York, 25.5.2000	7.9.2000	
Treaty concerning a European Vehicle and Driving Licence Information System	Luxembourg, 29.6.2000	29.6.2000	
Framework Agreement between the French Republic, the Federal Republic of Germany, the Italian Republic, the Kingdom of Spain, the Kingdom of Sweden, and the United Kingdom of Great Britain and Northern Ireland concerning Measures to Facilitate the Restructuring and Operation of the European Defence Industry	Farnborough, 27.7.2000	27.7.2000	Misc. No. 22 (2000) (Cm 4895)
Agreement on the Application of Article 65 of the Convention on the Grant of European Patents	London, 17.10.2000	17.10.2000	
Protocol drawn up on the basis of Article 43(1) of the Convention on the Establishment of a European Police Office (EUROPOL Convention) amending Article 2 and the Annex to that Convention	Brussels, 30.11.2000	30.11.2000	

II. European Communities Agreements Signed by the United Kingdom in 2000[1]

Title	*Place and Date*	*Text*[2]
PART 1 – SIGNED BY THE MEMBER STATES		
Convention, established by the Council in accordance with Article 34 of the Treaty on European Union, on Mutual Assistance in Criminal Matters between the Member States of the European Union	Brussels, 29.5.2000	
PART 2 – SIGNED BY THE COMMUNITY AND MEMBER STATES		
Partnership Agreement between the African, Caribbean and Pacific Group of States, of the one part, and the European Community and its Member States, of the other part	Cotonou, 23.6.2000	

[1] Information supplied by the Foreign and Commonwealth Office. The table includes some agreements signed by the United Kingdom before 2000, where information was not previously available. The information is correct as at January 2001, although in some cases information available since that time has been included. Treaties concluded by the European Community alone, to which the UK is not a separate party, are not included in this list.

[2] Publication is in the European Communities Series of UK Command Papers (EC). Cm = Command Paper number.

III. Bilateral Agreements Signed by the United Kingdom in 2000[1]

Country and Title	*Place and Date*	*Text*[2]
ANGOLA		
Agreement for the Promotion and Protection of Investments	London, 4.7.2000	
DENMARK		
Exchange of Notes extending the European Convention on Mutual Assistance in Criminal Matters to the Isle of Man	Copenhagen, 15.12.1999/ 25.2.2000	TS No. 44 (2000) (Cm 4689)
ESTONIA		
Exchange of Notes amending the Air Service Agreement done at London on 3.3.1993	Tallinn, 16.11.1999/ 25.7.2000	
FRANCE		
Additional Protocol to the Sangatte Protocol on the Establishment of Bureaux responsible for Controls on Persons travelling by train between the UK and France	Brussels, 29.5.2000	France No. 2 (2000) (Cm 5015)
Agreement concerning the Establishment of a Maritime Boundary between France and Jersey	St Helier, 4.7.2000	France No. 3 (2000) (Cm 5024)
Agreement concerning Fishing in the Bay of Granville, with Exchanges of Notes and Declaration	St Helier, 4.7.2000	France No. 4 (2000) (Cm 5025)
GUYANA		
Exchange of Notes concerning Certain Commercial Debts (UK Guyana Debt Agreement No. 5 (1999))	Georgetown, 11.9.2000	TS No. 130 (2000) (Cm 4929)

[1] Information supplied by the Foreign and Commonwealth Office. The table includes some agreements signed by the United Kingdom before 2000, where information was not previously available. The information is correct as at January 2001, although in some cases information available since that time has been included.

[2] Publication is in various series of UK Command Papers, including the Treaty Series (TS). Cm = Command Paper number.

Country and Title	*Place and Date*	*Text*
HONG KONG SAR		
Agreement for the Avoidance of Double Taxation on Revenues arising from the Business of Shipping Transport	Hong Kong, 25.10.2000	
INDONESIA		
Exchange of Notes concerning Certain Commercial Debts (UK Indonesia Debt Agreement No. 2 (1998))	Jakarta, 3/5.4.2000	TS No. 94 (2000) (Cm 4810)
IRELAND		
Exchange of Letters amending the Agreement concerning the International Fund for Ireland done at London and Dublin on 18.9.1986	Dublin/Belfast, 27.9/10.10.2000	TS No. 131 (2000) (Cm 5007)
ITALY		
Exchange of Notes extending the European Convention on Mutual assistance in Criminal Matters to the Isle of Man	London, 31.1.2000	TS No. 42 (2000) (Cm 4684)
JAPAN		
Agreement on Social Security	Tokyo, 29.2.2000	Japan No. 1 (2000) (Cm 4744)
JORDAN		
Exchange of Notes concerning Certain Commercial Debts (UK Jordan Debt Agreement No. 5 (1999))	Amman, 26.4/7.5.2000	TS No. 102 (2000) (Cm 4836)
LATVIA		
Exchange of Notes extending the Agreement for the Promotion and Protection of Investments done at London on 24.1.1994 to the Isle of Man and the Bailiwicks of Guernsey and Jersey	Riga, 13.3.2000	TS No. 85 (2000) (Cm 4775)
MACEDONIA, THE FYR OF		
Agreement on Co-operation in the fields of Education, Science and Culture	Skopje, 10.3.2000	Macedonia No. 2 (2000) (Cm 4788)

Country and Title	*Place and Date*	*Text*
MAURITANIA		
Exchange of Notes amending the UK/Mauritania Debt Agreement No. 6 (1995) (UK/Mauritania Debt Agreement No. 6 (1995) Amendment)	Rabat/ Nouakchott, 3.4/10.5.2000	TS No. 116 (2000) (Cm 4866)
MAURITIUS		
Exchange of Notes amending the Air Services Agreement done at Port Louis on 12.7.1973	Port Louis, 8.6/6.11.2000	
MONGOLIA		
Agreement concerning Air Services	London, 1.3.2000	TS No. 68 (2000) (Cm 4742)
NETHERLANDS		
Agreement concerning Air Services between and beyond the UK Overseas Territories of Anguilla, Bermuda, the British Virgin Islands, the Cayman Islands, Montserrat and Turks and Caicos Islands on the one hand, and the Netherlands Antilles on the other	London, 10.1.2000	Netherlands No. 1 (2000) (Cm 5850)
NORWAY		
Convention for the Avoidance of Double Taxation and the Prevention of Fiscal Evasion with Respect to Taxes on Income and Capital, with Exchange of Notes	London, 12.10.2000	
PAKISTAN		
Exchange of Notes concerning Commercial Debts (UK/Pakistan Debt Agreement No. 1 (1999))	Islamabad, 17/21.2.2000	TS No. 63 (2000) (Cm 4729)
RUSSIAN FEDERATION		
Exchange of Notes concerning Certain Commercial Debts (UK/Russia Debt Agreement No. 4 (1996))	London, 9.6.2000	TS No. 108 (2000) (Cm 4854)

Country and Title	*Place and Date*	*Text*
Exchange of Notes concerning Certain Commercial Debts (UK/Russia Debt Agreement No. 5 (1999))	London, 22.11.2000	TS No. 8 (2001) (Cm 5041)
SIERRA LEONE		
Agreement for the Promotion and Protection of Investments	Freetown, 13.1.2000	Sierra Leone No. 1 (2000) (Cm 4896)
SLOVENIA		
Agreement concerning Certain Commercial Debts (UK/ Slovenia Debt Agreement No. 1 (1999))	Ljubljana, 15/18.5.2000	
Agreement on International Road Transport	Prague, 30.5.2000	Slovenia No. 1 (2000) (Cm 4835)
SWEDEN		
Exchange of Notes extending the European Convention on Mutual Assistance in Criminal Matters to the Isle of Man	Stockholm, 4.1/28.2.2000	TS No. 62 (2000) (Cm 4726)
Agreement on the Reciprocal Holding of Stocks of Crude Oil and/or Petroleum Products	London, 8.3.2000	TS No. 60 (2000) (Cm 4720)
TURKEY		
Exchange of Notes concerning the Employment in Turkey and the UK of the Dependants of Diplomatic and Consular Personnel	Ankara, 12.1.2000	TS No. 98 (2000) (Cm 4826)
TURKMENISTAN		
Exchange of Notes terminating the Exchange of Notes between the Government of the UK and the Government of the Union of the Soviet Socialist Republics concerning the Mutual Abolition of Consular Fees on Visas, signed at Moscow, 13.4.1964	Ashgabat, 21.2/13.3.2000	TS No. 79 (2000) (Cm 4766)
Exchange of Notes amending the Air Services Agreement done at Ashgabat on 9.2.1995	Ashgabat, 14.8/11.9.2000	TS No. 9 (2001) (Cm 5042)

Country and Title	*Place and Date*	*Text*
VIETNAM		
Exchange of Notes amending the Air Services Agreement done at London on 19.8.1994	Hanoi, 8/26.9.2000	TS No. 129 (2000) (Cm 4927)
YUGOSLAVIA, FEDERAL REPUBLIC OF		
Exchange of Notes between the Federative Republic of Brazil, on behalf of the Government of the UK and the Government of the Federal Republic of Yugoslavia reviving the Agreement concerning Air Services signed at London on 3.2.1959, as amended	Belgrade, 9/17.3.2000	TS No. 96 (2000) (Cm 4815)
MISCELLANEOUS		
Agreement with the Organization for the Prohibition of Chemical Weapons on the Privileges and Immunities of the OPCW	The Hague, 26.10.2000	

IV. United Kingdom Legislation During 2000 Concerning Matters of International Law[1]

The Nuclear Safeguards Act 2000 (c. 5) implements the Vienna Protocol of 22 September 1998, additional to the Safeguards Agreement of 6 September 1976, between the UK and the International Atomic Energy Agency in connection with the Treaty on the Non-Proliferation of Nuclear Weapons of 1968. It provides for disclosure of information to the Secretary of State which he needs or will need to enable the obligations of the UK under the Protocol to be met, and gives the Agency's inspectors powers of entry and search to obtain evidence. Failure to provide information, failure to allow access to inspectors and provision of false or misleading information constitute criminal offences.

The Terrorism Act 2000 (c. 11) replaces the Prevention of Terrorism (Temporary Provisions) Act 1989 and the Northern Ireland (Emergency Provisions) Act 1996, and reforms the law in relation to the prevention of terrorism. It applies to any territory in or outside the UK, and includes in the definition of terrorism the use or threat of action designed to influence the government of the UK, of a part of the UK or of a country other than the UK. It makes provision to enable the UK to ratify the UN Convention on the Suppression of Terrorist Bombings of 1998 and the UN Convention for the Suppression of the Financing of Terrorism 2000. It provides for extra-territorial jurisdiction over terrorist offences and for extradition, and amends the Extradition Act 1989.

[1] Compiled by C. A. Hopkins.

TABLE OF CASES[1]

[1] The figures in heavier type indicate the pages on which cases are reviewed.

INDEX